Hands-On Design Patterns with C++

Solve common C++ problems with modern design patterns and build robust applications

Fedor G. Pikus

BIRMINGHAM—MUMBAI

Hands-On Design Patterns with C++

Associate Group Product Manager: Kunal Sawant

Publishing Product Manager: Kunal Sawant

Content Development Editor: Rosal Colaco

Technical Editor: Maran Fernandes

Copy Editor: Safis Editing

Project Manager: Prajakta Naik

Project Coordinator: Manisha Singh

Proofreader: Safis Editing

Indexer: Manju Arasan

Production Designer: Prashant Ghare

Business Development Executive: Kriti Sharma

Developer Relations Marketing Executives: Rayyan Khan and Sonia Chauhan

First published: June 2019

Second edition: June 2023

Production reference: 1300623

Published by Packt Publishing Ltd.

Livery Place

35 Livery Street

Birmingham

B3 2PB, UK.

ISBN 978-1-80461-155-5

www.packtpub.com

Contributors

About the author

Fedor G. Pikus is a Technical Fellow and head of the Advanced Projects Team in Siemens Digital Industries Software. His responsibilities include planning the long-term technical direction of Calibre products, directing and training the engineers who work on these products, design, and architecture of the software, and researching new design and software technologies.

His earlier positions included a Chief Scientist at Mentor Graphics (acquired by Siemens Software), a Senior Software Engineer at Google, and a Chief Software Architect for Calibre Design Solutions at Mentor Graphics. He joined Mentor Graphics in 1998 when he made a switch from academic research in computational physics to the software industry.

Fedor is a recognized expert in high-performance computing and C++. He is the author of two books on C++ and software design, has presented his works at CPPNow, CPPCon, SD West, DesignCon, and in software development journals, and is also an O'Reilly author. Fedor has over 30 patents and over 100 papers and conference presentations on physics, EDA, software design, and C++ language.

This book would not be possible without the support of my wife, Galina, who made me go on in moments of self-doubt. Thank you to my sons, Aaron and Benjamin, for their enthusiasm. I especially appreciate my cats, Pooh and Tux, for letting me use their warming pad as my laptop.

About the reviewer

Andrey Gavrilin is a senior software engineer working for an international company that provides treasury management cloud solutions. He has an MSc degree in engineering (industrial automation) and has worked in different areas such as accounting and staffing, road data bank, web and Linux distribution development, and fintech. His interests include mathematics, electronics, embedded systems, full-stack web development, retro gaming, and retro programming.

Table of Contents

Part 1: Getting Started with C++ Features and Concepts

1

An Introduction to Inheritance and Polymorphism   3

2

Class and Function Templates   21

3

Memory and Ownership 59

Part 2: Common C++ Idioms

4

Swap – from Simple to Subtle 79

5

A Comprehensive Look at RAII 95

6

Understanding Type Erasure   127

7

SFINAE, Concepts, and Overload Resolution Management   155

Part 3: C++ Design Patterns

8

The Curiously Recurring Template Pattern   197

9

Named Arguments, Method Chaining, and the Builder Pattern   225

10

Local Buffer Optimization   257

11

ScopeGuard   287

12

Friend Factory   317

13

Virtual Constructors and Factories   337

14

The Template Method Pattern and the Non-Virtual Idiom   367

Part 4: Advanced C++ Design Patterns

15

16

17

18

Patterns for Concurrency   537

Assessments   579

Index   593

Other Books You May Enjoy   602

Preface

When considering this book, some of you will ask: *Another book on design patterns in C++? Why that, and why now? Hasn't everything there is to know about design patterns been written already?*

There are several reasons why yet another book on *design patterns* has been written, but first of all, this is very much a C++ book—this is not a book on *design patterns* in C++ but a book on design patterns *in* C++, and the emphasis sets it apart. C++ has all the capabilities of a traditional object-oriented language, so all the classic object-oriented design patterns, such as Factory and Strategy, can be implemented in C++. A few of those are covered in this book. But the full power of C++ is realized when you utilize its generic programming capabilities. Remember that design patterns are frequently occurring design challenges and the commonly accepted solution—both sides are equally important in a pattern. It stands to reason that when new tools become available, new solutions become possible. Over time, the community settles on some of these solutions as the most advantageous overall, and a new variation of an old design pattern is born—the same challenge but a different preferred solution. But expanding capabilities also opens up new frontiers—with new tools at our disposal, new design challenges arise.

Others may expect to find a new coming of the classic book "*Design Patterns: Elements of Reusable Object-Oriented Software*". This 'isn't that book, and I do not believe that the time is right for such a book. The "*Gang of Four*" book was novel, even revolutionary, and it introduced the language of design patterns into the broad programming community. This has been done once and for all. It also established the neat taxonomy of design patterns, and that part has not aged nearly as well: as our pattern vocabulary expanded, we found patterns that do not fit easily into a particular category. We also extended the notion of design patterns beyond object-oriented programming and found that some of these patterns strongly resemble their object-oriented cousins while others are entirely new and different. Furthermore, in C++ and other languages with significantly different capabilities, a pattern that addresses the same need may look totally different. The bottom line is the original classification of patterns, while still useful, by now has more exceptions than typical examples, and the pattern landscape became too divergent for a new taxonomy that would not seem far too artificial. Maybe in time, as we develop the art further, new trends will emerge from the bird's eye view of the expanded pattern landscape, but it has not happened yet.

This book has less ambitious but very practical goals. In this book, we focus on design patterns where C++ has something essential to add to at least one of the two sides of the pattern. On the one hand, we have patterns such as Visitor, where the generic programming capabilities of C++ allow for a better solution. That better solution was made possible by new features that were added with the evolution of the language from C++11 to C++17. On the other hand, generic programming is still programming (only the execution of the program happens at compile time); programming requires design, and design has common challenges that are not all that dissimilar to the challenges of traditional programming. Thus, many of the traditional patterns have their twins, or at least close siblings, in generic programming, and we largely focus on those patterns in this book. A prime example is the Strategy pattern, better known in the generic programming community by its alternative name, the Policy pattern. Also, as new features are added to the language, it can offer solutions to new problems or new solutions to old problems, and both of these eventually develop into design patterns. This is the case with the C++ coroutines, which make an appearance in the last chapter.

Finally, a language as complex as C++ is bound to have a few idiosyncrasies of its own that often lead to C++-specific challenges that have common, or *standard*, solutions. While not quite deserving of being called *patterns*, these C++-specific idioms are also covered in this book.

A few words about the changes for the second edition: first of all, there is a new chapter on patterns for concurrency. All examples are updated to use C++17 or C++20 wherever it makes sense, but never gratuitously. Many patterns, idioms, and examples demonstrating their use were updated with recent developments and advances – the result of the work of the C++ programming community in the last few years.

All that said, there are three main reasons why this book has been written:

- To cover C++-specific solutions for otherwise general, *classic* design patterns

- To show C++-specific pattern variants that occur when old design challenges arise in the new domain of generic programming

- To keep our patterns up to date with the language's evolution

Who this book is for

This book is intended for C++ programmers who want to learn from *the wisdom of the community—* from commonly-recognized good solutions to frequently occurring design problems. Another way to put it is that this book is a way for a programmer to learn from someone else's mistakes.

This is not a *learn C++* book; the target audience is mostly programmers who are reasonably familiar with the tools and the syntax of the language, and who are more interested in learning how and why these tools should be used. However, this book will also be useful for programmers wanting to learn more about C++, but wishing that their study could be guided by concrete and practical examples (for such programmers, we recommend having a C++ reference book close to hand as well). Finally, programmers who want to learn not just what's new in C++17 or C++20, but what all these new features can be used for, will hopefully find this book illuminating as well.

What this book covers

Chapter 1, An Introduction to Inheritance and Polymorphism, provides a brief overview of the object-oriented features of C++. This chapter is not intended as a reference for object-oriented programming in C++, but, rather, highlights the aspects of it that are important for the subsequent chapters.

Chapter 2, Class and Function Templates, provides an overview of the generic programming facilities of C++—class templates, function templates, and lambda expressions. This chapter covers template instantiations and specializations, along with template function argument deduction and overload resolution, and prepares you for more complex uses of templates in later chapters.

Chapter 3, Memory and Ownership, describes modern idiomatic ways of expressing different kinds of memory ownership in C++. This is a collection of conventions or idioms—the compiler does not enforce these rules, but programmers will find it easier to understand each other if they use the shared idiomatic vocabulary.

Chapter 4, Swap - From Simple to Subtle, explores one of the most basic C++ operations, the swap, or exchange, of two values. This operation has surprisingly complex interactions with other C++ features that are discussed in the chapter.

Chapter 5, A Comprehensive Look at RAII, explores in detail one of the fundamental concepts of C++, that of resource management, and introduces what may be the most popular C++ idiom, RAII, which is the standard C++ approach to managing resources.

Chapter 6, Understanding Type Erasure, provides insight into a C++ technique that has been available in C++ for a long time but has grown in popularity and importance since the introduction of C++11. Type erasure allows the programmer to write abstract programs that do not explicitly mention certain types.

Chapter 7, SFINAE, Concepts, and Overload Resolution Management, discusses SFINAE—a C++ idiom that is, on the one hand, essential to the use of templates in C++ and *just happens* transparently, while on the other hand, requires a very thorough and subtle understanding of C++ templates when used purposefully.

Chapter 8, The Curiously Recurring Template Pattern, describes a *mind-wrapping* template-based pattern that combines the benefits of object-oriented programming with the flexibility of templates. The chapter explains the pattern and teaches you how to use it properly to solve practical problems. Lastly, this chapter prepares you for recognizing this pattern in later chapters.

Chapter 9, Named Arguments, Method Chaining, and the Builder Pattern, covers an unusual technique for calling functions in C++, using named arguments instead of positional ones. This is another one of those idioms we use implicitly in every C++ program, but its explicit purposeful use takes some thought.

Chapter 10, Local Buffer Optimization, is the only purely performance-oriented chapter in this book. Performance and efficiency are critical considerations that influence every design decision that affects the language itself—there is not a feature in the language that was not reviewed from the point of view of efficiency before being accepted into the standard. It is only fair that a chapter is dedicated to a common idiom used to improve the performance of C++ programs.

Chapter 11, ScopeGuard, introduces an old C++ pattern that has changed almost beyond recognition with the recent versions of C++. The chapter teaches you about a pattern for easily writing exception-safe, or, more generally, error-safe code in C++.

Chapter 12, Friend Factory, describes another old pattern that finds new uses in modern C++. This pattern is used to generate functions *associated* with templates, such as arithmetic operators for every type generated by a template.

Chapter 13, Virtual Constructors and Factories, covers another classic object-oriented programming pattern as applied to C++, the Factory pattern. In the process, the chapter also shows you how to get the appearance of polymorphic behavior from C++ constructors, even though constructors cannot be virtual.

Chapter 14, The Template Method Pattern and the Non-Virtual Idiom, describes an interesting crossover between a classic object-oriented pattern, the template, and a very C++-centric idiom. Together, they form a pattern that describes the optimal use of virtual functions in C++.

Chapter 15, Policy-Based Design, covers one of the jewels of C++ design patterns, the Policy pattern (more commonly known as the Strategy pattern), applied at compile time, that is, as a generic programming pattern instead of an object-oriented pattern.

Chapter 16, Adapters and Decorators, discusses the two very broad and closely related patterns as they apply to C++. The chapter considers the use of these patterns in object-oriented designs, as well as in generic programs.

Chapter 17, The Visitor Pattern and Multiple Dispatch, rounds off our gallery of classic object-oriented programming patterns with the perennially popular Visitor pattern. The chapter explains the pattern itself, then focuses on the ways that modern C++ makes the implementation of Visitor simpler, more robust, and less error-prone.

Chapter 18, Patterns for Concurrency, is a new addition to the book. While C++ has been used to write concurrent programs long before C++11 gave us the "official" tools for it, the wide range of problem-specific solutions makes identifying common patterns difficult. This chapter introduces the patterns that became the basic building blocks for designing concurrent software in C++.

To get the most out of this book

To run examples from this book, you will need a computer running Windows, Linux, or macOS (C++ programs can be built on something as small as a Raspberry Pi). You will also need a modern C++ compiler, such as GCC, Clang, Visual Studio, or another compiler that supports the C++ language up to C++20 (most examples need only C++14, some rely on C++17 features, and a few require up-to-date C++20 support). You will need a basic knowledge of GitHub and Git in order to clone a project with examples.

Download the example code files

You can download the example code files for this book from GitHub at https://github.com/
PacktPublishing/Hands-On-Design-Patterns-with-CPP-Second-Edition/.
If there's an update to the code, it will be updated in the GitHub repository.

We also have other code bundles from our rich catalog of books and videos available at https://
github.com/PacktPublishing/. Check them out!

Conventions used

There are a number of text conventions used throughout this book.

Code in text: Indicates code words in text, database table names, folder names, filenames, file
extensions, pathnames, dummy URLs, user input, and Twitter handles. Here is an example: "The
implementation of the insert() function must insert the record into both the storage and the
index, there is no way around it."

A block of code is set as follows:

```
class Database {
  class Storage { ... };    // Disk storage Storage S;
  class Index { ... };    // Memory index Index I;
  public:
  void insert(const Record& r);
  ...
};
```

Any command-line input or output is written as follows:

```
Benchmark                               Time
-------------------------------------------
BM_delete_explicit                   4.54 ns
BM_delete_type_erased                13.4 ns
BM_delete_type_erased_fast           12.7 ns
BM_delete_template                   4.56 ns
```

> **Tips or important notes**
> Appear like this.

Get in touch

Feedback from our readers is always welcome.

General feedback: If you have questions about any aspect of this book, email us at `customercare@packtpub.com` and mention the book title in the subject of your message.

Errata: Although we have taken every care to ensure the accuracy of our content, mistakes do happen. If you have found a mistake in this book, we would be grateful if you would report this to us. Please visit `www.packtpub.com/support/errata` and fill in the form.

Piracy: If you come across any illegal copies of our works in any form on the internet, we would be grateful if you would provide us with the location address or website name. Please contact us at `copyright@packt.com` with a link to the material.

If you are interested in becoming an author: If there is a topic that you have expertise in and you are interested in either writing or contributing to a book, please visit `authors.packtpub.com`.

Share Your Thoughts

Once you've read *Hands-On Design Patterns with C++ (Second Edition)*, we'd love to hear your thoughts! Scan the QR code below to go straight to the Amazon review page for this book and share your feedback.

https://packt.link/r/1-804-61155-7

Your review is important to us and the tech community and will help us make sure we're delivering excellent quality content.

Download a free PDF copy of this book

Thanks for purchasing this book!

Do you like to read on the go but are unable to carry your print books everywhere?

Is your eBook purchase not compatible with the device of your choice?

Don't worry, now with every Packt book you get a DRM-free PDF version of that book at no cost.

Read anywhere, any place, on any device. Search, copy, and paste code from your favorite technical books directly into your application.

The perks don't stop there, you can get exclusive access to discounts, newsletters, and great free content in your inbox daily

Follow these simple steps to get the benefits:

1. Scan the QR code or visit the link below

https://packt.link/free-ebook/9781804611555

2. Submit your proof of purchase

3. That's it! We'll send your free PDF and other benefits to your email directly

Part 1:
Getting Started with C++
Features and Concepts

This part introduces and explains the features of C++ object-oriented programming, generic programming, and some of the other advanced language tools that are necessary for you to understand the rest of the book. We also discuss some of the more annoying limitations imposed by the language: many of the patterns we show in the later chapters are nothing but universally recognized solutions to these limitations. This is not meant as a complete guide for any of the features, but helps make the book more self-contained as a hands-on guide for programmers. This part has the following chapters:

- *Chapter 1, An Introduction to Inheritance and Polymorphism*
- *Chapter 2, Class and Function Templates*
- *Chapter 3, Memory and Ownership*

1

An Introduction to Inheritance and Polymorphism

C++ is, first and foremost, an object-oriented language, and objects are the fundamental building blocks of a C++ program. Class hierarchies are used to express relationships and interactions between different parts of a software system, define and implement interfaces between components, and organize data and code. While this isn't a book for teaching C++, the aim of this chapter is to give the reader enough knowledge about C++ language features as they relate to classes and inheritance, which will be used in later chapters. To that end, we won't attempt to completely describe the C++ tools for working with classes but introduce the concepts and language constructs that will be used throughout this book.

The following topics will be covered in this chapter:

- What are classes and what is their role in C++?
- What are class hierarchies and how does C++ use inheritance?
- What is runtime polymorphism and how is it used in C++?

Classes and objects

Object-oriented programming is a way to structure a program by combining the algorithms and the data that the algorithms operate on into single entities called **objects**. Most object-oriented languages, including C++, are class-based. A **class** is a definition of an object—it describes the algorithms and the data, its format, and its relations to other classes. An object is a concrete instantiation of a class, that is, a variable. An object has an address, which is a location in memory. A class is a user-defined type. In general, any number of objects can be instantiated from the definition provided by the class (some classes limit the number of objects that can be created, but this is an exception, not the norm).

In C++, the data contained in a class is organized as a collection of data members, or variables, of different types. The algorithms are implemented as functions—the methods of the class. While there's no language requirement that the data members of a class should be somehow relevant to the implementation of its methods, it's one of the signs of good design when the data is well encapsulated in the classes, and the methods have limited interaction with external data.

This concept of **encapsulation** is central to the classes in C++—the language allows us to control which data members and methods are public—visible outside of the class, and which are internal—private to the class. A well-designed class has mostly, or only, private data members, and the only public methods are those needed to express the public interface of the class—in other words, what the class does. This public interface is like a contract—the class designer promises that this class provides certain features and operations. The private data and methods of the class are part of the implementation, and they can be changed as long as the public interface, the contract we've committed to, remains valid. For example, the following class represents a rational number and supports the increment operation, as exposed by its public interface:

```
class Rational { public:
   Rational& operator+=(const Rational& rhs);
};
```

A well-designed class doesn't expose any more of the implementation details than it has to through its public interface. The implementation isn't part of the contract, although the documented interface may impose some restrictions on it. For example, if we promise that all rational numbers don't contain any common multipliers in the numerator and denomination, the addition should include the step of canceling them. That would be a good use of a private member function—the implementation of several other operations will need to call it, but the client of the class never needs to call it because every rational number is already reduced to its lowest terms before it's exposed to the callers:

```
class Rational {
  public:
  Rational& operator+=(const Rational& rhs); private:
  long n_; // numerator
  long d_; // denominator
  void  reduce();
};
Rational& Rational::operator+=(const Rational& rhs) {
  n_ = n_*rhs.d_ + rhs.n_*d_;
  d_ = d_*rhs.d_; reduce();
  return *this;
}
Rational a, b; a += b;
```

The class methods have special access to the data members—they can access the private data of the class. Note the distinction between the class and the object here—`operator+=()` is a method of the `Rational` class and is invoked on the object, a. However, it has access to the private data of the b object as well, because a and b are objects of the same class. If a member function references a class member by name without any additional qualifiers, then it's accessing a member of the same class it's invoked on (we can make it explicit by writing `this->n_` and `this->d_`). Accessing members of another object of the same class requires a pointer or a reference to that object, but is otherwise not restricted, as would have been the case if we tried to access a private data member from a non-member function.

By the way, C++ also supports C-style structs. But in C++, a struct isn't limited to just an aggregate of data members—it can have methods, public and private access modifiers, and anything else classes have. From a language point of view, the only difference between a class and a struct is the default access—in a class, all members and methods are private by default, while in a struct they're public. Beyond that, the use of structs instead of classes is a matter of convention—traditionally, structs are used for C-style structs (structs that would be legal in C) as well as *almost* C-style structs, for example, a struct with only a constructor added. Of course, this boundary isn't precise and is a matter of coding styles and practices in each project or team.

In addition to the methods and data members we've seen, C++ also supports static data and methods. A static method is very similar to a regular non-member function—it isn't invoked on any particular object, and the only way it can get access to an object of any type is through its arguments. However, unlike a non-member function, a static method retains its privileged access to the private data of the class.

Classes by themselves are a useful way to group together (encapsulate) the algorithms and the data they operate on and to limit access to some data. However, the most powerful object-oriented features of C++ are inheritance and the resulting class hierarchies.

Inheritance and class hierarchies

Class hierarchies in C++ serve a dual purpose. On the one hand, they allow us to express relations between objects. On the other hand, they let us compose more complex types from simpler ones. Both uses are accomplished through inheritance.

The concept of inheritance is central to the C++ use of classes and objects. Inheritance allows us to define new classes as extensions of existing ones. When a derived class is inherited from the base class, it contains, in some form, all of the data and the algorithms that were in the base class, and it adds some of its own. In C++, it's important to distinguish between two primary types of inheritance—public and private.

Public inheritance inherits the public interface of the class. It also inherits the implementation—the data members of the base class are also a part of the derived class. But the inheritance of the interface is what distinguishes public inheritance—the derived class has, as a part of its public interface, the public member functions of the base class.

Remember that the public interface is like a contract—we promise to the clients of the class that it supports certain operations, maintains some invariants, and obeys the specified restrictions. By publicly inheriting from the base class, we bind the derived class to the same contract (plus any extensions of the contract, should we decide to define additional public interfaces). Because the derived class also respects the interface contract of the base class, we could use a derived class in any place in the code where a base class is expected—we would not be able to use any of the extensions to the interface (the code expects the base class, we don't know about any extensions at that point), but the base class interface and its restrictions have to be valid.

This is often expressed as the *is-a principle*—an instance of a derived class is also an instance of the base class. However, the way we interpret the *is-a* relationship in C++ isn't exactly intuitive. For example, is a square a rectangle? If it is, then we can derive the `Square` class from the `Rectangle` class:

```cpp
class Rectangle {
  public:
    double Length() const { return length_; }
    double Width() const { return width_; }
    ...
  private:
    double l_;
    double w_;
};
class Square : public Rectangle {
    ...
};
```

Right away, there's something that doesn't seem right—the derived class has two data members for dimensions, but it really needs only one. We would have to somehow enforce that they're always the same. This doesn't seem so bad—the `Rectangle` class has the interface that allows for any positive values of length and width, and the `Square` imposes additional restrictions. But it's worse than that—the `Rectangle` class has a contract that allows the user to make the dimensions different. This can be quite explicit:

```cpp
class Rectangle {
  public:
    void Scale(double sl, double sw) {
       // Scale the dimensions
      length_ *= sl;
      width_ *= sw;
    }
    ...
};
```

Now, we have a public method that allows us to distort the rectangle, altering its aspect ratio. As with any other public method, it's inherited by the derived classes, so now the Square class has it too. In fact, by using public inheritance, we assert that a Square object can be used anywhere a Rectangle object is used, without even knowing that it's really a Square. Clearly, this is a promise we can't keep—when the client of our class hierarchy tries to change the aspect ratio of a square, we can't do it. We could ignore the call or report an error at runtime. Either way, we've violated the contract provided by the base class. There's only one solution—in C++, a square isn't a rectangle. Note that a rectangle is usually not a square, either—the contract provided by the Square interface could contain any number of guarantees that we can't maintain if we derive the Rectangle class from Square.

Similarly, a penguin isn't a bird in C++ if the bird interface includes flying. The correct design for such cases usually includes a more abstract base class, Bird, that doesn't make any promises that at least one derived class can't keep (for example, a Bird object doesn't make a guarantee that it can fly). Then, we create intermediate-based classes, such as FlyingBird and FlightlessBird, that are derived from the common base class and serve as base classes for the more specific classes such as Eagle or Penguin. The important lesson here is that whether or not a penguin is a bird in C++ depends on how we define what a bird is, or, in C++ terms, what the public interface of the Bird class is.

Because the public inheritance implies the *is-a* relationship, the language allows a wide range of conversions between references and pointers to different classes in the same hierarchy. First of all, a conversion from a pointer to a derived class into a pointer to the base class is implicit (this is the same for references):

```
class Base { ... };
class Derived : public Base { ... };
Derived* d = new Derived;
Base* b = d;    // Implicit conversion
```

This conversion is always valid because an instance of the derived class is also an instance of the base class. The inverse conversion is possible but has to be made explicit:

```
Base* b = new Derived;      // *b is really Derived
Derived* d = b; // Does not compile, not implicit Derived*
Derived* d1 =
    static_cast<Derived*>(b);    // Explicit conversion
```

The reason this conversion isn't implicit is that it's valid only if the base class pointer really points to a derived object (otherwise, the behavior is undefined). The programmer, therefore, must explicitly assert, using the static cast, that somehow, through the logic of the program or a prior test or by some other means, it's known that this conversion is valid. If you aren't sure that the conversion is valid, there's a safer way to try it without causing undefined behavior; we'll learn about this in the next section.

Note that the static (or implicit) conversion between pointers to base and derived classes is not quite as straightforward as you might think. The first base of any object always has the same address as the derived object itself, but then it gets more complicated. There is generally no standard requirement on the memory layout of derived classes with multiple bases:

```
class Base1 { ... };
class Base2 { ... };
class Derived : public Base1, public Base2 { ... };
```

Most compilers will lay out the base classes first, then the data members of the derived class:

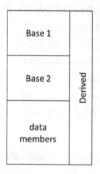

Figure 1.1 – Possible memory layout of a derived class

From *Figure 1.1*, it is evident that pointer conversion between the base and derived classes generally involves offset calculations. We can easily see this in an example:

```
// Example 01_cast.C
Derived d;
Derived* p = &d;
std::cout << "Derived: " << (void*)(p) <<
   " Base1: " << (void*)(static_cast<Base1*>(p)) <<
   " Base2: " << (void*)(static_cast<Base2*>(p)) <<
   std::endl;
```

The program prints something like this:

```
Derived: 0x7f97e550 Base1: 0x7f97e550 Base2: 0x7f97e560
```

You can see that the Base1 object is located at the same address as the Derived object, and Base2 starts with an offset (16 bytes, in our case). Seems like the cast is an easy calculation: If you have a pointer to Derived and you want to cast to Base2, add 16. The offsets between base classes are known at compile time, and the compiler knows the layout it is using. Pointer offset calculations are usually implemented in hardware (all modern CPUs support them and do not require a separate addition instruction). This doesn't sound so hard at all.

Now, what do you do if the pointer is `null`? The pointer has a value of 0. If you apply the same *conversion*, you get 16 (0x10), and now your check for `null` fails:

```
void f(Base2* p) {
   if (p != nullptr) do_work(*p);
}
Derived* p = nullptr;
f(p); // Will it try to dereference 0x10?
```

Obviously, this would be very bad, so we can assume that `null` pointers remain so. Indeed, they do:

```
Derived* p = nullptr;
std::cout << "Derived: " << (void*)(p) <<
   " Base1: " << (void*)(static_cast<Base1*>(p)) <<
   " Base2: " << (void*)(static_cast<Base2*>(p)) <<
   std::endl;
```

This prints the same values for all pointers:

```
Derived: 0x0 Base1: 0x0 Base2: 0x0
```

This is the only way to do casts, but it implies that a simple implicit cast from `Derived*` to `Base*` hides inside a conditional computation with a `null` pointer check.

The other kind of inheritance in C++ is **private inheritance**. When inheriting privately, the derived classes don't extend the public interface of the base class—all base class methods become private in the derived class. Any public interface has to be created by the derived class, starting from a clean slate. There's no assumption that an object of the derived class can be used in place of an object of the base class. What the derived class does get from the base class is the implementation details—both the methods and the data members can be used by the derived class to implement its own algorithms. It's said, therefore, that private inheritance implements a *has-a* relationship—the derived object has an instance of the base class contained inside of it.

The relation of the privately derived class to its base class is, therefore, similar to that of the relationship of a class to its data members. The latter implementation technique is known as **composition**—an object is composed of any number of other objects, which are all used as its data members. In the absence of any reason to do otherwise, the composition should be preferred to private inheritance. What, then, might be the reasons to use private inheritance? There are several possibilities. First of all, it's possible, within the derived class, to re-expose one of the public member functions of the base class with the help of a `using` declaration:

```
class Container : private std::vector<int> {
   public:
   using std::vector<int>::size;
   ...
};
```

This can be useful in rare cases, but it's also equivalent to an inline forwarding function:

```
class Container {
  private:
  std::vector<int> v_;
  public:
  size_t size() const { return v_.size(); }
  ...
};
```

Second, a pointer or reference to a derived object can be converted into a pointer or reference to the base object, but only inside a member function of the derived class. Again, the equivalent functionality for composition is provided by taking the address of a data member. So far, we haven't seen a good reason to use private inheritance, and indeed, the common advice is to prefer composition. But the next two reasons are more significant, and either one could be motivation enough to use private inheritance.

One good reason to use private inheritance has to do with the size of the composed or derived objects. It isn't uncommon to have base classes that provide only methods but no data members. Such classes have no data of their own and, therefore, should not occupy any memory. But in C++, they have to be given a non-zero size. This has to do with the requirement that any two different objects or variables have different and unique addresses. Typically, if we have two variables declared one after the other, the address of the second one is the address of the first one, plus the size of the first one:

```
int x;      // Created at address 0xffff0000, size is 4
int y;      // Created at address 0xffff0004
```

To avoid the need to handle zero-sized objects differently, C++ assigns an empty object the size of one. If such an object is used as a data member of a class, it occupies at least 1 byte (the alignment requirements for the next data member may increase this value). This is wasted memory; it'll never be used for anything. On the other hand, if an empty class is used as a base class, there's no requirement that the base part of an object must have a non-zero size. The entire object of the derived class must have a non-zero size, but the address of a derived object, its base object, and its first data member can all be at the same address. Therefore, it's legal in C++ to allocate no memory for an empty base class, even though `sizeof()` returns 1 for this class. While legal, such empty base class optimization isn't required and is considered an optimization. Nonetheless, most modern compilers do this optimization:

```
class Empty {
  public:
  void useful_function();
};
class Derived : private Empty {
  int i;
};      // sizeof(Derived) == 4
class Composed {
  int i;
```

```
    Empty e;
};      // sizeof(Composed) == 8
```

If we create many derived objects, the memory saved by the empty base optimization can be significant.

The second reason to possibly use private inheritance has to do with virtual functions, and this will be explained in the next section.

Polymorphism and virtual functions

When we discussed public inheritance earlier, we mentioned that a derived object can be used in any place where a base object is expected. Even with this requirement, it's often useful to know what the actual type of the object is—in other words, what type the object was created as:

```
Derived d;
Base& b = d;
...
b.some_method(); // b is really a Derived object
```

some_method() is a part of the public interface of the Base class and has to be valid for the Derived class as well. But, within the flexibility allowed by the contract of the base class interface, it can do something different. As an example, we've already used the avian hierarchy before to represent different birds, in particular, birds that can fly. The FlyingBird class can be assumed to have a fly() method, and every specific bird class derived from it has to support flight. But eagles fly differently from vultures, and so the implementation of the fly() method in the two derived classes, Eagle and Vulture, can be different. Any code that operates on arbitrary FlyingBird objects can call the fly() method, but the results will vary depending on the actual type of the object.

This functionality is implemented in C++ using virtual functions. A virtual public function must be declared in the base class:

```
class FlyingBird : public Bird {
  public:
  virtual void fly(double speed, double direction) {
     ... move the bird at the specified speed
         in the given direction ...
  }
  ...
};
```

A derived class inherits both the declaration and the implementation of this function. The declaration and the contract it provides must be respected. If the implementation meets the needs of the derived class, there's no need to do anything more. But if the derived class needs to change the implementation, it can override the implementation of the base class:

```
class Vulture : public FlyingBird {
  public:
```

```
virtual void fly(double speed, double direction) {
   ... move the bird but accumulate
       exhaustion if too fast ...
   }
};
```

Note that the keyword `virtual`, when used in a derived class for methods that override base class virtual functions, is entirely optional and has no effect; we will see later that there are good reasons to omit that.

When a virtual function is called, the C++ runtime system must determine what the real type of the object is. Usually, this information isn't known at compile time and must be determined at runtime:

```
void hunt(FlyingBird& b) {
  b.fly(...);     // Could be Vulture or Eagle
  ...
};
Eagle e;
hunt(e);    // Now b in hunt() is Eagle
            // FlyingBird::fly() is called
Vulture v;
hunt(v);    // Now b in hunt() is Vulture
            // Vulture::fly() is called
```

The programming technique where some code operates on any number of base objects and invokes the same methods, but the results depend on the actual type of these objects, is known as **runtime polymorphism**, and the objects that support this technique are **polymorphic**. In C++, polymorphic objects must have at least one virtual function, and only the parts of their interface that use virtual functions for some or all of the implementation are polymorphic.

It should be evident from this explanation that the declaration of the virtual function and its overrides should be identical—the programmer calls the function on a base object, but the version that's implemented in the derived class runs instead. This can happen only if the two functions have identical arguments and return types. One exception is that if a virtual function in the base class returns a pointer or a reference to an object of some type, the override can return a pointer or a reference to an object derived from that type (this is known as **covariant return types**).

A very common special case of polymorphic hierarchies is one where the base class doesn't have a good *default* implementation of the virtual function. For example, all flying birds fly, but they all fly at different speeds, so there's no reason to select one speed as the default. In C++, we can refuse to provide any implementation for a virtual function in the base class.

Such functions are called **pure virtual**, and any base class that contains a pure virtual function is known as an **abstract class**:

```
class FlyingBird {
  public:
    virtual void fly(...) = 0;      // Pure virtual function
};
```

An abstract class defines an interface only; it's the job of the concrete derived classes to implement it. If the base class contains a pure virtual function, every derived class that's instantiated in the program must provide an implementation. In other words, an object of a base class can't be created (a derived class could also be an abstract class, but then it cannot be instantiated directly either, we must derive another class from it). We can, however, have a pointer or a reference to an object of a base class—they really point to a derived class, but we can operate on it through the base class interface.

A few notes on the C++ syntax—when overriding a virtual function, it isn't required to repeat the `virtual` keyword. If the base class declares a virtual function with the same name and arguments, the one in the derived class will always be a virtual function and will override the one from the base class. Note that, if the arguments differ, the derived class function doesn't override anything and instead shadows the name of the base class function. This can lead to subtle bugs where the programmer intended to override a base class function but didn't copy the declaration correctly:

```
class Eagle : public FlyingBird {
  public:
    void fly(int speed, double direction);
};
```

Here, the types of the arguments are slightly different. The `Eagle::fly()` function is also virtual, but it doesn't override `FlyingBird::fly()`. If the latter is a pure virtual function, the bug will be caught because every pure virtual function must be implemented in a derived class. But if `FlyingBird::fly()` has the default implementation, then the bug will go undetected by the compiler. C++11 provides a very useful feature that greatly simplifies finding such bugs—any function that's intended to be an override of a base class virtual function can be declared with the `override` keyword:

```
class Eagle : public FlyingBird {
  public:
    void fly(int speed, double direction) override;
};
```

The `virtual` keyword is still optional, but if the `FlyingBird` class doesn't have a virtual function that we could be overriding with this declaration, this code won't compile.

It is also possible to prevent the derived classes from overriding a virtual function by declaring it `final`:

```
class Eagle : public FlyingBird {
  public:
  // All Eagles fly the same way, derived classes BaldEagle
  // and GoldenEagle cannot change this.
  void fly(int speed, double direction) final;
};
```

Note that the use of the `final` keyword is rare: it is unusual for the design to require that from this point on, the customizations should be disabled in the hierarchy. The `final` keyword can also be applied to the entire class: it means that no more classes can be derived from this one. Again, this is a rare situation.

So, should or shouldn't you use the `virtual` keyword on overrides? This is a matter of style, but the style affects the readability and maintainability of the code. The following is the recommended practice:

- Any virtual function that does not override one in the base class must use the `virtual` keyword. This includes both the functions in classes that have no bases and the functions added in derived classes.

- Any other virtual function should not use the `virtual` keyword. All overrides should use the `override` keyword, with the following exception, which is also another rule.

- A final override must use the `final` keyword and should not use the `override` keyword.

There are two advantages to this approach. The first is clarity and readability: if you see `virtual`, this is a virtual function that does not override anything. If you see `override`, this must be an override (otherwise the code would not compile). If you see `final`, this is also an override (again, the code would not compile otherwise) and it's the last such in the hierarchy. The second advantage shows up during code maintenance. One of the greatest problems with maintaining hierarchies is the base class fragility: you write a set of base and derived classes, someone else comes along and adds an argument to the base class function, and suddenly all your derived class functions don't override the base class ones and never get called. With consistent use of the `override` keyword, this will not happen.

The most common use of virtual functions, by far, is in hierarchies that use public inheritance—since every derived object is also a base object (*is-a* relationship), a program can often operate on a collection of derived objects as if they were all of the same types, and the virtual function overrides ensure that the right processing happens for every object:

```
void MakeLoudBoom(std::vector<FlyingBird*> birds)
  for (auto bird : birds) {
    bird->fly(...);    // Same action, different results
  }
}
```

But virtual functions can also be used with private inheritance. The use is less straightforward (and much less common)—after all, an object that's derived privately can't be accessed through a base class pointer (a private base class is referred to as an **inaccessible base**, and an attempt to cast a derived class pointer to the base class will fail). However, there's one context in which this cast is permitted, and that's within a member function of the derived class. Here's, then, the way to arrange a virtual function call from a privately inherited base class to the derived one:

```cpp
class Base {
  public:
  virtual void f() {
      std::cout << "Base::f()" << std::endl;
    }
  void g() { f(); }
};
class Derived : private Base {
  public:
  virtual void f() {
     std::cout << "Derived::f()" << std::endl;
  }
  void h() { g(); }
};
Derived d;
d.h(); // Prints "Derived::f()"
```

The public methods of the Base class become private in the Derived class, so we can't call them directly. We can, however, call them from another method of the Derived class, such as the public method h(). We can then call f() directly from h(), but that doesn't prove anything—it would come as no surprise if Derived::h() invoked Derived::f().

Instead, we call the Base::g() function that's inherited from the Base class. Inside that function, we're in the Base class—the body of this function may have been written and compiled long before the Derived class was implemented. And yet, in this context, the virtual function override works correctly and Derived::f() is called, just as it would if the inheritance were public.

In the previous section, we recommended that composition is preferred to private inheritance unless there's a reason to do otherwise. There's no good way to implement similar functionality using composition; so, if the virtual function behavior is desired, private inheritance is the only way to go.

A class with a virtual method has to have its type encoded into every object—this is the only way to know, at runtime, what was the type of the object when it was constructed, after we converted the pointer into a base class pointer and lost any other information about the original type. That type information isn't free; it takes space—a polymorphic object is always larger than an object with the same data members but no virtual methods (usually by the size of a pointer).

The extra size doesn't depend on how many virtual functions the class has—at long as it has one, the type information must be encoded in the object. Now, recall that a pointer to the base class can be converted into a pointer to the derived class, but only if we know the correct type of the derived class. With the static cast, there's no way to test whether our knowledge is correct. For non-polymorphic classes (classes without any virtual functions), there can be no better way; once their original type is lost, there is no way to recover it. But for polymorphic objects, the type is encoded in the object, so there has to be a way to use that information to check whether our assumption is correct about which derived object this really is. Indeed, there is a way. It's provided by the dynamic cast:

```
class Base { ... };
class Derived : public Base { ... };
Base* b1 = new Derived;      // Really Derived
Base* b2 = new Base;     // Not Derived
Derived* d1 = dynamic_cast<Derived*>(b1);   // Succeeds
Derived* d2 = dynamic_cast<Derived*>(b2);   // d2 == nullptr
```

The dynamic cast doesn't tell us what the real type of the object is; rather, it allows us to ask the question—Is the real type `Derived`? If our guess at the type is correct, the cast succeeds and returns the pointer to the derived object. If the real type is something else, the cast fails and returns a `null` pointer. The dynamic cast can also be used with references, with similar effects, save one—there's no *null reference*. A function that returns a reference must always return a reference to some valid object. Since the dynamic cast can't return a reference to a valid object if the requested type doesn't match the actual type. The only alternative is to throw an exception.

For performance-conscious code, it is important to be aware of the run-time cost of the dynamic cast. Naively, one might think that a virtual function call and a dynamic cast take about the same time: both boil down to the question – is this pointer to `Base` really a pointer to `Derived`? A simple benchmark shows that this is not so:

```
// Example 02_dynamic_cast.C
class Base {
  protected:
  int i = 0;
  public:
  virtual ~Base() {}
  virtual int f() { return ++i; }
};
class Derived : public Base {
  int f() override { return --i; }
};
Derived* p = new Derived;
// Measure the runtime of p->f();
// Measure the runtime of dynamic_cast<Derived*>(p);
```

The benchmark results should look something like this (the absolute numbers will depend on the hardware): 1 nanosecond for the virtual call, and 5 to 10 nanoseconds for the dynamic cast. Why is the dynamic cast so expensive? We need to learn more about the hierarchies before we can answer this question.

So far, we've limited ourselves to only one base class. While it's much easier to think about class hierarchies if we imagine them as trees, with the base class and the root and branches where multiple classes are derived from the same base, C++ doesn't impose such limitations. Next, we'll learn about inheriting from several base classes at once.

Multiple inheritance

In C++, a class can be derived from several base classes. Going back to our birds, let's make an observation—while flying birds have a lot in common with each other, they also have something in common with other flying animals, specifically, the ability to fly. Since flight isn't limited to birds, we may want to move the data and the algorithms related to processing flight into a separate base class. But there's also no denying that an eagle is a bird. We could express this relation if we used two base classes to construct the `Eagle` class:

```
class Eagle : public Bird, public FlyingAnimal { ... };
```

In this case, the inheritance from both base classes is public, which means that the derived class inherits both interfaces and must fulfill two separate contracts. What happens if both interfaces define a method with the same name? If this method isn't virtual, then an attempt to invoke it on the derived class is ambiguous, and the program doesn't compile. If the method is virtual and the derived class has an override for it, then there's no ambiguity since the method of the derived class is called. Also, `Eagle` is now both `Bird` and `FlyingAnimal`:

```
Eagle* e = new Eagle;
Bird* b = e;
FlyingAnimal* f = e;
```

Both conversions from the derived class into the base class pointer are allowed. The reverse conversions must be made explicitly using a static or a dynamic cast. There's another interesting conversion—if we have a pointer to a `FlyingAnimal` class that's also a `Bird` class, can we cast from one to the other? Yes, we can with a dynamic cast:

```
Bird* b = new Eagle;    // Also a FlyingAnimal
FlyingAnimal* f = dynamic_cast<FlyingAnimal*>(b);
```

When used in this context, the dynamic cast is sometimes called a **cross-cast**—we aren't casting up or down the hierarchy (between derived and based classes) but across the hierarchy—between the classes on different branches of the hierarchy tree.

Cross-cast is also mostly responsible for the high runtime cost of the dynamic cast we have seen in the previous section. While the most common use of dynamic_cast is to cast from Base* to Derived* to verify that a given object is really of the derived class, the cast could also be used to cast between bases of the same derived class. This is a much harder problem. If you just want to check that the base class object is really a derived one, the compiler knows the Derived type at this point (you cannot use the dynamic cast on incomplete types).

Therefore, the compiler knows exactly what base classes this derived type has and can trivially check if yours is one of them. But when casting across the hierarchy, the compiler knows only two base classes: at the time when this code was written, a derived class that combines both may not exist, it will be written later. But the compiler must generate the correct code now. So, the compiler has to generate code that, at run time, digs through all the possible classes that are derived from both base classes to see if yours is one of them (the actual implementation is less straightforward and more efficient than that, but the task to be accomplished remains the same).

In reality, this overhead is often unnecessary because, most of the time, the dynamic cast is indeed used to find out whether the base class pointer really points to a derived object. In many cases, the overhead is not significant. But if better performance is required, there is no way to make the dynamic cast faster. If you want a fast way to check whether a polymorphic object is really of a given type, you have to use virtual functions and, unfortunately, a list of all possible types (or at least all the ones you might be interested in):

```cpp
enum type_t { typeBase, typeDerived1, typeDerived2 };
class Base {
  virtual type_t type() const { return typeBase; }
};
class Derived1 : public Base {
  type_t type() const override { return typeDerived1; }
};
...
void process_derived1(Derived1* p);
void do_work(Base* p) {
  if (p->type() == typeDerived1) {
    process_derived1(static_cast<Derived1*>(p));
  }
}
```

Multiple inheritance is often maligned and disfavored in C++. Much of this advice is outdated and stems from the time when compilers implemented multiple inheritance poorly and inefficiently. Today, with modern compilers, this isn't a concern. It's often said that multiple inheritance makes the class hierarchy harder to understand and reason about. Perhaps it would be more accurate to say that it's harder to design a good multiple inheritance hierarchy that accurately reflects the relations between different properties, and that a poorly designed hierarchy is difficult to understand and reason about.

These concerns mostly apply to hierarchies that use public inheritance. Multiple inheritance can be private as well. There's even less reason to use multiple private inheritance instead of composition than there was to use single private inheritance. However, the empty base optimization can be done on multiple empty base classes and remains a valid reason to use private inheritance, if it applies:

```
class Empty1 {};
class Empty2 {};
class Derived : private Empty1, private Empty2 {
  int i;
};   // sizeof(Derived) == 4
class Composed {
  int i;
  Empty1 e1;
  Empty2 e2;
};   // sizeof(Composed) == 8
```

Multiple inheritance can be particularly effective when the derived class represents a system that combines several unrelated, non-overlapping attributes. We'll encounter such cases throughout this book when we explore various design patterns and their C++ representations.

Summary

While by no means a complete guide or reference to classes and objects, this chapter introduced and explained the concepts you will need to understand the examples and explanations in the rest of this book. As our interest is and will be in representing design patterns in C++, this chapter focused on the proper use of classes and inheritance. We paid particular attention to what relations are expressed through different C++ features—it's through these features we'll express relations and interactions between different components that form a design pattern.

The next chapter will similarly cover knowledge of C++ templates, which will be necessary to understand the subsequent chapters of this book.

Questions

- What is the importance of objects in C++?

- Which relation is expressed by public inheritance? Which relation is expressed by private inheritance? What is a polymorphic object?

- What is the difference between the dynamic cast and the static cast? Why is the dynamic cast so expensive?

Further reading

- *Deciphering Object-Oriented Programming with C++*: `https://www.packtpub.com/product/deciphering-object-oriented-programming-with-c/9781804613900`

- *Software Architecture with C++*: `https://www.packtpub.com/product/software-architecture-with-c/9781838554590`

- *C++ Fundamentals*: `https://www.packtpub.com/product/c-fundamentals`

- *C++ Data Structures and Algorithms*: `https://www.packtpub.com/product/c-data-structures-and-algorithm-design-principles`

- *Mastering C++ Programming*: `https://www.packtpub.com/product/mastering-c-programming`

- *Beginning C++ Programming*: `https://www.packtpub.com/product/beginning-c-programming`

2

Class and Function Templates

The template programming features of C++ form a large and complex subject, with many books dedicated exclusively to teaching these features. In this book, we will use many of the advanced C++ generic programming features. How, then, should we prepare ourselves to understand these language constructs as they make their appearance throughout this book? This chapter takes an informal approach—instead of precise definitions, we demonstrate the use of templates through examples and explain what the different language features do. If you find your knowledge lacking at this point, you're encouraged to seek a deeper understanding and read one or more of the books dedicated entirely to the C++ language that are focused on explaining its syntax and semantics. Of course, if you wish for a more precise, formal description, you can refer to the C++ standard or a reference book.

The following topics will be covered in this chapter:

- Templates in C++
- Class and function templates
- Template instantiations
- Template specializations
- Overloading of template functions
- Variadic templates
- Lambda expressions
- Concepts

Templates in C++

One of the greatest strengths of C++ is its support for generic programming. In generic programming, the algorithms and data structures are written in terms of generic types that will be specified later. This allows the programmer to implement a function or a class once, and later, instantiate it for many different types. Templates are a C++ feature that allows classes and functions to be defined on generic types. C++ supports three kinds of templates—function, class, and variable templates.

Function templates

Function templates are generic functions—unlike regular functions, a template function does not declare its argument types. Instead, the types are template parameters:

```
// Example 01
template <typename T>
T increment(T x) { return x + 1; }
```

This template function can be used to increment a value of any type by one, for which adding one is a valid operation:

```
increment(5);      // T is int, returns 6
increment(4.2);     // T is double, return 5.2 char c[10];
increment(c);      // T is char*, returns &c[1]
```

Most template functions have some limitations on the types that are used as their template parameters. For example, our `increment()` function requires that the expression $x + 1$ is valid for the type of x. Otherwise, the attempt to instantiate the template will fail, with a somewhat verbose compilation error.

Both non-member and class member functions can be function templates; however, virtual functions cannot be templates. The generic types can be used not only to declare function parameters but to declare any variables inside the body of the function:

```
template <typename T> T sum(T from, T to, T step) {
    T res = from;
    while ((from += step) < to) { res += from; }
    return res;
}
```

In C++20, simple template declarations can be abbreviated: instead of writing

```
template <typename T> void f(T t);
```

we can write

```
// Example 01a
void f(auto t);
```

Other than more terse declarations, there is no particular advantage to this abbreviation, and the feature is quite limited. First of all, `auto` can be used only as the "top-level" parameter type; for example, this is invalid (but allowed by some compilers):

```
void f(std::vector<auto>& v);
```

and must still be written as

```
template <typename T> void f(std::vector<T>& v);
```

Also, if you need to use template type parameters elsewhere in the function declaration, you can't abbreviate them:

```
template <typename T> T f(T t);
```

Of course, you could declare the return type as `auto` and use the trailing return type:

```
auto f(auto t) -> decltype(t);
```

but at this point, the template is not really "abbreviated."

We will see more of function templates later, but let's introduce class templates next.

Class templates

Class templates are classes that use generic types, usually to declare their data members, but also to declare methods and local variables inside them:

```
// Example 02
template <typename T> class ArrayOf2 {
  public:
  T& operator[](size_t i) { return a_[i]; }
  const T& operator[](size_t i) const { return a_[i]; }
  T sum() const { return a_[0] + a_[1]; }
  private:
  T a_[2];
};
```

This class is implemented once, and can then be used to define an array of two elements of any type:

```
ArrayOf2<int> i; i[0] = 1; i[1] = 5;
std::cout << i.sum();                      // 6
ArrayOf2<double> x; x[0] = -3.5; x[1] = 4;
std::cout << x.sum();                      // 0.5
ArrayOf2<char*> c; char s[] = "Hello";
c[0] = s; c[1] = s + 2;
```

Pay particular attention to the last example—you might expect the `ArrayOf2` template not to be valid with a type such as `char*`—after all, it has a method, `sum()`, that does not compile if the type of `a_[0]` and `a_[1]` is a pointer. However, our example compiles as written—a method of a class template does not have to be valid until we try to use it. If we never call `c.sum()`, then the fact that it would not compile never comes up, and the program remains valid. If we do call a member function that does not compile for the chosen template arguments, we get a syntax error in the body of the template (in our example, something about not being able to add two pointers). These error messages are rarely straightforward. Even if they were, it is unclear if the problem is in the body of the function, or if the function was not supposed to be called in the first place. Later in this chapter, we will see how to improve this situation.

Variable templates

The last kind of template in C++ is a variable template, which was introduced in C++14. This template allows us to define a variable with a generic type:

```
// Example 03
template <typename T> constexpr T pi =
T(3.14159265358979323846264338327950288419716939937510582097494459230
781L);
pi<float>;        // 3.141592
pi<double>;       // 3.141592653589793
```

Variable templates are, for the most part, very straightforward to use, mostly for defining your own constants, but there are some interesting patterns that take advantage of them; we will see one in the next section.

Non-type template parameters

Usually, template parameters are types, but C++ also allows for several kinds of non-type parameters. First of all, template parameters can be values of integer or enumeration types:

```
// Example 04
template <typename T, size_t N> class Array {
  public:
  T& operator[](size_t i) {
    if (i >= N) throw std::out_of_range("Bad index");
    return data_[i];
  }
  private:
  T data_[N];
};
Array<int, 5> a;        // OK
cin >> a[0];
Array<int, a[0]> b;     // Error
```

This is a template with two parameters—the first is a type, but the second is not. It is a value of type size_t that determines the size of the array; the advantage of such a template over a built-in C-style array is that it can do range checking. The C++ standard library has a std::array class template that should be used instead of implementing your own array in any real program, but it does make for an easy-to-follow example.

The values of non-type parameters that are used to instantiate a template must be compile-time constants or `constexpr` values—the last line in the preceding example is invalid because the value of a[0] is not known until the program reads it in at runtime. C++20 allows floating-point and user-defined types for non-type template parameters; until then, the parameters were limited to integral types, pointers (including function and member pointers), references, and enumerations. Of course, the value of a non-type parameter has to be a compile-time constant so, for example, pointers to local variables are not allowed.

The numeric template parameters used to be very popular in C++ because they allow complex compile-time calculations to be implemented, but in the recent versions of the standard, `constexpr` functions can be used to the same effect and are much easier to read. Of course, the standard takes with one hand and gives with the other, and so an interesting new use case emerged for non-template parameters combined with `constexpr` functions: these functions, first introduced in C++11, are used to define "immediate functions," or functions that are evaluated at compile time. The problem with `constexpr` functions is that they *may* evaluate at compile time but it's not required; they could also be evaluated at run time:

```
constexpr size_t length(const char* s) {
  size_t res = 0;
  while (*(s++)) ++res;
  return res;
}
std::cout << length("abc") << std::endl;
char s[] = "runtime";
std::cout << length(s) << std::endl;
```

Here we have a `constexpr` function `length()`. Does the length computation actually happen at compile time? There is no way to know short of examining the generated assembly code (which can differ from one compiler to another). The only way to be sure is to invoke the function in a compile-time context, for example:

```
static_assert(length("abc") == 3, ""); // OK
char s[] = "runtime";
static_assert(length(s) == 7, ""); // Fails
```

The first assert compiles, and the second does not even though the value 7 is correct: the argument is not a compile-time value, so the evaluation must happen at run time.

In C++20, the function may be declared `consteval` instead of `constexpr`: this guarantees that the evaluation happens at compile time or not at all (thus, the second `cout` statement in the preceding example will not compile). Prior to C++20, we have to get creative. Here is one way to enforce compile-time execution:

```
// Example 05c
template <auto V>
static constexpr auto force_consteval = V;
```

The `force_consteval` variable template can be used to enforce compile-time evaluation as follows:

```
std::cout << force_consteval<length("abc")> << std::endl;
char s[] = "runtime";
std::cout << force_consteval<length(s)> << std::endl;
```

The second `cout` statement does not compile because the function `length()` cannot be evaluated as an immediate function. The variable template `force_consteval` uses a non-type template parameter whose type is not specified but deduced from the template argument (an `auto` template parameter). This is a C++17 feature; in C++14 we have to use a rather unelegant macro to achieve the same result:

```
// Example 05d
template <typename T, T V>
static constexpr auto force_consteval_helper = V;
#define force_consteval(V)
force_consteval_helper<decltype(V), (V)>
std::cout << force_consteval(length("abc")) << std::endl;
```

If a non-type template parameter seems "less than a type," you will like the next option, a parameter that is definitely more than a simple type.

Template template parameters

The second kind of non-type template parameter worth mentioning is a *template template* parameter—a template parameter that is itself a template. We will need them in the later chapters of this book. This template parameter is substituted—not with a name of a class, but a name of an entire template.

Here is a class template with a template template parameter:

```
// Example 06a
template <typename T,
          template <typename> typename Container>
class Builder {
  Container<T> data_;
  public:
  void add(const T& t) { data_.push_back(t); }
  void print() const {
    for (const auto& x : data_) std::cout << x << " ";
    std::cout << std::endl;
  }
};
```

The `Builder` template declares a class that is used to construct (build) a container of an arbitrary type `T`. The container itself does not have a specific type, it's a template itself.

It can be instantiated with any container template that takes one type argument:

```
template <typename T> class my_vector { … };
Builder<int, my_vector> b;
b.add(1);
b.add(2);
b.print();
```

Of course, there are additional requirements on the `Container` template: it must have a single type parameter T (the rest may be defaulted), it should be default-constructible, it must have a `push_back()` method, and so on. C++20 gives us a concise way to state these requirements and make them a part of the template interface; we will learn about it later in this chapter, in the *Concepts* section.

Here is a function template that has two template template parameters:

```
// Example 06b
template <template <typename> class Out_container,
          template <typename> class In_container,
          typename T> Out_container<T>
resequence(const In_container<T>& in_container) {
  Out_container<T> out_container;
  for (auto x : in_container) {
    out_container.push_back(x);
  }
  return out_container;
}
```

This function takes an arbitrary container as an argument and returns another container, a different template, but instantiated on the same type, with the values copied from the input container:

```
my_vector<int> v { 1, 2, 3, 4, 5 };
template <typename T> class my_deque { … };
auto d = resequence<my_deque>(v);// my_deque with 1 … 5
```

Note that the compiler deduces both the type of the template argument (`In_container` as `my_vector`) and the type of its template parameter (T as int). Of course, the remaining template parameter `Out_container` cannot be deduced (it is not used in any parameters of the template function) and must be explicitly specified, which fits our intended use.

There is a major limitation on template template parameters that is made more complex by the fact that different compilers enforce it unevenly (i.e., some compilers let through the code that should not compile but you would really like to). The limitation is that the number of template parameters specified for the template template must match the number of the template parameters of the argument. Consider this template function:

```
template <template <typename> class Container, typename T>
void print(const Container<T>& container) {
```

```
    for (auto x : container) { std::cout << x << " "; }
    std::cout << std::endl;
}
std::vector<int> v { 1, 2, 3, 4, 5 };
print(v);
```

This code may compile, but it depends on the version of the standard and the compiler's strict adherence to the standard: the `std::vector` template has two template parameters, not one. The second parameter is the allocator; it has a default value, which is why we do not have to specify the allocator type when declaring a vector object. GCC, Clang, and MSVC all relax this requirement to some degree (but not to the same degree). Variadic templates, which we will see later in this chapter, offer another, more robust solution (at least in C++17 and later).

Templates are a kind of recipe for generating code. Next, we will see how we can convert these recipes into actual code we can run.

Template instantiations

The template name is not a type and cannot be used to declare a variable or call a function. To create a type or a function, the template must be instantiated. Most of the time, templates are instantiated implicitly when they are used. We will again start with function templates.

Function templates

To use a function template to generate a function, we have to specify which types should be used for all template type parameters. We can just specify the types directly:

```
template <typename T> T half(T x) { return x/2; }
int i = half<int>(5);
```

This instantiates the `half` function template with the `int` type. The type is explicitly specified; we could call the function with an argument of another type, as long as it is convertible to the type we requested:

```
double x = half<double>(5);
```

Even though the argument is an `int`, the instantiation is that of `half<double>`, and the return type is `double`. The integer value 5 is implicitly converted to `double`.

Even though every function template can be instantiated by specifying all its type parameters, this is rarely done. Most of the uses of function templates involve the automatic deduction of types. Consider the following:

```
auto x = half(8);     // int
auto y = half(1.5);    // double
```

The template type can be deduced only from the template function arguments—the compiler will attempt to select the type for the T parameter to match the type of the function argument that is declared with the same type. In our case, the function template has the argument x of the T type. Any call to this function has to provide some value for this argument, and this value must have a type. The compiler will deduce that T must be that type. In the first call in the preceding code block, the argument is 5, and its type is int. There is nothing better to do than to assume that T should be int in this particular template instantiation. Similarly, in the second call, we can deduce that T must be double.

After this deduction, the compiler performs type substitution: all other mentions of the T type are replaced by the type that was deduced; in our case, there is only one other use of T, which is the return type.

Template argument deduction is widely used to capture types that we cannot easily determine:

```
long x = ...;
unsigned int y = ...;
auto x = half(y + z);
```

Here, we deduce the T type to be whatever the type of the expression y + z is (it's long, but with template deduction, we don't need to specify that explicitly, and the deduced type will *follow* the argument type if we ever change the types of y and z). Consider the following example:

```
template <typename U> auto f(U);
half(f(5));
```

We deduce T to match whatever type the f() template function returns for an int argument (of course, the definition of the f() template function has to be provided before it can be called, but we do not need to dig into the header files where f() is defined, as the compiler will deduce the right type for us).

Only the types that are used to declare function arguments can be deduced. There is no rule that all template type parameters must be somehow present in the argument list, but any parameters that cannot be deduced must be explicitly specified:

```
template <typename U, typename V> U half(V x) {
    return x/2;
}
auto y = half<double>(8);
```

Here, the first template type parameter is explicitly specified, so U is double, and V is deduced to be int.

Sometimes, the compiler cannot deduce template type parameters, even if they are used to declare arguments:

```
template <typename T> T Max(T x, T y) {
    return (x > y) ? x : y;
```

```
}
auto x = Max(7L, 11); // Error
```

Here, we can deduce from the first argument that T must be long, but from the second argument, we deduce that T must be int. It is often surprising to programmers who learn their way around templates that the long type is not deduced in this case—after all, if we substitute long for T everywhere, the second argument will be implicitly converted, and the function will compile fine. So why isn't the *larger* type deduced? Because the compiler does not attempt to find a type for which all argument conversions are possible: after all, there is usually more than one such type. In our example, T could be double or unsigned long, and the function would still be valid. If a type can be deduced from more than one argument, the result of all these deductions must be the same.

Otherwise, the template instantiation is considered ambiguous.

The type deduction is not always as straightforward as using the type of the argument for a type parameter. The argument may be declared with a type that's more complex than a type parameter itself:

```
template <typename T> T decrement(T* p) {
    return --(*p);
}
int i = 7;
decrement(&i);      // i == 6
```

Here, the type of the argument is a *pointer to* int, but the type that is deduced for T is int. The deduction of types can be arbitrarily complex, as long as it's unambiguous:

```
template <typename T> T first(const std::vector<T>& v) {
    return v[0];
}
std::vector<int> v{11, 25, 67};
first(v);      // T is int, returns 11
```

Here, the argument is an instantiation of another template, std::vector, and we have to deduce the template parameter type from the type that was used to create this vector instantiation.

As we have seen, if a type can be deduced from more than one function argument, the result of these deductions must be the same. On the other hand, one argument can be used to deduce more than one type:

```
template <typename U, typename V>
std::pair<V, U> swap12(const std::pair<U, V>& x) {
    return std::pair<V, U>(x.second, x.first);
}
swap12(std::make_pair(7, 4.2)); // pair of 4.2, 7
```

Here, we deduce two types, U and V, from one argument, then use these two types to form a new type, std::pair<V, U>. This example is unnecessarily verbose, and we can take advantage of a few more C++ features to make it both more compact and easier to maintain. First of all, the standard already has a function that deduces the argument types and uses them to declare a pair, and we have even used this function—std::make_pair().

Secondly, the return type of the function can be deduced from the expression in the return statement (a C++14 feature). The rules of this deduction are similar to the rules of the template argument type deduction. With these simplifications, our example becomes the following:

```
template <typename U, typename V>
auto swap12(const std::pair<U, V>& x) {
  return std::make_pair(x.second, x.first);
}
```

Note that we don't explicitly use the types U and V anymore. We still need this function to be a template, since it operates on a generic type, that is, a pair of two types that we don't know until we instantiate the function. We could, however, use only one template parameter that would stand for the type of the argument:

```
template <typename T> auto swap12(const T& x) {
  return std::make_pair(x.second, x.first);
}
```

There is a significant difference between these two variants—the last function template will have its type deduced successfully from any call with one argument, no matter the type of that argument. If that argument is not std::pair, or, more generally, if the argument is not a class or a struct or it does not have the first and second data members, the deduction will still succeed, but the type substitution will fail. On the other hand, the previous version will not even be considered for arguments that are not a pair of some types. For any std::pair argument, the pair types are deduced, and the substitution should proceed without a problem. Can we use the last declaration and still restrict the type T to be a pair or another class with a similar interface? Yes, and we will see several ways to do so later in this book.

Member function templates are very similar to non-member function templates, and their arguments are similarly deduced. Member function templates can be used in classes or class templates, which we will review next.

Class templates

Instantiation of class templates is similar to that of function templates—the use of a template to create a type implicitly instantiates the template. To use a class template, we need to specify the type arguments for the template parameters:

```
template <typename N, typename D> class Ratio {
  public:
```

```
  Ratio() : num_(), denom_() {}
  Ratio(const N& num, const D& denom) :
    num_(num), denom_(denom) {}
  explicit operator double() const {
    return double(num_)/double(denom_);
  }
  private:
  N num_;
  D denom_;
};
Ratio<int, double> r;
```

The definition of the r variable implicitly instantiates the Ratio class template for the int and double types. It also instantiates the default constructor of this class. The second constructor is not used in this code and is not instantiated. It is this feature of class templates—instantiating a template instantiates all data members, but does not instantiate the methods until they are used—that allows us to write class templates where only some of the methods compile for certain types. If we use the second constructor to initialize the values of Ratio, then that constructor is instantiated, and must be valid for the given types:

```
Ratio<int, double> r(5, 0.1);
```

In C++17, these constructors can be used to deduce the types of the class template from the constructor arguments:

```
Ratio r(5, 0.1);
```

Of course, this works only if there are enough constructor arguments to deduce the types. For example, the default-constructed Ratio object has to be instantiated with explicitly specified types; there is simply no other way to deduce them. Prior to C++17, a helper function template was often used to construct an object whose type can be deduced from the arguments. Similarly to std::make_pair(), which we looked at previously, we can implement a make_ratio function that will do the same thing as the C++17 constructor argument deduction:

```
template <typename N, typename D>
Ratio<N, D> make_ratio(const N& num, const D& denom) {
  return { num, denom };
}
auto r(make_ratio(5, 0.1));
```

The C++17 way of deducing template arguments should be preferred, if it is available: it does not require writing another function that essentially duplicates the class constructor, and does not make an additional call to the copy or move constructor to initialize the object (although in practice most compilers will perform return value optimization and optimize away the call to the copy or move constructor).

When a template is used to generate a type, it is instantiated implicitly. Both class and function templates can be explicitly instantiated as well. Doing so instantiates a template without using it:

```
template class Ratio<long, long>;
template Ratio<long, long> make_ratio(const long&,
                                      const long&);
```

Explicit instantiations are rarely needed, and will not be used elsewhere in this book.

While instantiations of class templates with specific template parameters behave (mostly) like regular classes, static data members of class templates deserve special mention. First, let us recall the common challenge of static class data members: they must be defined somewhere, and only once:

```
// In the header:
class A {
  static int n;
};
// In a C file:
int A::n = 0;
std::cout << A::n;
```

Without such a definition, the program will not link: the name A::n is not defined. But if the definition is moved into the header and the header is included in several compilation units, the program also will not link, this time the name A::n is multiply defined.

The requirement to define static data members exactly once is not feasible for class templates: we need them defined for every set of template parameters the template is instantiated with, and we can't do that in any one compilation unit (other compilation units may instantiate the same template with different types). Fortunately, this is not necessary. Static members of class templates can (and should) be defined together with the template itself:

```
// In the header:
template <typename T> class A {
  static T n;
};
template <typename T> T A<T>::n {};
```

While this technically results in multiple definitions, it is the job of the linker to consolidate them so we are left with a single definition (there is only one value of a static member variable for all objects of the same type).

In C++17, inline variables offer a simpler solution:

```
// In the header:
template <typename T> class A {
  static inline T n {};
};
```

This also works for non-template classes:

```
// In the header:
class A {
  static inline int n = 0;
};
```

If the static data member of a class template has a non-trivial constructor, this constructor is invoked once for every instantiation of this template (not for every object – there is only one instance of a static member variable for all objects of the same type).

Class templates, as we have used them so far, allow us to declare generic classes, that is, classes that can be instantiated with many different types. So far, all of these classes look exactly the same, except for the types, and generate the same code. This is not always desirable—different types may need to be handled somewhat differently.

For example, let's say that we want to be able to represent not only a ratio of two numbers stored in the Ratio object but also a ratio of two numbers stored elsewhere, with the Ratio object containing pointers to these numbers. Clearly, some of the methods of the Ratio object, such as the conversion operator to double, need to be implemented differently if the object stores pointers to the numerator and denominator. In C++, this is accomplished by specializing the template, which we will do next.

Template specializations

Template specializations allow us to make the generated template code differently for some types— not just the same code with different types substituted, but completely different code. There are two kinds of template specializations in C++—explicit, or full, specializations and partial specialization. Let's start with the former.

Explicit specialization

Explicit template specialization defines a special version of the template for a particular set of types. In an explicit specialization, all generic types are replaced by specific, concrete types. Since an explicit specialization is not a generic class or function, it does not need to be instantiated later. For the same reason, it is sometimes called **full specialization**. If the generic types are fully substituted, there is nothing generic left. An explicit specialization should not be confused with an explicit template instantiation—while both create an instantiation of a template for a given set of type arguments, an explicit instantiation creates an instantiation of the generic code, with the generic types substituted by the specific types. An explicit specialization creates an instantiation of the function or class with the same name but it overrides the implementation, so the resulting code can be completely different. An example should help us understand this distinction.

Let's start with a class template. Let's say that, if both the numerator and the denominator of `Ratio` are `double`, we want to compute the ratio and store it as a single number. The generic `Ratio` code should remain the same, but for one particular set of types, we want the class to look entirely different. We can do this with an explicit specialization:

```
template <> class Ratio<double, double> {
  public:
  Ratio() : value_() {}
  template <typename N, typename D>
    Ratio(const N& num, const D& denom) :
      value_(double(num)/double(denom)) {}
  explicit operator double() const { return value_; }
  private:
  double value_;
};
```

Both template type parameters are specified to be `double`. The class implementation is totally unlike the generic version—instead of two data members, we have just one; the conversion operator simply returns the value, and the constructor now computes the ratio of the numerator and the denominator. But it is not even the same constructor—instead of the non-template constructor `Ratio(const double&, const double&)` that the generic version would have if it was instantiated for two `double` template arguments, we provided a template constructor that can take two arguments of any types as long as they are convertible to `double`.

Sometimes, we don't need to specialize the whole class template, because most of the generic code is still applicable. However, we may want to change the implementation of one or a few member functions. We can explicitly specialize the member function as well:

```
template <> Ratio<float, float>::operator double() const {
  return num_/denom_;
}
```

Template functions can be explicitly specialized as well. Again, unlike an explicit instantiation, we get to write the body of the function, and we can implement it any way we want:

```
template <typename T> T do_something(T x) {
  return ++x;
}
template <> double do_something<double>(double x) {
  return x/2;
}
do_something(3);        // 4
do_something(3.0);    // 1.5
```

We cannot, however, change the number or the types of arguments or the return type—they must match the result of the substitution of the generic types, so the following does not compile:

```
template <> long do_something<int>(int x) { return x*x; }
```

An explicit specialization must be declared before the first use of the template that would cause an implicit instantiation of the generic template for the same types. This makes sense—the implicit instantiation would create a class or a function with the same name and the same types as the explicit specialization. We would now have two versions of the same class or function in the program, and this violates the one definition rule and makes the program ill-formed (the exact rules can be found in the standard under *[basic.def.odr]*).

Explicit specializations are useful when we have one or a few types for which we need the template to behave very differently. However, this does not solve our problem with the ratio of pointers—we want a specialization that is still *somewhat generic*, that is, it can handle pointers to any types, just not any other types. This is accomplished by a partial specialization, which we will look at next.

Partial specialization

Now, we are getting to the really interesting part of C++ template programming—partial template specializations. When a class template is partially specialized, it remains as generic code, but *less generic* than the original template. The simplest form of a partial template is one where some of the generic types are replaced by concrete types, but other types remain generic:

```
template <typename N, typename D> class Ratio {
  .....
};
template <typename D> class Ratio<double, D> {
  public:
  Ratio() : value_() {}
  Ratio(const double& num, const D& denom) :
    value_(num/double(denom)) {}
  explicit operator double() const { return value_; }
  private:
  double value_;
};
```

Here, we convert Ratio to a double value if the numerator is double, regardless of the denominator type. More than one partial specialization can be defined for the same template. For example, we can also specialize for the case when the denominator is double and the numerator is anything:

```
template <typename N> class Ratio<N, double> {
  public:
  Ratio() : value_() {}
  Ratio(const N& num, const double& denom) :
```

```
    value_(double(num)/denom) {}
  explicit operator double() const { return value_; }
  private:
  double value_;
};
```

When the template is instantiated, the best specialization for the given set of types is selected. In our case, if neither the numerator nor the denominator is `double`, then the general template has to be instantiated—there are no other choices. If the numerator is `double`, then the first partial specialization is a better (more specific) match than the general template. If the denominator is `double`, then the second partial specialization is a better match. But what happens if both terms are `double`? In this case, the two partial specializations are equivalent; neither is more specific than the other. This situation is considered ambiguous and the instantiation fails. Note that only this particular instantiation, `Ratio<double, double>`, fails—it is not an error (at least, not a syntax error) to define both specializations, but it is an error to request an instantiation that cannot be uniquely resolved to the narrowest specialization. To allow any instantiation of our template, we have to remove this ambiguity, and the only way to do that is to provide an even more narrow specialization that would be preferred over the other two. In our case, there is only one option—a full specialization for `Ratio<double, double>`:

```
template <> class Ratio<double, double> {
  public:
  Ratio() : value_() {}
  template <typename N, typename D>
    Ratio(const N& num, const D& denom) :
      value_(double(num)/double(denom)) {}
  explicit operator double() const { return value_; }
  private:
  double value_;
};
```

Now, the fact that the partial specializations are ambiguous for the instantiation of `Ratio<double, double>` is no longer relevant—we have a more specific version of the template than either of them, so that version is preferred over both.

Partial specializations do not have to specify some of the generic types fully. Therefore, can keep all types generic, but impose some restrictions on them. For example, we still want a specialization where both the numerator and the denominator are pointers. They can be pointers to anything, so they are generic types, but *less generic* than the arbitrary types of the general template:

```
template <typename N, typename D> class Ratio<N*, D*> {
  public:
  Ratio(N* num, D* denom) : num_(num), denom_(denom) {}
  explicit operator double() const {
    return double(*num_)/double(*denom_);
```

```
    }
    private:
    N* const num_;
    D* const denom_;
};
int i = 5; double x = 10;
auto r(make_ratio(&i, &x));        // Ratio<int*, double*>
double(r);                // 0.5
x = 2.5;
double(r);                // 2
```

This partial specialization still has two generic types, but they are both pointer types, N* and D*, for any N and D types. The implementation is totally unlike that of the general template. When instantiated with two pointer types, the partial specialization is *more specific* than the general template and is considered a better match. Note that, in our example, the denominator is double. So why isn't a partial specialization for the double denominator considered? That is because, while the denominator is double as far as the program logic is concerned, technically it is double*, a completely different type, and we do not have a specialization for that.

To define a specialization, a general template must first be declared. It does not, however, need to be defined—it is possible to specialize a template that does not exist in the general case. To do so, we must forward-declare the general template, then define all the specializations we need:

```
template <typename T> class Value; // Declaration
template <typename T> class Value<T*> {
  public:
  explicit Value(T* p) : v_(*p) {} private:
  T v_;
};
template <typename T> class Value<T&> {
  public:
  explicit Value(T& p) : v_(p) {}
  private:
  T v_;
};
int i = 5; int* p = &i; int& r = i;
Value<int*> v1(p); // T* specialization
Value<int&> v2(r); // T& specialization
```

Here, we have no general Value template, but we have partial specializations for any pointer or reference types. If we try to instantiate the template on some other type, like int, we will get an error stating that the Value<int> type is incomplete—this is no different than trying to define an object with only a forward declaration of the class.

So far, we have seen only examples of partial specializations for class templates. Unlike the earlier discussion of full specializations, we have not seen a single function specialization here. There is a very good reason for that—a partial function template specialization does not exist in C++. What is sometimes incorrectly called a partial specialization is nothing more than overloading template functions. On the other hand, overloading template functions can get quite complex and is worth learning about—we will cover this next.

Template function overloading

We are used to regular functions, or class methods, being overloaded—multiple functions with the same name have different parameter types. Each call invokes the function with the best match of the parameter types to the call arguments, as shown in the following example:

```
// Example 07
void whatami(int x) {
  std::cout << x << " is int" << std::endl;
}
void whatami(long x) {
  std::cout << x << " is long" << std::endl;
}
whatami(5);      // 5 is int
whatami(5.0);     // Compilation error
```

If the arguments are a perfect match for one of the overloaded functions with the given name, that function is called. Otherwise, the compiler considers conversions to the parameter types of the available functions. If one of the functions offers *better* conversions, that function is selected. Otherwise, the call is ambiguous, just as in the last line of the preceding example. The precise definition of what constitutes the *best* conversion can be found in the standard (see the section *Overloading*, more specifically, subsection *[over.match]*). Generally, the *cheapest* conversions are the ones such as adding const or removing a reference; then, there are conversions between built-in types, conversions from derived to base class pointers, and so on. In the case of multiple arguments, each argument for the chosen function must have the best conversion. There is no *voting*—if a function has three arguments, and two are an exact match for the first overload, while the third one is an exact match for the second overload, then even if the remaining arguments are implicitly convertible to their corresponding parameter types, the overloaded call is ambiguous.

The presence of templates makes the overload resolution much more complex. Multiple function templates with the same name and, possibly, the same number of arguments, can be defined, in addition to non-template functions. All of these functions are the candidates for an overloaded function call, but the function templates can generate functions with different parameter types, so how do we decide what the actual overloaded functions are? The exact rules are even more complex than the ones for non-template functions, but the basic idea is this—if there is a non-template function that is a near-perfect match to the call arguments, that function is selected. The standard, of course, uses much more precise terms than *near-perfect*, but *trivial* conversions, such as adding const, fall under that category—you get them *at no cost*. If there is no such function, the compiler will attempt to instantiate all function templates with the same name to a near-perfect match, using the template argument deduction. If exactly one of the templates was instantiated, the function created by this instantiation is called. Otherwise, overload resolution continues the usual way among the non-template functions.

This is a very simplified description of a very complex process, but there are two important points—firstly, if there is an equally good match of a call to a template and a non-template function, the non-template function is preferred, and secondly, the compiler does not attempt to instantiate the function templates into something that might be convertible to the types we need. The template functions must match the call almost perfectly after the argument type deduction, or they are not called at all. Let's add a template to our previous example:

```
void whatami(int x); // Same as above
void whatami(long x); // Same as above
template <typename T> void whatami(T* x) {
  std::cout << x << " is a pointer" << std::endl;
}
int i = 5;
whatami(i);     // 5 is int
whatami(&i);    // 0x???? is a pointer
```

Here, we have what looks like a partial specialization of a function template. But it really isn't—it is just a function template—there is no general template for which it could be a specialization. Instead, it is simply a function template whose type parameter is deduced from the same arguments, but using different rules. The template can have its type deduced if the argument is a pointer of any kind. This includes a pointer to const—T could be a const type, so if we call whatami(ptr), where ptr is const int*, that first template overload is a perfect match when T is const int. If the deduction succeeds, the function generated by the template, that is, the template instantiation, is added to the overload set.

For the int* argument, it is the only overload that works, so it is called. But what happens if more than one function template can match the call, and both instantiations are valid overloads? Let's add one more template:

```
void whatami(int x); // Same as above
void whatami(long x); // Same as above
template <typename T> void whatami(T* x); // Same as above
template <typename T> void whatami(T&& x) {
  std::cout << "Something weird" << std::endl;
}
class C {    };
C c;
whatami(c);     // Something weird
whatami(&c);    // 0x???? is a pointer
```

This template function accepts its arguments by the universal reference, so it can be instantiated for any call to whatami() with one argument. The first call, whatami(c), is easy—the last overload, with T&&, is the only one that can be called. There are no conversions from c to a pointer or an integer. But the second call is tricky—we have not one, but two template instantiations that are a perfect match for the call, with no conversions needed. So why is this not an ambiguous overload? Because the rules for resolving overloaded function templates are different than the rules for non-template functions and resemble the rules for selecting the partial specialization of a class template (which is another reason why function template overloads are often confused with partial specializations). The template that is more specific is a better match.

In our case, the first template is more specific—it can accept any pointer argument, but only pointers. The second template can accept any argument at all, so any time the first template is a possible match, the second is too, but not the reverse. If a more specific template can be used to instantiate a function that is a valid overload, then this template is used.

Otherwise, we have to fall back to the more general template.

The very general template functions in the overload set sometimes lead to unexpected results. Let's say we have the following three overloads for int, double, and anything:

```
void whatami(int x) {
    std::cout << x << " is int" << std::endl;
}
void whatami(double x) {
    std::cout << x << " is double" << std::endl;
}
template <typename T> void whatami(T&& x) {
    std::cout << "Something weird" << std::endl;
}
int i = 5;
float x = 4.2;
whatami(i);     // i is int
whatami(x);     // Something weird
whatami(1.2);    // 1.2 is double
```

The first call has an int argument, so whatami(int) is a perfect match. The second call would have gone to whatami(double) if we did not have the template overload—the conversion from float to double is implicit (so is the conversion from float to int, but the conversion to double is preferred). But it's still a conversion, so when the function template instantiates to a perfect match of whatami(float&&), that is the best match and the chosen overload. The last call has a double argument, and again we have a perfect match to a non-template function whatami(double), so it is preferred over any alternative.

It should be noted that overloading pass-by-value and pass-by-reference functions for the same parameter types often creates ambiguities in overload resolution. For example, these two functions are almost always ambiguous:

```
template <typename T> void whatami(T&& x) {
    std::cout << "Something weird" << std::endl;
}
template <typename T> void whatami(T x) {
    std::cout << "Something copyable" << std::endl;
}
class C {};
C c;
whatami(c);
```

As long as the argument to the function can be copied (and our object c is copyable), the overload is ambiguous and the call will not compile. The problem does not happen when a more specific function overloads a more general one (in all our previous examples, whatami(int) used pass-by-value with no problems), but mixing the two types of parameter passing for similarly general functions is inadvisable.

Finally, there is one more kind of function that has a special place in the overload resolution order—a variadic function.

A variadic function is declared with ... instead of arguments, and it can be called with any number of arguments of any type (printf is one such function). This function is the overload of the last resort—it is called only if no other overloads can be used:

```
void whatami(...) {
    std::cout << "It's something or somethings" << std::endl;
}
```

As long as we have the overload whatami(T&& x) available, a variadic function will never be the preferred overload, at least not for any calls to whatami() with one argument. Without that template, whatami(...) is called for any argument that is not a number or a pointer. The variadic functions were around since the days of C, and are not to be confused with variadic templates that were introduced in C++11, and this is what we'll talk about next.

Variadic templates

Probably the greatest difference between generic programming in C and C++ is type safety. It is possible to write generic code in C—the standard function qsort() is a perfect example—it can sort values of any type and they are passed in using a void* pointer, which can really be a pointer to any type. Of course, the programmer has to know what the real type is and cast the pointer to the right type. In a generic C++ program, the types are either explicitly specified or deduced at the time of the instantiation, and the type system for generic types is as strong as it is for regular types. Unless we want a function with an unknown number of arguments, that is, prior to C++11, the only way was the old C-style variadic functions where the compiler had no idea what the argument types were; the programmer just had to know and unpack the variable arguments correctly.

C++11 introduced the modern equivalent to a variadic function—a variadic template. We can now declare a generic function with any number of arguments:

```
template <typename ... T> auto sum(const T& ... x);
```

This function takes one or more arguments, possibly of different types, and computes their sum. The return type is not easy to determine, but, fortunately, we can let the compiler figure it out—we just declare the return type as auto. How do we actually implement the function to add up the unknown number of values whose types we can't name, not even as generic types? In C++17, it's easy, because it has fold expressions:

```
// Example 08a
template <typename ... T> auto sum(const T& ... x) {
  return (x + ...);
}
sum(5, 7, 3);            // 15, int
sum(5, 7L, 3);           // 15, long
sum(5, 7L, 2.9);         // 14.9, double
```

You can verify that the type of the result is what we say it is:

```
static_assert(std::is_same_v<
  decltype(sum(5, 7L, 2.9)), double>);
```

In C++14, as well as in C++17, when a fold expression is not sufficient (and they are useful only in limited contexts, mostly when the arguments and combines using binary or unary operators), the standard technique is recursion, which is ever-popular in template programming:

```
// Example 08b
template <typename T1> auto sum(const T1& x1) {
  return x1;
}
template <typename T1, typename ... T>
auto sum(const T1& x1, const T& ... x) {
  return x1 + sum(x ...);
}
```

The first overload (not a partial specialization!) is for the sum() function with one argument of any type. That value is returned. The second overload is for more than one argument, and the first argument is explicitly added to the sum of the remaining arguments. The recursion continues until there is only one argument left, at which point the other overload is called and the recursion stops. This is the standard technique for unraveling the parameter packs in variadic templates, and we will see this many times in this book. The compiler will inline all the recursive function calls and generate straightforward code that adds all arguments together.

The class templates can also be variadic—they have an arbitrary number of type arguments and can build classes from a varying number of objects of different types. The declaration is similar to that of a function template. For example, let's build a class template, `Group`, that can hold any number of objects of different types and return the right object when it's converted to one of the types it holds:

```cpp
// Example 09
template <typename ... T> struct Group;
```

The usual implementation of such templates is again recursive, using deeply nested inheritance, although a non-recursive implementation is sometimes possible. We will see one in the next section. The recursion has to be terminated when there is only one type parameter left. This is done using a partial specialization, so we will leave the general template we showed previously as a declaration only, and define a specialization for one type parameter:

```cpp
template <typename ... T> struct Group;
template <typename T1> struct Group<T1> {
  T1 t1_;
  Group() = default;
  explicit Group(const T1& t1) : t1_(t1) {}
  explicit Group(T1&& t1) : t1_(std::move(t1)) {}
  explicit operator const T1&() const { return t1_; }
  explicit operator T1&() { return t1_; }
};
```

This class holds the value of one type, `T1`, initializes it by copy or move and returns a reference to it when converted to the `T1` type. The specialization for an arbitrary number of type parameters contains the first one as a data member, together with the corresponding initialization and conversion methods, and inherits from the `Group` class template of the remaining types:

```cpp
template <typename T1, typename ... T>
struct Group<T1, T ...> : Group<T ...> {
  T1 t1_;
  Group() = default;
  explicit Group(const T1& t1, T&& ... t) :
    Group<T ...>(std::forward<T>(t) ...), t1_(t1) {}
  explicit Group(T1&& t1, T&& ... t) :
    Group<T...>(std::forward<T>(t)...),
                t1_(std::move(t1)) {}
  explicit operator const T1&() const { return t1_; }
  explicit operator T1&() { return t1_; }
};
```

For every type contained in a `Group` class, there are two possible ways it can be initialized—copy or move. Fortunately, we do not have to spell out the constructors for every combination of copy and move operations. Instead, we have two versions of the constructor for the two ways to initialize the first argument (the one stored in the specialization); we use perfect forwarding for the remaining arguments.

Now, we can use our `Group` class template to hold some values of different types (it cannot handle multiple values of the same type since the attempt to retrieve this type would be ambiguous):

```
Group<int, long> g(3, 5);
int(g);      // 3
long(g);     // 5
```

It is rather inconvenient to write all the group types explicitly and to make sure they match the argument types. In C++17, we can use a deduction guide to enable class template parameter deduction from the constructor:

```
template <typename ... T> Group(T&&... t) -> Group<T...>;
Group g(3, 2.2, std::string("xyz"));
int(g);                // 3
double(g);             // 2.2
std::string(g);        // "xyz"
```

Before C++17, the usual solution to this problem is to use a helper function template (a variadic template, of course) to take advantage of the template argument deduction:

```
template <typename ... T> auto makeGroup(T&& ... t) {
    return Group<T ...>(std::forward<T>(t) ...);
}
auto g = makeGroup(3, 2.2, std::string("xyz"));
```

Note that the C++ standard library contains a class template, `std::tuple`, which is a much more complete and full-featured version of our `Group`.

Variadic templates can have non-type parameters as well; in this case, the `makeGroup` template can be instantiated with an arbitrary number of arguments. Often, these non-type parameter packs are used in combination with `auto` (deduced) types. For example, here is a template that holds a list of compile-time constant values of different types:

```
// Example 10
template <auto... Values> struct value_list {};
```

Without `auto` (i.e., prior to C++17) it is almost impossible to declare such a template since the types must be explicitly specified. Note that this is the entire template: it holds the constant values as a part of its definition. To extract them, we need another variadic template:

```
template <size_t N, auto... Values>
struct nth_value_helper;
```

```
template <size_t n, auto v1, auto... Values>
struct nth_value_helper<n, v1, Values...> {
  static constexpr auto value =
    nth_value_helper<n - 1, Values...>::value;
};
template <auto v1, auto... Values>
struct nth_value_helper<0, v1, Values...> {
  static constexpr auto value = v1;
};
template <size_t N, auto... Values>
constexpr auto nth_value(value_list<Values...>) {
  return nth_value_helper<N, Values...>::value;
}
```

The template function `nth_value` deduces the parameter pack `Values` from the type of the `value_list` argument (the argument itself contains no data and is of no interest except for its type). A recursive instantiation of partial class specializations is then used to iterate over the parameter pack until we get to the N-th value. Note that to store floating-point constants in this manner, we need C++20.

Variadic templates can be used in combination with template template parameters to resolve some of the problems created when, for example, standard library containers are used as arguments substituted for template template parameters. A simple solution is to declare the parameter as taking any number of types:

```
template <template <typename...> class Container,
          typename... T>
void print(const Container<T...>& container);
std::vector<int> v{ … };
print(v);
```

Note that the `std::vector` template has two type parameters. In C++17, a standard change made this a valid match for the parameter pack specified in the `Container` template template parameter. Most compilers allowed such matches even earlier.

The variadic templates, especially combined with perfect forwarding, are extremely useful for writing very general template classes—for example, a vector can contain objects of an arbitrary type, and, to construct these objects in place instead of copying them, we have to call constructors with a different number of arguments. When the vector template is written, there is no way to know how many arguments are needed to initialize the objects the vector will contain, so a variadic template has to be used (indeed, the in-place constructors of `std::vector`, such as `emplace_back`, are variadic templates).

There is one more kind of template-like entity in C++ that we have to mention, one that has the appearance of both a class and a function—a lambda expression. The next section is dedicated to this.

Lambda expressions

In C++, the regular function syntax is extended with the concept of a *callable*, short for *callable entity*—a callable is something that can be called in the same way as a function. Some examples of callables are functions (of course), function pointers, or objects with the `operator()`, also known as **functors**:

```
void f(int i); struct G {
  void operator()(int i);
};
f(5);            // Function
G g; g(5);       // Functor
```

It is often useful to define a callable entity in a local context, right next to the place it is used. For example, to sort a sequence of objects, we may want to define a custom comparison function. We can use an ordinary function for this:

```
bool compare(int i, int j) { return i < j; }
void do_work() {
  std::vector<int> v;
  .....
  std::sort(v.begin(), v.end(), compare);
}
```

However, in C++, functions cannot be defined inside other functions, so our `compare()` function may have to be defined quite far from the place it is used. If it is a single-use comparison function, such separation is inconvenient and reduces the readability and maintainability of the code.

There is a way around this limitation—while we cannot declare functions inside functions, we can declare classes, and classes can be callable:

```
void do_work() {
  std::vector<int> v;
  .....
  struct compare {
    bool operator()(int i, int j) const { return i < j; }
  };
  std::sort(v.begin(), v.end(), compare());
}
```

This is compact and local, but rather verbose. We do not actually need to give this class a name, and we only ever want one instance of this class. In C++11, we have a much better option, the lambda expression:

```
void do_work() {
  std::vector<int> v;
  .....
  auto compare = [](int i, int j) { return i < j; };
```

```
    std::sort(v.begin(), v.end(), compare);
}
```

If we use this comparison function for just one call to `std::sort`, we don't even need to give it a name and can define it inside the call:

```
std::sort(v.begin(), v.end(),
          [](int i, int j) { return i < j; });
```

This is as compact as it gets. The return type can be specified, but can usually be deduced by the compiler. The lambda expression creates an object, so it has a type, but that type is generated by the compiler, so the object declaration must use `auto`.

The lambda expressions are objects, so they can have data members. Of course, a local callable class can also have data members. Usually, they are initialized from the local variables in the containing scope:

```
// Example 11
void do_work() {
  std::vector<double> v;
  . . . . .
  struct compare_with_tolerance {
    const double tolerance;
    explicit compare_with_tolerance(double tol) :
      tolerance(tol) {}
    bool operator()(double x, double y) const {
      return x < y && std::abs(x - y) > tolerance;
    }
  };
  double tolerance = 0.01;
  std::sort(v.begin(), v.end(),
            compare_with_tolerance(tolerance));
}
```

Again, this is a very verbose way to do something simple. We have to mention the tolerance variable three times—as a data member, a constructor argument, and in the member initialization list. A lambda expression makes this code simpler as well because it can capture local variables. In local classes, we are not allowed to reference variables from the containing scope, except by passing them through the constructor arguments, but for lambda expressions, the compiler automatically generates a constructor to capture all local variables mentioned in the body of the expression:

```
void do_work() {
  std::vector<double> v;
  . . . . .
  double tolerance = 0.01;
  auto compare_with_tolerance = [=](auto x, auto y) {
    return x < y && std::abs(x - y) > tolerance;
```

```
  };
  std::sort(v.begin(), v.end(), compare_with_tolerance);
}
```

Here, the name `tolerance` inside the lambda expression refers to the local variable with the same name. The variable is captured by value, which is specified in the lambda expression's capture clause `[=]`. We could have captured by reference using `[&]` like this:

```
auto compare_with_tolerance = [&](auto x, auto y) {
  return x < y && std::abs(x - y) > tolerance;
};
```

The difference is that, when capturing by value, a copy of the captured variable is created inside the lambda object at the point where it is constructed. This local copy is `const` by default, although we can declare the lambda mutable, which would let us change the captured values:

```
double tolerance = 0.01;
size_t count = 0; // line 2
auto compare_with_tolerance = [=](auto x, auto y) mutable {
  std::cout << "called " << ++count << " times\n";
  return x < y && std::abs(x - y) > tolerance;
};
std::vector<double> v;
… store values in v …
// Counts calls but does not change the value on line 2
std::sort(v.begin(), v.end(), compare_with_tolerance);
```

On the other hand, capturing the variables from the outer scope by reference makes every mention of this variable inside the lambda a reference to the original variable. Values captured by reference can be changed:

```
double tolerance = 0.01;
size_t count = 0;
auto compare_with_tolerance = [&](auto x, auto y) mutable {
  ++count; // Changes count above
  return x < y && std::abs(x - y) > tolerance;
};
std::vector<double> v;
… store values in v …
std::sort(v.begin(), v.end(), compare_with_tolerance);
std::cout << "lambda called " << count << " times\n";
```

It is also possible to explicitly capture some variables by value or by reference; for example, the capture `[=, &count]` captures everything by value except `count`, which is captured by reference.

Instead of changing the arguments of the lambda expression from int in the earlier example to double, we can declare them as auto, which effectively makes the operator() of the lambda expression a template (this is a C++14 feature).

Lambda expressions are most commonly used as local functions. However, they are not really functions; they are callable objects, and so they are missing one feature that functions have—the ability to overload them. The last trick we will learn in this section is how to work around that and create an overload set from lambda expressions.

First, the main idea—it is indeed impossible to overload callable objects. On the other hand, it is very easy to overload several operator() methods in the same object—methods are overloaded like any other function. Of course, the operator() of a lambda expression object is generated by the compiler, not declared by us, so it is not possible to force the compiler to generate more than one operator() in the same lambda expression. But classes have their own advantages, the main one being that we can inherit from them.

Lambda expressions are objects—their types are classes, so we can inherit from them too. If a class inherits publicly from a base class, all public methods of the base class become public methods of the derived class. If a class inherits publicly from several base classes (multiple inheritance), its public interface is formed from all the public methods of all the base classes. If there are multiple methods with the same name in this set, they become overloaded and the usual overloading resolution rules apply (in particular, it is possible to create an ambiguous set of overloads, in which case the program will not compile).

So, we need to create a class that automatically inherits from any number of base classes. We have just seen the right tool for that—variadic templates. As we have learned in the previous section, the usual way to iterate over an arbitrary number of items in the parameter pack of a variadic template is through recursion:

```
// Example 12a
template <typename ... F> struct overload_set;
template <typename F1>
struct overload_set<F1> : public F1 {
  overload_set(F1&& f1) : F1(std::move(f1)) {}
  overload_set(const F1& f1) : F1(f1) {}
  using F1::operator();
};
template <typename F1, typename ... F>
struct overload_set<F1, F ...> :
    public F1, public overload_set<F ...> {
  overload_set(F1&& f1, F&& ... f) :
    F1(std::move(f1)),
    overload_set<F ...>(std::forward<F>(f) ...) {}
  overload_set(const F1& f1, F&& ... f) :
    F1(f1), overload_set<F ...>(std::forward<F>(f) ...) {}
```

```
   using F1::operator();
   using overload_set<F ...>::operator();
};
template <typename ... F> auto overload(F&& ... f) {
   return overload_set<F ...>(std::forward<F>(f) ...);
}
```

The overload_set is a variadic class template; the general template has to be declared before we can specialize it, but it has no definition. The first definition is for the special case of only one lambda expression—the overload_set class inherits from the lambda expression and adds its operator() to its public interface. The specialization for N lambda expressions (N>1) inherits from the first one and from the overload_set constructed from the remaining N-1 lambda expressions. Finally, we have a helper function that constructs the overload set from any number of lambda expressions—in our case, this is a necessity and not mere convenience since we cannot explicitly specify the types of the lambda expressions, but have to let the function template deduce them. Now, we can construct an overload set from any number of lambda expressions:

```
int i = 5;
double d = 7.3;
auto l = overload(
   [] (int* i) { std::cout << "i=" << *i << std::endl; },
   [] (double* d) { std::cout << "d=" << *d << std::endl; }
);
l(&i);     // i=5
l(&d);     // d=5.3
```

This solution is not perfect, because it does not handle ambiguous overloads well. In C++17, we can do better, and it gives us a chance to demonstrate an alternative way of using a parameter pack that does not need recursion. Here is the C++17 version:

```
// Example 12b
template <typename ... F>
struct overload_set : public F ... {
   overload_set(F&& ... f) : F(std::forward<F>(f)) ... {}
   using F::operator() ...;     // C++17
};
template <typename ... F> auto overload(F&& ... f) {
   return overload_set<F ...>(std::forward<F>(f) ...);
}
```

The variadic template does not rely on partial specializations anymore; instead, it inherits directly from the parameter pack (this part of the implementation works in C++14 as well, but the using declaration needs C++17). The template helper function is the same—it deduces the types of all lambda expressions and constructs an object from the overload_set instantiation with these types. The lambda expressions themselves are passed to the base classes using perfect forwarding, where they are used to initialize all the base objects of the `overload_set` objects (lambda expressions are movable). Without the need for recursion or partial specialization, this is a much more compact and straightforward template. Its use is identical to the previous version of `overload_set`, but it handles near-ambiguous overloads better.

We can get rid of the template function as well and use template deduction guides:

```
// Example 12c
template <typename ... F>
struct overload : public F ... {
  using F::operator() ...;
};
template <typename ... F> // Deduction guide
overload(F&& ... ) -> overload<F ...>;
```

The use of the `overload` template remains largely unchanged; note the curly braces used to construct an object:

```
int i = 5;
double d = 7.3;
auto l = overload{
  [](int* i) { std::cout << "i=" << *i << std::endl; },
  [](double* d) { std::cout << "d=" << *d << std::endl; },
};
l(&i);    // i=5
l(&d);    // d=5.3
```

We will see lambdas used extensively in later chapters of this book when we will need to write a fragment of code and attach it to an object so that it can be executed later.

Next, we are going to learn about a new C++ feature that, in a way, does the opposite of what we were trying to do so far: it makes templates *less* general. As we have seen already, it is easy to over-promise with a template: we can define templates whose definitions then do not compile in some cases. It would be better to make any restrictions on the template arguments to be a part of the declaration, so let us see how that is done.

Concepts

C++20 introduced a major enhancement to the C++ template machinery: concepts.

In C++20, templates (both class and function templates), as well as non-template functions (members of class templates, usually) may use a constraint to specify the requirements on template arguments. These constraints are useful to produce better error messages, but they are truly indispensable when there is a need to select a function overload or a template specialization based on some properties of template arguments.

The basic syntax for a constraint is quite simple: a constraint is introduced by the keyword `requires` which can be specified after the function declaration or before the return type (in this book, we use both ways interchangeably so the reader becomes familiar with different styles of writing code). The expression itself usually uses the template parameters and must evaluate to a boolean value, for example:

```
// Example 13a
template <typename T> T copy(T&& t)
   requires (sizeof(T) > 1)
{
   return std::forward<T>(t);
}
```

Here the function `copy()` requires that the type of its argument has a size of at least two bytes. If we attempt to call this function with a `char` argument, the call will not compile. Note that if a constraint is violated, it is as if the function did not exist for the purposes of a particular call: if there is another overload, it will be considered next even if, without the constraint, the overloads were ambiguous.

Here is a more complex (and more useful) example:

```
template <typename T1, typename T2>
std::common_type_t<T1, T2> min2(T1&& t1, T2&& t2)
{
   if (t1 < t2) return std::forward<T1>(t1);
   return std::forward<T2>(t2);
}
```

This is a function similar to `std::min`, except it takes two arguments of different types. This creates two potential issues: first, what is the return type? The return value is one of the two arguments, but there has to be a single return type. We can use the `std::common_type` trait from the `<type_traits>` header as a reasonable answer: for numeric types, it does the usual type promotion, for classes, it converts from base class to derived class if possible, and it respects implicit user-specified conversions. But there is a second problem: if the expression `t1 < t2` does not compile, we get an error in the body of the function. This is unfortunate because the error is hard to analyze and may be misleading: it suggests that the body of the function is implemented incorrectly. We can address the second concern by adding a static assert:

```
static_assert(sizeof(t1 < t2) > 0);
```

This at least makes clear that we intended for the code to not compile if there is no matching `operator<()`. Note the weird way we had to formulate the assert: the expression `t1 < t2` itself must, in general, evaluate at run time, and is just as likely to be false. We need a compile-time value, and we don't care which argument is less, just that they can be compared. So we assert something not about the result of the comparison but about the size of this result: `sizeof()` is always a compile-time value and the size of anything is at least 1 in C++. The only way this assertion can fail is if the expression does not compile at all.

This still does not solve the other part of the problem: the requirement on the argument types is not included in the interface of the function. The function can be called on any two types and then may or may not compile. With C++20 constraints, we can move the requirement from the implicit (compilation failure) or explicit (static assert) error in the function body to the function declaration and make it part of the function interface:

```
// Example 13b
template <typename T1, typename T2>
std::common_type_t<T1, T2> min2 (T1&& t1, T2&& t2)
  requires (sizeof(t1 < t2) > 0)
{
  if (t1 < t2) return std::forward<T1>(t1);
  return std::forward<T2>(t2);
}
```

As you learn to build more complex constraints, it is important to remember that the constraint expression must evaluate to a `bool` value; no conversions whatsoever are permitted, which is why a very similar expression does not work:

```
template <typename T1, typename T2>
std::common_type_t<T1, T2> min2 (T1&& t1, T2&& t2)
  requires (sizeof(t1 < t2));
```

The integer value of `sizeof()` is always non-zero and would have converted to `true`, but not in this context. The good news is that we don't have to use the `sizeof()` hack at all to write constraints. There is yet another type of constraint expression, a *requires expression*, that is much more powerful and expresses our intent much clearer:

```
// Example 13b
template <typename T1, typename T2>
std::common_type_t<T1, T2> min2 (T1&& t1, T2&& t2)
  requires (requires { t1 < t2; });
```

The requires expression begins with the `requires` keyword followed by braces { }; it can contain any number of expressions that have to compile, or the value of the entire requires expression is false (it does not matter what the results of these expressions are, they just have to be valid C++). You can also use types, type traits, and combinations of requirements of different kinds. By a quirk of the language, the parentheses around the requires expression are optional, which means you can see code like `requires requires { t1 < t2 }` where the first and the second `requires` are completely different keywords.

The requirements on template types can be quite complex; often, the same requirements apply in many different templates. Sets of such requirements can be given names and defined for later use; these named requirements are called concepts. Each concept is a condition that is evaluated at compile time when used in a constraint.

The syntax for a constraint is similar to a template:

```
// Example 13c
template <typename T1, typename T2> concept Comparable =
   requires(T1 t1, T2 t2) { t1 < t2; };
```

We are not going to cover the syntax in detail in this book – for that, use a reference source such as cppreference.com. A concept can be used instead of the requirement it contains:

```
template <typename T1, typename T2>
std::common_type_t<T1, T2> min2(T1&& t1, T2&& t2)
   requires Comparable<T1, T2>;
```

Concepts that constrain a single type can also be used as template parameter placeholders. Let us consider an example of a swap() function. For integral types, there is a trick that allows us to swap two values without using a temporary variable. It relies on the properties of a bitwise XOR operation. Let us assume, for the purposes of this demonstration, that, on a particular hardware, this version is faster than the usual way of implementing swap. We would like to write a swap template function MySwap(T& a, T& b) that automatically detects whether the type T supports an XOR operation and use it, if available; otherwise we fall back on the usual swap.

First, we need a concept for a type that supports XOR:

```
// Example 14a,b
template <typename T> concept HasXOR =
   requires(T a, T b) { a ^ b; };
```

The concept has a requires expression; every expression inside the curly braces must compile, otherwise, the requirement of the concept is not met.

Now, we can implement an XOR-based swap template. We could do it with a `requires` constraint, but there is a more compact way:

```
template <HasXOR T> void MySwap(T& x, T& y) {
    x = x ^ y;
    y = x ^ y;
    x = x ^ y;
}
```

The concept name HasXOR can be used instead of the typename keyword to declare the template parameter. This restricts our MySwap() function to the types that have operator^(). But we need a general case overload, too. We should also note that *general* does not mean *any* in our case: the type has to support move assignment and move construction. We need another concept:

```
template <typename T> concept Assignable =
   requires(T a, T b) {
     T(std::move(b));
```

```
    b = std::move(a);
  };
```

This is a very similar concept, except we have two expressions; both must be valid for the concept to be true.

The second `MySwap()` overload accepts all `Assignable` types. However, we must explicitly exclude the types with XOR, or we will have ambiguous overloads. This is a perfect example to show that we can combine concepts as template placeholders with concepts in requirements:

```
template <Assignable T> void MySwap(T& x, T& y)
  requires (!HasXOR<T>)
{
  T tmp(std::move(x));
  x = std::move(y);
  y = std::move(tmp);
}
```

Now a call to `MySwap()` will select the XOR-based overload if possible, otherwise, it will use the general overload (swapping non-assignable types will not compile at all).

Finally, let us return to one of the first examples in this chapter: that of a class template `ArrayOf2` in the section "*Class templates.*" Recall that it has a member function sum() which has much more strict requirements on the template type than the rest of the class: it adds the values of the array elements. If the elements do not have `operator+()`, there is no problem as long as we don't call `sum()`, but if we do, we get a syntax error. It would have been better if this function was not a part of the class interface at all unless the type supports it. We can accomplish this with a constraint:

```
// Example 15
template <typename T> class ArrayOf2 {
  public:
  T& operator[](size_t i) { return a_[i]; }
  const T& operator[](size_t i) const { return a_[i]; }
  T sum() const requires (requires (T a, T b) { a + b; }) {
    return a_[0] + a_[1];
  }
  private:
  T a_[2];
};
```

If the expression a + b does not compile, the code behaves as if there was no member function `sum()` declared in the class interface. Of course, we could also use a named concept for this.

We will see more ways to manage requirements on template parameters in *Chapter 7*. For now, let us review what we have learned and go on to use these tools to solve common C++ problems.

Summary

Templates, variadic templates, and lambda expressions are all powerful features of C++, offering simplicity in use, but are rich in complex details. The examples in this chapter should serve to prepare the reader for the later chapters of this book, where we use these techniques to implement design patterns, both classic and novel, with the tools of the modern C++ language. The reader wishing to learn the art of using these complex and powerful tools to their fullest potential is referred to other books that are dedicated to teaching these subjects, some of which can be found at the end of this chapter.

The reader is now ready to learn common C++ idioms, starting with idioms for expressing memory ownership, in the next chapter.

Questions

1. What is the difference between a type and a template?
2. What kind of templates does C++ have?
3. What kinds of template parameters do C++ templates have?
4. What is the difference between a template specialization and a template instantiation?
5. How can you access the parameter pack of a variadic template?
6. What are lambda expressions used for?
7. How do concepts refine template interfaces?

Further reading

- *C++ Fundamentals*: https://www.packtpub.com/product/c-fundamentals
- *C++ Data Structures and Algorithms*: https://www.packtpub.com/product/c-data-structures-and-algorithms
- *Mastering C++ Programming*: https://www.packtpub.com/product/mastering-c-programming

3

Memory and Ownership

Memory mismanagement is one of the most common problems in C++ programs. Many of these problems boil down to incorrect assumptions about which part of the code or which entity owns a particular memory. Then, we get memory leaks, accessing unallocated memory, excessive memory use, and other problems that are difficult to debug. Modern C++ has a set of memory ownership idioms that, taken together, allow the programmer to clearly express their design intent when it comes to memory ownership. This, in turn, makes it much easier to write code that correctly allocates, accesses, and deallocates memory.

The following topics are covered in this chapter:

- What is memory ownership and resource ownership?

- What are the characteristics of well-designed resource ownership? When and how should we be agnostic about resource ownership? How do we express exclusive memory ownership in C++?

- How do we express shared memory ownership in C++?

- What is the cost of different memory ownership language constructs?

Technical requirements

You can find the C++ Core Guidelines at https://github.com/isocpp/CppCoreGuidelines/blob/master/CppCoreGuidelines.md.

You can find the C++ **Guidelines Support Library** (**GSL**) at https://github.com/Microsoft/GSL. Examples are available at https://github.com/PacktPublishing/Hands-On-Design-Patterns-with-CPP-Second-Edition/tree/master/Chapter03.

What is memory ownership?

In C++, the term *memory ownership* refers to the entity that is responsible for enforcing the lifetime of a particular memory allocation. In reality, we rarely talk about the ownership of raw memory. Usually, we manage the ownership and the lifetime of the objects that reside in said memory and memory ownership is really just shorthand for *object ownership*. The concept of memory ownership is closely tied to that of *resource ownership*. First of all, memory is a resource. It is not the only resource a program can manage, but it is by far the most commonly used one. Second, the C++ way of managing resources is to have objects own them. Thus, the problem of managing resources is reduced to the problem of managing the owning objects, which, as we just learned, is what we really mean when we talk about memory ownership. In this context, memory ownership is about owning more than memory, and mismanaged ownership can leak, miscount, or lose track of any resource that can be controlled by the program—memory, mutexes, files, database handles, cat videos, airline seat reservations, or nuclear warheads.

Well-designed memory ownership

What does well-designed memory ownership look like? The naive answer that first comes up is that, at every point in the program, it is clear who owns which object. This, however, is overly constraining— most of the program does not deal with ownership of resources, including memory. These parts of the program merely use resources. When writing such code, it is sufficient to know that a particular function or class does not own the memory. It is completely irrelevant to know who does what:

```
struct MyValues { long a, b, c, d; }
void Reset(MyValues* v) {
  // Don't care who owns v, as long as we don't
  v->a = v->b = v->c = v->d = 0;
}
```

How about this, then—at every point in the program, is it clear who owns that object, or is it clear that the owner is not changing? This is better since most of the code will fall under the second part of our answer. However, it's still too constraining—when taking ownership of an object, it is usually not important to know who it is taken from:

```
class A {
  public:
  // Constructor transfers ownership from whomever
  A(std::vector<int>&& v) : v(std::move(v)) {}
  private:
  std::vector<int> v_;    // We own this now
};
```

Similarly, the whole point of shared ownership (expressed through the reference-counted `std::shared_ptr`) is that we don't need to know who else owns the object:

```cpp
class A {
  public:
  // No idea who owns v, don't care
  A(std::shared_ptr<std::vector<int>> v) : v_(v) {}
  // Sharing ownership with any number of owners
  private:
  std::shared_ptr<std::vector<int>> v_;
};
```

A more accurate description of well-designed memory ownership takes more than one quoted sentence. Generally, the following are the attributes of good memory ownership practices:

- If a function or a class does not alter memory ownership in any way, this should be clear to every client of this function or class, as well as the implementer.

- If a function or a class takes exclusive ownership of some of the objects passed to it, this should be clear to the client (we assume that the implementer knows this already since they have to write the code).

- If a function or a class shares ownership of an object passed to it, this should be clear to the client (or anyone who reads the client code, for that matter).

- For every object that is created, for every unit of code where it's used, it is clear whether this code is expected to delete the object or not.

Poorly designed memory ownership

Just as good memory ownership defies a simple description and instead is characterized by a set of criteria it satisfies, so can bad memory ownership practices be recognized by their common manifestations. In general, where a good design makes it clear whether a particular piece of code owns a resource or not, a bad design requires additional knowledge that cannot be deduced from the context. For example, who owns the object returned by the following `MakeWidget()` function?

```cpp
Widget* w = MakeWidget();
```

Is the client expected to delete the widget when it's no longer needed? If yes, how should it be deleted? If we decide to delete the widget and do it in the wrong way, for example, by calling `operator delete` on a widget that was not, in fact, allocated by `operator new`, memory corruption will certainly result. In the best-case scenario, the program will just crash:

```cpp
WidgetFactory WF;
Widget* w = WF.MakeAnother();
```

Does the Factory own the widgets it created? Will it delete them when the Factory object is deleted? Alternatively, is the client expected to do that? If we decide that the Factory probably knows what it created and will delete all such objects in due time, we may end up with a memory leak (or worse, if the objects owned some other resources):

```
Widget* w = MakeWidget();
Widget* w1 = Transmogrify(w);
```

Does `Transmogrify()` take ownership of the widget? Is the w widget still around after `Transmogrify()` is done with it? If the widget is deleted to construct a new, transmogrified, w1 widget, we now have a dangling pointer. If the widget is not deleted, but we assume it might be, we have a memory leak.

Lest you think that all bad memory management practices can be recognized by the presence of raw pointers somewhere, here is an example of a rather poor approach to memory management that often arises as a knee-jerk response to the problems caused by the use of raw pointers:

```
void Double(std::shared_ptr<std::vector<int>> v) {
  for (auto& x : *v) {
    x *= 2;
  }
};
...
std::shared_ptr<std::vector<int>> v(...);
Double(v);
...
```

The `Double()` function is claiming in its interface that it takes shared ownership of the vector. However, that ownership is entirely gratuitous—there is no reason for `Double()` to own its argument—it does not attempt to extend its lifetime and, it does not transfer ownership to anyone else; it merely modifies a vector passed in by the caller. We can reasonably expect that the caller owns the vector (or that somebody else even higher in the call stack does), and that the vector will still be around when `Double()` returns control to the caller—after all, the caller wanted us to double the elements, presumably so that they can do something else with them.

While this list is hardly complete, it serves to demonstrate the spectrum of problems that can be caused by a slap-dash approach to memory ownership. In the next section, we review the patterns and guidelines developed by the C++ community to help to avoid these problems and express the programmer's intent clearly.

Expressing memory ownership in C++

Throughout its history, the C++ language has evolved in its approach to expressing memory ownership. The same syntactic constructs have been, at times, imbued with different assumed semantics. This evolution was partially driven by new features added to the language (it's hard to talk about shared memory ownership if you don't have any shared pointers). On the other hand, most of the memory management tools added in C++ 11 and later were not new ideas or new concepts. The notion of a shared pointer has been around for a long time. This language support makes it easier to implement one (and having a shared pointer in the standard library makes most custom implementations unnecessary), but shared pointers were used in C++ long before C++ 11 added them to the standard. The more important change that has occurred was the evolution of the understanding of the C++ community and the emergence of common practices and idioms. It is in this sense, as a set of conventions and semantics commonly associated with different syntactic features, that we can talk about the set of memory management practices as a design pattern of the C++ language. Let's now learn the different ways that we can express different types of memory ownership.

Expressing non-ownership

Let's start with the most common kind of memory ownership. Most code does not allocate, deallocate, construct, or delete. It just does its work on objects that were created by someone else earlier and will be deleted by someone else later. How do you express the notion that a function is going to operate on an object but will not attempt to delete it or, conversely, extend its lifetime past the completion of the function itself?

Very easily, in fact, and every C++ programmer has done it many times:

```
// Example 01
void Transmogrify(Widget* w) {        // I will not delete w
  ...
}
void MustTransmogrify(Widget& w) {    // Neither will I
  ...
}
```

In a well-written program, a function with a raw pointer parameter signals that it is not involved with the ownership of the corresponding object in any way; the same goes for references. Similarly, a class that contains a member function pointer refers to an object but expects someone else to own it and manage its lifetime. Note that the destructor of the WidgetProcessor class in the next example does not delete the object the class points to – this is a sure sign that we refuse ownership of that object:

```
// Example 02
class WidgetProcessor {
  public:
  WidgetProcessor(Widget* w) : w_(w) {}
  WidgetProcessor() {} // DO NOT delete w_!!!

    ...

  private:
  Widget* w_;      // I do not own w_
};
```

Non-owning access to an object should be granted by using raw pointers or references. Yes—even in C++ 14, with all its smart pointers, there is a place for raw pointers. Not only that but in the bulk of the code, the majority of pointers will be raw pointers—all the non-owning ones (as we will see in the next section, C++17 and C++20 take this point much further).

You might reasonably point out at this time that the preceding example of recommended practices for granting non-owning access looks exactly like one of the examples of bad practices shown earlier. The distinction is in the context—in a well-designed program, only non-owning access is granted through raw pointers and references. Actual ownership is always expressed in some other way. Thus, it is clear that when a raw pointer is encountered, the function or class is not going to mess with the ownership of the object in any way. This, of course, creates some confusion when it comes to converting old legacy code, with raw pointers everywhere, to modern practices. As a matter of clarity, it is recommended to convert such code one part at a time, with clearly indicated transitions between code that follows the modern guidelines and code that does not.

Another issue to discuss here is the use of pointers versus references. As a matter of syntax, the reference is basically a pointer that is never null and cannot be left uninitialized. It is tempting to adopt a convention that any pointer passed to a function may be null and must, therefore, be checked, and any function that cannot accept a null pointer must instead take a reference. It is a good convention and widely used, but not widely enough to be considered an accepted design pattern. Perhaps in recognition of this, the C++ Core Guidelines library offers an alternative for expressing non-null pointers—not_null<T*>. Note that this is not a part of the language itself, but can be implemented in standard C++ without any language extension.

Expressing exclusive ownership

The second most common type of ownership is exclusive ownership—the code creates an object and will delete it later. The task of deletion will not be delegated to someone else, and no extension of the lifetime of the object is permitted. This type of memory ownership is so common that we do it all the time without even thinking about it:

```
void Work() {
  Widget w;
  Transmogrify(w);
  Draw(w);
}
```

All local (stack) variables express unique memory ownership! Note that ownership in this context does not mean that someone else will not modify the object. It merely means that when the creator of the w widget—the DoWork() function, in our case—decides to delete it; the deletion will succeed (nobody has deleted it already) and the object will actually be deleted (nobody attempted to keep the object alive after the end of its scope).

This is the oldest way to construct an object in C++, and it's still the best one. If a stack variable does what you need, use it. C++ 11 provides another way to express unique ownership, and it is mainly used in cases where an object cannot be created on the stack but must be allocated on the heap. Heap allocation often happens when ownership is shared or transferred—after all, the stack-allocated object will be deleted at the end of the containing scope; there is no way around it. If we need to keep the object alive for longer, it has to be allocated somewhere else. The other reason to create objects on the heap is that the size or type of the object may not be known at compile time. This usually happens when the object is polymorphic—a derived object is created, but the base class pointer is used. Whatever the reason for not allocating objects on the stack, we have a way of expressing the exclusive ownership of such objects using `std::unique_ptr`:

```
// Example 03
class FancyWidget : public Widget { ... };
std::unique_ptr<Widget> w(new FancyWidget);
```

There is also a technical reason why you may have to construct objects on the heap even when a stack-allocated object seems sufficient: the stack size is quite limited, usually anywhere between 2 MB and 10 MB. That is the space for all stack allocations in one thread, and when it is exceeded, the program crashes. A large enough object can exhaust the stack space or push it too close to the limit for subsequent allocations. Such objects must be created on the heap and owned by stack-allocated unique pointers or other resource-owning objects.

What if the way to create an object is more complex than just `operator new`, and we need a Factory function? That is the type of ownership we will consider next.

Expressing transfer of exclusive ownership

In the preceding example, a new object was created and immediately bound to a unique pointer, `std::unique_ptr`, which guarantees exclusive ownership. The client code looks exactly the same if the object is created by a Factory:

```
std::unique_ptr<Widget> w(WidgetFactory());
```

But what should the Factory function return? It could certainly return a raw pointer, `Widget*`. After all, that is what new returns. But this opens the way to incorrect use of `WidgetFactory`—for example, instead of capturing the returned raw pointer in a unique pointer, we could pass it to a function such as `Transmogrify` that takes a raw pointer because it does not deal with the ownership. Now, nobody owns the widget, and it ends up as a memory leak. Ideally, `WidgetFactory` would be written in a way that would force the caller to take ownership of the returned object.

What we need here is an ownership transfer—`WidgetFactory` is certainly an exclusive owner of the object it constructs, but at some point, it needs to hand off that ownership to a new, also exclusive, owner. The code to do so is very simple:

```
// Example 04
std::unique_ptr<Widget> WidgetFactory() {
```

```
    Widget* new_w = new Widget;
      ...
    return std::unique_ptr<Widget>(new_w);
}
std::unique_ptr<Widget> w(WidgetFactory());
```

This works exactly the way we want it to, but why? Doesn't the unique pointer provide exclusive ownership? The answer is, it does, but it is also a movable object (it has a move constructor). Moving the content of a unique pointer into another one transfers the ownership of the object; the original pointer is left in the moved-from state (its destruction will not delete any objects). What is so good about this idiom? It clearly expresses, and forces at compile time, that the Factory expects the caller to take exclusive (or shared) ownership of the object. For example, the following code, which would have left the new widget with no owner, does not compile:

```
void Transmogrify(Widget* w);
Transmogrify(WidgetFactory());
```

So, how do we call `Transmogrify()` on a widget after we properly assumed ownership? This is still done with a raw pointer:

```
std::unique_ptr<Widget> w(WidgetFactory());
Transmogrify(w.get());
Transmogrify(&*w);      // same as above if w is not null
```

But what about the stack variables? Can exclusive ownership be transferred to someone else before the variable is destroyed? This is going to be slightly more complicated—the memory for the object is allocated on the stack and is going away, so some amount of copying is involved. Exactly how much copying depends on whether the object is movable. Moving, in general, transfers the ownership from the moved-from object to the moved-to one. This can be used for return values but is more often used for passing arguments to functions that take exclusive ownership. Such functions must be declared to take the parameters by the `rvalue` reference T&&:

```
// Example 05
void Consume(Widget&& w) {
  auto my_w = std::move(w);
    ...
}
Widget w, w1;
Consume(std::move(w));      // No more w
// w is in a moved-from state now
Consume(w1);    // Does not compile - must consent to move
```

Note that the caller must explicitly give up ownership by wrapping the argument in `std::move`. This is one of the advantages of this idiom; without it, an ownership-transferring call would look exactly the same as a regular call.

Expressing shared ownership

The last type of ownership we need to cover is shared ownership, where multiple entities own the object equally. First, a word of caution—shared ownership is often misused, or over-used. Consider the preceding example, where a function was passed a shared pointer to an object it did not need to own. It is tempting to let the reference counting deal with the ownership of objects and *not worry about deletion*. However, this is often a sign of poor design. In most systems, at some level, there is clear ownership of resources, and this should be reflected in the chosen design of resource management. The *not worry about deletion* concern remains valid; explicit deletion of objects should be rare, but automatic deletion does not require shared ownership, merely a clearly expressed one (unique pointers, data members, and containers provide automatic deletion just as well).

That being said, there are definite cases for shared ownership. The most common valid applications of shared ownership are at a low level, inside data structures such as lists, trees, and more. A data element may be owned by other nodes of the same data structure, by any number of iterators currently pointing to it, and, possibly by some temporary variables inside data structure member functions that operate on the entire structure or a part of it (such as rebalancing a tree). The ownership of the entire data structure is usually clear in a well-thought-out design. But the ownership of each node, or data element, may be truly shared in the sense that any owner is equal to any other; none is privileged or primary.

In C++, the notion of shared ownership is expressed through a shared pointer, `std::shared_ptr`:

```
// Example 06
struct ListNode {
  T data;
  std::shared_ptr<ListNode> next, prev;
};
class ListIterator {
  ...
  std::shared_ptr<ListNode> node_;
};
class List {
  ...
  std::shared_ptr<ListNode> head_;
};
```

The advantage of this design is that a list element that was unlinked from the list remains alive for as long as there is a way to access it through an iterator. This is not the way `std::list` is done, and it does not provide such guarantees (deleting a `std::list` object invalidates all iterators). Note that the doubly linked list of shared pointers makes it so any two consecutive nodes in the list own each other and neither is deleted even when the list head is deleted; this leaks the owned objects. For this reason, a real design would likely use `std::weak_pointer` for one of next or prev.

Such complications aside, this may be a valid design for certain applications where the iterators need to own the data they refer to even after the list is deleted or some elements are erased from the list. One example is a thread-safe list, where it is very difficult to guarantee that one thread does not erase a list element while another still has an iterator pointing to it. Note that this particular application would also require atomic shared pointers, which are only available in C++ 20 (or you can write your own using C++ 11).

Now, what about functions taking shared pointers as parameters? In a program that follows good memory ownership practices, such a function conveys to the caller that it intends to take partial ownership that lasts longer than the function call itself—a copy of the shared pointer will be created. In the concurrent context, it may also indicate that the function needs to protect the object from deletion by another thread for at least as long as it's executing.

There are several disadvantages to shared ownership that you must keep in mind. The best-known one is the bane of shared pointers, that is, the circular dependency. If two objects with shared pointers point to each other, the entire pair remains *in use* indefinitely. C++ offers a solution to that in the form of std::weak_ptr, a counterpart to the shared pointer that provides a safe pointer to an object that may have already been deleted. If the previously mentioned pair of objects uses one shared and one weak pointer, the circular dependency is broken.

The circular dependency problem is real, but it happens more often in designs where shared ownership is used to conceal the larger problem of unclear resource ownership. However, there are other downsides to shared ownership. The performance of a shared pointer is always going to be lower than that of a raw pointer. On the other hand, a unique pointer can be just as efficient as a raw pointer (and in fact, std::unique_ptr is). When the shared pointer is first created, an additional memory allocation for the reference count must take place.

In C++ 11, std::make_shared can be used to combine the allocations for the object itself and the reference counter, but this implies that the object is created with the intent to share (often, the object Factory returns unique pointers, some of which are later converted to shared pointers). Copying or deleting a shared pointer must also increment or decrement the reference counter. Shared pointers are often attractive in concurrent data structures, where, at least at the low level, the notion of ownership may indeed be fuzzy, with several accesses to the same object happening at the same time. However, designing a shared pointer to be thread-safe in all contexts is not easy and carries additional runtime overhead.

So far, we have mostly restricted ourselves to pointers as means of owning objects (and their memory and other resources). Non-ownership has been similarly expressed through raw pointers and references or simple non-owning pointers. However, this is not the only way to own resources (and we did mention that the most common form of exclusive ownership is a stack variable). We are now going to see how resource-owning objects can be used directly to express both ownership and non-ownership.

Owning objects and views

C++ has not been limited to owning pointers since its creation: any object can own resources, and we already mentioned that the simplest way to express exclusive ownership is to create a local variable on the stack. Of course, any of such objects can also be owned by a pointer (unique or shared) and when non-owning access is desired, these objects are commonly accessed through raw pointers or references. However, in C++17 and C++20 a different pattern has emerged, and it is worth exploring.

Resource-owning objects

Every C++ programmer is familiar with resource-owning objects; perhaps the most common one is `std::string` – an object that owns a character string. Of course, it also has a lot of specialized member functions for operating on strings, but from the point of view of memory ownership, `std::string` is essentially an owning `char*` pointer. Similarly, `std::vector` is an owning object for an array of objects of arbitrary type.

The most common way to construct such objects is either as local variables or as data members of a class. In the latter case, the issue of who owns the entire class is managed elsewhere, but, within the class, all data members are owned exclusively by the object itself. Consider this simple example:

```
class C {
  std::string s_;
};

...
std::vector<int> v = … ;     // v owns the array of int
C c;                         // c owns the string s
```

So far, we have not said anything new compared to the section on exclusive ownership just a few pages earlier in this chapter. However, we have subtly changed the focus from owning pointers to owning objects. As long as we focus on the ownership aspect, these objects are essentially specialized owning (unique) pointers. There is an important difference, however: most such objects convey additional information, such as the length of the string for `std::string` or the size of the array for `std::vector`. Keep this in mind: it is going to come up again when we get to the changes brought by C++17/20.

While resource-owning objects have been around since the beginning of C++, they themselves have been often owned through pointers. There are, perhaps, two main reasons for this; both have been rendered obsolete by C++ advances. The first reason to own, for example, a string via an owning pointer is the need to transfer ownership. A stack object is destroyed at the end of the scope. A class data member is destroyed when the object is destroyed. In either case, there is no way to transfer the ownership of the object itself, such as `std::string`, to someone else. However, if we focus on the ownership aspect, then the string object itself is just a (decorated) owning pointer, and the goal is to transfer the ownership of the underlying resource (the character string for `std::string`) to another owner. When we put it this way, the answer is obvious: since C++11, the string has move semantics, and moving a string is barely more expensive than moving a pointer (remember, the string is an owning pointer that also knows the length, so that has to be moved too).

We can say, more generally, that there is no reason to own a cheap-to-move owning object via a pointer if the only reason is ownership transfer. For example, consider this string builder class:

```
class Builder {
  std::string* str_;
  public:
  Builder(…) : str_(new std::string){
    … construct string str_ …
  }
  std::string* get(){
    std::string* tmp = str_;
    str_ = nullptr;
    return tmp;
  }
};
```

While it gets the job done, a much better way to write the same class is to simply move the string:

```
// Example 07
class Builder {
  std::string str_;
  public:
  Builder(…){ … construct string str_ … }
  std::string get(){ return std::move(str_); }
};
std::string my_string = Builder(…).get();
```

The same is true for factories that construct owning cheap-to-move objects. Instead of returning them via `std::unique_ptr`, the factory can return the object itself:

```
std::string MakeString(…) {
  std::string str;
  … construct the string …
  return str;
}
std::string my_string = MakeString(…);
```

The return value may benefit from the return-value optimization (the compiler constructs the return value directly in the memory allocated for the final object, `my_string`). But even without this optimization, we have a guarantee that there is no copying of the string here, only moving (if this move is optimized away, the optimization is sometimes called **move elision**, similar to the better-known **copy elision**, which optimizes away copy constructors).

The second reason to use owning pointers for resource-owning objects is that the object's existence itself may be conditional:

```
std::unique_ptr<std::string*> str;
if (need_string) str.reset(new std::string(…args…));
```

In many cases, an *"empty"* object can be used instead, such as a zero-length string. Again, for many owning objects, and certainly for all cheap-to-move STL containers, the cost of constructing such an object is trivial. But there could be a meaningful difference between the empty string and no string at all (that is, an empty string could be a valid result, and an absence of any string signifies something to the rest of the program). In C++17, we have a straightforward way to express this behavior using std::optional:

```
std::optional<std::string> str;
if (need_string) str.emplace(…args…);
```

The object of the std::optional<std::string> type may contain a string or be empty. The non-empty std::optional owns the object it contains (deleting the std::optional will also delete the string). Unlike std::unique_pointer, there are no heap memory allocations here: the std::optional object contains enough space within it to store a std::string object. std::optional is also movable, just like the string itself, so this pattern can be combined with the previous one. In general, we can say that in modern C++ there is no reason to own lightweight owning objects such as std::string indirectly. However, expressing the non-ownership of such objects has not received as much attention until recently.

Non-owning access to resource-owning objects

We have seen how a std::string object can, for most purposes, replace an owning pointer to char* (or to std::string). How do we, then, express non-owning access? Let us say that we need to pass a string to a function that operates on the string but does not take ownership of it (does not destroy it). This is a trivial exercise:

```
void work_on_string(const std::string& str);
std::string my_string = …;
work_on_string(my_string);
```

This is what we have been doing since C++ was created. But this simplicity hides a profound distinction: remember that, as long as we don't care about all the extra methods and the features they provide, std::string is just an owning pointer to a character string that also knows its length. So, how would we handle the same situation if we used an owning pointer instead of a string? The corresponding pointer is std::unique_ptr<char[]>, so we would write something like this:

```
void work_on_string(const char* str);
std::unique_ptr<char[]> my_string(new char[…length…]);
```

```
… initialize the string …
work_on_string(my_string.get());
```

Following the earlier guidelines, we passed a non-owning raw pointer to the function. We definitely would not write this declaration:

```
void work_on_string(const std::unique_ptr<char[]>& str);
```

Yet we do this without a second thought when the same character array is owned by a std::string object. Why do we approach these very similar problems so differently? This is the time to remember why a string is not just an owning pointer restricted to character arrays; it contains more information than just the pointer: it also knows the length of the string. There was no good way in C++ to grant non-owning access to such *"rich"* owning pointers, short of passing the entire pointer object by reference. By contrast, a unique pointer (or any other owning pointer) contains the same information as a basic pointer, so when ownership is not required, the owning pointer naturally reduces to a raw pointer without any information loss.

The difference is about more than just symmetry. Consider that passing a string by a const reference prevents the function work_on_string from changing the content of the string. On the other hand, a non-const reference allows the function to clear the string (release the memory it owns), which is an ownership aspect. We are forced to muddle the clarity of intent by mixing together two unrelated types of access we can grant to a function: the ability to change the content of the data and the ownership of the data.

C++17 addressed this problem in a very limited context: specifically for strings, it introduced a new type std::string_view. A string view is a (const) non-owning pointer to a string that also stores the length of the string. In other words, it is a perfect non-owning equivalent to std::string: a string view to a string is exactly what a const raw pointer is to a unique pointer. Now, to grant non-owning access to a std::string object, we write:

```
// Example 09
void work_on_string(std::string_view str);
std::string my_string = …;
work_on_string(my_string);
```

In contrast, a function that takes ownership of a std::string object must still take it by reference. Specifically, use an rvalue reference to transfer the ownership:

```
// Example 09
void consume_string(std::string&& str);
std::string my_string = …;
consume_string(std::move(my_string));
// Do not use my_string anymore!
```

Use a non-`const` lvalue reference only to allow the function to change the string; in C++17, there is no good *rich pointer* equivalent to a non-`const` raw pointer. There is probably no need to use `const std::string&` except when the existing interfaces require it since `std::string_view` offers equivalent functionality.

There are other benefits and advantages of using `std::string_view` (in particular, it greatly simplifies writing common code for processing C and C++ strings), but in this chapter, we focus on the ownership aspect. Also, remember that the string view is limited to character strings. We could have the exact same discussion about another owning class, for example, `std::vector<int>`.

We now see a new pattern emerge: for a "*rich*" owning pointer that, in addition to owning memory, contains some information about the data it owns, the corresponding non-owning object (the equivalent of a raw pointer) should be a view object that contains the same information but does not own the resource. We find this view object in C++20 as `std::span`. Until then, the only good way to grant non-owning access to a vector of integers was to pass it by reference:

```
void work_on_data(std::vector<int>& data);
std::vector<int> my_data = …;
work_on_data(my_data);
```

In C++20, we can use the span to clearly differentiate the non-owning view (raw pointer equivalent) from the owning object (unique pointer equivalent):

```
// Example 10
void ModifyData(std::span<int> data);
std::vector<int> my_data = …;
ModifyData(my_data); // Can change my_data
```

Thus, `std::span<int>` is a *rich pointer* equivalent to `int*`—it contains a non-`const` pointer and the size is cheap to copy and does not own the resource it points to. Unlike `std::string_view`, we can modify the object accessed through a span. But if we want the equivalent to a `const` pointer, we can use `std::span<const int>`:

```
// Example 10
void UseData(std::span<const int> data);
std::vector<int> my_data = …;
UseData(my_data); // Cannot change my_data
```

Since `std::string` contains a contiguous array of characters, it too can be used with a span, in this case, `std::span<char>` or `std::span<const char>`. The latter is essentially the same as `std::string_view`, including the option to construct them from string literals. The former is the equivalent of a non-`const` pointer to `char`.

The span pairs well with a vector or a string because they offer a non-owning view of an array. But it does not work for other STL containers since they all allocate memory in multiple non-contiguous allocations. For that, we need to use the C++20 ranges library. For example, the generalization of the preceding non-owning vector access to an arbitrary container can be written like this:

```
// Example 11
void ModifyData(std::ranges::view auto data) { ... }
std::list<int> my_data = ...;
ModifyData(std::views::all(my_data));
```

If you have never seen a C++20 template, this takes some getting used to. The first line is a template function: `auto` parameters make "*ordinary*" functions into templates even without the `template` keyword. The incantation `std::ranges::view` before `auto` restricts the template parameters to those that satisfy the view concept. A view is a container-like object that has `begin()` and `end()` member functions and, in addition, must be cheap to move and either cheap to copy or non-copyable (this is, of course, a loose paraphrasing of the exact requirements enumerated by the standard). We could have written the same function with the `template` and `requires` keywords, but this compact syntax is idiomatic in C++20.

Note that, in this concept-based coding style, the restrictions on the function arguments are specified by the concept requirements. We could have written the same template function to require ranges instead of views:

```
void ModifyData(std::ranges::range auto data) { ... }
std::list<int> my_data = ...;
ModifyData(my_data);
```

Ranges are essentially arbitrary objects with `begin()` and `end()`, so `std::list` is a range (but not a view, it can be copied but not cheaply). Note that, as written, the function takes the argument by value, so a copy is made. Unless that was the intent (and in this case, it is not), the correct way to write this function is like this:

```
void ModifyData(std::ranges::range auto&& data) { ... }
```

A `const` reference would also work if we wanted to express non-modifying access. But the important point to note is that we did not have to do the same for views: by restricting the `work_on_data` function to accept only views, we have limited it to cheap-to-copy types similar to `std::string_view` (or a raw pointer, for that matter). Indeed, passing a range by reference is exactly like passing a string or a vector itself: this gives the callee access to the ownership. If we want to write a function that explicitly does not take ownership of a range, the view is the right way to express this.

It is still too early to talk about patterns for C++20 ranges: they have not been around long enough to establish commonly recognized and accepted use practices (a necessary requirement for a pattern) and the library is still incomplete. C++23 is expected to contain several significant enhancements (in particular, there is no good equivalent to `std::span<const char>` in C++20 ranges – it is going to be added in C++23).

However, we can confidently talk about the more general pattern becoming established in C++: resource ownership, including memory, should be handled by owning objects, while non-owning access should be granted through views. The owning objects can be smart pointers or more complex and specialized container objects. These containers, in addition to managing the memory in more complex ways, embed more information about the data they contain. In general, for each container, there should be a corresponding view that grants non-owning access while preserving all the additional information. For smart pointers, this view is a raw pointer or a reference. For `std::string`, this view is `std::string_view`. For `std::vector`, arrays, and any other containers that own contiguous memory, you will want `std::span`. For arbitrary containers, the corresponding views may be found in the C++20 ranges library; for a custom container, you may have to write your own view objects as well (just make sure they satisfy the relevant view concepts).

Summary

In C++, memory ownership is really just shorthand for object ownership, which, in turn, is the way to manage arbitrary resources, their ownership, and access. We have reviewed the contemporary idioms that the C++ community has developed to express different types of memory ownership. C++ allows the programmer to express exclusive or shared memory ownership. Just as important is expressing *non-ownership* in programs that are agnostic about the ownership of resources. We have also learned about the practices and attributes of resource ownership in a well-designed program.

We now have the idiomatic language to clearly express which entity in the program owns each object or resource, and when non-owning access is granted. The next chapter covers the idiom for the simplest operation on resources: the exchange, or swap.

Questions

1. Why is it important to clearly express memory ownership in a program?
2. What are the common problems that arise from unclear memory ownership?
3. What types of memory ownership can be expressed in C++?
4. How do you write non-memory-owning functions and classes?
5. Why should exclusive memory ownership be preferred to a shared one?
6. How do you express exclusive memory ownership in C++?
7. How do you express shared memory ownership in C++?
8. What are the potential downsides of shared memory ownership?
9. What are views? How is a string view better than passing a string by reference?

Further reading

- *C++20 STL Cookbook* by *Bill Weinman*: https://www.packtpub.com/product/c20-stl-cookbook/9781803248714

- *Template Metaprogramming with C++* by *Marius Bancila*: https://www.packtpub.com/product/template-metaprogramming-with-c/9781803243450

- *C++ Data Structures and Algorithms* by *Wisnu Anggoro*: https://www.packtpub.com/application-development/c-data-structures-and-algorithms

- *Expert C++ Programming* by *Jeganathan Swaminathan, Maya Posch*, and *Jacek Galowicz*: https://www.packtpub.com/application-development/expert-c-programming

Part 2:
Common C++ Idioms

This part describes some of the more common C++ idioms: established, universally recognized ways to express a specific idea or implement a frequently needed task. The boundary between "patterns" and "idioms" is fuzzy at best. In this book, we consider more complete design solutions to be patterns, while simpler techniques are idioms. In other words, choosing a pattern may influence the design of your entire application or its major component, while using an idiom is more of an implementation decision that has been learned from someone else's mistakes.

This part has the following chapters:

- *Chapter 4, Swap - From Simple to Subtle*

- *Chapter 5, A Comprehensive Look at RAII*

- *Chapter 6, Understanding Type Erasure*

- *Chapter 7, SFINAE, Concepts, and Overload Resolution Management*

4

Swap – from Simple to Subtle

We begin our exploration of basic C++ idioms with a very simple, even humble, operation—**swap**. The notion of swap refers to two objects exchanging places—after the swap, the first object keeps its name, but otherwise looks like the second object used to, and vice versa. This operation is so fundamental to C++ classes that the standard provides a template, `std::swap`, to do just that. Rest assured that C++ manages to turn even something as basic as a swap into a complex issue with subtle nuances.

The following topics are covered in this chapter:

- How is `swap` used by the standard C++ library?

- What are the applications of swap?

- How can we write exception-safe code using swap?

- How can we implement swap for our own types correctly?

- How can we correctly swap variables of an arbitrary type?

Technical requirements

Here is a link to all the example code of this chapter: `https://github.com/PacktPublishing/Hands-On-Design-Patterns-with-CPP-Second-Edition/tree/main/Chapter04`

This is a link to the C++ Core Guidelines: `https://github.com/isocpp/CppCoreGuidelines/blob/master/CppCoreGuidelines.md`

This is a link for the C++ **Guidelines Support Library (GSL)**: `https://github.com/Microsoft/GSL`

Swap and the standard template library

The swap operation is widely used in the C++ standard library. All **Standard Template Library (STL)** containers provide swap functionality, and there is a non-member function template, `std::swap`. There are also uses of swap in STL algorithms. The standard library is also a template for implementing custom features that resemble standard ones.

Therefore, we'll begin our study of the swap operation with a look at the functionality provided by the standard.

Swap and STL containers

Conceptually, swap is equivalent to the following operation:

```
template <typename T> void swap(T& x, T& y) { T tmp(x);
    x = y;
    y = tmp;
}
```

After the `swap()` is called, the contents of the x and y objects are swapped. This, however, is probably the worst possible way to actually implement swap. The first and most obvious problem with this implementation is that it copies both objects unnecessarily (it actually does three copy operations). The execution time of this operation is proportional to the size of the T type. For an STL container, the size would refer to the size of the actual container, not to the type of the element:

```
void swap(std::vector<int>& x, std::vector<int>& y) {
    std::vector<int> tmp(x);
    x = y;
    y = tmp;
}
```

Note that this code compiles, and, in most cases, even does the right thing. However, it copies every element of the vector several times. The second problem is that it temporarily allocates resources—for example, during the swap, we create a third vector that uses as much memory as one of the vectors being swapped. This allocation seems unnecessary, given that, in the final state, we have exactly as much data as we started with; only the names we use to access this data have been changed. The last problem with naive implementation is revealed when we consider what happens if, for example, the memory allocation we just mentioned fails.

The entire swap operation, which should have been as simple and foolproof as exchanging the names used to access vector elements, instead fails with a memory allocation failure.

But that's not the only way it can fail—the copy constructor and the assignment operator can both throw exceptions.

All STL containers, including `std::vector`, provide a guarantee that they can be swapped in constant time. The way this is accomplished is rather straightforward if you consider that the STL container objects themselves contain only pointers to the data, plus some state, such as object size. To swap these containers, we need only to swap the pointers (and the rest of the state, of course)—the elements of the container remain exactly where they always were, in dynamically allocated memory, and do not need to be copied or even accessed. The implementation of the swap needs only to swap the pointers, the sizes, and other state variables (in a real STL implementation, a container class, such as a vector, does not directly consist of data members of built-in types, such as pointers, but has one or more class data members that, in turn, are made from pointers and other built-in types).

Since any pointers or other vector data members are not publicly accessible, the swap has to be implemented as a member function of the container, or be declared a friend. The STL takes the former approach—all STL containers have a `swap()` member function that swaps the object with another object of the same type (see examples `01a` and `01b`).

The implementation of this by swapping pointers takes care, indirectly, of the two other problems we mentioned. First of all, because only the data members of the containers are swapped, there is no memory allocation. Secondly, copying pointers and other built-in types cannot throw an exception, and so the entire swap operation does not throw (and cannot otherwise fail).

The simple and consistent picture we have described so far is only mostly true. The first complication, and by far the simpler one, applies only to containers that are parameterized not just on the element type, but also on a callable object of some sort. For example, the `std::map` container accepts the optional comparison function for comparing the elements of the map, which, by default, is `std::less`. Such callable objects have to be stored with the container. Since they are invoked very often, it is highly desirable, for performance reasons, to keep them in the same memory allocation as the container object itself, and indeed they are made data members of the container class.

However, that optimization comes with a price—swapping two containers now requires exchanging the compare functions; that is, the actual objects, not the pointers to them. The comparison objects are implemented by the client of the library, so there is no guarantee that swapping them is possible, let alone that it will not throw an exception.

Therefore, for `std::map`, the standard provides the following guarantee—in order for the map to be swappable, the callable objects must also be swappable. Furthermore, swapping two maps does not throw an exception, unless swapping comparison objects may throw, in which case, any exception thrown by that swap is propagated from the `std::map` swap.

This consideration does not apply to containers, such as `std::vector`, that do not use any callable objects, and swapping these containers still does not throw an exception (as far as we know up to now).

The other complication in the otherwise consistent and natural behavior of the swap is due to the allocators, and that is a hard one to resolve. Consider the problem—the two swapped containers must, necessarily, have allocators of the same type, but not necessarily the same allocator object. Each container has its elements allocated by its own allocator, and they must be deallocated by the same allocator. After the swap, the first container owns the elements from the second one and must eventually deallocate them. This can only be done (correctly) using the allocator of the first container; therefore, the allocators must also be exchanged.

C++ standards prior to **C++11** ignore the problem entirely, and decree that any two allocator objects of the same type must be able to deallocate each other's memory. If it's true, then we do not have to swap allocators at all. If it is not true, then we have already violated the standard and are in undefined behavior territory. C++11 allows allocators to have a non-trivial state, which must, therefore, be swapped too. But the allocator objects do not have to be swappable. The standard addresses the problem in the following way—if, for any `allocator_type` allocator class, there is a `trait` class that defines, among other things, the `std::allocator_traits<allocator_type>::propagate_on_container_swap::value` trait property, and if this value is `true`, then the allocators are exchanged using an unqualified call to a non-member swap; that is, simply a `swap(allocator1, allocator2)` call (see the next section to learn what that call actually does). If this value is not `true`, then the allocators are not swapped at all, and both container objects must use the same allocator. If that is not `true` either, then we are back to undefined behavior. **C++17** puts a more formal veneer on this by declaring `swap()` member functions of STL containers to be conditionally `noexcept()`, with the same limitations.

The requirement that swapping two containers cannot throw an exception, at least as long as the allocators are not involved and the container does not use callable objects or uses non-throwing ones, ends up imposing a rather subtle limitation on the implementation of the container—it prevents the use of local buffer optimization.

We will talk about this optimization in great detail in *Chapter 10, Local Buffer Optimization*, but in a nutshell, the idea is to avoid dynamic memory allocation for containers of very few elements, such as short strings, by defining a buffer inside the container class itself. This optimization, however, is generally incompatible with the notion of a non-throwing swap, since the elements inside the container object can no longer be exchanged by merely swapping pointers, but have to be copied between the containers.

Non-member swap

The standard also provides a template `std::swap()` function. Prior to C++11, it was declared in the `<algorithm>` header; in C++11, it was moved to `<utility>`. The declaration of the function is as follows:

```
template <typename T>
  void swap (T& a, T& b);
template <typename T, size_t N>
  void swap(T (&a)[N], T (&b)[N]);      // Since C++11
```

The overload for arrays was added in C++11. In C++20, both versions are additionally declared `constexpr`. For STL containers, `std::swap()` calls the member function `swap()`. As we will see in the following section, the behavior of `swap()` can be customized for other types as well, but without any special efforts, the default implementation is used. This implementation does a swap using a temporary object. Before C++11, the temporary object was copy-constructed, and the swap was done with two assignments, just as we did in the preceding section. The type has to be copyable (both copy-constructible and copy-assignable), otherwise `std::swap()` will not compile (see examples 02a and 02b). In C++11, `std::swap()` has been redefined to use move construction and move assignment (see example 02c). As usual, if the class is copyable, but does not have move operations declared at all, then the copy constructor and assignment are used. Note that if the class has copy operations declared and move operations declared as deleted, there is no automatic fallback to copying—that class is a non-movable type and `std::swap()` will not compile for it (see example 02d).

Since copying an object can, in general, throw an exception, swapping two objects for which a custom swap behavior is not provided can throw an exception as well. Move operations do not usually throw exceptions, and in C++11, if the object has a move constructor and an assignment operator and neither throws an exception, `std::swap()` also provides a no-throw guarantee. That behavior has been formalized in C++17 with a conditional `noexcept()` specification.

Swapping like the standard

From the preceding review of how the standard library handles a swap, we can deduce the following guidelines:

- Classes that support swap should implement `swap()` member functions that perform the operation in constant time
- A free-standing `swap()` non-member function should also be provided for all types that can be swapped
- Swapping two objects should not throw exceptions or otherwise fail

The latter guideline is less strict, and it is not always possible to follow it. In general, if the type has move operations that do not throw an exception, a non-throwing swap implementation is also possible. Note also that many exception-safety guarantees, and in particular those provided by the standard library, require that move and swap operations do not throw an exception.

When and why to use swap

What is so important about the swap functionality that it deserves its own chapter? For that matter, why even use swap, and not continue to refer to an object by its original name?

Mostly, it has to do with exception safety, which is also why we keep mentioning when swap can and cannot throw an exception.

Swap and exception safety

The most important application of swap in C++ has to do with writing exception-safe code, or, more generally, error-safe code. Here is the problem, in a nutshell—in an exception-safe program, throwing an exception should never leave the program in an undefined state.

More generally, an error condition should never leave the program in an undefined state. Note that the error does not need to be handled by means of an exception—for example, returning an error code from a function should also be handled without creating undefined behavior. In particular, if an operation causes an error, the resources already consumed by the operation in progress should be released. Often, an even stronger guarantee is desired—every operation either succeeds or is entirely rolled back.

Let's consider an example where we will apply a transform to all elements of a vector, and store the results in a new vector:

```
// Example 03a
class C;                // Our element type
C transmogrify(C x) {    // Some operation on C
  return C(...);
}
void transmogrify(const std::vector<C>& in,
                  std::vector<C>& out) {
  out.resize(0);
  out.reserve(in.size());
  for (const auto& x : in) {
    out.push_back(transmogrify(x));
  }
}
```

Here, we return the vector via an output parameter. Let us assume that it is a requirement to use an already existing vector for output and we are not doing it for performance reasons. In all recent versions of C++, returning a vector by value is quite fast: the compiler will either apply the return-value optimization and elide the copy completely (copy elision is not guaranteed but likely) or replace copy by move (also fast, guaranteed). The vector is made empty at first, and grows to the same size as the input vector. Any data the out vector may have had is gone. Note the reserve() call that is used to avoid repeated deallocations of the growing vector.

This code works fine as long as there are no errors, that is, no exceptions are thrown. But this is not guaranteed. First of all, reserve() does a memory allocation, which may fail. If this happens, the transmogrify() function will exit via the exception, and the output vector will be empty since the resize(0) call has already been executed. The initial content of the output vector is lost, and nothing is written to replace it. Secondly, any iteration of the loop over the elements of the vector may throw an exception. An exception could be thrown by the copy constructor of the new element of the output vector, or by the transformation itself. Either way, the loop is interrupted. STL guarantees that the output vector is not left in an undefined state even if the copy constructor inside the push_back() call fails—the new element is not *partially* created, and the vector size is not increased.

However, the elements already stored will remain in the output vector (and any elements that were there originally are gone). This may not be what we intended—it is not unreasonable to request that the transmogrify() operation either succeeds and applies the transform to the entire vector, or fails and changes nothing.

The key to such exception-safe implementation is the swap:

```
// Example 03b
void transmogrify(const std::vector<C>& in,
                  std::vector<C>& out) {
  std::vector<C> tmp;
  tmp.reserve(in.size());
  for (const C& x : in) {
    tmp.push_back(transmogrify(x));
  }
  out.swap(tmp);     // Must not throw!
}
```

In this example, we have changed the code to operate on a temporary vector during the entire transformation. Note that, in a typical case of an output vector that is empty on input, this does not increase the amount of memory in use. If the output vector has some data in it, both the new data and the old data exist in memory until the end of the function. This is necessary to provide a guarantee that the old data will not be deleted unless the new data can be fully computed. If desired, this guarantee can be traded for lower overall memory use, and the output vector can be emptied at the beginning of the function (on the other hand, any caller who wants to make such a trade-off can just empty the vector before calling transmogrify()).

If an exception is thrown at any time during the execution of the transmogrify() function, right up until the last line, then the temporary vector is deleted, as would be any local variable allocated on the stack (see *Chapter 5, A Comprehensive Look at RAII*, later in this book). The last line is the key to exception safety—it swaps the content of the output vector with that of the temporary one. If that line can throw an exception, then our entire work is for nothing—the swap has failed, and the output vector is left in an undefined state since we do not know how much of the swap had succeeded before the exception was thrown. But if the swap does not throw an exception, as in the case for std::vector, then, as long as the control reached the last line, the entire transmogrify() operation has succeeded, and the result will be returned to the caller. What happens to the old content of the output vector? It is now owned by the temporary vector, which is about to be deleted, implicitly, on the next line (the closing brace). Assuming the destructor of C follows the C++ guidelines and does not throw an exception (to do otherwise would be to invite the dreaded specter of undefined behavior), our entire function has been made exception-safe.

This idiom is sometimes known as **copy-and-swap** and is, perhaps, the easiest way to implement an operation with commit-or-rollback semantics, or a strong exception-safety guarantee. The key to the idiom is the ability to swap objects cheaply and without exceptions being thrown.

Other common swap idioms

There are a few more commonly used techniques that rely on swap, although none are as critically important as the use of swap for exception safety.

Let's start with a very simple way to reset a container, or any other swappable object, to its default-constructed state:

```
// Example 04
class C {
    public:
    void swap(C& rhs) noexcept {
        … swap data members …
    }
};
C c = ....;    // Object with stuff in it
{
  C tmp;
  c.swap(tmp);    // c is now default-constructed
}               // Old c is now gone
```

Note that this code explicitly creates a default-constructed (*empty*) object just to swap with it, and uses an extra scope (a pair of curly braces) to ensure that that object is deleted as soon as possible. We can do better by using a temporary object, without a name, to swap with:

```
C c = ....;    // Object with stuff in it
C().swap(c);    // Temporary is created and deleted
```

The temporary object here is created and deleted within the same line of code and takes the old content of the object c with it. Note that the order of what is swapped with what is very important—the swap() member function is called on the temporary object. An attempt to do the reverse will not compile:

```
C c = ....;    // Object with stuff in it
c.swap(C());    // Close but does not compile
```

This is because the swap() member function takes its argument by a C& non-const reference, and non-const references cannot be bound to temporary objects (more generally, to r-values). Note that, for the same reason, the swap() non-member function cannot be used to swap an object with a temporary object either, so if the class does not have a swap() member function, then an explicitly named object must be created.

A more general form of this idiom is used to apply transforms to the original object without changing its name in the program. Let's suppose that we have a vector in our program to which we want to apply the preceding `transmogrify()` function; however, we do not want to create a new vector. Instead, we want to continue using the original vector (or at least its variable name) in the program, but with the new data in it. This idiom is an elegant way to achieve the desired result:

```
// Example 05
std::vector<C> vec;
...                        // Write data into the vector
{
    std::vector<C> tmp;
    transmogrify(vec, tmp);     // tmp is the result
    swap(vec, tmp);            // Now vec is the result!
}                          // and now old vec is destroyed
...                        // Keep using vec, with new data
```

Note that if `transmogrify()` can throw an exception, we have to use the entire scope, including swap, as a `try` block to achieve exception safety:

```
std::vector<C> vec;
...                        // Write data into the vector
try {
    std::vector<C> tmp;
    transmogrify(vec, tmp);     // throws an exception
    swap(vec, tmp);            // we never get here
} catch (...) {}            // vec is unchanged
...                        // Keep using vec, with old data
```

This pattern can be repeated as many times as needed, replacing the content of the object without introducing new names into the program. Contrast it with the more traditional, C-like way that does not use swap:

```
std::vector<C> vec;
...      // Write data into the vector std::vector<C> vec1;
transmogrify(vec, vec1);     // Must use vec1 from now on!
std::vector<C> vec2;
transmogrify(vec1, vec2);     // Must use vec2 from now on!
```

Note that the old names, `vec` and `vec1`, are still accessible after the new data is computed. It would be an easy mistake to use `vec` in the following code when `vec1` should be used instead. With the previously demonstrated swap technique, the program is not polluted with new variable names.

How to implement and use swap correctly

We have seen how the swap functionality is implemented by the standard library, and what the expectations are for a swap implementation. Let's now see how to correctly support swap for your own types.

Implementing swap

We have seen that all STL containers, and many other standard library types (for example, `std::thread`), provide a `swap()` member function. While not required, it is the easiest way to implement swap that needs access to the private data of the class, as well as the only way to swap an object with a temporary object of the same type. The proper way to declare the `swap()` member function is like this:

```
class C {
  public:
    void swap(C& rhs) noexcept;
};
```

Of course, the `noexcept` specification should only be included if a no-throw guarantee can indeed be given; in some cases, it may need to be conditional, based on properties of other types. The function may also be declared `constexpr`, if appropriate.

How should the swap be implemented? There are several ways. For many classes, we can simply swap the data members, one at a time. This delegates the problem of swapping the objects to their contained types, which, if they follow the pattern, will eventually end up swapping the built-in types that everything is made of. If you know that your data member has a `swap()` member function, then you can call that. Otherwise, you have to call the non-member swap. This is likely to call an instantiation of the `std::swap()` template, but you should not invoke it by that name for reasons that will be explained in the next section.

Instead, you should bring the name into the containing scope, and call `swap()` without the `std::` qualifier:

```
//Example 06a
#include <utility>      // <algorithm> before C++11
...
class C {
  public:
    void swap(C& rhs) noexcept {
      using std::swap;    // Brings in std::swap into this scope
      v_.swap(rhs.v_);
      swap(i_, rhs.i_);     // Calls std::swap
    }
    ...
    private:
```

```
  std::vector<int> v_;
  int i_;
};
```

A particular implementation idiom that is very swap-friendly is the so-called **pimpl idiom**, also known as the **handle-body idiom**. It is primarily used to minimize compilation dependencies and avoid exposing the implementation of the class in the header file. In this idiom, the entire declaration of a class in the header file consists of all the necessary public member functions, plus a single pointer that points to the actual implementation. The implementation and the body of the member functions are all in the .C file. The *pointer to implementation* data member is often called p_impl or pimpl, hence the name of the idiom. Swapping a pimpl-implemented class is as easy as swapping the two pointers:

```
// Example 06b
// In the header C.h:
class C_impl;           // Forward declaration
class C {
  public:
  void swap(C& rhs) noexcept {
    swap(pimpl_, rhs.pimpl_);
  }
  void f(...);          // Declaration only
  ...
  private:
  C_impl* pimpl_;
};
// In the C file:
class C_impl {
  ... real implementation ...
};
void C::f(...) {
  pimpl_->f(...);       // Actual implementation of C::f()
}
```

This takes care of the member function swap(). But what if someone calls a non-member swap() function on our custom types? As written, that call will invoke the default implementation of std::swap(), if it's visible (for example, due to a using std::swap declaration), that is, the one that uses the copy or move operations:

```
// Example 07a
class C {
  public:
  void swap(C& rhs) noexcept;
};
...
C c1(...), c2(...);
```

```
swap(c1, c2);     // Either does not compile
                  // or calls std::swap
```

Even though we have a `swap()` member function, `std::swap` does not use it. It is evident that we must also support a non-member `swap()` function. We can easily declare one, right after the class declaration. However, we should also consider what happens if the class is declared not in the global scope, but in a namespace:

```
// Example07b
namespace N {
  class C {
    public:
    void swap(C& rhs) noexcept;
  };
  void swap(C& lhs, C& rhs) noexcept { lhs.swap(rhs); }
}
...
N::C c1(...), c2(...);
swap(c1, c2);     // Calls non-member N::swap()
```

The unqualified call to `swap()` calls the `swap()` non-member function inside the N namespace, which in turn calls the member function `swap()` on one of the arguments (the convention adopted by the standard library is to call `lhs.swap()`). Note, however, that we did not invoke `N::swap()`, only `swap()`. Outside of the N namespace and without a `using namespace N;` specification, an unqualified call would not normally resolve to a function inside a namespace. However, in this case, it does, due to a feature in the standard called the **Argument-Dependent Lookup (ADL)**, also known as the **Koenig lookup**. The ADL adds to the overload resolution all functions declared in the scopes where the arguments of the function are declared.

In our case, the compiler sees the `c1` and `c2` arguments of the `swap(...)` function and recognizes their type as `N::C`, even before it figures out what the `swap` name refers to. Since the arguments are in the N namespace, all functions declared in that namespace are added to the overload resolution, and thus, the `N::swap` function becomes visible.

If the type has a `swap()` member function, then the easiest way to implement the non-member `swap()` function is to call that. However, such a member function is not required; if the decision was made to not support a `swap()` member function, then the `swap()` non-member has to have access to the private data of the class. It would have to be declared a `friend` function:

```
// Example 07c
class C {
  friend void swap(C& rhs) noexcept;
};
void swap(C& lhs, C& rhs) noexcept {
```

```
    ... swap data members of C ...
}
```

It is also possible to define the implementation of the swap() function inline, without a separate definition:

```
// Example 07d
class C {
  friend void swap(C& lhs, C& rhs) noexcept {
    ... swap data members of C ...
  }
};
```

This is particularly handy when we have a class template, instead of a single class. We consider this pattern in more detail later, in *Chapter 11, ScopeGuard*.

One often forgotten implementation detail is the self-swap—swap(x, x), or, in the case of a member function call, x.swap(x). Is it well-defined, but what does it do? The answer appears to be that it is, or should be, well-defined in both C++03 and C++11 (and later), but ends up doing nothing; that is, it does not change the object (although not necessarily at zero cost). A user-defined swap implementation should either be implicitly safe for self-swap or should explicitly test for it. If the swap is implemented in terms of copy or move assignments, it is important to note that the copy assignment is required by the standard to be safe against self-assignments, while the move assignment may change the object, but must leave it in a valid state, called a **moved-from** state (in this state, we can still assign something else to the object).

We should also note that similarly named STL functions std::iter_swap and std::swap_ranges are, in fact, algorithms that use swap() – possibly std::swap – to swap values pointed to by iterators or by entire ranges of iterators. They are also an example of how to correctly invoke swap() functions, not just in STL but everywhere in your code, as shown in the next section.

Using swap correctly

Up until now, we have switched between calling a swap() member function, a swap() non-member function, and the explicitly qualified std::swap() operation, without any pattern or reason. We should now bring some discipline to this matter.

First of all, it is always safe and appropriate to call the swap() member function as long as you know that it exists. The latter qualification usually comes up when writing template code—when dealing with concrete types, you typically know what interface they provide. This leaves us with just one question—when calling the swap() non-member function, should we use the std:: prefix?

Consider what happens if we do, as shown here:

```
// Example 08
namespace N {
```

```
  class C {
    public:
    void swap(C& rhs) noexcept;
  };
    void swap(C& lhs, C& rhs) noexcept { lhs.swap(rhs); }
}
...
N::C c1(...), c2(...);
std::swap(c1, c2);    // Calls std::swap()
swap(c1, c2);         // Calls N::swap()
```

Note that the argument-dependent lookup does not apply to qualified names, which is why the call to `std::swap()` still calls the instantiation of the template swap from the `<utility>` header file of the STL. For this reason, it is recommended never to call `std::swap()` explicitly, but to bring that overload into the current scope with a `using` declaration, then call the unqualified `swap`:

```
using std::swap;    // Makes std::swap() available
swap(c1, c2);    // Calls N::swap() if provided
              // Otherwise, calls std::swap()
```

This is exactly what STL algorithms do. For example, `std::iter_swap` is usually implemented something like this:

```
template <typename Iter1, typename Iter2>
void iter_swap(Iter1 a, ITer2 b) {
  using std::swap;
  swap(*a, *b);
}
```

Unfortunately, the fully qualified invocation of `std::swap()` is often found in many programs. To protect yourself against such code and to ensure that your custom swap implementation is called no matter what, you can instantiate the `std::swap()` template for your own type:

```
// Example 09
namespace std {
void swap(N::C& lhs, N::C& rhs) noexcept {
  lhs.swap(rhs); }
}
```

Generally, declaring your own functions or classes for the reserved `std::` namespace is not allowed by the standard. However, the standard makes an exception for explicit instantiations of certain template functions (`std::swap()` being among them). With such specialization in place, a call to `std::swap()` will invoke that instantiation, which forwards it to our custom swap implementation. Note that it is not sufficient to instantiate the `std::swap()` template, because such instantiations do not participate in the argument-dependent lookup. If the other non-member swap function is not provided, we have the reverse problem:

```
using std::swap;        // Makes std::swap() available
std::swap(c1, c2);      // Calls our std::swap() overload
swap(c1, c2);           // Calls default std::swap()
```

Now, the non-qualified call ends up calling the instantiation of the default `std::swap()` operation—the one with the move constructors and assignments. In order to ensure that every call to swap is correctly handled, both a non-member `swap()` function and the explicit `std::swap()` instantiation should be implemented (of course, they can, and should, all forward to the same implementation). Finally, note that the standard allows us to extend the `std::` namespace with template instantiations, but not with additional template overloads. Therefore, if, instead of a single type, we have a class template, we cannot specialize `std::swap` for it; such code will, in all likelihood, compile, but the standard does not guarantee that the desired overload will be selected (technically, the standard invokes the undefined behavior and guarantees nothing at all). For that reason alone, calling `std::swap` directly should be avoided.

Summary

The swap functionality in C++ is used to implement several important patterns. The most critical one is the copy-and-swap implementation of exception-safe transactions. All standard library containers, and most other STL objects, provide the swap member function that is fast and, when possible, does not throw exceptions. User-defined types that need to support swap should follow the same pattern. Note, however, that implementing a non-throwing swap function usually requires an extra indirection and goes against several optimization patterns. In addition to the member function swap, we have reviewed the use and implementation of the non-member swap. Given that `std::swap` is always available, and can be called on any copyable or movable objects, the programmer should take care to implement a non-member swap function too if a better way to swap exists for a given type (in particular, any type with a member function swap should also provide a non-member function overload that calls that member function).

Finally, while the preferred invocation of the non-member swap is without the `std::` prefix, the alternative use, although ill-advised, is common enough that an implicit instantiation of the `std::swap` template should be considered.

The next chapter takes us on a tour of one of the most popular, and powerful, C++ idioms—the C++ way of managing resources.

Questions

1. What does swap do?

2. How is swap used in exception-safe programs?

3. Why should a swap function be non-throwing?

4. Should a member or a non-member implementation of swap be preferred?

5. How do standard library objects implement swap?

6. Why should the non-member swap function be called without the `std::` qualifier?

A Comprehensive Look at RAII

Resource management is probably the second most frequent thing a program does, after computing. But just because it's frequently done does not mean it's visible—some languages hide most, or all, resource management from the user. And just because it is hidden, does not mean it's not there.

Every program needs to use some memory, and memory is a resource. A program would be of no use if it never interacted with the outside world in some way, at least to print the result, and input and output channels (files, sockets, and so on) are resources.

In this chapter, we will start by answering the following questions:

- What is considered a resource in a C++ program?

- What are the key concerns for managing resources in C++?

Then, we will introduce **Resource Acquisition is Initialization** (**RAII**) and explain how it helps in efficient resource management in C++ by answering these questions:

- What is the standard approach for managing resources in C++ (RAII)?

- How does RAII solve the problems of resource management?

We will end the chapter with a discussion about the implications and possible concerns of using RAII by providing the answers to these questions:

- What are the precautions that must be taken when writing RAII objects?

- What are the consequences of using RAII for resource management?

C++, with its zero-overhead abstraction philosophy, does not hide resources or their management at the core language level. But we would do well to not confuse hiding resources with managing them.

Technical requirements

Here are some useful links:

- Google Test unit testing framework: `https://github.com/google/googletest`
- Google Benchmark library: `https://github.com/google/benchmark`
- Example code: `https://github.com/PacktPublishing/Hands-On-Design-Patterns-with-CPP-Second-Edition/tree/master/Chapter05`

Resource management in C++

Every program operates on resources and needs to manage them. The most commonly used resource is memory, of course. Hence, you often read about **memory management** in C++. But really, resources can be just about anything. Many programs exist specifically to manage real, tangible physical resources, or the more ephemeral (but no less valuable) digital ones. Money in bank accounts, airline seats, car parts and assembled cars, or even crates of milk—in today's world, if it is something that needs to be counted and tracked, there is a piece of software somewhere that is doing it. But even in a program that does pure computations, there may be varied and complex resources, unless the program also eschews abstractions and operates at the level of bare numbers. For example, a physics simulation program may have particles as resources.

All of these resources have one thing in common—they need to be accounted for. They should not vanish without a trace, and a program should not just make up resources that don't really exist. Often, a specific instance of a resource is needed—you would not want someone else's purchase to be debited from your bank account; the specific instance of the resource matters. Thus, the most important consideration when evaluating different approaches to resource management is correctness—how well does the design ensure that resources are managed properly, how easy is it to make a mistake, and how hard would it be to find such a mistake? It should come as no surprise, then, that we use a testing framework to present the coding examples of resource management in this chapter.

Installing the microbenchmark library

In our case, we are interested in the efficiency of memory allocations and small fragments of code that may contain such allocations. The appropriate tool for measuring the performance of small fragments of code is a microbenchmark. There are many microbenchmark libraries and tools out there; in this book, we will use the Google Benchmark library. To follow along with the examples in this chapter, you must first download and install the library (follow the instructions in the Readme.md file). Then you can compile and run the examples. You can build the sample files included with the library to see how to build a benchmark on your particular system; you can also use the example benchmark from this chapter's repository:

```
// Example 01
#include <stdlib.h>
```

```
#include "benchmark/benchmark.h"
void BM_malloc(benchmark::State& state) {
  constexpr size_t size = 1024;
  for (auto _ : state) {
    void* p = malloc(size);
    benchmark::DoNotOptimize(p);
    free(p);
  }
  state.SetItemsProcessed(state.iterations());
}
BENCHMARK(BM_malloc);
BENCHMARK_MAIN();
```

Note the call to `DoNotOptimize()`: it's a special function that doesn't generate any code but tricks the compiler into thinking that its argument is necessary and cannot be optimized away. Without this, the compiler will probably figure out that the entire benchmark loop has no observable effect and can be optimized to nothing.

On a Linux machine, the command to build and run a benchmark program called `01_benchmark.C` might look something like this:

```
$CXX 01_benchmark.C -I. -I$GBENCH_DIR/include -O3 \
   --std=c++17 $GBENCH_DIR/lib/libbenchmark.a -lpthread \
   -o 01_benchmark && ./01_benchmark
```

Here, `$CXX` is your C++ compiler, such as `g++` or `clang++`, and `$GBENCH_DIR` is the directory where the benchmark is installed.

The preceding example should print something like this:

```
-------------------------------------------------------------------
Benchmark                Time           CPU   Iterations UserCounters...
-------------------------------------------------------------------
BM_malloc              6.54 ns       6.54 ns    110928398 items_per_second=152.995M/s
```

On this particular machine, a single iteration (one pair of calls to `malloc()` and `free()`) takes 6.37 nanoseconds, which translates into 157 million memory allocations per second.

Sometimes we have to benchmark very short operations:

```
void BM_increment(benchmark::State& state) {
  size_t i = 0;
  for (auto _ : state) {
    ++i;
    benchmark::DoNotOptimize(i);
  }
```

```
    state.SetItemsProcessed(state.iterations());
}
```

We may be reasonably concerned about the overhead of the benchmark loop itself. In such cases, we can execute multiple copies of the benchmarked operation within the body of the loop. We can even get the C++ preprocessor to make copies for us:

```
// Example 02
#define REPEAT2(x) x x
#define REPEAT4(x) REPEAT2(x) REPEAT2(x)
#define REPEAT8(x) REPEAT4(x) REPEAT4(x)
#define REPEAT16(x) REPEAT8(x) REPEAT8(x)
#define REPEAT32(x) REPEAT16(x) REPEAT16(x)
#define REPEAT(x) REPEAT32(x)
void BM_increment32(benchmark::State& state) {
  size_t i = 0;
  for (auto _ : state) {
    REPEAT(
      ++i;
      benchmark::DoNotOptimize(i);
    )
  }
  state.SetItemsProcessed(32*state.iterations());
}
```

The time of a "*single*" iteration now includes 32 iterations, so it is much easier to use the items per second value. Remember to include repeat count in the number of items processed:

```
Benchmark              Time           CPU    Iterations UserCounters...
-----------------------------------------------------------------------
BM_increment        0.210 ns      0.210 ns   1000000000 items_per_second=4.77094G/s
BM_increment32       6.75 ns       6.75 ns    103796866 items_per_second=4.7385G/s
```

Writing fast programs is all well and good, but they have to be correct first. To that end, we need to write tests, so we also need a testing framework.

Installing Google Test

We will be testing very small fragments of code for correctness. On the one hand, this is simply because each fragment illustrates a specific concept or idea. On the other hand, even in a large-scale software system, resource management is done by small building blocks of code. They may combine to form a quite complex resource manager, but each block performs a specific function and is testable. The appropriate testing system for this situation is a unit testing framework. There are many such frameworks to choose from; in this book, we will use the Google Test unit testing framework. To follow along with the examples in this chapter, you must first download and install the framework (follow the instructions in the README file). Once installed, you can compile and run the examples. You can build the sample tests included with the library to see how to build and link with Google Test on your particular system; you can also use the example from this chapter's repository:

```
#include <vector>
#include "gtest/gtest.h"
TEST(Memory, Vector) {
  std::vector<int> v(10);
  EXPECT_EQ(10u, v.size());
  EXPECT_LE(10u, v.capacity());
}
```

On a Linux machine, the command to build and run a 02_test.C test might look something like this:

```
$CXX 02_test.C -I. -I$GTEST_DIR/include -g -O0 -I. \
  -Wall -Wextra -Werror -pedantic --std=c++17 \
  $GTEST_DIR/lib/libgtest.a $GTEST_DIR/lib/libgtest_main.a\
  -lpthread -lrt -lm -o -2_test && ./02_test
```

Here, $CXX is your C++ compiler, such as g++ or clang++, and $GTEST_DIR is the directory where Google Test is installed. If all tests pass, you should get this output:

```
Running main() from gtest_main.cc
[==========] Running 1 test from 1 test case.
[----------] Global test environment set-up.
[----------] 1 test from Memory
[ RUN      ] Memory.Vector
[       OK ] Memory.Vector (0 ms)
[----------] 1 test from Memory (0 ms total)
[----------] Global test environment tear-down
[==========] 1 test from 1 test case ran. (0 ms total)
[  PASSED  ] 1 test.
```

Writing good tests is an art. We have to identify the aspects of our code that need to be validated and come up with ways to observe these aspects. In this chapter, we are interested in resource management, so let us see how we can test the utilization and release of resources.

Counting resources

A unit testing framework, such as Google Test, allows us to execute some code and verify that the results are what they should be. The results that we can look at include any variable or expression that we can access from the test program. That definition does not extend, for example, to the amount of memory that is currently in use. So, if we want to verify that resources are not disappearing, we have to count them.

In the following simple test fixture, we use a special resource class instead of, say, the `int` keyword. This class is instrumented to count how many objects of this type have been created, and how many are currently alive:

```
// Example 03
struct object_counter {
  static int count;
  static int all_count;
  object_counter() { ++count; ++all_count; }
  ~object_counter() { --count; }
};
int object_counter::count = 0;
int object_counter::all_count = 0;
```

Now we can test that our program manages resources correctly, as follows:

```
// Example 03
#include "gtest/gtest.h"
TEST(Memory, NewDelete) {
  object_counter::all_count = object_counter::count = 0;
  object_counter* p = new object_counter;
  EXPECT_EQ(1, object_counter::count);
  EXPECT_EQ(1, object_counter::all_count);
  delete p;
  EXPECT_EQ(0, object_counter::count);
  EXPECT_EQ(1, object_counter::all_count);
}
```

In Google Test, every test is implemented as a **test fixture**. There are several types; the simplest one is a standalone test function, such as the one we use here. Running this simple test program tells us that the test has passed, as follows:

```
[----------] 1 test from Memory
[ RUN      ] Memory.NewDelete
[       OK ] Memory.NewDelete (0 ms)
[----------] 1 test from Memory (0 ms total)
[  PASSED  ] 1 test.
```

The expected results are verified using one of the EXPECT_* macros and any test failures will be reported. This test verifies that, after creating and deleting an instance of the type object_counter, there are no such objects left, and that exactly one was constructed.

Dangers of manual resource management

C++ allows us to manage resources almost at the hardware level, and someone, somewhere, must indeed manage them at this level. The latter is actually true for every language, even the high-level ones that do not expose such details to the programmers. But *somewhere* does not have to be in your program! Before we learn the C++ solutions and tools for resource management, let's first understand the problems that arise from not using any such tools.

Manual resource management is error-prone

The first and most obvious danger of managing every resource manually, with explicit calls to acquire and release each one, is that it is easy to forget the latter. For example, see the following:

```
{
  object_counter* p = new object_counter;
  ... many more lines of code ...
  // Were we supposed to do something here?
  // Can't remember now...
}
```

We are now leaking a resource (the `object_counter` objects, in this case). If we did this in a unit test, it would fail, as follows:

```
// Example 04
TEST(Memory, Leak1) {
  object_counter::all_count = object_counter::count = 0;
  object_counter* p = new object_counter;
  EXPECT_EQ(1, object_counter::count);
  EXPECT_EQ(1, object_counter::all_count);
  //delete p;  // Forgot that
  EXPECT_EQ(0, object_counter::count); // This test fails!
  EXPECT_EQ(1, object_counter::all_count);
}
```

You can see the failing tests, and the location of the failures, as reported by the unit test framework:

```
[ RUN      ] Memory.Leak1
04_memory.C:31: Failure
Expected equality of these values:
  0
  object_counter::count
    Which is: 1
[  FAILED  ] Memory.Leak1 (0 ms)
```

In a real program, finding such errors is much harder. Memory debuggers and sanitizers can help with memory leaks, but they require that the program actually execute the buggy code, so they depend on the test coverage.

The resource leaks can be much subtler and harder to find, too. Consider this code, where we did not forget to release the resource:

```
bool process(... some parameters ... ) {
  object_counter* p = new object_counter;
  ... many more lines of code ...
  delete p;     // A-ha, we remembered!
  return true;  // Success
}
```

During subsequent maintenance, a possible failure condition was discovered, and the appropriate test was added:

```
bool process(... some parameters ... ) {
  object_counter* p = new object_counter;
  ... many more lines of code ...
  if (!success) return false;   // Failure, cannot continue
  ... even more lines of code ...
  delete p;     // Still here
  return true;  // Success
}
```

This change introduced a subtle bug—now, resources are leaked only if the intermediate computation has failed and triggered the early return. If the failure is rare enough, this mistake may escape all tests, even if the testing process employs regular memory sanitizer runs. This mistake is also all too easy to make since the edit could be made in a place far removed from both the construction and deletion of the object, and nothing in the immediate context gives the programmer a hint that a resource needs to be released.

The alternative to leaking a resource, in this case, is to release it. Note that this leads to some code duplication:

```
bool process(... some parameters ... ) {
  object_counter* p = new object_counter;
  ... many more lines of code ...
  if (!success) {
    delete p;
    return false;     // Failure, cannot continue
  }
  ... even more lines of code ...
  delete p;     // Still here
```

```
    return true;     // Success
}
```

As with any code duplication, there comes the danger of code divergence. Let's say that the next round of code enhancements required more than one `object_counter`, and an array of them is now allocated as follows:

```
bool process(... some parameters ... ) {
  object_counter* p = new object_counter[10]; // Array now
  ... many more lines of code ...
  if (!success) {
    delete p;
    return false;     // Old scalar delete
  }
  ... even more lines of code ...
  delete [] p;     // Matching array delete
  return true;     // Success
}
```

If we change new to the new array, we must change `delete` as well; the thought goes, there is probably one at the end of the function. Who knew that there was one more in the middle? Even if the programmer had not forgotten about the resources, manual resource management gets disproportionately more error-prone as the program becomes more complex. And not all resources are as forgiving as a counter object. Consider the following code that performs some concurrent computation, and must acquire and release mutex locks. Note the very words **acquire** and **release**, the common terminology for locks, suggest that locks are treated as a kind of resource (the resource here is exclusive access to the data protected by the lock):

```
std::mutex m1, m2, m3;
bool process_concurrently(... some parameters ... ) {
  m1.lock();
  m2.lock();
  ... need both locks in this section ...
  if (!success) {
    m1.unlock();
    m2.unlock();
    return false;
  } // Both locks unlocked
  ... more code ...
  m2.unlock();     // Don't need access to m1-guarded data
                   // Still need m1
  m3.lock();
  if (!success) {
    m1.unlock();
```

```
      return false;
   } // No need to unlock m2 here
   ... more code ...
   m1.unlock();
   m3.unlock();
   return true;
}
```

This code has both duplication and divergence. It also has a bug—see if you can find it (hint—count how many times m3 is unlocked, versus how many `return` statements there are after it's locked). As the resources become more numerous and complex to manage, such bugs are going to creep up more often.

Resource management and exception safety

Remember the code at the beginning of the previous section—the one we said is correct, where we did not forget to release the resource? Consider the following code:

```
bool process(... some parameters ... ) {
  object_counter* p = new object_counter;
  ... many more lines of code ...
  delete p;
  return true;     // Success
}
```

I have bad news for you—this code probably wasn't correct either. If any of the many more lines of code can throw an exception, then `delete p` is never going to be executed:

```
bool process(... some parameters ... ) {
  object_counter* p = new object_counter;
  ... many more lines of code ...
  if (!success) // Cannot continue
    throw process_exception();
  ... even more lines of code ...
  // Won't do anything if an exception is thrown!
  delete p;
  return true;
}
```

This looks very similar to the early `return` problem, only worse—the exception can be thrown by any code that the `process()` function calls. The exception can even be added later to some code that the `process()` function calls, without any changes in the function itself. It used to work fine, then one day it does not.

Unless we change our approach to resource management, the only solution is to use the `try` ... `catch` blocks:

```
bool process(... some parameters ... ) {
  object_counter* p = new object_counter;
  try {
    ... many more lines of code ...
    if (!success) // Cannot continue
      throw process_exception();
    ... even more lines of code ...
  } catch ( ... ) {
    delete p;    // For exceptional case
  }
  delete p;    // For normal case return true;
}
```

The obvious problem here is code duplication again, as well as the proliferation of the `try` ... `catch` blocks literally everywhere. Worse than that, this approach does not scale should we need to manage multiple resources, or even just manage anything more complex than a single acquisition with a corresponding release:

```
std::mutex m;
bool process(... some parameters ... ) {
  m.lock(); // Critical section starts here
  object_counter* p = new object_counter;
  // Problem #1: constructor can throw
  try {
    ... many more lines of code ...
    m.unlock();    // Critical section ends here
    ... even more lines of code ...
  } catch ( ... ) {
    delete p;    // OK, always needed
    m.unlock();    // Do we need this? Maybe...
    throw;    // Rethrow the exception for the client to handle
  }
  delete p;    // For normal case, no need to unlock mutex
  return true;
}
```

Now, we can't even decide whether the catch block should release the mutex or not—it depends on whether the exception was thrown before or after the `unlock()` operation that happens in the normal, non-exceptional control flow. Also, the `object_counter` constructor could throw an exception (not the simple one we had so far, but a more complex one that ours could evolve into). That would happen outside of the `try` ... `catch` block, and the mutex would never get unlocked.

It should be clear to us by now that we need an entirely different solution for the resource management problem, not some patchwork. In the next section, we will discuss the pattern that became the golden standard of resource management in C++.

The RAII idiom

We have seen in the previous section how ad hoc attempts to manage resources become unreliable, then error-prone, and eventually fail. What we need is to make sure that resource acquisition is always paired up with resource release, and that these two actions happen before and after the section of code that uses the resource respectively. In C++, this kind of bracketing of a code sequence by a pair of actions is known as the Execute Around design pattern.

> **Tip**
>
> For more information, see the article *C++ Patterns – Executing Around Sequences* by Kevlin Henney, available at `http://www.two-sdg.demon.co.uk/curbralan/papers/europlop/ExecutingAroundSequences.pdf`.

When specifically applied to resource management, this pattern is much more widely known as **Resource Acquisition is Initialization (RAII)**.

RAII in a nutshell

The basic idea behind RAII is very simple—there is one kind of function in C++ that is guaranteed to be called automatically, and that is the destructor of an object created on the stack, or the destructor of an object that is a data member of another object (in the latter case, the guarantee holds only if the containing class itself is destroyed). If we could hook up the release of the resource to the destructor of such an object, then the release could not be forgotten or skipped. It stands to reason that if releasing the resource is handled by the destructor, acquiring it should be handled by the constructor during the initialization of the object. Hence the full meaning of RAII as introduced in the title of this chapter—*A Comprehensive Look at RAII*.

Let's see how this works in the simplest case of memory allocation, via `operator new`. First, we need a class that can be initialized from a pointer to the newly allocated object, and whose destructor will delete that object:

```
// Example 05
template <typename T> class raii {
  public:
  explicit raii(T* p) : p_(p) {}
  ~raii() { delete p_; }
  private:
```

```
    T* p_;
};
```

Now it is very easy to make sure that deletion is never omitted, and we can verify that it works as expected with a test that uses `object_counter`:

```
// Example 05
TEST(RAII, AcquireRelease) {
  object_counter::all_count = object_counter::count = 0;
  {
    raii<object_counter> p(new object_counter);
    EXPECT_EQ(1, object_counter::count);
    EXPECT_EQ(1, object_counter::all_count);
  } // No need to delete p, it's automatic
  EXPECT_EQ(0, object_counter::count);
  EXPECT_EQ(1, object_counter::all_count);
}
```

Note that in C++17, the class template type is deduced from the constructor and we can simply write the following:

```
raii p(new object_counter);
```

The RAII resource release happens when the owning object is destroyed for any reason; thus, the cleanup after an exception is thrown and automatically taken care of:

```
// Example 05
struct my_exception {};
TEST(Memory, NoLeak) {
  object_counter::all_count = object_counter::count = 0;
  try {
    raii p(new object_counter);
    throw my_exception();
  } catch ( my_exception& e ) {
  }
  EXPECT_EQ(0, object_counter::count);
  EXPECT_EQ(1, object_counter::all_count);
}
```

Of course, we probably want to use the new object for more than just creating and deleting it, so it would be nice to have access to the pointer stored inside the RAII object. There is no reason to grant such access in any way other than the standard pointer syntax, which makes our RAII object a kind of pointer itself:

```
// Example 06
template <typename T> class scoped_ptr {
```

```cpp
public:
explicit scoped_ptr(T* p) : p_(p) {}
~scoped_ptr() { delete p_; }
T* operator->() { return p_; }
const T* operator->() const { return p_; }
T& operator*() { return *p_; }
const T& operator*() const { return *p_; }
private:
T* p_;
};
```

This pointer can be used to automatically delete, at the end of the scope, the object that it points to (hence the name):

```cpp
// Example 06
TEST(Scoped_ptr, AcquireRelease) {
  object_counter::all_count = object_counter::count = 0;
  {
    scoped_ptr p(new object_counter);
    EXPECT_EQ(1, object_counter::count);
    EXPECT_EQ(1, object_counter::all_count);
  }
  EXPECT_EQ(0, object_counter::count);
  EXPECT_EQ(1, object_counter::all_count);
}
```

The destructor is called when the scope containing the `scoped_ptr` object is exited. It does not matter how it is exited—an early `return` from a function, a `break` or `continue` statement in the loop, or an exception being thrown are all handled in exactly the same way, and without leaks. We can verify this with tests, of course:

```cpp
// Example 06
TEST(Scoped_ptr, EarlyReturnNoLeak) {
  object_counter::all_count = object_counter::count = 0;
  do {
    scoped_ptr p(new object_counter);
    break;
  } while (false);
  EXPECT_EQ(0, object_counter::count);
  EXPECT_EQ(1, object_counter::all_count);
}
TEST(Scoped_ptr, ThrowNoLeak) {
  object_counter::all_count = object_counter::count = 0;
  try {
    scoped_ptr p(new object_counter);
    throw 1;
```

```
  } catch ( ... ) {}
  EXPECT_EQ(0, object_counter::count);
  EXPECT_EQ(1, object_counter::all_count);
}
```

All tests pass, confirming that there is no leak:

```
[----------] 6 tests from Scoped_ptr
[ RUN      ] Scoped_ptr.AcquireRelease
[       OK ] Scoped_ptr.AcquireRelease (0 ms)
[ RUN      ] Scoped_ptr.EarlyReturnNoLeak
[       OK ] Scoped_ptr.EarlyReturnNoLeak (0 ms)
[ RUN      ] Scoped_ptr.ThrowNoLeak
[       OK ] Scoped_ptr.ThrowNoLeak (0 ms)
[ RUN      ] Scoped_ptr.DataMember
[       OK ] Scoped_ptr.DataMember (0 ms)
[ RUN      ] Scoped_ptr.Reset
[       OK ] Scoped_ptr.Reset (0 ms)
[ RUN      ] Scoped_ptr.Reseat
[       OK ] Scoped_ptr.Reseat (0 ms)
[----------] 6 tests from Scoped_ptr (0 ms total)
```

Similarly, we can use a scoped pointer as a data member in another class—a class that has secondary storage and must release it upon destruction:

```
class A {
  public:
  A(object_counter* p) : p_(p) {}
  private:
  scoped_ptr<object_counter> p_;
};
```

This way, we don't have to delete the object manually in the destructor of class A, and, in fact, if every data member of class A takes care of itself in a similar fashion, class A may not even need an explicit destructor.

Anyone familiar with C++11 should recognize our `scoped_ptr` as a very rudimentary version of `std::unique_ptr`, which can be used for the same purpose. As you might expect, the standard unique pointer's implementation has a lot more to it, and for good reasons. We will review some of these reasons later in this chapter, but, to be clear: you should use `std::unique_ptr` in your code and the only reason we implemented our own `scoped_ptr` here is to understand how an RAII pointer works.

One last issue to consider is that of performance. C++ strives for zero-overhead abstractions whenever possible. In this case, we are wrapping a raw pointer into a smart pointer object. However, the compiler does not need to generate any additional machine instructions; the wrapper only forces the compiler to generate the code that, in a correct program, it would have done anyway. We can confirm with a simple benchmark that both the construction/deletion and the dereference of our `scoped_ptr` (or `std::unique_ptr`, for that matter) take exactly the same time as the corresponding operations on a raw pointer. For example, the following microbenchmark (using the Google benchmark library) compares the performance of all three pointer types for dereferencing:

```
// Example 07
void BM_rawptr_dereference(benchmark::State& state) {
  int* p = new int;
  for (auto _ : state) {
    REPEAT(benchmark::DoNotOptimize(*p);)
  }
  delete p;
  state.SetItemsProcessed(32*state.iterations());
}
void BM_scoped_ptr_dereference(benchmark::State& state) {
  scoped_ptr<int> p(new int);
  for (auto _ : state) {
    REPEAT(benchmark::DoNotOptimize(*p);)
  }
  state.SetItemsProcessed(32*state.iterations());
}
void BM_unique_ptr_dereference(benchmark::State& state) {
  std::unique_ptr<int> p(new int);
  for (auto _ : state) {
    REPEAT(benchmark::DoNotOptimize(*p);)
  }
  state.SetItemsProcessed(32*state.iterations());
}
BENCHMARK(BM_rawptr_dereference);
BENCHMARK(BM_scoped_ptr_ dereference);
BENCHMARK(BM_unique_ptr_dereference);
BENCHMARK_MAIN();
```

The benchmark shows that the smart pointers indeed incur no overhead:

```
------------------------------------------------------------------------
Benchmark                      Time          CPU Iterations UserCounters...
BM_rawptr_dereference          3.42 ns  3.42 ns  817698667 items_per_
second=9.35646G/s
BM_scoped_ptr_dereference      3.37 ns  3.37 ns  826869427 items_per_
second=9.48656G/s
BM_unique_ptr_dereference      3.42 ns  3.42 ns  827030287 items_per_
second=9.36446G/s
```

We have covered in enough detail the applications of RAII for managing memory. But there are other resources that a C++ program needs to manage and keep track of, so we have to expand our view of RAII now.

RAII for other resources

The name, RAII, refers to *resources* and not *memory*, and indeed the same approach is applicable to other resources. For each resource type, we need a special object, although generic programming and lambda expressions may help us to write less code (we will learn more about this in *Chapter 11, ScopeGuard*). The resource is acquired in the constructor and released in the destructor. Note that there are two slightly different flavors of RAII. The first option is the one we have already seen—the actual acquisition of the resource is at initialization, but outside of the constructor of the RAII object.

The constructor merely captures the handle (such as a pointer) that resulted from this acquisition. This was the case with the `scoped_ptr` object that we just saw—memory allocation and object construction were both done outside of the constructor of the `scoped_ptr` object, but still during its initialization. The second option is for the constructor of the RAII object to actually acquire the resource. Let's see how this works, with the example of an RAII object that manages mutex locks:

```
// Example 08
class mutex_guard {
  public:
  explicit mutex_guard(std::mutex& m) : m_(m) {
    m_.lock();
  }
  ~mutex_guard() { m_.unlock(); }
  private:
  std::mutex& m_;
};
```

Here, the constructor of the `mutex_guard` class itself acquires the resource; in this case, exclusive access to the shared data protected by the mutex. The destructor releases that resource. Again, this pattern completely removes the possibility of *leaking* a lock (that is, exiting a scope without releasing the lock), for example, when an exception is thrown:

```
// Example 08
std::mutex m;
TEST(MutexGuard, ThrowNoLeak) {
  try {
    mutex_guard lg(m);
    EXPECT_FALSE(m.try_lock());    // Expect to be locked
    throw 1;
  } catch ( ... ) {}
  EXPECT_TRUE(m.try_lock());       // Expect to be unlocked
```

```
    m.unlock();      // try_lock() will lock, undo it
}
```

In this test, we check whether the mutex is locked or not by calling `std::mutex::try_lock()` —
we cannot call `lock()` if the mutex is already locked, as it will deadlock. By calling `try_lock()`,
we can check the state of the mutex without the risk of deadlock (but remember to unlock the mutex
if `try_lock()` succeeds since we're using `try_lock()` just to test and don't want to lock the
mutex again).

Again, the standard provides an RAII object for mutex locking, `std::lock_guard`. It is used
in a similar manner but can be applied to any mutex type that has the `lock()` and `unlock()`
member functions:

```
try {
    std::lock_guard lg(m);        // C++17 constructor
    EXPECT_FALSE(m.try_lock());   // Expect to be locked
    throw 1;
} catch ( ... ) {}
EXPECT_TRUE(m.try_lock());        // Expect to be unlocked
```

In C++17, we have a similar RAII object for locking multiple mutexes – `std::scoped_lock`. In
addition to the RAII release, it offers a deadlock avoidance algorithm when locking several mutexes
at once. Of course, there are many more kinds of resources that a C++ program may have to manage,
so we often end up writing our own RAII objects. Sometimes, the standard helps out, such as the
addition of `std::jthread` in C++20 (a thread is also a resource, and *"releasing"* it usually means
joining the thread, which is what `std::jthread` does in its destructor). With the wide variety
of resources that can be managed with RAII techniques, sometimes we have needs that go beyond
automatically releasing resources at the end of the scope.

Releasing early

The scope of a function or a loop body does not always match the desired duration of the holding
of the resource. If we do not want to acquire the resource at the very beginning of the scope, this is
easy—the RAII object can be created anywhere, not just at the beginning of the scope. Resources are
not acquired until the RAII object is constructed, as follows:

```
void process(...) {
    ... do work that does not need exclusive access ...
    mutex_guard lg(m);      // Now we lock
    ... work on shared data, now protected by mutex ...
} // lock is released here
```

However, the release still happens at the end of the function body scope. What if we only want to lock a short portion of code inside the function? The simplest answer is to create an additional scope:

```
void process(...) {
    ... do work that does not need exclusive access ...
    {
       mutex_guard lg(m);    // Now we lock
       ... work on shared data, now protected by mutex ...
    } // lock is released here
    ... more non-exclusive work ...
}
```

It may be surprising if you have never seen it before, but in C++, any sequence of statements can be enclosed in the curly braces, as { ... }. Doing so creates a new scope with its own local variables. Unlike the curly braces that come after loops or conditional statements, the only purpose of this scope is to control the lifetime of these local variables. A program that uses RAII extensively often has many such scopes, enclosing variables with different lifetimes that are shorter than the overall function or loop body. This practice also improves readability by making it clear that some variables will not be used after a certain point, so the reader does not need to scan the rest of the code looking for possible references to these variables. Also, the user cannot accidentally add such a reference by mistake if the intent is to *expire* a variable and never use it again.

And what if a resource may be released early, but only if certain conditions are met? One possibility is, again, to contain the use of the resource in a scope, and exit that scope when the resource is no longer needed. It would be convenient to be able to use break to get out of a scope. A common way to do just that is to write a *do once* loop:

```
// Example 08
void process(...) {
    ... do work that does not need exclusive access ...
    do {    // Not really a loop
       mutex_guard lg(m);    // Now we lock
       ... work on shared data, now protected by mutex ...
       if (work_done) break;    // Exit the scope
       ... work on the shared data some more ...
    } while (false);           // lock is released here
    ... more non-exclusive work ...
}
```

However, this approach does not always work (we may want to release the resources, but not other local variables we defined in the same scope), and the readability of the code suffers as the control flow gets more complex. Resist the impulse to accomplish this by allocating the RAII object dynamically, with operator new! This completely defeats the whole point of RAII, since you now must remember to invoke operator delete. We can enhance our resource-managing objects by adding a client-triggered release, in addition to the automatic release by the destructor. We just have to make sure that the same resource is not released twice. Consider the following example, using `scoped_ptr`:

```
// Example 06
template <typename T> class scoped_ptr {
  public:
  explicit scoped_ptr(T* p) : p_(p) {}
  ~scoped_ptr() { delete p_; }
  ...
  void reset() {
    delete p_;
    p_ = nullptr;        // Releases resource early private:
  }
  T* p_;
};
```

After calling `reset()`, the object managed by the `scoped_ptr` object is deleted, and the pointer data member of the `scoped_ptr` object is reset to null. Note that we did not need to add a condition check to the destructor, because calling delete on a null pointer is allowed by the standard—it does nothing. The resource is released only once, either explicitly by the `reset()` call, or implicitly at the end of the scope containing the `scoped_ptr` object. As we already noted, you do not need to write your own `scoped_ptr` except to learn how RAII pointers work: `std::unique_ptr` can be reset too.

For the `mutex_guard` class, we can't deduce from just the lock whether an early release was called or not, and we need an additional data member to keep track of that:

```
// Example 08
class mutex_guard {
  public:
  explicit mutex_guard(std::mutex& m) :
    m_(m), must_unlock_(true) { m_.lock(); }
  ~mutex_guard() { if (must_unlock_) m_.unlock(); }
    void reset() { m_.unlock(); must_unlock_ = false; }
  private:
  std::mutex& m_;
  bool must_unlock_;
};
```

Now we can verify that the mutex is released only once, at the right time, with this test:

```
TEST(MutexGuard, Reset) {
  {
    mutex_guard lg(m);
    EXPECT_FALSE(m.try_lock());
    lg.reset();
```

```
    EXPECT_TRUE(m.try_lock()); m.unlock();
  }
  EXPECT_TRUE(m.try_lock()); m.unlock();
}
```

The standard `std::unique_ptr` pointer supports `reset()`, whereas `std::lock_guard` does not, so if you need to release a mutex early, you need to use a different standard RAII object, `std::unique_lock`:

```
// Example 08
TEST(LockGuard, Reset) {
  {
    std::unique_lock lg(m);
    EXPECT_FALSE(m.try_lock());
    lg.unlock();
    EXPECT_TRUE(m.try_lock()); m.unlock();
  }
  EXPECT_TRUE(m.try_lock()); m.unlock();
}
```

For other resources, you may have to write your own RAII object, which is usually a pretty simple class, but finish reading this chapter before you start writing, as there are a few *gotchas* to keep in mind.

Note that the `reset()` method of `std::unique_ptr` actually does more than just delete the object prematurely. It can also be used to **reset** the pointer by making it point to a new object while the old one is deleted. It works something like this (the actual implementation in the standard is a bit more complex, because of the additional functionality the unique pointer has):

```
template <typename T> class scoped_ptr {
  public:
  explicit scoped_ptr(T* p) : p_(p) {}
  ~scoped_ptr() { delete p_; }
  ...
  void reset(T* p = nullptr) {
    delete p_; p_ = p;    // Reseat the pointer
  }
  private:
  T* p_;
};
```

Note that this code breaks if a scoped pointer is reset to itself (for example, if `reset()` is called with the same value as that stored in `p_`). We could check for this condition and do nothing; it is worth noting that the standard does not require such a check for `std::unique_ptr`.

Careful implementation of Resource Acquisition is Initialization objects

It is obviously very important that the resource management objects do not mismanage the resources they are entrusted to guard. Unfortunately, the simple RAII objects we have been writing so far have several glaring holes.

The first problem arises when someone tries to copy these objects. Each of the RAII objects we have considered in this chapter is responsible for managing a unique instance of its resource, and yet, nothing prevents us from copying this object:

```
scoped_ptr<object_counter> p(new object_counter);
scoped_ptr<object_counter> p1(p);
```

This code invokes the default copy constructor, which simply copies the bits inside the object; in our case, the pointer is copied to the object_counter. Now we have two RAII objects that both control the same resource. Two destructors will be called, eventually, and both will attempt to delete the same object. The second deletion is undefined behavior (if we are very fortunate, the program will crash at that point).

Assignment of RAII objects is similarly problematic:

```
scoped_ptr<object_counter> p(new object_counter);
scoped_ptr<object_counter> p1(new object_counter);
p = p1;
```

The default assignment operator also copies the bits of the object. Again, we have two RAII objects that will delete the same managed object. Equally troublesome are the facts that we have no RAII objects that manage the second object_counter, the old pointer inside p1 is gone, and there is no other reference to this object, so we have no way to delete it.

The mutex_guard does no better—an attempt to copy it results in two mutex guards that will unlock the same mutex. The second unlock will be done on a mutex that is not locked (at least not by the calling thread), which, according to the standard, is undefined behavior. Assignment of the mutex_guard object is not possible, though, because the default assignment operator is not generated for objects with reference data members.

As you may have probably noticed, the problem is created by the **default** copy constructor and default assignment operator. Does it mean that we should have implemented our own? What would they do? Only one destructor should be called for each object that was constructed; a mutex can only be unlocked once after it was locked. This suggests that an RAII object should not be copied at all, and we should disallow both copying and assignment:

```
template <typename T> class scoped_ptr {
  public:
    explicit scoped_ptr(T* p) : p_(p) {}
```

```
~scoped_ptr() { delete p_; }
...
private:
T* p_;
scoped_ptr(const scoped_ptr&) = delete;
scoped_ptr& operator=(const scoped_ptr&) = delete;
};
```

There are some RAII objects that can be copied. These are reference-counted resource management objects; they keep track of how many copies of the RAII object exist for the same instance of the managed resource. The last of the RAII objects has to release the resource when it is deleted. We discuss shared management of resources in more detail in *Chapter 3, Memory and Ownership*.

A different set of considerations exist for move constructor and assignment. Moving the object does not violate the assumption that there is only one RAII object that owns a particular resource. It merely changes which RAII object that is. In many cases, such as mutex guards, it does not make sense to move an RAII object (indeed, the standard does not make `std::lock_guard` or `std::scoped_lock` movable, but `std::unique_lock` is movable and can be used to transfer ownership of a mutex). Moving a unique pointer is possible and makes sense in some contexts, which we also explore in *Chapter 3, Memory and Ownership*.

However, for a scoped pointer, moving would be undesirable, as it allows the extension of the lifetime of the managed object beyond the scope where it was created. Note that we do not need to delete the move constructor or move assignment operators if we already deleted the copying ones (although doing so does no harm). On the other hand, `std::unique_ptr` is a movable object, which means using it as a scope-guarding smart pointer does not offer the same protection because the resource could be moved out. However, if you need a scoped pointer, there is a very simple way to make `std::unique_ptr` do this job perfectly—all you have to do is to declare a `const std::unique_ptr` object:

```
std::unique_ptr<int> p;
{
  // Can be moved out of the scope
  std::unique_ptr<int> q(new int);
  q = std::move(p);      // and here it happens
  // True scoped pointer, cannot be moved anywhere
  const std::unique_ptr<int> r(new int);
  q = std::move(r);      // Does not compile
}
```

So far, we have protected our RAII objects against duplicating or losing resources. But there is one more kind of resource management mistake that we have not yet considered. It seems obvious that a resource should be released in a way that matches its acquisition. And yet, nothing protects our `scoped_ptr` object from such a mismatch between construction and deletion:

```
scoped_ptr<int> p(new int[10]);
```

The problem here is that we have allocated multiple objects using an array version of `operator new`; it should be deleted with the array version of `operator delete` - `delete [] p_` must be called inside the `scoped_ptr` destructor, instead of `delete p_` that we have there now.

More generally, an RAII object that accepts a resource handle during initialization, instead of acquiring the resource itself (like the `mutex_guard` does) must somehow ensure that the resource is released in the right way that matches the way it was acquired. Obviously, this is not possible, in general. In fact, it is impossible to do automatically, even for the simple case of a mismatched `new` array and the `delete` scalar (`std::unique_ptr` does no better than our `scoped_ptr` here, although facilities such as `std::make_unique` make writing such code less error-prone).

In general, either the RAII class is designed to release resources in one particular way, or the caller must specify how the resource must be released. The former is certainly easier, and in many cases is quite sufficient. In particular, if the RAII class also acquires a resource, such as our `mutex_guard`, it certainly knows how to release it. Even for the `scoped_ptr`, it would not be too hard to create two versions, `scoped_ptr` and `scoped_array`; the second one is for objects allocated by the `operator new` array. The standard handles it by specializing the unique pointer for arrays: you can write `std::unique_ptr<int []>` and the array `delete` will be used (it is still up to the programmer to make sure that arrays allocated by `new []` are owned by the correct instantiation of the pointer).

A more general version of an RAII class is parameterized not just by the resource type, but also by a callable object used to release this type, usually known as the deleter. The deleter can be a function pointer, a member function pointer, or an object with `operator()` defined—basically, anything that can be called like a function. Note that the deleter has to be passed to the RAII object in its constructor, and stored inside the RAII object, which makes the object larger. Also, the type of the deleter is a template parameter of the RAII class, unless it is erased from the RAII type (this will be covered in *Chapter 6, Understanding Type Erasure*). The standard gives us examples of both: `std::unique_ptr` has the deleter template parameter, while `std::shared_ptr` uses type erasure.

Downsides of RAII

Honestly, there aren't any significant downsides to RAII. It is by far the most widely used idiom for resource management in C++. The only issue of significance to be aware of has to do with exceptions. Releasing a resource can fail, like anything else. The usual way in C++ to signal a failure is to throw an exception. When that is undesirable, we fall back on returning error codes from functions. With RAII, we can do neither of these things.

It is easy to understand why error codes are not an option—the destructor does not return anything. Also, we cannot write the error code into some status data member of the object, since the object is being destroyed and its data members are gone, as are the other local variables from the scope containing the RAII object. The only way to save an error code for future examination would be to write it into some sort of a global status variable, or at least a variable from the containing scope. This is possible in a bind, but such a solution is very inelegant and error-prone. This is exactly the problem that C++ was trying to solve when exceptions were introduced: manually-propagated error codes are error-prone and unreliable.

So, if the exceptions are the answer to error reporting in C++, why not use them here? The usual answer is *that the destructors in C++ cannot throw*. This captures the gist of it, but the real restriction is a bit more nuanced. First of all, prior to C++11, the destructors technically could throw, but the exception would propagate and (hopefully) eventually get caught and processed. In C++11, all destructors are, by default, `noexcept`, unless explicitly specified as `noexcept (false)`. If a `noexcept` function throws, the program immediately terminates.

So indeed, in C++11, destructors cannot throw unless you specifically allow them to do so. But what's wrong with throwing an exception in the destructor? If the destructor is executed because the object was deleted, or because the control reached the end of the scope for a stack object, then nothing is wrong. The *wrong* happens if the control did not reach the end of the scope normally and the destructor is executed because an exception was already thrown. In C++, two exceptions cannot propagate at the same time. If this happens, the program will immediately terminate (note that a destructor can throw and catch an exception, there is no problem with that, as long as that exception does not propagate out of the destructor). Of course, when writing a program, there is no way to know when some function called from something in a particular scope, could throw. If the resource release throws and the RAII object allows that exception to propagate out of its destructor, the program is going to terminate if that destructor was called during exception handling. The only safe way is never to allow exceptions to propagate from a destructor.

This does not mean that the function that releases the resource itself cannot throw, but, if it does, an RAII destructor has to catch that exception:

```
class raii {
    ...
  ~raii() {
    try {
      release_resource();     // Might throw
    } catch ( ... ) {
      ... handle the exception, do NOT rethrow ...
    }
  }
};
```

This still leaves us with no way to signal that an error happened during resource release—an exception was thrown, and we had to catch it and not let it escape.

How much of a problem is this? Not that much, really. First of all, releasing memory—the most frequently managed resource—does not throw an exception. Usually, the memory is released not as just memory, but by deleting an object. But remember that the destructors should not throw an exception in order that the entire process of releasing memory by deleting an object doesn't throw an exception either. At this point, the reader might, in search of a counter-example, look up in the standard what happens if unlocking a mutex fails (that would force the destructor of `std::lock_guard` to deal with the error). The answer is both surprising and enlightening—unlocking a mutex cannot throw, but if it fails, undefined behavior results instead. This is no accident; the mutex was intended to work with an RAII object. Such is, in general, the C++ approach to releasing the resources: an exception should not be thrown if the release fails, or at least not allowed to propagate. It can be caught and logged, for example, but the calling program will, in general, remain unaware of the failure, possibly at the cost of undefined behavior.

RAII is a really successful technique that has evolved very little even as the language changes significantly from pre-C++11 all the way to C++20 (aside from minor syntactic conveniences such as constructor argument deduction). That is because it really doesn't have any downsides of note. But, as the language gets new capabilities, sometimes we find ways to improve even the best and most established patterns, and here is one of those cases.

Very modern RAII

If we really want to be picky, we can make another complaint about RAII; realistically, this is only a downside when the acquisition or release code is long and complex. The acquisition and release are done in the constructor and the destructor of an RAII object, respectively, and this code can be quite removed from the place in the code where the resource is acquired (so we have to jump around the program a bit to figure out what it does).

Similarly, if the resource handling requires a lot of state (such as the appropriate actions depending on several factors and conditions), we have to capture all this state in the RAII object. An example that truly challenges the readability of RAII would also be completely unreadable on a book page, so we will have to condense it. Let us say that we want to have an RAII lock guard that performs several actions when locking and unlocking the mutex, and even the way it handles the resource depends on some external parameters:

```
// Example 09a
class lock_guard {
  std::mutex& m_;
  const bool log_;
  const bool mt_;
  public:
  lock_guard(std::mutex& m, bool log, bool mt);
  ~lock_guard();
};
lock_guard ::lock_guard(std::mutex& m, bool log, bool mt)
  : m_(m), log_(log), mt_(mt) {
  if (log_) std::cout << "Before locking" << std::endl;
  if (mt_) m.lock();
}
lock_guard::~lock_guard() {
```

```
  if (mt_) m.unlock();
  if (log_) std::cout << "After locking" << std::endl;
}
```

And here is how this guard object might be used:

```
#include <mutex>
std::mutex m;
const bool mt_run = true;
void work() {
  try {
    lock_guard lg(m, true, mt_run);
    … this code might throw …
    std::cout << "Work is happening" << std::endl;
  } catch (...) {}
}
```

Here we perform only one possible action in addition to locking and unlocking – we can optionally log these events; you can already see that the implementations of the constructor and the destructor, the two sections of code that must be closely matched, are somewhat separated from each other. Also, tracking the state (do we need to log the events? Are we running in a multi-threaded or single-threaded context?) is becoming somewhat verbose. Again, you have to remember that this is a simplified example: in a real program, this is still a fine RAII object. But, if the code gets even longer, you may wish for a better way.

In this case, the better way is borrowed from Python (specifically, from the contextmanager decorator). This technique used coroutines and, thus, requires C++20 (so we managed to couple one of the oldest tools in C++ with the most cutting-edge one). The detailed explanation of the coroutines in general and the C++ coroutine machinery in particular lies outside of the scope of this book (you can find it, for example, in my book "*The Art of Writing Efficient Programs*", (https://www.packtpub.com/product/the-art-of-writing-efficient-programs/9781800208117)).

For now, it is sufficient to remember two things:

- First, C++ coroutines are, essentially, regular functions except they suspend themselves at any time and return the control to the caller. The caller can resume the coroutine, and it continues to execute from the suspension point as if nothing happened.

- Second, C++ coroutines require a lot of standard boilerplate code. In the example that follows, we will highlight the important fragments; you can safely assume that the rest of the code is required by the standard to make the coroutine machinery work.

Let us first see what the code for a lock guard looks like with this new coroutine-based RAII approach:

```
#include <mutex>
std::mutex m;
```

```
const bool mt_run = true;
co_resource<std::mutex> make_guard(std::mutex& m, bool log)
{
    if (log) std::cout << "Before locking" << std::endl;
    if (mt_run) m.lock();
    co_yield m;
    if (mt_run) m.unlock();
    if (log) std::cout << "After locking" << std::endl;
}
void work () {
    try {
        co_resource<std::mutex> lg { make_guard(m, true) };
        … this code might throw …
        std::cout << "Work is happening" << std::endl;
    } catch (...) {}
}
```

Instead of the lock_guard object, we have the make_guard function. This function is a coroutine; you can tell because it has the co_yield operator – this is one of several ways C++ coroutines return values to the caller. The code before co_yield is resource acquisition, it is executed when the resource is acquired and is equivalent to the constructor of our lock_guard object. The code after co_yield is the same as the destructor of lock_guard. Arguably, this is easier to read and maintain (at least after you stop staring at the coroutine syntax) because all the code is in the same place you can think of co_yield as a placeholder for the work the caller is going to do while owning the resource (the mutex, in our case). Also, there are no class members and member initialization to write – the function parameters are accessible throughout the execution of the coroutine.

The coroutine returns an object of type co_resource<std::mutex>: that is our modern RAII type is implemented as the co_resource class template; it is implemented as follows:

```
// Example 09
#include <cassert>
#include <coroutine>
#include <cstddef>
#include <memory>
#include <utility>

template <typename T> class co_resource {
    public:
    using promise_type = struct promise_type<T>;
    using handle_type = std::coroutine_handle<promise_type>;
    co_resource(handle_type coro) : coro_(coro) {}
    co_resource(const co_resource&) = delete;
    co_resource& operator=(const co_resource&) = delete;
    co_resource(co_resource&& from)
```

```
      : coro_(std::exchange(from.coro_, nullptr)) {}
  co_resource& operator=(co_resource&& from) {
    std::destroy_at(this);
    std::construct_at(this, std::move(from));
    return *this;
  }
  ~co_resource() {
    if (!coro_) return;
    coro_.resume();      // Resume from the co_yield point
    coro_.destroy();     // Clean up
  }
  private:
  handle_type coro_;
};
```

This is the object that owns the resource, but you don't see the resource or its type T directly: it is hidden inside the coroutine handle `coro_`. This handle acts like a pointer to the state of the coroutine. If you focus on the handle as a resource for the moment, we have a fairly routine resource-owning object. It acquires the resource in the constructor and maintains the exclusive ownership: the handle is destroyed in the destructor of the `co_resource` object unless the ownership is transferred via move, and copying the resource is not allowed.

This resource-owning object is going to be returned by a coroutine function; every such object must contain a nested type named `promise_type`. Often, it is a nested class, but it can also be a separate type (in this example, we made it such largely to avoid a single very long code fragment). The standard imposes several requirements on the interface of the promise type, and here is the type that meets these requirements for our purposes:

```
template <typename T> struct promise_type {
  const T* yielded_value_p = nullptr;
  std::suspend_never initial_suspend() noexcept {
    return {};
  }
  std::suspend_always final_suspend() noexcept {
    return {};
  }
  void return_void() noexcept {}
  void unhandled_exception() { throw; }
  std::suspend_always yield_value(const T& val) noexcept {
    yielded_value_p = &val;
    return {};
  }
  using handle_type = std::coroutine_handle<promise_type>;
  handle_type get_return_object() {
```

```
        return handle_type::from_promise(*this);
    }
};
```

Our promise type contains a pointer to the value returned by the coroutine. How does the value get there? When the coroutine returns the result via co_yield, the member function yield_value() is called (the compiler generates this call). The value returned by co_yield is passed to this function, which, in turn, captures its address (the lifetime of the value is the same as that of the coroutine itself). The other important member function of the promise type is get_return_object(): it is invoked by the compiler to return the co_resource object itself to the caller of the make_guard() coroutine. Note that it does not return a co_resource object, but a handle that is implicitly convertible to co_resource (it has an implicit constructor from handle_type). The rest of the promise_type interface is, for our purposes, the boilerplate code required by the standard.

Here is how the co_resource RAII works: first, we call the function make_guard():

```
co_resource<std::mutex> make_guard(std::mutex& m, bool log)
{
    if (log) std::cout << "Before locking" << std::endl;
    if (mt_run) m.lock();
    co_yield m;
    if (mt_run) m.unlock();
    if (log) std::cout << "After locking" << std::endl;
}
```

From the caller's point of view, it starts executing like any other function, although the internal details are quite different. All the code we wrote before co_yield is executed, then the coroutine is suspended and the co_resource<std::mutex> object is constructed and returned to the caller, where it is moved into a stack variable:

```
co_resource<std::mutex> lg { make_guard(m, true) };
```

The execution proceeds as usual, protected by the locked mutex. At the end of the scope, the object lg is destroyed; this happens no matter whether we exit the scope normally or by throwing an exception. In the destructor of the co_resource object, the coroutine is resumed via the call to the member function resume() of the coroutine handle coro_. This causes the coroutine to resume execution right after the point where stopped before, so the control jumps to the next line after co_yield. The resource release code we wrote there is executed, and the coroutine exits through the bottom of the scope, now for the last time. The destructor of co_resource has some cleanup to do, but, otherwise, we are (mostly) done.

There are a few things we have left out to avoid overly extending the example. First of all, as written, the co_resource template does not work if the resource type T is a reference. This may be perfectly acceptable: handling references by RAII is not that common. In this case, a static assert or a concept check is sufficient. Otherwise, we have to carefully handle dependent types inside the template.

Second, the implicit requirement on the coroutine such as `make_guard()` is that it returns a value via `co_yield` exactly once (you can have more than one `co_yield` in the body of the coroutine, but only one can be executed for a particular call). To make the code robust, we have to verify that this requirement has been met using run-time asserts.

We now have the acquisition and release code right next to each other and we don't need to convert function arguments into data members like we did when constructors and destructors handled RAII. The only thing that might make it even better would be if we didn't have to write a separate `make_guard()` function, at least in cases where we have only one call to it. Turns out that we can combine coroutines and lambdas to just such a result:

```
void work(){
  try {
    auto lg { [&](bool log)->co_resource<std::mutex> {
      if (log) std::cout << "Before locking" << std::endl;
      if (mt_run) m.lock();
      co_yield m;
      if (mt_run) m.unlock();
      if (log) std::cout << "After locking" << std::endl;
    }(true) };
    ... this code might throw ...
    std::cout << "Work is happening" << std::endl;
  } catch (...) {}
}
```

Here the coroutine is the `operator()` of a lambda expression; note that we have to specify the return type explicitly. The lambda is invoked immediately; and; as usual in such cases, the use of captures or parameters boils down to what is more convenient in each case.

With the coroutine-based RAII resource management, we were able to keep all the relevant code portions very close to each other. Of course, there is a price: launching, suspending, and resuming coroutines takes time (and a bit of memory). The basic RAII object is always going to be faster, so don't try to replace `std::unique_pointer` with a `co_resource` class. But keep in mind that our original dissatisfaction with RAII started with the observation that when the code executed for the acquisition or release of resources is long, complex, and uses a lot of state variables, an RAII class might be hard to read. It is likely that in such cases the overhead of the coroutines is less important (we should also point out that the "scope guard" pattern described later in *Chapter 11, ScopeGuard*, addresses some of the same concerns and sometimes is a better option).

The RAII techniques we have learned are some of the most enduring C++ patterns; they were in use from the first day of C++ and continue to evolve and benefit from the latest language features. Throughout this book, we will casually and without a second thought use classes such as `std::unique_ptr` or `std::lock_guard`. For now, we leave you with these final thoughts.

Summary

After this chapter, you should be well aware of the dangers of an ad-hoc approach to resource management. Fortunately, we have learned the most widely used idiom for resource management in C++; the RAII idiom. With this idiom, each resource is owned by an object. Constructing (or initializing) the object acquires the resource, and deleting the object releases it. We saw how using RAII addresses the problems of resource management, such as leaking resources, accidentally sharing resources, and releasing resources incorrectly. We have also learned the basics of writing exception-safe code, at least as far as the leaking or otherwise mishandling of resources is concerned. Writing RAII objects is simple enough, but there are several caveats to keep in mind. Finally, we reviewed the complications that arise when error handling has to be combined with RAII.

RAII is a resource management idiom, but it can also be viewed as an abstraction technique: the complex resources are hidden behind simple resource handles. The next chapter introduces another kind of abstraction idiom, type erasure: instead of complex objects, we will now hide complex types.

Questions

1.   What are the resources that a program can manage?

2.   What are the main considerations when managing resources in a C++ program?

3.   What is RAII?

4.   How does RAII address the problem of leaking resources?

5.   How does RAII address the problem of dangling resource handles?

6.   What RAII objects are provided by the C++ standard library?

7.   What precautions must be taken when writing RAII objects?

8.   What happens if releasing a resource fails?

Further reading

- `https://www.packtpub.com/application-development/expert-c-programming`

- `https://www.packtpub.com/application-development/c-data-structures-and-algorithms`

- `https://www.packtpub.com/application-development/rapid-c-video`

6

Understanding Type Erasure

Type erasure is often seen as a mysterious, enigmatic programming technique. It is not exclusive to C++ (most tutorials on type erasure use Java for their examples). The goal of this chapter is to lift the shroud of mystery and teach you what type erasure is and how to use it in C++.

The following topics will be covered in this chapter:

- What is type erasure?
- Is type erasure a design pattern, or an implementation technique?
- How can we implement type erasure?
- What design and performance considerations must be taken into account when deciding to use type erasure? What other guidelines can be offered for the use of type erasure?

Technical requirements

Example code can be found at the following link: `https://github.com/PacktPublishing/Hands-On-Design-Patterns-with-CPP-Second-Edition/tree/main/Chapter06`

You will need the Google Benchmark library installed and configured, details for which can be found here: `https://github.com/google/benchmark` (see *Chapter 4, Swap - From Simple to Subtle*)

What is type erasure?

Type erasure, in general, is a programming technique by which the explicit type information is removed from the program. It is a type of abstraction that ensures that the program does not explicitly depend on some of the data types.

This definition, while perfectly correct, also serves perfectly to surround type erasure in mystery. It does so by employing a sort of circular reasoning—it dangles before you the hope for something that, at first glance, appears impossible—a program written in a strongly typed language that does not use the actual types. How can this be? Why, by abstracting away the type, of course! And so, the hope and the mystery lives on.

It is hard to imagine a program that uses types without explicitly mentioning them (at least a C++ program; there are certainly languages where all types are not final until runtime).

So, we begin by demonstrating what is meant by type erasure using an example. This should allow us to gain an intuitive understanding of type erasure, which, in the later sections of this chapter, we will develop and make more rigorous. The aim here is to increase the level of abstraction—instead of writing some type-specific code, perhaps several versions of it for different types, we can write just one version that is more abstract, and expresses the concept—for example, instead of writing a function whose interface expresses the concept *sort an array of integers*, we want to write a more abstract function, *sort any array*.

Type erasure by example

We will go through a detailed explanation of what type erasure is and how it is accomplished in C++. But first, let's see what a program that has had the explicit type information removed from it looks like.

We start with a very simple example of using a unique pointer, `std::unique_ptr`:

```
std::unique_ptr<int> p(new int(0));
```

This is an owning pointer (see *Chapter 3, Memory and Ownership*)—the entity containing this pointer, such as an object or a functional scope, also controls the lifetime of the integer we allocated, and is responsible for its deletion. The deletion is not explicitly visible in the code and will happen when the p pointer is deleted (for example, when it goes out of scope). The way this deletion will be accomplished is also not explicitly visible—by default, `std::unique_ptr` deletes the object it owns using `operator delete`, or, more precisely, by invoking `std::default_delete`, which, in turn, calls `operator delete`. What if we do not want to use the regular standard `delete`? For example, we may have objects that are allocated on our own heap:

```
class MyHeap {
  public:
    ...
    void* allocate(size_t size);
    void deallocate(void* p);
    ...
};
void* operator new(size_t size, MyHeap* heap) {
    return heap->allocate(size);
}
```

Allocation is no problem, with the help of the overloaded `operator new`:

```
MyHeap heap;
std::unique_ptr<int> p(new(&heap) int(0));
```

This syntax invokes the two-argument `operator new` function; the first argument is always the size and is added by the compiler, and the second argument is the heap pointer. Since we have such an overload declared, it will be invoked and will return the memory allocated from the heap. But we have not done anything to change the way the object is deleted. The regular `operator delete` function will be called and will attempt to return to the global heap some memory that wasn't allocated from there. The result is likely to be memory corruption, and probably a crash. We could define an `operator delete` function with the same additional argument, but it does us no good here—unlike `operator new`, there is no place to pass arguments to `delete` (you will often see such an `operator delete` function defined anyway, and it should behave as such, but it has nothing to do with any `delete` you see in the program; it is used in the stack unwinding if the constructor throws an exception).

Somehow, we need to tell the unique pointer that this particular object is to be deleted differently. It turns out that `std::unique_ptr` has a second `template` argument. You usually don't see it because it defaults to `std::default_delete`, but that can be changed and a custom `deleter` object can be defined to match the allocation mechanism. The `deleter` has a very simple interface—it needs to be callable:

```
template <typename T> struct MyDeleter {
  void operator()(T* p);
};
```

The `std::default_delete` policy is implemented pretty much like that and simply calls `delete` on the p pointer. Our custom `deleter` will need a non-trivial constructor to store the pointer to the heap. Note that, while the `deleter` needs, in general, to be able to delete an object of any type that can be allocated, it does not have to be a template class. A non-template class with a template member function will do just as well, as long as the data members of the class do not depend on the deleted type. In our case, the data members depend only on the type of the heap, but not on what is being deleted:

```
class MyDeleter {
  MyHeap* heap_;
  public:
  MyDeleter(MyHeap* heap) : heap_(heap) {}
  template <typename T> void operator()(T* p) {
    p->~T();
    heap_->deallocate(p);
  }
};
```

The `deleter` has to perform the equivalent of both functions of the standard `operator delete` function—it has to invoke the destructor of the object being deleted, then it must deallocate the memory that was allocated for this object.

Now that we have the appropriate `deleter`, we can finally use `std::unique_ptr` with our own heap:

```
// Example 01
MyHeap heap;
MyDeleter deleter(&heap);
std::unique_ptr<int, MyDeleter> p(
  new(&heap) int(0), deleter);
```

Note that `deleter` objects are often created on demand, at the point of allocation:

```
MyHeap heap;
std::unique_ptr<int, MyDeleter> p(
  new(&heap) int(0), MyDeleter(&heap));
```

Either way, the `deleter` must be no-throw-copyable or no-throw-movable; that is, it must have a copy constructor or a move constructor, and the constructor must be declared `noexcept`. The built-in types, such as raw pointers, are, of course, copyable, and the default compiler-generated constructor does not throw. Any aggregate type combining one or more of these types as data members, such as our `deleter`, has a default constructor that also does not throw (unless it has been redefined, of course).

Note that the `deleter` is a part of the unique pointer's type. Two unique pointers that own objects of the same type, but have different deleters, are different types:

```
// Example 02
MyHeap heap;
std::unique_ptr<int, MyDeleter> p(
  new(&heap) int(0), MyDeleter(&heap));
std::unique_ptr<int> q(new int(0));
p = std::move(q);    // Error: p and q are different types
```

Similarly, the unique pointer must be constructed with the `deleter` of the right type:

```
std::unique_ptr<int> p(new(&heap) int(0),
  MyDeleter(&heap));    // Does not compile
```

As an aside, while experimenting with unique pointers of different types, you might notice that the two pointers in the preceding code, p and q, while not assignable, are comparable: p `==` q compiles. This happens because the `comparison` operator is actually a template—it accepts two unique pointers of different types and compares the underlying raw pointers (if that type differs as well, the compilation error is likely to not mention the unique pointer at all, but instead, to say something about comparing pointers to distinct types without a cast).

Now let's do the same example, but with the shared pointer, std::shared_ptr. First, we point the shared pointer to an object constructed with the regular operator new function as follows:

```
std::unique_ptr<int> p(new int(0));
std::shared_ptr<int> q(new int(0));
```

For comparison, we left the unique pointer declaration there as well. The two smart pointers are declared and constructed in exactly the same way. And now, in the following code block, the shared pointer to an object allocated on our heap:

```
MyHeap heap;
std::unique_ptr<int, MyDeleter> p(
  new(&heap) int(0), MyDeleter(&heap));
std::shared_ptr<int> q(
  new(&heap) int(0), MyDeleter(&heap));
```

Now you see a difference—the shared pointer that was created with a custom deleter is, nonetheless, of the same type as the one that uses the default deleter! In fact, all shared pointers to int have the same type, std::shared_ptr<int>—the template does not have another argument. Think this through—the deleter is specified in the constructor but is used only in the destructor, therefore it must be stored inside the smart pointer object until needed. There is no way to recover it later if we lose the object that was given to us during construction. Both std::shared_ptr and std::unique_ptr must store the deleter object of an arbitrary type inside the pointer object itself. But only the std::unique_ptr class has the deleter information in its type. The std::shared_ptr class is the same for all deleter types. Going back to the very beginning of this section, the program that uses std::shared_ptr<int> does not have any explicit information about the deleter type.

This type has been erased from the program. This, then, is what a type-erased program looks like:

```
// Example 03
void some_function(std::shared_ptr<int>);       // no deleter
MyHeap heap;
{
  std::shared_ptr<int> p(      // No deleter in the type
    new(&heap) int(0),
    MyDeleter(&heap));       // Deleter in constructor only
  std::shared_ptr<int> q(p);       // No deleter type anywhere
  some_function(p);      // uses p, no deleter
}      // Deletion happens, MyDeleter is invoked
```

We spent so much time dissecting std::shared_ptr because it provides a very simple example of type erasure, especially since we can contrast it with std::unique_ptr which has to solve exactly the same problem but chooses the opposite approach. This simple example, however, does not highlight the design implications of choosing type erasure and does not illustrate what design problems this pattern solves. For that, we should look at the quintessential type-erased object in C++: `std::function`.

From example to generalization

In C++, `std::function` is a general-purpose polymorphic function wrapper, or a general callable object. It is used to store any callable entity such as a function, a lambda expression, a functor (an object with the `operator()`), or a member function pointer. The only requirement for these different callable entities is that they must have the same call signature, i.e., accept the same arguments and return the result of the same type. The signature is specified when a particular `std::function` object is declared:

```
std::function<int(long, double)> f;
```

We have just declared a callable that can be invoked with two arguments, `long` and `double` (or, to be more precise, with any two arguments convertible to `long` and `double`), and returns a result that can be converted to `int`. What does it do with the arguments and what is the result? That is determined by the concrete callable entity that is assigned to `f`:

```
// Example 04
std::function<size_t(const std::string&)> f;
size_t f1(const std::string& s) { return s.capacity(); }
f = f1;
std::cout << f("abcde");    // 15
char c = 'b';
f = [=](const std::string& s) { return s.find(c); };
std::cout << f("abcde");    // 1
f = &std::string::size;
std::cout << f("abcde");    // 5
```

In this example, we first assign a non-member function `f1` to `f`; now calling `f(s)` returns the capacity of the string `s` since that's what `f1` does. Next, we change `f` to contain a lambda expression; calling `f(s)` now invokes that expression. The only thing these two functions have in common is the interface: they accept the same arguments and have the same result types. Finally, we assign a member function pointer to `f`; while the function `std::string::size()` takes no arguments, all member functions have an implicit first argument which is a reference to the object itself, so it fits the requirement on the interface.

We can now see type erasure in its more general form: it is an abstraction for many different implementations that all provide the same behavior. Let us consider what design capabilities it opens.

Type erasure as a design pattern

We have already seen how type erasure manifests itself in a program: the code expects certain semantics behavior, but, instead of dealing with specific types that provide it, we use an abstraction and "erase" the properties of those types that are not relevant to the task at hand (starting with the name of the type).

In this way, type erasure has attributes of several other design patterns, but it's not equivalent to any of them. It could reasonably be considered a design pattern in its own right. So, what does type erasure offer as a design pattern?

In type erasure, we find an abstract expression of certain behavior, such as a function call, that can be used to separate the interface from the implementation. So far, this sounds very similar to inheritance. Recall now how, at the end of the last section, we made a `std::function` object invoke several completely different callables: a function, a lambda expression, and a member function. This illustrates the fundamental difference between type erasure and inheritance: with inheritance, the base class determines the abstract behavior (the interface), and any class that needs to implement that interface must be derived from the same base. With type erasure, there is no such requirement: the types that provide the common behavior do not have to form any particular hierarchy; in fact, they need not be classes at all.

It can be said that type erasure offers a non-intrusive way to separate the interface from the implementation. By "intrusive" we mean the fact that we must change a type in order to use the abstraction: for example, we may have a class that has the desired behavior, but, in order to be used polymorphically, it must also inherit from the common base class. This is the "intrusion" – the enforced change we must make to the otherwise perfectly good class in order to make it usable as a concrete implementation of a certain abstract interface. As we have just seen, type erasure has no such need. As long as the class (or any other type) has the desired behavior – usually, a way to invoke it in a function call-like manner with certain arguments – it can be used to implement this behavior. The other properties of the type are not relevant for supporting the interface we are focusing on and are "erased."

We can also say that type erasure provides "external polymorphism:" there is no unifying hierarchy required, and the set of types that can be used to implement a particular abstraction is extensible, not limited to just classes derived from a common base.

So, why doesn't type erasure completely replace inheritance in C++? To some extent, it is tradition; don't be too fast to kick tradition, though – the other name for tradition is "convention," and conventional code is also familiar, easy-to-understand code. But there are two "real" reasons as well. The first one is performance. We will study the implementations of type erasure and their respective performance later in this chapter; however, without spoiling anything, we can say that high-performance implementations of type erasure became available only recently. The second one is convenience, and we can see that already. If we need to declare an abstraction for a whole set of related operations, we can declare a base class with the necessary virtual member functions. If we use a `std::function` approach, a type-erased implementation would have to handle each of these operations separately. As we will see soon, this is not a requirement – we can implement a type-erased abstraction for a whole set of operations at once. However, doing it with inheritance is easier. Also, remember that all concrete types hiding behind the type erasure must provide the required behavior; if we require that all these types support several different member functions, it is more likely that they are going to be coming from the same hierarchy for other reasons.

Type erasure as an implementation technique

Not every use of type erasure has a grand design idea behind it. Often, type erasure is used purely as an implementation technique (the same is true for inheritance, and we are about to see one such use). In particular, type erasure is a great tool for breaking dependencies between components of a large system.

Here is a simple example. We are building a large distributed software system, so one of our core components is the network communication layer:

```
class Network {
    ...
    void send(const char* data);
    void receive(const char* buffer);
    ...
};
```

This is, of course, a very simplified and abstract view of a component that is, at best, non-trivial, but sending data across the network is not what we want to focus on now. The important point is that this is one of our foundational components, the rest of the system depends on it. We may have several different programs built as a part of our software solution; all of them include this communication library.

Now, in one specific application, we have a need to process the data packets before and after they are sent across the network; it could be a high-security system that requires advanced encryption, or it could be the only tool in our system that is designed to work over unreliable networks and needs to insert error correction codes. The point is, the designer of the network layer is now asked to introduce a dependency on some external code that comes from a higher-level application-specific component:

```
class Network {
    ...
    bool needs_processing;
    void send(const char* data) {
        if (needs_processing) apply_processing(buffer);
        ...
    }
    ...
};
```

While this code looks simple, it is a dependency nightmare: the low-level library now has to be built with the `apply_processing()` function from the specific application. Even worse, all other programs that do not require this functionality must still be compiled and linked with this code, even if they never set `needs_processing`.

While this problem can be handled the "old school" way – with some function pointers or (worse) global variables, type erasure offers an elegant solution:

```cpp
// Example 05
class Network {
  static const char* default_processor(const char* data) {
    std::cout << "Default processing" << std::endl;
    return data;
  }
  std::function<const char*(const char*)> processor =
    default_processor;
  void send(const char* data) {
    data = processor(data);
    ...
  }
  public:
  template <typename F>
  void set_processor(F&& f) { processor = f; }
};
```

This is an example of the strategy design pattern, where the implementation of a particular behavior can be chosen at run-time. Now, any higher-level component of the system can specify its own processor function (or a lambda expression, or a callable object) without forcing the rest of the software to link with their code:

```cpp
Network N;
N.set_processor([](const char* s){ char* c; ...; return c; };
```

Now that we know what type erasure looks like and how it can help decouple components, both as a design pattern and as a convenient implementation technique, there is only one more question left - how does it work?

How is type erasure implemented in C++?

We have seen what type erasure looks like in C++. Now we understand what it means for a program to not explicitly depend on a type. But the mystery remains—the program makes no mention of the type, and yet, at the right time, invokes an operation on the type it knows nothing about. How? That is what we are about to see.

Very old type erasure

The idea of writing a program without explicit type information is certainly not new. In fact, it predates object-oriented programming and the notion of objects by a long time. Consider this C program (no C++ here) as an example:

```
// Example 06
int less(const void* a, const int* b) {
  return *(const int*)a - *(const int*)b;
}
int main() {
  int a[10] = { 1, 10, 2, 9, 3, 8, 4, 7, 5, 0 };
  qsort(a, 10, sizeof(int), less);
}
```

Now remember the function declaration for qsort from the standard C library:

```
void qsort(void *base, size_t nmemb, size_t size,
  int (*compare)(const void *, const void *));
```

Note that, while we are using it to sort an array of integers, the qsort function itself does not have any explicit types—it uses void* to pass in the array to be sorted. Similarly, the comparison function takes two void* pointers and has no explicit type information in its declaration. Of course, at some point, we need to know how to compare the real types. In our C program, the pointers that could, in theory, point to anything, are reinterpreted as pointers to integers. This action, which reverses the abstraction, is known as **reification**.

In C, restoring concrete types is entirely the responsibility of the programmer—our less() comparison function does, in fact, only compare integers, but it is impossible to deduce so from the interface. Neither is it possible to validate, at runtime, that the correct types are used throughout the program, and it is certainly not possible for the program to automatically select the right comparison operation for the actual type at runtime.

Nonetheless, this simple example lets us penetrate the magic of type erasure: the general code indeed does not depend on the concrete type that was erased, but that type is hidden in the code of a function called through the type-erased interface. In our example, it was the comparison function:

```
int less(const void* a, const int* b) {
  return *(const int*)a - *(const int*)b;
}
```

The calling code knows nothing about the type int, but the implementation of less() operates on this type. The type is "hidden" in the code of a function invoked through the type-agnostic interface.

The major downside of this C approach is that the programmer is wholly responsible for ensuring that all the pieces of the type-erased code are consistent; in our example, it is the sorted data and the comparison function that must refer to the same type.

In C++, we can do a lot better, but the idea is still the same: the erased type is reified by the implementation of some type-specific code that is invoked through the type-agnostic interface. The key difference is that we are going to force the compiler to generate this code for us. There are, fundamentally, two techniques that can be used. The first one relies on run-time polymorphism (inheritance), and the second one uses template magic. Let us start with the polymorphic implementation.

Type erasure using inheritance

We're now going to see how `std::shared_ptr` does its magic. We will do it with a simplified example of a smart pointer that focuses specifically on the type erasure aspect. It should not surprise you to learn that this is done with a combination of generic and object-oriented programming:

```cpp
// Example 07
template <typename T> class smartptr {
  struct destroy_base {
    virtual void operator()(void*) = 0;
    virtual ~deleter_base() {}
  };
  template <typename Deleter>
  struct destroy : public destroy_base {
    destroy (Deleter d) : d_(d) {}
    void operator()(void* p) override {
      d_(static_cast<T*>(p));
    }
    Deleter d_;
  };
  public:
  template <typename Deleter> smartptr(T* p, Deleter d) :
    p_(p), d_(new destroy<Deleter>(d)) {}
  ~smartptr() { (*d_)(p_); delete d_; }
  T* operator->() { return p_; }
  const T* operator->() const { return p_; }
  private:
  T* p_;
  destroy_base* d_;
};
```

The `smartptr` template has only one type parameter. Since the erased type is not part of the smart pointer's type, it has to be captured in some other object. In our case, this object is an instantiation of the nested `smartptr<T>::destroy` template. This object is created by the constructor, which is the last point in the code where the deleter type is explicitly present. But `smartptr` must refer to the `destroy` instance through a pointer whose type does not depend on `destroy` (since the `smartptr` object has the same type for all deleters). Therefore, all instances of the `destroy` template inherit from the same base class, `destroy_base`, and the actual deleter is invoked through a virtual function. The constructor is a template that deduces the type of deleter, but the type is only hidden, as it's part of the actual declaration of the specific instantiation of this template. The smart pointer class itself, and, in particular, its destructor, where the deleter is actually used, really have the deleter type erased. The compile-time type detection is used to create a correct-by-construction polymorphic object that will rediscover the deleter type at runtime and perform the correct action. For that reason, we do not need a dynamic cast, and can use the static cast instead, which only works if we know the real derived type (and we do).

The same technique can be used to implement `std::function` and other type-erased types, such as the ultimate type-erased class, `std::any` (in C++17 and above). This is a class, not a template, but it can hold a value of any type:

```
// Example 08
std::any a(5);
int i = std::any_cast<int>(a);      // i == 5
std::any_cast<long>(a);             // throws bad_any_cast
```

Of course, without knowing the type, `std::any` cannot provide any interfaces. You can store any value in it, and get it back if you know the right type (or you can ask for the type and get back a `std::type_info` object).

Before we learn the other (usually more efficient) way to implement type erasure, we have to address one glaringly obvious inefficiency in our design: every time we create or delete a shared pointer or a `std::function` object that is implemented as described above, we must allocate and deallocate memory for the derived object that conceals the erased type.

Type erasure without memory allocation

There are, however, ways to optimize the type-erased pointers (as well as any other type-erased data structures) and avoid the additional memory allocation that happens when we construct the polymorphic `smartptr::destroy` object. We can avoid this allocation, at least sometimes, by pre-allocating a memory buffer for these objects. The details of this optimization, as well as its limitations, are discussed in *Chapter 10, Local Buffer Optimization*. Here is the gist of the optimization:

```
// Example 07
template <typename T> class smartptr {
  ...
  public:
  template <typename Deleter> smartptr(T* p, Deleter d) :
    p_(p) {
```

```
      static_assert(sizeof(Deleter) <= sizeof(buf_));
      ::new (static_cast<void*>(buf_)) destroy<Deleter>(d));
    }
    ~smartptr() {
      destroy_base* d = (destroy_base*)buf_;
      (*d)(p_);
      d->~destroy_base();
    }
    private:
    T* p_;
    alignas(8) char buf_[16];
};
```

The local buffer optimization does make type-erased pointers and functions a lot more efficient, as we will see later in this chapter. Of course, it imposes restrictions on the size of the deleter; for this reason, most real-life implementations use a local buffer for small enough erased types and dynamic memory for types that don't fit into the buffer. The alternative solution - to assert as shown above and force the programmer to increase the buffer – is often embraced in very high-performance applications.

There are some subtler consequences of the use of this optimization: the deleter (or another erased object) is now stored as a part of the class and must be copied with the rest of the class. How do we copy an object whose type we no longer know? This and other details will have to wait until *Chapter 10, Local Buffer Optimization*. For now, we will use the local buffer optimization in the rest of the examples, both to show its use and to simplify the code.

Type erasure without inheritance

There is an alternative implementation of type erasure that does not use an internal hierarchy of classes to store the erased type. Instead, the type is captured in the implementation of a function, just like it was done in C:

```
void erased_func(void* p) {
  TE* q = static_cast<T*>(p);
  … do work on type TE …
}
```

In C++, we make the function a template so the compiler generates instantiations for every type TE we need:

```
template <typename TE> void erased_func(void* p) {
  TE* q = static_cast<T*>(p);
  … do work on type TE …
}
```

This is a somewhat unusual template function: the type parameter cannot be deduced from the arguments and must be explicitly specified. We already know that this will be done in the constructor of a type-erased class, such as our smart pointer: there, we still know the type that is about to be erased. The other very important point is that any function generated by the preceding template can be invoked through the same function pointer:

```
void(*)(void*) fp = erased_func<int>; // or any other type
```

Now we can see how the type erasure magic works: we have a function pointer whose type does not depend on the type TE we are erasing. We are going to generate a function with an implementation that uses this type and assign it to this pointer. When we need to use the erased type TE, such as deleting the object with the specified deleter, we are going to call a function through this pointer; we can do that without knowing what TE is. We just have to put this all together into a correct-by-construction implementation, and here is our type-erased smart pointer:

```
// Example 07
template <typename T>
class smartptr_te_static {
  T* p_;
  using destroy_t = void(*)(T*, void*);
  destroy_t destroy_;
  alignas(8) char buf_[8];
  template<typename Deleter>
  static void invoke_destroy(T* p, void* d) {
    (*static_cast<Deleter*>(d))(p);
  }
public:
  template <typename Deleter>
  smartptr_te_static(T* p, Deleter d)
    : p_(p), destroy_(invoke_destroy<Deleter>)
  {
    static_assert(sizeof(Deleter) <= sizeof(buf_));
    ::new (static_cast<void*>(buf_)) Deleter(d);
  }
  ~smartptr_te_static() {
    this->destroy_(p_, buf_);
  }
  T* operator->() { return p_; }
  const T* operator->() const { return p_; }
};
```

We store the user-given deleter in a small local buffer; in this example, we do not show the alternative implementation for a larger deleter that would require dynamic memory allocation. The function template that retains the information about the erased type is invoke_destroy(). Note that it is a static function; static functions can be invoked through a regular function pointer instead of a more cumbersome member function pointer.

In the constructor of the smartptr class, we instantiate invoke_destroy<Deleter> and assign it to the destroy_ function pointer. We also need a copy of the deleter object, since the deleter may contain a state (for example, a pointer to the allocator that provided the memory for the object owned by the smart pointer). We construct this deleter in the space provided by the local buffer buf_. At this point, the original Deleter type is erased: all we have is a function pointer that does not depend on the Deleter type and a character array.

When the time comes to destroy the object owned by the shared pointer, we need to invoke the deleter. Instead, we invoke the function through the destroy_ pointer and pass to it the object to be destroyed and the buffer where the deleter resides. The erased Deleter type is nowhere to be seen, but it is hiding inside the specific implementation of invoke_destroy(). There, the pointer to the buffer is cast back to the type that is actually stored in the buffer (Deleter) and the deleter is invoked.

This example is, perhaps, the most concise demonstration of type erasure machinery in C++. But it is not quite equivalent to the example in the previous section where we used inheritance. While we invoke the deleter on the object of type T owned by the smart pointer, we do nothing to destroy the deleter object itself, specifically, the copy we stored inside the local buffer. The local buffer is not the problem here: if we dynamically allocated the memory instead, it would still be accessed through a generic pointer such as char* or void*, and we would now know how to properly delete it. For that, we need another function that can reify the original type. Well, maybe: trivially destructible deleters (and, in general, trivially destructible callable objects) are very common. All function pointers, member function pointers, stateless objects, and lambdas that do not capture any non-trivial objects by value are all trivially destructible. So we could simply add a static assert to our constructor and restrict our smart pointer to trivially destructible deleters, and, in reality, it would serve us fine in most cases. But I also want to show you a more general solution.

We can, of course, use another pointer to a static function that destroys the deleter and is instantiated with the right type in the constructor. But the destructor is not the end of what we need: in general, we also need to copy and move deleters, and maybe even compare them. That's a lot of function pointers making our smartptr class bloated. By comparison, the inheritance-based implementation did everything with just the pointer to the destroy object (stored as a pointer to the base class destroy_base). There is a way we can do the same. For this example, there is no good way to gradually reveal the magic, so we have to jump right in and follow up with a line-by-line explanation:

```cpp
// Example 07
template <typename T>
class smartptr_te_vtable {
    T* p_;
    struct vtable_t {
        using destroy_t = void(*)(T*, void*);
        using destructor_t = void(*)(void*);
```

```
      destroy_t destroy_;
      destructor_t destructor_;
  };
  const vtable_t* vtable_ = nullptr;
  template <typename Deleter>
  constexpr static vtable_t vtable = {
    smartptr_te_vtable::template destroy<Deleter>,
    smartptr_te_vtable::template destructor<Deleter>
  };
  template <typename Deleter>
  static void destroy(T* p, void* d) {
    (*static_cast<Deleter*>(d))(p);
  }
  template <typename Deleter>
  static void destructor(void* d) {
    static_cast<Deleter*>(d)->~Deleter();
  }
  alignas(8) char buf_[8];
public:
  template <typename Deleter>
  smartptr_te_vtable(T* p, Deleter d)
    : p_(p), vtable_(&vtable<Deleter>)
  {
    static_assert(sizeof(Deleter) <= sizeof(buf_));
    ::new (static_cast<void*>(buf_)) Deleter(d);
  }
  ~smartptr_te_vtable() {
    this->vtable_->destroy_(p_, buf_);
    this->vtable_->destructor_(buf_);
  }
  T* operator->() { return p_; }
  const T* operator->() const { return p_; }
};
```

Let us explain how this code works. First of all, we declare a `struct vtable_t` that contains function pointers to every operation we need to implement on the erased `Deleter` type. In our case, there are just two: invoke the deleter on an object to be destroyed and destroy the deleter itself. In general, we would have at least copy and move operations there as well (you will find such implementation in *Chapter 10, Local Buffer Optimization*). Next, we have the `vtable_` pointer. After the object is constructed, it will point to an object of the type `vtable_t`. While this may suggest dynamic memory allocation ahead, we are going to do much better than that. Next is a variable template `vtable`; instantiating it on a concrete `Deleter` type will create a static instance of a variable of type `vtable_t`. This is, perhaps, the most tricky part: usually, when we have a static data member of a class, it's just a variable, and we can access it by name. But here is something different: the name `vtable` can refer to many objects, all of the same type, `vtable_t`. None of them are explicitly created by us: we do not allocate memory for them, do not call `operator new` to construct them. The compiler creates one of these objects for every `Deleter` type we use. For every smartptr object, the address of the specific `vtable` object we want it to use is stored in the `vtable_` pointer.

An object of type `vtable_t` contains pointers to static functions. Our `vtable` must do so as well: as you can see, we initialized the function pointers in `vtable` to point to instantiations of static member functions of the `smartptr` class. These instantiations are for the same `Deleter` type that the `vtable` itself is instantiated with.

The name `vtable` was not chosen lightly: we have indeed implemented a virtual table; the compiler builds a very similar structure with function pointers for every polymorphic hierarchy, and every virtual class has a virtual pointer that points to the table for its original type (the one it was constructed with).

After the `vtable`, we have two static function templates. That is where the erased type is really hidden and later reified. As we have seen before, the function signatures do not depend on the `Deleter` type, but their implementations do. Finally, we have the same buffer for storing deleter objects locally.

As before, the constructor ties everything together; this must be so since the constructor is the only place in this code where the `Deleter` type is explicitly known. Our constructor does three things: first, it stores the pointer to the object, as any other smart pointer does. Second, it points the `vtable_` pointer to an instance of the static `vtable` variable for the right `Deleter` type. Finally, it constructs a copy of the deleter in the local buffer. At this point, the `Deleter` type is erased: nothing in the `smartptr` object explicitly depends on it.

The deleter, and its true type, come into play again when the destructor of the smart pointer is called and we need to destroy the owned object and the deleter itself. Each of these actions is done by means of an indirect function call. The functions to call are stored in the `*vtable_` object (just like for polymorphic classes, the correct virtual function overrides are found in the virtual table of function pointers). The deleter is passed into these functions using the address of the buffer – no type information there. But the functions were generated for the specific `Deleter` type, so they cast the `void*` buffer address to the right type and use the deleter that was stored in the buffer.

This implementation allows us to have multiple type-erased operations while storing just one `vtable_` pointer in the object itself.

We can also combine the two approaches: invoke some operations through a virtual table and have dedicated function pointers for others. Why? Performance, possibly: invoking a function through a virtual table may be a little slower. This needs to be measured for any specific application.

So far, we used type erasure to provide abstract interfaces for very specific behaviors. We already know that type erasure does not need to be so restricted – we have seen the example of the `std::function`. The last example in this section will be our own generic type-erased function.

Efficient type erasure

After the examples and explanations of the last section, a type-erased function is not going to be much of a challenge. Nonetheless, there is value in showing it here. We are going to demonstrate a very efficient implementation of type erasure (the implementation you find in this book was inspired by the works of Arthur O'Dwyer and Eduardo Magrid).

The template for a generic function looks like this:

```
template<typename Signature> class Function;
```

Here `Signature` is something like `int(std::string)` for a function that takes a string and returns an integer. This function can be constructed to invoke any `Callable` type as long as an object of this type can be invoked like a function with the specified signature.

We are going to use a local buffer again, but instead of hard-coding it into the class, we will add template parameters to control buffer size and alignment:

```
template<typename Signature, size_t Size = 16,
         size_t Alignment = 8> struct Function;
```

For ease of coding, it is convenient to unpack the function signature into the argument types `Args...` and the return type `Res`. The easiest way to do so is with a class template specialization:

```
// Example 09
template<typename Signature, size_t Size = 16,
         size_t Alignment = 8> struct Function;
template<size_t Size, size_t Alignment,
         typename Res, typename... Args>
struct Function<Res(Args...), Size, Alignment> {...};
```

Now all that is left is the small matter of the implementation. First, we need the buffer to store the `Callable` object in it:

```
// Example 09
alignas(Alignment) char space_[Size];
```

Second, we need a function pointer `executor_` to store the address of the static function `executor` generated from a template with the type of the `Callable` object:

```
// Example 09
using executor_t = Res(*)(Args..., void*);
executor_t executor_;
template<typename Callable>
static Res executor(Args... args, void* this_function) {
  return (*reinterpret_cast<Callable*>(
```

```
      static_cast<Function*>(this_function)->space_))
    (std::forward<Args>(args)...);
}
```

Next, in the constructor we must initialize the executor and store the callable in the buffer:

```
// Example 09
template <typename CallableArg,
          typename Callable = std::decay_t<CallableArg>>
  requires(!std::same_as<Function, Callable>)
Function(CallableArg&& callable) :
  executor_(executor<Callable>)
{
    ::new (static_cast<void*>(space_))
      Callable(std::forward<CallableArg>(callable));
}
```

The constructor has two subtle details. The first is the treatment of the type of the callable: we deduce it as `CallableArg` but then use it as `Callable`. This is because `CallableArg` may be a reference to the type of the callable, such as the function pointer, and we don't want to construct a copy of a reference. The second is the concept restriction: the `Function` itself is a callable object with the same signature, but we do not want this constructor to apply in such a case – that is the job of the copy constructor. If you don't use C++20, you have to use SFINAE to achieve the same effect (see *Chapter 7, SFINAE, Concepts, and Overload Resolution Management,* for details). If you like the concept style, you can emulate it to some degree:

```
#define REQUIRES(...) \
  std::enable_if_t<__VA_ARGS__, int> = 0
template <typename CallableArg,
          typename Callable = std::decay_t<CallableArg>,
          REQUIRES(!std::is_same_v<Function, Callable>)>
Function(CallableArg&& callable) …
```

Speaking of copying, our `Function` is correct only for trivially copyable and trivially destructible `Callable` types since we did not provide any means to destroy or copy the callable objects stored in the buffer. This still covers a lot of ground, but we can handle non-trivial callables as well using the vtable approach (you will find an example in *Chapter 10, Local Buffer Optimization*).

There is one more detail we need to take care of right now: `std::function` can be default-constructed without any callable; calling such a "null" function throws a `std::bad_function_call` exception. We can do this too if we initialize the executor to a pre-defined function that does nothing except throw this exception:

```
// Example 09
static constexpr Res default_executor(Args..., void*) {
```

```
    throw std::bad_function_call();
}
constexpr static executor_t default_executor_ =
    default_executor;
executor_t executor_ = default_executor_;
```

Now we have a generic function that is very similar to `std::function` (or would have been if we added support for calling member functions, copy and move semantics, and the few missing member functions). It does work the same way:

```
Function<int(int, int, int, int)> f =
    [](int a, int b, int c, int d) { return a + b + c + d; };
int res = f(1, 2, 3, 4);
```

And just what did that convenience cost us? All performance should be measured, but we can also get some idea by examining the machine code generated by the compiler when it has to call a type-erased function. Here is what it takes to invoke `std::function` with the same signature as we just used:

```
// Example 09
using Signature = int(int, int, int, int);
using SF = std::function<Signature>;
auto invoke_sf(int a, int b, int c, int d, const SF& f) {
    return f(a, b, c, d);
}
```

The compiler (GCC-11 with O3) turns this code into this:

```
endbr64
sub     $0x28,%rsp
mov     %r8,%rax
mov     %fs:0x28,%r8
mov     %r8,0x18(%rsp)
xor     %r8d,%r8d
cmpq    $0x0,0x10(%rax)
mov     %edi,0x8(%rsp)
mov     %esi,0xc(%rsp)
mov     %edx,0x10(%rsp)
mov     %ecx,0x14(%rsp)
je      62 <_Z9invoke_sfiiiiRKSt8functionIFiiiiiEE+0x62>
lea     0xc(%rsp),%rdx
lea     0x10(%rsp),%rcx
mov     %rax,%rdi
lea     0x8(%rsp),%rsi
lea     0x14(%rsp),%r8
callq   *0x18(%rax)
mov     0x18(%rsp),%rdx
```

```
sub     %fs:0x28,%rdx
jne     67 <_Z9invoke_sfiiiiRKSt8functionIFiiiiiEE+0x67>
add     $0x28,%rsp
retq
callq   67 <_Z9invoke_sfiiiiRKSt8functionIFiiiiiEE+0x67>
callq   6c <_Z9invoke_sfiiiiRKSt8functionIFiiiiiEE+0x6c>
```

Now our function:

```
// Example 09
using F = Function<Signature>;
auto invoke_f(int a, int b, int c, int d, const F& f) {
  return f(a, b, c, d);
}
```

This time, the compiler can do much better:

```
endbr64
jmpq    *0x10(%r8)
```

What we see here is the so-called tail call: the compiler simply redirects the execution to the actual callable that needs to be invoked. You might ask, doesn't it always? Not usually: most function calls are implemented with `call` and `ret` instructions. To call a function, its arguments must be stored in a predefined location, then the return address is pushed onto the stack and the execution is transferred to the function entry point by the `call` instruction. The return instruction `ret` takes the address off the stack and transfers execution to it. The beauty of the tail call is this: while we want the call to `Function` to call the original callable in the end, we don't need the execution to return to the `Function` object. If there is nothing to do in the `Function` executor except to return the control to the caller, we might as well simply leave the original return address as-is and have the callable return the control to the right place without an additional indirection. Of course, this assumes that the executor has nothing to do after the call.

There are two key optimizations in our code that enable this compact implementation. The first one is the way we handle the null function: most implementations of `std::function` initialize the executor to `nullptr` and do a pointer comparison on every call. We did no such comparison; we always invoke the executor. But then, our executor is never null: unless otherwise initialized, it points to the default executor.

The second optimization is more subtle. You might have noticed that the executor has one more argument than the callable: to call a function with the signature `int(int, int)` our executor needs the two original function arguments (of course) and the pointer to the callable object (stored in the local buffer in our case). So our executor's signature is `int(int, int, void*)`. Why not pass the object first? That's what the `std::function` does (at least the one whose assembly we have just seen). The problem is that the original function arguments are also sitting on the stack. Adding one more argument at the end of the stack is easy. But to insert the new first argument, we have to shift all the existing arguments by one (this is why the code generated for `std::function` becomes longer the more arguments you have).

As convincing as it sounds, any speculations about performance are hardly worth the electrons expanded to have them written down. Performance must always be measured, and this is the last task left for us to do in this chapter.

Performance of type erasure

We are going to measure the performance of a type-erased generic function and a type-erased smart pointer deleter. First, we need the right tools; in this case, a micro-benchmarking library.

Installing the micro-benchmark library

In our case, we are interested in the efficiency of very small fragments of code that construct and delete objects using different kinds of smart pointers. The appropriate tool for measuring the performance of small fragments of code is a micro-benchmark. There are many micro-benchmark libraries and tools out there; in this book, we will use the Google Benchmark library. To follow along with the examples in this section, you must first download and install the library (to do this, follow the instructions in the `Readme.md` file). Then you can compile and run the examples. You can build the sample files included with the library to see how to build a benchmark on your particular system. For example, on a Linux machine, the command to build and run a `smartptr.C` benchmark program might look something like this:

```
$CXX smartptr.C smartptr_ext.C -o smartptr -g -O3 \
  -I. -I$GBENCH_DIR/include \
  -Wall -Wextra -Werror -pedantic --std=c++20 \
  $GBENCH_DIR/lib/libbenchmark.a -lpthread -lrt -lm && \
./smartptr
```

Here, `$CXX` is your C++ compiler, such as `clang++` or `g++-11`, and `$GBENCH_DIR` is the directory where the benchmark is installed.

The overhead of type erasure

Every benchmark needs a baseline. In our case, the baseline is a raw pointer. We can reasonably assume that no smart pointer will be able to outperform a raw pointer, and the best smart pointer will have zero overhead. Thus, we begin by measuring how long it takes to construct and destroy a small object using a raw pointer:

```
// Example 07
struct deleter {
  template <typename T> void operator()(T* p) { delete p; }
```

```
};
deleter d;
void BM_rawptr(benchmark::State& state) {
  for (auto _ : state) {
    int* p = new int(0);
    d(p);
  }
  state.SetItemsProcessed(state.iterations());
}
```

A good optimizing compiler can do a great deal of damage to a microbenchmark like this by optimizing the "unnecessary" work (which is, really, all the work done by this program). We can prevent such optimizations by moving the allocation into a different compilation unit:

```
// 07_smartptr.C:
void BM_rawptr(benchmark::State& state) {
  for (auto _ : state) {
    int* p = get_raw_ptr()
    d(p);
  }
  state.SetItemsProcessed(state.iterations());
}
// 07_smartptr_ext.C:
int* get_raw_ptr() { return new int(0); }
```

If you have a compiler that can do whole program optimizations, turn them off for this benchmark. But don't turn off the optimization of each file: we want to profile the optimized code since that's what the real program will use.

The actual numbers reported by the benchmark depend, of course, on the machine that it runs on. But we are interested in the relative changes, so any machine will do, as long as we stay with it for all measurements:

Benchmark	Time
BM_rawptr	8.72 ns

We can now verify that `std::unique_ptr` indeed has zero overhead (as long as we construct and delete objects the same way, of course):

```
// smartptr.C
void BM_uniqueptr(benchmark::State& state) {
  for (auto _ : state) {
    auto p(get_unique_ptr());
  }
  state.SetItemsProcessed(state.iterations());
```

```
    }
    // smartptr_ext.C
    auto get_unique_ptr() {
      return std::unique_ptr<int, deleter>(new int(0), d);
    }
```

The result is within the measurement noise from the raw pointer, as can be seen here:

Benchmark	Time
BM_uniqueptr	8.82 ns

We can similarly measure the performance of std::shared_ptr as well as different versions of our own smart pointer:

Benchmark	Time
BM_sharedptr	22.9 ns
BM_make_sharedptr	17.5 ns
BM_smartptr_te	19.5 ns

The first line, BM_sharedptr, constructs and deletes a std::shared_ptr<int> with our custom deleter. The shared pointer is much more expensive than the unique pointer. Of course, there is more than one reason for that—std::shared_ptr is a reference-counting smart pointer, and maintaining a reference count has its own overhead. Using std::make_shared to allocate shared pointers makes its creation and deletion considerably faster, as we can see in the BM_make_sharedptr benchmark, but, to make sure that we measure only the overhead of type erasure, we should implement a type-erased unique pointer. But we already did—it's our smartptr that we saw in the *How is type erasure implemented in C++?* section of this chapter. It has just enough functionality to measure the performance of the same benchmark that we used for all other pointers:

```
    void BM_smartptr_te(benchmark::State& state) {
      for (auto _ : state) {
        auto get_smartptr_te();
      }
      state.SetItemsProcessed(state.iterations());
    }
```

Here, smartptr_te stands for the type-erased version of the smart pointer implemented using inheritance. It is slightly faster than std::shared_ptr, proving our suspicion that the latter has more than one source of overhead. Just like std::shared_ptr, deleting smartptr_te touches two memory locations: in our case, it is the object that is being deleted and the deleter (embedded in a polymorphic object). This is exactly what std::make_shared avoids by consolidating both memory locations for std::shared_ptr, and it definitely pays off. We can reasonably assume that the second memory allocation is also the reason for the poor performance of our type-erased smart pointer (approximately twice as slow as the raw or unique pointers). We can avoid this allocation if we use an internal buffer reserved inside the smart pointer object. We have already seen a local buffer implementation of the smart pointer in the section *Type erasure without memory allocation* (in this benchmark, it is renamed as `smartptr_te_lb0`). Here it is benchmarked under the name `BM_smartptr_te_lb0`. The version that uses the local buffer when possible but switches to dynamic allocation for larger deleters is named `smartptr_te_lb` and is slightly slower (`BM_smartptr_te_lb`):

Benchmark	Time
BM_smartptr_te_lb	11.3 ns
BM_smartptr_te_lb0	10.5 ns
BM_smartptr_te_static	9.58 ns
BM_smartptr_te_vtable	10.4 ns

We have also benchmarked the two type-erased smart pointers implemented without inheritance. The static function version `BM_smartptr_te_static` is slightly faster than the version that uses the vtable (`BM_smartptr_te_vtable`). Both of these use local buffers; it should not come as a surprise that the compiler-generated vtable performs exactly as well as the equivalent structure we crafted using static variable templates.

Overall, there is some overhead even for the best type erasure implementation, just under 10 percent in our case. Whether or not this is acceptable, depends on the application.

We should also measure the performance of the generic type-erased function. We can measure its performance with any callable entity, for example, a lambda expression:

```
// Example 09
void BM_fast_lambda(benchmark::State& state) {
  int a = rand(), b = rand(), c = rand(), d = rand();
  int x = rand();
  Function<int(int, int, int, int)> f {
    [=](int a, int b, int c, int d) {
      return x + a + b + c + d; }
  };
  for (auto _ : state) {
    benchmark::DoNotOptimize(f(a, b, c, d));
    benchmark::ClobberMemory();
  }
}
```

We can do the same measurement for `std::function` as well, and compare the results:

Benchmark	Time
BM_fast_lambda	0.884 ns
BM_std_lambda	1.33 ns

While it may seem like a great success, this benchmark also hides the warning against going overboard with type erasure. All we have to do to reveal this warning is to measure the performance of the direct call to the same lambda:

```
Benchmark                    Time
BM_lambda                    0.219 ns
```

How do we reconcile this major slowdown with the minor cost of type erasure we have seen earlier when we were comparing smart and raw pointers?

It is important to pay attention to what is being erased. A well-implemented type-erased interface can deliver performance very similar to that of a virtual function call. A non-inlined non-virtual function call is going to be slightly faster (in our case, a call that took just under 9 nanoseconds incurred about 10 percent overhead). But a type-erased invocation is always indirect. The one competition it can't come close to is an inlined function call. This is exactly what we observed when we compared the performance of type-erased and direct invocations of lambdas.

With what we learned about the performance of type erasure, when can we recommend it?

Guidelines for using type erasure

What problems does type erasure solve, and when is the cost of the solution acceptable? First of all, it is important to not lose sight of the original goal: type erasure is a design pattern that helps with the separation of concerns, a very powerful design technique. It is used to create an abstraction for a certain behavior when the implementation of said behavior can be provided by an open set of possibly unrelated types.

It is also used as an implementation technique, mostly to aid in breaking dependencies between compilation units and other program components.

Before we can answer the question "*Is type erasure worth the cost?*", we need to consider the alternatives. In many cases, the alternative is another way to implement the same abstraction: polymorphic class hierarchies or function pointers. The performance of either option is similar to that of the type erasure (in its optimal implementation), so it comes down to convenience and code quality. For a single function, using a type-erased function is easier than developing a new class hierarchy, and more flexible than using a function pointer. For a class with many member functions, it is usually easier and less error-prone to maintain a class hierarchy.

The other possible alternative is to do nothing and allow tighter coupling between parts of the design. The downsides of such a decision are often inversely proportional to its performance benefit: closely coupled parts of the system often need to coordinate implementation to achieve good performance, but they are closely coupled for a reason. Components that are logically well separated should not interact extensively, therefore, the performance of such interaction should not be critical.

What do we do when performance is important but we still need an abstraction? Often, the direct opposite of type erasure: we make everything into templates.

Consider C++20 ranges. On one hand, they are abstract sequences. We can write a function that operates on a range and invoke it with a vector, a deque, a range created from one of these containers, a subrange of that range, or a filtered view. Anything is a range as long as it can be iterated from `begin()` to `end()`. But ranges created from a vector and a deque are different types, even though they are abstractions for sequences, interface-wise. The standard library provides multiple range adapters and range views, and they are all templates. So are the functions operating on the ranges.

Could we implement a type-erased range? Yes, it is not even that hard. We end up with a single type, `GenericRange`, that can be constructed from a vector, a deque, a list, or anything else that has `begin()`, `end()`, and a forward iterator. We also get something that is about twice as slow as most container iterators, except for vectors: their iterators are really just pointers, and vectorizing compilers can do optimizations that speed up the code by at least an order of magnitude. The possibility of such optimizations is lost when we erase the type of the original container.

The C++ designers made the decision that, on the one hand, ranges provide an abstraction for certain behavior and let us separate the interface from the implementation. On the other hand, they were unwilling to sacrifice performance. So they chose to make ranges and all code that operates on them into templates.

As a designer of a software system, you may have to make similar decisions. The general guideline is to prefer tighter coupling for closely related components where such coupling is essential for performance. Conversely, prefer better separation for loosely coupled components whose interaction does not require high efficiency. When in that domain, type erasure should be considered at least equally to polymorphism and other decoupling techniques.

Summary

In this chapter, we have, hopefully, demystified the programming technique known as type erasure. We have shown how a program can be written without all of the type information being explicitly visible, and some of the reasons why this may be a desirable implementation. We have also demonstrated that, when implemented efficiently and used wisely, it is a powerful technique that may lead to much simpler and more flexible interfaces and clearly separated components.

The next chapter is a change of direction—we are done with the abstraction idioms for some time and now move on to C++ idioms that facilitate the binding of template components into complex interacting systems. We start with the SFINAE idiom.

Questions

1. What is type erasure, really?
2. How is type erasure implemented in C++?
3. What is the difference between hiding a type behind `auto` and erasing it?
4. How is the concrete type reified when the program needs to use it?
5. What is the performance overhead of type erasure?

7

SFINAE, Concepts, and Overload Resolution Management

The idiom we study in this chapter, **Substitution Failure Is Not An Error** (**SFINAE**), is one of the more complex in terms of the language features it uses. Thus, it tends to get inordinate amounts of attention from C++ programmers. There is something in this feature that appeals to the mindset of a typical C++ programmer - a normal person thinks that, if it isn't broken, don't mess with it. A programmer, especially one writing in C++, tends to think that, if it isn't broken, you're not using it to its full potential. Let's just say that SFINAE has a lot of potential.

We will cover the following topics in this chapter:

- What are function overloading and overload resolution? What are type deduction and substitution?
- What is SFINAE, and why was it necessary in C++?
- How can SFINAE be used to write insanely complex, and sometimes useful, programs?

Technical requirements

The example code for this chapter can be found at `https://github.com/PacktPublishing/Hands-On-Design-Patterns-with-CPP-Second-Edition/tree/master/Chapter07`.

Overload resolution and overload sets

This section will test your knowledge of the latest and most advanced additions to the C++ standard. We will start with one of the most basic features of C++, functions, and their overloads.

C++ function overloading

Function overloading is a very straightforward concept in C++; multiple different functions can have the same name. That's it, that is all there is to overloading - when the compiler sees syntax that indicates a function call, formatted as f(x), then there must be more than one function named f. If this happens, we are in an overload situation, and overload resolution must take place to find out which of these functions should be called.

Let's start with a simple example:

```
// Example 01
void f(int i) { cout << "f(int)" << endl; }          // 1
void f(long i) { cout << "f(long)" << endl; }      // 2
void f(double i) { cout << "f(double)" << endl; }     // 3
f(5);          // 1
f(5l);      // 2
f(5.0);     // 3
```

Here, we have three function definitions for the same name, f, and three function calls. Note that the function signatures are all different (in that the parameter types are different). This is a requirement - overloaded functions must differ somehow in their parameters. It is not possible to have two overloads that take the exact same arguments but differ in the return type or the function body. Also, note that, while the example is for a regular function, the exact same rules apply to the overloaded member functions, so we will not pay special attention to member functions exclusively.

Back to our example, which of the f() functions is called on each line? To understand that, we need to know how overloaded functions are resolved in C++. The exact rules for overload resolution are fairly complex and differ in subtle ways between different versions of the standard, but for the most part, they are designed so that the compiler does what you would expect it to do in the most commonly encountered cases. We would expect f(5) to call the overload that accepts an integer argument since 5 is an int variable. And so it does. Similarly, 5l has the long type, and so f(5l) calls the second overload. Finally, 5.0 is a floating-point number, and so the last overload is called.

That wasn't so hard, was it? But what happens if the argument does not match the parameter type exactly? Then, the compiler has to consider type conversions. For example, the type of the 5.0 literal is double. Let's see what happens if we call f() with an argument of the float type:

```
f(5.0f);
```

Now we have to convert the argument from the float type to one of the int, long, or double types. Again, the standard has rules, but it should come as no surprise that the conversion to double is preferred and that the overload is called.

Let's see what happens with a different integer type, say, unsigned int:

```
f(5u);
```

Now we have two options; convert unsigned int to a signed int, or to signed long. While it may be argued that the conversion to long is *safer*, and thus better, the two conversions are considered so close by the standard that the compiler cannot choose. This call does not compile because the overload resolution is considered ambiguous; the error message should say as much. If you encounter such a problem in your code, you have to help the compiler by casting the arguments to a type that makes the resolution unambiguous. Usually, the simplest way is to cast the type of the parameter for the overload you want to call:

```
unsigned int i = 5u;
f(static_cast<int>(i));
```

So far, we have dealt with a situation where the types of parameters were different, but their number was the same. Of course, if the number of parameters differs between different function declarations for the same name, only the functions that can accept the required number of arguments need to be considered. Here is an example of two functions with the same name but a different number of arguments:

```
void f(int i) { cout << "f(int)" << endl; }              // 1
void f(long i, long j) { cout << "f(long2)" << endl; }   // 2
f(5.0, 7);
```

Here, the overload resolution is very simple - we need a function that can accept two arguments, and there is only one choice. Both arguments will have to be converted to long. But what if there is more than one function with the same number of parameters? Let's see what happens in the following example:

```
// Example 02
void f(int i, int j) { cout << "f(int, int)" << endl; }// 1
void f(long i, long j) { cout << "f(long2)" << endl; }    // 2
void f(double i) { cout << "f(double)" << endl; }        // 3
f(5, 5);       // 1
f(5l, 5l);     // 2
f(5, 5.0);     // 1
f(5, 5l);      // ?
```

First of all, the obvious case - if the types of all arguments match exactly the types of the parameters for one of the overloads, that overload is called. Next, things start to get interesting - if there is no exact match, we can have conversions on each argument. Let's consider the third call, f(5, 5.0). The first argument, int, matches the first overload exactly but could be converted to long if necessary. The second argument, double, does not match either overload but could be converted to match both. The first overload is a better match - it requires fewer argument conversions. Finally, what about the last line? The first overload can be called, with a conversion on the second argument. The second overload can also be made to work, with a conversion on the first argument. Again, this is an ambiguous overload, and this line will not compile. Note that it is not, in general, true that the overload with the fewer conversions always wins; in more complex cases, it is possible to have ambiguous overloads even if one requires fewer conversions (the general rule is, if there is an overload that has the best conversion on every argument, it wins; otherwise, the call is ambiguous). To resolve this ambiguity, you have to change the types of some of the arguments (by casting, in general, or by changing the type of the numeric literal, in our case) to make the intended overload be the preferred one.

Note how the third overload was completely left out because it has the wrong number of parameters for all function calls. It's not always that simple, though - functions can have default arguments, which means the number of arguments does not always have to match the number of parameters.

Consider the following code block:

```
// Example 03
void f(int i) { cout << "f(int)" << endl; }              // 1
void f(long i, long j) { cout << "f(long2)" << endl; }   // 2
void f(double i, double j = 0) {                         // 3
  cout << "f(double, double = 0)" << endl;
}
f(5);        // 1
f(51, 5);    // 2
f(5, 5);     // ?
f(5.0);      // 3
f(5.0f);     // 3
f(51);       // ?
```

We now have three overloads. The first and the second can never be confused because they have a different number of parameters. The third overload, however, can be called with either one or two arguments; in the former case, the second argument is assumed to be zero. The first call is the simplest - one argument, where the type matches the parameter type of the first overload exactly. The second call reminds us of the case we have seen before - two arguments, where the first is an exact match to one of the overloads, but the second requires a conversion. The alternative overload needs conversions on both arguments, so the second function definition is the best match.

The third call seems straightforward enough with its two integer arguments, but this simplicity is deceptive - there are two overloads that accept two arguments, and in both overload cases, both arguments need conversions. While the conversion from int to long may seem better than the one from int to double, C++ does not see it this way. This call is ambiguous. The next call, f(5.0), has only one argument, which can be converted to int, the type of the parameter in the one-argument overload. But it is still a better match for the third overload, where it needs no conversion at all. Change the argument type from double to float, and we get the next call. The conversion to double is better than that to int, and utilizing the default argument is not considered a conversion and so does not carry any other *penalty* when overloads are compared. The last call is again ambiguous - both conversions to double and to int are considered of equal weight, thus the first and third overloads are equally good. The second overload offers an exact match to the first parameter; however, there is no way to call that overload without the second argument, so it is not even considered.

So far, we have considered only ordinary C++ functions, although everything we have learned applies equally to member functions as well. Now, we need to add template functions to the mix.

Template functions

In addition to regular functions, for which the parameter types are known, C++ also has `template` functions. When these functions are called, the parameter types are deduced from the types of the arguments at the call site. The template functions can have the same name as non-template functions, and several template functions can have the same name as well, so we need to learn about overload resolution in the presence of templates.

Consider the following example:

```
// Example 04
void f(int i) { cout << "f(int)" << endl; }          // 1
void f(long i) { cout << "f(long)" << endl; }      // 2
template <typename T>
void f(T i) { cout << "f(T)" << endl; }          // 3
f(5);          // 1
f(51);      // 2
f(5.0);      // 3
```

The `f` function name can refer to any of the three functions, one of which is a template. The best overload will be chosen from these three each time. The set of functions that are considered for the overload resolution of a particular function call is known as the **overload set**. The first call to `f()` matches exactly the first non-template function in the overload set - the argument type is `int`, and the first function is `f(int)`. If an exact match to a non-template function is found in the overload set, it is always considered the best overload.

The template function can also be instantiated with an exact match - the process of replacing template parameters with concrete types is known as template argument substitution (or type substitution), and, if `int` is substituted for the `T` template parameter, then we arrive at another function that exactly matches the call. However, a non-template function that matches exactly is considered a better overload. The second call is processed similarly, but it is an exact match to the second function in the overload set, so that is the function that will be called. The last call has an argument of the `double` type that can be converted to `int` or `long`, or substituted for `T` to make the template instantiation an exact match. Since there is no exactly matching non-template function, the template function instantiated to an exact match is the next best overload and is selected.

But what happens when there are multiple template functions that can have their template parameters substituted to match the argument types of the call? Let's find out:

```
// Example 05
void f(int i) { cout << "f(int)" << endl; }      // 1
template <typename T>
```

```
void f(T i) { cout << "f(T)" << endl; }        // 2
template <typename T>
void f(T* i) { cout << "f(T*)" << endl; }       // 3
f(5);          // 1
f(5l);        // 2
int i = 0;
f(&i);        // 3
```

The first call is again an exact match to the non-template function, and so is resolved. The second call matches the first, non-template, overload, with a conversion, or the second overload exactly if the right type, `long`, is substituted for T. The last overload does not match either of these calls - there is no substitution that would make the `T*` parameter type match either `int` or `long`. The last call, however, can be matched to the third overload if `int` is substituted for T. The problem is that it could also match the second overload if `int *` were substituted for T. So which template overload is chosen? The answer is the more specific one - the first overload, `f(T)`, can be made to match any one-argument function call, while the second overload, `f(T*)`, can only match calls with pointer arguments. The more specific, narrower overload is considered a better match and is selected. This is a new notion, specific to templates - instead of choosing better conversions (in general, *fewer* or *simpler* conversions), we select the overload that is *harder* to instantiate.

This rule seemingly breaks for null pointers: `f(NULL)` can call either the first or the second overload (`f(int)` or `f(T)`), and `f(nullptr)` call the second overload, `f(T)`. The pointer overload is never called, even though both `NULL` and `nullptr` are supposedly null pointers. However, this is actually the case of the compiler strictly following the rules. NULL in C++ is an integer zero, it's actually a macro:

```
#define NULL 0 // Or 0L
```

Depending on whether it is defined as `0` or `0L`, `f(int)` or `f(T)` with T==`long` are called. The constant `nullptr`, despite having "ptr" in its name, is actually a constant value of type `nullptr_t`. It is *convertible* to any pointer type but it is not of any pointer type. This is why, when dealing with functions accepting pointers of different types, an overload with a `nullptr_t` parameter is often declared.

Finally, there is one more kind of function that can match just about any function call with the same name, and that is the function that takes variable arguments:

```
// Example 06
void f(int i) { cout << "f(int)" << endl; }     // 1
void f(...) { cout << "f(...)" << endl; }        // 2
f(5);          // 1
f(5l);        // 1
f(5.0);        // 1
struct A {};
```

```
A a;
f(a);      {};      // 2
```

The first of the overloads can be used for the first three function calls - it is an exact match for the first call, and conversions exist to make the other two calls fit the signature of the first overload for `f()`. The second function in this example can be called with any number of arguments of any type. This is considered the choice of last resort - a function with specific arguments that can be made to match the call with the right conversions is preferred. This includes user-defined conversions, as follows:

```
struct B {
   operator int() const { return 0; }
};
B b;
f(b);           // 1
```

Only if there are no conversions that allow us to avoid calling the `f(...)` variadic function, then it has to be called.

Now we know the order of the overload resolution - first, a non-template function that matches the arguments exactly is chosen. If there is no such match in the overload set, then a template function is chosen if its parameters can be substituted with concrete types in a way that gives an exact match. If there is more than one option for such a template function, then a more specific overload is preferred over the more general one. If the attempt to match a template function in this manner also fails, then a non-template function is called if the arguments can be converted to its parameter types. Finally, if everything else fails, but a function with the right name that takes variable arguments is available, then that function is called. Note that certain conversions are considered *trivial* and are included in the notion of the *exact* match, for example, the conversion from T to `const T`. At every step, if there is more than one equally good option, the overload is considered ambiguous and the program is ill-formed.

The process of type substitution in a template function is what determines the final types of the template function parameters, and how good a match they are to the arguments of the function call. This process can lead to somewhat unexpected results and must be considered in more detail.

Type substitution in template functions

We must carefully differentiate between the two steps in instantiating a template function to match a particular call - first, the types of the template parameters are deduced from the argument types (a process referred to as type deduction). Once the types are deduced, the concrete types are substituted for all parameter types (this is a process called **type substitution**). The difference becomes more obvious when the function has multiple parameters.

Type deduction and substitution

Type deduction and substitution are closely related, but not exactly the same. The deduction is the process of "*guessing:*" what should the template type, or types, be in order to match the call? Of course, the compiler does not really guess but applies a set of rules defined in the standard. Consider the following example:

```
// Example 07
template <typename T>
void f(T i, T* p) { std::cout << "f(T, T*)" << std::endl; }
int i;
f(5, &i);      // T == int
f(51, &i);     // ?
```

When considering the first call, we can deduce from the first argument that the T template parameter should be int. Thus, int is substituted for T in both parameters of the function. The template is instantiated as f(int, int*) and is an exact match for the argument types. When considering the second call, we could deduce that T should be long from the first argument. Alternatively, we could deduce that T should be int from the second argument. This ambiguity leads to the failure of the type deduction process. If this is the only overload available, neither option is chosen, and the program does not compile. If more overloads exist, they are considered in turn, including possibly the overload of last resort, the f(...) variadic function. One important detail to note here is that conversions are not considered when deducing template types - the deduction of T as int would have yielded f(int, int*) for the second call, which is a viable option for calling f(long, int*) with the conversion of the first argument. However, this option is not considered at all, and instead, type deduction fails as ambiguous.

The ambiguous deduction can be resolved by explicitly specifying the template types, which removes the need for type deduction:

```
f<int>(51, &i);     // T == int
```

Now, type deduction is not done at all: we know what T is from the function call, as it is explicitly specified. Type substitution, on the other hand, still has to happen - the first parameter is of the int type, and the second is of the int* type. The function call succeeds with a conversion on the first argument. We could also force deduction the other way:

```
f<long>(51, &i);     // T == long
```

Again, deduction is not necessary, as we know what T is. Substitution proceeds in a straightforward way, and we end up with f(long, long*). This function cannot be called with int* as the second argument since there is no valid conversion from int* to long*. Thus, the program does not compile. Note that, by explicitly specifying the types, we have also specified that f() must be a template function. The non-template overloads for f() are no longer considered. On the other hand, if there is more than one f() template function, then these overloads are considered as usual, but this time with the results of the argument deduction forced by our explicit specification.

Template functions can have default arguments, just like non-template functions, however, the values of these arguments are not used to deduce types (in C++11, template functions can have default values for their type parameters, which provides an alternative). Consider the following example:

```
// Example 08
void f(int i, int j = 1) {                              // 1
  cout << "f(int2)" << endl;
}
template <typename T> void f(T i, T* p = nullptr) {     // 2
  cout << "f(T, T*)" << endl;
}
int i;
f(5);         // 1
f(5l);      // 2
```

The first call is an exact match to the f(int, int) non-template function, with the default value of 1 for the second argument. Note that it would have made no difference if we had declared the function as f(int i, int j = 1L), with the default value as long. The type of the default argument does not matter - if it can be converted to the specified parameter type, then that's the value that is used, otherwise, the program would not compile from line 1. The second call is an exact match to the f(T, T*) template function, with T == long and the default value of NULL for the second argument. Again, it does not matter at all that the type of that value is not long*.

We now understand the difference between type deduction and type substitution. Type deduction can be ambiguous when different concrete types can be deduced from different arguments. If this happens, it means we have failed to deduce the argument types and cannot use this template function. Type substitution is never ambiguous - once we know what T is, we simply substitute that type every time we see T in the function definition. This process can also fail, but in a different way.

Substitution failure

Once we have deduced the template parameter types, type substitution is a purely mechanical process:

```
// Example 09
template <typename T> T* f(T i, T& j) {
  j = 2*i;
  return new T(i);
}
int i = 5, j = 7;
const int* p = f(i, j);
```

In this example, the T type can be deduced from the first argument as int. It can also be deduced from the second argument, also as int. Note that the return type is not used for type deduction. Since there is only one possible deduction for T, we now proceed to substitute T with int every time we see T in the function definition:

```
int* f(int i, int& j) {
    j = 2*i;
    return new int(i);
}
```

Not all types, however, are created equal, and some allow more liberties than others. Consider this code:

```
// Example 10
template <typename T>
void f(T i, typename T::t& j) {
    std::cout << "f(T, T::t)" << std::endl;
}
template <typename T>
void f(T i, T j) {
    std::cout << "f(T, T)" << std::endl;
}
struct A {
struct t { int i; }; t i; };
A a{5};
f(a, a.i);     // T == A
f(5, 7);       // T == int
```

When considering the first call, the compiler deduces the T template parameter as being of the A type, from both the first and second argument - the first argument is a value of the A type, and the second one is a reference to the value of the A::t nested type, which matches T::t if we stick with our original deduction of T as A. The second overload yields conflicting values for T from the two arguments and, therefore, cannot be used. Thus, the first overload is called.

Now, look closely at the second call. The T type can be deduced as int from the first argument for both overloads. Substituting int for T, however, yields something strange in the second argument of the first overload - int::t. This, of course, would not compile - int is not a class and does not have any nested types. In fact, we could expect that the first template overload will fail to compile for every T type that is not a class, or that does not have a nested type called t. Indeed, the attempt to substitute int for T in the first template function fails with an invalid type for the second argument. However, this substitution failure does not mean that the entire program cannot compile. Instead, it is silently ignored, and the overload that would otherwise be ill-formed is removed from the overload set. The overload resolution then continues as usual. Of course, we could discover that none of the overloads match the function call, and the program will still not compile, but the error message will not mention anything about int::t being invalid; it'll just say that there are no functions that can be called.

Again, it is important to differentiate between type deduction failure and type substitution failure. We can remove the former from consideration entirely:

```
f<int>(5, 7);     // T == int
```

Now, the deduction is unnecessary, but the substitution of int for T must still take place, and this substitution yields an invalid expression in the first overload. Again, this substitution failure drops this candidate for f() from the overload set, and the overload resolution continues (in this case, successfully) with the remaining candidates. Ordinarily, this would be the end of our exercise in overloading: the template produces code that can't compile, so the entire program should not compile either. Fortunately, C++ is more forgiving in this one situation and has a special exception that we need to know about.

Substitution Failure Is Not An Error

The rule that a substitution failure arising from an expression that would be invalid with the specified or deduced types does not make the whole program invalid is known as **Substitution Failure Is Not An Error** (**SFINAE**). This rule is essential for using template functions in C++; without SFINAE, it would be impossible to write many otherwise perfectly valid programs. Consider the following template overload, which differentiates between regular pointers and member pointers:

```
// Example 11
template <typename T> void f(T* i) {          // 1
  std::cout << "f(T*)" << std::endl;
}
template <typename T> void f(int T::* p) {    // 2
  std::cout << "f(T::*)" << std::endl;
}
struct A { int i; };
A a;
f(&a.i);      // 1
f(&A::i);     // 2
```

So far, so good - the first time, the function is called with a pointer to a specific variable, a.i, and the T type is deduced as int. The second call is with a pointer to a data member of the A class, where T is deduced as A. But now, let's call f() with a pointer to a different type:

```
int i;
f(&i);     // 1
```

The first overload still works fine and is what we want to call. But the second overload isn't just less suitable, it is altogether invalid - it would cause a syntax error if we tried to substitute int for T. This syntax error is observed by the compiler and silently ignored, together with the overload itself.

Note that the SFINAE rule is not limited to invalid types, such as references to non-existing class members. There are many ways in which substitution can fail:

```
// Example 12
template <size_t N>
void f(char(*)[N % 2] = nullptr) {      // 1
    std::cout << "N=" << N << " is odd" << std::endl;
}
template <size_t N>
void f(char(*)[1 - N % 2] = nullptr) { // 2
    std::cout << "N=" << N << " is even" << std::endl;
}
f<5>();
f<8>();
```

Here, the template parameter is a value, not a type. We have two template overloads that both take a pointer to an array of characters, and array size expressions are valid only for some values of N. Specifically, a zero-size array is invalid in C++. Therefore, the first overload is valid only if N % 2 is non-zero, that is, if N is odd. Similarly, the second overload is valid only if N is even. No arguments are given to the function, so we intend to use the default arguments. The two overloads would have been ambiguous in every way, were it not for the fact that, for both calls, one of the overloads fails during template argument substitution and is silently removed.

The preceding example is very condensed - in particular, the template parameter value deduction, the equivalent of type deduction for numeric parameters is disabled by the explicit specification. We can bring the deduction back and still have the substitution fail, or not, depending on whether an expression is valid:

```
// Example 13
template <typename T, size_t N = T::N>
void f(T t, char(*)[N % 2] = NULL) {
    std::cout << "N=" << N << " is odd" << std::endl;
}
template <typename T, size_t N = T::N>
void f(T t, char(*)[1 - N % 2] = NULL) {
    std::cout << "N=" << N << " is even" << std::endl;
}
struct A { enum {N = 5}; };
struct B { enum {N = 8}; };
A a;
B b;
f(a);
f(b);
```

Now, the compiler has to deduce the type from the first argument. For the first call, f(a), the A type is easily deduced. There is no way to deduce the second template parameter, N, so the default value is used (we are now in C++11 territory). Having deduced both template parameters, we now proceed to the substitution, where T is replaced by A, and N is replaced by 5. This substitution fails for the second overload but succeeds for the first one. With only one remaining candidate in the overload set, the overload resolution concludes. Similarly, the second call, f(b), ends up calling the second overload.

Note that there is a subtle but very important difference between the preceding example and the earlier example where we had this function:

```
template <typename T> void f(T i, typename T::t& j);
```

In this template, the substitution failure is "*natural:*" the parameter that may cause the failure is needed and is intended to be of a pointer to member type. In the previous case, the template parameter N is gratuitous: it is not needed for anything other than artificially causing substitution failures and disabling some overloads. Why would you ever want to cause an artificial substitution failure? We have seen one reason, forcing the selection of otherwise ambiguous overloads. The more general reason has to do with the fact that type substitution sometimes can lead to errors.

When substitution failure is still an error

Note that SFINAE does not protect us from any and all syntax errors that might happen during template instantiation. For example, if the template parameters are deduced, and the template arguments are substituted, we may still end up with an ill-formed template function:

```
// Example 14
template <typename T> void f(T) {
  std::cout << sizeof(T::i) << std::endl;
}
void f(...) { std::cout << "f(...)" << std::endl; }
f(0);
```

This code fragment is very similar to those we considered earlier, with one exception - we do not learn that the template overload presupposes that the T type is a class, and has a data member named T::i, until we examine the function body. By then, it is too late, as the overload resolution is done only on the basis of the function declaration - the parameters, the default arguments, and the return type (the latter is not used to deduce types or select a better overload, but still undergoes type substitution and is covered by SFINAE). Once the template is instantiated and chosen by the overload resolution, any syntax errors, such as an invalid expression in the body of the function, are not ignored - such a failure is very much an error. The exact list of contexts where a substitution failure is, or is not, ignored, is defined in the standard; it was significantly expanded in C++11, with subsequent standards making a few subtle tweaks.

There is another case where an attempt to use SFINAE leads to an error instead. Here is an example:

```
// Example 15a
template <typename T> struct S {
  typename T::value_type f();
};
```

Here we have a class template. If the type T does not have a nested type value_type, type substitution leads to an error, and this is a real error, it is not ignored. You can't even instantiate this class template with a type that does not have value_type. Making the function into a template does not solve the problem:

```
template <typename T> struct S {
  template <typename U> typename T::value_type f();
};
```

It is very important to remember that SFINAE applies only when the error occurs during the substitution of the types that were deduced for the template function. In the last example, the substitution error does not depend on the template type parameter U, so it is always going to be an error. If you really need to work around this, you have to use a member function template and use a template type parameter to trigger the substitution error. Since we do not need an additional template parameter, we can default it to be the same as the class template type parameter T:

```
// Example 15b
template <typename T> struct S {
  template <typename U = T>
  std::enable_if_t<std::is_same_v<U, T>
  typename U::value_type f();
};
```

Now the substitution error, if any, will happen with a type dependent on the template type parameter U::value_type. We do not need to specify type U since it is defaulted to T, and it can't be anything else because of the requirement that types U and T are the same (otherwise the return type of the function is invalid, which is a SFINAE error). Thus, our template member function f() does (almost) exactly what the original non-template function f() did (there are subtle differences if the function has overloads within the class). So, if you really need to "hide" a substitution error caused by a class template parameter, you can do so by introducing a redundant function template parameter and restricting the two to always be the same.

Before continuing, let's review the three kinds of substitution failures we encountered.

Where and why does substitution failure happen?

To understand the rest of this chapter, it is essential that we clearly differentiate between several kinds of substitution failures that can occur in template functions.

The first kind happens when the template declaration uses dependent types or other constructs that can cause a failure, and their use is necessary to declare the template properly. Here is a template function that is intended to be called with a container argument (all STL containers have a nested type `value_type`):

```
// Example 16
template <typename T>
bool find(const T& cont, typename T::value_type val);
```

If we try to call this function with an argument that does not define the nested type, `value_type`, the function call will not compile (assuming we have no other overloads). There are many more examples where we naturally use dependent types and other expressions that may be invalid for some values of template parameters. Such invalid expressions cause a substitution failure. It does not have to happen in the argument declaration. Here is a template whose return type may be undefined:

```
// Example 16
template <typename U, typename V>
std::common_type_t<U, V> compute(U u, V v);
```

In this template, the return type is the common type of the two template parameter types. But what if the template arguments are such that the types U and V have no common type? Then the type expression `std::common_type_t<U, V>` is invalid and the type substitution fails. Here is yet another example:

```
// Example 15
template <typename T>
auto process(T p) -> decltype(*p);
```

Here, again, the substitution failure may occur in the return type, but we use the trailing return type so that we can directly check whether the expression `*p` compiles (or, more formally, is valid). If it is, the type of the result is the return type. Otherwise, the substitution fails. Note that there is a difference between this declaration and something like this:

```
template <typename T> T process(T* p);
```

If the function argument is a raw pointer, both versions amount to the same thing. But the first variant also compiles for any type that can be dereferenced, such as container iterators and smart pointers, while the second version works only for raw pointers.

The second kind of substitution failure happens when the function declaration compiles successfully, including the type substitution, and then we get a syntax error in the function body. We can easily modify each of these examples to see how this might have happened. Let's start with the `find()` function:

```
// Example 17
template <typename T, typename V>
bool find(const T& cont, V val) {
  for (typename T::value_type x : cont) {
    if (x == val) return true;
  }
  return false;
}
```

This time, we decided to accept a value of any type. This is not necessarily wrong in itself, but the body of our template function is written in the assumption that the container type T has the nested type `value_type` and that this type is comparable with the type V. If we call the function with a wrong argument, the call will still compile because nothing particular is required of the argument types by the substitution that happens in the declaration of the template. But then we get a syntax error in the body of the template itself, rather than at the call site.

Here is how a similar thing can happen with the `compute()` template:

```
// Example 17
template <typename U, typename V>
auto compute(U u, V v) {
  std::common_type_t<U, V> res = (u > v) ? u : v;
  return res;
}
```

This template function can be called for any two arguments, but then it won't compile unless there is a common type for both.

Note the very significant difference between the two kinds of substitution failures: if the failure happens in SFINAE context, the function is removed from the overload resolution as if it does not exist. If there is another overload (a function with the same name), it will be considered and may end up being called. If there is not, we will get a syntax error at the call site that boils down to "there is no such function." On the other hand, if the failure happens in the body of the template (or in some other place not covered by SFINAE rules) then, assuming the function is the best, or the only, overload, it will be called. The client's code – the call itself – will compile fine, but the template will not.

There are several reasons why the first option is preferable. First of all, the caller may have wanted to call a different overload, the one that would have compiled fine, but the rules for overload resolution among templates are complex and the wrong overload was chosen. It may be very difficult for the caller to fix this error and force the choice of the intended overload. Second, the error messages you get when the body of the template fails compilation are often incomprehensible. Our examples were simple, but in a more realistic case, you may see an error that involves some internal types and objects that you know nothing about. The last reason is more of a conceptual statement: the interface of the template function, like any other interface, should describe the requirements on the caller as completely as possible. An interface is a contract; if the caller has complied with it, the implementer of the function must deliver as promised.

Let's assume that we have a template function whose body has some requirements on the type parameters and that these requirements are not captured by the interface written in a natural, straightforward way (the type substitution succeeds but the template does not compile). The only way to convert the hard substitution failure into an SFINAE failure is to make it happen in SFINAE context. To do this, we need to add something to the interface that is not necessary to declare the function. The only purpose of this addition is to trigger a substitution failure and remove the function from the overload resolution set before it could lead to a compilation error in the body of the function. Such "artificial" failure is the third kind of substitution failure. Here is an example where we enforce the requirement that the types are pointers even though the interface itself would be just fine without it:

```
// Example 18
template <typename U, typename V>
auto compare(U pu, V pv) -> decltype(bool(*pu == *pv)) {
  return *pu < *pv;
}
```

This function takes two pointers (or any other pointer-like objects that can be dereferenced) and returns the Boolean result of comparing the values they point to. In order for the body of the function to compile, both arguments must be something that can be dereferenced. Furthermore, the results of dereferencing them must be comparable for equality. Finally, the result of the comparison must be convertible to bool. The trailing return type declaration is unnecessary: we could have just declared the function to return `bool`. But it does have an effect: it moves a possible substitution failure from the body of the function to its declaration, where it becomes an SFINAE failure. The return type is always `bool` unless the expression inside `decltype()` is invalid. That could happen for any of the same reasons the function body would not compile: one of the arguments cannot be dereferenced, the values are not comparable, or the result of the comparison is not convertible to `bool` (the latter is usually redundant, but we might as well enforce the entire contract).

Notice that the line between the "natural" and "artificial" substitution failures is not always clear. For example, one could have argued that using `std::common_type_t<U, V>` as the return type earlier was artificial (the third kind of substitution failure, not the first kind) and that the "natural" way would be to declare the return type as `auto` and let the function body fail if the common type could not be deduced. Indeed, the difference often boils down to the programmer's style and intent: if it wasn't for the need to enforce the type restriction, would the programmer have written the type expression in the template declaration anyway?

The failures of the first kind are straightforward: the template interface itself forms a contract, the attempted call violated the contract, and the function wasn't called. The failures of the second kind are, ideally, to be avoided altogether. But to do that, we have to employ the failures of the third kind, the artificial substitution failures in SFINAE context. The rest of this chapter deals with the ways to code such interface-limiting template contracts. Since the first days of C++, SFINAE techniques were used to artificially cause a substitution failure that would remove such functions from the overload set. C++20 added a totally different mechanism for solving this problem: concepts. Before we discuss controlling overload resolution with SFINAE, we need to learn more about this latest addition to the language.

Concepts and constraints in C++20

The rest of this chapter is all about the "artificial" substitution failures that are added to the template declaration to impose restrictions on the template arguments. In this section, we are going to learn about the new, C++20, way of coding these restrictions. In the next section, we will show what you can do if you can't use C++20 but still want to constrain your templates.

Constraints in C++20

C++20 changed the way we are using SFINAE to restrict template arguments by introducing concepts and constraints. Even though the overall feature is usually referred to as "concepts," it is the constraints that are the most important part. What follows is not a complete or formal description of these features, but rather a demonstration of the best practices (it may be too early to say "patterns" since the community is still in the process of establishing what is and isn't sufficiently widely accepted).

The first way to specify a constraint is by writing a `requires` clause that has the form:

```
requires(constant-boolean-expression)
```

The keyword `requires` and the constant (compile-time) expression in parentheses must appear either immediately after the template parameters or as the last element of the function declaration:

```
// Example 19
template <typename T> requires(sizeof(T) == 8) void f();
template <typename T> void g(T p) requires(sizeof(*p) < 8);
```

Just like in the last section, the constraint written at the end of the declaration can refer to the function arguments by name, while the constraint written after the parameter list can refer only to the template parameters (other, more subtle differences between the two syntaxes are outside of the scope of this chapter). Unlike the last section, if a constraint fails, the compiler usually issues a clear diagnostic instead of simply reporting that "no function f was found" and template deduction failed.

What can be used in the constant expression in a `requires` clause? Anything that can be computed at compile time, really, as long as the overall result is a `bool`. Type traits such as `std::is_` convertible_v or std::is_default_constructible_v are often used to restrict types. If the expressions are complex, constexpr functions can help to simplify them:

```
template <typename V> constexpr bool valid_type() {
  return sizeof(T) == 8 && alignof(T) == 8 &&
    std::is_default_constructible_v<T>;
}
template <typename T> requires(valid_type<T>()) void f();
```

But there is one special expression that we have not seen before – the requires expression. This expression can be used to check if some arbitrary expression compiles (technically, it "is valid"):

```
requires { a + b; }
```

Assuming the values a and b are defined in the context where the expression is used, this expression evaluates to true if the expression a + b is valid. What if we know the types we want to test but don't have the variables? Then we can use the second form of the requires expression:

```
requires(A a, B b) { a + b; }
```

The types A and B usually refer to the template parameters or some dependent types.

Note that we said "arbitrary expression is valid" and not "arbitrary code is valid." This is an important difference. For example, you can't write

```
requires(C cont) { for (auto x: cont) {}; }
```

And require that the type C meets all requirements for a range-for loop. Most of the time, you test expressions such as cont.begin() and cont.end() instead. However, you can also come up with a more complex requirement by hiding the code in a lambda expression:

```
requires(C cont) {
  [](auto&& c) {
    for (auto x: cont) { return x; };
  }(cont);
}
```

Woe is you if such code ever fails and you have to figure out the error message.

When a requires expression is used in a template constraint, the template is restricted not by a specific trait but by the required behavior of the types:

```
// Example 20
template <typename T, typename P>
void f(T i, P p) requires( requires { i = *p; } );
template <typename T, typename P>
void f(T i, P p) requires( requires { i.*p; } );
```

First of all, yes, there are two keywords `requires` (by the way, parentheses are optional in this case and you can find this constraint written as `requires requires`). The first `requires` introduces a constraint, a `requires` clause. The second `requires` begins the `requires` expression. The expression in the first function `f()` is valid if the second template argument `p` can be dereferenced (it can be a pointer, but it doesn't have to be) and the result can be assigned to the first argument `i`. We don't require that the types on both sides of the assignment be the same or even that `*p` can be convertible to `T` (usually it would be, but it's not required). We just need the expression `i = *p` to compile. Finally, if we did not have the right variables readily available, we could have declared them as parameters to the `requires` expression:

```
// Example 20
template <typename T, typename P>
requires(requires(T t, P p) { t = *p; }) void f(T i, P p);
template <typename T, typename P>
requires(requires(T t, P p) { t.*p; }) void f(T i, P p);
```

These two examples also demonstrate that we can do SFINAE overload control with constraints: if a constraint fails, the template function is removed from the overload resolution set and the resolution continues.

As we have seen already, sometimes we need to check not an expression but a dependent type; we can do that inside the `requires` expression as well:

```
requires { typename T::value_type; }
```

A requires expression evaluates to bool, so it can be used in a logical expression:

```
requires(
    requires { typename T::value_type; } &&
    sizeof(T) <= 32
)
```

We could combine multiple requires expressions this way, but we can also write more code inside a single expression:

```
requires(T t) { typename T::value_type; t[0]; }
```

Here we require that the type `T` has a nested type `value_type` and an index operator that accepts integer indices.

Finally, sometimes we need to check not just that some expression compiles but that its result has a certain type (or satisfies some type requirements). This can be done with the compound form of the `requires` expression:

```
requires(T t) { { t + 1 } -> std::same_as<T>; }
```

Here we require that the expression t + 1 compiles and yields the result of the same type as the variable t itself. The last part is done using a concept; you will read about them in the next section, but for now, think of it as an alternative way to write the std::is_same_v type trait.

Speaking of concepts… Everything we have described so far can be found under the heading of "concepts" in any C++20 book, except we have not mentioned the concepts themselves. That is about to change.

Concepts in C++20

Concepts are simply a named set of requirements – the same requirements we were just learning about. In a way, they are similar to constexpr functions, except they operate on types, not values.

You use a concept when there is a set of requirements that you refer to often, or one that you want to give a meaningful name to. For example, a range is defined by a very simple requirement: it must have a begin iterator and an end iterator. We can write a simple requires expression every time we declare a function template that accepts a range argument, but it is both more convenient and more readable to give this requirement a name:

```
// Example 21
template <typename R> concept Range = requires(R r) {
    std::begin(r);
    std::end(r);
};
```

We have just introduced a concept named Range with one template type parameter R; this type must have begin and end iterators (the reason we use std::begin() instead of the member function begin() is that C arrays are also ranges but they have no member functions).

Note that C++20 has a ranges library and a corresponding set of concepts (including std::ranges::range that should be used instead of our homemade Range in any real code) but the idea of ranges makes for convenient teaching material and we will use it to drive the examples.

Once we have a named concept, we can use it instead of spelling out the requirements in any template constraint:

```
// Example 21
template <typename R> requires(Range<R>) void sort(R&& r);
```

As you can see, the concept can be used inside a requires clause as if it was a constexpr variable of type bool. Indeed, a concept can also be used in contexts such as static assert:

```
static_assert(Range<std::vector<int>>);
static_assert(!Range<int>);
```

For simple template declarations where the concept is the whole requirement, the language provides a much simpler way to state it:

```
// Example 21
template <Range R> void sort(R&& r);
```

In other words, the concept name can be used instead of the `typename` keyword in a template declaration. Doing so automatically restricts the corresponding type parameter to types that satisfy the concept. If necessary, a `requires` clause can still be used to define additional constraints. Finally, the concepts can also be used with the new C++20 template syntax:

```
// Example 21
void sort(Range auto&& r);
```

All three declarations have the same effect and the choice is largely a matter of style and convenience.

Concepts and type restrictions

We have already seen how concepts and constraints are used to impose restrictions on the parameters of function templates. The `requires` clauses can appear after the template parameters or at the end of the function declaration; both places are SFINAE contexts and a substitution failure in either location does not stop the compilation of the entire program. In this regard, concepts are not fundamentally different from substitution failures: while you can use a constraint outside of an SFINAE context, a substitution failure would still be an error. For example, you cannot assert that a type does not have a nested type `value_type` by using a constraint:

```
static_assert(!requires{ typename T::value_type; });
```

You may expect that the `requires` expression evaluates to false if the requirement is not met, but in this case, it simply does not compile (you get the error that `T::value_type` does not refer to a valid type).

However, there are restrictions you can enforce with concepts that were impossible to implement before. These are requirements for class templates. In the simplest form, we can use a concept to restrict class template type parameters:

```
// Example 21
template <Range R> class C { … };
```

This class template can only be instantiated with types that satisfy the concept `Range`.

Then, we can constrain individual member functions, whether they are templates or not:

```
// Example 21
template <typename T> struct holder {
  T& value;
```

```
  holder(T& t) : value(t) {}
  void sort() requires(Range<T>) {
    std::sort(std::begin(value), std::end(value));
  }
};
```

Now the class template itself can be instantiated on any type. However, its interface includes a member function `sort()` only if the type satisfies the `Range` constraint.

This is a very important difference between constraints and the old SFINAE: the artificial substitution failure helps only if it happens when substituting deduced type parameters in function templates. Earlier in this chapter, we had to add a dummy template type parameter to a member function just so we could create an SFINAE failure. With concepts, there is no need for any of that.

Concepts and constraints are the best way to specify restrictions on template parameters. They make a lot of the SFINAE tricks invented over the years obsolete. But not everyone has access to C++20 yet. Also, some of the SFINAE techniques are still used even with concepts. In the last section, we will learn about these techniques as well as see what can be done if you do not have C++20 but still want to constraint template types.

SFINAE techniques

The rule that a failure of the template argument substitution is not an error - the SFINAE rule - had to be added to the language simply to make certain narrowly defined template functions possible. But the ingenuity of a C++ programmer knows no bounds, and so SFINAE was repurposed and exploited to manually control the overload set by intentionally causing substitution failures. A huge variety of SFINAE-based techniques were invented over the years until the C++20 concepts made most of them obsolete.

Still, some use of SFINAE remains even in C++20, and then there is the vast body of pre-C++20 code that you may need to read, understand, and maintain.

Let's start with the applications of SFINAE that are still useful even when concepts are available.

SFINAE in C++20

First of all, even in C++20, there are still "natural" type substitution failures. For example, you may want to write this function:

```
template <typename T> typename T::value_type f(T&& t);
```

This is still fine, assuming you really want to return a value of the type given by the nested `value_type`. However, before you rush to answer "yes" you should examine closely what is the type you really want to return. What is the contract with the caller that you want to enforce? Maybe the existence of `value_type` was used as a proxy for the real requirements, such as the type T has the index operator or can be used as a range to iterate over. In this case, you can now state the requirements directly, for example:

```
template <typename T> auto f(T&& t)
requires( requires { *t.begin(); t.begin() != t.end(); } );
```

This says that what you really need is a type with member functions `begin()` and `end()`. The values returned by these functions (presumably, the iterators) are dereferenced and compared; if these operations are supported, the return values are close enough to iterators for our purposes. Finally, in the preceding example, we let the compiler determine the return type. This is often convenient, but the downside is that the interface – our contract – does not say what the return type is; the client of our code must read the implementation. Assuming we return a value we get by dereferencing an iterator, we can be explicit about it:

```
template <typename T> auto f(T&& t)->decltype(*t.begin())
requires( requires {
  *t.begin();
  t.begin() != t.end();
  ++t.begin();
} );
```

This is a very comprehensive contract with the client, assuming, of course, that we as implementers guarantee that the body of the function will compile if the stated requirements are met. Otherwise, the contract is incomplete: for example, if we do use `T::value_type` in the body of the function, we should add `typename T::value_type` to the list of requirements, whether or not this is the type we eventually return (if it is, we could still use SFINAE for the return type, nothing wrong with that).

Similar considerations exist when a dependent type is used to declare a template function argument, for example:

```
template <typename T>
bool find(const T& t, typename T::value_type x);
```

Again, we should ask ourselves if these really are the requirements we want to impose. Assuming the function is looking for the value x in the container t, do we really care what the type of x is as long as it can be compared with the values stored in the container? Consider this alternative:

```
template <typename T, typename X>
bool find(const T& t, X x)
requires( requires {
  *t.begin() == x;
  t.begin() == t.end();
  ++t.begin();
} );
```

Now we require that the container has everything needed for a range-for loop and that the values stored in the container can be compared with x for equality. Assuming that all we do is iterate over the container and return true if a value equal to x is found, this is all we need to require from the caller.

You should not infer that the "natural" SFINAE should no longer be used in C++20 and be replaced by independent template parameters bound together by constraints. All we suggest is that you examine your code to determine whether the contract expressed by the interface and enforced through SFINAE is really what you want, or merely what was convenient to code. In the latter case, concepts offer a way to express what you really wanted to require but could not (but do read on, because there are concept-inspired techniques that can be used before C++20 and meet the same need). On the other hand, if the template function is best written in a way that triggers a substitution failure when the client supplies an invalid argument, then, by all means, continue to use SFINAE – there is no need to rewrite everything to use concepts.

Even the "artificial" SFINAE still has uses in C++20, as we are about to see.

SFINAE and type traits

The most important application of "artificial" SFINAE in C++20 is writing type traits. Type traits are not going anywhere: even if you replace `std::is_same_v` (trait) with `std::same_as` (concept) in your code, you should know that the concept's implementation uses the very trait it replaces.

Not all type traits require the use of SFINAE, but many do. These are the traits that check for the presence of some syntactic feature, such as the existence of a nested type. The implementation of these traits faces a common problem: if the type does not have the required feature, some code does not compile. But we don't want a compilation error. We want an expression that evaluates to `false`. So how do we get the compiler to ignore an error? By making it occur in an SFINAE context, of course.

Let's start with an example that was getting in our way throughout the entire chapter: we are going to write a trait to check whether a type has the nested type `value_type`. We are going to use SFINAE, so we need a template function. This function must use the nested type in an SFINAE context. There are several options for that. Often, it is convenient to add a template argument that depends on the expression that may fail, for example:

```
template <typename T, typename = T::value_type> void f();
```

Note that the second parameter has no name – we never use it. If we attempt to instantiate this template with any type T that does not have a nested `value_type`, for example, `f<int>()`, the substitution will fail, but this is not an error (SFINAE!). Of course, not having a function to call when we write `f(ptr)` is an error, so we must provide a fallback overload:

```
template <typename T> void f(…);
```

You may find the notion of the "doubly universal" `template f(...)` function curious - it takes any arguments of any type, even without the template, so why use the template? Of course, it is so a call with an explicitly specified type, such as f<int>(), considers this function as a possible overload (remember that, by specifying the template parameter type, we also exclude all non-template functions from consideration). However, we want the priority of this overload to be as low as possible, so the first overload is preferred as long as it exists. That's why we use f(...) which is the "overload of the last resort." Alas, the overload of f() and f(...) is still considered ambiguous, so we need to have at least one argument. The type of the argument doesn't matter as long as we can readily construct an object of that type:

```
template <typename T, typename = T::value_type>
void f(int);
template <typename T> void f(...);
```

Now a call to f<T>(0) will choose the first overload if T::value_type is a valid type. Otherwise, there is only one overload to choose from, the second one. All we need is a way to figure out which overload would be chosen if we made the call, without actually making it.

This turns out to be pretty easy: we can use decltype() to check the type of the result of the function (prior to C++11, sizeof() was used instead). Now, all we need is to give the two overloads different return types. Any two different types can be used. We can then write some conditional code on these types. However, remember that we are writing a type trait, and the traits that check for the existence of something usually end up being std::true_type if the value exists and std::false_type if it does not. There's no reason to overcomplicate our implementation – we can just return the desired type from both overloads and use it as the trait:

```
// Example 22
namespace detail {
template <typename T, typename = T::value_type>
void test_value_type(int);
template <typename T> void test_value_type (...);
}
template <typename T> using has_value_type =
  decltype(detail::test_value_type <T>(0));
```

Since the functions are never called but used only inside decltype(), we do not need to provide the definition of the functions, only their declarations (but see the next section for a more complete and nuanced explanation). To avoid polluting the global namespace with the test functions that the client should not ever have to worry about, it is customary to hide them in a namespace such as detail or internal. Speaking of customary, we should define the two aliases:

```
template <typename T>
using has_value_type_t = has_value_type<T>::type;
template <typename T> inline constexpr
bool has_value_type_v = has_value_type<T>::value;
```

Now we can use our trait like any standard trait, for example:

```
static_assert(has_value_type_v<T>, "I require value_type");
```

As we have seen earlier, there are several other SFINAE contexts we could have used to "hide" the potential error arising from using `T::value_type`. The trailing return type could be used but is not convenient since we already have a return type we need (there is a way around that, but it's more complex than the alternatives). Also, if we ever need to use SFINAE with a constructor, the return type is not an option there.

The other common technique is adding extra arguments to the function; the substitution error occurs in the argument type and the arguments must have default values so the caller doesn't even know they exist. This used to be more popular in the past, but we are moving away from this practice: the dummy arguments can interfere with the overload resolution and it may be hard to come up with a reliable default value for such arguments.

The one other technique that is becoming standard practice is to have the substitution failure occur in an optional non-type template parameter:

```
// Example 22a
template <typename T, std::enable_if_t<
  sizeof(typename T::value_type) !=0, bool> = true>
std::true_type test_value_type(int);
```

Here we have a non-type template parameter (a value of type `bool`) with a default value `true`. The substitution of type T in this parameter can fail in the same way all the earlier failures in this section occurred: if the nested type `T::value_type` does not exist (if it does, the logical expression `sizeof (...)  !=  0` never fails since the size of any type is non-negative). The advantage of this approach is that it's easier to combine multiple expressions if we need to check for several failures at once, for example:

```
template <typename T, std::enable_if_t<
  sizeof(typename T::value_type) !=0 &&
  sizeof(typename T::size_type) !=0, bool> = true>
std::true_type test_value_type(int);
```

This technique is sometimes used with the failing expression in the default value instead of the type:

```
template <typename T,
          bool = sizeof(typename T::value_type)>
std::true_type test_value_type(int);
```

This is a bad habit to get into: while it sometimes works and may seem easier to write, it has a major drawback. Often, you need to declare several overloads with different conditions such that only one of these succeeds. You can do so using the earlier approach:

```
template <typename T, std::enable_if_t<cond1, bool> = true>
res_t func();
template <typename T, std::enable_if_t<cond2, bool> = true>
res_t func(); // OK as long as only one cond1,2 is true
```

But you cannot do this:

```
template <typename T, bool = cond1> = true>
res_t func();
template <typename T, bool = cond2 > = true>
res_t func();
```

Two templates that have the same parameters but different default values are considered duplicate declarations, even if one of the conditions `cond1` or `cond2` always causes a substitution failure. It is better to get into the habit of writing such code with the (possibly failing) condition in the type of the non-type parameter.

To review everything we have learned about SFINAE, let's write another trait. This time, we are going to check whether a type is a class:

```
// Example 23
namespace detail {
template <typename T> std::true_type test(int T::*);
template <typename T> std::false_type test(...);
}
template <typename T>
using is_class = decltype(detail::test<T>(nullptr));
```

The key difference between a class and not a class is that a class has members and, thus, member pointers. This time the easiest way is to declare a member function argument that is a member pointer (doesn't matter what kind of member, we're not going to call the function). The substitution failure occurs in the parameter type `T::*` if the type T does not have any members.

This is almost exactly how the standard trait `std::is_class` is defined except it also checks for unions: unions are not considered classes by `std::is_class`, but implementing `std::is_union` requires compiler support, not SFINAE.

The techniques we have learned allow us to write any trait that checks for a particular property of a type: whether it is a pointer, whether it has a nested type or a member, etc. On the other hand, the concepts make it easy to check for behaviors: can a type be dereferenced, can two types be compared, etc? Note that I said "easy" not "possible:" you can use concepts to check for very narrowly defined features, and you can use traits to detect behaviors, but it is not as straightforward.

This chapter mainly targets a programmer who writes templates and template libraries in application code: if you write a library with the complexity and rigor of STL, you need to be very precise in your definitions (you also need a standard committee to debate and hash out those definitions to the necessary degree of precision). For the rest of us, the degree of formality provided by "call f (p) if *p compiles" is usually sufficient. In C++20, we can do this with concepts. If you do not use C++20 yet, you have to use one of the SFINAE techniques. Several such were discussed in this chapter; the community has developed many more over the years. However, the development of concepts had an interesting effect on these practices: in addition to the tools we can use directly in C++20, the standard offers us a way of thinking about this problem that is applicable much more broadly. Thus, several SFINAE techniques that somewhat resemble the concepts (for example, testing behaviors in a trailing decltype()) are becoming more popular, while other practices are falling out of favor. There have even been several attempts to implement a concept library using pre-C++20 language features. Of course, it is not possible to replicate concepts; in many ways, we can't even get close. However, we can still benefit from the thinking that went into developing the concepts language even if we cannot use the language itself. Thus, we can use SFINAE "in the spirit" of concepts, which provides a consistent way to implement SFINAE-based restrictions instead of an ad hoc collection of techniques. What follows is one such approach to implementing concept-like restrictions without the use of C++20.

Concepts before concepts

Our goal is not so much to implement a full concept library here: you can find such libraries online, and this book is about design patterns and best practices, not writing specific libraries. The aim of this section is to select the few best SFINAE-based techniques among the multitude of available options. These techniques also fit the concept-based mindset, as much as possible anyway. The methods and tricks we have not chosen are not necessarily inferior, but this section offers a set of SFINAE tools and practices that is consistent, uniform, and sufficient for the absolute majority of an application programmer's needs.

Just like with real concepts, we will need two kinds of entities: concepts and restrictions.

If you look at the way concepts are used, they strongly resemble constant Boolean variables:

```
template <typename R> concept Range = ...;
template <typename R> requires(Range<R>) void sort(...);
```

The requires() clause needs a Boolean value, it is not restricted to concepts (consider the expression requires(std::is_class_v<T>)). The concept Range<R> thus acts like a Boolean value. Perforce, we are going to use constexpr bool variables instead of concepts in our attempt to emulate their behavior. From the comparison of Range<R> with std::is_class_v<T> we can also deduce that a trait-like mechanism is probably our best bet to implement concepts: std::is_class_v is also a constexpr bool variable, after all.

From the implementations of the traits we learned in the last section, we know that we are going to need two overloads:

```
template <typename R> constexpr yes_t RangeTest(some-args);
template <typename R> constexpr no_t RangeTest(...);
```

The first overload is going to be valid and preferred for any type R that satisfies the requirements of Range (once we figure out how to do it). The second overload is always available but never preferred, so it is called only if this is the only overload left.

We can figure out which overload was called from the return types (yes_t and no_t are just placeholders for some types we haven't chosen yet). But there is a much simpler way; all we need for our Range "concept" is a constant Boolean value, so why not let the constexpr function return the right value directly, like so:

```
template <typename R> constexpr bool RangeTest(some-args) {
    return true;
}
template <typename R> constexpr bool RangeTest(...) {
    return false;
}
template <typename R>
constexpr inline bool Range = RangeTest<R>(0);
```

The last two statements (the variable and the fallback overload) are complete. "All" we need is to make it so the first overload suffers a substitution failure when R is not a range. So, what is a range for our purposes? Just like we did in the section *Concepts in C++20*, we are going to define a range as any type that has begin() and end(). Since we are testing for a specific behavior, which may fail to compile but should not cause an error, we should trigger this failure in an SFINAE context. As we have seen already, the easiest place for this possibly invalid code is the trailing return type:

```
template <typename R>
constexpr auto RangeTest(??? r) -> decltype(
    std::begin(r),         // Ranges have begin()
    std::end(r),           // Ranges have end()
    bool{}                 // But return type should be bool
) { return true; }
```

The trailing return type lets us write code that uses parameter names. All we need is a parameter r of type R. This is easy to do when using SFINAE in any template function that is meant to be called. But this function is never going to be called with an actual range. We could try to declare an argument of type R& and then call the function with a default-constructed range R{}, but this is not going to work because constexpr functions must have constexpr arguments (otherwise they can still be called but not in a constant expression, i.e. not at compile time), and R{} is not going to be a constexpr value for most ranges.

We could give up on using references altogether and use pointers instead:

```cpp
// Example 24
template <typename R>
constexpr auto RangeTest(R* r) -> decltype(
  std::begin(*r),      // Ranges have begin()
  std::end(*r),            // Ranges have end()
  bool{}              // But return type should be bool
) { return true; }
template <typename R> constexpr bool RangeTest(...) {
  return false;
}
template <typename R>
constexpr inline bool Range = RangeTest<R>(nullptr);
```

While you may have expected that "concept-like" SFINAE is going to be incredibly complex, this is actually all you need to define a concept such as `Range`:

```cpp
static_assert(Range<std::vector<int>>);
static_assert(!Range<int>);
```

These two statements look exactly like their C++20 equivalents! Our "concept" even works in C++14 except there are no `inline` variables there so we have to use `static` instead.

Having finished with concepts for now, we also need to do something about constraints. Here our success is going to be much more limited. First of all, since we are using SFINAE, we can apply restrictions only to template function parameters (as we have seen, the C++20 constraints can apply even to non-template functions, such as member functions of class templates). Also, we are very limited in where we can write these constraints. The most universal way is to add a non-template parameter to the template and test the constraint there:

```cpp
template <typename R,
    std::enable_if_t<Range<R>, bool> = true>
void sort(R&& r);
```

We can hide the boilerplate code in a macro:

```cpp
// Example 24
#define REQUIRES(...) \
  std::enable_if_t<(__VA_ARGS__), bool> = true
template <typename R, REQUIRES(Range<R>)> void sort(R&& r);
```

The variadic macro neatly solves the common problem macros have when their arguments are code: commas are interpreted as separators between arguments. This is by no means as convenient as C++20 constraints, but it's as close as you're going to get.

Now let us come back to the concepts. What we wrote earlier works, but has two problems: first, there is a lot of boilerplate code there too. Second, we had to use pointers to introduce function parameter names we could later use to test the required behaviors. This limits what behaviors we can require because functions can pass arguments by reference and the behavior can depend on what type of reference is used, while we cannot form pointers to references. In fact, the code we just wrote won't compile in many cases because the type of the argument R to the template function `sort()` is deduced as a reference. To use it reliably, we have to check the underlying type instead:

```
// Example 24
template <typename R, REQUIRES(Range<std::decay_t<R>>)>
void sort(R&& r);
```

It would be much more convenient if we could use reference arguments, but then we are back to the problem we already faced: how to invoke such a function? We can't use a value of the corresponding type, such as R{} because it is not a constant expression. The same problem happens if we try to use R{} as the default argument value – it is still not a constant expression.

As with most problems in software engineering, this one can be solved by adding another level of indirection:

```
template <typename R>
constexpr static auto RangeTest(R& r = ???) ->
    decltype(std::begin(r), std::end(r));
template <typename R>            // Overload for success
constexpr static auto RangeTest(int) ->
    decltype(RangeTest<R>(), bool{}) { return true; }
template <typename R>            // Fallback overload
constexpr bool RangeTest(...) { return false; }
template <typename R>
constexpr static bool Range = RangeTest<R>(0);
```

Our fallback overload remains the same, but the overload that is going to be called if the SFINAE test succeeds now attempts to call `RangeTest(r)` in a `decltype` context (also, we are back to using `int` instead of a pointer as the dummy argument). The last problem is what to use as the default value for the argument `r`.

The usual way of getting references to objects in code that is never going to be called is `std::declval`, so we might want to write this:

```
template <typename R>
constexpr static auto RangeTest(R& r=std::declval<R>()) ->
    decltype(std::begin(r), std::end(r));
```

Unfortunately, this is not going to compile, and the error message is going to be something like "`std::declval` must not be used." This is strange, we are not really using it (the entire function is used only inside `decltype()`) but let's try to work around it. After all, there is no magic in `std::declval`, we just need a function that returns a reference to our object:

```
template <typename T> constexpr T& lvalue();
template <typename R>
constexpr static auto RangeTest(R& r = lvalue<R>()) ->
  decltype(std::begin(r), std::end(r));
```

On a standard-compliant compiler, this is not going to compile either, but the error is going to be different, this time the compiler will say something like this:

```
inline function 'lvalue<std::vector<int>>' is used but not defined."
```

OK, we can define the function but make sure it is never called:

```
template <typename T> constexpr T& lvalue() { abort(); }
template <typename R>
constexpr static auto RangeTest(R& r = lvalue<R>()) ->
  decltype(std::begin(r), std::end(r));
```

Adding `{ abort(); }` makes all the difference – the program now compiles and (after you add the rest of the missing pieces) it runs without aborting. That is as it should be: the function `lvalue()` is used only inside `decltype`, and its implementation should not matter at all. I'm not going to keep you in suspense any longer, this is an issue with the standard itself; if you want to want to dive into the thorny details, you can follow *Core Issue 1581* here: `https://www.open-std.org/jtc1/sc22/wg21/docs/papers/2017/p0859r0.html`. For now, we will just have to keep the useless function body (it doesn't hurt anything). Of course, we can define similar functions for initializing default rvalue arguments as well as `const` lvalue references, and contain them in some implementation-only namespace:

```
namespace concept_detail {
template <typename T>
  constexpr const T& clvalue() { abort(); }
template <typename T> constexpr T& lvalue() { abort(); }
template <typename T> constexpr T&& rvalue() { abort(); }
}
```

Now we can define concepts that test behaviors for the type of reference we want:

```
// Example 24a
template <typename R>
constexpr static auto RangeTest(
  R& r = concept_detail::lvalue<R>()) ->
  decltype(std::begin(r), std::end(r));
template <typename R>
```

```
constexpr static auto RangeTest(int) ->
  decltype(RangeTest<R>(), bool{}) { return true; }
template <typename R>
constexpr bool RangeTest(...) { return false; }
template <typename R>
constexpr static bool Range = RangeTest<R>(0);
```

The constraints, including our REQUIRES macro, still work exactly the same way (after all, the concept itself did not change – Range is still a constant Boolean variable).

There is still the issue of the boilerplate; in fact, we have even more of it with the unwieldy default argument values. That's the easiest to take care of, though, with the help of some macros:

```
// Example 25
#define CLVALUE(TYPE, NAME) const TYPE& NAME = \
  Concepts::concept_detail::clvalue<TYPE>()
#define LVALUE(TYPE, NAME) TYPE& NAME = \
  Concepts::concept_detail::lvalue<TYPE>()
#define RVALUE(TYPE, NAME) TYPE&& NAME = \
  Concepts::concept_detail::rvalue<TYPE>()
```

Of the three template functions (such as RangeTest), the first function is the equivalent of the C++20 concept declaration – that's where the behaviors we want to require are coded. Other than these macros, it can't really be made any shorter:

```
// Example 25
template <typename R> CONCEPT RangeTest(RVALUE(R, r)) ->
  decltype(std::begin(r), std::end(r));
```

Here we also defined a macro:

```
#define CONCEPT constexpr inline auto
```

This is done not so much to shorten the code but to make it clear to the reader (if not the compiler) that we are defining a concept. Compare it with the C++20 statement:

```
template <typename R> concept Range =
  requires(R r) { std::begin(r); std::end(r); };
```

The other two overloads (RangeTest(int) and RangeTest(...)), as well as the definition of the concept variable itself, can easily be made universal for any concept (except for the name, of course). In fact, the only declaration that varies from one concept to another is the first one:

```
template <typename R>
constexpr static auto RangeTest(int) ->
  decltype(RangeTest<R>(), bool{}) { return true; }
```

We can make it work for any concept-testing function if we use a variadic template:

```
// Example 25
template <typename… T>
constexpr static auto RangeTest(int) ->
  decltype(RangeTest<T…>(), bool{}) { return true; }
```

Since all of our argument macros, such as `LVALUE()`, include the default value for each argument, the function can always be called without arguments. We have to be mindful of the possibility that the test function we define conflicts with the function `RangeTest(int)`. This does not happen here because `int` is not a valid range, but it could happen for other arguments. Since we control these common overloads and the definition of the concept variable itself, we could make sure that they use an argument that will not conflict with anything we could ever write in regular code:

```
// Example 25
struct ConceptArg {};
template <typename… T>
constexpr static auto RangeTest(ConceptArg, int) ->
  decltype(RangeTest<T…>(), bool{}) { return true; }
template <typename T>
constexpr bool RangeTest(ConceptArg, ...) { return false; }
template <typename R>
constexpr static bool Range = RangeTest<R>(ConceptArg{},0);
```

This code is going to be the same for all concepts, except for the names such as `Range` and `RangeTest`. A single macro can generate all these lines from just two naming arguments:

```
// Example 25
#define DECLARE_CONCEPT(NAME, SUFFIX) \
template <typename... T> constexpr inline auto      \
  NAME ## SUFFIX(ConceptArg, int) -> \
  decltype(NAME ## SUFFIX<T...>(), bool{}){return true;} \
template <typename... T> constexpr inline bool \
  NAME ## SUFFIX(ConceptArg, ...) { return false; } \
template <typename... T> constexpr static bool NAME = \
  NAME ## SUFFIX<T...>(ConceptArg{}, 0)
```

We did not do so for brevity, but if you want to use these concept-like utilities in your code, you should hide all the implementation details in a namespace.

Now we can define our range concept as follows:

```
// Example 25
template <typename R> CONCEPT RangeTest(RVALUE(R, r)) ->
  decltype(std::begin(r), std::end(r));
DECLARE_CONCEPT(Range, Test);
```

Thanks to the variadic template, we are not limited to concepts with just one template parameter. Here is a concept for two types that can be added together:

```
// Example 25
template <typename U, typename V> CONCEPT
  AddableTest(CLVALUE(U, u), CLVALUE(V, v)) ->
  decltype(u + v);
DECLARE_CONCEPT(Addable, Test);
```

For comparison, this is what the C++20 version looks like:

```
template <typename U, typename V> concept Addable =
  require(U u, V v) { u + v; }
```

Of course, it is much shorter and more powerful. But the C++14 version is about as close as you can get (this is not the only approach but they all yield similar results).

These "fake concepts" can be used to constrain templates, just like C++20 concepts:

```
// Example 25
template <typename R, REQUIRES(Range<R>)> void sort(R&& r);
```

OK, not quite like the C++20 concepts – we are limited to template functions, and any requirement must involve at least one template parameter. So, if you want to restrict a non-template member function of a template class, you have to play the template game:

```
template <typename T> class C {
  template <typename U = T, REQUIRE(Range<U>)> void f(T&);
  ...
};
```

But we do get the same result in the end: a call to sort with a vector compiles and sort of something that is not a range does not:

```
std::vector<int> v = ...;
sort(v);          // OK
sort(0);          // Does not compile
```

Unfortunately, one place where our pseudo-concepts really come up short is the error messages – a C++20 compiler would usually tell us which concept was not satisfied and why, while the template substitution error messages are not easy to decipher.

By the way, when you write a test to make sure that something does not compile, you can now use a concept (or a pseudo-concept) to do that:

```
// Example 25
template <typename R>
CONCEPT SortCompilesTest(RVALUE(R, r))->decltype(sort(r));
DECLARE_CONCEPT(SortCompiles, Test);
static_assert(SortCompiles<std::vector<int>>);
static_assert(!SortCompiles<int>);
```

The C++20 version is left as an exercise for you.

Before we end this chapter, let's look at the recommendations and the best practices for use of SFINAE and concepts in templates.

Constrained templates – the best practices

We have recommended the most useful SFINAE and concept-based techniques as we encountered them throughout the chapter, but we had a lot of material to cover, so it may be helpful to concisely restate these guidelines. These guidelines are here mainly for a programmer who uses templates in their application code. That includes the foundational code such as core template libraries of the applications, but a programmer writing a library such as STL, written for the widest possible use under extremely varied conditions and documented very precisely in a formal standard, would find these guidelines lacking in precision and formality:

- Learn the basic rules of SFINAE: in which contexts it applies (declarations) and in which it does not (function body).

- The "natural" use of SFINAE that arises from using parameter-dependent types in the template declarations and argument-dependent expressions in the trailing return type is almost always the simplest way to express constraints on the template parameters (but see the next guideline).

- Ask yourself whether you use a dependent type such as `T::value_type` because this is precisely the right type for the context where you use it, or is it just simpler than writing the real constraint on the interface (such as "any type that converts to `T::value_type`)? In the latter case, this chapter should have convinced you that such restrictions are not that hard to express.

- Whenever it makes sense, make your templates more general by using additional template parameters and necessary constraints on them (instead of using `T::value_type` as an argument type, use another template parameter and constrain it to be convertible to `T::value_type`).

- If you use C++20 and have access to concepts, avoid using "artificial" SFINAE, i.e. do not create substitution failures whose only purpose is to constrain the template. Use the `requires` clauses, with or without concepts, as needed.

- If you can't use C++20 concepts, choose a common uniform approach to SFINAE-based constraints and follow it. Take advantage of the concept-based approach developed for C++20 even if you can't use the language tools: follow the same style and patterns when applying SFINAE-based techniques. The previous section presented one such approach.

- Ideally, if a template declaration meets all specified restrictions, there should be no substitution errors in the body of the template (i.e. if the function invokes, it compiles). This is a difficult goal in practice: the restrictions may end up being verbose and sometimes difficult to write up, and you may not even be aware of all the constraints your implementation implicitly demands. Even STL, designed with the benefit of the committee scrutinizing every word in its requirements, does not fully meet this goal. Nonetheless, it is a good practice to aim for. Also, if you must allow a function to be invoked but not compile, at least have the requirements codified by static asserts in the body of the function – they are much easier for your users to understand than the strange substitution errors in types they never even heard of.

After reading this chapter, these guidelines should not be too daunting for you.

Summary

SFINAE is a somewhat esoteric feature of the C++ standard - it is complex and has many subtle details. While it is usually mentioned in the context of *manual control of the overload resolution*, its main purpose is actually not to enable very elaborate guru-level code but to make the regular (automatic) overload resolution work the way the programmer intended. In this role, it usually works exactly as desired and with no additional effort - in fact, the programmer usually does not need to even be aware of this feature. Most of the time, when you write a generic overload and a special overload for the pointers, you expect the latter not to be called for types that are not pointers. Most of the time, you probably don't even pause to notice that the rejected overload would be ill-formed - who cares, it's not supposed to be used. But to find out that it's not supposed to be used, the type has to be substituted, which would result in an invalid code. SFINAE breaks this chicken-and-egg problem - to find out that the overload should be rejected, we have to substitute types, but that would create code that should not compile, which should not be a problem, because the overload should be rejected in the first place, but we do not know that until we substitute the types, and so on. This is what we call "natural" SFINAE.

Of course, we did not go through a few dozen pages just to learn that the compiler magically does the right thing and you don't have to worry about it. The more elaborate use of SFINAE is to create an artificial substitution failure, and thus take control of the overload resolution by removing some of the overloads. In this chapter, we learned the *safe* contexts for these *temporary* errors that are eventually suppressed by SFINAE. With careful application, this technique can be used to inspect and differentiate, at compile time, anything from the simple features of different types (*is this a class?*) to complex behaviors that can be provided by any number of C++ language features (*is there any way to add these two types?*). In C++20, such code is greatly simplified by introducing constraints and concepts. However, we can apply concept-inspired thinking even to the code written for earlier standards.

In the next chapter, we will introduce another advanced template pattern that is used to greatly increase the power of class hierarchies in C++: class inheritance lets us pass information from the base class to the derived, and the Curiously Recurring Template Pattern does the opposite, it makes the base class aware of the derived.

Questions

1. What is an overload set?

2. What is overload resolution?

3. What are type deduction and type substitution?

4. What is SFINAE?

5. In what contexts can potentially invalid code be present and not trigger a compilation error, unless that code is actually needed?

6. How can we determine which overload was chosen without actually calling it?

7. How is SFINAE used to control conditional compilation?

8. Why are C++20 constraints superior to SFINAE for constraining templates?

9. How does the C++20 concepts standard benefit the programmers using earlier language versions?

Part 3: C++ Design Patterns

This part begins with the main portion of the book. It introduces the most important, frequently used C++ design patterns. Each pattern is generally used as a commonly accepted approach to solving a certain type of problem. Exactly what the problem is, varies a great deal: some are system architecture challenges, others are interface design problems, yet others deal with program performance.

This part has the following chapters:

The Curiously Recurring Template Pattern

We are already familiar with the concepts of inheritance, polymorphism, and virtual functions. A derived class inherits from the base class and customizes the behavior of the base class by overriding its virtual functions. All operations are done on an instance of the base class, polymorphically. When the base object is actually an instance of the derived class, the right customized overrides are called. The base class knows nothing about the derived class, which may not even have been written when the base class code was written and compiled. The **Curiously Recurring Template Pattern** (CRTP) turns this well-ordered picture on its head, and inside out.

The following topics will be covered in this chapter:

- What is CRTP?

- What is static polymorphism and how does it differ from dynamic polymorphism?

- What are the downsides of virtual function calls, and why may it be preferable to resolve such calls at compile time?

- What are the other uses of CRTP?

Technical requirements

The Google Benchmark library: https://github.com/google/benchmark

Example code: https://github.com/PacktPublishing/Hands-On-Design-Patterns-with-CPP-Second-Edition/tree/master/Chapter08

Wrapping your head around CRTP

CRTP was first introduced, under this name, by James Coplien in 1995, in his article in *C++ Report*. It is a particular form of a more general bounded polymorphism (Peter S. Canning et al., *F-bounded polymorphism for object-oriented programming*, Conference on Functional Programming Languages and Computer Architecture, 1989). While not a general replacement for virtual functions, it provides the C++ programmer with a similar tool that, under the right circumstances, offers several advantages.

What is wrong with a virtual function?

Before we can talk about a *better* alternative to a virtual function, we should consider why we would want to have an alternative at all. What is not to like about virtual functions?

The problem is the performance overhead. A virtual function call can be several times more expensive than a non-virtual call, more for very simple functions that would have been inlined were they not virtual (recall that a virtual function can never be inlined). We can measure this difference with a microbenchmark, the ideal tool for measuring the performance of small fragments of code. There are many microbenchmark libraries and tools out there; in this book, we will use the Google Benchmark library. To follow along with the examples in this chapter, you must first download and install the library (the detailed instructions can be found in *Chapter 5, A Comprehensive Look at RAII*). Then, you can compile and run the examples.

Now that we have the microbenchmark library ready, we can measure the overhead of a virtual function call. We are going to compare a very simple virtual function, with the minimum amount of code, against a non-virtual function doing the same thing. Here is our virtual function:

```
// Example 01
class B {
  public:
  B() : i_(0) {}
  virtual ~B() {}
  virtual void f(int i) = 0;
  int get() const { return i_; }
  protected:
  int i_;
};
class D : public B {
  public:
  void f(int i) override { i_ += i; }
};
```

And, here is the equivalent non-virtual one:

```
// Example 01
class A {
```

```
  public:
  A() : i_(0) {}
  void f(int i) { i_ += i; }
  int get() const { return i_; }
  protected:
  int i_;
};
```

We can now call both of them in a micro-benchmark fixture and measure how long each call takes:

```
void BM_none(benchmark::State& state) {
  A* a = new A;
  int i = 0;
  for (auto _ : state) a->f(++i);
  benchmark::DoNotOptimize(a->get());
  delete a;
}
void BM_dynamic(benchmark::State& state) {
  B* b = new D;
  int i = 0;
  for (auto _ : state) b->f(++i);
  benchmark::DoNotOptimize(b->get());
  delete b;
}
```

The benchmark::DoNotOptimize wrapper prevents the compiler from optimizing away the unused object, and, along with it, removing the entire set of function calls as unnecessary. Note that there is a subtlety in measuring the virtual function call time; a simpler way to write the code would be to avoid the new and delete operators and simply construct the derived object on the stack:

```
void BM_dynamic(benchmark::State& state) {
  D d;
  int i = 0;
  for (auto _ : state) d.f(++i);
  benchmark::DoNotOptimize(b->get());
}
```

However, this benchmark is likely to yield the same time as the non-virtual function call. The reason is not that a virtual function call has no overhead. Rather, in this code, the compiler is able to deduce that the call to the virtual function, f(), is always a call to D::f() (it helps that the call is not done through the base class pointer, but rather the derived class reference, so it could hardly be anything else). A decent optimizing compiler will de-virtualize such a call, for instance, generating a direct call to D::f() without the indirection and the reference to the *v-table*. Such a call can even be inlined.

Another possible complication is that both microbenchmarks, especially the non-virtual call, may be too fast—the body of the benchmark loop is likely to take less time than the overhead of the loop. We can remedy that by making several calls inside the body of the loop. This can be accomplished with the copy-paste feature of your editor, or with the C++ preprocessor macros:

```
#define REPEAT2(x) x x
#define REPEAT4(x) REPEAT2(x) REPEAT2(x)
#define REPEAT8(x) REPEAT4(x) REPEAT4(x)
#define REPEAT16(x) REPEAT8(x) REPEAT8(x)
#define REPEAT32(x) REPEAT16(x) REPEAT16(x)
#define REPEAT(x) REPEAT32(x)
```

Now, inside the benchmark loop, we can write the following:

```
REPEAT(b->f(++i);)
```

The per-iteration time reported by the benchmark now refers to 32 function calls. While this does not matter for comparing the two calls, it may be convenient to make the benchmark itself report the true number of calls per second by adding this line to the end of the benchmark fixture, after the loop:

```
state.SetItemsProcessed(32*state.iterations());
```

We can now compare the results of the two benchmarks:

```
Benchmark            Time UserCounters...
BM_none           1.60 ns items_per_second=19.9878G/s
BM_dynamic        9.04 ns items_per_second=3.54089G/s
```

We see that the virtual function call is almost 10 times more expensive than the non-virtual one. Note that this is not exactly a fair comparison; the virtual call provides additional functionality. However, some of this functionality can be implemented in other ways, without paying the performance overhead.

Introducing CRTP

Now, we will introduce CRTP, which turns inheritance on its head:

```
template <typename D> class B {
    ...
};
class D : public B<D> {
    ...
};
```

The first change that jumps out is that the base class is now a `class` template. The derived class still inherits from the base class, but now from the specific instantiation of the base class template—on its own! Class B is instantiated on class D, and class D inherits from that instantiation of class B, which is instantiated on class D, which inherits from class B, which... that's recursion in action. Get used to it because you will see it often in this chapter.

What is the motivation for this mind-twisting pattern? Consider that now the base class has compile-time information about the derived class. Therefore, what used to be a virtual function call can now be bound to the right function at compile time:

```cpp
// Example 01
template <typename D> class B {
  public:
  B() : i_(0) {}
  void f(int i) { static_cast<D*>(this)->f(i); }
  int get() const { return i_; }
  protected:
  int i_;
};
class D : public B<D> {
  public:
  void f(int i) { i_ += i; }
};
```

The call itself can still be done on the base class pointer:

```cpp
B<D>* b = ...;
b->f(5);
```

There is no indirection and no overhead for the virtual call. The compiler can, at compile time, track the call all the way to the actual function called, and even inline it:

```cpp
void BM_static(benchmark::State& state) {
  B<D>* b = new D;
  int i = 0;
  for (auto _ : state) {
    REPEAT(b->f(++i);)
  }
  benchmark::DoNotOptimize(b->get());
  state.SetItemsProcessed(32*state.iterations());
}
```

The benchmark shows that the function call made through the CRTP takes exactly as much time as a regular function call:

```
Benchmark              Time UserCounters...
BM_none             1.60 ns items_per_second=19.9878G/s
BM_dynamic          9.04 ns items_per_second=3.54089G/s
BM_static           1.55 ns items_per_second=20.646G/s
```

The main restriction on the CRTP is that the size of the base class, B, cannot depend on its template parameter, D. More generally, the template for class B has to instantiate with type D being an incomplete type. For example, this will not compile:

```
template <typename D> class B {
  using T = typename D::T;
  T* p_;
};
class D : public B<D> {
  using T = int;
};
```

The realization that this code will not compile may come somewhat as a surprise, given how similar it is to many widely used templates that refer to the nested types of their template parameters. For example, consider this template, which converts any sequence container with push_back() and pop_back() functions to a stack:

```
template <typename C> class stack {
  C c_;
public:
  using value_type = typename C::value_type;
  void push(const valuetype& v) { c.push_back(v); }
  value_type pop() {
    value_type v = c.back();
    c.pop_back();
    return v;
  }
};
stack<std::vector<int>> s;
```

Note that the using type alias for value_type looks exactly the same as the preceding one, in our attempt to declare class B. So, what is wrong with the one in B? Actually, nothing is wrong with class B itself. It would compile just fine in a context similar to that of our stack class:

```
class A {
  public:
  using T = int;
```

```
   T x_;
};
B<A> b; // Compiles with no problems
```

The problem lies not with class B itself, but with our intended use of it:

```
class D : public B<D> ...
```

At the point where B<D> has to be known, type D has not been declared yet. It cannot be—the declaration of class D requires us to know exactly what the base class B<D> is. So, if class D has not been declared yet, how does the compiler know that the identified D even refers to a type? After all, you cannot instantiate a template on a completely unknown type. The answer lies somewhere in between—class D is forward-declared, the same as if we had this code:

```
class A;
B<A> b; // Now does not compile
```

Some templates can be instantiated on forward-declared types, while others cannot. The exact rules can be painstakingly gathered from the standard, but the gist is this—anything that might affect the size of the class has to be fully declared. A reference to a type declared inside an incomplete type, such as our using T = typename D::T, would be a forward declaration of a nested class, and those are not allowed either.

On the other hand, the body of a member function of a class template is not instantiated until it's called. In fact, for a given template parameter, a member function does not even have to compile, as long as it's not called. Therefore, references to the derived class, its nested types, and its member functions, inside the member functions of the base class are perfectly fine. Also, since the derived class type is considered forward-declared inside the base class, we can declare pointers and references to it. Here is a very common refactoring of the CRTP base class that consolidates the uses of the static cast in one place:

```
template <typename D> class B {
  ...
  void f(int i) { derived()->f(i); }
  D* derived() { return static_cast<D*>(this); }
};
class D : public B<D> {
  ...
  void f(int i) { i_ += i; }
};
```

The base class declaration owns a pointer to the incomplete (forward-declared) type D. It works like any other pointer to an incomplete type; by the time the pointer is de-referenced, the type has to be complete. In our case, this happens inside the body of the member function; B::f(), which, as we discussed, is not compiled until it's called by the client code.

So what do we do if we need to use a nested type of the derived class while writing the base class? Inside a function body, there is no problem. If we need to use the nested type in the base class itself, it is usually for one of two reasons. The first is to declare the return type of a member function:

```
// Example 01a
template <typename D> class B {
  typename D::value_type get() const {
    return static_cast<const D*>(this)->get();
  }
  …
};
D : public B<D> {
  using value_type = int;
  value_type get() const { … };
  …
};
```

As we have just discussed, this will not compile. Fortunately, this problem is easy to solve, all we have to do is let the compiler deduce the return type:

```
// Example 01a
template <typename D> class B {
  auto get() const {
    return static_cast<const D*>(this)->get();
  }
  …
};
```

The second case is more difficult: the nested type is needed to declare a data member or a parameter. In this case, there is only one option left: the type should be passed into the base class as an additional template parameter. Of course, it introduces some redundancy into the code, but it can't be helped:

```
// Example 01a
template <typename T, typename value_type> class B {
  value_type value_;
  …
};
class D : public B<D, int> {
  using value_type = int;
  value_type get() const { … }
  …
};
```

Now that we know what is CRTP and how to code it, let us see what design problems can be solved with it.

CRTP and static polymorphism

Since CRTP allows us to override base class functions with those of the derived class, it implements polymorphic behavior. The key difference is that polymorphism happens at compile time, not at runtime.

Compile-time polymorphism

As we have just seen, CRTP can be used to allow the derived class to customize the behavior of the base class:

```
template <typename D> class B {
  public:
  ...
  void f(int i) { static_cast<D*>(this)->f(i); }
  protected:
  int i_;
};
class D : public B<D> {
  public:
  void f(int i) { i_ += i; }
};
```

If the base class B::f() method is called, it dispatches the call to the derived class method for the real derived class, just like a virtual function does. Of course, in order to fully take advantage of this polymorphism, we have to be able to call the methods of the base class through the base class pointer. Without this ability, we are simply calling methods of the derived class whose type we already know:

```
D* d = ...; // Get an object of type D
d->f(5);
B<D>* b = ...; // Also has to be an object of type D
b->f(5);
```

Note that the function call looks exactly like any virtual function class, with the base class pointer. The actual function, f(), that is called comes from the derived class, D::f(). There is, however, a significant difference—the actual type of the derived class, D, has to be known at compile time—the base class pointer is not B* but rather B<D>*, which implies that the derived object is of type D. There does not seem to be much point to such *polymorphism* if the programmer has to know the actual type. But, that is because we have not fully thought through what *compile-time polymorphism* really means. Just as the benefit of a virtual function is that we can call member functions of a type we don't even know exists, the same has to be true for *static polymorphism* to be useful.

How do we write a function that has to compile for parameters of an unknown type? With a function template, of course:

```
// Example 01
template <typename D> void apply(B<D>* b, int& i) {
    b->f(++i);
}
```

This is a template function that can be called on any base class pointer, and it automatically deduces the type of the derived class, D. Now, we can write what looks like regular polymorphic code:

```
B<D>* b = new D;      // 1
apply(b);             // 2
```

Note that, on line one, the object has to be constructed with the knowledge of the actual type. This is always the case; the same is true for regular runtime polymorphism with virtual functions:

```
void apply(B* b) { ... }
B* b = new D;         // 1
apply(b);             // 2
```

In both cases, on line two, we invoke some code that was written only with the knowledge of the base class. The difference is that, with run-time polymorphism, we have a common base class and some functions that operate on it. With CRTP and static polymorphism, there is a common base class template but no single common base class (a template is not a type) and every function that operates on this base template becomes a template itself. To make the symmetry (not equivalence!) between the two types of polymorphism complete, we just need to figure out two more special cases: pure virtual functions and polymorphic destruction. Let's start with the former.

The compile-time pure virtual function

What would be the equivalent of the pure virtual function in the CRTP scenario? A pure virtual function must be implemented in all derived classes. A class that declares a pure virtual function, or inherits one and does not override it, is an abstract class; it can be further derived from, but it cannot be instantiated.

When we contemplate the equivalent of a pure virtual function for static polymorphism, we realize that our CRTP implementation suffers from a major vulnerability. What happens if we forget to override the *compile-time virtual function,* f(), in one of the derived classes?

```
// Example 02
template <typename D> class B {
  public:
    ...
    void f(int i) { static_cast<D*>(this)->f(i); }
```

```
};
class D : public B<D> {
  // no f() here!
};
...
B<D>* b = ...;
b->f(5); // 1
```

This code compiles with no errors or warnings—on line one, we call B::f(), which, in turn, calls D::f(). Class D does not declare its own version of the member f(), so the one inherited from the base class is the one that is called. That is, of course, the member function, B::f(), that we have already seen, which again calls D::f(), which is really B::f() ... and we have an infinite loop.

The problem here is that nothing requires us to override the member function f() in the derived class, but the program is malformed if we don't. The root of the problem is that we are mixing together the interface and the implementation—the public member function declaration in the base class says that all derived classes must have a function, void f(int), as a part of their public interface. The derived class's version of the same function provides the actual implementation. We will cover separating the interface and the implementation in *Chapter 14, The Template Method Pattern and the Non-Virtual Idiom*, but for now, suffice it to say that our life would be a lot easier if these functions had different names:

```
// Example 03
template <typename D> class B {
  public:
    ...
    void f(int i) { static_cast<D*>(this)->f_impl(i); }
};
class D : public B<D> {
  void f_impl(int i) { i_ += i; }
};
...
B<D>* b = ...;
b->f(5);
```

What happens now if we forget to implement D::f_impl()? The code does not compile, because there is no such member function in class D, either directly or through inheritance. So, we have implemented a compile-time pure virtual function! Note that the virtual function is actually f_impl(), not f().

With that accomplished, how would we implement a regular virtual function, with a default implementation that can be optionally overridden? If we follow the same pattern of separating the interface and the implementation, we only have to provide the default implementation for B::f_impl():

```
// Example 03
template <typename D> class B {
```

```
  public:
  ...
  void f(int i) { static_cast<D*>(this)->f_impl(i); }
  void f_impl(int i) {}
};
class D1 : public B<D1> {
  void f_impl(int i) { i_ += i; }
};
class D2 : public B<D2> {
  // No f() here
};
...
B<D1>* b = ...;
b->f(5); // Calls D1::f_impl()
B<D2>* b1 = ...;
b1->f(5); // Calls B::f_impl() by default
```

The last special case we need to cover is polymorphic destruction.

Destructors and polymorphic deletion

So far, we have willfully avoided tackling the issue of deleting objects implemented with CRTP in some sort of polymorphic fashion. In fact, if you go back and reread the examples that presented complete code, such as the benchmark fixture, BM_static, in the *Introducing CRTP* section, we either avoided deleting the object altogether or constructed a derived object on the stack. This is because polymorphic deletion presents an additional complication that we are finally ready to deal with.

First of all, let's note that, in many cases, polymorphic deletion is not a concern. All objects are created with their actual types known. If the code that constructs the objects also owns and eventually deletes them, the question *what is the type of the deleted object?* is never really asked. Similarly, if the objects are stored in a container, they are not deleted through the base class pointer or reference:

```
template <typename D> void apply(B<D>& b) {
  ... operate on b ...
}
{
  std::vector<D> v;
  v.push_back(D(...)); // Objects created as D
  ...
  apply(v[0]); // Objects processed as B&
} // Objects deleted as D
```

In many cases, as shown in the preceding example, the objects are constructed and deleted with their actual type known and no polymorphism involved, but the code that works on them in between is universal, written to work on the base type and, therefore, any class derived from that base type.

But, what if we need to actually delete the object through the base class pointer? Well, that is not easy. First of all, a simple call to the delete operator will do the wrong thing:

```
B<D>* b = new D;
...
delete b;
```

This code compiles. Worse, even the compilers that normally warn when a class has a virtual function but a non-virtual destructor do not generate any warnings in this case, because there are no virtual functions, and CRTP polymorphism is not recognized by the compiler as a potential source of trouble. However, the trouble there is that only the destructor of the base class, B<D>, itself is called; the destructor of D is never called!

You may be tempted to resolve this problem the same way as we deal with other *compile-time virtual* functions, by casting to the known derived type and calling the indented member function of the derived class:

```
template <typename D> class B {
  public:
    ~B() { static_cast<D*>(this)->~D(); }
};
```

Unlike the regular functions, this attempt at polymorphism is badly broken, for not one but two reasons—first of all, in the destructor of the base class, the actual object is not of the derived type anymore, and calling any member functions of the derived class on it results in undefined behavior. Secondly, even if this somehow worked, the destructor of the derived class is going to do its work and then call the destructor of the base class, which results in an infinite loop.

There are two solutions to this problem. One option is to extend the compile-time polymorphism to the act of deletion in the same way as we do for any other operation, with a function template:

```
template <typename D> void destroy(B<D>* b) {
  delete static_cast<D*>(b);
}
```

This is well-defined. The delete operator is called on the pointer of the actual type, D, and the right destructor is called. However, you must take care to always delete these objects using this destroy() function, instead of calling the delete operator.

The second option is to actually make the destructor virtual. This does bring back the overhead of the virtual function call, but only for the destructor. It also increases the object size by the size of the virtual pointer. If neither of these two sources of overhead is a concern, you could use this hybrid static-dynamic polymorphism, where all virtual function calls are bound at compile time and with no overhead, except the destructor.

CRTP and access control

When implementing CRTP classes, you do have to worry about access—any method you want to call has to be accessible. Either the method has to be public, or the caller has to have special access. This is a little different from the way virtual functions are called—when calling a virtual function, the caller must have access to the member function that is named in the call. For example, a call to the base class function, B::f(), requires that either B::f() is public or the caller has access to non-public member functions (another member function of class B can call B::f() even if it's private). Then, if B::f() is virtual and overridden by the derived class D, the override D::f() is actually called at **runtime**. There is no requirement that D::f() be accessible from the original call site; for example, D::f() can be private.

The situation with CRTP polymorphic calls is somewhat different. All calls are explicit in the code, and the callers must have access to the functions they call. Usually, it means that the base class must have access to the member functions of the derived class. Consider the following example from an earlier section, but now with explicit access control:

```
template <typename D> class B {
  public:
  ...
    void f(int i) { static_cast<D*>(this)->f_impl(i); }
  private:
    void f_impl(int i) {}
};
class D : public B<D> {
  private:
    void f_impl(int i) { i_ += i; }
    friend class B<D>;
};
```

Here, both functions, B::f_impl() and D::f_impl(), are private in their respective classes. The base class has no special access to the derived class, and cannot call its private member functions. Unless we want to change the member function, D::f_impl(), from private to public and allow any caller access to it, we have to declare the base class to be a friend of the derived class.

There is also some benefit in doing the reverse. Let's create a new derived class, D1, with a different override of the implementation function, f_impl():

```
class D1 : public B<D> {
  private:
    void f_impl(int i) { i_ -= i; }
```

```
   friend class B<D1>;
};
```

This class has a subtle error—it is not actually derived from B<D1> but from the old class, B<D>; a mistake that is easy to make when creating a new class from an old template. This mistake will be found if we attempt to use the class polymorphically:

```
B<D1>* b = new D1;
```

This does not compile because B<D1> is not a base class of D1. However, not all uses of CRTP involve a polymorphic call. In any case, it would be better if the error was caught when class D1 was first declared. We can accomplish that by making class B into a sort of abstract class, only in the sense of static polymorphism. All it takes is to make the constructor of class B private and to declare the derived class to be a friend:

```
template <typename D> class B {
  int i_;
  B() : i_(0) {}
  friend D;
  public:
  void f(int i) { static_cast<D*>(this)->f_impl(i); }
  private:
  void f_impl(int i) {}
};
```

Note the somewhat unusual form of the friend declaration—friend D and not friend class D. This is how you write a friend declaration for the template parameter. Now, the only type that can construct an instance of class B<D> is that specific derived class, D, which is used as the template parameter, and the erroneous code, class D1 : public B<D>, does not compile any longer.

Now that we know how CRTP works, let us see what it is useful for.

CRTP as a delegation pattern

So far, we have used CRTP as a compile-time equivalent of dynamic polymorphism, including virtual-like calls through the base pointer (compile-time, of course, with a template function). This is not the only way CRTP can be used. In fact, more often than not, the function is called directly on the derived class. This is a very fundamental difference—typically, public inheritance expresses the *is-a* relationship—the derived object is a kind of a base object. The interface and the generic code are in the base class, while the derived class overrides the specific implementation. This relation continues to hold when a CRTP object is accessed through the base class pointer or reference. Such use of CRTP is sometimes also called a **static interface**.

When the derived object is used directly, the situation is quite different—the base class is no longer the interface, and the derived class is not just the implementation. The derived class expands the interface of the base class, and the base class delegates some of its behavior to the derived class.

Expanding the interface

Let's consider several examples where CRTP is used to delegate behavior from the base class to the derived one.

The first example is a very simple one—for any class that provides `operator+=()`, we want to generate `operator+()` automatically that used the former:

```
// Example 04
template <typename D> struct plus_base {
  D operator+(const D& rhs) const {
    D tmp = rhs;
    tmp += static_cast<const D&>(*this);
    return tmp;
  }
};
class D : public plus_base<D> {
  int i_;
  public:
  explicit D(int i) : i_(i) {}
  D& operator+=(const D& rhs) {
    i_ += rhs.i_;
    return *this;
  }
};
```

Any class that inherits from `plus_base` in this manner automatically acquires the addition operator that is guaranteed to match the provided increment operator. The observant among you might point out that the way we have declared the operator + here is, well, strange. Aren't two-argument operators supposed to be non-member functions? Indeed, they usually are. Nothing in the standard requires them to be, and the preceding code is technically valid. The reason binary operators such as ==, +, and so on are usually declared as non-member functions has to do with implicit conversions—if we have an addition, x + y, and the intended `operator+` is a member function, it has to be a member function of the x object. Not any object implicitly convertible to the type of x, but x itself—it's a member function call on x. In contrast, the y object has to be implicitly convertible to the type of the argument of that member `operator+` usually, the same type as x. To restore the symmetry and allow implicit conversions (if any are provided) on both the left- and right-hand side of the + sign, we have to declare `operator+` as a non-member function. Usually, such a function needs to have access to the private data members of the class, as in the example previously, so it has to be declared a friend. Putting all of this together, we arrive at this alternative implementation:

```
// Example 05
template <typename D> struct plus_base {
  friend D operator+(const D& lhs, const D& rhs) {
    D tmp = lhs;
    tmp += rhs;
    return tmp;
  }
};
class D : public plus_base<D> {
  int i_;
  public:
  explicit D(int i) : i_(i) {}
  D& operator+=(const D& rhs) {
    i_ += rhs.i_;
    return *this;
  }
};
```

There is a significant difference between this use of CRTP and the one we saw earlier—the object that is going to be used in the program is of type C, and it will never be accessed through a pointer to plus_base<C>. The latter isn't a complete interface for anything but is really an implementation that makes use of the interface provided by the derived class. CRTP here is used as an implementation technique, not as a design pattern. However, the boundary between the two is not always clear: some implementation techniques are so powerful that they can alter design choices.

One example is the generated comparison and ordering operations. In C++20, the recommended choice for designing interfaces of value types (or any other comparable and ordered types) is to provide only two operators, operator==() and operator<=>(). The compiler will generate the rest. If you like this approach to interface design and want to use it in earlier versions of C++, you need a way to implement it. CRTP offers us a possible implementation. We will need a base class that will generate operator!=() from the operator==() of the derived class. It will also generate all ordering operators; of course, we cannot use operator<=>() before C++20, but we can use any member function name we agree on, such as cmp():

```
template <typename D> struct compare_base {
  friend bool operator!=(const D& lhs, const D& rhs) {
    return !(lhs == rhs); }
  friend bool operator<=(const D& lhs, const D& rhs) {
    return lhs.cmp(rhs) <= 0;
  }
  friend bool operator>=(const D& lhs, const D& rhs) {
```

```
      return lhs.cmp(rhs) >= 0;
  }
  friend bool operator< (const D& lhs, const D& rhs) {
    return lhs.cmp(rhs) <  0;
  }
  friend bool operator> (const D& lhs, const D& rhs) {
    return lhs.cmp(rhs) >  0;
  }
};
class D : public compare_base<D> {
  int i_;
  public:
  explicit D(int i) : i_(i) {}
  auto cmp(const D& rhs) const {
    return (i_ < rhs.i_) ? -1 : ((i_ > rhs.i_) ? 1 : 0);
  }
  bool operator==(const D& rhs) const {
    return i_ == rhs.i_;
  }
};
```

There are many such examples to be found in the literature on CRTP. Along with these examples, you can find discussions on whether C++20 concepts offer a better alternative. The next section explains what this is about.

CRTP and concepts

At the first glance, it is unclear how concepts could replace CRTP. Concepts (which you can read more about in *Chapter 7, SFINAE, Concepts, and Overload Resolution Management*) are all about restricting interfaces, while CRTP extends the interfaces.

There are discussions inspired by cases where both concepts and CRTP can solve the same problem by totally different means. Recall our use of CRTP to automatically generate operator+() from operator+=(); all we had to do was to inherit from the special base class template:

```
// Example 05
template <typename D> struct plus_base {
  friend D operator+(const D& lhs, const D& rhs) { … }
};
class D : public plus_base<D> {
  D& operator+=(const D& rhs) { … }
};
```

Our base class serves two purposes. First, it generates `operator+()` from `operator+=()`. Second, it provides a mechanism for classes to opt into this automation: to receive the generated `operator+()`, a class must inherit from `plus_base`.

The first problem by itself is easy to solve, we can just define a global `operator+()` template:

```
template <typename T>
T operator+(const T& lhs, const T& rhs) {
  T tmp = lhs;
  tmp += rhs;
  return tmp;
}
```

There is a "slight" problem with this template: we just provided a global `operator+()` for every type in our program, whether it needs one or not. Furthermore, most of the time it won't even compile since not all classes define `operator+=()`.

This is where the concepts come in: we can restrict the applicability of our new `operator+()` so, in the end, it is generated for the same types that we would have otherwise inherited from `plus_base` and no other.

One way to do this is to require that the template parameter type T at least have the increment operator:

```
template <typename T>
requires( requires(T a, T b) { a += b; } )
T operator+(const T& lhs, const T& rhs) { … }
```

However, this is not the same result as what we got with CRTP. In some cases, it may be a better result: instead of having to opt every class into the automatic generation of `operator+()`, we did it for every class that satisfies certain restrictions. But in other cases, any reasonable description of these restrictions produces overly broad results, and we have to opt into our types one by one. This is easy to do with concepts as well, but the technique used is not widely known. All you need to do is to define a concept whose general case is false (a Boolean variable will suffice):

```
template <typename T>
constexpr inline bool gen_plus = false; // General
template <typename T>
requires gen_plus<T>
T operator+(const T& lhs, const T& rhs) { … }
```

Then, for every type that needs to opt in, we specialize the concept:

```
class D { // No special base
  D& operator+=(const D& rhs) { … }
};
template <>
constexpr inline bool generate_plus<D> = true; // Opt-in
```

There are some advantages to both approaches: CRTP uses a base class that can be more complex than just a wrapper for a definition of an operator; while concepts can combine explicit opt-in with some more general restrictions when appropriate. However, these discussions miss a much more important distinction: CRTP can be used to expand class interface with both member and non-member functions, while concepts can be used only with non-member functions, including non-member operators. When both concepts and CRTP-based solutions are applicable, you should choose the most appropriate one (for simple functions such as `operator+()`, concepts are probably easier to read). Also, you don't have to wait until C++20 to use the concept-based restrictions: the methods of emulating concepts shown in *Chapter 7, SFINAE, Concepts, and Overload Resolution Management*, are more than adequate here.

Of course, we can use concepts with CRTP instead of trying to replace CRTP: if the CRTP base class template has some requirements on the type we want to derive from it, we can enforce these with concepts. The use of concepts here is no different from what we find in the chapter dedicated to them. But we are going to stay with CRTP and what else can be done with it.

CRTP as an implementation technique

As we pointed out earlier, CRTP is often used as a purely implementation pattern; however, even in this role, it can influence design: some design choices are desirable but hard to implement, and, if a good implementation technique comes along, the design choices often change. So, let us see what problems can be solved with CRTP.

CRTP for code reuse

Let us start with a specific implementation issue: we have multiple classes that have some common code. Ordinarily, we would write a base class for them. But the common code is not really common: it does the same thing for all classes except it for the types it uses. What we need is not a common base class but a common base class template. And that brings us to CRTP.

An example is an object registry. It may be desirable, often for debugging purposes, to know how many objects of a certain type are currently in existence, and perhaps even to maintain a list of such objects. We definitely do not want to instrument every class with the registry mechanism, so we want to move it to the base class. But, now we have a problem—if we have two derived classes, C and D, both inherit from the same base class, B, and the count of instances of B will be the total for both C and D. The problem is not that the base class can't determine what the real type of the derived class is—it can, if we're willing to pay the cost of runtime polymorphism. The problem is that the base class has only one counter (or however many are coded in the class), while the number of different derived classes is unlimited. We could implement a very complex, expensive, and non-portable solution that uses **Run-Time Type Information (RTTI)**, such as `typeid`, to determine the class name and maintain a map of names and counters. But, what we really need is one counter per derived type, and the only way to do it is to make the base class aware of the derived class type at compile time. This brings us back to CRTP:

```cpp
// Example 08
template <typename D> class registry {
  public:
  static size_t count;
  static D* head;
  D* prev;
  D* next;
  protected:
  registry() {
    ++count;
    prev = nullptr;
    next = head;
    head = static_cast<D*>(this);
    if (next) next->prev = head;
  }
  registry(const registry&) {
    ++count;
    prev = nullptr;
    next = head;
    head = static_cast<D*>(this);
    if (next) next->prev = head;
  }
  ~registry() {
    --count;
    if (prev) prev->next = next;
    if (next) next->prev = prev;
    if (head == this) head = next;
  }
};
template <typename D> size_t registry<D>::count(0);
template <typename D> D* registry<D>::head(nullptr);
```

We have declared the constructor and the destructor protected because we don't want any registry objects created, except by the derived classes. It is also important to not forget the copy constructor, otherwise, the default one is generated by the compiler, and it does not increment the counter or update the list (but the destructor does, so the counter will go negative and overflow). For each derived class, D, the base class is `registry<D>`, which is a separate type with its own static data members, `count` and `head` (the latter is the head of the list of currently active objects). Any type that needs to maintain the runtime registry of active objects now only needs to inherit from `registry`:

```
// Example 08
class C : public registry<C> {
  int i_;
  public:
  C(int i) : i_(i) {}
};
```

A similar example, where the base class needs to know the type of the derived class and use it to declare its own members, can be found in *Chapter 9, Named Arguments, Method Chaining, and Builder Pattern*. Next, we will see another example of CRTP, and this time the availability of the implementation opens the door to a particular design choice.

CRTP for generic interfaces

Another scenario where it is often necessary to delegate behavior to derived classes is the problem of visitation. Visitors, in a general sense, are objects that are invoked to process a collection of data objects and execute a function on each one in turn. Often, there are hierarchies of visitors, where the derived classes customize or alter some aspect of the behavior of the base classes. While the most common implementation of visitors uses dynamic polymorphism and virtual function calls, a static visitor offers the same sort of performance benefits we saw earlier. Visitors are not usually invoked polymorphically; you create the visitor you want and run it. The base visitor class, however, does call the member functions that may be dispatched, at compile time, to the derived classes if they have the right overrides. Consider this generic visitor for a collection of animals:

```
// Example 09
struct Animal {
  public:
  enum Type { CAT, DOG, RAT };
  Animal(Type t, const char* n) : type(t), name(n) {}
  const Type type;
  const char* const name;
};
template <typename D> class GenericVisitor {
  public:
  template <typename it> void visit(it from, it to) {
    for (it i = from; i != to; ++i) {
      this->visit(*i);
    }
  }
}
```

```
  private:
  D& derived() { return *static_cast<D*>(this); }
  void visit(const Animal& animal) {
    switch (animal.type) {
      case Animal::CAT:
        derived().visit_cat(animal); break;
      case Animal::DOG:
        derived().visit_dog(animal); break;
      case Animal::RAT:
        derived().visit_rat(animal); break;
    }
  }
  void visit_cat(const Animal& animal) {
    cout << "Feed the cat " << animal.name << endl;
  }
  void visit_dog(const Animal& animal) {
    cout << "Wash the dog " << animal.name << endl;
  }
  void visit_rat(const Animal& animal) {
  cout << "Eeek!" << endl;
}
  friend D;
  GenericVisitor() = default;
};
```

Note that the main visitation method is a template member function (a template within a template!), and it accepts any kind of iterator that can iterate over a sequence of `Animal` objects. Also, by declaring a private default constructor at the bottom of the class, we are protecting ourselves from making a mistake where the derived class incorrectly specifies its own type for the inheritance. Now, we can start creating some visitors. The default visitor simply accepts the default actions provided by the generic visitor:

```
class DefaultVisitor :
  public GenericVisitor<DefaultVisitor> {
};
```

We can visit any sequence of `Animal` objects, for example, a vector:

```
std::vector<Animal> animals {
  {Animal::CAT, "Fluffy"},
  {Animal::DOG, "Fido"},
  {Animal::RAT, "Stinky"}};
DefaultVisitor().visit(animals.begin(), animals.end());
```

The visitation yields the expected result:

```
Feed the cat Fluffy
Wash the dog Fido
Eeek!
```

But, we don't have to constrain ourselves to the default actions—we can override the visitation actions for one or more animal types:

```cpp
class TrainerVisitor :
  public GenericVisitor<TrainerVisitor> {
  friend class GenericVisitor<TrainerVisitor>;
  void visit_dog(const Animal& animal) {
    cout << "Train the dog " << animal.name << endl;
  }
};
class FelineVisitor :
  public GenericVisitor<FelineVisitor> {
  friend class GenericVisitor<FelineVisitor>;
  void visit_cat(const Animal& animal) {
    cout << "Hiss at the cat " << animal.name << endl;
  }
  void visit_dog(const Animal& animal) {
    cout << "Growl at the dog " << animal.name << endl;
  }
  void visit_rat(const Animal& animal) {
    cout << "Eat the rat " << animal.name << endl;
  }
};
```

When a dog trainer chooses to visit our animals, we use `TrainerVisitor`:

```
Feed the cat Fluffy
Train the dog Fido
Eeek!
```

Finally, a visiting cat would have a set of actions all of its own:

```
Hiss at the cat Fluffy
Growl at the dog Fido
Eat the rat Stinky
```

We will learn a lot more about different kinds of visitors later, in *Chapter 17, The Visitor Pattern and Multiple Dispatch*. Now, however, we are going to explore the use of CRTP in conjunction with another common pattern.

CRTP and policy-based design

Policy-based design is a compile-time variant of the well-known Strategy pattern; we have an entire chapter dedicated to it, *Chapter 15*, aptly named *Policy-Based Design*. Here, we're going to stay focused on the use of CRTP to provide additional functionality to the derived classes. Specifically, we are going to generalize the use of CRTP base classes to extend the interface of the derived class.

So far, we have used one base class to add features to the derived class:

```
template <typename D> struct plus_base {…};
class D : public plus_base<D> {…};
```

However, if we want to extend the interface of the derived class in multiple ways, a single base class presents an unnecessary restriction. First of all, if we add several member functions, the base class can get quite large. Second, we may want a more modular approach to the interface design. For example, we can have one base class template that adds factory construction methods to any derived class:

```
// Example 10
template <typename D> struct Factory {
  template <typename... Args>
  static D* create(Args&&... args) {
    return new D(std::forward<Args>(args)...);
  }
  static void destroy(D* d) { delete d; }
};
```

We can even have several different factories that present the same interface but allocate memory differently. We can have another base class template that adds the conversion to string to any class that has the stream inserter operator:

```
// Example 10
template <typename D> struct Stringify {
  operator std::string() const {
    std::stringstream S;
    S << *static_cast<const D*>(this);
    return S.str();
  }
};
```

It makes no sense to combine the two into a single base. In a large system, there can be many more of these classes, each adds a specific feature to the derived class and uses CRTP to implement it. But not every derived class needs every one of these features. With multiple base classes to choose from, it is easy to construct a derived class that has a specific set of features:

```
// Example 10
class C1 : public Stringify<C1>, public Factory<C1> {…};
```

This works, but we are in danger of repeating nearly identical code if we need to implement several derived classes that have very similar behavior, except for the features provided by the CRTP bases. For example, if we have another factory that constructs objects in thread-local memory to speed up the performance of concurrent programs (let's call it TLFactory), we might have to write this:

```
class C2 : public Stringify<C2>, public TLFactory<C2> {…};
```

But the two classes C1 and C2 are exactly the same except for the base classes, and yet, as written we would have to implement and maintain two copies of identical code. It would be better if we could write a single class template and plug different base classes into it as needed. This is the main idea of policy-based design; there are different approaches to it and you can learn about them in *Chapter 15, Policy-Based Design*. For now, let us focus on using CRTP base classes in a template. Since we now need a class template that accepts multiple base class types, we will need to use a variadic template. We need something like this:

```
template <typename… Policies>
class C : public Policies… {};
```

There are versions of the policy-based design that use this exact template; but in our case, it won't compile if we try to use Factory or Stringify as policies. The reason is that they are not types (classes) and, therefore, cannot be used as a type name. They are templates, so we have to declare the template parameters of the template C as templates themselves (this is known as a template template parameter). The syntax is easier to understand if we first recall how to declare a single template template parameter:

```
template <template <typename> class B> class C;
```

If we wanted to inherit from a specific instantiation of this class template B, we would write

```
template <template <typename> class B>
class C : public B<template argument> {…};
```

When using CRTP, the template argument is the type of the derived class itself, C<B>:

```
template <template <typename> class B>
class C : public B<C<B>> {…};
```

Generalizing this to a parameter pack is straightforward:

```
// Example 11
template <template <typename> class... Policies>
class C : public Policies<C<Policies...>>... {…};
```

The template parameter is a pack (any number of templates instead of a single class). The derived class inherits from the entire pack `Policies...`, except `Policies` are templates and we need to specify the actual instantiations of these templates. Each template in the pack is instantiated on the derived class, whose type is `C<Policies...>`.

If we need additional template parameters, for example, to enable using different value types in the class C, we can combine them with policies:

```
// Example 11
template <typename T,
          template <typename> class... Policies>
class C : public Policies<C<T, Policies...>>... {
  T t_;
  public:
  explicit C(T t) : t_(t) {}
  const T& get() const { return t_; }
  friend std::ostream&
  operator<<(std::ostream& out, const C c) {
    out << c.t_;
    return out;
  }
};
```

To use this class with a particular set of policies, it is convenient to define some aliases:

```
using X = C<int, Factory, Stringify>;
```

If we want to use several classes with the same Policies, we can define a template alias as well:

```
template <typename T> using Y = C<T, Factory, Stringify>;
```

We will learn more about policies in the *Chapter 15, Policy-Based Design*. We will encounter the technique we just studied, CRPT, there and in other chapters of this book – it is a flexible and powerful tool.

Summary

We have examined a rather convoluted design pattern that combines both sides of C++—generic programming (templates) and object-oriented programming (inheritance). True to its name, the Curiously Recurring Template Pattern creates a circular loop, where the derived class inherits the interface and the implementation from the base class, while the base class has access to the interface of the derived class through the template parameters. CRTP has two main use modes—true static polymorphism, or *static interface*, where the object is primarily accessed as the base type, and expanding the interface, or delegation, where the derived class is accessed directly but the implementation uses CRTP to provide common functionality. The latter can vary from a simple addition of one or two methods to a complex task of composing the interfaces of derived classes from multiple building blocks or policies.

The next chapter introduces an idiom that makes use of the pattern we have just learned. This idiom also changes the standard way we pass arguments to functions, in order of the parameters, and lets us have order-independent named arguments instead. Read on to find out how!

Questions

1. How expensive is a virtual function call, and why?
2. Why does a similar function call, resolved at compile time, have no such performance overhead?
3. How would you make compile-time polymorphic function calls?
4. How would you use CRTP to expand the interface of the base class?
5. What is necessary to use multiple CRTP base classes in a single derived class?.

9

Named Arguments, Method Chaining, and the Builder Pattern

In this chapter, we are going to examine a solution to a very common C++ problem: too many arguments. No, we are not talking about the arguments between C++ programmers, such as whether to put curly braces at the end of the line or the start of the next one (we have no solution to that problem). This is the problem of C++ functions with too many arguments. If you have maintained a large C++ system long enough, you have seen it—functions start with simple declarations and, over time, grow additional arguments, often defaulted, to support new features.

The following topics will be covered in this chapter:

- What are the problems with long function declarations?
- What is the alternative?
- What are the downsides of using the named arguments idiom?
- How can the named arguments idiom be generalized?

Technical requirements

Here is the example code: https://github.com/PacktPublishing/Hands-On-Design-Patterns-with-CPP-Second-Edition/tree/master/Chapter09.

Here is the Google Benchmark library: https://github.com/google/benchmark (see *Chapter 4, Swap – From Simple to Subtle*, for installation instructions).

The problem with arguments

Everyone who has worked on a sufficiently large C++ system at some point have had to add arguments to a function. To avoid breaking the existing code, the new argument is often given a default value which usually retains the old functionality. That works great the first time, is OK the second time, and then one has to start counting arguments on every function call. There are other problems with long function declarations as well, and if we want a better solution, it is worth our time to understand what they are before trying to solve them. We begin this section with a more in-depth analysis of the problem before moving on to the solution.

What's wrong with many arguments?

Whether the code that passes around a lot of arguments was written this way from the start or has grown *organically*, it is fragile and vulnerable to programmer mistakes. The main problem is that there are, usually, many arguments of the same type, and they can be miscounted. Consider designing a civilization-building game—when a player creates a new city, a corresponding object is constructed. The player gets to choose what facilities to build in the city, and the game sets the options for available resources:

```cpp
class City {
  public:
    enum center_t { KEEP, PALACE, CITADEL };
    City(size_t number_of_buildings,
         size_t number_of_towers,
         size_t guard_strength,
         center_t center,
         bool with_forge,
         bool with_granary,
         bool has_fresh_water,
         bool is_coastal,
         bool has_forest);
    ...
};
```

It looks like we have taken care of everything. To start the game, let's give each player a city with a keep, a guard tower, two buildings, and a guard company:

```cpp
City Capital(2, 1, 1, City::KEEP,
             false, false, false, false);
```

Can you see the mistake? The compiler, fortunately, can—not enough arguments. Since the compiler won't let us make a mistake here, this is no big deal, we just need to add the argument for has_forest. Also, let's say the game placed the city near a river, so it has water now:

```
City Capital(2, 1, 1, City::KEEP,
             false, true, false, false, false);
```

That was easy ... Oops! We now have the city on the river but without fresh water (just what is in that river?). At least the townsfolk won't starve, thanks to the free granary they accidentally received. That error—where the true value was passed to the wrong parameter—will have to be found during debugging. Also, this code is quite verbose, and we may find ourselves typing the same values over and over. Maybe the game tries to place cities near the rivers and forests by default? OK then:

```
class City {
  public:
  enum center_t { KEEP, PALACE, CITADEL };
  City(size_t number_of_buildings,
       size_t number_of_towers,
       size_t guard_strength,
       enter_t center,
       bool with_forge,
       bool with_granary,
       bool has_fresh_water = true,
       bool is_coastal = false,
       bool has_forest = true);
    ...
};
```

Now, let's go back to our first attempt to create a city—it now compiles, one argument short, and we are none the wiser that we miscounted the arguments. The game is a great success, and, in the next update, we get an exciting new building—a temple! We need to add a new argument to the constructor, of course. It makes sense to add it after with_granary, with all the other buildings, and before the terrain features. But then we have to edit every call to the City constructor. What is worse, it is very easy to make a mistake since the false for *no temple* looks, to both the programmer and the compiler, exactly like the false for *no fresh water*. The new argument has to be inserted in the right place, in a long line of very similarly-looking values.

Of course, the existing game code works without temples, so they are only needed in the new updated code. There is some value in not disturbing existing code unless necessary. We could do that if we added the new argument at the end and gave it the default value, so any constructor call that was not changed still creates the exact same city as before:

```
class City {
  public:
```

```
      enum center_t { KEEP, PALACE, CITADEL };
    City(size_t number_of_buildings,
         size_t number_of_towers,
         size_t guard_strength,
         center_t center,
         bool with_forge,
         bool with_granary,
         bool has_fresh_water = true,
         bool is_coastal = false,
         bool has_forest = true,
         bool with_temple = false);
    ...
};
```

But now, we let short-term convenience dictate our long-term interface design. The parameters no longer have even a logical grouping, and in the long run, mistakes are even more likely. Also, we did not fully solve the problem of not updating the code that does not need to change—the next release adds a new terrain, desert, and with it, another argument:

```
class City {
  public:
  enum center_t { KEEP, PALACE, CITADEL };
  City(size_t number_of_buildings,
       size_t number_of_towers,
       size_t guard_strength,
       center_t center,
       bool with_forge,
       bool with_granary,
       bool is_coastal = false,
       bool has_forest = true,
       bool with_temple = false,
       bool is_desert = false);
  ...
};
```

Once started, we have to give default values to all new arguments added at the end. Also, in order to create a city in the desert, we also have to specify whether it has a temple. There is no logical reason why it has to be this way, but we are bound by the process in which the interface evolved. The situation gets even worse when you consider that many types we used are convertible to each other:

```
City Capital(2, 1, false, City::KEEP,
             false, true, false, false, false);
```

This creates a city with zero guard companies and not whatever the programmer expected to disable when they set the third argument to `false`. Even `enum` types do not offer full protection. You probably noticed that all new cities usually start as a keep, so it would make sense to have that as the default as well:

```
// Example 01
class City {
  public:
  enum center_t { KEEP, PALACE, CITADEL };
  City(size_t number_of_buildings,
       size_t number_of_towers,
       size_t guard_strength,
       center_t center = KEEP,
       bool with_forge = false,
       bool with_granary = false,
       bool has_fresh_water = true,
       bool is_coastal = false,
       bool has_forest = true,
       bool with_temple = false,
       bool is_desert = false);
  ...
};
```

Now, we don't have to type as many arguments and might even avoid some mistakes (if you don't write arguments, you can't write them in the wrong order). But, we can make new ones:

```
City Capital(2, 1, City::CITADEL);
```

The two guard companies we just hired (because the numerical value of CITADEL is 2) will find themselves quite short on space in the lowly keep (which we intended to change but did not). The `enum class` of C++11 offers better protection since each one is a different type without conversions to integers, but the overall problem remains. As we have seen, there are two problems with passing a lot of values to C++ functions as separate arguments. First, it creates very long declarations and function calls that are error-prone. Second, if we need to add a value or change the type of a parameter, there is a lot of code to be edited. The solution to both problems existed even before C++ was created; it comes from C—use aggregates—that is, structs—to combine many values into one parameter.

Aggregate parameters

With aggregate parameters, we create a struct or a class that contains all the values, instead of adding one parameter per value. We don't have to be limited to one aggregate; for example, our city may take several structs, one for all terrain-related features that the game sets, and another for all features that the player controls directly:

```
struct city_features_t {
  size_t number_of_buildings = 1;
  size_t number_of_towers = 0;
  size_t guard_strength = 0;
  enum center_t { KEEP, PALACE, CITADEL };
  center_t center = KEEP;
  bool with_forge = false;
  bool with_granary = false;
  bool with_temple = false;
};
struct terrain_features_t {
  bool has_fresh_water = true;
  bool is_coastal = false;
  bool has_forest = true;
  bool is_desert = false;
};
class City {
  public:
  City(city_features_t city_features,
       terrain_features_t terrain_features);
  ...
};
```

This solution has many advantages. First of all, assigning values to the arguments can be done explicitly, by name, and is very visible (and very verbose):

```
city_features_t city_features;
city_features.number_of_buildings = 2;
city_features.center = city_features::KEEP;
...
terrain_features_t terrain_features;
terrain_features.has_fresh_water = true;
...
City Capital(city_features, terrain_features);
```

It is much easier to see what each argument's value is, and mistakes are much less likely (the alternative, aggregate initialization of the structs, only moves the problem from one initialization to the other).

If we need to add a new feature, most of the time we just have to add a new data member to one of the aggregate types. Only the code that actually deals with the new argument has to be updated; all the functions and classes that simply pass the arguments and forward them do not need to change at all. We can even give the aggregate types default values to provide default values for all arguments, as we have done in the last example.

This is, overall, an excellent solution to the problem of functions with many parameters. However, it has one drawback: the aggregates have to be explicitly created and initialized, line by line. This works out fine for many cases, especially when these classes and structs represent state variables that we are going to keep for a long time. But, when used purely as parameter containers, they create unnecessarily verbose code, starting from the fact that the aggregate variable must have a name. We don't really need that name, as we are going to use it only once to call the function, but we have to make one up. It would be tempting just to use a temporary variable:

```cpp
struct city_features_t {
  size_t number_of_buildings = 1;
  size_t number_of_towers = 0;
  size_t guard_strength = 0;
  enum center_t { KEEP, PALACE, CITADEL };
  center_t center = KEEP;
  bool with_forge = false;
  bool with_granary = false;
  bool with_temple = false;
};
struct terrain_features_t {
  bool has_fresh_water = true;
  bool is_coastal = false;
  bool has_forest = true;
  bool is_desert = false;
};
City Capital({2, 1, 0, KEEP, true, false, false},
             {true, false, false, true});
```

This works, but it brings us full circle, right to where we started; a function with a long list of easily mixed Boolean arguments. The fundamental problem we encounter is that C++ functions have positional arguments, and we are trying to come up with something that would let us specify arguments by name. Aggregate objects resolve this problem mostly as a side effect, and if the overall design benefits from collecting a group of values into one class, you should certainly do it. However, as a solution specifically for the problem of named arguments, with no other, more permanent reason to group the values together, they fall short. We will now see how this deficiency can be addressed.

Named arguments in C++

We have seen how collecting logically related values into aggregate objects gives us a side benefit; we can pass these values to functions and access them by name instead of by their order in a long list. The key is *logically related*, though; aggregating values for no reason other than they happen to be used together in one function call creates unnecessary objects with names we would rather not have to invent. We need a way to create temporary aggregates, preferably without explicit names or declarations. We have a solution to this problem, and had it for a long time in C++; all it needs is a fresh look from a different perspective, which we are about to take now.

Method chaining

Method chaining is a borrowed C++ technique; it originates in **Smalltalk**. Its main purpose is to eliminate unnecessary local variables. You have used method chaining already, although you may not have realized it. Consider this code that you have probably written many times:

```
// Example 02
int i, j;
std::cout << i << j;
```

The last line invoked the inserter operator `<<` twice. The first time it is invoked on the object on the left-hand side of the operator, `std::cout`. What object is the second call on? In general, the operator syntax is just a way to call a function named `operator<<()`. Usually, this particular operator is a non-member function, but the `std::ostream` class has several member function overloads as well, and one of them is for `int` values. So, the last line really is this:

```
// Example 02-
std::cout.operator<<(i).operator<<(j);
```

The second call to `operator<<()` is done on the result of the first one. The equivalent C++ code is this:

```
// Example 02
auto& out1 = std::cout.operator(i);
out1.operator<<(j);
```

This is the method chaining—the call to one method function returns the object on which the next method should be called. In the case of `std::cout`, the member `operator<<()` returns a reference to the object itself. By the way, the non-member `operator<<()` does the same, only instead of the implicit argument `this`, it has the stream object as an explicit first argument. Now, we can use method chaining to eliminate the explicitly named argument object.

Method chaining and named arguments

As we have seen before, the aggregate argument objects work well when they are not used mainly to hold arguments; if we need an object to hold the state of the system, and we build it over time and keep it for a long time, we can also pass this object as a single argument to any function that needs this state. It's creating aggregates for just one function call that we have a problem with. On the other hand, we do not like to write functions with many arguments either. This is particularly true for functions that usually have most arguments left as default, with only a few changes. Going back to our game, let's say that each day, game time, is processed by a function call.

The function is called, once per game day, to advance the city through the day and process the consequences of various random events the game can generate:

```
class City {
  ...
  void day(bool flood = false, bool fire = false,
    bool revolt = false, bool exotic_caravan = false,
    bool holy_vision = false, bool festival = false, ... );
  ...
};
```

A lot of different events can happen over time, but rarely more than one happens on any particular day. We set all arguments to false by default, but this does not really help; there is no particular order to these events, and if the festival happens, all the previous arguments must be specified even though they are still equal to their default values.

An aggregate object helps a lot, but we need to create and name it:

```
class City {
  ...
  struct DayEvents {
    bool flood = false;
    bool fire = false;
    ...
  };
  void day(DayEvents events);
  ...
};
City capital(...);
City::DayEvents events;
events.fire = true;
capital.day(events);
```

We would like to create a temporary `DayEvents` object just for the call to `City::day()`, but we need a way to set its data members. This is where method chaining comes in:

```
// Example 03
class City {
  ...
  class DayEvents {
    friend City;
    bool flood = false;
    bool fire = false;
    public:
    DayEvents() = default;
    DayEvents& SetFlood() { flood = true; return *this; }
    DayEvents& SetFire() { fire = true; return *this; }
    ...
  };
  void day(DayEvents events);
  ...
};
City capital(...);
capital.day(City::DayEvents().SetFire());
```

The default constructor constructs an unnamed temporary object. On that object, we invoke the `SetFire()` method. It modifies the object and returns a reference to itself. We pass the created and modified temporary object to the `day()` function, which processes the events of the day, displays the updated graphics of the city in flames, plays the sound of fire, and updates the status of the city to reflect that some buildings were damaged by fire.

Since each of the `Set()` methods return a reference to the same object, we can invoke more than one in a method chain, to specify multiple events. Also, the `Set()` methods can take arguments, of course; for example, instead of `SetFire()` that always changes the fire event to `true` from its default `false`, we could have a method that can set the event flag either way:

```
DayEvents& SetFire(bool value = true) {
  fire = value;
  return *this;
}
```

Today is the market day in our city, which coincides with a major festival, so the king hired an extra guard company in addition to the two already stationed in the city:

```
City capital(...);
capital.day(City::DayEvents().
            SetMarket().
```

```
                SetFestival().
                SetGuard(3));
```

Note that we did not have to specify anything for all the events that did not happen. We now have true named arguments; when we call a function, we pass the arguments in any order, by name, and we do not need to explicitly mention any arguments we wish to leave at their default values. This is the C++ named arguments idiom. A call with named arguments is, of course, more verbose than a call with positional arguments; each argument must have the name explicitly written. That was the point of the exercise. On the other hand, we come out ahead if there is a long list of default arguments we did not have to change. One question that could be asked is that of performance—we have a lot of extra function calls, the constructor, and a `Set()` call for every named argument, and that must cost something. Let's find out exactly what it costs.

Performance of the named arguments idiom

There is definitely more going on with the named argument call, as more functions are called. On the other hand, the function calls are really simple and, if they are defined in the header file, and the entire implementation is visible to the compiler, there is no reason for the compiler not to inline all the `Set()` calls and eliminate the unnecessary temporary variables. With good optimization, we could expect similar performance from the named arguments idiom and the explicitly named aggregate object.

The appropriate tool to measure the performance of a single function call is the micro benchmark. We use the Google microbenchmark library for this purpose. While the benchmarks are usually written in one file, we need another source file if we want the function we call to be external, not inlined. On the other hand, the `Set()` methods should definitely be inlined, so they should be defined in the header file. The second source file should contain the definition of the function we are calling with named or positional arguments. Both files are combined at link time:

```
$CXX named_args.C named_args_extra.C -g -O4 -I. \
   -Wall -Wextra -Werror -pedantic --std=c++14 \
   -I$GBENCH_DIR/include $GBENCH_DIR/lib/libbenchmark.a \
   -lpthread -lrt -lm -o named_args
```

We can compare the positional arguments, the named arguments, and the arguments aggregate. The result will depend on the type and number of arguments. For example, for a function with four Boolean arguments, we can compare these calls:

```
// Example 04
// Positional arguments:
Positional p(true, false, true, false);
// Named arguments idiom:
Named n(Named::Options().SetA(true).SetC(true));
// Aggregate object:
Aggregate::Options options;
```

```
options.a = true;
options.c = true;
Aggregate a(options));
```

The performance measured by the benchmark will depend greatly on the compiler and on the options that control optimization. For example, these numbers were collected on GCC12 with -O3:

```
Benchmark                  Time   UserCounters...
BM_positional_const   0.233 ns   items_per_second=138.898G/s
BM_named_const        0.238 ns   items_per_second=134.969G/s
BM_aggregate_const    0.239 ns   items_per_second=135.323G/s
```

There is no noticeable performance hit for the explicitly named aggregate object that the compiler was able to inline and optimize away. The named and positional arguments perform similarly. Note that the performance of the function calls depends greatly on what else is going on in the program at the same time, since the arguments are passed on registers, and register availability is affected by the context.

In our benchmark, we have used compile-time constants as argument values. This is not uncommon, especially for arguments that specify certain options—very often, at each call site, many of the options will be static, unchanging (the values are different in other places in the code where the same function is called, but on this line, many of the values are fixed at compile time). For example, if we have a special code branch to process natural disasters in our game, the ordinary branch will always call our day simulation with a flood, fire, and other disaster flags set to false. But, just as often the arguments are computed at runtime. How does this affect the performance? Let's create another benchmark where the values of the arguments are retrieved, for example, from a vector:

```
// Example 04
std::vector<int> v; // Fill v with random values
size_t i = 0;
// ... Benchmark loop ...
const bool a = v[i++];
const bool b = v[i++];
const bool c = v[i++];
const bool d = v[i++];
if (i == v.size()) i = 0; // Assume v.size() % 4 == 0
Positional p(a, b, c, d); // Positional arguments
Named n(Named::Options().
   SetA(a).SetC(b).SetC(c).SetD(d)); // Named arguments
Aggregate::Options options;
options.a = a;
options.b = b;
options.c = c;
options.d = d;
Aggregate a(options)); // Aggregate object
```

By the way, it would be ill-advised to shorten the preceding code in this manner:

```
Positional p(v[i++], v[i++], v[i++], v[i++]);
```

The reason is that the order in which the arguments are evaluated is undefined, so it is arbitrary which of the `i++` calls is executed first. If `i` starts from 0, this call may end up calling `Positional(v[0], v[1], v[2], v[3])` or `Positional(v[3], v[2], v[1], v[0])` or any other permutation.

On the same compiler and hardware, we now get different numbers:

```
Benchmark                Time   UserCounters...
BM_positional_vars      50.8 ns  items_per_second=630.389M/s
BM_named_vars           49.4 ns  items_per_second=647.577M/s
BM_aggregate_vars       45.8 ns  items_per_second=647.349M/s
```

We can see from the results that the compiler completely eliminated the overhead of the unnamed temporary object (or the named aggregate) and generated similarly performing code for all three ways to pass arguments into the function. In general, the result of the compiler optimizations is difficult to predict. For example, CLANG produces significantly different results (named argument calls are faster when most parameters are compile-time constants but slower when they are run-time values).

The benchmark does not favor any particular argument-passing mechanism. We can say that the named arguments idiom performs no worse than an explicitly named aggregate object or the equivalent positional parameters, at least, if the compiler were able to eliminate the unnamed temporary especially. On some compilers, the named arguments may be faster if the function has many arguments. If the optimization does not happen, the call may be a bit slower. On the other hand, in many cases the performance of the function call itself is not critical; for example, our cities are constructed only when the player builds one, a few times during the game. The day events are processed once per game day, which probably takes more than a few seconds of real-time, not least so the player can enjoy interacting with the game. On the other hand, the functions that are repeatedly called in performance-critical code should be inlined whenever possible, and we can expect better optimizations for argument passing in this case as well. Overall, we can conclude that, unless the performance of the particular function call is critical for program performance, one should not be concerned with the overhead of named arguments. For performance-critical calls, performance should be measured on a case-by-case basis, and it is possible for named arguments to be faster than positional ones.

General method chaining

Applications of method chaining in C++ are not limited to argument passing (we have already seen another application, although a well-hidden one, in the form of streaming I/O). For use in other contexts, it is helpful to consider some more general forms of method chaining.

Method chaining versus method cascading

The term *method cascading* is not often found in the context of C++, and for a good reason—C++ does not really support it. Method cascading refers to calling a sequence of methods on the same object. For example, in *Dart*, where method cascading is supported explicitly, we can write the following:

```
var opt = Options();
opt.SetA()..SetB();
```

This code first calls `SetA()` on the opt object, then calls `SetB()` on the same object. The equivalent code is this:

```
var opt = Options();
opt.SetA()
opt.SetB();
```

But wait, did we not just do the same with C++ and our options object? We did, but we skimmed over an important difference. In method chaining, the next method is applied to the result of the previous one. This is a chained call in C++:

```
Options opt;
opt.SetA().SetB();
```

This chained call is equivalent to the following code:

```
Options opt;
Options& opt1 = opt.SetA();
Options& opt2 = opt1.SetB();
```

C++ does not have the cascading syntax, but the code equivalent to a cascade would be this:

```
Options opt;
opt.SetA();
opt.SetB();
```

But this is exactly what we did earlier, and the short form was the same:

```
Options opt;
opt.SetA().SetB();
```

What makes the C++ cascading possible in this case is that the methods return the reference to the same object. We can still say that the equivalent code is this:

```
Options opt;
Options& opt1 = opt.SetA();
Options& opt2 = opt1.SetB();
```

And, it's technically true. But, because of the way the methods are written, we have the additional guarantee that opt, opt1, and opt2 all refer to the same object. Method cascading can always be implemented through method chaining, but it restricts the interfaces because all calls must return a reference to this. This implementation technique is sometimes called by the somewhat unwieldy name **cascading-by-chaining by returning self**. The method chaining, in general, is not restricted to return *self,* or the reference to the object itself (*this in C++). What can be accomplished with more general chaining? Let's see.

General method chaining

If the chained method does not return a reference to the object itself, it should return a new object. Usually, this object is of the same type, or at least a type from the same class hierarchy, if the methods are polymorphic. For example, let's consider a class that implements data collection. It has a method to filter the data using a predicate (a callable object, an object with an operator() that returns true or false). It also has a method to sort the collection. Each of these methods creates a new collection object and leaves the original object intact. Now, if we want to filter all valid data in our collection, and assuming that we have an is_valid predicate object, we can create a sorted collection of valid data:

```
Collection c;
... store data in the collection ...
Collection valid_c = c.filter(is_valid);
Collection sorted_valid_c = valid_c.sort();
```

The intermediate object can be eliminated using method chaining:

```
Collection c;
...
Collection sorted_valid_c = c.filter(is_valid).sort();
```

It should be clear after reading the last section that this is an example of method chaining, and a more general one than what we saw earlier—each method returns an object of the same type, but not the same object. The difference between chaining and cascading is very clear in this example—a cascade of methods would filter and sort the original collection (assuming we decided to support such operations).

Method chaining in class hierarchies

When applied to class hierarchies, method chaining runs into a particular problem; let's say that our sort() method returns a sorted data collection that is an object of a different type, SortedCollection, which is derived from the Collection class. The reason it is a derived class is that after sorting we can support efficient search, and so the SortedCollection class has a search() method that the base class does not have. We can still use method chaining, and even call the base class methods on the derived class, but doing so breaks the chain:

```
// Example 05
class SortedCollection;
```

```
class Collection {
  public:
  Collection filter();
  // sort() converts Collection to SortedCollection.
  SortedCollection sort();
};
class SortedCollection : public Collection {
  public:
  SortedCollection search();
  SortedCollection median();
};
SortedCollection Collection::sort() {
  SortedCollection sc;
  ... sort the collection ...
  return sc;
}
Collection c;
auto c1 = c.sort().search().filter.median();
```

In this example, the chaining worked for a while: we were able to sort a Collection, search the result, and filter the result of the search. The call to sort() operates on a Collection and returns a SortedCollection. The call to search() needs a SortedCollection, so it works as intended. The call to filter() needs a Collection; the method can be invoked on a derived class such as SortedCollection, but the return result is still going to be a Collection. Then the chain breaks: the call to median() needs a SortedCollection, which we have, except filter() effectively cast it back to a Collection. There is no way to tell median() that the object is really a SortedCollection (other than casting).

Polymorphism, or virtual functions, does not help here; first of all, we would need to define virtual functions for search() and median() in the base class, even though we don't intend to support this functionality there, as only the derived class supports them. We cannot declare them pure virtual because we use the Collection as a concrete class, and any class with a pure virtual function is an abstract class, so objects of this class cannot be instantiated. We can make these functions abort at runtime, but at the very least we have moved the detection of a programming error—searching in an unsorted collection—from compile time to runtime. Worse, it does not even help:

```
class SortedCollection;
class Collection {
  public:
  Collection filter();
  // Converts Collection to SortedCollection
  SortedCollection sort();
  virtual SortedCollection median();
};
```

```
class SortedCollection : public Collection {
  public:
  SortedCollection search();
  SortedCollection median() override;
};
SortedCollection Collection::sort() {
  SortedCollection sc;
  ... sort the collection ...
  return sc;
}
SortedCollection Collection::median() {
  cout << "Collection::median called!!!" << endl;
  abort();
  return {};       // Still need to return something
}
Collection c;
auto c1 = c.sort().search().filter().median();
```

This is not going to work because `Collection::filter` returns a copy of the object, not a reference to it. The object it returns is the base class, `Collection`. If called on a `SortedCollection` object, it rips out the base class portion from the derived object and returns that. If you think that making `filter()` virtual as well, and overriding it in the derived class, solves this problem at the expense of overriding every function in the base class, you have another surprise coming—virtual functions must have identical return types, except for *covariant return types*. References to the base and derived classes are covariant return types. Classes themselves, returned by value, are not.

Note that this problem would not have happened if we were returning object references. However, we can only return references to the object we are called on; if we create a new object in the body of a method function and return a reference to it, it's a dangling reference to a temporary object that is deleted the moment the function returns. The result is undefined behavior (the program is likely to crash). On the other hand, if we always return the reference to the original object, we cannot change its type from based to derived in the first place.

The C++ solution to this problem involves the use of templates and a curious design pattern. In fact, it is so mind-twisting that the word *curious* is even in its name—the Curiously Recurring Template Pattern. We have a whole chapter on the CRTP pattern in this book. The application of the pattern to our case is relatively straightforward—the base class needs to return the right type from its functions, but can't because it does not know what the type is. The solution—pass the right type into the base class as the template argument. Of course, the base class would have to be a base class template for this to work:

```
template <typename T> class Collection {
  public:
  Collection() {}
  T filter(); // "*this" is really a T, not a Collection
```

```
  T sort() {
    T sc; // Create new sorted collection
    ...
    return sc;
  }
};
class SortedCollection :
  public Collection<SortedCollection> {
  public:
  SortedCollection search();
  SortedCollection median();
};
Collection<SortedCollection> c;
auto c1 = c.sort().search().filter().median();
```

The chain here starts similarly to our initial example: sort() is invoked on a Collection and returns a SortedCollection, then search() applies to the SortedCollection and returns another SortedCollection, then filter() is called. This time, filter() from the base class Collection knows what the real type of the object is because Collection itself is a template instantiated on the type of the derived object. So, filter() works on any collection but returns an object of the same type as the initial collection – in our case, both are SortedCollection objects. Finally, median() needs a SortedCollection and gets it.

This is a complex solution. While it works, its complexity suggests that method chaining should be used judiciously when the object type has to change in the middle of the chain. There is a good reason for that—changing the object type is fundamentally different than calling a sequence of methods. It is a more significant event that perhaps should be made explicit, and the new object should get its own name.

Now that we know what method chaining is, let us see where else it can be useful.

The Builder pattern

Let us go almost all the way back to the start of the chapter and take another look at the way we pass named arguments to a C++ function. Instead of a constructor with many arguments, we settled on an options object where each argument is explicitly named:

```
City GreensDale(City::Options()
  .SetCenter(City::KEEP)
  .SetBuildings(3)
  .SetGuard(1)
  .SetForge()
);
```

Let us now focus on the `Options` object itself, specifically, the way we construct it. The constructor does not create a finished object (that would just move the problem from the `City` constructor to the `Options` constructor). Instead, we build the object piece by piece. This is a particular case of a very general design pattern – the Builder.

Basics of the Builder pattern

The Builder design pattern is used whenever we decide that an object cannot be constructed in what we consider a complete state by the constructor alone. Instead, we write a helper class, or builder class, that builds these objects and hands them out to the program.

The first question you might ask is "Why?" – isn't the constructor supposed to do exactly that job? There could be several reasons. One very common reason is that we use a more general object to represent some more specific data set. For example, we want an object that holds Fibonacci numbers or prime numbers, and we decided to use a `std::vector` to store them. Now we have a problem: the vector has whatever constructors the STL provides, but we need to ensure that our vector has the right numbers in it, and we can't write a new constructor. We could create a special class to hold only prime numbers, but we will end up with a lot of classes that, after being constructed differently, are used in very similar ways. We would have to write new code to process prime numbers, odd numbers, square numbers, etc when using a vector for all of them would be perfectly sufficient. Alternatively, we could just use vectors everywhere and write the right values into them whenever our program needs it. This is no good too: we expose and duplicate a lot of low-level code that we would like to encapsulate and reuse (which is why we wanted a constructor for each kind of number).

The solution is the Builder pattern: the code for computing and storing the numbers is encapsulated in a builder class, but the object created by the builder is a generic vector. For example, here is a builder for Fibonacci numbers (the sequence of numbers that starts with 1, 1, and every subsequent number is a sum of the last two numbers):

```
// Example 08
class FibonacciBuilder {
  using V = std::vector<unsigned long>;
  V cache_ { 1, 1, 2, 3, 5 };
  public:
  V operator()(size_t n) {
    while (cache_.size() < n) {      // Cache new numbers
      cache_.push_back(cache_[cache_.size() - 1] +
                       cache_[cache_.size() - 2]);
    }
    return V{cache_.begin(), cache_.begin() + n};
  }
};
```

Suppose our program needs to get sequences of the first n Fibonacci numbers for some algorithm (the value of n varies at run time). We may need these numbers more than once, sometimes for larger values of n than before and sometimes for smaller ones. All we need to do is to ask the builder:

```
FibonacciBuilder b;
auto fib10 = b(10);
```

We could keep the already known values somewhere in the program, but that complicates the program with the additional job of tracking them. It is better to move that work to a class dedicated to constructing Fibonacci numbers and nothing else - a builder. Is it worth it to cache Fibonacci numbers? Probably not really, but remember that this is a concise example: if we needed, say, prime numbers instead, reusing already known values would be very much worth it (but the code would be much longer).

The other common reason to use the builder is that the code necessary to build an object may be too complex for a constructor. Often, it manifests itself in the large number of arguments we would have to pass to a constructor if we tried to write one. The way we build the Options argument for our City at the start of this section is a trivial example of that, with the Options object acting as its own builder. Particular situations where builders are most useful include cases where the construction process is conditional and the data needed to fully construct an object varies in both the number and the type depending on some run-time variables. Again, our City is a trivial example of that: no single City needs every constructor argument, but without the Options and its (trivial) builder, we would have to provide a parameter for every one of them.

The approach we have seen for our Fibonacci vector builder is a common variant of the Builder pattern in C++; it's not very exciting but it works. In this chapter, we are going to see some alternative ways to implement a Builder. The first one generalizes the way we built our Options.

The fluent Builder

The way we build the Options object is through method chaining. Each method takes a small step toward constructing the final object. There is a general name for this approach: the fluent interface. While it is not limited to designing builders, the fluent interface became popular in C++ mostly as a way to build complex objects.

The fluent builder relies on method chaining: each member function of the builder class contributes to constructing the object that is being built and returns the builder itself, so the work can continue. For example, here is an Employee class (possibly for some workplace database):

```cpp
// Example 09
class Employee {
  std::string prefix_;
  std::string first_name_;
  std::string middle_name_;
  std::string last_name_;
```

```
  std::string suffix_;
  friend class EmployeeBuilder;
  Employee() = default;
  public:
  friend std::ostream& operator<<(std::ostream& out,
                                  const Employee& e);
};
```

We are going to add even more data to the class later, but already it has enough data members to make a single constructor hard to use (too many arguments of the same type). We could use a constructor with an `Options` object, but, going forward, we expect the need to do some computations during the construction of the object: we may need to validate certain data, and other parts of the employee record may be conditional: two fields that cannot be set at the same time, a field whose default value depends on other fields, etc. So let's start designing a builder for this class.

The `EmployeeBuilder` needs to construct an `Employee` object first, then provide several chained methods to set different fields of the object, and, finally, hand over the constructed object. There may be some error checking involved, or more complex operations affecting other multiple fields, but a basic builder looks like this:

```
// Example 09
class EmployeeBuilder {
  Employee e_;
  public:
  EmployeeBuilder& SetPrefix(std::string_view s) {
    e_.prefix_ = s; return *this;
  }
  EmployeeBuilder& SetFirstName(std::string_view s) {
    e_.first_name_ = s ; return *this;
  }
  EmployeeBuilder& SetMiddleName(std::string_view s) {
    e_.middle_name_ = s; return *this;
  }
  EmployeeBuilder& SetLastName(std::string_view s) {
    e_.last_name_ = s; return *this;
  }
  EmployeeBuilder& SetSuffix(std::string_view s) {
    e_.suffix_ = s; return *this;
  }
  operator Employee() {
    assert(!e_.first_name_.empty() &&
           !e_.last_name_.empty());
    return std::move(e_);
  }
};
```

Several design decisions had to be made along the way. First, we decided to make the constructor `Employee::Employee()` private, so only friends such as `EmployeeBuilder` can create these objects. This ensures that a partially initialized or otherwise invalid `Employee` object cannot appear in the program: the only way to get one is from a builder. This is usually the safer choice, but sometimes we need to be able to default-construct the objects (for example, to use them in containers or for many serialization/deserialization implementations). Second, the builder holds the object that is being built until it can be moved to the caller. This is the common approach, but we have to be careful to use each builder object only once. We could also provide a way to reinitialize the builder; this is often done when the builder needs to do a lot of computations whose results are reused for building multiple objects. Finally, in order to construct an `Employee` object, we need to construct a builder first:

```
Employee Homer = EmployeeBuilder()
  .SetFirstName("Homer")
  .SetMiddleName("J")
  .SetLastName("Simpson")
;
```

The other common approach is to provide a static function `Employee::create()` that constructs a builder; in this case, the builder constructor is made private, with friends.

As we mentioned in the section on *Method chaining in class hierarchies*, the chained methods do not have to all return references to the same class. If our `Employee` object has an internal structure such as separate sub-records for the home address, job location, and so on, we could have a more structured approach to the builder as well.

The goal here is to design an interface so the client code could look like this:

```
// Example 09
Employee Homer = EmployeeBuilder()
  .SetFirstName("Homer")
  .SetMiddleName("J")
  .SetLastName("Simpson")
  .Job()
    .SetTitle("Safety Inspector")
    .SetOffice("Sector 7G")
  .Address()
    .SetHouse("742")
    .SetStreet("Evergreen Terrace")
    .SetCity("Springfield")
  .Awards()
    .Add("Remorseless Eating Machine")
;
```

To do this, we need to implement a hierarchy of builders with a common base class:

```
// Example 09
class JobBuilder;
class AwardBuilder;
class AbstractBuilder {
  protected:
  Employee& e_;
  public:
  explicit AbstractBuilder(Employee& e) : e_(e) {}
  operator Employee() {
    assert(!e_.first_name_.empty() &&
           !e_.last_name_.empty());
    return std::move(e_);
  }
  JobBuilder Job();
  AddressBuilder Address();
  AwardBuilder Awards();
};
```

We still start with `EmployeeBuilder` which constructs the `Employee` object; the rest of the builders hold a reference to it, and, by calling the corresponding member function on `AbstractBuilder` we can switch to a different type of builder for the same `Employee` object. Note that, while `AbstractBuilder` serves as the base class for all other builders, there are no pure virtual functions (or any other virtual functions): as we have seen earlier, run-time polymorphism is not particularly useful in method chaining:

```
class EmployeeBuilder : public AbstractBuilder {
  Employee employee_;
  public:
  EmployeeBuilder() : AbstractBuilder(employee_) {}
  EmployeeBuilder& SetPrefix(std::string_view s){
    e_.prefix_ = s; return *this;
  }
  ...
};
```

To add the job information, we switch to the `JobBuilder`:

```
// Example 09
class JobBuilder : public AbstractBuilder {
  public:
  explicit JobBuilder(Employee& e) : AbstractBuilder(e) {}
  JobBuilder& SetTitle(std::string_view s) {
```

```
      e_.title_ = s; return *this;
  }
  ...
  JobBuilder& SetManager(std::string_view s) {
    e_.manager_ = s; return *this;
  }
  JobBuilder& SetManager(const Employee& manager) {
    e_.manager_ = manager.first_name_ + " " +
                    manager.last_name_;
      return *this;
  }
  JobBuilder& CopyFrom(const Employee& other) {
    e_.manager_ = other.manager_;
      ...
    return *this;
  }
};
JobBuilder AbstractBuilder::Job() {
  return JobBuilder(e_);
}
```

Once we have a `JobBuilder`, all its chained methods return a reference to itself; of course, a `JobBuilder` is also an `AbstractBuilder`, so we could switch to another builder type such as `AddressBuilder` any time. Note that we can declare the `AbstractBuilder::Job()` method with just the forward declaration of the `JobBuilder`, but the implementation has to be deferred until the type itself is defined.

In this example, we also see the flexibility of the Builder pattern that would be very difficult to implement using constructors only. For example, there are two ways to define an employee's manager: we can provide the name, or use another employee record. Also, we can copy the workplace information from another employee's records, and still use `Set` methods to modify the fields that are not the same.

Other builders such as `AddressBuilder` are likely to be similar. But there may be very different builders as well. For example, an employee could have an arbitrary number of awards:

```
// Example 09
class Employee {
  ... name, job, address, etc ...
  std::vector<std::string> awards_;
};
```

The corresponding builder needs to reflect the nature of the information that it is adding to the object:

```cpp
// Example 09
class AwardBuilder : public AbstractBuilder {
  public:
  explicit AwardBuilder(Employee& e) : AbstractBuilder(e)
  {}
  AwardBuilder& Add(std::string_view award) {
    e_.awards_.emplace_back(award); return *this;
  }
};
AwardBuilder AbstractBuilder::Awards() {
  return AwardBuilder(e_);
}
```

We can call `AwardBuilder::Add()` as many times as we need to build the particular `Employee` object.

Here is our builder in action. Note how, for different employees, we can use different ways to supply the required information:

```cpp
Employee Barry = EmployeeBuilder()
  .SetFirstName("Barnabas")
  .SetLastName("Mackleberry")
;
```

We can use one employee record to add the manager's name to another employee:

```cpp
Employee Homer = EmployeeBuilder()
  .SetFirstName("Homer")
  .SetMiddleName("J")
  .SetLastName("Simpson")
  .Job()
    .SetTitle("Safety Inspector")
    .SetOffice("Sector 7G")
    .SetManager(Barry) // Writes "Barnabas Mackleberry"
  .Address()
    .SetHouse("742")
    .SetStreet("Evergreen Terrace")
    .SetCity("Springfield")
  .Awards()
    .Add("Remorseless Eating Machine")
;
```

We can copy employment records between employees:

```
Employee Lenny = EmployeeBuilder()
  .SetFirstName("Lenford")
  .SetLastName("Leonard")
  .Job()
    .CopyFrom(Homer)
  ;
```

Some of the fields, such as first and last name, are optional, and the builder checks the finished records for completeness before they can be accessed (see the `AbstractBuilder::operator Employee()` above). Other fields, such as name suffixes, are optional:

```
Employee Smithers = EmployeeBuilder()
  .SetFirstName("Waylon")
  .SetLastName("Smithers")
  .SetSuffix("Jr") // Only when needed!
  ;
```

The fluent builder is a powerful C++ pattern for constructing complex objects with many components, particularly when parts of the object are optional. However, it can get quite verbose for objects containing large amounts of highly structured data. There are alternatives, of course.

The implicit builder

We have already seen a case where the Builder pattern was employed without a dedicated builder object: all `Options` objects for named argument passing act as their own builders. We are going to see another version which is particularly interesting because there is no explicit builder object here. This design is particularly suitable for building nested hierarchical data such as XML files. We are going to demonstrate its use to build a (very simplified) HTML writer.

In this design, HTML records are going to be represented by the corresponding classes: a class for the `<P>` tag, another for the `<UL>` tag, and so on. All of these classes elaborate the common base class, `HTMLElement`:

```
class HTMLElement {
  public:
  const std::string name_;
  const std::string text_;
  const std::vector<HTMLElement> children_;
  HTMLElement(std::string_view name, std::string_view text)
    : name_(name), text_(text) {}
  HTMLElement(std::string_view name, std::string_view text,
              std::vector<HTMLElement>&& children)
    : name_(name), text_(text),
```

```
        children_(std::move(children)) {}
    friend std::ostream& operator<<(std::ostream& out,
        const HTMLElement& element);
};
```

There is, of course, a lot more to an HTML element, but we have to keep things simple. Also, our base element allows unlimited nesting: any element can have a vector of child elements, each of which can have child elements, and so on. Printing of an element is, therefore, recursive:

```
std::ostream& operator<<(std::ostream& out,
                         const HTMLElement& element) {
  out << "<" << element.name_ << ">\n";
  if (!element.text_.empty())
    out << "  " << element.text_ << "\n";
  for (const auto& e : element.children_) out << e;
  out << "</" << element.name_ << ">" << std::endl;
  return out;
}
```

Note that, in order to add child elements, we have to supply them in a `std::vector` which is then moved into the `HTMLElement` object. The rvalue reference means that the vector argument is going to be a temporary value or a result of `std::move`. However, we are not going to add the child elements to vectors ourselves: this is the job of the derived classes for the specific elements (`<P>`, `<UL>`, etc). The specific element classes can prevent the addition of child elements when the syntax does not allow it, as well as enforce other restrictions on the fields of an HTML element.

What do these specific classes look like? The simpler ones are going to look like this:

```
class HTML : public HTMLElement {
  public:
  HTML() : HTMLElement("html", "") {}
  HTML(std::initializer_list<HTMLElement> children) :
    HTMLElement("html", "", children) {};
};
```

This HTML class represents the `<html>` tag. Classes such as `Body`, `Head`, `UL`, `OL`, and many more, are written exactly the same way. The class `P` for the `<P>` tag is similar except it does not allow nested objects, so it has only one constructor that takes the text argument. It is very important that these classes do not add any data members; they must initialize the base `HTMLElement` object and nothing else. The reason should be obvious if you look at the base class again: we store a vector of `HTMLElement` child objects. However, they were constructed – as HTML or as `UL`, or as anything else – they are only `HTMLElement` objects now. Any extra data is going to be lost.

You may also notice that the vector parameter of the HTMLElement constructor is initialized from a std::initializer_list argument. This conversion is done implicitly by the compiler from the list of the constructor arguments:

```
// Example 10
auto doc = HTML{
  Head{
    Title{"Mary Had a Little Lamb"}
  },
  Body{
    P{"Mary Had a Little Lamb"},
    OL{
      LI{"Its fleece was white as snow"},
      LI{"And everywhere that Mary went"},
      LI{"The lamb was sure to go"}
    }
  }
};
```

This statement begins with a call to construct an HTML object using two arguments. They are Head and Body objects, but they get converted to HTMLElement and put into std::initializer_list<HTMLElement> by the compiler. The list is then used to initialize a vector, which is moved into the children_ vector in the HTML object. Both Head and Body objects themselves have child objects, one of which (OL) has its own child objects.

Note it gets a little tricky if you want to have additional constructor arguments because you cannot mix regular arguments with initializer list elements. This problem happens, for example, with the LI class. The straightforward way to implement this class, based on what we learned so far, is as follows:

```
//Example 10
class LI : public HTMLElement {
  public:
  explicit LI(std::string_view text) :
    HTMLElement("li", text) {}
  LI(std::string_view text,
      std::initializer_list<HTMLElement> children) :
    HTMLElement("li", text, children) {}
};
```

Unfortunately, you can't call this constructor with something like this:

```
//Example 10
LI{"A",
  UL{
    LI{"B"},
```

```
    LI{"C"}
  }
}
```

It seems obvious that what the programmer wanted is for the first argument to be "A" and the second argument (and any more arguments, if we had them) should go into the initializer list. But that doesn't work: generally, to form an initializer list, we have to enclose the element sequence in braces {...}. Only when the entire argument list matches an initializer list can these braces be omitted. With some arguments not being part of the initializer list, we have to be explicit:

```
//Example 10
LI{"A",
  {UL{          // Notice { before UL!
    LI{"B"},
    LI{"C"}
  }}            // And closing } here
}
```

If you don't want to write the extra braces, you have to change the constructor slightly:

```
//Example 11
class LI : public HTMLElement {
  public:
  explicit LI(std::string_view text) :
    HTMLElement("li", text) {}
  template <typename ... Children>
  LI(std::string_view text, const Children&... children) :
    HTMLElement("li", text,
          std::initializer_list<HTMLElement>{children...})
  {}
};
```

Instead of using an initializer list parameter, we use a parameter pack and explicitly convert it to an initializer list (which is then converted to a vector). Of course, the parameter pack will accept an arbitrary number of arguments of any type, not just HTMLElement and its derived classes, but the conversion to the initializer list will fail. If you want to follow the practice that any template that did not fail to instantiate should not produce compilation errors in its body, you have to restrict the types in the parameter pack to classes derived from HTMLElement. This is easily done using C++20 concepts:

```
// Example 12
class LI : public HTMLElement {
  public:
  explicit LI(std::string_view text) :
    HTMLElement("li", text) {}
```

```
    LI(std::string_view text,
       const std::derived_from<HTMLElement>
       auto& ... children) :
      HTMLElement("li", text,
              std::initializer_list<HTMLElement>{children...})
    {}
};
```

If you don't use C++20 but still want to restrict the parameter types, you should read the *Chapter 7, SFINAE, Concepts, and Overload Resolution Management* in this book.

With the parameter pack used as an intermediary for constructing an initializer list, we can avoid the extra braces and write our HTML document like this:

```
// Examples 11, 12
auto doc = HTML{
  Head{
    Title{"Mary Had a Little Lamb"}
  },
  Body{
    P{"Mary Had a Little Lamb"},
    OL{
      LI{"Its fleece was white as snow"},
      LI{"And everywhere that Mary went"},
      LI{"The lamb was sure to go"}
    },
    UL{
      LI{"It followed her to school one day"},
      LI{"Which was against the rules",
        UL{
          LI{"It made the children laugh and play"},
          LI{"To see a lamb at school"}
        }
      },
      LI{"And so the teacher turned it out"}
    }
  }
};
```

This does look like an application of the Builder pattern: even though the final construction is done by a single call to the HTMLElement constructor, that constructor just moves the already constructed vector of child elements into its final location. The actual construction is done in steps like all builders do. But where is the builder object? There isn't one, not explicitly. Part of the builder functionality is provided by all the derived objects, such as HTML, UL, etc. They may look like they represent the corresponding HTML constructs, but they really don't: after the entire document is constructed, we only have HTMLElement objects. The derived objects are used only to build the document. The rest of the builder code is generated by the compiler when it does all the implicit conversions between parameter packs, initializer lists, and vectors. By the way, any half-decent optimizing compiler is going to get rid of all the intermediate copies and copy the input strings straight into the final vector where they are going to be stored.

Of course, this is a very simplified example, and for any practical use, we would need to store more data with HTML elements and give the programmer a way to initialize this data. We could combine the implicit builder approach with the fluent interface to provide an easy way to add optional values such as style, type, etc, to all HTMLElement objects.

By now you have seen three distinct Builder designs: there is the "traditional" builder with a single builder object, the fluent builder that employs method chaining, and the implicit builder that uses many small builder helper objects and relies heavily on compiler-generated code. There are other designs, but they are mostly variants and combinations of the approaches you have learned. Our study of the Builder pattern has drawn to a close.

Summary

Yet again, we have seen the power of C++ to essentially create a new language out of the existing one; C++ does not have named function arguments, only positional ones. That is part of the core language. And yet, we were able to extend the language and add support for named arguments in a reasonable-looking way, using the method chaining technique. We have also explored the other applications of method chaining beyond the named arguments idiom.

One of these applications, the fluent builder, is again an exercise in creating new languages: the power of the fluent interface, in general, is that it can be used to create domain-specific languages to execute sequences of instructions on some data. And so the fluent builder can be used to allow the programmer to describe the construction of objects as a sequence of steps that are familiar in a particular domain. Then, of course, there is the implicit builder that (with the right indents) even makes C++ code look a bit like the HTML document that is being built.

The next chapter introduces the only purely performance-oriented idiom in this book. We have discussed in several chapters the performance cost of memory allocation, and its impact on the implementation of several patterns. The next idiom, local buffer optimization, attacks the problem head-on, by avoiding memory allocation altogether.

Questions

1. Why do functions with many arguments of the same or related types lead to fragile code?

2. How do aggregate argument objects improve code maintainability and robustness?

3. What is the named argument idiom and how does it differ from aggregate arguments?

4. What is the difference between method chaining and cascading?

5. What is the Builder pattern?

6. What is the fluent interface and when is it used?

10

Local Buffer Optimization

Not all design patterns are concerned with designing class hierarchies. For commonly occurring problems, a software design pattern is the most general and reusable solution, and, for those programming in C++, one of the most commonly occurring problems is inadequate performance. One of the most common causes of such poor performance is inefficient memory management. Patterns were developed to deal with these problems. In this chapter, we will explore one such pattern that addresses, in particular, the overhead of small, frequent memory allocations.

The following topics will be covered in this chapter:

- What is the overhead of small memory allocations, and how can it be measured?

- What is local buffer optimization, how does it improve performance, and how can the improvements be measured?

- When can the local buffer optimization pattern be used effectively?

- What are the possible downsides of, and restrictions on, the use of the local buffer optimization pattern?

Technical requirements

You will need the Google Benchmark library installed and configured, details for which can be found here: `https://github.com/google/benchmark` (see *Chapter 4, Swap – From Simple to Subtle*, for installation instructions).

Example code can be found at the following link: `https://github.com/PacktPublishing/Hands-On-Design-Patterns-with-CPP-Second-Edition/tree/main/Chapter10`.

The overhead of small memory allocations

The local buffer optimization is just that - an optimization. It is a performance-oriented pattern, and we must, therefore, keep in mind the first rule of performance - never guess anything about performance. Performance, and the effect of any optimization, must be measured.

The cost of memory allocations

Since we are exploring the overhead of memory allocations and the ways to reduce it, the first question we must answer is how expensive a memory allocation is. After all, nobody wants to optimize something so fast that it needs no optimization. We can use Google Benchmark (or any other microbenchmark, if you prefer) to answer this question. The simplest benchmark to measure the cost of memory allocation might look like this:

```
void BM_malloc(benchmark::State& state) {
  for (auto _ : state) {
    void* p = malloc(64);
    benchmark::DoNotOptimize(p);
  }
  state.SetItemsProcessed(state.iterations());
}
BENCHMARK(BM_malloc_free);
```

The `benchmark::DoNotOptimize` wrapper prevents the compiler from optimizing away the unused variable. Alas, this experiment is probably not going to end well; the microbenchmark library needs to run the test many times, often millions of times, to accumulate a sufficiently accurate average runtime. It is highly likely that the machine will run out of memory before the benchmark is complete. The fix is easy enough, we must also free the memory we allocated:

```
// Example 01
void BM_malloc_free(benchmark::State& state) {
  const size_t S = state.range(0);
  for (auto _ : state) {
    void* p = malloc(S);
    benchmark::DoNotOptimize(p); free(p);
  }
  state.SetItemsProcessed(state.iterations());
}
BENCHMARK(BM_malloc_free)->Arg(64);
```

We must note that we now measure the cost of both allocation and deallocation, which is reflected in the changed name of the function. This is not an unreasonable change; any allocated memory will need to be deallocated sometime later, so the cost must be paid at some point. We have also changed the benchmark to be parameterized by the allocation size. If you run this benchmark, you should get something like this:

```
Benchmark                   Time    Items per second
BM_malloc_free/64           19.2 ns 52.2041M/s
```

This tells us that the allocation and deallocation of 64 bytes of memory cost about 19 nanoseconds on this particular machine, which adds up to 52 million allocations/deallocations per second. If you're curious whether the *64 bytes* size is special in some way, you can change the size value in the argument of the benchmark, or run the benchmark for a whole range of sizes:

```
void BM_malloc_free(benchmark::State& state) {
  const size_t S = state.range(0);
  for (auto _ : state) {
    void* p = malloc(S);
    benchmark::DoNotOptimize(p); free(p);
  }
  state.SetItemsProcessed(state.iterations());
}
BENCHMARK(BM_malloc_free)->
  RangeMultiplier(2)->Range(32,    256);
```

You might also note that, so far, we have measured the time it takes to make the very first memory allocation in the program since we have not allocated anything else. The C++ runtime system probably did some dynamic allocations at the startup of the program, but still, this is not a very realistic benchmark. We can make the measurement more relevant by reallocating some amount of memory:

```
// Example 02
#define REPEAT2(x) x x
#define REPEAT4(x) REPEAT2(x) REPEAT2(x)
#define REPEAT8(x) REPEAT4(x) REPEAT4(x)
#define REPEAT16(x) REPEAT8(x) REPEAT8(x)
#define REPEAT32(x) REPEAT16(x) REPEAT16(x)
#define REPEAT(x) REPEAT32(x)
void BM_malloc_free(benchmark::State& state) {
  const size_t S = state.range(0);
  const size_t N = state.range(1);
  std::vector<void*> v(N);
  for (size_t i = 0; i < N; ++i) v[i] = malloc(S);
  for (auto _ : state) {
    REPEAT({
      void* p = malloc(S);
      benchmark::DoNotOptimize(p);
      free(p);
```

```
    });
  }
  state.SetItemsProcessed(32*state.iterations());
  for (size_t i = 0; i < N; ++i) free(v[i]);
}
BENCHMARK(BM_malloc_free)->
  RangeMultiplier(2)->Ranges({{32, 256}, {1<<15, 1<<15}});
```

Here, we make N calls to `malloc` before starting the benchmark. Further improvements can be achieved by varying the allocation size during the reallocations. We have also replicated the body of the benchmark loop 32 times (using the C preprocessor macro) to reduce the overhead of the loop itself on the measurement. The time reported by the benchmark is now the time it takes to do 32 allocations and deallocations, which is not very convenient, but the allocation rate remains valid, since we have accounted for the loop unrolling, and multiplied the number of iterations by 32 when setting the number of processed items (in Google Benchmark, an item is whatever you want it to be, and the number of items per second is reported at the end of the benchmark, so we have declared one allocation/deallocation to be an item).

Even with all these modifications and improvements, the final result is going to be pretty close to our initial measurement of 54 million allocations per second. This seems very fast, just 18 nanoseconds. Remember, however, that a modern CPU can do dozens of instructions in this time. As we are dealing with small allocations, it is highly likely that the processing time spent on each allocated memory fragment is also small, and the overhead of allocation is non-trivial. This, of course, represents guessing about performance and is something I warned you against, and so we will confirm this claim via direct experiments.

First, however, I want to show you another reason why small memory allocations are particularly inefficient. So far, we have explored the cost of memory allocations on only one thread. Today, most programs that have any performance requirements at all are concurrent, and C++ supports concurrency and multi-threading. Let's take a look at how the cost of memory allocations changes when we do it on several threads at once:

```
// Example 03
void BM_malloc_free(benchmark::State& state) {
  const size_t S = state.range(0);
  const size_t N = state.range(1);
  std::vector<void*> v(N);
  for (size_t i = 0; i < N; ++i) v[i] = malloc(S);
  for (auto _ : state) {
    REPEAT({
      void* p = malloc(S);
      benchmark::DoNotOptimize(p);
      free(p);
    });
```

```
  }
  state.SetItemsProcessed(32*state.iterations());
  for (size_t i = 0; i < N; ++i) free(v[i]);
}
BENCHMARK(BM_malloc_free)->
  RangeMultiplier(2)->Ranges({{32, 256}, {1<<15, 1<<15}})
  ->ThreadRange(1, 2);
```

The result greatly depends on the hardware and the version of malloc used by the system. Also, on large machines with many CPUs, you can have many more than two threads.

Nonetheless, the overall trend should look something like this:

```
Benchmark                              Time    Items per second
BM_malloc_free/32/32768/threads:1   778 ns   41.1468M/s
BM_malloc_free/32/32768/threads:2   657 ns   24.3749M/s
BM_malloc_free/32/32768/threads:4   328 ns   24.3854M/s
BM_malloc_free/32/32768/threads:8   242 ns   16.5146M/s
```

This is quite dismal; the cost of allocations increased several times when we went from one thread to two (on a larger machine, a similar increase is going to happen, but probably with more than two threads). The system memory allocator appears to be the bane of effective concurrency. There are better allocators that can be used to replace the default malloc() allocator, but they have their own downsides. Plus, it would be better if our C++ program did not depend on a particular, non-standard, system library replacement for its performance. We need a better way to allocate memory. Let's have a look at it.

Introducing local buffer optimization

The least amount of work a program can do to accomplish a certain task is no work at all. Free stuff is great. Similarly, the fastest way to allocate and deallocate memory is this - don't. Local buffer optimization is a way to get something for nothing; in this case, to get some memory for no additional computing cost.

The main idea

To understand local buffer optimization, you have to remember that memory allocations do not happen in isolation. Usually, if a small amount of memory is needed, the allocated memory is used as a part of some data structure. For example, let's consider a very simple character string:

```
// Example 04
class simple_string {
  public:
  simple_string() = default;
```

```
  explicit simple_string(const char* s) : s_(strdup(s)) {}
  simple_string(const simple_string& s)
    : s_(strdup(s.s_)) {}
  simple_string& operator=(const char* s) {
    free(s_);
    s_ = strdup(s);
    return *this;
  }
  simple_string& operator=(const simple_string& s) {
    if (this == &s) return *this;
    free(s_);
    s_ = strdup(s.s_);
    return *this;
  }
  bool operator==(const simple_string& rhs) const {
    return strcmp(s_, rhs.s_) == 0;
  }
  ~simple_string() { free(s_); }
  private:
  char* s_ = nullptr;
};
```

The string allocates its memory from `malloc()` via a `strdup()` call and returns it by calling `free()`. To be in any way useful, the string would need many more member functions, but these are sufficient for now to explore the overhead of memory allocation. Speaking of allocation, every time a string is constructed, copied, or assigned, an allocation happens. To be more precise, every time a string is constructed, an additional allocation happens; the string object itself has to be allocated somewhere, which may be on the stack for a local variable, or on the heap if the string is a part of some dynamically allocated data structure. In addition to that, an allocation for the string data happens, and the memory is always taken from `malloc()`.

This, then, is the idea of the local buffer optimization - why don't we make the string object larger so it can contain its own data? That really would be getting something for nothing; the memory for the string object has to be allocated anyway, but the additional memory for the string data we would get at no extra cost. Of course, a string can be arbitrarily long, so we do not know in advance how much larger we need to make the string object to store any string the program will encounter. Even if we did, it would be a tremendous waste of memory to always allocate an object of that large size, even for very short strings.

We can, however, make an observation - the longer the string is, the longer it takes to process it (copy, search, convert, or whatever we need to do with it).

For very long strings, the cost of allocations is going to be small compared to the cost of processing. For short strings, on the other hand, the cost of the allocation could be significant. Therefore, the most performance benefit can be obtained by storing short strings in the object itself, while any string that is too long to fit in the object will be stored in allocated memory as before. This is, in a nutshell, local buffer optimization, which for strings is also known as **short string optimization**; the object (string) contains a local buffer of a certain size, and any string that fits into that buffer is stored directly inside the object:

```
// Example 04
class small_string {
  public:
  small_string() = default;
  explicit small_string(const char* s) :
    s_((strlen(s) + 1 < sizeof(buf_)) ? strcpy(buf_, s)
                                      : strdup(s)) {}
  small_string(const small_string& s) :
    s_((s.s_ == s.buf_) ? strcpy(buf_, s.buf_)
                        : strdup(s.s_)) {}
  small_string& operator=(const char* s) {
    if (s_ != buf_) free(s_);
    s_ = (strlen(s) + 1 < sizeof(buf_)) ? strcpy(buf_, s)
                                        : strdup(s);
    return *this;
  }
  small_string& operator=(const small_string& s) {
    if (this == &s) return *this;
    if (s_ != buf_) free(s_);
    s_ = (s.s_ == s.buf_) ? strcpy(buf_, s.buf_)
                          : strdup(s.s_);
    return *this;
  }
  bool operator==(const small_string& rhs) const {
    return strcmp(s_, rhs.s_) == 0;
  }
  ~small_string() {
    if (s_ != buf_) free(s_);
  }
  private:
  char* s_ = nullptr;
  char buf_[16];
};
```

In the preceding code example, the buffer size is set statically at 16 characters, including the null character used to terminate the string. Any string that is longer than 16 is allocated from `malloc()`. When assigning or destroying a string object, we must check whether the allocation was done or the internal buffer was used, in order to appropriately release the memory used by the string.

Effect of local buffer optimization

How much faster is `small_string` compared to `simple_string`? That depends, of course, on what you need to do with it. Let's start with just creating and deleting the strings. To avoid typing the same benchmark code twice, we can use the template benchmark, as follows:

```
// Example 04
template <typename T>
void BM_string_create_short(benchmark::State& state) {
  const char* s = "Simple string";
  for (auto _ : state) {
    REPEAT({
      T S(s);
      benchmark::DoNotOptimize(S);
    })
  }
  state.SetItemsProcessed(32*state.iterations());
}
BENCHMARK_TEMPLATE1(BM_string_create_short, simple_string);
BENCHMARK_TEMPLATE1(BM_string_create_short, small_string);
```

The result is quite impressive:

Benchmark	Time	Items per sec
BM_string_create_short<simple_string>	835 ns	38.34M/s
BM_string_create_short<small_string>	18.7 ns	1.71658G/s

It gets even better when we try the same test on multiple threads:

Benchmark	Time	Items per sec
BM_create<simple_string>/threads:2	743 ns	21.5644M/s
BM_create<simple_string>/threads:4	435 ns	18.4288M/s
BM_create<small_string>/threads:2	9.34 ns	1.71508G/s
BM_create<small_string>/threads:4	4.77 ns	1.67998G/s

Regular string creation is slightly faster on two threads, but creating short strings is almost exactly twice as fast (and again twice as fast on four threads). Of course, this is pretty much the best-case scenario for small string optimization - firstly because all we do is create and delete strings, which is the very part we optimized, and secondly because the string is a local variable its memory is allocated as a part of the stack frame, so there is no additional allocation cost.

However, this is not an unreasonable case; after all, local variables are not rare at all, and if the string is a part of some larger data structure, the allocation cost for that structure has to be paid anyway, so allocating anything else at the same time and without additional cost is effectively free.

Nonetheless, it is unlikely that we only allocate the strings to immediately deallocate them, so we should consider the cost of other operations. We can expect similar improvements for copying or assigning strings, as long as they stay short, of course:

```
template <typename T>
void BM_string_copy_short(benchmark::State& state) {
  const T s("Simple string");
  for (auto _ : state) {
    REPEAT({
      T S(s);
      benchmark::DoNotOptimize(S);
    })
  }
  state.SetItemsProcessed(32*state.iterations());
}
template <typename T>
void BM_string_assign_short(benchmark::State& state) {
  const T s("Simple string");
  T S;
  for (auto _ : state) {
    REPEAT({ benchmark::DoNotOptimize(S = s); })
  }
  state.SetItemsProcessed(32*state.iterations());
}
BENCHMARK_TEMPLATE1(BM_string_copy_short, simple_string);
BENCHMARK_TEMPLATE1(BM_string_copy_short, small_string);
BENCHMARK_TEMPLATE1(BM_string_assign_short, simple_string);
BENCHMARK_TEMPLATE1(BM_string_assign_short, small_string);
```

Indeed, a similar dramatic performance gain is observed:

```
Benchmark                               Time Items per sec
BM_string_copy_short<simple_string>     786 ns 40.725M/s
BM_string_copy_short<small_string>      53.5 ns 598.847M/s
BM_string_assign_short<simple_string>   770 ns 41.5977M/s
BM_string_assign_short<small_string>    46.9 ns 683.182M/s
```

We are also likely to need to read the data in the strings at least once, to compare them or search for a specific string or character, or compute some derived value. We do not expect improvements of a similar scale for these operations, of course, since none of them involves any allocations or deallocations. You might ask why, then, should we expect any improvements at all?

Indeed, a simple test of string comparison, for example, shows no difference between the two versions of the string. In order to see any benefit, we have to create many string objects and compare them:

```
template <typename T>
void BM_string_compare_short(benchmark::State& state) {
  const size_t N = state.range(0);
  const T s("Simple string");
  std::vector<T> v1, v2;
  ... populate the vectors with strings ...
  for (auto _ : state) {
    for (size_t i = 0; i < N; ++i) {
      benchmark::DoNotOptimize(v1[i] == v2[i]);
    }
  }
  state.SetItemsProcessed(N*state.iterations());
}
BENCHMARK_TEMPLATE1(BM_string_compare_short,
                    simple_string)->Arg(1<<22);
BENCHMARK_TEMPLATE1(BM_string_compare_short,
                    small_string)->Arg(1<<22);
```

For small values of N (a small total number of strings), there won't be any significant benefit from the optimization. But when we have to process many strings, comparing strings with the small string optimization can be approximately twice as fast:

```
Benchmark                               Time Items per sec
BM_compare<simple_string>/4194304   30230749 ns 138.855M/s
BM_compare<small_string>/4194304    15062582 ns 278.684M/s
```

Why is that happening, if there are no allocations at all? This experiment shows the second, very important, benefit of local buffer optimization - improved cache locality. The string object itself has to be accessed before the string data can be read; it contains the pointer to the data. For the regular string, accessing the string characters involves two memory accesses at different, generally unrelated addresses. If the total amount of data is large, then the second access, to the string data, is likely to miss the cache and wait for the data to be brought from the main memory. On the other hand, the optimized string keeps the data close to the string object, so that once the string itself is in the cache, so is the data. The reason that we need a sufficient amount of different strings to see this benefit is that with few strings, all string objects and their data can reside in the cache permanently. Only when the total size of the strings exceeds the size of the cache will the performance benefits manifest themselves. Now, let's dive deeper into some additional optimizations.

Additional optimizations

The `small_string` class we have implemented has an obvious inefficiency - when the string is stored in the local buffer, we do not really need the pointer to the data. We know exactly where the data is, in the local buffer. We do need to know, somehow, whether the data is in the local buffer or in the externally allocated memory, but we don't need to use 8 bytes (on a 64-bit machine) just to store that. Of course, we still need the pointer for storing longer strings, but we could reuse that memory for the buffer when the string is short:

```
// Example 05
class small_string {
  ...
  private:
  union {
    char* s_;
    struct {
      char buf[15];
      char tag;
    } b_;
  };
};
```

Here, we use the last byte as a `tag` to indicate whether the string is stored locally (`tag == 0`) or in a separate allocation (`tag == 1`). Note that the total buffer size is still `16` characters, `15` for the string itself and `1` for the tag, which also doubles at the trailing zero if the string needs all `16` bytes (this is why we have to use `tag == 0` to indicate local storage, as it would cost us an extra byte to do otherwise). The pointer is overlaid in memory with the first 8 bytes of the character buffer. In this example, we have chosen to optimize the total memory occupied by the string; this string still has a 16-character local buffer, just like the previous version, but the object itself is now only 16 bytes, not 24. If we were willing to keep the object size the same, we could have used a larger buffer and stored longer strings locally. The benefit of the small string optimization does, generally, diminish as the strings become longer. The optimal crossover point from local to remote strings depends on the particular application and must of course be determined by benchmark measurements.

Local buffer optimization beyond strings

The local buffer optimization can be used effectively for much more than just short strings. In fact, any time a small dynamic allocation of a size that is determined at runtime is needed, this optimization should be considered. In this section, we will consider several such data structures.

Small vector

Another very common data structure that often benefits from local buffer optimization is vectors. Vectors are essentially dynamic contiguous arrays of data elements of the specified type (in this sense, a string is a vector of bytes, although null termination gives strings their own specifics). A basic vector, such as `std::vector` found in the C++ standard library, needs two data members, a data pointer and the data size:

```
// Example 06
class simple_vector {
  public:
  simple_vector() = default;
  simple_vector(std::initializer_list<int> il) :
    n_(il.size()),
    p_(static_cast<int*>(malloc(sizeof(int)*n_)))
  {
    int* p = p_;
    for (auto x : il) *p++ = x;
  }
  ~simple_vector() { free(p_); }
  size_t size() const { return n_; }
  private:
  size_t n_ = 0;
  int* p_ = nullptr;
};
```

Vectors are usually templates, like the standard `std::vector`, but we have simplified this example to show a vector of integers (converting this vector class to a template is left as an exercise for you, and does not in any way alter the application of the local buffer optimization pattern). We can apply *small vector optimization* and store the vector data in the body of the vector object as long as it is small enough:

```
// Example 06
class small_vector {
  public:
  small_vector() = default;
  small_vector(std::initializer_list<int> il) :
    n_(il.size()), p_((n_ < sizeof(buf_)/sizeof(buf_[0]))
      ? buf_ : static_cast<int*>(malloc(sizeof(int)*n_)))
  {
    int* p = p_;
    for (auto x : il) *p++ = x;
  }
  ~small_vector() {
```

```
    if (p_ != buf_) free(p_);
  }
  private:
  size_t n_ = nullptr;
  int* p_ = nullptr;
  int buf_[16];
};
```

We can further optimize the vector in a similar manner to the string and overlay the local buffer with the pointer. We cannot use the last byte as a `tag`, as we did before, since any element of the vector can have any value, and the value of zero is, in general, not special. However, we need to store the size of the vector anyway, so we can use it at any time to determine whether the local buffer is used or not. We can take further advantage of the fact that if the local buffer optimization is used, the size of the vector cannot be very large, so we do not need a field of the `size_t` type to store it:

```
// Example 07
class small_vector {
  public:
  small_vector() = default;
  small_vector(std::initializer_list<int> il) {
    int* p;
    if (il.size() < sizeof(short_.buf)/
                        sizeof(short_.buf[0]))) {
      short_.n = il.size();
      p = short_.buf;
    } else {
      short_.n = UCHAR_MAX;
      long_.n = il.size();
      p = long_.p = static_cast<int*>(
        malloc(sizeof(int)*long_.n));
    }
    for (auto x : il) *p++ = x;
  }
  ~small_vector() {
    if (short_.n == UCHAR_MAX) free(long_.p);
  }
  private:
  union {
    struct {
      int buf[15];
      unsigned char n;
    } short_ = { {}, '\0' };
    struct {
      size_t n;
```

```
      int* p;
    } long_;
  };
};
```

Here, we store the vector size either in `size_t long_.n` or in `unsigned char short_.n`, depending on whether or not the local buffer is used. A remote buffer is indicated by storing UCHAR_MAX (that is, 255) in the short size. Since this value is larger than the size of the local buffer, this `tag` is unambiguous (were the local buffer increased to store more than 255 elements, the type of `short_.n` would need to be changed to a longer integer).

We can measure the performance gains from small vector optimization using a benchmark similar to the one we used for the strings. Depending on the actual size of the vector, gains of about 10x can be expected in creating and copying the vectors, and more if the benchmark runs on multiple threads. Of course, other data structures can be optimized in a similar manner when they store small amounts of dynamically allocated data. The optimizations of these data structures are fundamentally similar, but there is one noteworthy variant we should highlight.

Small queue

The small vector we have just seen uses a local buffer to store a small array of vector elements. This is the standard way of optimizing data structures that store a variable number of elements when this number is often small. A particular version of this optimization is used for data structures based on a queue, where the buffer grows on one end and is consumed on the other end. If there are only a few elements in the queue at any time, the queue can be optimized with a local buffer. The technique commonly employed here is a **circular buffer**: our buffer is an array of fixed size `buffer[N]`, so, as the elements are added to the end of the queue, we are going to reach the end of the array. By then some elements were taken from the queue, so the first few elements of the array are no longer used. When we reach the end of the array, the next enqueued value goes into the first element of the array, `buffer[0]`. The array is treated like a ring, after the element `buffer[N-1]` comes the element `buffer[0]` (hence another name for this technique, a *ring buffer*).

The circular buffer technique is commonly used for queues and other data structures where data is added and removed many times while the total volume of data stored at any given time is limited. Here is one possible implementation of a circular buffer queue:

```
// Example 08
class small_queue {
  public:
  bool push(int i) {
    if (front_ - tail_ > buf_size_) return false;
    buf_[(++front_) & (buf_size_ - 1)] = i;
    return true;
```

```
  }
  int front() const {
    return buf_[tail_ & (buf_size_ - 1)];
  }
  void pop() { ++tail_; }
  size_t size() const { return front_ - tail_; }
  bool empty() const { return front_ == tail_; }
private:
  static constexpr size_t buf_size_ = 16;
  static_assert((buf_size_ & (buf_size_ - 1)) == 0,
                "Buffer size must be a power of 2");
  int buf_[buf_size_];
  size_t front_ = 0;
  size_t tail_ = 0;
};
```

In this example, we support only the local buffer; if the number of elements the queue must hold exceeds the size of the buffer, the call to push() returns false. We could have switched to a heap-allocated array instead, just like we did in Example 07 for small_vector.

In this implementation, we increment the indices front_ and tail_ without bounds, but when these values are used as indices into the local buffer, we take the index value modulo buffer size. Of note is the optimization that is very common when dealing with circular buffers: the size of the buffer is a power of two (enforced by the assert). This allows us to replace the general (and slow) modulo calculation such as front_ % buf_size_ by much faster bitwise arithmetic. We do not have to worry about integer overflow either: even if we call push() and pop() more than 2^64 times, the unsigned integer index values will overflow and go back to zero and the queue continues to work fine.

As expected, the queue with the local buffer optimization far outperforms a general queue such as std::queue<int> (as long as the optimization remains valid and the number of elements in the queue is small, of course):

Benchmark	Time	items_per_second
BM_queue<std::queue<int>>	472 ns	67.787M/s
BM_queue<small_queue>	100 ns	319.857M/s

The circular local buffer can be used very effectively in many situations where we need to process large volumes of data but hold only a few elements at a time. Possible applications include network and I/O buffers, pipelines for exchanging data between threads in concurrent programs, and many more.

Let us now look at applications of local buffer optimizations beyond common data structures.

Type-erased and callable objects

There is another, very different, type of application where the local buffer optimization can be used very effectively - storing callable objects, which are objects that can be invoked as functions. Many template classes provide an option to customize some part of their behavior using a callable object. For example, `std::shared_ptr`, the standard shared pointer in C++, allows the user to specify a custom deleter. This deleter will be called with the address of the object to be deleted, so it is a callable with one argument of the `void*` type. It could be a function pointer, a member function pointer, or a functor object (an object with an `operator()` defined) - any type that can be called on a p pointer; that is, any type that compiles in the `callable(p)` function call syntax can be used. The deleter, however, is more than a type; it is an object and is specified at runtime, and so it needs to be stored someplace where the shared pointer can get to it. Were the deleter a part of the shared pointer type, we could simply declare a data member of that type in the shared pointer object (or, in the case of the C++ shared pointer, in its reference object that is shared between all copies of the shared pointer). You could consider it a trivial application of the local buffer optimization, as in the following smart pointer that automatically deletes the object when the pointer goes out of scope (just like `std::unique_ptr`):

```
// Example 09
template <typename T, typename Deleter> class smartptr {
  public:
  smartptr(T* p, Deleter d) : p_(p), d_(d) {}
  ~smartptr() { d_(p_); }
  T* operator->() { return p_; }
  const T* operator->() const { return p_; } private:
  T* p_;
  Deleter d_;
};
```

We are after more interesting things, however, and one such thing can be found when we deal with type-erased objects. The details of such objects were considered in the chapter dedicated to type erasure, but in a nutshell, they are objects where the callable is not a part of the type itself (as in, it is *erased* from the type of the containing object). The callable is instead stored in a polymorphic object, and a virtual function is used to call the object of the right type at runtime. The polymorphic object, in turn, is manipulated through the base class pointer.

Now, we have a problem that is, in a sense, similar to the preceding small vector - we need to store some data, in our case the callable object, whose type, and therefore size, is not statically known. The general solution is to dynamically allocate such objects and access them through the base class pointer. In the case of a smart pointer `deleter`, we could do it like this:

```
// Example 09
template <typename T> class smartptr_te {
  struct deleter_base {
```

```
    virtual void apply(void*) = 0;
    virtual ~deleter_base() {}
  };
  template <typename Deleter>
  struct deleter : public deleter_base {
    deleter(Deleter d) : d_(d) {}
    void apply(void* p) override {
      d_(static_cast<T*>(p));
    }
    Deleter d_;
  };
public:
  template <typename Deleter>
  smartptr_te(T* p, Deleter d) : p_(p),
    d_(new deleter<Deleter>(d)) {}
  ~smartptr_te() {
    d_->apply(p_);
    delete d_;
  }
  T* operator->() { return p_; }
  const T* operator->() const { return p_; }
private:
  T* p_;
  deleter_base* d_;
};
```

Note that the `Deleter` type is no longer a part of the smart pointer type; it was *erased*. All smart pointers for the same T object type have the same type, `smartptr_te<T>` (here, `te` stands for *type-erased*). However, we have to pay a steep price for this syntactic convenience - every time a smart pointer is created, there is an additional memory allocation. How steep? The first rule of performance must again be remembered - *steep* is only a guess until confirmed by an experiment, such as the following benchmark:

```
// Example 09
struct deleter {     // Very simple deleter for operator new
  template <typename T> void operator()(T* p) { delete p; }
};
void BM_smartptr(benchmark::State& state) {
  deleter d;
  for (auto _ : state) {
    smartptr<int, deleter> p(new int, d);
  }
  state.SetItemsProcessed(state.iterations());
```

```
}
void BM_smartptr_te(benchmark::State& state) {
  deleter d;
  for (auto _ : state) {
    smartptr_te<int> p(new int, d);
  }
  state.SetItemsProcessed(state.iterations());
}
BENCHMARK(BM_smartptr);
BENCHMARK(BM_smartptr_te);
BENCHMARK_MAIN();
```

For a smart pointer with a statically defined deleter, we can expect the cost of each iteration to be very similar to the cost of calling `malloc()` and `free()`, which we measured earlier:

Benchmark	Time	Items per second
BM_smartptr	21.0 ns	47.5732M/s
BM_smartptr_te	44.2 ns	22.6608M/s

For a type-erased smart pointer, there are two allocations instead of one, and so the time it takes to create the pointer object is doubled. By the way, we can also measure the performance of a raw pointer, and it should be the same as the smart pointer within the accuracy of the measurements (this was, in fact, a stated design goal for the `std::unique_ptr` standard).

We can apply the same idea of local buffer optimization here, and it is likely to be even more effective than it was for strings; after all, most callable objects are small. We can't completely count on that, however, and must handle the case of a callable object that is larger than the local buffer:

```
// Example 09
template <typename T> class smartptr_te_lb {
  struct deleter_base {
    virtual void apply(void*) = 0;
    virtual ~deleter_base() {}
  };
  template <typename Deleter>
    struct deleter : public deleter_base {
    deleter(Deleter d) : d_(d) {}
    void apply(void* p) override {
      d_(static_cast<T*>(p));
    }
    Deleter d_;
  };
  public:
```

```
template <typename Deleter>
  smartptr_te_lb(T* p, Deleter d) : p_(p),
    d_((sizeof(Deleter) > sizeof(buf_))
        ? new deleter<Deleter>(d)
        : new (buf_) deleter<Deleter>(d)) {}
~smartptr_te_lb() {
  d_->apply(p_);
  if ((void*)(d_) == (void*)(buf_)) {
    d_->~deleter_base();
  } else {
    delete d_;
  }
}
T* operator->() { return p_; }
const T* operator->() const { return p_; }
private:
T* p_;
deleter_base* d_;
char buf_[16];
};
```

Using the same benchmark as before, we can measure the performance of the type-erased smart pointer with local buffer optimization:

```
Benchmark                  Time Items per second
BM_smartptr             21.0 ns 47.5732M/s
BM_smartptr_te          44.2 ns 22.6608M/s
BM_smartptr_te_lb       22.3 ns 44.8747M/s
```

While the construction and deletion of a smart pointer without type erasure took 21 nanoseconds, and 44 nanoseconds with type erasure, the optimized type-erased shared pointer test takes 22 nanoseconds on the same machine. The slight overhead comes from checking whether the `deleter` is stored locally or remotely.

Local buffer optimization in the standard library

We should note that the last application of local buffer optimization, storing callables for type-erased objects, is widely used in the C++ standard template library. For example, `std::shared_ptr` has a type-erased deleter, and most implementations use the local buffer optimization; the deleter is stored with the reference object and not with each copy of the shared pointer, of course. The `std::unique_pointer` standard, on the other hand, is not type-erased at all, to avoid even a small overhead, or potentially a much larger overhead should the deleter not fit into the local buffer.

The *"ultimate"* type-erased object of the C++ standard library, `std::function`, is also typically implemented with a local buffer for storing small callable objects without the expense of an additional allocation. The universal container object for any type, `std::any` (since C++17), is also typically implemented without a dynamic allocation when possible.

Local buffer optimization in detail

We have seen the applications of local buffer optimization; for simplicity, we stayed with the most basic implementation of it. This simple implementation misses several important details, which we will now highlight.

First of all, we completely neglected the alignment of the buffer. The type we used to reserve the space inside an object is `char`; therefore, our buffer is byte-aligned. Most data types have higher alignment requirements: the exact requirements are platform-specific, but most built-in types are aligned on their own size (double is 8-byte-aligned on a 64-bit platform such as x86). Higher alignments are needed for some machine-specific types such as packed integer or floating-point arrays for AVX instructions.

Alignment is important: depending on the processor and the code generated by the compiler, accessing memory not aligned as required by the data type can result in poor performance or memory access violations (crashes). For example, most AVX instructions require 16- or 32-byte alignment, and the unaligned versions of these instructions are significantly slower. Another example is atomic operations such as the ones used in mutexes and other concurrent data structures: they also don't work if the data type is not properly aligned (for example, an atomic `long` must be aligned on an 8-byte boundary).

Specifying the minimum alignment for our buffer is not hard, at least if we know the type we want to store in the buffer. For example, if we have a small vector for an arbitrary type T, we can simply write:

```
template <typename T>
class small_vector {
  alignas(T) char buffer_[buffer_size_];
  ...
};
```

If the buffer is used for storing an object of one of several types, we have to use the highest alignment of all possible types. Finally, if the type of the object to be stored is unknown – the typical case for type-erased implementations – we have to select a *"high enough"* alignment and add a compile-time check at the point where a specific object is constructed in the buffer.

The second important subtlety to remember is how the buffer is defined. Usually, it is an aligned array of characters (or `std::byte_t`). In the previous section, we used an array of `int` for the small vector of integers. Again, there is a subtlety here: declaring the buffer as an object or an array of objects of the right type will cause these objects to be destroyed automatically when the object containing the buffer is destroyed. For trivially destructible types such as integers, it makes no difference at all – their destructors do nothing.

In general, this is not so, and an arbitrary destructor can be invoked only if an object was constructed at this location. For our small vector, this is not always the case: the vector may be empty or contain fewer objects than the buffer can hold. This is the most common case by far: usually, if we employ local buffer optimization, we cannot be sure that an object was constructed in the buffer. In this case, declaring the buffer as an array of non-trivially-destructible objects would be a mistake. However, if you have a guarantee that, in your particular case, the buffer always contains an object (or several objects, for an array), declaring them with the corresponding type greatly simplifies the implementation of the destructor, as well as the copy/move operations.

You should have noticed by now that a typical implementation of a local buffer needs a lot of boilerplate code. There are `reinterpret_cast` casts everywhere, you have to remember to add the alignment, there are some compile-time checks you should always add to make sure only suitable types are stored in the buffer, and so on. It is good to combine these details together in a single general reusable implementation. Unfortunately, as is often the case, there is a tension between reusability and complexity, so we will have to settle for several general reusable implementations.

If we put together everything we have learned about local buffers, we can come up with something like this:

```
// Example 10
template<size_t S, size_t A = alignof(void*)>
struct Buffer {
  constexpr static auto size = S, alignment = A;
  alignas(alignment) char space_[size];
  ...
};
```

Here we have a buffer of arbitrary size and alignment (both are template parameters). Now that we have a space to store objects, we have to make sure the type we want to erase fits into this space. To this end, it is convenient to add a `constexpr` validator function (it's used only in compile-time syntax checks):

```
template<size_t S, size_t A = alignof(void*)>
struct Buffer {
  template <typename T> static constexpr bool valid_type()
  {
    return sizeof(T) <= S && (A % alignof(T)) == 0;
  }
  ...
};
```

The buffer can be used as if it contained an object of type T by calling the member function as<T>():

```
template<size_t S, size_t A = alignof(void*)>
struct Buffer {
  ...
  template <typename T> requires(valid_type<T>())
    T* as() noexcept {
    return reinterpret_cast<T*>(&space_);
  }
  template <typename T> requires(valid_type<T>())
    const T* as() const noexcept {
    return const_cast<Buffer*>(this)->as<T>();
  }
};
```

The buffer can be constructed empty (default-constructed) or with an immediately constructed object. In the former case, the object can be emplaced later. Either way, we validate that the type fits into the buffer and meets the alignment requirements (if C++20 and concepts are not available, SFINAE can be used instead). The default constructor is trivial, but the emplacing constructor and the emplace() method have constraints on the type and the constructor arguments:

```
template<size_t S, size_t A = alignof(void*)>
struct Buffer {
  ...
  Buffer() = default;
  template <typename T, typename... Args>
    requires(valid_type<T>() &&
             std::constructible_from<T, Args...>)
  Buffer(std::in_place_type_t<T>, Args&& ...args)
    noexcept(std::is_nothrow_constructible_v<T, Args...>)
  {
    ::new (static_cast<void*>(as<T>()))
      T(std::forward<Args>(args)...);
  }
  template<typename T, typename... Args>
    requires(valid_type<T>() &&
             std::constructible_from<T, Args...>)
  T* emplace(Args&& ...args)
    noexcept(std::is_nothrow_constructible_v<T, Args...>)
  {
    return ::new (static_cast<void*>(as<T>()))
      T(std::forward<Args>(args)...);
  }
};
```

Note that we do check that the requested type can be stored in the buffer but no checking is done at run time to ensure that the buffer does indeed contain such an object. Such checking can be added at the cost of additional space and run-time computations and might make sense as a debugging instrumentation. We do not do anything special for copying, moving, or deleting the buffer. As-is, this implementation is suitable for trivially copyable and trivially destructible objects. In this case, we will want to assert these restrictions when an object is constructed in the buffer (in both the constructor and the `emplace()` method):

```
template<size_t S, size_t A = alignof(void*)>
struct Buffer {
  template <typename T>
  Buffer(std::in_place_type_t<T>, Args&& ...args) … {
    static_assert(std::is_trivially_destructible_v<T>, "");
    static_assert(std::is_trivially_copyable_v<T>, "");

    …
  }
};
```

In this case, it may also make sense to add a `swap()` method to the class:

```
template<size_t S, size_t A = alignof(void*)>
struct Buffer {

  …
  void swap(Buffer& that) noexcept {
    alignas(alignment) char tmp[size];
    ::memcpy(tmp, this->space_, size);
    ::memcpy(this->space_, that.space_, size);
    ::memcpy(that.space_, tmp, size);
  }
};
```

On the other hand, if we're using this buffer for storing objects of a single known type and that type is not trivially destructible, we end up writing something like this all the time:

```
buffer_.as<T>()->~T();
```

We can simplify the client code by adding another generally usable method:

```
template<size_t S, size_t A = alignof(void*)>
struct Buffer {

  …
  template <typename T> void destroy() {
    this->as<T>()->~T();
  }
};
```

We can add similar methods to copy and move objects stored in the buffer, or leave that to the client.

Our general local buffer implementation works for all trivially copyable and destructible types, as well as for all cases where the type is known and the client of our code handles copying and destroying the objects stored in the buffer. There is one special case that is left out but is nonetheless worth considering: when a local buffer is used in type-erased classes, the stored (erased) type may require non-trivial copying or deletion but the client cannot do these operations since the whole point of type erasure is that the client code does not know the erased type after it was emplaced into the buffer. In this special case, we need to capture the type at the point when it was stored and generate the corresponding copy, move, and deletion operations. In other words, we have to combine our local buffer with the techniques we learned earlier, in *Chapter 6, Understanding Type Erasure*, about type erasure. The most suitable variant of type erasure, in this case, is `vtable` – a table of function pointers we generate using templates. The `vtable` itself is an aggregate (`struct`) holding function pointers that will do the deletion, copying, or moving:

```
// Example 11
template<size_t S, size_t A = alignof(void*)>
struct Buffer {
  ...
  struct vtable_t {
    using deleter_t = void(Buffer*);
    using copy_construct_t = void(Buffer*, const Buffer*);
    using move_construct_t = void(Buffer*, Buffer*);
    deleter_t*  deleter_;
    copy_construct_t* copy_construct_;
    move_construct_t* move_construct_;
  };
  const vtable_t* vtable_ = nullptr;
};
```

We need one class member, `vtable_`, to store a pointer to the `vtable`. The object that we will point to needs to be created by the constructor or the `emplace()` method, of course – that is the only time we know the real type and how to delete or copy it. But we are not going to do dynamic memory allocation for it. Instead, we create a static template variable and initialize it with pointers to static member functions (also templates). The compiler creates an instance of this static variable for every type we store in the buffer. Of course, we also need static template functions (a pointer to a static member function is the same as a regular function pointer, rather than a member function pointer). These functions are instantiated by the compiler with the same type `T` of the object that is stored in the buffer:

```
template<size_t S, size_t A = alignof(void*)>
struct Buffer {
  ...
  template <typename U, typename T>
```

```
  constexpr static vtable_t vtable = {
    U::template deleter<T>,
    U::template copy_construct<T>,
    U::template move_construct<T>
  };
  template <typename T>
    requires(valid_type<T>() &&
    std::is_nothrow_destructible_v<T>)
  static void deleter(Buffer* space) {
    space->as<T>()->~T();
  }
  template <typename T>
    requires(valid_type<T>())
  static void copy_construct(Buffer* to,
                             const Buffer* from)
    noexcept(std::is_nothrow_copy_constructible_v<T>)
  {
    ::new (static_cast<void*>(to->as<T>()))
      T(*from->as<T>());
    to->vtable_ = from->vtable_;
  }
  template <typename T>
    requires(valid_type<T>())
    static void move_construct(Buffer* to, Buffer* from)
    noexcept(std::is_nothrow_move_constructible_v<T>)
  {
    ::new (static_cast<void*>(to->as<T>()))
      T(std::move(*from->as<T>()));
    to->vtable_ = from->vtable_;
  }
};
```

As shown in *Chapter 6, Understanding Type Erasure*, we first use template static functions to generate copy, move, and delete operations for any type T we need. We store the pointers to these functions in an instance of a static template variable `vtable`, and a pointer to that instance in a (non-static) data member `vtable_`. The latter is our only cost, size-wise (the rest is static variables and functions that are generated by the compiler once for each type stored in the buffer).

This `vtable_` has to be initialized at the time the object is emplaced in the buffer since this is the last time we explicitly know the type of the stored object:

```
// Example 11
template<size_t S, size_t A = alignof(void*)>
struct Buffer {
```

```
template <typename T, typename... Args>
  requires(valid_type<T>() &&
  std::constructible_from<T, Args...>)
Buffer(std::in_place_type_t<T>, Args&& ...args)
  noexcept(std::is_nothrow_constructible_v<T, Args...>)
  : vtable_(&vtable<Buffer, T>)
{
  ::new (static_cast<void*>(as<T>()))
    T(std::forward<Args>(args)...);
}
template<typename T, typename... Args>
  requires(valid_type<T>() &&
  std::constructible_from<T, Args...>)
T* emplace(Args&& ...args)
  noexcept(std::is_nothrow_constructible_v<T, Args...>)
{
  if (this->vtable_) this->vtable_->deleter_(this);
  this->vtable_ = &vtable<Buffer, T>;
  return ::new (static_cast<void*>(as<T>()))
    T(std::forward<Args>(args)...);
}
...
};
```

Note the initialization of the `vtable_` member in the constructor. In the `emplace()` method, we also have to delete the object previously constructed in the buffer, if one exists.

With the type erasure machinery in place, we can finally implement the destructors and the copy/move operations. They all use a similar approach – call the corresponding function in the `vtable`. Here are the copy operations:

```
// Example 11
template<size_t S, size_t A = alignof(void*)>
struct Buffer {
  ...
  Buffer(const Buffer& that) {
    if (that.vtable_)
      that.vtable_->copy_construct_(this, &that);
  }
  Buffer& operator=(const Buffer& that) {
    if (this == &that) return *this;
    if (this->vtable_) this->vtable_->deleter_(this);
    if (that.vtable_)
```

```
      that.vtable_->copy_construct_(this, &that);
    else this->vtable_ = nullptr;
    return *this;
  }
};
```

The move operations are similar, only they use the `move_construct_` function:

```
template<size_t S, size_t A = alignof(void*)>
struct Buffer {
  ...
  Buffer(Buffer&& that) {
    if (that.vtable_)
      that.vtable_->move_construct_(this, &that);
  }
  Buffer& operator=(Buffer&& that) {
    if (this == &that) return *this;
    if (this->vtable_) this->vtable_->deleter_(this);
    if (that.vtable_)
      that.vtable_->move_construct_(this, &that);
    else this->vtable_ = nullptr;
    return *this;
  }
};
```

Note that the move-assignment operator is not required to check for self-assignment, but it's also not wrong to do so. It is highly desirable for the move operations to be `noexcept`; unfortunately, we cannot guarantee that because we do not know the erased type at compile time. We can make a design choice and declare them `noexcept` anyway. If we do, we can also assert, at compile-time, that the object we store in the buffer is `noexcept` movable.

Finally, we have the destruction operations. Since we allow the caller to destroy the contained object without destroying the buffer itself (by calling `destroy()`), we have to take care to ensure that the object gets destroyed only once:

```
template<size_t S, size_t A = alignof(void*)>
struct Buffer {
  ...
  ~Buffer() noexcept {
    if (this->vtable_) this->vtable_->deleter_(this);
  }
  // Destroy the object stored in the aligned space.
  void destroy() noexcept {
```

```
        if (this->vtable_) this->vtable_->deleter_(this);
        this->vtable_ = nullptr;
    }
};
```

Having the type-erased `vtable` allows us to reconstruct, at run time, the type stored in the buffer (it is embedded in the code generated for the static functions such as `copy_construct()`). There is, of course, a cost to it; we already noted the additional data member `vtable_`, but there is also some run-time cost arising from the indirect function calls. We can estimate it by using both implementations of the local buffer (with and without type erasure) to store and copy some trivially copyable object, for example, a lambda with a captured reference:

```
Benchmark                        Time
BM_lambda_copy_trivial           5.45 ns
BM_lambda_copy_typeerased        4.02 ns
```

The overhead of (well-implemented) type erasure is non-negligible but modest. An added advantage is that we could also verify at run-time whether or not our calls to `as<T>()` refer to a valid type and that the object is indeed constructed. Relatively to the very cheap implementation of an unchecked method, this would add significant overhead, so probably should be restricted to debug builds.

We have seen significant, sometimes dramatic, improvements to the performance of many different data structures and classes provided by the local buffer optimization. With the easy-to-use general implementations we just learned, why would you not use this optimization all the time? As is the case for any design pattern, our exploration is not complete without mentioning the trade-offs and the downsides.

Downsides of local buffer optimization

Local buffer optimization is not without its downsides. The most obvious one is that all objects with a local buffer are larger than they would be without one. If the typical data stored in the buffer is smaller than the chosen buffer size, then every object is wasting some memory, but at least the optimization is paying off. Worse, if our choice of buffer size is badly off and most data is, in fact, larger than the local buffer, the data is stored remotely but the local buffers are still created inside every object, and all that memory is wasted.

There is an obvious trade-off between the amount of memory we are willing to waste and the range of data sizes where the optimization is effective. The size of the local buffer should be carefully chosen with the application in mind.

The more subtle complication is this - the data that used to be external to the object is now stored inside the object. This has several consequences, in addition to the performance benefits we were so focused on. First of all, every copy of the object contains its own copy of the data as long as it fits into the local buffer. This prevents designs such as the reference counting of data; for example, a

Copy-On-Write (**COW**) string, where the data is not copied as long as all string copies remain the same, cannot use the small string optimization.

Secondly, the data must be moved if the object itself is moved. Contrast this with `std::vector`, which is moved or swapped, essentially like a pointer - the pointer to the data is moved but the data remains in place. A similar consideration exists for the object contained inside `std::any`. You could dismiss this concern as trivial; after all, local buffer optimization is used primarily for small amounts of data, and the cost of moving them should be comparable to the cost of copying the pointer. However, more than performance is at stake here - moving an instance of `std::vector` (or `std::any`, for that matter) is guaranteed not to throw an exception. However, no such guarantees are offered when moving an arbitrary object. Therefore, `std::any` can be implemented with a local buffer optimization only if the object it contains is `std::is_nothrow_move_constructible`.

Even such a guarantee does not suffice for the case of `std::vector`, however; the standard explicitly states that moving, or swapping, a vector does not invalidate iterators pointing to any element of the vector. Obviously, this requirement is incompatible with local buffer optimization, since moving a small vector would relocate all its elements to a different region of memory. For that reason, many high-efficiency libraries offer a custom vector-like container that supports small vector optimization, at the expense of the standard iterator invalidation guarantees.

Summary

We have just introduced a design pattern aimed solely at improved performance. Efficiency is an important consideration for the C++ language; thus, the C++ community developed patterns to address the most common inefficiencies. Repeated or wasteful memory allocation is perhaps the most common of all. The design pattern we have just seen - local buffer optimization - is a powerful tool that can greatly reduce such allocations. We have seen how it can be applied to compact data structures, as well as to store small objects, such as callables. We have also reviewed the possible downsides of using this pattern.

With the next chapter, *Chapter 11, ScopeGuard*, we move on to study more complex patterns that address broader design issues. The idioms we have learned so far are often used in the implementation of these patterns.

Questions

1. How can we measure the performance of a small fragment of code?
2. Why are small and frequent memory allocations particularly bad for performance?
3. What is local buffer optimization, and how does it work?
4. Why is an allocation of an additional buffer inside an object effectively *free*?
5. What is short string optimization?

6. What is small vector optimization?

7. Why is local buffer optimization particularly effective for callable objects?

8. What are the trade-offs to consider when using local buffer optimization?

9. When should an object not be placed in a local buffer?

11

ScopeGuard

This chapter covers a pattern that can be seen as a generalization of the RAII idiom we studied earlier. In its earliest form, it is an old and established C++ pattern, however, it is also one that has particularly benefited from the language additions in C++11, C++14, and C++17. We will witness the evolution of this pattern as the language becomes more powerful. The ScopeGuard pattern exists at the intersection of declarative programming (say what you want to happen, not how you want it done) and error-safe programs (especially exception safety). We will have to learn a bit about both before we fully understand ScopeGuard.

The following topics will be covered in this chapter:

- How can we write error-safe and exception-safe code? How does RAII make error handling easier?

- What is composability as applied to error handling?

- Why is RAII not powerful enough for error handling, and how is it generalized? How can we implement declarative error handling in C++?

Technical requirements

Here is the example code: https://github.com/PacktPublishing/Hands-On-Design-Patterns-with-CPP-Second-Edition/tree/master/Chapter11.

You will also need the Google Benchmark library installed and configured: https://github.com/google/benchmark (see *Chapter 4, Swap – From Simple to Subtle*, for installation instructions).

This chapter is rather heavy on advanced C++ features, so keep a C++ reference nearby (https://en.cppreference.com unless you want to dig through the standard itself).

Finally, a very thorough and complete implementation of ScopeGuard can be found in the Folly library: https://github.com/facebook/folly/blob/master/folly/ScopeGuard.h; it includes C++ library programming details beyond those covered in this book.

Error handling and resource acquisition is initialization

We begin by reviewing the concepts of error handling, and, in particular, writing exception-safe code in C++. The **Resource Acquisition Is Initialization (RAII)** idiom is one of the primary methods of error handling in C++. We have already dedicated an entire chapter to it, and you will need it here to make sense of what we are about to do. Let's first recognize the problem we are facing.

Error safety and exception safety

For the rest of this chapter, we will consider the following problem—suppose we are implementing a database of records. The records are stored on disk, but there is also an in-memory index for fast access to the records. The database API offers a method to insert records into the database:

```
class Record { ... };
class Database {
  public:
    void insert(const Record& r);
    ...
};
```

If the insertion succeeds, both the index and the disk storage are updated and consistent with each other. If something goes wrong, an exception is thrown.

While it appears to the clients of the database that the insertion is a single transaction, the implementation has to deal with the fact that it is done in multiple steps—we need to insert the record into the index and write it to disk. To facilitate this, the database contains two classes, each responsible for its type of storage:

```
class Database {
  class Storage { ... };    // Disk storage Storage S;
  class Index { ... };      // Memory index Index I;
  public:
  void insert(const Record& r);
  ...
};
```

The implementation of the insert() function must insert the record into both the storage and the index, there is no way around it:

```
//Example 01
void Database::insert(const Record& r) {
  S.insert(r);
  I.insert(r);
}
```

Unfortunately, either of these operations can fail. Let's see first what happens if the storage insertion fails. Let's assume that all failures in the program are signaled by throwing exceptions. If the storage insertion fails, the storage remains unchanged, the index insertion is not attempted at all, and the exception is propagated out of the `Database::insert()` function. That is exactly what we want—the insertion failed, the database is unchanged, and an exception is thrown.

So, what happens if the storage insertion succeeds but the index fails? Things are not looking so good this time—the disk is altered successfully, then the index insertion fails, and the exception propagates to the caller of `Database::insert()` to signal the insertion failure, but the truth is the insertion did not completely fail. It did not completely succeed either.

The database is left in an inconsistent state; there is a record on disk that is not accessible from the index. This is a failure to handle an error condition, exception-unsafe code, and it just won't do.

The impulsive attempt to change the order of the sub-operations does not help:

```
void Database::insert(const Record& r) {
    I.insert(r);
    S.insert(r);
}
```

Sure, everything is now fine if the index fails. But we have the same problem if the storage insertion throws an exception—we now have an entry in the index that is pointing to nowhere since the record was never written to disk.

Obviously, we cannot just ignore the exceptions thrown by `Index` or `Storage`; we have to somehow deal with them to maintain the consistency of the database. We know how to handle exceptions; that's what the `try-catch` block is for:

```
// Example 02
void Database::insert(const Record& r) {
    S.insert(r);
    try {
        I.insert(r);
    } catch (...) {
        S.undo();
        throw;     // Rethrow
    }
}
```

Again, if the storage fails, we don't need to do anything special. If the index fails, we have to undo the last operation on the storage (let's assume that it has the API to do that). Now the database is again consistent as if the insertion never happened. Even though we caught the exception thrown by the index, we still need to signal to the caller that the insertion fails, so we re-throw the exception. So far, so good.

The situation is not much different if we choose to use error codes instead of exceptions; let's consider the variant where all `insert()` functions return `true` if they succeed and `false` if they fail:

```
bool Database::insert(const Record& r) {
  if (!S.insert(r)) return false;
  if (!I.insert(r)) {
    S.undo();
    return false;
  }
  return true;
}
```

We have to check the return value of every function, undo the first action if the second one fails, and return `true` only if both actions succeed.

So far, so good; we were able to fix the simplest two-stage problem, so the code is error-safe. Now, it is time to up the complexity. Suppose that our storage needs some cleanup to be performed at the end of the transaction, for example, the inserted record is not in its final state until we call the `Storage::finalize()` method (maybe this is done so `Storage::undo()` can work, and after the insertion is finalized it can no longer be undone). Note the difference between `undo()` and `finalize()`; the former must be called only if we want to roll back the transaction, while the latter must be called if the storage insertion succeeded, regardless of what happens after.

Our requirements are met with this flow of control:

```
// Example 02a:
void Database::insert(const Record& r) {
  S.insert(r);
  try {
    I.insert(r);
  } catch (...) {
    S.undo();
    S.finalize();
    throw;
  }
  S.finalize();
}
```

Or we have something similar in the case of returning error codes (for the rest of this chapter, we will use exceptions in all our examples, but conversion to error codes is not hard).

This is already getting ugly, particularly the part about getting the cleanup code (in our case, `S.finalize()`) to run in every execution path. It's only going to get worse if we have a more complex sequence of actions that must all be undone unless the entire operation succeeds. Here is the control flow for three actions, each with its own rollback and cleanup:

```
if (action1() == SUCCESS) {
  if (action2() == SUCCESS) {
```

```
      if (action3() == FAIL) {
        rollback2();
        rollback1();
      }
      cleanup2();
    } else {
      rollback1();
    }
    cleanup1();
}
```

The obvious problem is the explicit tests for success, either as conditionals or as try-catch blocks. The more serious problem is that this way of error handling is not composable. The solution for N+1 actions is not the code for N actions with some bits added to it; no, we have to go deep inside the code and add the right pieces there. But we have already seen the C++ idiom for solving this very problem.

Resource Acquisition Is Initialization

The RAII idiom binds resources to objects. The object is constructed when the resource is acquired, and the resource is deleted when the object is destroyed. In our case, we are interested only in the second half, the destruction. The advantage of the RAII idiom is that the destructors of all local objects must be called when the control reaches the end of the scope, regardless of how it happens (`return`, `throw`, `break`, and so on). Since we struggled with the cleanup, let's hand that off to an RAII object:

```
// Example 02b:
class StorageFinalizer {
  public:
  StorageFinalizer(Storage& S) : S_(S) {}
  ~StorageFinalizer() { S_.finalize(); }
  private:
  Storage& S_;
};
void Database::insert(const Record& r) {
  S.insert(r);
  StorageFinalizer SF(S);
  try {
    I.insert(r);
  } catch (...) {
    S.undo();
    throw;
  }
}
```

The `StorageFinalizer` object binds to the `Storage` object when it is constructed and calls `finalize()` when it is destroyed. Since there is no way to exit the scope in which the `StorageFinalizer` object is defined without calling its destructor, we do not need to worry about the control flow, at least for the cleanup; it is going to happen. Note that the `StorageFinalizer` is properly constructed after the storage insertion succeeds; if the first insertion fails, there is nothing to finalize.

This code works, but it looks somehow half-done; we have two actions that are performed at the end of the function, and the first one (cleanup, or `finalize()`) is automated while the second one (rollback, or `undo()`) is not. Also, the technique is still not composable; here is the flow of control for three actions:

```
class Cleanup1() {
  ~Cleanup1() { cleanup1(); }
  ...
};
class Cleanup2() {
  ~Cleanup2() { cleanup2(); }
  ...
};

action1();
Cleanup1 c1;
try {
  action2();
  Cleanup2 c2;
  try {
    action3();
  } catch (...) {
    rollback2();
    throw;
  }
} catch (...) {
  rollback1();
}
```

Again, to add another action, we have to add a try-catch block deep in the code. On the other hand, the cleanup part by itself is perfectly composable. Consider what the previous code looks like if we don't need to do a rollback:

```
action1();
Cleanup1 c1;
action2();
Cleanup2 c2;
```

If we need one more action, we simply add two lines at the end of the function, and the cleanup happens in the right order. If we could do the same for the rollback, we would be all set.

We cannot simply move the call to undo() into a destructor of another object; the destructors are always called, but the rollback happens only in the case of an error. But we can make the destructor call the rollback conditionally:

```cpp
// Example 03:
class StorageGuard {
  public:
  StorageGuard(Storage& S) : S_(S) {}
  ~StorageGuard() {
    if (!commit_) S_.undo();
  }
  void commit() noexcept { commit_ = true; }
  private:
  Storage& S_;
  bool commit_ = false;
};
void Database::insert(const Record& r) {
  S.insert(r);
  StorageFinalizer SF(S);
  StorageGuard SG(S);
  I.insert(r);
  SG.commit();
}
```

Examine the code now; if the storage insertion fails, the exception is thrown and the database is unchanged. If it succeeds, two RAII objects are constructed. The first one will unconditionally call S.finalize() at the end of the scope. The second one will call S.undo() unless we commit the change first by calling the commit() method on the StorageGuard object. That will happen unless the index insertion fails, in which case an exception is thrown, the rest of the code in the scope is bypassed, and the control jumps straight to the end of the scope (the closing }) where the destructors of all local objects are called. Since we never called commit() in this scenario, the StorageGuard is still active and will undo the insertion. Note also that there are no explicit try-catch blocks at all: the actions that used to be in the catch clause are now done by the destructors. The exception should be, of course, caught eventually (in all examples that accompany this chapter, the exception is caught in main()).

The destructors of the local objects are called in reverse construction order. This is important; if we have to undo the insertion, this can be done only until the action is finalized, so the rollback has to happen before the cleanup. Therefore, we construct the RAII objects in the correct order—first, the cleanup (to be done last), then the rollback guard (to be done first, if necessary).

The code now looks very nice, with no try-catch blocks at all. In some ways, it does not look like regular C++. This programming style is called **declarative programming**; it is a programming paradigm in which the program logic is expressed without explicitly stating the flow of control (the opposite, and the more common in C++, is **imperative programming**, where the program describes which steps to do and in what order, but not necessarily why). There are declarative programming languages (the prime example is SQL), but C++ is not one of them. Nonetheless, C++ is very good at implementing constructs that allow the creation of higher-order languages on top of C++, and so we have implemented a declarative error-handling language. Our program now says that after the record was inserted into storage, two actions are pending—the cleanup and the rollback.

The rollback is disarmed if the entire function succeeds. The code looks linear, without the explicit flow of control, in other words, declarative.

Nice as it is, it is also far from perfect. The obvious problem is that we have to write a guard or a finalizer class for every action in our program. The less obvious one is that writing these classes correctly is not easy, and we have not done a particularly good job so far. Take a moment to figure out what is missing before looking at the fixed version here:

```cpp
class StorageGuard {
  public:
  StorageGuard(Storage& S) : S_(S), commit_(false) {}
  ~StorageGuard() { if (!commit_) S_.undo(); }
  void commit() noexcept { commit_ = true; }
  private:
  Storage& S_;
  bool commit_;
  // Important: really bad things happen if
  // this guard is copied!
  StorageGuard(const StorageGuard&) = delete;
  StorageGuard& operator=(const StorageGuard&) = delete;
};
void Database::insert(const Record& r) {
  S.insert(r);
  StorageFinalizer SF(S);
  StorageGuard SG(S);
  I.insert(r);
  SG.commit();
}
```

What we need is a general framework that lets us schedule an arbitrary action to be executed at the end of the scope, unconditionally or conditionally. The next section presents the pattern that provides such a framework, ScopeGuard.

The ScopeGuard pattern

In this section, we learn how to write the on-exit action RAII classes such as the ones we implemented in the previous section, but without all the boilerplate code. This can be done in C++03 but is much improved in C++14, and again in C++17.

ScopeGuard basics

Let's start with the more difficult problem—how to implement a generic rollback class, a generic version of `StorageGuard` from the last section. The only difference between that and the cleanup class is that the cleanup is always active, but the rollback is canceled after the action is committed. If we have the conditional rollback version, we can always take out the condition check, and we get the cleanup version, so let's not worry about that for now.

In our example, the rollback is a call to the `S.undo()` method. To simplify the example, let's start with a rollback that calls a regular function, not a member function:

```
void undo(Storage& S) { S.undo(); }
```

Once the implementation is finished, the program should look something like this:

```
{
  S.insert(r);
  ScopeGuard SG(undo, S);      // Approximate desired syntax
  ...
  SG.commit();                 // Disarm the scope guard
}
```

This code tells us (in a declarative manner!) that if the insert action succeeded, we schedule the rollback to be done upon exiting the scope. The rollback will call the `undo()` function with the argument S, which in turn will undo the insertion. If we made it to the end of the function, we disarm the guard and disable the rollback call, which commits the insertion and makes it permanent.

A much more general and reusable solution was proposed by Andrei Alexandrescu in the *Dr. Dobbs* article in 2000 (`http://www.drdobbs.com/cpp/generic-change-the-way-you-write-excepti/184403758?`). Let's look at the implementation and analyze it:

```
// Example 04
class ScopeGuardImplBase {
  public:
  ScopeGuardImplBase() = default;
  void commit() const noexcept { commit_ = true; }
  protected:
  ScopeGuardImplBase(const ScopeGuardImplBase& other) :
    commit_(other.commit_) { other.commit(); }
  ~ScopeGuardImplBase() {}
```

```
    mutable bool commit_ = false;
};

template <typename Func, typename Arg>
class ScopeGuardImpl : public ScopeGuardImplBase {
  public:
  ScopeGuardImpl(const Func& func, Arg& arg) :
    func_(func), arg_(arg) {}
  ~ScopeGuardImpl() { if (!commit_) func_(arg_); }
  private:
  const Func& func_;
  Arg& arg_;
};


template <typename Func, typename Arg>
ScopeGuardImpl<Func, Arg>
MakeGuard(const Func& func, Arg& arg) {
  return ScopeGuardImpl<Func, Arg>(func, arg);
}
```

From the top, we have the base class for all the scope guards, `ScopeGuardImplBase`. The base class holds the commit flag and the code to manipulate it; the constructor initially creates the guard in the armed state, so the deferred action will happen in the destructor. The call to `commit()` will prevent that from happening and make the destructor do nothing. Finally, there is a copy constructor that creates a new guard in the same state as the original but then disarms the original guard. This is so the rollback does not happen twice, from the destructors of both objects. The object is copyable but not assignable. We use C++03 features for everything here, including the disabled assignment operator. This implementation is fundamentally C++03; the few C++11 twists are just icing on the cake (that is about to change in the next section).

There are several details of the implementation of `ScopeGuardImplBase` that may seem odd and need elaboration. First of all, the destructor is not virtual; this is not a typo or a bug, this is intentional, as we will see later. Second, the `commit_` flag is declared `mutable`. This is, of course, so that it can be changed by the `commit()` method, which we declared `const`. So, why is `commit()` declared `const`? One reason is so we can call it on the source object from the copy constructor, to transfer the responsibility for the rollback from the other object to this one. In this sense, the copy constructor really does a move and will be officially declared as such later. The second reason for `const` will become obvious later (it is related to the non-virtual destructor, of all things).

Let's now turn to the derived class, `ScopeGuardImpl`. This is a class template with two type parameters—the first is the type of the function or any other callable object we are going to call for the rollback, and the second is the type of the argument. Our rollback function is restricted, for now, to having only one argument. That function is called in the destructor of the `ScopeGuard` object unless the guard was disarmed by calling `commit()`.

Finally, we have a factory function template, `MakeGuard`. This is a very common idiom in C++; if you need to create an instantiation of a class template from the constructor arguments, use a template function that can deduce the type of the parameters and that of the return value from the arguments (in C++17 class templates can do that too, as we will see later).

How is this all used to create a guard object that will call undo (S) for us? Like this:

```
void Database::insert(const Record& r) {
  S.insert(r);
  const ScopeGuardImplBase& SG = MakeGuard(undo, S);
  I.insert(r);
  SG.commit();
}
```

The `MakeGaurd` function deduces the types of the undo () function and the argument S and returns a `ScopeGuard` object of the corresponding type. The return is by value, so there is a copy involved (the compiler may choose to elide the copy as an optimization, but is not required to). The returned object is a temporary variable, it has no name and binds it to the base class reference SG (casting from the derived class to the base class is implicit for both pointers and references). The lifetime of the temporary variable is until the closing semicolon of the statement that created it, as everyone knows. But then, what does the SG reference point to after the end of the statement? It has to be bound to something, as references cannot be unbound, they are not like NULL pointers. The truth is, "everyone" knows wrong, or rather only mostly right—usually, the temporaries indeed live until the end of the statement. However, binding a temporary to a const reference extends its lifetime to coincide with the lifetime of the reference itself. In other words, the unnamed temporary `ScopeGuard` object created by `MakeGuard` will not be destroyed until the SG reference goes out of scope. Const-ness is important here, but do not worry, you can't forget it; the language does not permit binding non-const references to temporary variables, so the compiler will let you know. So this explains the commit () method; it has to be const since we are going to call it on the const reference (and, therefore, the commit_ flag has to be mutable).

But what about the destructor? At the end of the scope, the destructor of the `ScopeGuardImplBase` class will be called, since that is the type of reference that goes out of scope. The base class destructor itself does nothing, it's the derived class that has the destructor we want. A polymorphic class with a virtual destructor would have served us right, but we did not take that route. Instead, we availed ourselves of yet another special rule in the C++ standard concerning the const references and temporary variables—not only is the lifetime of the temporary variable extended but also the destructor of the derived class, that is the actual class that was constructed, is going to be called at the end of the scope.

Note that this rule applies only to destructors; you still cannot call derived class methods on the base class SG reference. Also, the lifetime extension works only when the temporary variable is directly bound to a const reference. It does not work if, for example, we initialize another const reference from the first one. This is why we had to return the `ScopeGuard` object from the MakeGuard function by value; if we tried to return it by reference, the temporary would be bound to that reference, which is going to go away at the end of the statement. The second reference, SG, initialized from the first one, would not have extended the lifetime of the object.

The function implementation we just saw comes very close to the original goal, it is just a bit more verbose (and it mentions `ScopeGuardImplBase` instead of the promised `ScopeGuard`). Fear not, for the last step is merely syntactic sugar:

```
using ScopeGuard = const ScopeGuardImplBase&;
```

Now, we can write this:

```
// Example 04a
void Database::insert(const Record& r) {
  S.insert(r);
  ScopeGuard SG = MakeGuard(undo, S);
  I.insert(r);
  SG.commit();
}
```

This is as far as we are going to get with the language tools we've used so far. Ideally, the desired syntax would be as follows (and we are not very far off):

```
ScopeGuard SG(undo, S);
```

We can tidy up our `ScopeGuard` a bit by making use of the C++11 features. First of all, we can properly disable the assignment operator. Second, we can stop pretending that our copy constructor is anything other than a move constructor:

```
// Example 05
class ScopeGuardImplBase {
  public:
  ScopeGuardImplBase() = default;
  void commit() const noexcept { commit_ = true; }
  protected:
  ScopeGuardImplBase(ScopeGuardImplBase&& other) :
    commit_(other.commit_) { other.commit(); }
  ~ScopeGuardImplBase() {}
  mutable bool commit_ = false;
  private:
  ScopeGuardImplBase& operator=(const ScopeGuardImplBase&)
    = delete;
};
using ScopeGuard = const ScopeGuardImplBase&;

template <typename Func, typename Arg>
class ScopeGuardImpl : public ScopeGuardImplBase {
```

```
  public:
  ScopeGuardImpl(const Func& func, Arg& arg) :
    func_(func), arg_(arg) {}
  ~ScopeGuardImpl() { if (!commit_) func_(arg_); }

  ScopeGuardImpl(ScopeGuardImpl&& other) :
    ScopeGuardImplBase(std::move(other)),
    func_(other.func_),
    arg_(other.arg_) {}
  private:
  const Func& func_;
  Arg& arg_;
};

template <typename Func, typename Arg>
ScopeGuardImpl<Func, Arg>
MakeGuard(const Func& func, Arg& arg) {
  return ScopeGuardImpl<Func, Arg>(func, arg);
}
```

Moving to C++14, we can make one more simplification and deduce the return type of the
MakeGuard function:

```
// Example 05a
template <typename Func, typename Arg>
auto MakeGuard(const Func& func, Arg& arg) {
  return ScopeGuardImpl<Func, Arg>(func, arg);
}
```

There is still one concession we had to make—we did not really need the undo(S) function what we
really wanted was to call S.undo(). This is done just as easily with a member function variant of
ScopeGuard. In fact, the only reason we have not done so from the beginning is to make the example
easier to follow; the member function pointer syntax is not the most straightforward aspect of C++:

```
// Example 06
template <typename MemFunc, typename Obj>
class ScopeGuardImpl : public ScopeGuardImplBase {
  public:
  ScopeGuardImpl(const MemFunc& memfunc, Obj& obj) :
    memfunc_(memfunc), obj_(obj) {}
  ~ScopeGuardImpl() { if (!commit_) (obj_.*memfunc_)(); }
  ScopeGuardImpl(ScopeGuardImpl&& other) :
    ScopeGuardImplBase(std::move(other)),
    memfunc_(other.memfunc_),
    obj_(other.obj_) {}
  private:
```

```
    const MemFunc& memfunc_; Obj& obj_;
};

template <typename MemFunc, typename Obj>
auto MakeGuard(const MemFunc& memfunc, Obj& obj) {// C++14
    return ScopeGuardImpl<MemFunc, Obj>(memfunc, obj);
}
```

Of course, if both versions of the ScopeGuard template are used in the same program, we have to rename one of them. Also, our function guard is limited to calling functions with only one argument, while our member function guard can call only member functions with no arguments. In C++03, this problem is solved in a tedious but reliable way—we have to create versions of the implementation, ScopeGuardImpl0, ScopeGuardImpl1, ScopeGuardImpl2, and so on, for functions with zero, one, two, and so on arguments. We then create ScopeObjGuardImpl0, ScopeObjGuardImpl1, and so on, for member functions with zero, one, two, and so on arguments. If we do not create enough, the compiler will let us know. The base class remains the same for all these variants of the derived class, and so is the ScopeGuard typedef.

In C++11, we have variadic templates that are designed to address this exact problem, but we're not going to see such an implementation here. There is no reason for it; we can do so much better than that, as you are about to see.

Generic ScopeGuard

We are now firmly in C++11 territory, nothing that you are about to see has a C++03 equivalent of any practical worth.

Our ScopeGuard has, so far, allowed us to all arbitrary functions as rollback for any action. Just like the hand-crafted guard objects, the scope guards are composable and guarantee exception safety. But our implementation, so far, is somewhat limited in what exactly we can call to implement the rollback; it has to be a function or a member function. While this seems to cover a lot, we may want to call, for example, two functions to do a single rollback. We could, of course, write a wrapper function for that, but that sets us back on the path toward single-purpose hand-crafted rollback objects.

There is, in truth, another problem with our implementation. We decided to capture the function argument by reference:

```
    ScopeGuardImpl(const Func& func, Arg& arg);
```

This mostly works, unless the argument is a constant or a temporary variable; then, our code will not compile.

C++11 gives us another way to create arbitrary callable objects: lambda expressions. Lambdas are actually classes, but they behave like functions in that they can be called with parentheses. They can take arguments, but they can also capture any arguments from the containing scope, and that often obviates the need to pass arguments to the function call itself. We can also write arbitrary code and package it in a lambda expression. This sounds ideal for the scope guard; we could just write something that says, *at the end of the scope run this code.*

Let's see what a lambda expression ScopeGuard looks like:

```
// Example 07
class ScopeGuardBase {
  public:
  ScopeGuardBase() = default;
  void commit() noexcept { commit_ = true; }
  protected:
  ScopeGuardBase(ScopeGuardBase&& other) noexcept :
    commit_(other.commit_) { other.commit(); }
  ~ScopeGuardBase() = default;
  bool commit_ = false;
  private:
  ScopeGuardBase& operator=(const ScopeGuardBase&)
    = delete;
};

template <typename Func>
class ScopeGuard : public ScopeGuardBase {
  public:
  ScopeGuard(Func&& func) : func_(std::move(func)) {}
  ScopeGuard(const Func& func) : func_(func) {}
  ~ScopeGuard() { if (!commit_) func_(); }
  ScopeGuard(ScopeGuard&& other) = default;
  private:
  Func func_;
};

template <typename Func>
ScopeGuard<Func> MakeGuard(Func&& func) {
  return ScopeGuard<Func>(std::forward<Func>(func));
}
```

The base class is essentially the same as before, except we are not going to use the const reference trick anymore, and so the Impl suffix is gone; what you see is not an implementation aid but the base of the guard class itself; it contains the reusable code dealing with the commit_ flag. Since we do not use the const reference, we can stop pretending that the commit() method is const, and drop the mutable declaration from commit_.

The derived class, on the other hand, is much different. First of all, there is only one class for all types of rollback, and the argument type parameter is gone; instead, we have a functional object that is going to be a lambda, and it'll contain all the arguments that it needs. The destructor is the same as before (except for the missing argument to the callable `func_`), and so is the move constructor. But the primary constructor of the object is quite different; the callable object is stored by value, and initialized from either a `const` reference or an r-value reference, with a suitable overload selected automatically by the compiler.

The `MakeGuard` function is largely unchanged, and we do not need two of them; we can use perfect forwarding (`std::forward`) to forward the argument of any type to one of the constructors of `ScopeGuard`.

Here is how this ScopeGuard is used:

```
void Database::insert(const Record& r) {
  S.insert(r);
  auto SG = MakeGuard([&] { S.undo(); });
  I.insert(r);
  SG.commit();
}
```

The punctuation-rich construct that is used as an argument to `MakeGuard` is the lambda expression. It creates a callable object, and calling this object will run the code in the body of the lambda, in our case `S.undo()`. There is no S variable declared in the lambda object itself, so it has to be captured from the containing scope. All captures are done by reference (`[&]`). Finally, the object is called with no arguments; the parentheses can be omitted, although `MakeGuard([&]() { S.undo(); });` is also valid. The function does not return anything, that is, the return type is `void`; it does not have to be explicitly declared. Note that, so far, we have used C++11 lambdas and have not taken advantage of the more powerful C++14 lambdas. This will usually be the case with ScopeGuard, although in practice, you would probably use C++14 just for auto-deduced return types, if nothing else.

We have, until now, intentionally set aside the matter of the regular cleanup and focused on error handling and the rollback. Now that we have a decent working ScopeGuard, we can tie up loose ends quite easily:

```
// Example 07a
void Database::insert(const Record& r) {
  S.insert(r);
  auto SF = MakeGuard([&] { S.finalize(); });
  auto SG = MakeGuard([&] { S.undo(); });
  I.insert(r);
  SG.commit();
}
```

As you can see, nothing special needs to be added to our framework to support the cleanup. We simply create another ScopeGuard that we never disarm.

We should also point out that, in C++17, we no longer need the `MakeGuard` function since the compiler can deduce the template arguments from the constructor:

```
// Example 07b
void Database::insert(const Record& r) {
    S.insert(r);
    ScopeGuard SF = [&] { S.finalize(); };    // C++17
    ScopeGuard SG = [&] { S.undo(); };
    I.insert(r);
    SG.commit();
}
```

As long as we are on the subject of making ScopeGuard use prettier, we should consider some helpful macros. We can easily write a macro for the cleanup guard, the one that is always executed. We would like the resulting syntax to look something like this (if this isn't declarative enough, I don't know what is):

```
ON_SCOPE_EXIT { S.finalize(); };
```

We can, in fact, get that very syntax. First of all, we need to generate a name for the guard, what used to be called `SF`, and we need it to be something unique. From the cutting edge of modern C++, we are now reaching decades back, to classic C and its preprocessor tricks, to generate a unique name for an anonymous variable:

```
#define CONCAT2(x, y) x##y
#define CONCAT(x, y) CONCAT2(x, y)
#ifdef __COUNTER__
#define ANON_VAR(x) CONCAT(x, __COUNTER__)
#else
#define ANON_VAR(x) CONCAT(x, __LINE__)
#endif
```

The `__CONCAT__` macros are how you concatenate two tokens in the preprocessor (and yes, you need two of them, that's the way the preprocessor works). The first token will be a user-specified prefix, and the second one is something unique. Many compilers support a preprocessor variable, `__COUNTER__`, that is incremented every time it's used, so it's never the same. However, it is not in the standard. If `__COUNTER__` is not available, we have to use the line number `__LINE__` as a unique identifier. Of course, it is only unique if we don't put two guards on the same line, so don't.

Now that we have a way to generate an anonymous variable name, we can implement the ON_SCOPE_EXIT macro. It would be trivial to implement one where the code is passed as a macro argument, but it would not give us the syntax we want; the argument has to be in parentheses, so at best we could get `ON_SCOPE_EXIT(S.finalize();)`. Also, commas in the code confuse the preprocessor, since it interprets them as a separator between the macro arguments. If you look carefully at the syntax we requested, `ON_SCOPE_EXIT { S.finalize(); };`, you will realize that this macro has no arguments at all, and the body of the lambda expression is just typed after the no-argument macro.

The macro expansion, therefore, ends on something that can be followed by an opening curly brace. Here is how this is done:

```
// Example 08
struct ScopeGuardOnExit {};
template <typename Func>
ScopeGuard<Func> operator+(ScopeGuardOnExit, Func&& func) {
    return ScopeGuard<Func>(std::forward<Func>(func));
}
#define ON_SCOPE_EXIT auto ANON_VAR(SCOPE_EXIT_STATE) = \
    ScopeGuardOnExit() + [&]()
```

The macro expansion declares an anonymous variable that starts with SCOPE_EXIT_STATE, followed by a unique number, and it ends on the incomplete lambda expression, [&](), that is completed by the code in the curly braces. In order to not have a closing parenthesis of the former MakeGuard function, which the macro cannot generate (the macro is expanded before the lambda body, so it cannot generate any code after that), we have to replace the MakeGuard function (or the ScopeGuard constructor in C++17) with an operator. The choice of the operator does not matter; we use +, but we could use any binary operator. The first argument to the operator is a temporary object of a unique type, it limits the overload resolution only to the operator+() defined previously (the object itself is not used at all, we only need its type). The operator+() itself is exactly what MakeGuard used to be, it deduces the type of the lambda expression and creates the corresponding ScopeGuard object. The only downside of this technique is that the closing semicolon at the end of the ON_SCOPE_EXIT statement is required, and should you forget it, the compiler will remind you in the most obscure and opaque way possible.

Our program code can now be further tidied up:

```
// Example 08
void Database::insert(const Record& r) {
    S.insert(r);
    ON_SCOPE_EXIT { S.finalize(); };
    auto SG = ScopeGuard([&] { S.undo(); });
    I.insert(r);
    SG.commit();
}
```

It is tempting to apply the same technique to the second guard. Unfortunately, this is not so simple; we have to know the name of this variable so we can call commit() on it. We can define a similar macro that does not use an anonymous variable but instead takes the user-specified name:

```
// Example 08a
#define ON_SCOPE_EXIT_ROLLBACK(NAME) \
    auto NAME = ScopeGuardOnExit() + [&]()
```

We can use it to complete the conversion of our code:

```
// Example 08a
void Database::insert(const Record& r) {
  S.insert(r);
  ON_SCOPE_EXIT { S.finalize(); };
  ON_SCOPE_EXIT_ROLLBACK(SG){ S.undo(); };
  I.insert(r);
  SG.commit();
}
```

At this point, we should revisit the issue of composability. For three actions, each with its own rollback and cleanup, we now have the following:

```
action1();
ON_SCOPE_EXIT { cleanup1; };
ON_SCOPE_EXIT_ROLLBACK(g2){ rollback1(); };
action2();
ON_SCOPE_EXIT { cleanup2; };
ON_SCOPE_EXIT_ROLLBACK(g4){ rollback2(); };
action3();
g2.commit();
g4.commit();
```

One can see how this pattern is trivially extended to any number of actions. An observant reader might wonder whether they have noticed a bug in the code, though—should not the rollback guards be dismissed in reverse construction order? This is not a bug, although neither is the reverse order of all commit() calls. The reason is that commit() cannot throw an exception, it was declared noexcept, and indeed its implementation is such that no exception can be thrown. This is vitally important for the ScopeGuard pattern to work; if commit() could throw, then there would be no way to guarantee that all rollback guards are properly disarmed. At the end of the scope, some actions would be rolled back, and others would not, leaving the system in an inconsistent state.

While ScopeGuard was primarily designed to make exception-safe code easier to write, the interaction of the ScopeGuard pattern with exceptions is far from trivial, and we should spend more time on it.

ScopeGuard and exceptions

The ScopeGuard pattern is designed to correctly run various cleanup and rollback operations automatically upon exiting a scope, no matter what caused the exit—normal completion by reaching the end of the scope, an early return, or an exception. This makes writing error-safe code in general, and exception-safe code in particular, much easier; as long as we queued up the right guards after every action, the correct cleanup and error handling will automatically happen. That is, of course, assuming that ScopeGuard itself is functioning correctly in the presence of exceptions. We are going to learn how to make sure it does and how to use it to make the rest of the code error-safe.

What must not throw an exception

We have already seen that the `commit()` function that is used to commit an action and disarm the rollback guard must never throw an exception. Fortunately, that is easy to guarantee since all this function does is set a flag. But what happens if the rollback function also fails, and throws an exception?

```
// Example 09
void Database::insert(const Record& r) {
  S.insert(r);
  auto SF = MakeGuard([&] { S.finalize(); });
  auto SG = MakeGuard([&] { S.undo(); });
              // What if undo() can throw?
  I.insert(r);     // Let's say this fails
  SG.commit();     // Commit never happens
}               // Control jumps here and undo() throws
```

The short answer is *nothing good*. In general, we have a conundrum—we cannot allow the action, in our case the storage insertion, to remain, but we also cannot undo it, since that also fails. Specifically, in C++, two exceptions cannot propagate at the same time. For that reason, the destructors are not allowed to throw exceptions; a destructor may be called when an exception is thrown, and if that destructor also throws, we now have two exceptions propagating at the same time. If this happens, the program immediately terminates. This is not so much a shortcoming of the language as a reflection on the unsolvable nature of the problem in general; we cannot let things stay the way they are, but we also failed in an attempt to change something. There aren't any good options left.

In general, there are three ways a C++ program can handle this situation. The best option is not to fall into this trap—if the rollback cannot throw, none of this will happen. A well-written exception-safe program thus goes to great lengths to provide non-throwing rollback and cleanup. For example, the main action can produce the new data and have it ready, then making the data available to the callers is as simple as swapping a pointer, definitely a non-throwing operation. The rollback involves only swapping the pointer back and maybe deleting something (as we already said, destructors should not throw exceptions; if they do, the program behavior is undefined).

The second option is to suppress the exception in the rollback. We tried to undo the operation, it didn't work, there is nothing else we can do about it, so let's push on. The danger here is that the program may be in an undefined state, and every operation from this point forward may be incorrect. This is, however, the worst-case scenario. In practice, the consequences may be less severe. For example, for our database, we may know that if the rollback fails, there is a chunk of disk space that is claimed by the record but is unreachable from the index. The caller will be correctly informed that the insertion failed, but we have wasted some disk space. This may be preferable to terminating the program outright. If this is what we want, we have to catch any exceptions that might be thrown by the ScopeGuard action:

```
// Example 09a
template <typename Func>
class ScopeGuard : public ScopeGuardBase {
```

```
public:
  ...
  ~ScopeGuard() {
    if (!commit_) try { func_(); } catch (...) {}
  }
  ...
};
```

The `catch` clause is empty; we catch everything but do nothing. This implementation is sometimes called a *shielded ScopeGuard*.

The final option is to allow the program to fail. That will happen with no effort on our part if we just let two exceptions happen, but we could also print a message or otherwise signal to the user what is about to happen and why. If we want to insert our own dying action before the program terminates, we have to write code that is very similar to previously:

```
template <typename Func>
class ScopeGuard : public ScopeGuardBase {
  public:
  ...
  ~ScopeGuard() {
    if (!commit_) try { func_(); } catch (...) {
      std::cout << "Rollback failed" << std::endl;
      throw;    // Rethrow
    }
  }
  ...
};
```

The key difference is the `throw;` statement without any arguments. This re-throws the exception we caught and allows it to continue propagating.

The difference between the last two code fragments highlights a subtle detail that we have glossed over earlier, but one that will become important later. It is imprecise to say that in C++ the destructors should not throw exceptions. The correct statement is that an exception should not propagate out of the destructor. The destructor can throw anything it wants as long as it also catches it:

```
class LivingDangerously {
  public:
  ~LivingDangerously() {
    try {
      if (cleanup() != SUCCESS) throw 0;
      more_cleanup();
    } catch (...) {
      std::cout << "Cleanup failed, proceeding anyway" <<
```

```
        std::endl;
        // No rethrow - this is critical!
      }
    }
  };
```

Up until now, we have dealt with exceptions mostly as a nuisance; the program has to remain in a well-defined state if something somewhere throws something, but other than that, we have no use for these exceptions; we just pass them on. On the other hand, our code could work with any type of error handling, be it exceptions or error codes. If we knew for sure that errors are always signaled by exceptions and that any return from a function other than an exception thrown is a success, we could take advantage of that to automate the detection of success or failure and therefore allow a commit or rollback to happen as needed.

Exception-driven ScopeGuard

We are now going to assume that if a function returns without throwing an exception, the operation has succeeded. If the function throws, it obviously failed. The objective now is to get rid of the explicit call to commit() and instead detect whether the destructor of ScopeGuard is executed because an exception was thrown, or because the function returned normally.

There are two parts to this implementation. The first part is specifying when we want the action to be taken. The cleanup guard must be executed regardless of how we exit the scope. The rollback guard is executed only in case of failure. For completeness, we can also have a guard that is executed only if the function has succeeded. The second part is determining what actually happened.

We will start with the second part. Our ScopeGuard now needs two additional parameters that will tell us whether it should be executed on success and whether it should be executed on failure (both can be enabled at the same time). Only the destructor of ScopeGuard needs to be modified:

```
template <typename Func, bool on_success, bool on_failure>
class ScopeGuard {
  public:
    ...
    ~ScopeGuard() {
      if ((on_success && is_success()) ||
          (on_failure && is_failure())) func_();
    }
    ...
};
```

We still need to figure out how to implement the pseudo-functions is_success() and is_failure(). Remember that failure means that an exception was thrown. In C++, we have a function for that: `std::uncaught_exception()`. It returns true if an exception is currently propagating, and false otherwise. Armed with this knowledge, we can implement our guard:

```
// Example 10
template <typename Func, bool on_success, bool on_failure>
class ScopeGuard {
  public:
  ...
  ~ScopeGuard() {
    if ((on_success && !std::uncaught_exception()) ||
        (on_failure && std::uncaught_exception())) func_();
  }
  ...
};
```

Now, back to the first part: `ScopeGuard` will execute the delayed action if the conditions are right, so how do we tell it what conditions are right? Using the macro approach we developed earlier, we can define three versions of the guard—ON_SCOPE_EXIT is always executed, ON_SCOPE_SUCCESS is executed only if no exceptions were thrown, and ON_SCOPE_FAILURE is executed if an exception was thrown. The latter replaces our ON_SCOPE_EXIT_ROLLBACK macro, only now it too can use an anonymous variable name, since there are no explicit calls to `commit()`. The three macros are defined in a very similar way, we just need three different unique types instead of one ScopeGuardOnExit, so we can decide which `operator+()` to call:

```
// Example 10
struct ScopeGuardOnExit {};
template <typename Func>
auto operator+(ScopeGuardOnExit, Func&& func) {
  return
    ScopeGuard<Func, true, true>(std::forward<Func>(func));
}
#define ON_SCOPE_EXIT auto ANON_VAR(SCOPE_EXIT_STATE) = \
  ScopeGuardOnExit() + [&]()

struct ScopeGuardOnSuccess {};
template <typename Func>
auto operator+(ScopeGuardOnSuccess, Func&& func) {
  return
    ScopeGuard<Func, true, false>(std::forward<Func>(func));
}
#define ON_SCOPE_SUCCESS auto ANON_VAR(SCOPE_EXIT_STATE) =\
  ScopeGuardOnSuccess() + [&]()

struct ScopeGuardOnFailure {};
template <typename Func>
auto operator+(ScopeGuardOnFailure, Func&& func) {
```

```
    return
      ScopeGuard<Func, false, true>(std::forward<Func>(func));
}
#define ON_SCOPE_FAILURE auto ANON_VAR(SCOPE_EXIT_STATE) =\
    ScopeGuardOnFailure() + [&]()
```

Each overload of operator+() constructs a ScopeGuard object with different Boolean arguments that control when it does and does not execute. Each macro directs the lambda expression to the desired overload by specifying the type of the first argument to the operator+() using one of the unique tree types we defined just for this purpose: ScopeGuardOnExit, ScopeGuardOnSuccess, and ScopeGuardOnFailure.

This implementation can pass simple and even fairly elaborate tests and appears to work. Unfortunately, it has a fatal flaw—it does not correctly detect success or failure. To be sure, it works fine if our Database::insert() function was called from the normal control flow, where it may or may not succeed. The problem is we may call Database::insert() from a destructor of some other object, and that object may be used in a scope where an exception is thrown:

```
class ComplexOperation {
  Database db_;
  public:
  ...
  ~ComplexOperation() {
    try {
      db_.insert(some_record);
    } catch (...) {}    // Shield any exceptions from insert()
  }
};


{
  ComplexOperation OP;
  throw 1;
}    // OP.~ComplexOperation() runs here
```

Now, db_.insert() runs in the presence of an uncaught exception, and so std::uncaught_exception() will return true. The problem is this is not the exception we were looking for. This exception does not indicate that insert() failed, but it will be treated as such and the database insertion will be undone.

What we really need is to know how many exceptions are currently propagating. This may seem a strange statement since C++ does not allow multiple exceptions to propagate at the same time. However, we have already seen that this is an oversimplification; the second exception can propagate just fine as long as it does not escape the destructor. In the same manner, three or more exceptions can propagate if we have nested destructor calls, we just have to catch them all in time. To solve this problem correctly, we need to know how many exceptions were propagating when the Database::insert()

function was called. Then, we can compare it with the number of exceptions propagating at the end of the function, however we got there. If these numbers are the same, insert() did not throw any exceptions, and any preexisting ones are not our concern. If a new exception was added, insert() has failed, and the exit handling must change accordingly.

C++17 lets us implement this detection; in addition to the previous std::uncaught_exception(), which is deprecated (and removed in C++20), we now have a new function, std::uncaught_exceptions(), which returns the number of currently propagating exceptions. We can now implement this UncaughtExceptionDetector to detect new exceptions:

```
// Example 10a
class UncaughtExceptionDetector {
  public:
  UncaughtExceptionDetector() :
    count_(std::uncaught_exceptions()) {}
  operator bool() const noexcept {
    return std::uncaught_exceptions() > count_;
  }
  private:
  const int count_;
};
```

With this detector, we can finally implement the automatic ScopeGuard:

```
// Example 10a
template <typename Func, bool on_success, bool on_failure>
class ScopeGuard {
  public:
  ...
  ~ScopeGuard() {
  if ((on_success && !detector_) ||
      (on_failure && detector_)) func_();
  }
  ...
  private:
  UncaughtExceptionDetector detector_;
  ...
};
```

The need to use C++17 may present a (hopefully short-term) obstacle to using this technique in programs constrained to older versions of the language. While there is no other standard-compliant, portable way to solve this problem, most modern compilers have ways to get to the uncaught exception counter. This is how it is done in GCC or Clang (the names starting with ___ are GCC internal types and functions):

```
// Example 10b
namespace __cxxabiv1 {
```

```
    struct cxa_eh_globals;
    extern "C" cxa_eh_globals* cxa_get_globals() noexcept;
}
class UncaughtExceptionDetector {
  public:
  UncaughtExceptionDetector() :
    count_(uncaught_exceptions()) {}
  operator bool() const noexcept {
    return uncaught_exceptions() > count_;
  }
  private:
  const int count_;
  int uncaught_exceptions() const noexcept {
    return *(reinterpret_cast<int*>(
      static_cast<char*>( static_cast<void*>(
        cxxabiv1::cxa_get_globals())) + sizeof(void*)));
  }
};
```

Whether we use the exception-driven ScopeGuard or the explicitly named ScopeGuard (perhaps to handle error codes as well as exceptions), we have accomplished our goals—we now can specify deferred actions that must be taken at the end of a function or any other scope.

At the end of this chapter, we will show another implementation of ScopeGuard that can be found in several sources on the web. This implementation deserves some consideration, but you should be aware of the downsides as well.

Type-erased ScopeGuard

If you search online for a ScopeGuard example, you may chance upon an implementation that uses `std::function` instead of a class template. The implementation itself is quite simple:

```
// Example 11
class ScopeGuard {
  public:
  template <typename Func> ScopeGuard(Func&& func) :
    func_(std::forward<Func>(func)) {}
  ~ScopeGuard() { if (!commit_) func_(); }
  void commit() const noexcept { commit_ = true; }
  ScopeGuard(ScopeGuard&& other) :
    commit_(other.commit_), func_(std::move(other.func_)) {
    other.commit();
  }
  private:
  mutable bool commit_ = false;
```

```
    std::function<void()> func_;
    ScopeGuard& operator=(const ScopeGuard&) = delete;
};
```

Note that this ScopeGuard is a class, not a class template. It has template constructors that can accept the same lambda expression or another callable object as the other guard. But the variable used to store that expression has the same type no matter what the type of the callable is. That type is `std::function<void()>`, a wrapper for any function that takes no arguments and returns nothing. How can a value of any type be stored in an object of some fixed type? That is the magic of type erasure, and we have a whole chapter dedicated to it (*Chapter 6, Understanding Type Erasure*). This non-template ScopeGuard makes the code that uses it simpler (at least in the pre-C++17 version) because there are no types to deduce:

```
void Database::insert(const Record& r) {
    S.insert(r);
    ScopeGuard SF([&] { S.finalize(); });
    ScopeGuard SG([&] { S.undo(); });
    I.insert(r);
    SG.commit();
}
```

There is, however, a serious downside to this approach—a type-erased object has to do a non-trivial amount of computation to achieve its magic. As a minimum, it involves an indirect or a virtual function call, and often some memory is allocated and deallocated as well.

Using the lessons of *Chapter 6, Understanding Type Erasure*, we can come up with a slightly more efficient type erasure implementation; in particular, we can insist that the on-exit callable fits into the guard's buffer:

```
// Example 11
template <size_t S = 16>
class ScopeGuard : public CommitFlag {
    alignas(8) char space_[S];
    using guard_t = void(*)(void*);
    guard_t guard_ = nullptr;
    template<typename Callable>
    static void invoke(void* callable) {
        (*static_cast<Callable*>(callable))();
    }
    mutable bool commit_ = false;
public:
    template <typename Callable,
              typename D = std::decay_t<Callable>>
    ScopeGuard(Callable&& callable) :
        guard_(invoke<Callable>) {
```

```
      static_assert(sizeof(Callable) <= sizeof(space_));
      ::new(static_cast<void*>(space_))
        D(std::forward<Callable>(callable));
    }
    ScopeGuard(ScopeGuard&& other) = default;
    ~ScopeGuard() { if (!commit_) guard_(space_); }
};
```

We can compare the runtime cost of the type-erased ScopeGuard versus the template ScopeGuard using the Google Benchmark library. The results will depend on what operation we are guarding, of course: for long computations and expensive on-exit actions, a slight difference in ScopeGuard's run time makes no difference. The difference is going to be more pronounced if the computations in the scope and upon exiting the scope are fast:

```
void BM_nodelete(benchmark::State& state) {
  for (auto _ : state) {
    int* p = nullptr;
    ScopeGuardTypeErased::ScopeGuard SG([&] { delete p; });
    p = rand() < 0 ? new int(42) : nullptr;
  }
  state.SetItemsProcessed(state.iterations());
}
```

Note that the memory is never allocated (rand() returns non-negative random numbers) and the pointer p is always null, so we are benchmarking the call to rand() plus the overhead of ScopeGuard. For comparison, we can call delete explicitly, without the guard. The result shows that the template version of the guard has no measurable overhead, while both type-erased implementations have some:

```
Benchmark                                   Time
-------------------------------------------------
BM_nodelete_explicit                      4.48 ns
BM_nodelete_type_erased                   6.29 ns
BM_nodelete_type_erased_fast              5.48 ns
BM_nodelete_template                      4.50 ns
```

Our own type-erased version adds about 1 nanosecond to each iteration, and the one based on std::function takes almost twice as long. Benchmarks of this sort are strongly affected by compiler optimizations and can produce very different results in response to even slight changes in the code. For example, let us change the code to always construct the new object:

```
void BM_nodelete(benchmark::State& state) {
  for (auto _ : state) {
    int* p = nullptr;
    ScopeGuardTypeErased::ScopeGuard SG([&] { delete p; });
    p = rand() >= 0 ? new int(42) : nullptr;
```

```
  }
  state.SetItemsProcessed(state.iterations());
}
```

Now we call the operator new on each iteration of the loop, so the corresponding deletion must happen as well. This time, the compiler was able to optimize the template ScopeGuard much better than the type-erased one:

```
Benchmark                               Time
---------------------------------------------
BM_delete_explicit                     4.54 ns
BM_delete_type_erased                  13.4 ns
BM_delete_type_erased_fast             12.7 ns
BM_delete_template                     4.56 ns
```

Overall, there isn't much of a reason to use type erasure here. The runtime cost may be negligible or significant, but there is usually nothing to gain in exchange. The only advantage of the type-erased version is that the guard itself is always of the same type. But the type of the guard is almost always irrelevant: we create the variable as auto or using constructor template argument deduction, and the only explicit operation we may need to do on the guard is to disarm it. Thus, we never need to write any code that depends on the guard's type. Overall, the template-based ScopeGuard, with or without macros, remains the pattern of choice for automatically releasing resources and performing other actions at the end of a scope.

Summary

In this chapter, we have studied, in detail, one of the best C++ patterns for writing exception-safe and error-safe code. The ScopeGuard pattern allows us to schedule an arbitrary action, a fragment of C++ code, to be executed upon completion of a scope. The scope may be a function, the body of a loop, or just a scope inserted into the program to manage the lifetime of local variables. The actions that are executed to the end may be conditional on the successful completion of the scope, however, that is defined. The ScopeGuard pattern works equally well when success or failure are indicated by return codes or exceptions, although in the latter case we can automatically detect the failure (with return codes, the programmer has to explicitly specify which return values mean success and which do not). We have observed the evolution of the ScopeGuard pattern as more recent language features are used. In its optimal form, ScopeGuard provides a simple declarative way to specify post-conditions and deferred actions, such as cleanup or rollback, in a manner that is trivially composable for any number of actions that need to be committed or undone.

The next chapter describes another very C++-specific pattern, the Friends Factory, which is a kind of Factory, only instead of objects during the execution of a program, it manufactures functions during its compilation.

Questions

1. What is an error-safe or exception-safe, program?

2. How can we make a routine that performs several related actions be error-safe?

3. How does RAII assist in writing error-safe programs?

4. How does the ScopeGuard pattern generalize the RAII idiom?

5. How can the program automatically detect when a function exits successfully and when it fails?

6. What are the advantages and drawbacks of a type-erased ScopeGuard

12

Friend Factory

In this chapter, we are going to talk about making friends. We mean C++ friends here, not friends of C++ (you find those in your local C++ users group). In C++, friends of classes are functions or other classes that are granted special access to the class. In that way, they are not so different from your friends. But C++ can just manufacture friends as needed, on demand!

The following topics will be covered in this chapter:

- How do friend functions work in C++ and what do they do?

- When should you use friend functions versus class member functions?

- How to combine friends and templates

- How to generate friend functions from templates

Technical requirements

The example code for this chapter can be found at the following GitHub link: `https://github.com/PacktPublishing/Hands-On-Design-Patterns-with-CPP-Second-Edition/tree/master/Chapter12`.

Friends in C++

Let's start by reviewing the way in which C++ grants friendship to classes, and the effects of this action, as well as when and for what reasons the friendship should be used ("my code does not compile until I add `friend` everywhere" is not a valid reason, but an indication of a poorly designed interface - redesign your classes instead).

How to grant friendship in C++

A *friend* is a C++ concept that applies to classes and affects the access to class members (*access* is what `public` and `private` control). Usually, public member functions and data members are accessible to anyone, and private ones are only accessible to other member functions of the class itself. The following code does not compile because the data member C:x_ is private:

```
// Example 01
class C {
  int x_;
  public:
  C(int x) : x_(x) {}
};
C increase(C c, int dx) {
  return C(c.x_ + dx);      // Does not compile
}
```

The easiest way to solve this particular problem is to make increase() a member function, but let's stay with this version for a moment. The other option is to relax access and make C::x_ public. That is a bad idea because it exposes x_ - not just to increase(), but to any other code out there that wants to directly modify an object of type C. What we need is to make x_ public, or at least accessible, to increase() and to nobody else. This is done with a friend declaration:

```
// Example 02
class C {
  int x_;
  public:
  C(int x) : x_(x) {}
  friend C increase(C c, int dx);
};
C increase(C c, int dx) {
  return C(c.x_ + dx);      // Now it compiles
}
```

The friend declaration does nothing more than give the specified function the same access as the class member functions get. There is also a form of friend declaration that grants friendship not to a function, but to a class; this is just a way to grant friendship to all member functions of that class.

Friends versus member functions

We do have to come back to the question, why not just make increase() a member function of the C class? In the example given in the preceding section, there's no reason to, really - increase() is clearly meant to be a part of the public interface of the C class since it's one of the operations C supports. It needs special access to do its work, so it should be a member function. There are, however, cases where member functions come with limitations, or even cannot be used at all.

Let us consider an addition operator for the same C class - it's what is needed to make an expression such as c1 + c2 compile if both variables are of type C. The addition, or operator+(), can be declared as a member function:

```
// Example 03
class C {
  int x_;
  public:
  C(int x) : x_(x) {}
  C operator+(const C& rhs) const {
    return C(x_ + rhs.x_);
  }
};
...
C x(1), y(2);
C z = x + y;
```

This code compiles and does exactly what we want; there does not seem to be anything obviously wrong with it. That's because there isn't - so far. But we can add more than just objects of type C:

```
// Example 03
C x(1);
C z = x + 2;
```

This also compiles, and points to a subtle detail in the declaration of the C class - we did not make the C(int) constructor explicit. This constructor now introduces an implicit conversion from int to C, and that is how the expression x + 2 compiles - first, 2 is converted into a temporary object, C(2), using the constructor we provided, and second the member function, x.operator+(const C&), is called - the right-hand side is the temporary object we just created. The temporary object itself is deleted right after the expression is evaluated. The implicit conversion from integers is rather broad and might have been an oversight. Let's assume that it wasn't and that we really want the expression such as x + 2 to compile. What's not to like, then? Again, nothing so far. The objectionable feature of our design is what comes next:

```
// Example 03
C x(1);
C z = 2 + x; // Does NOT compile
```

If x + 2 compiles, you would reasonably expect 2 + x to compile and give the same result (there are areas of math where the addition is not commutative, but let's stick with the arithmetic here). The reason it does not compile is that the compiler cannot get to operator+() in the C class from here, and no other operator+() is available for these arguments. The x + y expression, when used with member function operators, is just syntactic sugar for the equivalent, if verbose, call to x.operator+(y). The same is true for any other binary operator such as multiplication or comparison.

The point is, the member function operator is invoked on the first argument of the expression (so technically, x + y and y + x are not identical; the member function is called on different objects, but the implementation is such that both give the same result). In our case, the member function would have to be invoked on the number 2, which is an integer and has no member functions at all. So, how did the expression x + 2 compile? Quite simple, really: x + by itself implies x.operator+(), and the argument is whatever comes after +. In our case, it's 2. So, either x.operator+(2) compiles, or it does not, but in either case, the search for operator+ to the call is over. The implicit conversion from int in our C class makes this call compile. So, why doesn't the compiler attempt a conversion on the first argument? The answer is, it never does because it has no guidance on what to convert it into - there may be any number of other types that have the operator+() member function, and some of them may accept the C class as their argument, or something C can be converted to. The compiler does not attempt to explore the almost infinite number of such possible conversions.

If we want to use plus in expressions where the first type may be a built-in type or any other type that does not have or cannot have a member function of operator+(), then we have to use a non-member function. No problem; we know how to write those:

```
C operator+(const C& lhs, const C& rhs) {
   return C(lhs.x_ + rhs.x_);
}
```

But now we have lost access to the private data member C::x_, so our non-member operator+() does not compile either. We have seen the solution to that problem in the previous section - we need to make it a friend:

```
// Example 04
class C {
   int x_;
   public:
   C(int x) : x_(x) {}
   friend C operator+(const C& lhs, const C& rhs);
};
C operator+(const C& lhs, const C& rhs) {
   return C(lhs.x_ + rhs.x_);
}

...

C x(1), y(2);
C z1 = x + y;
C z2 = x + 2;
C z3 = 1 + y;
```

Now, everything compiles and works as intended - the non-member function operator+() is simply a non-member function with two arguments of type const C&. The rules for it are the same as for any other such function.

We can avoid typing the declaration of the `operator+()` twice if we define its body *in situ* (immediately following the declaration, inside the class):

```
// Example 05
class C {
   int x_;
   public:
   C(int x) : x_(x) {}
   friend C operator+(const C& lhs, const C& rhs) {
     return C(lhs.x_ + rhs.x_);
   }
};
```

The latter example is subtly different from the previous one, but usually, you won't be able to see the difference, so it is simply a matter of style - moving the body of the function into the object makes the object itself longer, but defining the function outside of the class is more typing (as well as a possible divergence between the friend declaration and the actual function, if the code is ever changed). We will explain the intricacies of in situ friend declarations in the next section.

Either way, the friend function is really a part of the class public interface, but, for technical reasons, we prefer a non-member function in this case. There is even a case when the non-member function is the only choice. Consider the C++ input/output operators, such as the inserter, or `operator<<()`, which are used to write objects out into a stream (for example, `std::cout`). We want to be able to print an object of type C like so:

```
C c1(5);
std::cout << c1;
```

There is no standard `operator<<()` for our type C, so we have to declare our own. The inserter is a binary operator, just like plus (it has parameters on either side), so, were it a member function, it would have to be one on the left-hand side object. Look at the preceding statement - the left-hand side object in the `std::cout << c1` expression is not our object, `c1`, but the standard out stream, `std::cout`. That's the object we would have to add a member function to, but we cannot - `std::cout` is declared somewhere in the C++ standard library headers, and there is no way to extend its interface, at least not in a direct manner. Member functions on the C class can be declared by us, but this does not help - only the member functions of the left-hand side object are considered. The only alternative is a non-member function. The first argument has to be `std::ostream&`:

```
// Example 06
class C {
   ...
   friend std::ostream& operator<<(std::ostream& out,
                                   const C& c);
};
```

```
std::ostream& operator<<(std::ostream& out, const C& c) {
  out << c.x_;
  return out;
}
```

This function has to be declared as a friend since it also needs access to the private data of the C class. It can also be defined *in situ*:

```
// Example 07
class C {
  int x_;
  public:
  C(int x) : x_(x) {}
  friend std::ostream& operator<<(std::ostream& out,
                                  const C& c) {
    out << c.x_;
    return out;
  }
};
```

By convention, the return value is the same stream object, so the inserter operators can be chained:

```
C c1(5), c2(7);
std::cout << c1 << c2;
```

The way the last statement is interpreted is (std::cout << c1) << c2, which boils down to operator<<(operator<<(std::cout, c1), c2). The outer operator<<() is called on the return value of the inner operator<<(), which is the same: std::cout. Again, the inserter is part of the public interface of the C class - it makes the objects of type C printable. However, it has to be a non-member function.

The introduction to the use of friend in C++ glossed over several subtle details that are occasionally important, so let us spend some time to elucidate them.

Subtle details of friendship

First, let us talk about the effect of declaring a friend function without defining it (i.e., without the in situ implementation):

```
// Example 08
class C {
  friend C operator+(const C& lhs, const C& rhs);
  ...
};
C operator+(const C& lhs, const C& rhs) { ... }
```

By the way, it makes no difference whatsoever whether you put the friend declaration into the public or private part of the class. But about the friend declaration itself: which function did we grant access to? This is the first mention of an operator+() with this signature in our program (its definition must come later, after class C itself was declared). Turns out that the friend statement does double duty: it also acts as a forward declaration for the function.

Of course, there is no rule that prevents us from forward-declaring the same function ourselves:

```
// Example 09
class C;
C operator+(const C& lhs, const C& rhs);
class C {
    friend C operator+(const C& lhs, const C& rhs);
    ...
};
C operator+(const C& lhs, const C& rhs) { ... }
```

There is no need to use a separate forward declaration just to use friend, but it may be necessary for other reasons if we want to use operator+() earlier in our program.

Note that the compiler does not warn you if the friend forward declaration does not match the function definition, or if the friend statement does not match the forward declaration. If the function signature in the friend statement differs from the actual function, you will have granted friendship to some other function that is forward-declared but not defined anywhere. It is highly likely that you will get a syntax error compiling the real function because it now has no special access to the class and can't access its private members. But the error message won't say anything about a mismatch between the friend statement and the function definition. You just have to know that if you granted friendship to a function and the compiler doesn't see it, there is a discrepancy between the function signature in the friend statement and the one in the function definition.

Of course, if the friend statement also defines the function instead of just declaring it, then it is not acting as a forward declaration at all. But in this case, there is another subtlety, namely, in which scope is the new function defined? Consider that if you declare a static function inside a class, that function exists in the scope of the class itself. If we have a class C with a static function f(), the proper name of this function outside of the class is C::f:

```
class C {
    static void f(const C& c);
    ...
};
C c;
C::f(c);     // Must be called as C::f() not f()
```

It is easy to see that the same does not apply to the `friend` functions:

```
class C {
  friend void f(const C& c);
  ...
};
C c;
C::f(c);      // Does not compile - not a member
```

This makes sense, considering that we already saw that the `friend` statement without a definition forward-declared a function that is defined outside of the class. So, if the `friend` declaration forward-declared a function in the scope containing the class (in our case, the global scope, but could have been a `namespace`), then the `friend` statement with an in situ definition must define a function in the same scope, i.e., it injects a function into the outer scope of the class. Right? Yes, but not entirely.

In practice, odds are good that you would never notice the "not entirely" part, and everything behaves as if the function was simply injected into the containing scope. It takes a rather contrived example to demonstrate what really happens:

```
// Example 10
class C {
  static int n_;
  int x_;
  public:
  C(int x) : x_(x) {}
  friend int f(int i) { return i + C::n_; }
  friend int g(const C& c) { return c.x_ + C::n_; }
};
int C::n_ = 42;
...
C c(1);
f(0);         // Does not comppile - no ADL
g(c);         // Compiles fine
```

Here we have two `friend` functions, `f()` and `g()`, both are defined at the point of declaration. The function `g()` behaves as if it was declared in the global scope (or the scope containing the class C, if we used a `namespace`). But a call to `f()` in the same scope does not compile, and the error message is going to be "function f is not declared in this scope" or something to that effect. The wording of compiler error messages varies widely, but that is the gist of the error: the call to `f()` did not find a function to call. The only difference between the functions `f()` and `g()` is their arguments; that turns out to be key.

To understand this, we have to know how the compiler looks up a function name when you write a function call such as `f(0)`. First of all, this is a non-member function, so the compiler looks only for those (it could also be a functor – a class with `operator()`, but that is not important right now since we don't have any). Second, the compiler searches the current scope, the one where the call is made, and all containing scopes such as nested function bodies, classes, and namespaces) all the way to the global scope. But this is not the end of it: the compiler also looks at the arguments of the function and searches the scope (or scopes) where each of these argument types is declared. This step is called the **argument-dependent lookup (ADL)**, also known as the **Koenig lookup** after Andrew Koenig (who denies inventing it). After all these lookups are done and the compiler finds every function with the matching name in one of the scopes we just listed, the compiler does the overload resolution on all the functions it found (i.e., there is no priority given to any particular scope).

So, what does this have to do with the `friend` functions? Only this: according to the standard, a function defined by the `friend` statement is injected into the scope containing the class, but *it can be found only by the argument-dependent lookup.*

This explains the behavior we just saw: both the functions `f()` and `g()` are injected into the global scope since that is the scope containing class C. Function `g()` has an argument of type `const C&`, so it is found by the ADL in the scope containing the class C. Function `f()` has an argument of type `int`, and the built-in types are not considered to be declared in any scope, they "just are." Since no ADL can be performed and the functions defined as friends are only found by ADL, function `f()` cannot be found at all.

Note that this situation is very fragile. For example, if we forward-declare the same function, it can be found in the scope where it is forward-declared and does not need the ADL:

```
// Example 11
int f(int i);      // Forward declaration
class C {
  ...
  friend int f(int i) { return i + C::n_; }
};
f(0);          // No problem
```

The same happens if the `friend` statement only declared the function, to be defined later:

```
// Example 12
class C {
  ...
  friend int f(int i);      // Forward declaration
};
int f(int i) { return i + C::n_; }
f(0);          // No problem
```

Why don't we see this as a problem more often? Because most of the time, functions declared as friends inside classes have at least one argument of the type related to the class itself (such as a pointer or a reference). Both `operator+()` and `operator<<()` we have seen earlier fall into that category. After all, the only reason to declare a function as a friend is so it can access private members of the class, but the function would not need this access if it did not operate on an object of the class type. As a non-member function, how would it get access to such an object if not through its arguments? Of course, there are ways, but these situations rarely happen in practice.

Yet another subtle and potentially dangerous case happens when a program defines its own operator new. This is not illegal, class-specific memory allocation operators are often necessary. But declaring one is not that simple. There are two common uses of a custom operator new: the first one is where the operator is defined for the class that is being allocated, usually inside the class itself. These are called class-specific operators, and they aren't the subject of our interest now. We need to explain the second common case, where the custom operator new is defined to allocate memory using a specific allocator class. This is how it is usually done:

```
// Example 13
class Alloc {
  void* alloc(size_t s);      // Allocates memory
  void dealloc(void* p);       // Releases memory
  friend void* operator new (size_t s, Alloc* a);
  friend void operator delete(void* p, Alloc* a);
};
void* operator new (size_t s, Alloc* a) {
  return a->alloc(s);
}
void operator delete(void* p, Alloc* a) {
  a->dealloc(p);
}
class C { ... };
Alloc a;
C* c = new (&a) C;
```

There are several details to note: first, our allocator class Alloc has an overload for operator new: the first argument of every operator new is mandatory and must be the size of the allocation (the compiler fills that in). The second argument (and the third, etc, if necessary) are arbitrary; in our case, it's the pointer to the allocator class that is going to provide memory for this allocation. The operator new itself is a function in the global scope, and it is declared as a friend of class Alloc. If you are wondering how you can call the matching operator delete that we also declared, the answer is you cannot; this operator is used only by the compiler itself in case the allocation by operator new succeeded but the constructor of the new object throws an exception. The compiler will use operator delete with the arguments matching those of operator new. But this is not how you will delete this object when its lifetime is over: there is no way to add extra arguments to a delete expression, so you'll have to call the destructor yourself and then explicitly return the memory to the allocator.

This works exactly as intended. The compiler looks for the best match for the call to operator new(size_t, Alloc*) and finds our custom operator new in the global scope as intended.

Now, you may decide to move the body of the operator into the `friend` statement to save some typing as well as avoid the possibility of the `friend` declaration and the actual `operator new` definition ever getting out of sync. This is done with only a minor change:

```cpp
// Example 14
class Alloc {
  void* alloc(size_t s);      // Allocates memory
  void dealloc(void* p);        // Releases memory
  friend void* operator new (size_t s, Alloc* a) {
    return a->alloc(s);
  }
  friend void operator delete(void* p, Alloc* a) {
    a->dealloc(p);
  }
};
class C { ... };
Alloc a;
C* c = new (&a) C;
```

This program will almost certainly compile. It will work correctly on some compilers and produce horrible memory corruption on others. Unfortunately, those other compilers are correct. This is what is going on: the *new expression* (which is the standard name for the syntax "new ... some-type") has special rules for looking up the matching `operator new`. Specifically, the lookup is done in the scope of the class that is being constructed (class C in our case) and in the global scope (these rules are defined in the section [expr.new] of the standard). Note that there is no lookup in the scope of the arguments to `operator new` itself, i.e., no argument-dependent lookup. Since the function defined in situ by the `friend` statement can be found only by the argument-dependent lookup, it is not found at all. But how does the program compile then? This happens because of another overload for `operator new`, the so-called *placement new*. This overload has the form:

```cpp
void* new(size_t size, void* addr) { return addr; }
```

It is declared in the standard header `<new>`, which is included by so many other headers that your program is very likely to include it even if you did not do so explicitly.

The intent for the placement new is to construct an object in memory that was allocated earlier (we used this to construct objects in the space reserved inside a class when we studied type erasure in the eponymous chapter earlier). But it is also a possible match to our call of operator new(`size_t`, `Alloc*`) because `Alloc*` can be implicitly converted to `void*`. Our own overload, which does not require this conversion, would be a better match, but, unfortunately, when defined in situ, it is not found by the lookup. The result is that the object of type C is constructed in the memory already occupied by the allocator object itself, corrupting the latter object in the process.

You can test your compilers using our examples: when defined outside of the class, the custom `operator new` should be invoked and the program should work as intended. But when defined by the `friend` statement, only the placement new should be found (some compilers will also issue a warning about overwriting an already constructed object).

So far, our classes are just regular classes, not templates, and our non-member functions have declared friends that were just regular non-template functions. Now, let's consider what, if anything, needs to change if the class becomes a template.

Friends and templates

Both classes and functions in C++ can be templates, and we can have several different combinations - a class template can grant friendship to a non-template function if its parameter types don't depend on the template parameters; this is not a particularly interesting case, and certainly does not solve any of the problems we're dealing with now. When the friend function needs to operate on the template parameter types, making the right friends becomes trickier.

Friends of template classes

Let's start by making our C class into a template:

```
template <typename T> class C {
   T x_;
   public:
   C(T x) : x_(x) {}
};
```

We still want to add objects of type C and print them out. We have already considered reasons why the former is better accomplished with a non-member function, and the latter cannot be done in any other way. These reasons remain valid for class templates as well.

No problem - we can declare template functions to go with our template classes and do the work that the non-template functions used to do in the previous section. Let's start with `operator+()`:

```
template <typename T>
C<T> operator+(const C<T>& lhs, const C<T>& rhs) {
   return C<T>(lhs.x_ + rhs.x_);
}
```

This is the same function that we saw previously, only made into a template that can accept any instantiation of the class template C. Note that we parameterized this template on the type T, that is, the template parameter of C. We could, of course, simply declare the following:

```
template <typename C>
C operator+(const C& lhs, const C& rhs) { // NEVER do this!
```

```
    return C<T>(lhs.x_ + rhs.x_);
}
```

However, this introduces - into the global scope no less - an `operator+()` that claims to accept two arguments of any type. Of course, it really only handles types that have an `x_` data member. So, what are we going to do when we have a template class, `D`, that is also addable but has a `y_` data member instead?

The earlier version of the template is at least restricted to all possible instantiations of the class template `C`. Of course, it suffers from the same problem as our very first attempt at a non-member function - it does not have access to the private data member `C<T>::x_`. No problem - this chapter is about friends, after all. But friends to what? The entire class template, `C`, is going to have a friend declaration, just one for all `T` types, and that has to work for every instantiation of the template function `operator+()`. It appears that we have to grant friendship to the entire function template:

```
// Example 15
template <typename T> class C {
  T x_;
  public:
  C(T x) : x_(x) {}
  template <typename U>
  friend C<U> operator+(const C<U>& lhs, const C<U>& rhs);
};
template <typename T>
C<T> operator+(const C<T>& lhs, const C<T>& rhs) {
  return C<T>(lhs.x_ + rhs.x_);
}
```

Note the correct syntax - the keyword `friend` appears after the template and its parameters but before the return type of the function. Also, note that we had to rename the template parameter of the nested friend declaration - the `T` identifier is already used for the class template parameter. Similarly, we could rename the template parameter `T` in the definition of the function itself, but we don't have to - just like in function declarations and definitions, the parameter is just a name; it is only meaningful within each declaration - two declarations for the same function can use different names for the same parameter. What we can do instead is move the function body inline, into the class:

```
// Example 16
template <typename T> class C {
  int x_;
  public:
  C(int x) : x_(x) {}
  template <typename U>
  friend C<U> operator+(const C<U>& lhs, const C<U>& rhs) {
    return C<U>(lhs.x_ + rhs.x_);
```

```
        }
    };
```

You might point out that we have blown a rather wide hole in the encapsulation of the template class C – by granting friendship of any instantiation of C<T> to the entire template function, we have, for example, made the operator+(const C&<double>, const C&<double>) instantiation a friend of C<int>. This is clearly not necessary, although it may not be immediately obvious where the harm is in that (an example that shows actual harm would be rather convoluted, as necessary). But this misses a much more serious problem with our design, which becomes apparent as soon as we start using it to add something. It works, up to a point:

```
C<int> x(1), y(2);
C<int> z = x + y; // So far so good...
```

But only up to a point:

```
C<int> x(1), y(2);
C<int> z1 = x + 2; // This does not compile!
C<int> z2 = 1 + 2; // Neither does this!
```

But was this not the very reason to use a non-member function? What happened to our implicit conversions? This used to work! The answer is in the details - it used to work, but for a non-template function, operator+(). The conversion rules for a template function are very different. The exact technical details can be gleaned from the standard, with great diligence and effort, but this is the gist of it - when considering non-member, non-template functions, the compiler will look for all functions with the given name (operator+, in our case), then check if they accept the right number of parameters (possibly considering default arguments), then check if, for each such function, for each of its parameters, a conversion from the supplied argument to the specified parameter type exists (the rules on which conversions, exactly, are considered, and again fairly complex, but let's say that both user-given implicit conversions and built-in conversions such as non-const to const are considered). If this process yields only one function, that function is called (otherwise the compiler either selects the *best* overload or complains that several candidates are equally possible and the call is ambiguous).

For template functions, this process would again yield an almost unlimited number of candidates - every template function with the name operator+() would have to be instantiated on every known type just to check if enough type conversions are available to make it work. Instead, a much simpler process is attempted - in addition to all non-template functions described in the previous paragraph (in our case, none), the compiler also considers instantiations of template functions with the given name (again, operator+) and the types of all parameters equal to the types of the function arguments at the call site (so-called trivial conversions, such as adding const, are allowed).

In our case, the argument types in the x + 2 expression are C<int> and int, respectively. The compiler looks for an instantiation of the template function, operator+, that accepts two arguments of this type, and the user-given conversions are not considered. There is no such function, of course, and so the call to operator+() cannot be resolved.

The root of the problem is that we really want the user-given conversions to be used by the compiler automatically, but this is not going to happen as long as we are trying to instantiate a template function. We could declare a non-template function for `operator+(const C<int>&, const C<int>&)`, but, with a C template class, we would have to declare one for every T type that the C class might be instantiated on.

The template friend factory

What we need is to automatically generate a non-template function for every T type that's used to instantiate the class template C. Of course, it is impossible to generate all of these functions in advance - there is a nearly unlimited number of T types that could, in theory, be used with the template class C. Fortunately, we do not need to generate `operator+()` for every one of such types - we only need them for the types that were actually used with this template in our program.

Generating friends on demand

The pattern that we are about to see is a very old one, and was introduced by John Barton and Lee Nackman in 1994 for a completely different purpose - they used it to work around certain limitations of the compilers that existed at the time. The inventors proposed the name *Restricted Template Expansion*, which was never widely used. Years later, Dan Sacks coined the name *Friends Factory*, but the pattern is also sometimes referred to simply as the *Barton-Nackman trick*.

The pattern looks very simple and very similar to the code we wrote earlier throughout this chapter:

```
// Example 17
template <typename T> class C {
  int x_;
  public:
  C(int x) : x_(x) {}
  friend C operator+(const C& lhs, const C& rhs) {
    return C(lhs.x_ + rhs.x_);
  }
};
```

We are taking advantage of a very specific C++ feature, and so the code must be written precisely. A non-template friend function is defined inside the class template. This function must be defined inline; it cannot be declared a friend and then defined later, except as an explicit template instantiation - we could have declared the friend function inside the class and then defined `operator+<const C<int>>&, const C<int>&)`, which would work for C<int> but not C<double> (since we do not know what types the callers may instantiate later, this is not very useful). It may have the parameters of the T type, the template parameter, the C<T> type (which, inside the class template, can be referred to as simply C), and any other type that is either fixed or depends only on the template parameters, but it may not be a template itself. Every instantiation of the C class template, with any combination of template parameter types, generates exactly one non-template, non-member function with the specified name. Note that the generated functions are non-template functions; they are regular functions, and the usual conversion rules apply to them. We are now back to the non-template `operator+()`, and all conversions work exactly the way we want them to:

```
C<int> x(1), y(2);
C<int> z1 = x + y; // This works
C<int> z2 = x + 2; // and this too
C<int> z3 = 1 + 2; // so does this
```

This is it - this is the whole pattern. There are a few details we must note. First of all, the keyword `friend` cannot be omitted. A class cannot normally generate a non-member function, except for declaring a friend. Even if the function does not need access to any private data, in order to automatically generate non-template functions from instantiations of class templates, these functions have to be declared friends (static non-member functions can be generated in a similar manner, but the binary operators cannot be static functions - the standard explicitly forbids it). Second, the generated function is placed in the scope containing the class but must be found by the argument-dependent lookup, as we learned earlier in this chapter. For example, let's define the inserter operator for our C template class, but not before wrapping the entire class in a namespace:

```
// Example 18
namespace NS {
template <typename T> class C {
  int x_;
  public:
  C(int x) : x_(x) {}
  friend C operator+(const C& lhs, const C& rhs) {
    return C(lhs.x_ + rhs.x_);
  }
  friend std::ostream&
  operator<<(std::ostream& out, const C& c) {
    out << c.x_;
    return out;
  }
};
} // namespace NS
```

We can now both add and print the objects of the C type:

```
NS::C<int> x(1), y(2);
std::cout << (x + y) << std::endl;
```

Note that, even though the C class template is now in the namespace NS, and has to be used as such (NS::C<int>), we did not need to do anything special to invoke either `operator+()` or `operator<<()`. This does not mean that they were generated in the global scope. No, they are still in the namespace NS, but what we see is the argument-dependent lookup in action - when looking for a function named `operator+()`, for example, the compiler considers the candidates in the current scope (that is, the global scope, and there aren't any), as well as the scope in which the arguments to the function are defined. In our case, at least one of the arguments to `operator+()` is of type `NS::C<int>`, which automatically brings all functions declared in the `NS` namespace into play. The friend factory generates its functions in the scope containing the class template, which is, of course, also the `NS` namespace. Thus, the lookup finds the definition, and both the + and << operations are resolved exactly the way we would want them to be. Rest assured that this is by design and is no accident; the argument lookup rules are fine-tuned to produce this desired and expected result.

It is easy to prove that, even though friend functions are generated in the scope containing the class (in our case namespace `NS`), they can only be found by the argument-dependent lookup. A straightforward attempt to find the function without using an argument-dependent lookup will fail:

```
auto p = &NS::C<int>::operator+; // Does not compile
```

There is also a connection between the friend factory pattern and one of the patterns we studied earlier.

The friend factory and the Curiously Recurring Template Pattern

The friend factory is a pattern that synthesizes a non-template, non-member function from every instantiation of a class template - every time the template is instantiated on a new type, a new function is generated. For its parameters, this function can use any types we can declare in that instantiation of the class template. Usually, this is the class itself, but it can be any type the template knows about.

In this manner, the friend factory can be employed together with the **Curiously Recurring Template Pattern (CRTP)** that we studied in *Chapter 8, The Curiously Recurring Template Pattern*. Recall that the main idea of the CRTP is that a class inherits from an instantiation of a base class template that is parameterized by the derived class type. Consider what we have here - a template for a base class that is automatically instantiated with every class derived from it, and it knows what that type is. This seems like an ideal place to put a friend factory. Of course, the operators generated by the base class have to not only know what the type of the object is that they operate on but also what to do with it (for example, how to print it). Sometimes, the necessary data actually resides in the base class, and then the base class can provide complete implementations. But it is rare that the derived class adds so little to the base class. The more common use of CRTP, together with the friend factory, is to implement some operators in a standard way through some other functionality. For example, `operator!=()` can be implemented through `operator==()`:

```
// Example 19
template <typename D> class B {
  public:
  friend bool operator!=(const D& lhs, const D& rhs) {
    return !(lhs == rhs);
```

```
  }
};
template <typename T> class C : public B<C<T>> {
  T x_;
  public:
  C(T x) : x_(x) {}
  friend bool operator==(const C& lhs, const C& rhs) {
    return lhs.x_ == rhs.x_;
  }
};
```

Here, the derived class C uses the friend factory pattern to generate a non-template function for the binary operator==() directly from the instantiation of the class template. It also inherits from the base class B, which triggers an instantiation of that template as well, which in turn generates a non-template function for operator!=() for every type for which we have generated operator==().

The second use of CRTP is to convert member functions to non-member functions. For example, the binary operator+() is sometimes implemented in terms of operator+=(), which is always a member function (it acts on its first operand). To implement the binary operator+(), someone has to take care of the conversions to that object's type, and then operator+=() can be called. These conversions are provided by the binary operators that are generated by the common CRTP base class when using the friend factory. Similarly, the inserter operator can be generated if we establish the convention that our classes have a print() member function:

```
// Example 20
template <typename D> class B {
  public:
  friend D operator+(const D& lhs, const D& rhs) {
    D res(lhs);
    res += rhs; // Convert += to +
    return res;
  }
  friend std::ostream&
  operator<<(std::ostream& out, const D& d) {
    d.print(out);
    return out;
  }
};
template <typename T> class C : public B<C<T>> {
  T x_;
  public:
  C(T x) : x_(x) {}
  C operator+=(const C& incr) {
    x_ += incr.x_;
    return *this;
```

```
  }
  void print(std::ostream& out) const {
    out << x_;
  }
};
```

In this fashion, CRTP can be used to add boilerplate interfaces while delegating the implementation to the derived classes. It is, after all, a static (compile-time) delegation pattern.

Summary

In this chapter, we have learned about a very C++-specific pattern that was originally introduced as a workaround for the buggy early C++ compilers but found new use years later. The friend factory is used to generate non-template functions from instantiations of class templates. As non-template functions, these generated friends have much more flexible rules with regard to argument conversions compared to template functions. We have also learned how the argument-dependent lookup, type conversions, and the friend factory work together to deliver a result that looks very natural, by a process that is far from intuitive.

The next chapter describes a totally different kind of Factory - a C++ pattern that's based on the classic Factory pattern and addresses a certain asymmetry in the language - all member functions, even destructors, can be virtual, except the constructors.

Questions

1. What is the effect of declaring a function as a *friend*?
2. What is the difference between granting friendship to a function versus a function template?
3. Why are binary operators usually implemented as non-member functions?
4. Why is the inserter operator always implemented as a non-member function?
5. What is the main difference between argument conversions for template and non-template functions?
6. How can we make the act of instantiating the template also generate a unique non-template, non-member function?

13

Virtual Constructors and Factories

In C++, any member function of any class, including its destructor, can be made virtual - any member function except one—the constructor. Without virtual functions, the exact type of object on which the member function is invoked is known at compile time. Therefore, the type of object that is constructed is always known at compile time, at the point of the constructor call. Nonetheless, we often need to construct objects whose type is not known until runtime. This chapter describes several related patterns and idioms that address this design problem in various ways, including the Factory pattern.

The following topics will be covered in this chapter:

- Why there is no way to make a constructor virtual
- How to use the Factory pattern to defer the choice of the constructed object type until compile time
- Using C++ idioms to construct and copy objects polymorphically

Technical requirements

The example code for this chapter can be found at the following GitHub link: https://github.com/PacktPublishing/Hands-On-Design-Patterns-with-CPP_Second_Edition/tree/master/Chapter13.

Why constructors cannot be virtual

We already understand how polymorphism works—when a virtual function is called through a pointer or a reference to the base class, that pointer or reference is used to access the v-pointer in the class. The v-pointer is used to identify the true type of the object, that is, the type that the object was created with. It could be the base class itself, or any one of the derived classes. The member function on that object is actually called. So, why can't the same be done for constructors? Let's investigate this.

When does an object get its type?

It is pretty easy to understand why the process that we described previously cannot work for creating *virtual constructors*. First of all, it is evident from the description of the preceding process—as a part of it, we *identify the type that the object was created with*. That can only happen after the object is constructed—before construction, we don't have an object of this type yet, just some uninitialized memory. Another way to look at it is this—before the virtual function is dispatched to the correct type, the v-pointer needs to be looked up. Who puts the right value into the v-pointer? Considering that the v-pointer uniquely identifies the type of object, it can only be initialized during construction. This implies that it wasn't initialized before construction. But if it wasn't initialized, it can't be used to dispatch virtual function calls. And so again, we realize that constructors cannot be virtual.

For derived classes in the hierarchy, the process of establishing the type is even more complex. We can try to observe the type of an object as it is being constructed. The easiest way to do this is to use the `typeid` operator, which returns information about the object's type, including the name of the type:

```cpp
// Example 01
#include <iostream>
#include <typeinfo>
using std::cout;
using std::endl;
template <typename T>
auto type(T&& t) { return typeid(t).name(); }
class A {
  public:
  A() { cout << "A::A(): " << type(*this) << endl; }
  virtual
  ~A() { cout << "A::~A(): " << type(*this) << endl; }
};
class B : public A {
  public:
  B() { cout << "B::B(): " << type(*this) << endl; }
  ~B() { cout << "B::~B(): " << type(*this) << endl; }
};
class C : public B {
  public:
  C() { cout << "C::C(): " << type(*this) << endl; }
  ~C() { cout << "C::~C(): " << type(*this) << endl; }
};
int main() {
  C c;
}
```

Running this program produces the following result:

```
A::A(): 1A
B::B(): 1B
C::C(): 1C
C::~C(): 1C
B::~B(): 1B
A::~A(): 1A
```

The type name returned by the `std::typeinfo::name()` call is the so-called mangled type name—it's the internal name that the compiler uses to identify types, instead of human-readable names such as `class A`. If you want to know the unmangled type, you can use a demangler such as the `c++filt` program that comes with GCC:

```
$ c++filt -t 1A
A
```

We can also write a small C++ function to demangle type names, but the way to do it varies from one compiler to another (there is no portable version). For example, this is what you would write for GCC:

```
// Example 2
#include <cxxabi.h>
template <typename T> auto type(T&& p) {
  int r;
  std::string name;
  char* mangled_name =
    abi::__cxa_demangle(typeid(p).name(), 0, 0, &r);
  name += mangled_name;
  ::free(mangled_name);
  return name;
}
```

Note that the demangler function returns a C string (a `char*` pointer) that must be explicitly freed by the caller. The program now prints demangled names such as A, B, and C. This is enough for our use, but in some cases, you might notice that the type is not printed exactly as it should be:

```
class A {
  public:
    void f() const { cout << type(*this) << endl; }
};
...
C c;
c.f();
```

If we call the function f(), the type is reported as C but not const C as we might expect (the object is const inside a const member function). This is because the typeid operator removed the const and volatile qualifiers as well as any references from the type. To print those, you have to figure them out by yourself:

```
// Example 03
template <typename T> auto type(T&& p) {
  std::string name;
  using TT = std::remove_reference_t<T>;
  if (std::is_const<TT>::value) name += "const ";
  if (std::is_volatile<TT>::value) name += "volatile ";
  int r;
  name += abi::__cxa_demangle(typeid(p).name(), 0, 0, &r);
  return name;
}
```

Regardless of how you choose to print the types, how many objects were constructed in these examples? The source code says just one, the c object of type C:

```
int main() {
  C c;
}
```

The runtime output says three, that is, one of each type. Both answers are correct—when an object of type C is constructed, the base class, A, has to be constructed first, and so its constructor is called. Then, the intermediate base class, B, is constructed, and only then will C be. The destructors are executed in reverse order. The type of the object inside its constructor or destructor, as reported by the typeid operator, is the same as the type of object whose constructor or destructor is running.

It appears that the type, as indicated by the virtual pointer, is changing during the construction! That is, of course, assuming that the typeid operator returns the dynamic type, the type indicated by the virtual pointer, and not the static type that can be determined at compile time. The standard says that this is, indeed, the case. Does this mean that, if we called the same virtual method from each constructor, we would really be calling three different overrides of this method? It's easy enough to find out:

```
// Example 04
class A {
  public:
  A() { whoami(); }
  virtual ~A() { whoami(); }
  virtual void whoami() const {
    std::cout << "A::whoami" << std::endl;
  }
};
```

```cpp
class B : public A {
  public:
  B() { whoami(); }
  ~B() { whoami(); }
  void whoami() const override {
    std::cout << "B::whoami" << std::endl;
  }
};
class C : public B {
  public:
  C() { whoami(); }
  ~C() { whoami(); }
  void whoami() const override {
    std::cout << "C::whoami" << std::endl;
  }
};

int main() {
  C c;
  c.whoami();
}
```

Now, we will create the object of type C, and the call to whoami() after the creation confirms it – the dynamic type of the object is C. That was true from the beginning of the construction process; we asked the compiler to construct one object of type C, but the dynamic type of the object changed during construction:

```
A::whoami
B::whoami
C::whoami
C::whoami
C::whoami
B::whoami
A::whoami
```

It is clear that the virtual pointer value has changed as the construction of the object progressed. In the beginning, it was identifying the object type as A, even though the final type is C. Is this because we created the object on the stack? Would it be any different if the object was created on the heap? We can easily find out:

```cpp
C* c = new C;
c->whoami();
delete c;
```

Running the modified program produces exactly the same results as the original.

Another reason that the constructor cannot be virtual, or, more generally, why the type of the object being constructed has to be known at compile time at the point of construction, is that the compiler has to know how much memory to allocate for the object. The amount of memory is determined by the size of the type, that is, by the `sizeof` operator. The result of `sizeof(C)` is a compile-time constant, so the amount of memory allocated for the new object is always known at compile time. This is true whether we create the object on the stack or on the heap.

The bottom line is this—if the program creates an object of the T type, somewhere in the code there is an explicit call to the `T::T` constructor. After that, we can hide the T type in the rest of the program, for example, by accessing the object through a base class pointer, or by erasing the type (see *Chapter 6, Understanding Type Erasure*). But there has to be at least one explicit mention of the T type in the code, and that is at the point of construction.

On the one hand, we now have a very reasonable explanation of why constructing objects can never be polymorphic. On the other hand, this does nothing to address a design challenge that may require constructing an object whose type is not known at compile time. Consider designing a game—a player can recruit or summon any number of adventurers for their party and build settlements and cities. It would be reasonable to have a separate class for each creature kind and each building type, but then we have to construct an object of one of these types when an adventurer joins the party, or a building is erected, and until the player selects it, the game cannot know which object to construct.

As usual in software, the solution involves adding another level of indirection.

The Factory pattern

The problem we are faced with, that is, how to decide at runtime to create an object of a particular type, is obviously a very common design problem. Design patterns are the solutions for just such problems, and there is a pattern for this problem as well—it's called the Factory pattern. The Factory pattern is a creational pattern, and it provides solutions for several related problems—how to delegate the decision of which object to create to a derived class, how to create objects using a separate factory method, and so on. We will review these variations of the Factory pattern one by one, starting with the basic factory method.

The basics of the Factory method

In its simplest form, the factory method constructs an object of a type that's specified at runtime:

```
class Base { ... };
class Derived : public Base { ... };
Base* p = ClassFactory(type_identifier, ... arguments );
```

How do we identify at runtime which object to create? We need a runtime identifier for each type that the factory can create. In the simplest case, the list of these types is known at compile time.

Consider a game design where a player selects the type of building to construct from a menu. The program has a list of buildings that can be constructed, each represented by an object, with an identifier for each one:

```
// Example 05
enum Buildings {
  FARM, FORGE, MILL, GUARDHOUSE, KEEP, CASTLE
};
class Building {
  public:
  virtual ~Building() {}
};
class Farm : public Building { ... };
class Forge : public Building { ... };
```

When the player selects the building type, the corresponding identifier value is also selected by the game program. Now, the program can construct the building using the factory method:

```
Building* new_farm = MakeBuilding(FARM);
```

Note that the factory takes the type identifier argument and returns the pointer to the base class. The returned object should have the type that corresponds to the type identifier. How is the factory implemented? Remember the conclusion of the last section—somewhere in the program, every object has to be explicitly constructed with its true type. The Factory pattern does not remove this requirement; it merely hides the place where the construction happens:

```
// Example 05
Building* MakeBuilding(Buildings building_type) {
  switch (building_type) {
    case FARM: return new Farm;
    case FORGE: return new Forge;
    ...
  }
}
```

The correspondence between the type identifier and the object type is encoded in the switch statement inside the factory. The return type has to be the same for all types that are constructed by the factory since there is only one factory method, and its type is declared at compile time. In the simplest case, it is the base class pointer, although if you follow the modern memory ownership idioms described in *Chapter 3, Memory and Ownership*, of this book, the factory should return a unique pointer to the base class, std::unique_ptr<Building>.

```
// Example 06:
class Building {
```

```
  public:
    enum Type {FARM, FORGE, ...};
    virtual ~Building() {}
    auto MakeBuilding(Type building_type);
};
auto Building::MakeBuilding(Type building_type) {
  using result_t = std::unique_ptr<Building>;
  switch (building_type) {
    case FARM: return result_t{new Farm};
    case FORGE: return result_t{new Forge};
    ...
  }
}
```

In rare cases when the shared ownership is really needed, the shared pointer, `std::shared_ptr<Building>`, can be constructed by moving the object from the unique pointer (but this is the decision to be made by the caller, not the factory itself).

The other design choice that we made here (independently of using the owning pointer) is to move the type identifiers and the factory function into the base class. This is useful for encapsulation and to keep all related code and types closer together.

This is the basic form of the factory method. There are many variations that make it more suitable for a particular problem. We will review some of these variations here.

Factory clarification

Note that there is some ambiguity in the use of the term "factory method." In this chapter, we use it to describe the function that creates objects of different types based on some run-time information. There is another, not related, design pattern that is sometimes introduced with the same name: instead of constructing different classes, this pattern constructs the same class but in different ways. Here is a brief example: suppose we have a class to represent a point on a plain. The point is described by its coordinates, x and y:

```
class Point {
  double x_ {};
  double y_ {};
  public:
  Point(double x, double y) : x_(x), y_(y) {}
};
```

So far, so good. But the same point can be described using, for example, polar coordinates. Because these are two ways to describe the same point, we do not need a separate class, but we may want a new constructor that creates a cartesian point from the specified polar coordinates:

```
class Point() {
  ...
```

```
    Point(double r, double angle);
};
```

But this is not going to work: the new constructor and the original constructor from x and y both take exactly the same arguments, so there is no way for the overload resolution to figure out which one you meant. One solution is to use different types for quantities that are measured in different units (length and angle, in our case). But they have to be truly different types, not just aliases. Sometimes, such a unit template library is just what you need, but if you're staying with doubles, you need some other way of invoking different constructors based on the caller's intent and not just the arguments.

One way to handle this problem is to switch to factory construction. Instead of using the constructors, we will construct all `Point` objects using static factory methods. Note that the constructor itself is usually made private when using this approach:

```
// Example 07
class Point {
  double x_ {};
  double y_ {};
  Point(double x, double y) : x_(x), y_(y) {}
  public:
  static Point new_cartesian(double x, double y) {
    return Point(x, y);
  }
  static Point new_polar(double r, double phi) {
    return Point(r*std::cos(phi), r*std::sin(phi));
  }
};
Point p1(Point::new_cartesian(3, 4));
Point p2(Point::new_polar(5, 0.927295));
```

This design works, but in modern C++, the more popular alternative is to use multiple constructors and disambiguate them with uniquely defined type tags:

```
// Example 08
class Point {
  double x_ {};
  double y_ {};
  public:
  struct cartesian_t {} static constexpr cartesian {};
  Point(cartesian_t, double x, double y) : x_(x), y_(y) {}
  struct polar_t {} static constexpr polar {};
  Point(polar_t, double r, double phi) :
    Point(cartesian, r*std::cos(phi), r*std::sin(phi)) {}
};
Point p1(Point::cartesian, 3, 4);
Point p2(Point::polar, 5, 0.927295);
```

In this example, we create two unique types, `Point::polar_t` and `Point::cartesian_t`, along with the corresponding variables, and use them as tags to specify what kind of construction we want. The constructor overloads are no longer ambiguous since each one has a unique first parameter type. Delegating constructors makes this approach even more attractive.

While the use of static functions to construct objects of the same type in different ways is sometimes called a factory method, it can also be seen as a variant of the builder pattern (especially when, instead of static methods, we use a separate builder class with similar methods). In any case, the more modern pattern – using tags – can replace both of these patterns. Having clarified the terminology, let us return to the original problem of constructing objects of different types based on run-time information.

Arguments for factory methods

In our simple example, the constructor took no arguments. Passing arguments to the constructor presents a bit of a problem if the constructors of different types have different parameters—after all, the `MakeBuilding()` function has to be declared with some specific parameters. One option that appears straightforward is to make the factory a variadic template and simply forward the arguments to each constructor. The straightforward implementation might look like this:

```
// Example 09
template <typename... Args>
auto Building::MakeBuilding(Type type, Args&&... args) {
  using result_t = std::unique_ptr<Building>;
  switch (type) {
    case FARM: return
      result_t{new Farm(std::forward<Args>(args)...)};
    case FORGE: return
      result_t{new Forge(std::forward<Args>(args)...)};
    ...
  }
}
```

This code might even compile for a while, but, sooner or later, you are going to run into the following error. Let us give the two classes we build some constructor arguments:

```
// Example 09
class Farm : public Building {
  public:
  explicit Farm(double size);
};
class Forge : public Building {
  public:
  static constexpr size_t weaponsmith = 0x1;
  static constexpr size_t welder = 0x2;
  static constexpr size_t farrier = 0x4;
  Forge(size_t staff, size_t services);
```

```
};
std::unique_ptr<Building> forge =
  Building::MakeBuilding(Building::FORGE, 2,
    Forge::weaponsmith | Forge::welder | Forge::farrier);
```

The `Forge` class uses a bitmask as flags to mark which services are provided at the forge (a simple and efficient solution to handle a small number of non-exclusive options). For example, if (`services & Forge::farrier`) is `true`, one of the 2 craftsmen working at the forge can shoe horses. Simple, elegant, and ... doesn't compile.

The compiler error will mention that there is no matching constructor for the `Farm` class that could be used to construct a `Farm` from two integers. But we are not trying to construct a `Farm`! This error gets everybody sooner or later. The problem is that, at compile-time, it is impossible to be sure that we are not trying to construct a `Farm`: that is a run-time decision. The function `MakeBuilding()` must compile, which means its entire implementation must compile, including the line starting with `case FARM`. Your first thought might be to replace the `switch` statement with `if constexpr`, but that's not going to work because the condition we use to select which class to build is not `constexpr`, it's a run-time value – that's the whole point of the factory pattern.

Trying to construct a `Farm` with the arguments meant for a `Forge` is an error. However, it is a run-time error, and it can only be detected at run time. This still leaves us with the problem of how to make valid the code we never want to run. The problem is that the Farm doesn't have a constructor we could use for all the wrong arguments (but hopefully never will). The easiest workaround is to provide one:

```
// Example 09
class Farm : public Building {
  public:
  explicit Farm(...) { abort(); }
  ...
};
```

We have to do the same for all types we may construct with our factory. The variadic function constructor is an "overload of the last resort" – it is selected only if no other overload matches the arguments. Since it matches any arguments, the compilation errors will be gone, replaced by run-time errors if something does go wrong in the program. Why not simply add this constructor to the base class? We could, but base class constructors are not visible in derived classes without a `using` statement, so we still have to add something to every derived class.

Having to modify every class just so it can be used with the factory creation pattern is definitely a disadvantage, especially since the new constructor could be used anywhere, not just in the factory function (with unfortunate consequences). As usual, with one more layer of indirection, we could solve this problem as well by introducing an overloaded template for constructing our objects:

```
// Example 10
template <typename T, typename... Args>
```

```
auto new_T(Args&&... args) ->
  decltype(T(std::forward<Args>(args)...))* {
  return new T(std::forward<Args>(args)...);
}
template <typename T>
T* new_T(...) { abort(); return nullptr; }
template <typename... Args>
auto Building::MakeBuilding(Type type, Args&&... args) {
  using result_t = std::unique_ptr<Building>;
  switch (type) {
    case FARM: return
      result_t{new_T<Farm>(std::forward<Args>(args)...)};
    case FORGE: return
      result_t{new_T<Forge>(std::forward<Args>(args)...)};
    ...
  }
}
```

The good news is that now we do not need to modify any of the classes: any factory call with the correct arguments compiles and is forwarded to the right constructor, while any attempt to create an object with the wrong arguments is a run-time error. The bad news is that any attempt to create an object with the wrong arguments is a run-time error. That includes the dead code we never plan to run (such as creating a Farm with Forge's arguments), but it also includes any mistakes we could make when calling the factory.

If the variadic template solution looks much less attractive once you start implementing it, there is a simpler option: create a parameter object with the hierarchy matching the hierarchy of the objects we create. Let's assume that, in our game, the player can select upgrades for each building to be constructed. The user interface will have to offer building-specific options, of course, and the results of the user selections are stored in a building-specific object:

```
// Example 11
struct BuildingSpec {
  virtual Building::Type type() const = 0;
};
struct FarmSpec : public BuildingSpec {
  Building::Type type() const override {
    return Building::FARM;
  }
  bool with_pasture;
  int number_of_stalls;
};
struct ForgeSpec : public BuildingSpec {
  Building::Type type() const override {
    return Building::FORGE;
```

```
  }
  bool magic_forge;
  int number_of_apprentices;
};
```

Note that we included the type identifier with the argument object, there is no reason to call the factory method with two arguments that must always correctly match each other; it only creates the possibility of an error occurring. This way, we are guaranteed that the type identifier and the arguments match in every factory call:

```
// Example 11
auto Building::MakeBuilding(const BuildingSpec& spec) {
  using result_t = std::unique_ptr<Building>;
  switch (spec.type()) {
    case FARM: return result_t{
      new Farm(static_cast<const FarmSpec&>(spec))};
    case FORGE: return result_t{
      new Forge(static_cast<const ForgeSpec&>(spec))};
    ...
  }
}
```

Note that the factory pattern often works well with the named arguments pattern we saw in *Chapter 9, Named Arguments, Method Chaining, and the Builder Pattern* to avoid having to specify long argument lists. The spec objects themselves become the options objects we can use to specify named arguments:

```
// Example 11
class FarmSpec {
  ...
  bool with_pasture {};
  int number_of_stalls {};
  FarmSpec() = default;
  FarmSpec& SetPasture(bool with_pasture) {
    this->with_pasture = with_pasture;
    return *this;
  }
  FarmSpec& SetStalls(int number_of_stalls) {
    this->number_of_stalls = number_of_stalls;
    return *this;
  }
};
struct ForgeSpec : public BuildingSpec {
  ...
  bool magic_forge {};
  int number_of_apprentices {};
  ForgeSpec() = default;
  ForgeSpec& SetMagic(bool magic_forge) {
```

```
        this->magic_forge = magic_forge;
        return *this;
    }
    ForgeSpec& SetApprentices(int number_of_apprentices) {
        this->number_of_apprentices = number_of_apprentices;
        return *this;
    }
};
...
std::unique_ptr<Building> farm =
    Building::MakeBuilding(FarmSpec()
                                .SetPasture(true)
                                .SetStalls(2));
std::unique_ptr<Building> forge =
    Building::MakeBuilding(ForgeSpec()
                                .SetMagic(false)
                                .SetApprentices(4));
```

This technique can be combined with some of the other factory variations that are shown in the following sections so that we can pass arguments when the constructors require them.

Dynamic type registry

So far, we have assumed that the complete list of the types is known at compile time and can be encoded in the type identifier correspondence table (implemented with a switch statement, in our example). The former requirement is unavoidable in the scope of the entire program: since every constructor call is explicit somewhere, the total list of types that can be constructed is known at compile time. However, our solution is more constrained than that—we have a list of all types that are hard-coded in the factory method. No additional derived classes can be created without also adding them to the factory. Sometimes, this restriction is not as bad as it appears—for example, the list of buildings in the game may not change very often, and even when it does, there is a complete list that must be manually updated for the right menu to be generated, the pictures and sounds to appear in the right places, and so on.

Nonetheless, one of the advantages of the hierarchical designs is that derived classes can be added later without modifying any of the code written to operate on the hierarchy. The new virtual function simply plugs into the existing control flow and provides the necessary customized behavior. We can implement the same idea for the factory constructor.

First of all, each derived class has to be responsible for constructing itself. This is necessary because, as we have already learned, the explicit call to the constructor has to be written somewhere. If it's not in the generic code, it has to be a part of the code that is added when a new derived class is created. For example, we can have a static factory function:

```
class Forge : public Building {
  public:
```

```
    static Building* MakeBuilding() { return new Forge; }
};
```

Second, the list of the types has to be extensible at runtime instead of being fixed at compile time. We could still use an `enum`, but then it would have to be updated every time a new derived class is added. Alternatively, we could assign each derived class an integer identifier at runtime, making sure that the identifiers are unique. Either way, we need a map of these identifiers to the factory functions, and it cannot be a `switch` statement or anything else that is fixed at compile time. The map has to be extensible. We could use `std::map` for this, but, if the type identifiers are integers, we can also use a `std::vector` of function pointers indexed by the type identifier:

```
class Building;
using BuildingFactory = Building*(*)();
std::vector<BuildingFactory> building_registry;
```

Now, to register a new type, we just need to generate a new identifier and add the corresponding factory function to the vector:

```
size_t building_type_count = 0;
void RegisterBuilding(BuildingFactory factory) {
  building_registry.push_back(factory));
  ++building_type_count;
}
```

This registration machinery can be encapsulated in the base class itself:

```
// Example 12
class Building {
  static size_t building_type_count;
  using BuildingFactory = Building* (*)();
  static std::vector<BuildingFactory> registry;
  public:
  static size_t (BuildingFactory factory) {
    registry.push_back(factory);
    return building_type_count++;
  }
  static auto MakeBuilding(size_t building_type) {
    BuildingFactory RegisterBuilding factory =
        registry[building_type];
    return std::unique_ptr<Building>(factory());
  }
};
std::vector<Building::BuildingFactory> Building::registry;
size_t Building::building_type_count = 0;
```

This base class has the factory function table and the count of registered derived types as static data members. It also has two static functions: one to register new types and one to construct an object of one of the types registered with the class. Note that the registration function returns the type identifier it has associated with the factory function. We are going to use this momentarily.

Now, we just need to add every new building type to the registry. This is done in two steps—first, we need to add a registration method to every building class, like so:

```
class Forge : public Building {
  public:
  static void Register() {
    RegisterBuilding(Forge::MakeBuilding);
  }
};
```

Second, we need to arrange for all `Register()` methods to be called before the game begins and make sure we know the right identifier for every building type. This is where the value returned by the `RegisterBuilding()` function becomes important because we are going to store it as the type identifier inside the class itself:

```
// Example 12
class Forge : public Building {
  public:
  static void Register() {
    RegisterBuilding(Forge::MakeBuilding);
  }
  static const size_t type_tag;
};
const size_t Forge::type_tag =
  RegisterBuilding(Forge::MakeBuilding);
```

The registration happens during the initialization of the static variables, sometime before `main()` is started.

The factory functions do not have to be static member functions: anything that can be invoked via a function pointer will work. For example, we could use a lambda without captures:

```
// Example 12
class Farm : public Building {
  public:
  static const size_t type_tag;
};
const size_t Farm::type_tag =
  RegisterBuilding([]()->Building* { return new Farm; });
```

We have to explicitly specify the return type because the function pointer type is defined as a function with no argument that returns `Building*`, while the lambda is deduced as a function returning `Farm*` unless we cast the return value or specify the return type.

Now, a call to `Building::MakeBuilding(tag)` will construct an object of the type that's registered with the identifier `tag`. The value of the tag – the type identifier – is stored as a static member in every class, so we don't have to know what it is and can't make a mistake:

```
std::unique_ptr<Building> farm =
  Building::MakeBuilding(Farm::type_tag);
std::unique_ptr<Building> forge =
  Building::MakeBuilding(Forge::type_tag);
```

In our solution, the correspondence between the identifier values and the types is not known until runtime—we cannot say what building has the ID of 5 until we run the program. Usually, we do not need to know that since the right value is automatically stored in each class.

Note that this implementation is very similar to the code that the compilers generate for true virtual functions—virtual function calls are done through function pointers that are stored in tables and accessed by means of a unique identifier (the virtual pointer). The main difference is that the unique identifier is the static data member associated with each type. Nonetheless, this is as close to a *virtual constructor* as you can get.

There are many variants of this dynamic type registry pattern. In some cases, it is preferable to explicitly specify the type identifiers instead of generating them at the program startup time. In particular, readable names such as "farm" and "forge" can be useful. In this case, instead of a vector, we can store the factory function pointers in a `std::map` container indexed by strings (`std::map<std::string, BuildingFactory>`).

Another modification is to allow more general callable objects as factory functions. We can generalize the `BuildingFactory` type by using `std::function` instead of the function pointer:

```
using BuildingFactory = std::function<Building*()>;
```

We can still register and use static factory methods as factories for our derived classes, but we can also use lambdas and custom functors:

```
// Example 13
class Forge : public Building {
  public:
    static const size_t type_tag;
};
class ForgeFactory {
  public:
    Building* operator()() const { return new Forge; }
};
```

```
const size_t Forge::type_tag =
  RegisterBuilding(ForgeFactory{});
```

The implementation of these dynamic factories, whether it is done with a function pointer or a more general std::function, strongly resembles the type erasure pattern we have explored in *Chapter 6*, *Understanding Type Erasure*. The concrete type of object to construct is embedded in the code of the function or functor whose declaration makes no mention of these types. This allows us to store these functions in a single function table or map. Other implementations of type erasure from *Chapter 6*, *Understanding Type Erasure*, can be used as well.

For simplicity, we did not use any arguments for our factory methods. We did, however, explore the options for passing arguments in the previous section. The variadic templates do not work well with function pointers (we have to declare the signature of the factory function upfront), so the most likely pattern for passing arguments is going to be the parameter spec object:

```
// Example 14
struct BuildingSpec {};
class Building {
  ...
  using BuildingFactory =
    Building* (*)(const BuildingSpec&);
  static auto MakeBuilding(size_t building_type,
                           const BuildingSpec& spec) {
    BuildingFactory factory = registry[building_type];
    return std::unique_ptr<Building>(factory(spec));
  }
};
struct FarmSpec : public BuildingSpec {
  bool with_pasture {};
  int number_of_stalls {};
  FarmSpec() = default;
  FarmSpec& SetPasture(bool with_pasture) {
    this->with_pasture = with_pasture;
    return *this;
  }
  FarmSpec& SetStalls(int number_of_stalls) {
    this->number_of_stalls = number_of_stalls;
    return *this;
  }
};
class Farm : public Building {
  public:
  explicit Farm(const FarmSpec& spec);
  ...
};
```

```
const size_t Farm::type_tag = RegisterBuilding(
   [](const BuildingSpec& spec)->Building* {
      return new Farm(static_cast<const FarmSpec&>(spec));
   });
struct ForgeSpec : public BuildingSpec { ... };
class Forge : public Building { ... };
std::unique_ptr<Building> farm =
   Building::MakeBuilding(FarmSpec()
                               .SetPasture(true)
                               .SetStalls(2));
std::unique_ptr<Building> forge =
   Building::MakeBuilding(ForgeSpec()
                               .SetMagic(false)
                               .SetApprentices(4));
```

In all of our factory constructors so far, the decision about which object to construct was driven by the external input to the program, and the construction was done by the same factory method (possibly using delegation to the derived classes). We will now see a different variant of the factory, which is used to address a slightly different scenario.

Polymorphic factory

Consider a slightly different problem—imagine that, in our game, each building produces a unit of some kind, and the type of the unit is uniquely associated with the type of the building. The Castle recruits knights, the Wizard Tower trains mages, and the Spider Mound produces giant spiders. Now, our generic code not only constructs a building of the type that is selected at runtime but also creates new units whose types are also not known at compile time. We already have the building factory. We could implement the Unit factory in a similar way, where every building has a unique unit identifier associated with it. But this design exposes the correspondence between the units and the buildings to the rest of the program, and that is really not necessary—each building knows how to build the *right* unit; there is no reason for the rest of the program to know it too.

This design challenge calls for a slightly different factory—the factory method determines that a unit is created, but exactly which unit is decided by the building. This is the Template pattern in action, combined with the Factory pattern—the overall design is the Factory, but the unit type is customized by the derived classes:

```
// Example 15
class Unit {};
class Knight : public Unit { ... };
class Mage : public Unit { ... };
class Spider : public Unit { ... };
```

```
class Building {
  public:
  virtual Unit* MakeUnit() const = 0;
};
class Castle : public Building {
  public:
  Knight* MakeUnit() const { return new Knight; }
};
class Tower : public Building {
  public:
  Mage* MakeUnit() const { return new Mage; }
};
class Mound : public Building {
  public:
  Spider* MakeUnit() const { return new Spider; }
};
```

Each building has a factory for creating the corresponding unit, and we can access these factory methods through the base class Building:

```
std::vector<std::unique_ptr<Building>> buildings;
std::vector<std::unique_ptr<Unit>> units;
for (const auto& b : buildings) {
  units.emplace_back(b->MakeUnit());
}
```

The factory that uses polymorphism and is accessed via a virtual function in the base class – usually a pure virtual function – is known as the Abstract Factory pattern.

The factory methods for the buildings themselves are not shown in this example—the Unit factory can coexist with any of the building factory implementations we have learned (the source code example that accompanies this chapter uses the building factory from Example 12). The generic code that constructs units from buildings is written once and does not need to change when new derived classes for buildings and units are added.

Note that the return types of all MakeUnit() functions are different. Nonetheless, they are all overrides of the same virtual Building::MakeUnit() function. These are known as the *covariant return types*—the return type of the override method may be a derived class of the return type of the overridden method. In our case, return types match the class types, but in general, this is not required. Any base and derived classes can be used as covariant types, even if they come from a different hierarchy. However, only such types can be covariant, and, other than that exception, the return type of the override must match the base class virtual function.

The strict rules for covariant return types present some problems when we try and make factories return anything other than a raw pointer. For example, let's assume that we want to return `std::unique_ptr` instead of the raw pointer. But, unlike `Unit *` and `Knight *`, `std::unique_ptr<Unit>` and `std::unique_ptr<Knight>` are not covariant types and cannot be used as return types for a virtual method and its override.

We will consider solutions for this, and several other C++-specific problems related to factory methods, in the next section.

Factory-like patterns in C++

There are many variations of the basic Factory patterns used in C++ to address specific design needs and constraints. In this section, we will consider several of them. This is by no means an exclusive list of factory-like patterns in C++, but understanding these variants should prepare the reader for combining the techniques that they have learned from this book to address various design challenges related to object factories.

Polymorphic copy

So far, we have considered factory alternatives to the object constructor—either the default constructor or one of the constructors with arguments. However, a similar pattern can be applied to the copy constructor—we have an object, and we want to make a copy.

This is a similar problem in many ways—we have an object that's accessed through the base class pointer, and we want to call its copy constructor. For the reasons we discussed earlier, not the least of which is that the compiler needs to know how much memory to allocate, the actual constructor call has to be done on the statically determined type. However, the control flow that gets us to a particular constructor call can be determined at runtime, and that, again, calls for an application of the Factory pattern.

The factory method we will use to implement a polymorphic copy is somewhat similar to the Unit factory example from the previous section—the actual construction has to be done by each derived class, and the derived class knows what type of object to construct. The base class implements the control flow that dictates that someone's copy will be constructed, and the derived class customizes the construction part:

```
// Example 16
class Base {
  public:
    virtual Base* clone() const = 0;
};
class Derived : public Base {
  public:
    Derived* clone() const override {
```

```
        return new Derived(*this);
    }
};
Base* b0 = ... get an object somewhere ...
Base* b1 = b->clone();
```

We can use the typeid operator (possibly with the demangling function we used earlier in this chapter) to verify that the pointer b1 does indeed point to a Derived object.

We have just implemented polymorphic copying using inheritance. Earlier, in *Chapter 6, Understanding Type Erasure*, we have seen another way to copy objects whose type was known at construction time but later lost (or erased). The two approaches are not fundamentally different: when implementing type-erased copying, we built a virtual table ourselves. In this chapter, we had the compiler do it for us. The preferred implementation in any particular case will depend mostly on what else is going on in the code around it.

Note that, once again, we are using covariant return types, and, therefore, are limited to the raw pointers. Let's say that we want to return unique pointers instead. Since only the raw pointers to the base and derived types are considered covariant, we have to always return the unique pointer to the base class:

```
class Base {
  public:
    virtual std::unique_ptr<Base> clone() const = 0;
};
class Derived : public Base {
  public:
    std::unique_ptr<Base> clone() const override {
      return std::unique_ptr<Base>(new Derived(*this));
    }
};
std::unique_ptr<Base> b(... make an object ...);
std::unique_ptr<Base> b1 = b->clone();
```

In many cases, this is not a significant limitation. Sometimes, however, it can lead to unnecessary conversions and casts. If returning a smart pointer to the exact type is important, there is another version of this pattern that we will consider next.

CRTP Factory and return types

The only way we could return std::unique_ptr<Derived> from the factory copy constructor of the derived class is to make the virtual clone() method of the base class return the same type. But this is impossible, at least if we have more than one derived class—for each derived class, we would need the return type of Base::clone() to be that class. But there is only one Base::clone()! Or is there? Fortunately, in C++, we have an easy way of making many out of one—the templates. If we template the base class, we could make the base of each derived class return the right type. But to do this, we need the base class to somehow know the type of the class that will be derived from it. Of course, there is a pattern for that, too—in C++, it is called the Curiously Recurring Template Pattern, which we looked at in *Chapter 8, The Curiously Recurring Template Pattern*. Now, we can combine the CRTP and the Factory patterns:

```cpp
// Example 18
template <typename Derived> class Base {
  public:
  virtual std::unique_ptr<Derived> clone() const = 0;
};
class Derived : public Base<Derived> {
  public:
  std::unique_ptr<Derived> clone() const override {
    return std::unique_ptr<Derived>(new Derived(*this));
  }
};
std::unique_ptr<Derived> b0(new Derived);
std::unique_ptr<Derived> b1 = b0->clone();
```

auto return types make writing code like this significantly less verbose. In this book, we generally don't use them to make it clear which function returns what.

The template parameter of the Base class is one of the classes derived from it, hence the naming. If you wish, you can even enforce this restriction with a static assert:

```cpp
template <typename Derived> class Base {
  public:
  virtual std::unique_ptr<Derived> clone() const = 0;
  Base() {
    static_assert(std::is_base_of_v<Base, Derived>;
  }
};
```

The reason we had to hide the static assert in the class constructor is that within the declaration of the class itself, the type Derived is incomplete.

Note that, since the Base class now knows the type of the derived class, we don't even need the clone() method to be virtual:

```cpp
// Example 19
template <typename Derived> class Base {
  public:
  std::unique_ptr<Derived> clone() const {
    return std::unique_ptr<Derived>(
      new Derived(*static_cast<const Derived*>(this)));
  }
};
class Derived : public Base<Derived> { ... };
```

There are significant downsides to this method, at least regarding the way we have implemented it so far. First of all, we had to make the base class a template, which means that we no longer have a common pointer type to use in our general code (or we have to make an even wider use of templates). Second, this approach only works if no more classes are derived from the Derived class, because the type of the base class does not track the second derivation—only the one that instantiated the Base template. Overall, except for the specific cases where it is very important to return the exact type instead of the base type, this approach cannot be recommended.

On the other hand, there are some attractive features of this implementation that we may want to preserve. Specifically, we got rid of the multiple copies of the clone() function, one per each derived class, and got a template to generate them for us automatically. In the next section, we will show you how to retain that useful feature of the CRTP implementation, even if we have to give up on extending the notion of *covariant return types* to cover smart pointers by playing template tricks.

CRTP for Factory implementation

We have mentioned several times by now that, while CRTP is sometimes used as a design instrument, it is just as likely to be used as an implementation technique. We will now focus on using CRTP to avoid writing the clone() function in every derived class. This is not just done to reduce typing—the more code is written—especially very similar code that gets copied and modified—the more likely you are to make an error. We have already seen how to use CRTP to generate a version of clone() for every derived class automatically. We just don't want to give up the common (non-template) base class to do so. We don't really have to do so if we delegate the cloning to the special base class that handles only that:

```
// Example 20
class Base {
  public:
  virtual Base* clone() const = 0;
};
template <typename Derived> class Cloner : public Base {
  public:
  Base* clone() const {
    return new Derived(*static_cast<const Derived*>(this));
  }
};
class Derived : public Cloner<Derived> {
  ...
};
Base* b0(new Derived);
Base* b1 = b0->clone();
```

Here, for simplicity, we went back to returning raw pointers, although we could also return `std::unique_ptr<Base>`. What we cannot do is return `Derived*` since, at the time when the template for the `Cloner` is parsed, it is not known that `Derived` is always derived from `Base`.

This design allows us to derive any number of classes from `Base`, indirectly through `Cloner`, and not have to write another `clone()` function ever again. It still has the limitation that, if we derive another class from `Derived`, it will not be copied correctly. In many designs, this is not an issue—enlightened self-interest should guide you to avoid deep hierarchies and make all classes be one of two kinds: abstract base classes that are never instantiated, and concrete classes that are derived from one of these base classes, but never from another concrete class.

Factory and Builder

So far, we have been using mostly factory functions, or, more generally, functors such as lambdas. In practice, it is just as likely that we will need a factory class. This usually happens because the run-time information needed to construct an object is more complex than just the type identifier and a few arguments. These are the same reasons we may choose to use the Builder pattern to create objects, so a factory class can also be viewed as a builder class with a factory method used to create the concrete objects. The Unit factory we have seen earlier in this chapter is an example of such a pattern: the Building class and all of its derived classes act like a builder for the unit objects (and the fact that the building objects themselves are created by another factory only serves as yet another demonstration that even a simple piece of code can rarely be reduced to a single pattern). In that case, however, we had a special motive for using the factory class: each derived building class constructs its own unit objects.

Let us now consider a more common case for using a factory class: the overall complexity of the run-time data that goes into deciding which class to construct and how, as well as the non-trivial amount of code we need to do so. While it is possible to handle it all with a factory function and some global objects, it would be a poor design, lacking in cohesion and encapsulation. It is going to be error-prone and difficult to maintain. It is much better to encapsulate all related code and data into one class or a small number of related classes.

For this example, we are going to tackle the very common (and still very challenging) serialization/deserialization problem. In our case, we have a number of objects derived from the same base class. We want to implement the framework necessary to serialize them by writing them into a file and then restoring the objects from this file. In this final example of the chapter, we are going to combine several methods we have learned to design and implement the factory.

We are going to start with the base class. The base class is going to utilize the dynamic type registry we learned earlier. Also, it is going to declare a pure virtual `Serialize()` function that every derived class needs to implement to serialize itself into a file:

```
// Example 21
class SerializerBase {
  static size_t type_count;
```

```
    using Factory = SerializerBase* (*)(std::istream& s);
    static std::vector<Factory> registry;
    protected:
    virtual void Serialize(std::ostream& s) const = 0;
    public:
    virtual ~SerializerBase() {}
    static size_t RegisterType(Factory factory) {
      registry.push_back(factory);
      return type_count++;
    }
    static auto Deserialize(size_t type, std::istream& s) {
      Factory factory = registry[type];
      return std::unique_ptr<SerializerBase>(factory(s));
    }
};
std::vector<SerializerBase::Factory>
  SerializerBase::registry;
size_t SerializerBase::type_count = 0;
```

Any derived class needs to implement the `Serialize()` function as well as register the deserialization function:

```
// Example 21
class Derived1 : public SerializerBase {
  int i_;
  public:
  Derived1(int i) : i_(i) {...}
  void Serialize(std::ostream& s) const override {
    s << type_tag << " " << i_ << std::endl;
  }
  static const size_t type_tag;
};
const size_t Derived1::type_tag =
  RegisterType([](std::istream& s)->SerializerBase* {
    int i; s >> i; return new Derived1(i); });
```

Only the derived class itself has the information about its state, what must be saved in order to reconstitute the object, and how to do so. In our example, the serialization is always done in the `Serialize()` function, while the deserialization is done in the lambda we register with the type registry. Needless to say, the two must be consistent with each other. There are template-based tricks that can ensure this consistency, but they aren't relevant to the factory construction we are studying now.

We have the serialization part handled – all we need to do is call Serialize on any object we have:

```
std::ostream S ... - construct the stream as needed
Derived1 d(42);
d.Serialize(S);
```

The deserialization itself is not particularly hard (most of the work is done by the derived classes), but there is enough boilerplate code there to justify a factory class. A factory object will read the entire file and deserialize (re-create) all objects recorded there. There are, of course, many options for the destination of such objects. Since we are constructing objects whose types are not known at compile-time, we have to access them through the base class pointers. For example, we can store them in a container of unique pointers:

```cpp
// Example 21
class DeserializerFactory {
  std::istream& s_;
  public:
  explicit DeserializerFactory(std::istream& s) : s_(s) {}
  template <typename It>
  void Deserialize(It iter) {
    while (true) {
      size_t type;
      s_ >> type;
      if (s_.eof()) return;
      iter = SerializerBase::Deserialize(type, s_);
    }
  }
};
```

This factory reads the entire file, line by line. First, it reads just the type identifier (which each object must write during serialization). Based on that identifier, it dispatches the rest of the deserialization process to the correct function registered for the corresponding type. The factory uses an inserter iterator (such as a back-inserter) to store all deserialized objects in a container:

```cpp
// Example 21
std::vector<std::unique_ptr<SerializerBase>> v;
DeserializerFactory F(S);
F.Deserialize(std::back_inserter(v));
```

With this approach, we can handle any class derived from SerializerBase, as long as we can come up with a way to write it into a file and restore it. We can handle a more complex state and constructors with multiple arguments:

```cpp
// Example 21
class Derived2 : public SerializerBase {
  double x_, y_;
  public:
  Derived2(double x, double y) : x_(x), y_(y) {...}
  void Serialize(std::ostream& s) const override {
    s << type_tag << " " << x_ << " " << y_ << std::endl;
  }
```

```
    static const size_t type_tag;
};
const size_t Derived2::type_tag =
  RegisterType([](std::istream& s)->SerializerBase* {
    double x, y; s >> x >> y;
    return new Derived2(x, y);
});
```

We can equally easily deal with classes that have multiple constructors as long as we know how a particular object should be constructed again:

```
// Example 21
class Derived3 : public SerializerBase {
  bool integer_;
  int i_ {};
  double x_ {};
public:
  Derived3(int i) : integer_(true), i_(i) {...}
  Derived3(double x) : integer_(false), x_(x) {...}
  void Serialize(std::ostream& s) const override {
    s << type_tag << " " << integer_ << " ";
    if (integer_) s << i_; else s << x_;
    s << std::endl;
  }
  static const size_t type_tag;
};
const size_t Derived3::type_tag =
  RegisterType([](std::istream& s)->SerializerBase* {
    bool integer; s >> integer;
    if (integer) {
      int i; s >> i; return new Derived3(i);
    } else {
      double x; s >> x; return new Derived3(x);
    }
});
```

There are many more variations of the factory pattern in C++. If you understood the explanations and followed through with the examples in this chapter, none of these alternatives should present a particular challenge for you.

Summary

In this chapter, we have learned why constructors cannot be made virtual, and what to do when we really want a virtual constructor anyway. We have learned how to construct and copy objects whose type becomes known at runtime by using the Factory pattern and one of its variations. We also explored several implementations of the Factory constructor that differ in the way that the code is organized and that the behavior is delegated to different components of the system, and compared their advantages and trade-offs. We have also seen how multiple design patterns interact with each other.

While in C++, the constructor has to be invoked with the true type of the object to construct—always—this does not mean that the application code has to specify the complete type. The Factory pattern allows us to write code that specifies the type indirectly, using an identifier that is associated with the type elsewhere (*create an object of the third kind*), or an associated object type (*create a unit that goes with this building type*), or even the same type (*make me a copy of this, whatever it is*).

The next design pattern we will study in the following chapter is the Template Method pattern, one of the classic object-oriented patterns that, in C++, has additional implications for the way we design class hierarchies.

Questions

1. Why does C++ not allow a virtual constructor?
2. What is the Factory pattern?
3. How do you use the Factory pattern to achieve the effect of a virtual constructor?
4. How do you achieve the effect of a virtual copy constructor?
5. How do you use the Template and Factory patterns together?
6. How do you use the Builder and the Factory patterns together?

The Template Method Pattern and the Non-Virtual Idiom

The Template Method is one of the classic *Gang of Four* design patterns, or, more formally, one of the 24 patterns described in the book *Design Patterns – Elements of Reusable Object-Oriented Software* by Erich Gamma, Richard Helm, Ralph Johnson, and John Vlissides. It is a behavioral design pattern, meaning that it describes a way for communicating between different objects. As an object-oriented language, C++, of course, fully supports the Template Method pattern, although there are some implementation details that are specific or unique to C++ that this chapter will elucidate.

The following topics will be covered in this chapter:

- What is the Template Method pattern, and what problems does it solve?
- What is the non-virtual interface?
- Should you make virtual functions public, private, or protected by default?
- Should you always make destructors virtual and public in polymorphic classes?

Technical requirements

The example code for this chapter can be found at the following GitHub link: `https://github.com/PacktPublishing/Hands-On-Design-Patterns-with-CPP-Second-Edition/tree/master/Chapter14`.

The Template Method pattern

The Template Method pattern is a common way to implement an algorithm whose overall structure is pre-determined, but some of the details of the implementation need to be customized. If you are thinking about a solution that goes something like this—first, we do *X*, then *Y*, and then *Z*, but how exactly we do *Y* depends on the data we process—you are thinking about the Template Method.

As a pattern that allows the behavior of a program to change dynamically, the Template Method is somewhat similar to the strategy pattern. The key difference is that the strategy pattern changes the entire algorithm at runtime, while the Template Method lets us customize specific parts of the algorithm. This section deals with the latter, while we have a separate *Chapter 16, Policy-Based Design*, dedicated to the former.

The Template Method in C++

The Template Method pattern is easily implemented in any object-oriented language. The C++ implementation uses inheritance and virtual functions. Note that this has nothing to do with C++ templates, as in generic programming. The *template* here is the skeleton implementation of the algorithm:

```
// Example 01
class Base {
  public:
  bool TheAlgorithm() {
    if (!Step1()) return false; // Step 1 failed
    Step2();
    return true;
  }
};
```

The *template* here is the structure of the algorithm—all implementations must first do *step 1*, which may fail. If this happens, the entire algorithm is considered to have failed, and nothing more is done. If *step 1* succeeded, we must do *step 2*. By design, *step 2* cannot fail, and the overall algorithm computation is considered a success once *step 2* is completed.

Note that the `TheAlgorithm()` method is public but not virtual—any class derived from `Base` has it as a part of its interface but cannot override what it does. What the derived classes can override are the implementations of *step 1* and *step 2*, within the restrictions of the algorithm template – *step 1* may fail and must signal the failure by returning `false`, while *step 2* may not fail:

```
// Example 01
class Base {
  public:
  ...
  virtual bool Step1() { return true };
  virtual void Step2() = 0;
};
class Derived1 : public Base {
  public:
  void Step2() override { ... do the work ... }
};
class Derived2 : public Base {
  public:
```

```
  bool Step1() override { ... check preconditions ... }
  void Step2() override { ... do the work ... }
};
```

In the preceding example, overriding the potentially failing *step 1* is optional, and the default implementation is trivial; it does nothing and never fails. *Step 2* must be implemented by every derived class—there is no default, and it is declared as a pure virtual function.

You can see that the overall flow of control—the framework—remains invariant, but it has *placeholders* for customizable options, possibly with a default offered by the framework itself. Such a flow is known as the inversion of control. In a traditional control flow, its specific implementation determines the flow of computation and sequence of operations and makes calls to library functions or other lower-level functions to implement the necessary general algorithms. In the Template Method, it is the framework that calls specific implementations in the custom code.

Applications of the Template Method

There are many reasons to use the Template Method. In general, it is used to control what can and cannot be sub-classed—as opposed to a general polymorphic override, where the entire virtual function can be replaced, the base class here determines what can and cannot be overridden. Another common use of the Template Method is to avoid code duplication, and in this context, you can arrive at the use of the Template Method as follows. Suppose that you start with the regular polymorphism—a virtual function—and it overrides. For example, let's consider this toy design for a turn-based combat system for a game:

```cpp
// Example 02
class Character {
  public:
  virtual void CombatTurn() = 0;
  protected:
  int health_;
};
class Swordsman : public Character {
  bool wielded_sword_;
  public:
  void CombatTurn() override {
    if (health_ < 5) { // Critically injured
      Flee();
      return;
    }
    if (!wielded_sword_) {
      Wield();
      return; // Wielding takes a full turn
    }
```

```
      Attack();
    }
};
class Wizard : public Character {
  int mana_;
  bool scroll_ready_;
  public:
  void CombatTurn() override {
    if (health_ < 2 ||
        mana_ == 0) { // Critically injured or out of mana
      Flee();
      return;
    }
    if (!scroll_ready_) {
      ReadScroll();
      return; // Reading takes a full turn
    }
    CastSpell();
  }
};
```

Note how this code is highly repetitive—all characters may be forced to disengage from combat on their turn, then they must take a turn to get ready for combat, and only then, if they are ready and strong enough, can they use their offensive capabilities. If you see this pattern repeating over and over, it is a strong hint that the Template Method may be called for. With the Template Method, the overall sequence of the combat turn is fixed, but how each character advances to the next step and what he/she does once he/she gets there remains character-specific:

```
// Example 03
class Character {
  public:
  void CombatTurn() {
    if (MustFlee()) {
      Flee();
      return;
    }
    if (!Ready()) {
      GetReady();
      return; // Getting ready takes a full turn
    }
    CombatAction();
  }
  virtual bool MustFlee() const = 0;
  virtual bool Ready() const = 0;
  virtual void GetReady() = 0;
```

```
  virtual void CombatAction() = 0;
  protected:
  int health_;
};
```

Now each derived class must implement only the part of the code that is unique to this class:

```
// Example 03
class Swordsman : public Character {
  bool wielded_sword_;
  public:
  bool MustFlee() const override { return health_ < 5; }
  bool Ready() const override { return wielded_sword_; }
  void GetReady()override { Wield(); }
  void CombatAction()override { Attack(); }
};
class Wizard : public Character {
  int mana_;
  bool scroll_ready_;
  public:
  bool MustFlee() const override { return health_ < 2 ||
                                          mana_ == 0; }
  bool Ready() const override { return scroll_ready_; }
  void GetReady() override { ReadScroll(); }
  void CombatAction() override { CastSpell(); }
};
```

Note how this code is much less repetitive. The advantage of the Template Method goes beyond good looks, though. Let's say that in the next revision of the game, we have added healing potions, and at the beginning of the turn, each character may drink a potion. Now, imagine going through every derived class and adding code like if (health_ < ... some class-specific value ... && potion_count_ > 0) .... If the design already used the Template Method, the logic of potion-quaffing needs to be coded only once, and different classes implement their specific conditions for using a potion, as well as the consequences of drinking one. However, don't rush to implement this solution until you get to the end of this chapter, as this is not the best C++ code you can do.

Pre-and post-conditions and actions

Another common use of the Template Method is dealing with pre-and post-conditions or actions. In a class hierarchy, pre- and post-conditions generally verify that the design invariants of an abstraction provided by an interface are not violated by any specific implementation at any point during execution. Such verification naturally submits to the Template Method's design:

```
// Example 04
class Base {
```

```
public:
void VerifiedAction() {
  assert(StateIsValid());
  ActionImpl();
  assert(StateIsValid());
}
virtual void ActionImpl() = 0;
};
class Derived : public Base {
  public:
  void ActionImpl() override { ... real implementation ...}
};
```

The invariants are the requirements that the object must satisfy when it's accessible to the client, i.e., before any member function is called on it or after it returns. The member functions themselves often have to temporarily break the invariants, but they must restore the correct state of the class before returning control to the caller. Let us say that our classes from the preceding example keep track of how many actions have been executed. Each action is registered when it starts and again when it's done, and the two counts must be the same: once an action is initiated, it has to complete before control is returned to the caller. Of course, inside the `ActionImpl()` member function this invariant is violated since an action is in progress:

```
// Example 04
class Base {
  bool StateIsValid() const {
    return actions_started_ == actions_completed_;
  }
  protected:
  size_t actions_started_ = 0;
  size_t actions_completed_ = 0;
  public:
  void VerifiedAction() {
    assert(StateIsValid());
    ActionImpl();
    assert(StateIsValid());
  }
  virtual void ActionImpl() = 0;
};
class Derived : public Base {
  public:
  void ActionImpl() override {
    ++actions_started_;
    ... perform the action ...
    ++actions_completed_;
  }
};
```

Of course, any practical implementation of pre- and post-conditions must take into account several additional factors. First, some member functions may have additional invariants, i.e., they can be called only when the object is in a restricted state. Such functions would have specific pre-conditions to test. Second, we have not considered the possibility that an action is aborted due to an error (this may or may not involve throwing an exception). A well-designed implementation of error handling must guarantee that the class invariants are not violated after such an error. In our case, a failed action may be ignored altogether (in which case, we need to decrement the count of started actions) or our invariant may have to be more complex: all started actions must end up as completed or failed, and we need to count both:

```cpp
// Example 05
class Base {
  bool StateIsValid() const {
    return actions_started_ ==
      actions_completed_ + actions_failed_;
  }
  protected:
  size_t actions_started_ = 0;
  size_t actions_completed_ = 0;
  size_t actions_failed_ = 0;
  ...
};
class Derived : public Base {
  public:
  void ActionImpl() override {
    ++actions_started_;
    try {
      ... perform the action - may throw ...
      ++actions_completed_;
    } catch (...) {
      ++actions_failed_;
    }
  }
};
```

In a real program, you must ensure that a failed transaction isn't just counted correctly but is handled correctly too (often, it must be undone). We have discussed it in great detail in *Chapter 5, A Comprehensive Look at RAII*, and again in *Chapter 11, ScopeGuard*. Finally, in a concurrent program, it is no longer true that an object cannot be observed while a member function is being executed, and the entire subject of class invariants becomes much more complex and intertwined with thread-safety guarantees.

Of course, in software design, one man's invariants are another's customization points. Sometimes, it is the main code that remains the same, but what happens right before and right after depends on the specific application. In this case, we probably wouldn't be verifying any invariants, but instead executing initial and final actions:

```cpp
// Example 06
class FileWriter {
  public:
  void Write(const char* data) {
    Preamble(data);
    ... write data to a file ...
    Postscript(data);
  }
  virtual void Preamble(const char* data) {}
  virtual void Postscript(const char* data) {}
};
class LoggingFileWriter : public FileWriter {
  public:
  using FileWriter::FileWriter;
  void Preamble(const char* data) override {
    std::cout << "Writing " << data << " to the file" <<
      std::endl;
  }
  void Postscript (const char*) override {
    std::cout << "Writing done" << std::endl;
  }
};
```

There is, of course, no reason why pre- and post-conditions cannot be combined with opening and closing actions – the base class can have several "standard" member function calls before and after the primary implementation.

While this code gets the job done, it still has some deficiencies that we are about to expose.

The Non-Virtual Interface

The implementation of the dynamically customizable parts of the templated algorithm is usually done with virtual functions. For a general Template Method pattern, this is not a requirement, but in C++, we rarely need another way. Now, we are going to focus specifically on using the virtual functions and improving on what we have learned.

Virtual functions and access

Let's start with a general question—should virtual functions be public or private? The textbook object-oriented design style uses public virtual functions, so we often make them public without a second thought. Within the Template Method, this practice needs to be reevaluated—a public function is part of the class interface. In our case, the class interface includes the entire algorithm, and the framework we put in place in the base class. This function should be public, but it is also non-virtual. The customized implementations of some parts of the algorithm were never meant to be called directly by the clients of the class hierarchy. They are used in one place only—in the non-virtual public function, where they replace the placeholders we put in the template of the algorithm.

This idea may seem trivial, but it comes as a surprise to many programmers. I've had this question asked more than once—*does C++ even allow virtual functions to be anything other than public?* In fact, the language itself makes no restrictions on access to virtual functions; they can be private, protected, or public, just like any other class member functions. This can take some time to wrap your mind around; perhaps an example would help:

```
// Example 07
class Base {
  public:
  void method1() { method2(); method3(); }
  virtual void method2() { ... }
  private:
  virtual void method3() { ... }
};
class Derived : public Base {
  private:
  void method2() override { ... }
  void method3() override { ... }
};
```

Here, `Derived::method2()` and `Derived::method3()` are both private. Can the base class even call private methods of its derived classes? The answer is, it doesn't have to—`Base::method1()` only calls `Base::method2()` and `Base::method3()` which are its own member functions (public and private, respectively); there is no problem with calling private member functions of the same class. But if the actual class type is `Derived`, the virtual override of `method2()` is called at runtime instead. These two decisions, *can I call* `method2()`? and *which* `method2()`?, happen at totally different times—the former happens when the module containing the `Base` class is compiled (and the `Derived` class may not have even been written yet), while the latter happens when the program is executed (and the words *private* or *public* don't mean anything at that point). Also note that, as shown by `method3()` in the preceding example, a virtual function and its override can have different access. Again, the function invoked at compile time (`Base::method3()` in our case) must be accessible at the point of the call; the override that ends up executed at runtime doesn't have to be (however, if we were to call `Derived::method3()` directly outside of the class itself, we would be trying to call a private method of that class).

```
// Example 07
Derived* d = new Derived;
Base* b = d;
b->method2();     // OK, calls Derived::method2()
d->method2();     // Does not compile - private function
```

There is another, more fundamental reason, to avoid public virtual functions. A public method is a part of the class interface. A virtual function override is a customization of the implementation. A public virtual function inherently does both of these tasks, at once. The same entity performs two very different functions that should not be coupled—declaring the public interface and providing an alternative implementation. Each of these functions has different constraints—the implementation can be altered in any way, as long as the hierarchy invariants hold. But the interface cannot be actually changed by the virtual function (except for returning covariant types, but even that does not really change the interface). All the public virtual function does is restate that yes, indeed, the public interface still looks like what the base class has declared. Such a mixing of two very distinct roles calls for a better separation of concerns. The Template Method pattern is an answer to that design problem, and in C++, it takes the form of the **Non-Virtual Interface (NVI)**.

The NVI idiom in C++

The tension between the two roles of a public virtual function, and the unnecessary exposure of the customization points created by such functions, lead us to the idea of making the implementation-specific virtual functions private. Herb Sutter in his article, *Virtuality* (`http://www.gotw.ca/publications/mill18.htm`), suggests that most, if not all, virtual functions should be private.

For the Template Method, moving virtual functions from public to private comes with no consequences (other than the initial shock of seeing a private virtual function, if you have never realized that C++ allows them):

```
// Example 08 (NVI version of example 01)
class Base {
  public:
  bool TheAlgorithm() {
    if (!Step1()) return false; // Step 1 failed
    Step2();
    return true;
  }
  private:
  virtual bool Step1() { return true };
  virtual void Step2() = 0;
};
```

```
class Derived1 : public Base {
  void Step2() override { ... do the work ... }
};
class Derived2 : public Base {
  bool Step1() override { ... check preconditions ... }
  void Step2() override { ... do the work ... }
};
```

This design nicely separates the interface and the implementation—the client interface is, and always was, the one call to run the entire algorithm. The possibility to change parts of the algorithm's implementation is not reflected in the interface. Therefore, the user of this class hierarchy who only accesses it through the public interface and does not need to extend the hierarchy (write more derived classes), remains unaware of such implementation details. To see how this works in practice, you can convert every example in this chapter from public virtual functions to NVI; we are going to do just one, example 06, and leave the rest as an exercise to the reader.

```
// Example 09 (NVI version of example 06)
class FileWriter {
  virtual void Preamble(const char* data) {}
  virtual void Postscript(const char* data) {}
  public:
  void Write(const char* data) {
    Preamble(data);
    ... write data to a file ...
    Postscript(data);
  }
};
class LoggingFileWriter : public FileWriter {
  using FileWriter::FileWriter;
  void Preamble(const char* data) override {
    std::cout << "Writing " << data << " to the file" <<
      std::endl;
  }
  void Postscript (const char*) override {
    std::cout << "Writing done" << std::endl;
  }
};
```

The NVI gives complete control of the interface to the base class. The derived classes can only customize the implementation of this interface. The base class can determine and verify the invariants, impose the overall structure of the implementation, and specify which parts can, must, and cannot be customized. The NVI also separates the interface from the implementation explicitly. The implementers of the derived classes do not need to be concerned with exposing part of their implementation to the callers unintentionally—the implementation-only private methods cannot be called by anyone except the base class.

Note that it is still possible for a derived class such as `LoggingFileWriter` to declare its own non-virtual function named `Write`. This is known as "shadowing" in C++: a name introduced in a derived class shadows (or makes inaccessible) all functions with the same name that would have been otherwise inherited from the base class. This causes the interfaces of the base and derived classes to diverge and is a very bad practice. Unfortunately, there is no good way for the base class implementer to protect from intentional shadowing. Accidental shadowing sometimes occurs when a function that is intended as a virtual override is declared with slightly different arguments; this can be avoided if the `override` keyword is used for all overrides.

So far, we have made all virtual functions that customize the implementation private. That, however, is not exactly the main point of the NVI—this idiom, and the more general Template Method, focus on making the public interface non-virtual. It follows, by extension, that the implementation-specific overrides should not be public since they are not part of the interface. It does not necessarily follow that they should be private. That leaves *protected*. So, should the virtual functions that provide customizations for the algorithm be private or protected? The Template Method allows both—the client of the hierarchy cannot directly call either one, so the framework of the algorithm remains unaffected. The answer depends on whether the derived classes may need to sub-invoke the implementations provided by the base class. For an example of the latter, consider a class hierarchy that can be serialized and sent to a remote machine through a socket:

```
// Example 10
class Base {
  public:
    void Send() { // Template Method used here
      ... open connection ...
      SendData(); // Customization point
      ... close connection ...
    }
  protected:
    virtual void SendData() { ... send base class data ... }
  private:
    ... data ...
};
class Derived : public Base {
  protected:
    void SendData() {
      Base::SendData();
      ... send derived class data ...
    }
};
```

Here, the framework is provided by the public non-virtual method `Base::Send()`, which handles the connection protocol and, at the right time, sends the data across the network. Of course, it can only send the data that the base class knows about. That is why `SendData` is a customization point and is made virtual. The derived class must send its own data, of course, but someone must still send the base class data, and so the derived class makes a call to the protected virtual function in the base class.

If this example looks like it's missing something, there is a good reason for it. While we provided the general template for how to send data and a customization point for each class to handle its own data, there is another behavior aspect that should be user-configurable: *how* to send data. This is a great place to show the (sometimes obscure) difference between the template method pattern and the strategy pattern.

Template Method vs Strategy

While this chapter is not about the Strategy pattern, it is sometimes confused with the Template Method, so we will now clarify the difference. We can use the example from the previous section to do this.

We have already used the Template Method to provide an overall template for the execution of the "send" operation in `Base::Send()`. There are three steps to the operation: open the connection, send the data, and close the connection. Sending data is the step that depends on the actual type of the object (which derived class it really is), and so it is explicitly designated as a customization point. The rest of the template is set in stone.

However we need another kind of customization: the `Base` class, in general, is not the right place to define how to open and close the connection. Neither is the derived class: the same objects could be sent across different types of connections (sockets, files, shared memory, etc). This is where we can use the Strategy pattern to define communication strategy. The strategy is provided by a separate class:

```
// Example 11
class CommunicationStrategy {
  public:
  virtual void Open() = 0;
  virtual void Close() = 0;
  virtual void Send(int v) = 0;
  virtual void Send(long v) = 0;
  virtual void Send(double v) = 0;
  ... Send other types ...
};
```

Isn't it frustrating that template functions cannot be virtual? For a better solution to this problem, you have to wait until *Chapter 15, Policy-Based Design*. Anyway, now that we have the communication strategy, we can use it to parametrize the `Send()` operation template:

```
// Example 11
class Base {
  public:
  void Send(CommunicationStrategy* comm) {
    comm->Open();
```

```
      SendData(comm);
      comm->Close();
   }
   protected:
   virtual void SendData(CommunicationStrategy* comm) {
      comm->Send(i_);
      ... send all data ...
   }
   private:
   int i_;
   ... other data members ...
};
```

Note that the template for sending the data is basically unchanged, but we delegated the implementation of the specific steps to another class – the strategy. This is the key difference: the Strategy pattern allows us to choose (generally, at runtime) which implementation should be used for a particular operation. The public interface is fixed but the entire implementation is up to the specific strategy. The Template Method pattern enforces the overall implementation flow as well as the public interface. Only the specific steps of the algorithm can be customized.

The second difference is where the customization happens: `Base::Send()` is customized in two ways. The customizations to the template are done in the derived classes; the implementations of the strategy are provided by the classes outside of the `Base` hierarchy.

As we pointed out at the beginning of this section, there are good reasons to make all virtual member functions, by default, private (or protected), and they go beyond the applications of the Template Method pattern. However, there is one particular member function – the destructor - that deserves separate consideration because the rules for destructors are somewhat different.

A note about destructors

The entire discussion of the NVI is an elaboration on a simple guideline—make virtual functions private (or protected), and present the public interface through non-virtual base class functions. This sounds fine until it runs head-on into another well-known guideline—if the class has at least one virtual function, its destructor must also be made virtual. Since the two are in conflict, some clarification is needed.

The reason to make destructors virtual is that if the object is deleted polymorphically - for example, a derived class object is deleted through a pointer to the base class - the destructor must be virtual; otherwise, only the base part of the class will be destructed (the usual result is the *slicing* of the class, partial deletion, although the standard simply states that the results are undefined). So, if the objects are deleted through the base class pointers, the destructors must be virtual; there is no way around it. But that is the only reason. If the objects are always deleted with the correct derived type, then this reason does not apply. This situation is not uncommon: for example, if derived class objects are stored in a container, they will be deleted as their true type.

The container has to know how much memory to allocate for the object, so it can't store a mix of base and derived objects, or delete them as base objects (note that a container of pointers to the base class object is a different construct altogether, and is usually created specifically so that we can store and delete objects polymorphically).

Now, if the derived class has to be deleted as itself, its destructor does not need to be virtual. However, bad things will still happen if someone calls the destructor of the base class when the actual object is of the derived class type. To safely prevent that from happening, we can declare the non-virtual base class destructor as protected instead of public. Of course, if the base class is not abstract, and there are objects of both base and derived types around, then both destructors must be made public, and the safer option is to make them virtual (a runtime check can be implemented to verify that the base class destructor is not called to destroy a derived class object).

By the way, if polymorphic deletion (deletion through the base class pointer) is the only reason you need to write a destructor in the base class, writing `virtual ~Base() = default;` is perfectly acceptable – a destructor can be both `virtual` and `default` at the same time.

We must also caution the reader against trying to employ the Template Method, or the non-virtual interface idiom, for class destructors. It may be tempting to do something like this:

```cpp
// Example 12
class Base {
  public:
  ~Base() { // Non-virtual interface!
    std::cout << "Deleting now" << std::endl;
    clear(); // Employing Template Method here
    std::cout << "Deleting done" << std::endl;
  }
  protected:
  virtual void clear() { ... } // Customizable part
};
class Derived : public Base {
  private:
  void clear() override {
    ...
    Base::clear();
  }
};
```

However, this is not going to work (if the base class has a pure virtual `Base::clear()` instead of a default implementation, it is not going to work in a rather spectacular fashion). The reason for this is that, inside the destructor of the base class, `Base::~Base()`, the actual, real, and true type of the object is not `Derived` anymore. It's `Base`. That's right—when the `Derived::~Derived()` destructor is done with its work and the control is transferred to the base class destructor, the dynamic type of the object changes to `Base`.

The only other class member that works this way is the constructor—the type of the object is `Base` as long as the base constructor is running, and then changes to `Derived` when the derived constructor has started. For all other member functions, the type of the object is always the type it was created with. If the object was created as `Derived`, then that is the type, even if a method of the base class is called. So, what happens if, in the preceding example, `Base::clear()` is pure virtual? It's called anyway! The result depends on the compiler; most compilers will generate code that aborts the program, with some diagnostic that *a pure virtual function was called.*

Drawbacks of the Non-Virtual Interface

There aren't many drawbacks regarding the use of the NVI. That is why the guideline to always make virtual functions private, and use the NVI to call them, is widely accepted. However, there are some considerations that you must be aware of when deciding whether the Template Method is the right design pattern to follow. The use of the template pattern may lead to fragile hierarchies. Also, there is some overlap between design problems that can be solved using the template pattern and the ones better served by the strategy pattern, or, in C++, policies. We will review both considerations in this section.

Composability

Consider the earlier design for `LoggingFileWriter`. Now, suppose that we want to also have `CountingFileWriter` that counts how many characters were written into the file:

```
class CountingFileWriter : public FileWriter {
  size_t count_ = 0;
  void Preamble(const char* data) {
    count_ += strlen(data);
  }
};
```

That was easy. But there is no reason a counting file writer cannot also log. How would we implement a `CountingLoggingFileWriter`? No problem, we have the technology—change the private virtual functions to protected and call the base class version from the derived class:

```
class CountingLoggingFileWriter : public LoggingFileWriter {
  size_t count_ = 0;
  void Preamble(const char* data) {
    count_ += strlen(data);
    LoggingFileWriter::Preamble(data);
  }
};
```

Or should it be `LoggingCountingFileWriter` that inherits from `CountingFileWriter`? Note that, either way, some code is duplicated—in our case, the counting code is present in both `CountingLoggingFileWriter` and `CountingFileWriter`. This duplication is only going to get worse as we add more variations. The Template Method just isn't the right pattern if you need composable customizations. For that, you should read *Chapter 15, Policy-Based Design*.

The Fragile Base Class problem

The Fragile Base Class problem is not limited to the Template Method, but is, to some degree, inherent in all object-oriented languages. The problem arises when changes to the base class break the derived class. To see how this can happen, specifically when using the non-virtual interface, let's go back to the file writer and add the ability to write many strings at once:

```
class FileWriter {
  public:
  void Write(const char* data) {
    Preamble(data);
    ... write data to a file ...
    Postscript(data);
  }
  void Write(std::vector<const char*> huge_data) {
    Preamble(huge_data);
    for (auto data: huge_data) {
      ... write data to file ...
    }
    Postscript(huge_data);
  }
  private:
  virtual void Preamble(std::vector<const char*> data) {}
  virtual void Postscript(std::vector<const char*> data) {}
  virtual void Preamble(const char* data) {}
  virtual void Postscript(const char* data) {}
};
```

The counting writer is kept up to date with the changes:

```
class CountingFileWriter : public FileWriter {
  size_t count_ = 0;
  void Preamble(std::vector<const char*> huge_data) {
    for (auto data: huge_data) count_ += strlen(data);
  }
  void Preamble(const char* data) {
    count_ += strlen(data);
  }
};
```

So far, so good. Later, a well-intentioned programmer notices that the base class suffers from some code duplication and decides to refactor it:

```
class FileWriter {
  public:
  void Write(const char* data) { ... no changes here ... }
  void Write(std::vector<const char*> huge_data) {
    Preamble(huge_data);
    for (auto data: huge_data) Write(data); // Code reuse!
    Postscript(huge_data);
  }
  private:
  ... no changes here ...
};
```

Now, the derived class is broken—the counting customizations of both versions of `Write` are called when a vector of strings is written, and the data size is counted twice. Note that we are not talking about the more basic kind of fragility where an override method in a derived class can stop being an override if the signature of the base class method is changed: this kind of fragility is largely avoided by the proper use of the `override` keyword as recommended in *Chapter 1, An Introduction to Inheritance and Polymorphism.*

While there is no general solution to the Fragile Base Class problem as long as inheritance is used at all, the guideline that helps to avoid it when using the Template Method is straightforward—when changing the base class and the structure of the algorithms, or the framework, avoid changing which customization points are invoked. Specifically, do not skip any customization options that were already invoked, and do not add new calls to already existing ones (it's OK to add new customization points, as long as the default implementation is sensible). If such a change cannot be avoided, you will need to review every derived class to see whether it relied on the implementation override that is now removed or replaced, and what the consequences of such a change are.

A cautionary note about template customization points

This brief section is not a drawback of the Template Method, but rather a warning about a somewhat arcane corner of C++. Many of the design patterns that were originally developed as run-time behaviors (object-oriented patterns) found their compile-time analogs in C++ generic programming. So, is there a compile-time template method?

Of course, there is an obvious one: we can have a function or a class template that accepts function parameters, or, more generally, callable parameters, for a certain step of the otherwise fixed algorithm. The standard library has a plethora of examples, such as `std::find_if`:

```
std::vector<int> v = ... some data ...
auto it = std::find_if(v.begin(), v.end(),
```

```
                                [](int i) { return i & 1; });
 if (it != v.end()) { ... } // even value found
```

The algorithm of `std::find_if` is known and cannot be altered, except for the step where it checks whether a particular value satisfies the caller's predicate.

If we want to do the same for class hierarchies, we can use member function pointers (although it is easier to invoke member functions through lambdas), but there is no way to say *"call a member function with the same name but on a different class"* except by using virtual functions and their overrides. There is no equivalent to that in generic programming.

Unfortunately, there is a case where a template can be customized by accident, usually with unintended results. Consider this example:

```
// Example 15
void f() { ... }
template <typename T> struct A {
  void f() const { ... }
};
template <typename T> struct B : public A<T> {
  void h() { f(); }
};
B<int> b;
b.h();
```

Which function `f()` is called from inside `B<T>::h()`? On a standard-compliant compiler, it should be the free-standing function, i.e. `::f()`, and not the member function of the base class! This may come as a surprise: if A and B were non-template classes, the base class method `A::f()` would have been called. This behavior arises from the complexities of parsing templates in C++ (if you want to learn more about this, `two-phase template parse` or `two-stage name lookup` are the terms to search for, but the matter is far outside the subject of this book).

What would have happened if the global function `f()` was not available in the first place? Then we have to call the one in the base class, don't we?

```
// Example 15
// No f() here!
template <typename T> struct A {
  void f() const { ... }
};
template <typename T> struct B : public A<T> {
  void h() { f(); } // Should not compile!
};
B<int> b;
b.h();
```

If you tried this code and it has called A<T>::f(), then you have a buggy compiler: the standard says that this should not compile at all! But what should you do if you want to call a member function of your own base class? The answer is very simple but looks strange if you haven't written a lot of template code:

```
// Example 15
template <typename T> struct A {
  void f() const { ... }
};
template <typename T> struct B : public A<T> {
  void h() { this->f(); } // Definitely A::f()
};
B<int> b;
b.h();
```

That's right, you have to explicitly call this->f() to ensure that you're calling a member function. If you do this, A<T>::f() gets called whether or not there is a global f() declared. By the way, if you intended to call the global function, the way to do this unambiguously is ::f(), or, if the function is in a namespace NS, NS::f().

The compilation error where the compiler cannot find a member function that is clearly present in the base class is one of the more confusing C++ errors; it is even worse if the compiler does not issue this error and compiles the code "as intended" instead: if someone adds a global function with the same name later (or it is declared in another header you include), the compiler will switch to that function with no warning. The general guideline is to always qualify member function calls in a class template with this->.

Overall, the Template Method is one of the few patterns that remain purely object-oriented in C++: the template form we saw employed by std::find_if (and many more templates) usually falls under the general umbrella of Policy-Based designs that we're going to study in the next chapter.

Summary

In this chapter, we have reviewed a classic object-oriented design pattern, the Template Method, as it applies to C++ programs. This pattern works in C++ as well as in any other object-oriented language, but C++ also has its own flavor of the Template Method—the non-virtual interface idiom. The advantages of this design pattern lead to a rather broad guideline—make all virtual functions private or protected. Be mindful, however, of the specifics of the destructors with regard to polymorphism. Here are the general guidelines for access (public vs private) to virtual functions:

1. Prefer to make interfaces nonvirtual, using the Template Method design pattern

2. Prefer to make virtual functions private

3. Only if derived classes need to invoke the base implementation of a virtual function, make the virtual function protected.

4. A base class destructor should be either public and virtual (if objects are deleted through the base class pointer) or protected and nonvirtual (if derived objects are deleted directly).

We already mentioned the Strategy pattern in this chapter by way of clarifying how it differs from the Template Method pattern. Strategy is also a popular pattern in C++, in particular, its generic programming equivalent. This is going to be the subject of the next chapter.

Questions

1. What is a behavioral design pattern?

2. What is the Template Method pattern?

3. Why is the Template Method considered a behavioral pattern?

4. What is the inversion of control, and how does it apply to the Template Method?

5. What is the non-virtual interface?

6. Why is it recommended to make all virtual functions in C++ private?

7. When should virtual functions be protected?

8. Why can't the Template Method be used for destructors?

9. What is the Fragile Base class problem, and how can we avoid it when employing the Template Method?

Part 4:
Advanced C++
Design Patterns

This part continues with the description and detailed explanation of C++ design patterns, moving on to the more advanced patterns. Some of these patterns use advanced features of the C++ language. Others represent complex concepts and address more difficult design problems. Yet other patterns implement very open-ended designs, where part of the solution can be factored out into a commonly accepted pattern, but the entire system must be customizable within very wide limits.

This part has the following chapters:

- *Chapter 15, Policy-Based Design*
- *Chapter 16, Adapters and Decorators*
- *Chapter 17, The Visitor Pattern and Multiple Dispatch*
- *Chapter 18, Patterns for Concurrency*

15

Policy-Based Design

Policy-based design is one of the most well-known C++ patterns. Since the introduction of the standard template library in 1998, few new ideas have been more influential on the way we design C++ programs than the invention of policy-based design.

A policy-based design is all about flexibility, extensibility, and customization. It is a way to design software that can evolve and can be adapted to the changing needs, some of which could not even be anticipated at the time when the initial design was conceived. A well-designed policy-based system can remain unchanged at the structural level for many years, and serve the changing needs and new requirements without compromise.

Unfortunately, it is also a way to build software that could do all of those things if only there was someone who could figure out how it works. The aim of this chapter is to teach you to design and understand the systems of the former kind while avoiding the excesses that lead to the disasters of the latter one.

The following topics will be covered in this chapter:

- Strategy pattern and policy-based design
- Compile time policies in C++
- Implementations of policy-based classes
- Guidelines for the use of policies

Technical requirements

The example code for this chapter can be found at the following GitHub link: https://github.com/PacktPublishing/Hands-On-Design-Patterns-with-CPP_Second_Edition/tree/master/Chapter15.

Strategy pattern and policy-based design

The classic Strategy pattern is a behavioral design pattern that enables the runtime selection of a specific algorithm for a particular behavior, usually from a predefined family of algorithms. This pattern is also known as the *policy pattern*; the name predates its application to generic programming in C++. The aim of the Strategy pattern is to allow for more flexibility in the design.

> **Note**
>
> In the classic object-oriented Strategy pattern, the decision about which specific algorithm to use is deferred until runtime.

As is the case with many classic patterns, the generic programming in C++ applies the same approach to algorithm selection at compile time - it allows for compile-time customization of specific aspects of the system behavior by selecting from a family of related, compatible algorithms. We will now learn the basics of implementing classes with policies in C++, then proceed to study more complex and varied approaches to policy-based design.

Foundations of policy-based design

The Strategy pattern should be considered whenever we design a system that does certain operations, but the exact implementation of these operations is uncertain, varied, or can change after the system is implemented - in other words, when we know the answer to *what the system must do*, but not *how*. Similarly, the compile-time strategy (or a policy) is a way to implement a class that has a specific function (*what*), but there is more than one way to implement that function (*how*).

Throughout this chapter, we will design a smart pointer class to illustrate different ways to use policies. A smart pointer has many other required and optional features besides policies, and we will not cover all of them - for a complete implementation of a smart pointer, you will be referred to such examples as the C++ standard smart pointers (`unique_ptr` and `shared_ptr`), Boost smart pointers, or the Loki smart pointer (`http://loki-lib.sourceforge.net/`). The material presented in this chapter will help you to understand the choices made by the implementers of these libraries, as well as how to design their own policy-based classes.

A very minimal initial implementation of a smart pointer may look like this:

```
// Example 01
template <typename T>
  T* p_;
  class SmartPtr {
  public:
  explicit SmartPtr(T* p = nullptr) : p_(p) {}
  ~SmartPtr() {
    delete p_;
```

```
  }
  T* operator->() { return p_; }
  const T* operator->() const { return p_; }
  T& operator*() { return *p_; }
  const T& operator*() const { return *p_; }
  SmartPtr(const SmartPtr&) = delete;
  SmartPtr& operator=(const SmartPtr&) = delete;
  SmartPtr(SmartPtr&& that) :
    p_(std::exchange(that.p_, nullptr)) {}
  SmartPtr& operator=(SmartPtr&& that) {
    delete p_;
    p_ = std::exchange(that.p_, nullptr);
  }
};
```

This pointer has a constructor from the raw pointer of the same type and the usual (for a pointer) operators, that is, * and ->. The most interesting part here is the destructor - when the pointer is destroyed, it automatically deletes the object as well (it is not necessary to check the pointer for the null value before deleting it; the operator delete is required to accept a null pointer and do nothing). It follows, therefore, that the expected use of this smart pointer is as follows:

```
// Example 01
Class C { ... };
{
  SmartPtr<C> p(new C);
  ... use p ...
} // Object *p is deleted automatically
```

This is a basic example of the RAII class. The RAII object - the smart pointer, in our case - owns the resource (the constructed object) and releases (deletes) it when the owning object itself is deleted. The common applications, which were considered in detail in *Chapter 5, A Comprehensive Look at RAII*, focus on ensuring that the object that was constructed in the scope is deleted when the program exits this scope, no matter how the latter is accomplished (for example, if an exception is thrown somewhere in the middle of the code, the RAII destructor guarantees that the object is destroyed).

Two more member functions of the smart pointer are noted, not for their implementation, but for their absence - the pointer is made non-copyable as both its copy constructor and the assignment operator are disabled. This detail, which is sometimes overlooked, is of crucial importance for any RAII class - since the destructor of the pointer deletes the owned object, there should never be two smart pointers that point to, and will attempt to delete, the same object. On the other hand, moving the pointer is a valid operation: it transfers the ownership from the old pointer to the new one. Move constructor is necessary for factory functions to work (at least prior to C++17).

The pointer we have here is functional, but the implementation is constraining. In particular, it can own and delete only an object that was constructed with the standard `operator new`, and only a single object. While it could capture a pointer that was obtained from a custom `operator new` or a pointer to an array of elements, it does not properly delete such objects.

We could implement a different smart pointer for objects that are created on a user-defined heap, and another one for objects that are created in client-managed memory, and so on, one for every type of object construction with its corresponding way of deletion. Most of the code for these pointers would be duplicated - they are all pointers, and the entire pointer-like API will have to be copied into every class. We can observe that all of these different classes are, fundamentally, of the same kind - the answer to the question *what is this type?* is always the same - *it's a smart pointer.*

The only difference is in how the deletion is implemented. This common intent with a difference in one particular aspect of the behavior suggests the use of the Strategy pattern. We can implement a more general smart pointer where the details of how to handle the deletion of the object are delegated to one of any number of deletion policies:

```
// Example 02
template <typename T, typename DeletionPolicy>
class SmartPtr {
  T* p_;
  DeletionPolicy deletion_policy_;
  public:
  explicit SmartPtr(
    T* p = nullptr,
    const DeletionPolicy& del_policy = DeletionPolicy()) :
    p_(p), deletion_policy_(del_policy)
  {}
  ~SmartPtr() {
    deletion_policy_(p_);
  }
  T* operator->() { return p_; }
  const T* operator->() const { return p_; }
  T& operator*() { return *p_; }
  const T& operator*() const { return *p_; }
  SmartPtr(const SmartPtr&) = delete;
  SmartPtr& operator=(const SmartPtr&) = delete;
  SmartPtr(SmartPtr&& that) :
    p_(std::exchange(that.p_, nullptr)),
    deletion_policy_(std::move(deletion_policy_))
  {}
  SmartPtr& operator=(SmartPtr&& that) {
    deletion_policy_(p_);
    p_ = std::exchange(that.p_, nullptr);
```

```
    deletion_policy_ = std::move(deletion_policy_);
  }
};
```

The deletion policy is an additional template parameter, and an object of the type of the deletion policy is passed to the constructor of the smart pointer (by default, such an object is default-constructed). The deletion policy object is stored in the smart pointer and is used in its destructor to delete the object that's being pointed to by the pointer.

Care must be taken when implementing copy and move constructors for such policy-based classes: it is very easy to forget that the policy also needs to be moved or copied to the new object. In our case, copying is disabled, but move operations are supported. They must move not just the pointer itself but also the policy object. We do this as we would any other class: by moving the object (moving pointers is more involved since they are built-in types, but all classes are assumed to handle their own move operations correctly or delete them). In the assignment operator, remember that the current object owned by the pointer must be deleted by the corresponding, i.e. old, policy; only then do we move the policy from the right-hand side of the assignment.

The only requirement on the deletion policy type is that it should be callable - the policy is invoked, just like a function with one argument, and the pointer to the object that must be deleted. For example, the behavior of our original pointer that called `operator delete` on the object can be replicated with the following deletion policy:

```
// Example 02
template <typename T>
struct DeleteByOperator {
  void operator()(T* p) const {
    delete p;
  }
};
```

To use this policy, we must specify its type when constructing the smart pointer, and, optionally, pass an object of this type to the constructor, although in this case, the default constructed object will work fine:

```
class C { ... };
SmartPtr<C, DeleteByOperator<C>> p(new C(42));
```

In C++17, the **constructor template argument deduction (CTAD)** can usually deduce the template parameters:

```
class C { ... };
SmartPtr p(new C(42));
```

If the deletion policy does not match the object type, a syntax error will be reported for the invalid call to `operator()`. This is usually undesirable: the error message is not particularly friendly, and, in general, the requirements on the policy have to be inferred from the use of the policy throughout the template (our policy has only one requirement, but this is our first and simplest policy). A good practice for writing classes with policies is to verify and document all requirements on the policy explicitly and in one place. In C++20, this can be done with concepts:

```
// Example 03
template <typename T, typename F> concept Callable1 =
  requires(F f, T* p) { { f(p) } -> std::same_as<void>; };
template <typename T, typename DeletionPolicy>
requires Callable1<T, DeletionPolicy>
class SmartPtr {
  ...
};
```

Before C++20, we can accomplish the same result with compile-time asserts:

```
// Example 04
template <typename T, typename DeletionPolicy>
requires Callable1<T, DeletionPolicy>
class SmartPtr {
  ...
  static_assert(std::is_same<
    void, decltype(deletion_policy_(p_))>::value, "");
};
```

Even in C++20, you may prefer the assert error messages. Both options accomplish the same goal: they verify that the policies meet all requirements and also express these requirements in a readable way and in one place in the code. It is up to you whether to include "movable" in these requirements: strictly speaking, the policy needs to be movable only if you need to move the smart pointer itself. It is reasonable to allow non-movable policies and require move operations only if they are needed.

Other deletion policies are needed for objects that were allocated in different ways. For example, if an object is created on a user-given heap object whose interface includes the member functions `allocate()` and `deallocate()` to, respectively, allocate and free memory, we can use the following heap deletion policy:

```
// Example 02
template <typename T> struct DeleteHeap {
  explicit DeleteHeap(Heap& heap) : heap_(heap) {}
  void operator()(T* p) const {
    p->~T();
    heap_.deallocate(p);
  }
  private:
  Heap& heap_;
};
```

On the other hand, if an object is constructed in some memory that is managed separately by the caller, then only the destructor of the object needs to be called:

```
// Example 02
template <typename T> struct DeleteDestructorOnly {
  void operator()(T* p) const {
    p->~T();
  }
};
```

We mentioned earlier that, because the policy is used as a callable entity, `deletion_policy_(p_)`, it can be of any type that can be called like a function. That includes the actual function:

```
// Example 02
using delete_int_t = void (*)(int*);
void delete_int(int* p) { delete p; }
SmartPtr<int, delete_int_t> p(new int(42), delete_int);
```

A template instantiation is also a function and can be used in the same way:

```
template <typename T> void delete_T(T* p) { delete p; }
SmartPtr<int, delete_int_t> p(new int(42), delete_T<int>);
```

Of all the possible deletion policies, one is often the most commonly used. In most programs, it will likely be deletion by the default `operator delete` function. If this is so, it makes sense to avoid specifying this one policy every time it's used and make it the default:

```
// Example 02
template <typename T,
          typename DeletionPolicy = DeleteByOperator<T>>
class SmartPtr {
  ...
};
```

Now, our policy-based smart pointer can be used in exactly the same way as the original version, with only one deletion option:

```
SmartPtr<C> p(new C(42));
```

Here, the second template parameter is left to its default value, `DeleteByOperator<C>`, and a default constructed object of this type is passed to the constructor as the default second argument.

At this point, I must caution you against a subtle mistake that could be made when implementing such policy-based classes. Note that the policy object is captured in the constructor of the smart pointer by a `const` reference:

```
explicit SmartPtr(T* p = nullptr,
  const DeletionPolicy& del_policy = DeletionPolicy());
```

The const reference here is important since a non-const reference cannot be bound to a temporary object (we will consider the r-value references later in this section). However, the policy is stored in the object itself by value, and, thus, a copy of the policy object must be made:

```
template <typename T,
          typename DeletionPolicy = DeleteByOperator<T>>
class SmartPtr {
  T* p_;
  DeletionPolicy deletion_policy_;
  ...
};
```

It may be tempting to avoid the copy and capture the policy by reference in the smart pointer as well:

```
// Example 05
template <typename T,
          typename DeletionPolicy = DeleteByOperator<T>>
class SmartPtr {
  T* p_;
  const DeletionPolicy& deletion_policy_;
  ...
};
```

In some cases, this will even work, for example:

```
Heap h;
DeleteHeap<C> del_h(h);
SmartPtr<C, DeleteHeap<C>> p(new (&heap) C, del_h);
```

However, it won't work for the default way to create smart pointers or any other smart pointer that is initialized with a temporary policy object:

```
SmartPtr<C> p(new C, DeleteByOperator<C>());
```

This code will compile. Unfortunately, it is incorrect - the temporary `DeleteByOperator<C>` object is constructed just before the `SmartPtr` constructor is called, but is destroyed at the end of the statement. The reference inside the `SmartPtr` object is left dangling. At first glance, this should not surprise anyone - of course, the temporary object does not outlive the statement in which it was created - it is deleted at the closing semicolon at the latest. A reader who is more versed in subtle language details may ask - *doesn't the standard specifically extend the lifetime of a temporary bound to a constant reference?* Indeed, it does; for example:

```
{
  const C& c = C();
  ... c is not dangling! ...
} // the temporary is deleted here
```

In this code fragment, the temporary object C() is not deleted at the end of the sentence, but only at the end of the lifetime of the reference to which it is bound. So, why didn't the same trick work for our deletion policy object? The answer is, it sort of did - the temporary object that was created when the argument to the constructor was evaluated and bound to the const reference argument was not destroyed for the lifetime of that reference, which is the duration of the constructor call. Actually, it would not have been destroyed anyway - all temporary objects that are created during the evaluation of the function arguments are deleted at the end of the sentence containing the function call, that is, at the closing semicolon. The function, in our case, is the constructor of the object, and so the lifetime of the temporaries spans the entire call to the constructor. It does not, however, extend to the lifetime of the object - the const reference member of the object is not bound to the temporary object, but to the constructor parameter, which itself is a const reference.

The lifetime extension works only once - the reference bound to a temporary object extends its lifetime. Another reference that's bound to the first one does nothing else and may be left dangling if the object is destroyed (the **address sanitizer (ASAN)** of GCC and CLANG helps to find such bugs). Therefore, if the policy object needs to be stored as a data member of the smart pointer, it has to be copied.

Usually, policy objects are small, and copying them is trivial. However, sometimes, a policy object may have a non-trivial internal state that is expensive to copy. You could also imagine a policy object that is non-copyable. In these cases, it may make sense to move the argument object into the data member object. This is easy to do if we declare an overload that is similar to a move constructor:

```
// Example 06
template <typename T,
          typename DeletionPolicy = DeleteByOperator<T>>
class SmartPtr {
  T* p_;
  DeletionPolicy deletion_policy_;
  public:
  explicit SmartPtr(T* p = nullptr,
      DeletionPolicy&& del_policy = DeletionPolicy())
    : p_(p), deletion_policy_(std::move(del_policy))
  {}
  ...
};
```

As we said, the policy objects are usually small, so copying them is rarely an issue. If you do need both constructors, make sure that only one has default arguments, so the call to a constructor with no arguments or with no policy argument is not ambiguous.

We now have a smart pointer class that has been implemented once, but whose deletion implementation can be customized at compile time by specifying the deletion policy. We could even add a new deletion policy that did not exist at the time the class was designed, and it will work as long as it conforms to the same calling interface. Next, we will consider different ways to implement policy objects.

Implementation of policies

In the previous section, we learned how to implement the simplest policy object. The policy can be of any type as long as it conforms to the interface convention, and is stored in the class as a data member. The policy object is most commonly generated by a template; however, it could be a regular, non-template, object that's specific to a particular pointer type, or even a function. The use of the policy was limited to a specific behavioral aspect, such as the deletion of the object owned by the smart pointer.

There are several ways in which such policies can be implemented and used. First of all, let's review the declaration of a smart pointer with a deletion policy:

```
template <typename T,
          typename DeletionPolicy = DeleteByOperator<T>>
class SmartPtr { ... };
```

Next, let's look at how we can construct a smart pointer object:

```
class C { ... };
SmartPtr<C, DeleteByOperator<C>> p(
  new C(42), DeleteByOperator<C>());
```

One disadvantage of this design jumps out at once - the type C is mentioned four times in the definition of the object p - it must be consistent in all four places, or the code will not compile. C++17 allows us to simplify the definition somewhat:

```
SmartPtr p(new C, DeleteByOperator<C>());
```

Here, the constructor is used to deduce the parameters of the class template from the constructor arguments, in a manner similar to that of function templates. There are still two mentions of the type C that must be consistent.

One alternative implementation that works for stateless policies as well as for policy objects whose internal state does not depend on the types of the primary template (in our case, the type T of the SmartPtr template) is to make the policy itself a non-template object but give it a template member function. For example, the DeleteByOperator policy is stateless (the object has no data members) and can be implemented without a class template:

```
// Example 07
struct DeleteByOperator {
  template <typename T> void operator()(T* p) const {
    delete p;
  }
};
```

This is a non-template object, so it does not need a type parameter. The member function template is instantiated on the type of object that needs to be deleted - the type is deduced by the compiler. Since the type of the policy object is always the same, we do not have to worry about specifying consistent types when creating the smart pointer object:

```
// Example 07
SmartPtr<C, DeleteByOperator> p(
   new C, DeleteByOperator());          // Before C++17
SmartPtr p(new C, DeleteByOperator());    // C++17
```

This object can be used by our smart pointer as it is, with no changes to the `SmartPtr` template, although we may want to change the default template argument:

```
template <typename T,
          typename DeletionPolicy = DeleteByOperator>
class SmartPtr { ... };
```

A more complex policy, such as the heap deletion policy, can still be implemented using this approach:

```
struct DeleteHeap {
   explicit DeleteHeap(SmallHeap& heap) : heap_(heap) {}
   template <typename T> void operator()(T* p) const {
      p->~T();
      heap_.deallocate(p);
   }
   private:
   Heap& heap_;
};
```

This policy has an internal state - the reference to the heap - but nothing in this policy object depends on the type T of the object we need to delete, except for the `operator()` member function. Therefore, the policy does not need to be parameterized by the object type.

Since the main template, `SmartPtr`, did not have to be changed when we converted our policies from class templates to non-template classes with template member functions, there is no reason why we cannot use both types of policies with the same class. Indeed, any of the template class policies from the previous subsection would still work, so we can have some deletion policies implemented as classes and others as class templates. The latter is useful when the policy has data members whose type depends on the object type of the smart pointer.

If the policies are implemented as class templates, we have to specify the correct type to instantiate the policy for use with each specific policy-based class. In many cases, this is a very repetitive process - the same type is used to parameterize the main template and its policies. We can get the compiler to do this job for us if we use the entire template and not its particular instantiation as a policy:

```
// Example 08
template <typename T,
```

```
            template <typename> class DeletionPolicy =
                                    DeleteByOperator>
class SmartPtr {
  public:
  explicit SmartPtr(T* p = nullptr,
    const DeletionPolicy<T>& del_policy =
                          DeletionPolicy<T>())
  : p_(p), deletion_policy_(deletion_policy)
  {}
  ~SmartPtr() {
    deletion_policy_(p_);
  }
  ...
};
```

Note the syntax for the second template parameter - `template <typename> class DeletionPolicy`. This is known as a *template template* parameter - the parameter of a template is itself a template. The `class` keyword is necessary in C++14 and earlier; in C++17, it can be replaced with `typename`. To use this parameter, we need to instantiate it with some type; in our case, it is the main template type parameter T. This ensures the consistency of the object type in the primary smart pointer template and its policies, although the constructor argument still must be constructed with the correct type:

```
SmartPtr<C, DeleteByOperator> p(
  new C, DeleteByOperator<C>());
```

Again, in C++17, the class template parameters can be deduced by the constructor; this works for template template parameters as well:

```
SmartPtr p(new C, DeleteByOperator<C>());
```

The template template parameters seem like an attractive alternative to the regular type parameters when the types are instantiated from a template anyway. Why don't we always use them? First of all, as you can see, they are somewhat less flexible than template class parameters: they save typing in the common case when the policy is a template with the same first argument as the class itself, but they don't work in any other case (the policy may be a non-template or a template that requires more than one argument). The other issue is that, as written, the template template parameter has one significant limitation - the number of template parameters has to match the specification precisely, including the default arguments. In other words, let's say I have the following template:

```
template <typename T, typename Heap = MyHeap> class DeleteHeap { ...
};
```

This template cannot be used as a parameter of the preceding smart pointer - it has two template parameters, while we only specified only one in the declaration of `SmartPtr` (a parameter with a default value is still a parameter). This limitation is easy to work around: all we have to do is define the template template parameter as a variadic template:

```
// Example 09
template <typename T,
          template <typename...> class DeletionPolicy =
                                        DeleteByOperator>
class SmartPtr {
    ...
};
```

Now the deletion policy template can have any number of type parameters as long as they have default values (`DeletionPolicy<T>` is what we use in the `SmartPtr` and it has to compile). In contrast, we can use an instantiation of the `DeleteHeap` template for a smart pointer where the `DeletionPolicy` is a type parameter, not a template template parameter - we just need a class, and `DeleteHeap<int, MyHeap>` will do as good as any.

So far, we have always captured the policy object as a data member of the policy-based class. This approach to integrating classes into a larger class is known as **composition**. There are other ways in which the primary template can get access to the customized behavior algorithms provided by the policies, which we will consider next.

Use of policy objects

All of our examples until now have stored the policy object as a data member of the class. This is generally the preferred way of storing the policies, but it has one significant downside - a data member always has a non-zero size. Consider our smart pointer with one of the deletion policies:

```
template <typename T> struct DeleteByOperator {
  void operator()(T* p) const {
    delete p;
  }
};
template <typename T,
          typename DeletionPolicy = DeleteByOperator<T>>
class SmartPtr {
  T* p_;
  DeletionPolicy deletion_policy_;
  ...
};
```

Note that the policy object has no data members. However, the size of the object is not zero, but one byte (we can verify that by printing the value of `sizeof(DeleteByOperator<int>)`). This is necessary because every object in a C++ program must have a unique address:

```
DeleteByOperator<int> d1;    // &d1 = ....
DeleteByOperator<long> d2; // &d2 must be != &d1
```

When two objects are laid out consecutively in memory, the difference between their addresses is the size of the first object (plus padding, if necessary). To prevent both the d1 and d2 objects from residing at the same address, the standard mandates that their size is at least one byte.

When used as a data member of another class, an object will occupy at least as much space as its size requires, which in our case, is one byte. Assuming that the pointer takes 8 bytes, the entire object is, therefore, 9 bytes long. But the size of an object also has to be padded to the nearest value that meets the alignment requirements - if the address of the pointer has to be aligned on 8 bytes, the object can be either 8 bytes or 16 bytes, but not in-between. So, adding an empty policy object to the class ends up changing its size from 8 bytes to 16 bytes. This is purely a waste of memory and is often undesirable, especially for objects that are created in large numbers, such as pointers. It is not possible to coax the compiler into creating a data member of zero size; the standard forbids it. But there is another way in which policies can be used without the overhead.

The alternative to composition is inheritance - we can use the policy as a base class for the primary class:

```
// Example 10
template <typename T,
          typename DeletionPolicy = DeleteByOperator<T>>
class SmartPtr : private DeletionPolicy {
  T* p_;
  public:
  explicit SmartPtr(T* p = nullptr,
    DeletionPolicy&& deletion_policy = DeletionPolicy())
  : DeletionPolicy(std::move(deletion_policy)), p_(p)
  {}
  ~SmartPtr() {
    DeletionPolicy::operator()(p_);
  }
  ...
};
```

This approach relies on a particular optimization - if a base class is empty (has no non-static data members), it can be completely optimized out of the layout of the derived class. This is known as the **empty base class optimization**. It is allowed by the standard, but usually isn't required (C++11 requires this optimization for certain classes, but not for the classes we are using in this chapter). Even though it is not required, it is almost universally done by modern compilers. With empty base class optimization, the size of the derived `SmartPtr` class is only as large as necessary to hold its data members - in our case, 8 bytes.

When using inheritance for policies, the choice must be made between public or private inheritance. Usually, the policies are used to provide an implementation for a particular aspect of behavior. Such inheritance for implementation is expressed through private inheritance. In some cases, a policy may be used to change the public interface of the class; in this case, public inheritance should be used. For the deletion policy, we are not changing the interface of the class - the smart pointer always deletes the object at the end of its life; the only question is how. Therefore, the deletion policy should use private inheritance.

While the deletion policy using the `operator delete` is stateless, some policies have data members that must be preserved from the object given to the constructor. Therefore, in general, the base class policy should be initialized from the constructor argument by copying or moving it into the base class, similarly to the way we initialized the data members. The base classes are always initialized on the member initialization list before the data members of the derived class. Finally, the `base_type::function_name()` syntax can be used to call a member function of a base class; in our case, `DeletionPolicy::operator()(p_)`.

Inheritance or composition are the two choices for integrating the policy class into the primary class. In general, the composition should be preferred, unless there is a reason to use inheritance. We have already seen one such reason - the empty base class optimization. Inheritance is also a necessary choice if we want to affect the public interface of the class.

Our smart pointer is, so far, missing several important features that are commonly found in most smart pointer implementations. One such feature is the ability to release the pointer, that is, to prevent the automatic destruction of the object from taking place. This can be useful if, in some cases, the object is destroyed by some other means, or, alternatively, if the lifetime of the object needs to be extended and its ownership is passed to another resource-owning object. We can easily add this feature to our smart pointer:

```
template <typename T,
          typename DeletionPolicy>
class SmartPtr : private DeletionPolicy {
  T* p_;
  public:
  ~SmartPtr() {
    if (p) DeletionPolicy::operator()(p_);
  }
  void release() { p_ = nullptr; }
  ...
};
```

Now, we can call `p.release()` on our smart pointer, and the destructor will do nothing. We can hard-code the release feature into the pointer, but sometimes you may want to enforce the deletion as it is done in the pointer, with no release. This calls for making the release feature optional, controlled by another policy. We can add a `ReleasePolicy` template parameter to control whether the `release()` member function is present, but what should it do? We could, of course, move the implementation of `SmartPtr::release()` into the policy:

```
// Example 11
template <typename T> struct WithRelease {
  void release(T*& p) { p = nullptr; }
};
```

Now, the `SmartPtr` implementation only has to call `ReleasePolicy::release(p_)` to delegate the appropriate handling of `release()` to the policy. But what is the appropriate handling if we do not want to support the release functionality? Our no-release policy can simply do nothing, but this is misleading - the user has the expectation that, if `release()` was called, the object would not be destroyed. We could assert at runtime and terminate the program. This converts a logic error on the part of the programmer - trying to release a no-release smart pointer - into a runtime error. The best way would be for the `SmartPtr` class to not have the `release()` member function at all if it is not wanted. This way, the incorrect code would be impossible to compile. The only way to do this is to make the policy inject a new public member function into the public interface of the primary template. This can be accomplished using public inheritance:

```
template <typename T,
          typename DeletionPolicy,
          typename ReleasePolicy>
class SmartPtr : private DeletionPolicy,
                 public ReleasePolicy {
  ...
};
```

Now, if the release policy has a public member function called `release()`, then so does the `SmartPtr` class.

This solves the interface problem. Now, there is a small matter of implementation. The `release()` member function has now moved into the policy class, but it must operate on the data member p_ of the parent class. One way to do this would be to pass a reference to this pointer from the derived class to the base policy class during construction. This is an ugly implementation - it wastes 8 bytes of memory to store a reference to a data member that is almost "right there," which is stored in the derived class right next to the base class itself. A much better way is to cast from the base class to the correct derived class. Of course, for this to work, the base class needs to know what the correct derived class is. The solution to this problem is the **Curiously Recurring Template Pattern (CRTP)** that we studied in this book: the policy should be a template (so we will need a template template parameter) that is instantiated on the derived class type.

This way, the `SmartPtr` class is both the derived class of the release policy and the template parameter of it:

```
// Example 11
template <typename T,
          typename DeletionPolicy = DeleteByOperator<T>,
          template <typename...> class ReleasePolicy =
                                        WithRelease>
class SmartPtr : private DeletionPolicy,
                 public ReleasePolicy<SmartPtr<T,
                       DeletionPolicy, ReleasePolicy>>
{ ... };
```

Note that the `ReleasePolicy` template is specialized with the concrete instantiation of the `SmartPtr` template, including all its policies, and including the `ReleasePolicy` itself.

Now, the release policy knows the type of the derived class and can cast itself to that type. This case is always safe because the correct derived class is guaranteed by construction:

```
// Example 11
template <typename P> struct WithRelease {
  void release() { static_cast<P*>(this)->p_ = nullptr; }
};
```

The template parameter P will be substituted with the type of the smart pointer. Once the smart pointer publicly inherits from the release policy, the public member function, `release()`, of the policy is inherited and becomes a part of the smart pointer public interface.

The last detail concerning the implementation of the release policy has to do with the access. As we've written so far, the data member `p_` is private in the `SmartPtr` class and cannot be accessed by its base classes directly. The solution to this is to declare the corresponding base class to be a friend of the derived class:

```
// Example 11
template <typename T,
          typename DeletionPolicy = DeleteByOperator<T>,
          template <typename...> class ReleasePolicy =
                                        WithRelease>
class SmartPtr : private DeletionPolicy,
   public ReleasePolicy<SmartPtr<T, DeletionPolicy,
                             ReleasePolicy>>
{
   friend class ReleasePolicy<SmartPtr>;
   T* p_;
   ...
};
```

Note that inside the body of the SmartPtr class, we do not need to repeat all the template parameters. The shorthand SmartPtr refers to the currently instantiated template. This does not extend to the part of the class declaration before the opening brace of the class, so we had to repeat the template parameters when specifying the policy as a base class.

The no-release policy is just as easy to write:

```
// Example 11
template <typename P> struct NoRelease {};
```

There is no release() function here, so an attempt to call release() on a smart pointer with this policy will not compile. This solves our stated requirement to have a release() public member function only when it makes sense to call one. The policy-based design is a complex pattern, and it is rare to be limited to just one way to do something. There is another way to accomplish the same objective, we are going to study it later in this chapter, in the section, *Using policies to control the public interface*.

There is yet another way in which policy objects can sometimes be used. This applies only to policies that have no internal state in any version of the policy, by design. For example, our deletion policies are sometimes stateless, but the one with the reference to the caller's heap is not, so this is a policy that is not always stateless. The release policy can always be considered stateless; there is no reason for us to add a data member to it, but it is constrained to be used through public inheritance because its primary effect is to inject a new public member function.

Let's consider another aspect of behavior that we may want to customize - debugging or logging. For debugging purposes, it may be convenient to print when an object is owned by a smart pointer and when it is deleted. We could add a debugging policy to the smart pointer to support this. The debug policy has to do only one thing, and that is to print something when a smart pointer is constructed or destroyed. It does not need access to the smart pointer if we pass the value of the pointer to the printing function. Therefore, we can make the print functions static in the debug policy and not store this policy in the smart pointer class at all:

```
// Example 12
template <typename T,
          typename DeletionPolicy,
          typename DebugPolicy = NoDebug>
class SmartPtr : private DeletionPolicy {
  T* p_;
  public:
  explicit SmartPtr(T* p = nullptr,
    DeletionPolicy&& deletion_policy = DeletionPolicy())
  : DeletionPolicy(std::move(deletion_policy)), p_(p) {
    DebugPolicy::constructed(p_);
  }
  ~SmartPtr() {
    DebugPolicy::deleted(p_);
```

```
    DeletionPolicy::operator()(p_);
  }
  ...
};
```

For simplicity, we have omitted the release policy, but multiple policies are easy to combine. The debugging policy implementation is straightforward:

```
// Example 12
struct Debug {
  template <typename T>
  static void constructed(const T* p) {
    std::cout << "Constructed SmartPtr for object " <<
      static_cast<const void*>(p) << std::endl;
  }
  template <typename T>
  static void deleted(const T* p) {
    std::cout << "Destroyed SmartPtr for object " <<
      static_cast<const void*>(p) << std::endl;
  }
};
```

We have chosen to implement the policy as a non-template class with template static member functions. Alternatively, we could have implemented it as a template, parametrized with the object type T. The no-debug version of the policy, which is the default, is even simpler. It must have the same functions defined, but they don't do anything:

```
// Example 12
struct NoDebug {
  template <typename T>
    static void constructed(const T* p) {}
  template <typename T> static void deleted(const T* p) {}
};
```

We can expect the compiler to inline the empty template functions at the call site and optimize the entire call away since no code needs to be generated.

Note that by choosing this implementation of policies, we made a somewhat restrictive design decision - all versions of the debug policy must be stateless. We may, in time, come to regret this decision if we need to, for example, store a custom output stream inside a debug policy, instead of the default std::cout. But even in that case, only the implementation of the smart pointer class will have to change - the client code will continue to work with no changes.

We have considered three different ways to incorporate the policy objects into the policy-based class - by composition, by inheritance (public or private), and by compile-time incorporation only, where the policy object does not need to be stored inside the main object at runtime. We will now move on to more advanced techniques for policy-based design.

Advanced policy-based design

The techniques we have introduced in the previous section form the foundation of policy-based design - policies can be classes, template instantiations, or templates (used by template template parameters). The policy classes can be composed, inherited, or used statically at compile time. If a policy needs to know the type of the primary policy-based class, the CRTP can be used. The rest is largely variations on the same theme, as well as tricky ways to combine several techniques to accomplish something new. We will now consider some of these more advanced techniques.

Policies for constructors

Policies can be used to customize almost any aspect of the implementation, as well as to alter the class interface. However, there are unique challenges that arise when we attempt to customize class constructors using policies.

As an example, let's consider another limitation of our current smart pointer. As it stands so far, the object owned by the smart pointer is always deleted when the smart pointer is deleted. If the smart pointer supports release, then we can call the `release()` member function and be wholly responsible for the deletion of the object. But how are we going to ensure this deletion? The most likely way is, we will let another smart pointer own it:

```
SmartPtr<C> p1(new C);
SmartPtr<C> p2(&*p1); // Now two pointers own one object
p1.release();
```

This approach is verbose and error-prone - we temporarily let two pointers own the same object. If something were to happen at this moment that causes both pointers to be deleted, we would destroy the same object twice. We also have to remember to always release one of these pointers, but only one. We should take the higher-level view of the problem - we are trying to pass the ownership of the object from one smart pointer to another.

The better way to do this is by moving the first pointer into the second:

```
SmartPtr<C> p1(new C);
SmartPtr<C> p2(std::move(p1));
```

Now, the first pointer is left in the moved-from state, which we can define (the only requirement is that the destructor call must be valid). We choose to define it to be a pointer that does not own any object, that is, a pointer in the released state. The second pointer receives the ownership of the object and will delete it in due time.

To support this functionality, we must implement the move constructor. However, there may be a reason to sometimes prevent the transfer of ownership. Therefore, we may want to have both movable and non-movable pointers. This calls for yet another policy to control whether moving is supported:

```
template <typename T,
  typename DeletionPolicy = DeleteByOperator<T>,
  typename MovePolicy = MoveForbidden
>
class SmartPtr ...;
```

For simplicity, we have reverted to just one other policy - the deletion policy. The other policies we have considered can be added alongside the new MovePolicy. The deletion policy can be implemented in any of the ways we have learned already. Since it is likely to benefit from the empty base optimization, we will stay with the inheritance-based implementation for it. The move policy can be implemented in several different ways, but inheritance is probably the easiest:

```
// Example 13
template <typename T,
  typename DeletionPolicy = DeleteByOperator<T>,
  typename MovePolicy = MoveForbidden>
class SmartPtr : private DeletionPolicy,
                 private MovePolicy {
  T* p_;
  public:
  explicit SmartPtr(T* p = nullptr,
    DeletionPolicy&& deletion_policy = DeletionPolicy())
    : DeletionPolicy(std::move(deletion_policy)),
      MovePolicy(), p_(p) {}
  ... SmartPtr code unchanged ...
  SmartPtr(SmartPtr&& that) :
    DeletionPolicy(std::move(that)),
    MovePolicy(std::move(that)),
    p_(std::exchange(that.p_, nullptr)) {}
  SmartPtr(const SmartPtr&) = delete;
};
```

With both policies integrated using private inheritance, we now have a derived object with several base classes. Such multiple inheritance is fairly common in policy-based design in C++, and should not alarm you. This technique is sometimes known as *mix-in* since the implementation of the derived class is *mixed* from the pieces provided by the base classes. In C++, the term *mix-in* is also used to refer to a totally different inheritance scheme that is related to the CRTP, so the use of this term often creates confusion (in most object-oriented languages, *mix-in* unambiguously refers to the application of multiple inheritance that we can see here).

The new feature in our smart pointer class is the move constructor. The move constructor is unconditionally present in the `SmartPtr` class. However, its implementation requires that all base classes be movable. This gives us a way to disable move support with a non-movable move policy:

```
// Example 13
struct MoveForbidden {
  MoveForbidden() = default;
  MoveForbidden(MoveForbidden&&) = delete;
  MoveForbidden(const MoveForbidden&) = delete;
  MoveForbidden& operator=(MoveForbidden&&) = delete;
  MoveForbidden& operator=(const MoveForbidden&) = delete;
};
```

The movable policy is much simpler:

```
// Example 13
struct MoveAllowed {
};
```

We can now construct a movable pointer and a non-movable pointer:

```
class C { ... };
SmartPtr<C, DeleteByOperator<C>, MoveAllowed> p = ...;
auto p1(std::move(p)); // OK
SmartPtr<C, DeleteByOperator<C>, MoveForbidden> q = ...;
auto q1(std::move(q)); // Does not compile
```

An attempt to move a non-movable pointer does not compile because one of the base classes, `MoveForbidden`, is non-movable (does not have a move constructor). Note that the moved-from pointer p in the preceding example can be safely deleted, but cannot be used in any other way. In particular, it cannot be dereferenced.

While we are dealing with movable pointers, it would make sense to provide a move assignment operator as well:

```
// Example 13
template <typename T,
  typename DeletionPolicy = DeleteByOperator<T>,
  typename MovePolicy = MoveForbidden>
class SmartPtr : private DeletionPolicy,
                 private MovePolicy {
  T* p_;
  public:
```

```
explicit SmartPtr(T* p = nullptr,
  DeletionPolicy&& deletion_policy = DeletionPolicy())
  : DeletionPolicy(std::move(deletion_policy)),
    MovePolicy(), p_(p) {}
... SmartPtr code unchanged ...
SmartPtr& operator=(SmartPtr&& that) {
  if (this == &that) return *this;
  DeletionPolicy::operator()(p_);
  p_ = std::exchange(that.p_, nullptr);
  DeletionPolicy::operator=(std::move(that));
  MovePolicy::operator=(std::move(that));
  return *this;
}
SmartPtr& operator=(const SmartPtr&) = delete;
};
```

Note the check for the self-assignment. Unlike the copy assignment, which is required to do nothing for self-assignment, the move assignment is less constrained by the standard. The only certain requirement is that the self-move should always leave an object in a well-defined state (the moved-from state is an example of such a state). A no-op self-move is not required but is valid as well. Also, note the way in which the base classes are move-assigned - the easiest way is to invoke the move assignment operator of each base class directly. There is no need to cast the derived class that to each of the base types - this is an implicitly performed cast. We must not forget to set the moved-from pointer to nullptr, otherwise, the object owned by these pointers will be deleted twice.

For simplicity, we have ignored all of the policies we introduced earlier. This is fine – not all designs need everything to be controlled by a policy, and, in any case, it is quite straightforward to combine multiple policies. However, it is a good opportunity to point out that different policies are sometimes related - for example, if we use both a release policy and a move policy, the use of a movable move policy strongly suggests that the object must support release (a released pointer is similar to a moved-from pointer). Using template metaprogramming, we can force such dependence between the policies, if need be.

Note that a policy that needs to disable or enable constructors does not automatically have to be used as a base class - move assignment or construction also moves all data members, and, therefore, a non-movable data member will disable the move operations just as well. The more important reason to use inheritance here is the empty base class optimization: if we introduced a MovePolicy data member into our class, it would double the object size from 8 to 16 bytes on a 64-bit machine.

We have considered making our pointers movable. But what about copying? So far, we have disallowed copying outright - both the copy constructor and the copy assignment operator are deleted in our smart pointer from the very beginning. This makes sense so far - we do not want to have two smart pointers own the same object and delete it twice. But there is another type of ownership where the copy operation makes perfect sense - the shared ownership, such as what's implemented by a reference-counting shared pointer. With this type of pointer, copying the pointer is allowed, and both pointers now equally own the pointed-to object. A reference count is maintained to count how many pointers to the same object exist in the program. When the very last pointer owning a particular object is deleted, so is the object itself, since there are no more references to it.

There are several ways to implement a reference-counted shared pointer, but let's start with the design of the class and its policies. We still need a deletion policy, and it makes sense to have a single policy control the move and copy operations. For simplicity, we will again limit ourselves to just the policies we are currently exploring:

```cpp
// Example 14
template <typename T,
  typename DeletionPolicy = DeleteByOperator<T>,
  typename CopyMovePolicy = NoMoveNoCopy
>
class SmartPtr : private DeletionPolicy,
                 public CopyMovePolicy {
  T* p_;
  public:
  explicit SmartPtr(T* p = nullptr,
    DeletionPolicy&& deletion_policy = DeletionPolicy())
    : DeletionPolicy(std::move(deletion_policy)), p_(p)
  {}
  SmartPtr(SmartPtr&& other) :
    DeletionPolicy(std::move(other)),
    CopyMovePolicy(std::move(other)),
    p_(std::exchange(that.p_, nullptr)) {}
  SmartPtr(const SmartPtr& other) :
    DeletionPolicy(other),
    CopyMovePolicy(other),
    p_(other.p_) {}
  ~SmartPtr() {
    if (CopyMovePolicy::must_delete())
      DeletionPolicy::operator()(p_);
  }
};
```

The copy operations are no longer unconditionally deleted. Both the copy and the move constructor are provided (the two assignment operators are omitted for brevity, but should be implemented in the same way it was done earlier).

The deletion of the object in the destructor of the smart pointer is no longer unconditional - in the case of the reference-counted pointer, the copying policy maintains the reference count and knows when there is only one copy of the smart pointer for a particular object.

The smart pointer class itself provides the requirements for the policy classes. The no-move, no-copy policy must disallow all copy and move operations:

```
// Example 14
class NoMoveNoCopy {
  protected:
  NoMoveNoCopy() = default;
  NoMoveNoCopy(NoMoveNoCopy&&) = delete;
  NoMoveNoCopy(const NoMoveNoCopy&) = delete;
  NoMoveNoCopy& operator=(NoMoveNoCopy&&) = delete;
  NoMoveNoCopy& operator=(const NoMoveNoCopy&) = delete;
  constexpr bool must_delete() const { return true; }
};
```

In addition to that, the non-copyable smart pointer always deletes the object it owns in its destructor, so the `must_delete()` member function should always return `true`. Note that this function must be implemented by all copying policies, even if it is trivial, otherwise, the smart pointer class will not compile. However, we can fully expect the compiler to optimize the call away and unconditionally call the destructor when this policy is used.

The move-only policy is similar to the movable policy we had earlier, but now we must explicitly enable the move operations and disable the copy operations:

```
// Example 14
class MoveNoCopy {
  protected:
  MoveNoCopy() = default;
  MoveNoCopy(MoveNoCopy&&) = default;
  MoveNoCopy(const MoveNoCopy&) = delete;
  MoveNoCopy& operator=(MoveNoCopy&&) = default;
  MoveNoCopy& operator=(const MoveNoCopy&) = delete;
  constexpr bool must_delete() const { return true; }
};
```

Again, the deletion is unconditional (the pointer inside the smart pointer object can be null if the object was moved, but this does not prevent us from calling `operator delete` on it). This policy allows the move constructor and the move assignment operator to compile; the `SmartPtr` class provides the correct implementation for these operations, and no additional support from the policy is required.

The reference-counting copying policy is much more complex. Here, we have to decide on the shared pointer implementation. The simplest implementation allocates the reference counter in a separate memory allocation, which is managed by the copying policy. Let's start with a reference-counted copying policy that does not allow move operations:

```
// Example 14
class NoMoveCopyRefCounted {
```

```
  size_t* count_;
protected:
NoMoveCopyRefCounted() : count_(new size_t(1)) {}
NoMoveCopyRefCounted(const NoMoveCopyRefCounted& other) :
  count_(other.count_)
{
  ++(*count_);
}
NoMoveCopyRefCounted(NoMoveCopyRefCounted&&) = delete;
~NoMoveCopyRefCounted() {
  --(*count_);
  if (*count_ == 0) {
    delete count_;
  }
}
  bool must_delete() const { return *count_ == 1; }
};
```

When a smart pointer with this copying policy is constructed, a new reference counter is allocated and initialized to one (we have one smart pointer pointing to the particular object - the one we are now constructing). When a smart pointer is copied, so are all its base classes, including the copy policy. The copy constructor of this policy simply increments the reference count. When a smart pointer is deleted, the reference count is decremented. The very last smart pointer to be deleted also deletes the count itself. The copying policy also controls when the pointed-to object is deleted - it happens when the reference count reaches one, which means that we are about to delete the very last pointer for this object. It is, of course, very important to make sure that the counter is not deleted before the `must_delete()` function is called. This is guaranteed to be true since the destructors of the base classes run after the destructor of the derived class - the derived class of the last smart pointer will see the counter value of one and will delete the object; then, the destructor of the copying policy will decrement the counter once more, see it drop to zero, and delete the counter itself.

With this policy, we can implement shared ownership of an object:

```
SmartPtr<C, DeleteByOperator<C>, NoMoveCopyRefCounted> p1{new C};
auto p2(p1);
```

Now, we have two pointers to the same object, with the reference count of two. The object is deleted when the last of the two pointers is, assuming that no more copies are created beforehand. The smart pointer is copyable, but not movable:

```
SmartPtr<C, DeleteByOperator<C>, NoMoveCopyRefCounted> p1{new C};
auto p2(std::move(p1)); // Does not compile
```

In general, once reference-counted copying is supported, there is probably no reason to disallow move operations, unless they are simply not needed (in which case, the no-move implementation can be slightly more efficient). To support the move, we must give some thought to the moved-from state of the reference-counting policy – clearly, it must not decrement the reference counter when it is deleted, since a moved-from pointer no longer owns the object. The simplest way is to reset the pointer to the reference counter so that it is no longer accessible from the copying policy, but then the copying policy must support the special case of a null counter pointer:

```cpp
// Example 15
class MoveCopyRefCounted {
  size_t* count_;
  protected:
  MoveCopyRefCounted() : count_(new size_t(1)) {}
  MoveCopyRefCounted(const MoveCopyRefCounted& other) :
    count_(other.count_)
  {
    if (count_) ++(*count_);
  }
  ~MoveCopyRefCounted() {
    if (!count_) return;
    --(*count_);
    if (*count_ == 0) {
      delete count_;
    }
  }
  MoveCopyRefCounted(MoveCopyRefCounted&& other) :
    count_(std::exchange(other.count_, nullptr)) {}
  bool must_delete() const {
    return count_ && *count_ == 1;
  }
};
```

Finally, a reference-counting copying policy must support the assignment operations as well. These are implemented similarly to the copy or move constructors (but take care to use the left-hand-side policies for the deletion of the left-hand-side objects before assigning the new values to the policies).

As you have seen, some of the policy implementations can get pretty complex, and their interactions are even more so. Fortunately, the policy-based design is particularly well-suited for writing testable objects. This application of policy-based design is so important that it deserves special mention.

Policies for test

We will now show the reader how to use policy-based design to write better tests. In particular, policies can be used to make the code more testable by means of unit tests. This can be done by substituting a special test-only version of a policy instead of the regular one. Let us demonstrate this with the example of the reference-counting policy from the previous subsection.

The main challenge of that policy is, of course, maintaining the correct reference count. We can easily develop some tests that should exercise all of the corner cases of reference counting:

```
// Test 1: only one pointer
{
  SmartPtr<C, ... policies ...> p(new C);
} // C should be deleted here

// Test 2: one copy
{
  SmartPtr<C, ... policies ...> p(new C);
  {
    auto p1(p); // Reference count should be 2
  } // C should not be deleted here
} // C should be deleted here
```

The hard part is actually testing that all of this code works the way it is supposed to. We know what the reference count should be, but we have no way of checking what it really is (adding the public function count() to the smart pointer solves that problem, but it is the least of the difficulties). We know when the object is supposed to be deleted, but it is hard to verify that it actually was. We will probably get a crash if we delete the object twice, but even that is not certain. It is even harder to catch the case when the object is not deleted at all. A sanitizer can find such issues, at least if we use standard memory management, but they are not available in all environments and, unless the tests are designed to be run with the sanitizer, can produce very noisy output.

Fortunately, we can use policies to give our tests a window into the internal working of the object. For example, if we did not implement a public count() method in all our reference-counting policies, we can create a testable wrapper for the reference-counting policy:

```
class NoMoveCopyRefCounted {
  protected:
  size_t* count_;
  ...
};
class NoMoveCopyRefCountedTest :
  public NoMoveCopyRefCounted {
  public:
  using NoMoveCopyRefCounted::NoMoveCopyRefCounted;
  size_t count() const { return *count_; }
};
```

Note that we had to change the count_ data member from private to protected in the main copy policy. We could also declare the test policy a friend, but then we would have to do this for every new test policy. Now, we can actually implement our tests:

```
// Test 1: only one pointer
{
```

```
  SmartPtr<C, ... NoMoveCopyRefCountedTest> p(new C);
  assert(p.count() == 1);
} // C should be deleted here
// Test 2: one copy
{
  SmartPtr<C, ... NoMoveCopyRefCountedTest> p(new C);
  {
  auto p1(p); // Reference count should be 2
    assert(p.count() == 2);
    assert(p1.count() == 2);
    assert(&*p == &*p1);
  } // C should not be deleted here
  assert(p.count == 1);
} // C should be deleted here
```

Similarly, we can create an instrumented deletion policy that checks whether the object will be deleted, or record in some external logging object that it was actually deleted and test that the deletion was properly logged. We would need to instrument our smart pointer implementation to make calls to the debugging or testing policy:

```
// Example 16:
template <... template parameters ...,
          typename DebugPolicy = NoDebug>
class SmartPtr : ... base policies ... {
  T* p_;
  public:
  explicit SmartPtr(T* p = nullptr,
    DeletionPolicy&& deletion_policy = DeletionPolicy()) :
    DeletionPolicy(std::move(deletion_policy)), p_(p)
  {
    DebugPolicy::construct(this, p);
  }
  ~SmartPtr() {
    DebugPolicy::destroy(this, p_,
                         CopyMovePolicy::must_delete());
  if (CopyMovePolicy::must_delete())
    DeletionPolicy::operator()(p_);
  }
  ...
};
```

Both debug and production (non-debug) policies must have all the methods referenced in the class, but the empty methods of the non-debug policy are going to be inlined and optimized down to nothing.

```
// Example 16
struct NoDebug {
```

```
  template <typename P, typename T>
  static void construct(const P* ptr, const T* p) {}
  template <typename P, typename T>
  static void destroy(const P* ptr, const T* p,
                      bool must_delete) {}
  ... other events ...
};
```

The debug policies vary, the basic ones simply log all debuggable events:

```
// Example 16
struct Debug {
  template <typename P, typename T>
  static void construct(const P* ptr, const T* p) {
    std::cout << "Constructed SmartPtr at " << ptr <<
      ", object " << static_cast<const void*>(p) <<
      std::endl;
  }
  template <typename P, typename T>
  static void destroy(const P* ptr, const T* p,
                      bool must_delete) {
    std::cout << "Destroyed SmartPtr at " << ptr <<
      ", object " << static_cast<const void*>(p) <<
      (must_delete ? " is" : " is not") << " deleted" <<
      std::endl;
  }
};
```

The more complex policies can validate that the internal state of the objects is consistent with the requirements and that the class invariants are maintained.

By now, the reader has likely noticed that the declarations of the policy-based objects can be quite long:

```
SmartPtr<C, DeleteByOperator<T>, MoveNoCopy,
        WithRelease, Debug> p( ... );
```

This is one of the most frequently observed problems with policy-based design, and we should consider some ways to mitigate this problem.

Policy adapters and aliases

Perhaps the most obvious drawback of the policy-based design is the way we have to declare the concrete objects - specifically, the long list of policies that must be repeated every time. Judicious use of default parameters helps to simplify the most commonly used cases. For example, let us look at the following long declaration:

```
SmartPtr<C, DeleteByOperator<T>, MoveNoCopy,
```

```
        WithRelease, NoDebug>
p( ... );
```

Sometimes, this can be reduced to the following:

```
SmartPtr<C> p( ... );
```

This can be done if the defaults represent the most common case of a movable non-debug pointer that uses the `operator delete`. However, what is the point of adding the policies if we are not going to use them? A well-thought-out order of policy parameters helps to make the more common policy combinations shorter. For example, if the most common variation is the deletion policy, then a new pointer with a different deletion policy and default remaining policies can be declared without repeating the policies we do not need to change:

```
SmartPtr<C, DeleteHeap<T>> p( ... );
```

This still leaves the problem of the less commonly used policies. Also, policies are often added later as additional features must be added to the design. These policies are almost always added to the end of the parameter list. To do otherwise would require rewriting every bit of code where a policy-based class is declared to reorder its parameters. However, the late-coming policies are not necessarily less often used, and this evolution of the design may lead to a case where many policy arguments have to be explicitly written, even at their default values, so that one of the trailing arguments can be changed.

While there is no general solution to this problem within the confines of the traditional policy-based design, in practice, there are often few commonly used groups of policies, and then there are some frequent variations. For example, most of our smart pointers may be using `operator delete` and support move and release, but we frequently need to alternate between the debug and non-debug versions. This can be accomplished by creating adapters that convert a class with many policies to a new interface that exposes only the policies we want to change often and pins the rest of the policies to their commonly used values. Any large design will likely need more than one such adapter, as the commonly used sets of policies can vary.

The simplest way to write such an adapter is with the `using` alias:

```
// Example 17
template <typename T, typename DebugPolicy = NoDebug>
using SmartPtrAdapter =
    SmartPtr<T, DeleteByOperator<T>, MoveNoCopy,
                WithRelease, DebugPolicy>;
```

The other option is to use inheritance:

```
// Example 18
template <typename T, typename DebugPolicy = NoDebug>
class SmartPtrAdapter : public SmartPtr<T,
    DeleteByOperator<T>, MoveNoCopy,
```

```
    WithRelease, DebugPolicy>
{...};
```

This creates a derived class template that pins some of the parameters of the base class template while leaving the rest parameterized. The entire public interface of the base class is inherited, but some care needs to be taken about the constructors of the base class. By default, they are not inherited, and so the newly derived class will have the default compiler-generated constructors. This is probably not something we want, so we have to bring the base class constructors (and possibly the assignment operators) into the derived class:

```
// Example 18
template <typename T, typename DebugPolicy = NoDebug>
class SmartPtrAdapter : public SmartPtr<T,
  DeleteByOperator<T>, MoveNoCopy,
  WithRelease, DebugPolicy>
{
  using base_t = SmartPtr<T, DeleteByOperator<T>,
    MoveNoCopy, WithRelease, DebugPolicy>;
  using base_t::SmartPtr;
  using base_t::operator=;
};
```

The using alias is definitely easier to write and maintain, but the derived class adapter offers more flexibility if it is necessary to also adapt some of the member functions, nested types, etc.

We can now use the new adapter when we need a smart pointer with the preset policies, but quickly change the debug policy:

```
SmartPtrAdapter<C, Debug> p1{new C}; // Debug pointer
SmartPtrAdapter<C> p2{new C}; // Non-debug pointer
```

As we said from the beginning, the most common application of policies is to select a specific implementation for some aspect of the behavior of the class. Sometimes, such variations in the implementation are reflected in the public interface of the class as well - some operations may make sense only for some implementations, and not for others, and the best way to make sure that an operation that is not compatible with the implementation is not invoked is to simply not provide it.

Now, let us revisit the issue of selectively enabling parts of the public interface using policies.

Using policies to control the public interface

We have previously used policies to control the public interface in one of two ways - first, we were able to inject a public member function by inheriting from a policy. This approach is reasonably flexible and powerful, but has two drawbacks - first, once we inherit publicly from a policy, we have no control over what interface gets injected - every public member function of the policy becomes a part of the derived class interface. Second, to implement anything useful this way, we have to let the policy class cast itself to the derived class, and then it has to have access to all of the data members and possibly other policies of the class. The second approach we tried relied on a particular property of the constructors - to copy or move a class, we have to copy or move all of its base classes or data members; if one of them is non-copyable or non-movable, the entire constructor will fail to compile. Unfortunately, it usually fails with a rather non-obvious syntax error - nothing as straightforward as *no copy constructor found in this object*. We can extend this technique to other member functions, for example, to assignment operators, but it gets uglier.

We will now learn a more direct way to manipulate the public interface of a policy-based class. First of all, let's differentiate between conditionally disabling existing member functions and adding new ones. The former is reasonable and generally safe: if a particular implementation cannot support certain operations offered by the interface, they should not be offered in the first place. The latter is dangerous as it allows for the essentially arbitrary and uncontrolled extension of the public interface of the class. Therefore, we will focus on providing the interface for all possible intended uses of a policy-based class, and then disabling parts of that interface when they do not make sense for some choice of policies.

There is already a facility in the C++ language to selectively enable and disable member functions. Prior to C++20, this facility is most commonly implemented through concepts (if they are available) or `std::enable_if`, but the foundation behind it is the SFINAE idiom that we studied in *Chapter 7, SFINAE, Concepts, and Overload Resolution Management*. In C++20, the much more powerful concepts can replace `std::enable_if` in many cases.

To illustrate the use of SFINAE to let the policies selectively enable a member function, we're going to reimplement the policy controlling the public `release()` member function. We have done this once already in this chapter by inheriting from a `ReleasePolicy` that may or may not provide the `release()` member function; if one is provided, CRTP had to be used to implement it. We are now going to do the same but using C++20 concepts.

As we just said, a policy that relies on SFINAE and concepts cannot add any new member functions to the interface of a class; it can only disable some of them. Therefore, the first step is to add the `release()` function to the `SmartPtr` class itself:

```
// Example 19
template <typename T,
          typename DeletionPolicy = DeleteByOperator<T>,
          typename ReleasePolicy = NoRelease>
class SmartPtr : private DeletionPolicy {
  T* p_;
  public:
  void release() { p_ = nullptr; }
  ...
};
```

Right now, it is always enabled, so we need to conditionally enable it using some property of the `ReleasePolicy`. Since this policy controls a single behavior, all we need is a constant value that tells us whether the release feature should be supported:

```
// Example 19
struct WithRelease {
  static constexpr bool enabled = true;
};
struct NoRelease {
  static constexpr bool enabled = false;
};
```

Now, we need to conditionally enable the `release()` member function with a constraint:

```
// Example 19
template <...> class SmartPtr ... {
  ...
  void release() requires ReleasePolicy::enabled {
    p_ = nullptr;
  }
};
```

That's all we need in C++20. Note that we did not need to inherit from `ReleasePolicy` because there is nothing in it except for a constant value. We also do not need to move or copy this policy, for the same reason.

Before C++20 and concepts, we have to use `std::enable_if` to enable or disable a particular member function - in general, the expression `std::enable_if<value, type>` will compile and yield the specified `type` if the `value` is `true` (it must be a compile-time, or `constexpr`, Boolean value). If the `value` is `false`, the type substitution fails (no type result is produced). The proper use for this template metafunction is in an SFINAE context, where the failure of type substitution does not result in a compilation error, but simply disables the function that causes the failure (to be more precise, it removes it from the overload resolution set).

The policies themselves do not have to change at all: both SFINAE and constraints need a `constexpr bool` value. What changes is the expression used to disable a member function. It is tempting to write it simply as:

```
template <...> class SmartPtr ... {
  ...
  std::enable_if_t<ReleasePolicy::enabled> release() {
    p_ = nullptr;
  }
};
```

Unfortunately, this is not going to work: for the `NoRelease` policy, this fails to compile even if we do not try to call `release()`. The reason is that SFINAE works only when template parameter substitution is done (**S** stands for **Substitution**) and applies only to function templates. Therefore, our `release()` function must be a template, and, furthermore, the potential substitution failure has to occur during the substitution of template parameters. We do not need any template parameters to declare `release()`, but we have to introduce a dummy one to use SFINAE:

```
// Example 20
template <...> class SmartPtr ... {
  ...
  template<typename U = T>
  std::enable_if_t<sizeof(U) != 0 &&
                   ReleasePolicy::enabled> release() {
    p_ = nullptr;
  }
};
```

We have seen such "fake templates" when we were describing the "concept utilities" – a way to mimic concepts before C++20 – in *Chapter 7, SFINAE, Concepts, and Overload Resolution Management*. Now we have a template type parameter; the fact that it is never going to be used and is always set to its default value changes nothing. The conditional expression in the return type uses this template parameter (never mind that the part of the expression that depends on the parameter can never fail). Therefore, we are now within the SFINAE rules.

Now that we have a way to disable a member function selectively, we can revisit the conditionally enabled constructors to see how we can enable and disable constructors as well.

In C++20, the answer is "exactly the same way." We need a policy with a `constexpr` Boolean value and a `restrict` constraint to disable any constructor:

```
// Example 21
struct MoveForbidden {
  static constexpr bool enabled = false;
};
struct MoveAllowed {
  static constexpr bool enabled = true;
};
```

We can use this policy to constrain any member function, constructors included:

```
// Example 21
template <typename T,
          typename DeletionPolicy = DeleteByOperator<T>,
          typename MovePolicy = MoveForbidden>
class SmartPtr : private DeletionPolicy {
  public:
  SmartPtr(SmartPtr&& other)
```

```
        requires MovePolicy::enabled :
        DeletionPolicy(std::move(other)),
        p_(std::exchange(other.p_, nullptr)) {}
    ...
};
```

Prior to C++20, we have to use SFINAE. The one complication here is that the constructors have no return type and we have to hide the SFINAE test somewhere else. In addition, we again have to make the constructor a template. We can use a dummy template parameter again:

```
// Example 22
template <typename T,
          typename DeletionPolicy = DeleteByOperator<T>,
          typename MovePolicy = MoveForbidden>
class SmartPtr : private DeletionPolicy {
  public:
  template <typename U = T,
    std::enable_if_t<sizeof(U) != 0 && MovePolicy::enabled,
                     bool> = true>
  SmartPtr(SmartPtr&& other) :
    DeletionPolicy(std::move(other)),
    p_(std::exchange(other.p_, nullptr)) {}
  ...
};
```

If you use the concept utilities from *Chapter 7, SFINAE, Concepts, and Overload Resolution Management*, the code is going to look simpler and more straightforward, although a dummy template parameter is still needed:

```
// Example 22
template <typename T,
          typename DeletionPolicy = DeleteByOperator<T>,
          typename MovePolicy = MoveForbidden>
class SmartPtr : private DeletionPolicy {
  public:
  template <typename U = T,
    REQUIRES(sizeof(U) != 0 && MovePolicy::enabled)>
  SmartPtr(SmartPtr&& other) :
    DeletionPolicy(std::move(other)),
    p_(std::exchange(other.p_, nullptr)) {}
  ...
};
```

Now that we have a fully general way to enable or disable specific member functions that work for constructors as well, the reader may be wondering, what was the point of introducing the earlier way? Firstly, for simplicity - the enable_if expression has to be used in the right context, and the compiler errors that are generated if anything is even slightly wrong are not pretty. On the other hand, the notion that a non-copyable base class makes the entire derived class non-copyable is very basic and works every time. This technique can even be used in C++03, where SFINAE is much more limited and even harder to get to work correctly.

Also, we have already seen that sometimes policies need to add member variables to the class instead of (or in addition to) member functions. Our reference-counting pointer is a perfect example: if one of the policies provides reference counting, it must also contain the count. Member variables cannot be restricted with constraints, so they have to come from the base policy class.

Yet another reason to at least know the way to inject public member functions through policies is that sometimes the `enable_if` alternative requires that the entire set of possible functions be declared in the primary class template, and then some can be selectively disabled. Sometimes, that set of functions is self-contradicting and cannot be present all at once. An example is a set of conversion operators. Right now, our smart pointer cannot be converted back into a raw pointer. We could enable such conversions and require them to be explicit, or allow implicit conversions:

```
void f(C*);
SmartPtr<C> p(...);
f((C*)(p));        // Explicit conversion
f(p);              // Implicit conversion
```

The conversion operators are defined as follows:

```
template <typename T, ...>
class SmartPtr ... {
  T* p_;
  public:
  explicit operator T*() { return p_; } // Explicit
  operator T*() { return p_; }          // Implicit
  ...
};
```

We already decided that we do not want these operators to be unconditionally present; instead, we want them controlled by a raw conversion policy. Let us start with the same approach we used the last time for a policy that enables a member function:

```
// Example 23
struct NoRaw {
  static constexpr bool implicit_conv = false;
  static constexpr bool explicit_conv = false;
};
struct ExplicitRaw {
  static constexpr bool implicit_conv = false;
  static constexpr bool explicit_conv = true;
};
```

```
struct ImplicitRaw {
  static constexpr bool implicit_conv = true;
  static constexpr bool explicit_conv = false;
};
```

Again, we will write C++20 code first, where we can restrict both the explicit and the implicit operators using constraints:

```
// Example 23
template <typename T, ..., typename ConversionPolicy>
class SmartPtr : ... {
  T* p_;
  public:
  explicit operator T*()
    requires ConversionPolicy::explicit_conv
    { return p_; }
  operator T*()
    requires ConversionPolicy::implicit_conv
    { return p_; }
  explicit operator const T*()
    requires ConversionPolicy::explicit_conv const
    { return p_; }
  operator const T*()
    requires ConversionPolicy::implicit_conv const
    { return p_; }
};
```

For completeness, we also provided conversions to a `const` raw pointer. Note that in C++20, there is a simpler way to provide these operators using the conditional explicit specifier (another C++20 feature):

```
// Example 24
template <typename T, ..., typename ConversionPolicy>
class SmartPtr : ... {
  T* p_;
  public:
  explicit (ConversionPolicy::explicit_conv)
  operator T*()
    requires (ConversionPolicy::explicit_conv ||
              ConversionPolicy::implicit_conv)
    { return p_; }
  explicit (ConversionPolicy::explicit_conv)
  operator const T*()
    requires (ConversionPolicy::explicit_conv const ||
              ConversionPolicy::implicit_conv const)
    { return p_; }
};
```

Prior to C++20, we can attempt to enable one of these operators using `std::enable_if` and SFINAE, again based on a conversion policy. The problem is, we cannot declare both implicit and explicit conversion to the same type, even if one is later disabled. These operators cannot be in the same overload set to begin with:

```
// Example 25 - does not compile!
template <typename T, ..., typename ConversionPolicy>
class SmartPtr : ... {
  T* p_;
  public:
  template <typename U = T,
            REQUIRES(ConversionPolicy::explicit_conv)>
  explicit operator T*() { return p_; }
  template <typename U = T,
            REQUIRES(ConversionPolicy::implicit_conv)>
  operator T*() { return p_; }
  ...
};
```

If we want to have the option to select one of these operators in our smart pointer class, we have to have them generated by the base class policy. Since the policy needs to be aware of the smart pointer type, we have to use the CRTP again. Here is a set of policies to control the conversion from smart pointers to raw pointers:

```
// Example 26
template <typename P, typename T> struct NoRaw {
};
template <typename P, typename T> struct ExplicitRaw {
  explicit operator T*() {
    return static_cast<P*>(this)->p_;
  }
  explicit operator const T*() const {
    return static_cast<const P*>(this)->p_;
  }
};
template <typename P, typename T> struct ImplicitRaw {
  operator T*() {
    return static_cast<P*>(this)->p_;
  }
  operator const T*() const {
    return static_cast<const P*>(this)->p_;
  }
};
```

These policies add the desired public member function operators to the derived class. Since they are templates that need to be instantiated with the derived class type, the conversion policy is a template template parameter, and its use follows the CRTP:

```
// Example 26
template <typename T, ... other policies ...
          template <typename, typename>
          class ConversionPolicy = ExplicitRaw>
class SmartPtr : ... other base policies ...,
  public ConversionPolicy<SmartPtr<... paramerers ...>, T>
{
  T* p_;
  template<typename, typename>
  friend class ConversionPolicy;
  public:
  ...
};
```

Once again, note the use of the template template parameter: the template parameter `ConversionPolicy` is not a type but a template. When inheriting from an instantiation of this policy, we have to write the complete type of our `SmartPtr` class, with all its template arguments. We made the conversion policy a template of two arguments (the second one is the object type T). We could also deduce the type T from the first template parameter (the smart pointer type), it's largely a matter of style.

The selected conversion policy adds its public interface, if any, to that of the derived class. One policy adds a set of explicit conversion operators, while the other one provides implicit conversions. Just like in the earlier CRTP example, the base class needs access to the private data members of the derived class. We can either grant friendship to the entire template (and every instantiation of it) or, more verbosely, to the specific instantiation used as the base class for each smart pointer:

```
friend class ConversionPolicy<
  SmartPtr<T, ... parameters ..., ConversionPolicy>, T>;
```

We have learned several different ways to implement new policies. Sometimes, the challenge comes in reusing the ones we already have. The next section shows one way to do it.

Rebinding policies

As we have already seen, the policy lists can get quite long. Often, we want to change just one policy and create a class *just like that other one, but with a small change*. There are at least two ways to do this.

The first way is very general but somewhat verbose. The first step is to expose the template parameters as aliases, inside the primary template. This is a good practice, anyway - without such aliases, it is very difficult to find out, at compile time, what a template parameter was in case we ever need to use it outside of the template. For example, we have a smart pointer, and we want to know what the deletion policy was. The easiest way, by far, is with some help from the smart pointer class itself:

```
template <typename T,
          typename DeletionPolicy = DeleteByOperator<T>,
          typename CopyMovePolicy = NoMoveNoCopy,
          template <typename, typename>
            class ConversionPolicy = ExplicitRaw>
class SmartPtr : ... base policies ... {
  T* p_;
  public:
  using value_type = T;
  using deletion_policy_t = DeletionPolicy;
  using copy_move_policy_t = CopyMovePolicy;
  template <typename P, typename T1>
  using conversion_policy_t = ConversionPolicy<P, T1>;
  ...
};
```

Note that we're using two different types of aliases here - for the regular template parameters such as `DeletionPolicy`, we can use a `using` alias. For a template template parameter, we have to use the template alias, sometimes called template `typedef` - to reproduce the same policy with another smart pointer, we need to know the template itself, not the template instantiation, such as `ConversionPolicy<SmartPtr, T>`. Now, if we need to create another smart pointer with some of the same policies, we can simply query the policies of the original object:

```
// Example 27
SmartPtr<int,
  DeleteByOperator<int>, MoveNoCopy, ImplicitRaw>
  p1(new int(42));
using ptr_t = decltype(p1); // The exact type of p1
SmartPtr<ptr_t::value_type,
  ptr_t::deletion_policy_t, ptr_t::copy_move_policy_t,
  ptr_t::conversion_policy_t> p2;
SmartPtr<double,
  ptr_t::deletion_policy_t, ptr_t::copy_move_policy_t,
  ptr_t::conversion_policy_t> p3;
```

Now, p2 and p1 have exactly the same type. There is, of course, an easier way to accomplish that. But the point is, we could alter any one of the types in the list and keep the rest, and get a pointer just like p1, *except for one change*. For example, the pointer p2 has the same policies but points to a `double`.

The latter turns out to be a pretty common case, and there is a way to facilitate the *rebinding* or a template to a different type while keeping the rest of the arguments intact. To do this, the primary template and all its policies need to support such rebinding:

```cpp
// Example 27
template <typename T> struct DeleteByOperator {
  void operator()(T* p) const { delete p; }
  template <typename U>
    using rebind_type = DeleteByOperator<U>;
};
template <typename T,
          typename DeletionPolicy = DeleteByOperator<T>,
          typename CopyMovePolicy = NoMoveNoCopy,
          template <typename, typename>
            class ConversionPolicy = ExplicitRaw>
class SmartPtr : private DeletionPolicy,
  public CopyMovePolicy,
  public ConversionPolicy<SmartPtr<T, DeletionPolicy,
    CopyMovePolicy, ConversionPolicy>, T> {
  T* p_;
  public:
  ...
  template <typename U>
  using rebind = SmartPtr<U,
    typename DeletionPolicy::template rebind<U>,
    CopyMovePolicy, ConversionPolicy>;
};
```

The rebind alias defines a new template that has only one parameter - the type we can change. The rest of the parameters come from the primary template itself. Some of these parameters are types that also depend on the primary type T, and themselves need rebinding (in our example, the deletion policy). By choosing not to rebind the copy/move policy, we impose a requirement that none of these policies depend on the primary type, otherwise this policy, too, needs to be rebound. Finally, the template conversion policy does not need rebinding - we have access to the entire template here, so it will be instantiated with the new primary type. We can now use the rebinding mechanism to create a *similar* pointer type:

```cpp
SmartPtr<int,
  DeleteByOperator<int>, MoveNoCopy, ImplicitRaw>
p(new int(42));
using dptr_t = decltype(p)::rebind<double>;
dptr_t q(new double(4.2));
```

If we have direct access to the smart pointer type, we can use it for rebinding (for example, in a template context). Otherwise, we can get the type from a variable of this type using `decltype()`. The pointer q has the same policies as p but points to a `double`, and the type-dependent policies such as the deletion policy have been updated accordingly.

We have covered the main ways in which the policies can be implemented and used to customize policy-based classes. It is now time to review what we have learned and state some general guidelines for the use of policy-based designs.

Recommendations and guidelines

The policy-based design allows for exceptional flexibility in the creation of finely customizable classes. Sometimes, this flexibility and power become the enemy of a good design. In this section, we will review the strengths and weaknesses of the policy-based design and come up with some general recommendations.

Strengths of the policy-based design

The main advantages of the policy-based design are flexibility and extensibility of the design. At a high level, these are the same benefits the Strategy pattern offers, only realized at compile-time. The policy-based design allows the programmer to select, at compile time, one of several algorithms for each specific task or operation performed by the system. Since the only constraints on the algorithms are the requirements on the interface that binds them into the rest of the system, it is equally possible to extend the system by writing new policies for the customizable operations.

At a high level, the policy-based design allows the software system to be built from components. At a high level, this is hardly a novel idea, certainly not limited to policy-based design. The focus of the policy-based design is the use of components to define behavior and the implementation of individual classes. There is some similarity between policies and callbacks - both allow a user-specified action to be taken when a particular event takes place. However, the policies are much more general than callbacks - while a callback is a function, policies are entire classes, with multiple functions and, possibly, a non-trivial internal state.

These general concepts translate into a unique set of advantages for the design, mostly centered around the ideas of flexibility and extensibility. With the overall structure of the system and its high-level components determined by the high-level design, the policies allow for a variety of low-level customizations within the constraints that were imposed by the original design. Policies can extend the class interface (add public member functions), implement or extend the state of the class (add data members), and specify implementations (add private member functions). The original design, in setting the overall structure of the classes and their interactions, in effect authorizes each policy to have one or more of these roles.

The result is an extensible system that can be modified to address evolving requirements, even ones that have not been anticipated or known at the time when the system was designed. The overall architecture remains stable, while the selection of possible policies and the constraints on their interfaces offers a systematic, disciplined way to modify and extend the software.

Disadvantages of policy-based design

The first problem with the policy-based design that comes to mind is the one we have already encountered - declarations of policy-based classes with a specific set of policies are extremely verbose, especially if one of the policies at the end of the list has to be changed. Consider the declaration of a smart pointer with all of the policies we have implemented in this chapter, put together:

```
SmartPtr<int, DeleteByOperator<int>, NoMoveNoCopy, ExplicitRaw,
WithoutArrow, NoDebug> p;
```

That's just for a smart pointer - a class with a fairly simple interface and limited functionality. Even though it is unlikely that someone will need one pointer with all of these customization possibilities, the policy-based classes tend to have a lot of policies. This problem may be the most evident, but it is actually not the worst. The template aliases help to give concise names to the few policy combinations that are actually used by a particular application. In the template context, the types of smart pointers used as function arguments are deduced and do not need to be explicitly specified. In regular code, auto can be used to save a lot of typing and also make the code more robust - when the complex type declarations that must be consistent are replaced with an automatic way to generate these consistent types, the errors caused by typing something slightly different in two different places disappear (in general, if there is a recipe to make the compiler generate correct-by-construction code, use it).

The much more significant, if slightly less visible, problem is that all of these policy-based types with different policies are actually different types. Two smart pointers that point to the same object type but have different deletion policies are different types. Two smart pointers that are otherwise the same but have different copying policies are different types. Why is that a problem? Consider a function that is called to work on an object that is passed into the function using a smart pointer. This function does not copy the smart pointer, so it should not matter what the copying policy is - it is never used. And yet, what should the argument type be? There is no one type that can accommodate all smart pointers, even the ones with very similar functionality.

There are several possible solutions here. The most straightforward one is to make all functions that use policy-based types into templates. This does simplify the coding, and it reduces code duplication (at least the source code duplication), but it has its own downsides - the machine code becomes larger since there are multiple copies of every function, and all template code must be in the header files.

The other option is to erase the policy types. We saw the type erasure technique in *Chapter 6, Understanding Type Erasure*. Type erasure solves the problem of having many similar types - we could make all smart pointers, regardless of their policies, be of the same type (only to the extent that the policies determine the implementation and not the public interface, of course). However, this comes at a very high cost.

One of the main drawbacks of the templates in general, and the policy-based design, in particular, is that templates provide a zero-overhead abstraction - we can express our programs in terms of convenient high-level abstractions and concepts, but the compiler strips it all away, inlines all of the templates, and generates the minimum necessary code. Type erasure not only negates this advantage but has the opposite effect - it adds a very high overhead of memory allocations and indirect function calls.

The last option is to avoid using policy-based types, at least for some operations. Sometimes, this choice carries a little extra cost - for example, a function that needs to operate on an object but not delete or own it should take the object by reference instead of a smart pointer (see *Chapter 3, Memory and Ownership*). In addition to clearly expressing the fact that the function is not going to own the object, this neatly solves the problem of what type the argument should be - the reference is the same type, no matter which smart pointer it came from. This is, however, a limited approach - more often than not, we do need to operate on the entire policy-based objects, which are usually much more complex than a simple pointer (for example, custom containers are often implemented using policies).

The final disadvantage is the general complexity of the policy-based types, although such claims should be made with care - the important question is, complexity compared to what? Policy-based designs are usually invoked to solve complex design problems where a family of similar types serves the same overall purpose (*what*), but does so in slightly different ways (*how*). This leads us to the recommendations on the use of policies.

Guidelines for policy-based designs

The guidelines for policy-based designs boil down to managing the complexity and making sure the ends justify the means - the flexibility of the design and the elegance of the resulting solutions should justify the complexity of the implementation and its use.

Since most of the complexity comes from the increasing number of policies, this is the focus of most of the guidelines. Some policies end up putting together very different types that happen to have a similar implementation. The goal of such a policy-based type is to reduce code duplication. While a worthwhile objective, this is generally not a good enough reason to expose a multitude of disparate policy options to the end user of the type. If two different types or type families happen to have similar implementations, that implementation can be factored out. The private, hidden, implementation-only part of the design can itself use policies if it makes the implementation easier.

However, these hidden policies should not be selected by the client - the client should specify the types that make sense in the application and the policies that customize the visible behavior. From these types and policies, the implementation can derive additional types as needed. This is no different than calling a common function to, say, find the minimum element in a sequence from several different unrelated algorithms that all happen to need that operation. The common code is not duplicated, but neither is it exposed to the user.

So, when should a policy-based type be broken up into two or more pieces? A good way to look at it is to ask whether the primary type, with a particular set of policies, has a good specific name that describes it. For example, a non-copyable owning pointer, movable or not, is a *unique pointer* - there is only one such pointer for each object at any given time. This is true for any deletion or conversion policy.

On the other hand, a reference-counted pointer is a *shared pointer*, again, with any choice of other policies. This suggests that our one smart pointer to end all smart pointers would be, perhaps, better split into two - a non-copyable unique pointer and a copyable shared pointer. We still get some code reuse because the deletion policy, for example, is common to both pointer types, and does not have to be implemented twice. This is, indeed, the choice the C++ standard makes. The `std::unique_ptr` has only one policy, the deletion policy. The `std::shared_ptr` also has the same policy and can use the same policy objects, but it is type-erased, so all shared pointers to a particular object are of one type.

But what about other policies? Here, we come to the second guideline - the policies that restrict the use of the class should be justified by the cost of possible errors that are caused by the incorrect use they are trying to prevent. For example, do we really need a non-movable policy? On the one hand, it could prevent a programming error if the ownership of the object absolutely must not be transferred. On the other hand, in many cases, the programmer will simply change the code to use a movable pointer. Also, we are forced to use movable pointers to return them by value from factory functions. However, a non-copyable policy is often justified and should be the default. For example, there are good reasons to make most containers non-copyable by default: copying a large collection of data is almost always the result of sloppy coding, usually when passing arguments to functions.

Similarly, while it is probably desirable to prevent implicit casting to the raw pointer as a matter of basic coding discipline, there is always a way to convert the smart pointer to the raw one explicitly - if nothing else, `&*p` should always work. Again, the benefits of the carefully restricted interface probably do not justify adding this policy. However, it makes a great compact learning example for a set of techniques that can be used to create more complex and more useful policies, and so the time we spent learning how this policy works is entirely justified.

When a policy affecting the public interface is justified, we have to make a choice between a constraint-based policy that restricts the existing member functions and a CRTP-based policy that adds them. As a rule, a design that relies on constraints is preferable, even prior to C++20 where we have to use the "pseudo-concepts." However, this approach cannot be used to add member variables to the class, only member functions.

Another way to look at the question of what the right set of policies is and what policies should be broken up into separate groups is to go back to the fundamental strength of the policy-based design - the composability of the behavior expressed by different policies. If we have a class with four different policies, each of which can have four different implementations, that is 256 different versions of the class. It is, of course, unlikely that we will need all 256. But the point is, at the time when we implement the class, we do not know which of these versions we will actually need later. We could make a guess and implement only a few most likely ones. If we are wrong, this will result in much code duplication and copy-pasting. With the policy-based design, we have the potential to implement any combination of the behavior, without actually having to write them all explicitly up front.

Now that we understand this strength of policy-based designs, we can use it to evaluate a particular set of policies - do they need to be composable? Would we ever need to combine them in different ways? If some policies always come in certain combinations or groups, this calls for automatically deducing these policies from one primary user-specified policy. On the other hand, a set of largely independent policies that can be combined arbitrarily is probably a good set of policies.

Another way to address some of the weaknesses of policy-based design is to try and accomplish the same goal by different means. There is no substitute for the entirety of the capabilities offered by the policies - the Strategy pattern is there for a reason. However, there are alternative patterns that offer somewhat superficial similarities and may be used to solve some of the same problems as the policy-based design addresses. We will see one such alternative in *Chapter 16, Adapters and Decorators* when we talk about decorators. It is not as general, but when it works, it can provide all the advantages of the policies, in particular, the composability, without some of the problems.

Summary

In this chapter, we have studied, extensively, the applications of the Strategy pattern (also known as the policy pattern) to C++ generic programming. The combination of the two gives rise to one of the most powerful tools in the arsenal of a C++ programmer - the policy-based design of classes. This approach provides great flexibility by allowing us to compose the behavior of the class from many building blocks, or policies, each of which is responsible for a particular aspect of the behavior.

We have learned different ways to implement policies - these can be templates, classes with template member functions, classes with static functions, and even classes with constant values. Just as varied are the ways that we can use policies through composition, inheritance, or direct access to static members. Policy parameters can be types or templates, each with its own advantages and limitations.

A tool as powerful as the policy-based design is also easily misused or applied in poor judgment. Often, such situations arise from the gradual evolution of the software toward more and more complexity. To mitigate such mischance, we have provided a set of guidelines and recommendations that focus on the key advantages that the policy-based design offers to the programmer and suggested the techniques and constraints that maximize such advantages.

In the next chapter, we will consider a more limited design pattern that can sometimes be used to mimic the policy-based approach, without some of its drawbacks. This chapter is dedicated to the Decorator pattern and the more general Adapter pattern. Both are sort of C++ magic tricks - they make an object appear as something it's not.

Questions

1. What is the Strategy pattern?

2. How is the Strategy pattern implemented at compile time using C++ generic programming?

3. What types can be used as policies?

4. How can policies be integrated into the primary template?

5. Should I use policies with public member functions or policies with constraint variables?

6. What are the main drawbacks of policy-based design?

16

Adapters and Decorators

This chapter takes on two classic patterns in **object-oriented programming** (**OOP**) - the Adapter pattern and the decorator pattern. These patterns are just two of the original twenty-three design patterns that were introduced in the *Design Patterns – Elements of Reusable Object-Oriented Software* book by Erich Gamma, Richard Helm, Ralph Johnson, and John Vlissides. As an object-oriented language, C++ can take advantage of these patterns as well as any other language. But, as is often the case, generic programming brings some advantages, variations, and, with it, new challenges to the classic patterns.

The following topics are covered in this chapter:

- What are the adapter and decorator patterns?

- What is the difference between the two?

- What design problems can be solved by these patterns?

- How are these patterns used in C++?

- How does generic programming help to design adapters and decorators?

- What other, different, patterns offer alternative solutions to similar problems?

Technical requirements

The example code for this chapter can be found on GitHub at the following link: `https://github.com/PacktPublishing/Hands-On-Design-Patterns-with-CPP-Second-Edition/tree/master/Chapter16`.

The decorator pattern

We will begin this study with the definitions of the two classic patterns. As we will see, on paper, the patterns, as well as the differences between them, are quite clear. Then, C++ comes in and blurs the lines by allowing design solutions that fall somewhere in-between the two. Still, the clarity of these simple cases is helpful, even if it gets muddled as we pile on the complexity. Let's start with what is clear, then.

The decorator pattern is also a structural pattern; it allows a behavior to be added to an object. The classic decorator pattern extends the behavior of an existing operation that's performed by a class. It *decorates* the class with the new behavior and creates an object of the new, decorated type. The decorator implements the interface of the original class and forwards the requests from its own interface to that class, but it also performs additional actions before and after these forwarded requests - these are the *decorations*. Such decorators are sometimes called "class wrappers".

Basic decorator pattern

We will begin with a C++ example of the decorator pattern that follows the classic definition as closely as possible. For this example, we will imagine designing a fantasy game that's set in medieval times (true to life, only with dragons and elves and so on). Of course, what are medieval times without fighting? And so, in our game, the player has a choice of units appropriate for his/her side, and they can do battle when called on. Here is the basic `Unit` class - at least the combat-related part:

```
// Example 01
class Unit {
  public:
  Unit(double strength, double armor) :
    strength_(strength), armor_(armor) {}
  virtual bool hit(Unit& target) {
    return attack() > target.defense();
  }
  virtual double attack() = 0;
  virtual double defense() = 0;
  protected:
  double strength_;
  double armor_;
};
```

The unit has `strength`, which determines its attack, and `armor`, which provides defense. The actual values of the attack and the defense are computed by the derived classes - the concrete units - but the combat mechanism itself is right here - if the attack is stronger than the defense, the unit successfully hits the target (this is a very simplistic approach to gaming, of course, but we want to make the examples as concise as possible).

Now, what are the actual units in the game? The pillar of the human armies is the valorous `Knight`. This unit has strong armor and a sharp sword, giving it bonuses to both attack and defend:

```
// Example 01
class Knight : public Unit {
  public:
  using Unit::Unit;
  double attack() { return strength_ + sword_bonus_; }
  double defense() { return armor_ + plate_bonus_; }
  protected:
  static constexpr double sword_bonus_ = 2;
  static constexpr double plate_bonus_ = 3;
};
```

Fighting against the knights are the brutish ogres. The ogres swing simple wooden clubs and wear ragged leather, neither of which are great implements of war, giving them some combat penalties:

```
// Example 01
class Ogre : public Unit {
  public:
  using Unit::Unit;
  double attack() { return strength_ + club_penalty_; }
  double defense() { return armor_ + leather_penalty_; }
  protected:
  static constexpr double club_penalty_ = -1;
  static constexpr double leather_penalty_ = -1;
};
```

On the other hand, ogres are remarkably strong, to begin with:

```
Knight k(10, 5);
Ogre o(12, 2);
k.hit(o); // Yes!
```

Here the knight, aided by his attack bonus and the enemy's weak armor, will successfully hit the ogre. But the game is far from over. As the units fight, the surviving ones gain experience and eventually become veterans. A veteran unit is still the same kind of unit, but it gains attack and defense bonuses, reflecting its combat experience. Here, we do not want to change any of the class interfaces, but we want to modify the behavior of the `attack()` and `defense()` functions. This is the job of the decorator pattern, and what follows is the classic implementation of the `VeteranUnit` decorator:

```
// Example 01
class VeteranUnit : public Unit {
  public:
  VeteranUnit(Unit& unit,
```

```
                double strength_bonus,
                double armor_bonus)  :
   Unit(strength_bonus, armor_bonus), unit_(unit) {}
  double attack() { return unit_.attack() + strength_; }
  double defense() { return unit_.defense() + armor_; }
  private:
  Unit& unit_;
};
```

Note that this class inherits directly from the Unit class, so in the class hierarchy, it is *to the side* of concrete unit classes such as Knight or Ogre. We still have the original unit that is decorated and becomes the veteran - the VeteranUnit decorator contains a reference to it. The way it is used, then, is to decorate a unit and use the decorated unit from then on, but it does not delete the original unit:

```
// Example 01
Knight k(10, 5);
Ogre o(12, 2);
VeteranUnit vk(k, 7, 2);
VeteranUnit vo(o, 1, 9);
vk.hit(vo); // Another hit!
```

Here, both our old enemies reached their first veterancy levels, and the victory again goes to the knight. But experience is the best teacher, and our ogre gains another level, and, with it, enchanted runic armor with a massive defense bonus:

```
VeteranUnit vvo(vo, 1, 9);
vk.hit(vvo); // Miss!
```

Note that we can decorate a decorated object in this design! This is intentional, and the bonuses stack up as the unit gains levels. This time, the experienced fighter's defense proves to be too much for the knight.

As we already mentioned, this is the classic decorator pattern, straight out of the textbook. It works in C++ but with some limitations. The first one is rather evident even though we want to use the decorated unit once we have it, the original unit must be kept around, and the lifetimes of these objects must be carefully managed. There are practical solutions to such practical problems, but the focus of this book is on combining design patterns with generic programming, and the new design possibilities that pairing creates. Therefore, our creative path takes us elsewhere.

The second problem is more endemic to C++. It is best illustrated by an example. The game's designers have added a special ability to the `Knight` unit - it can charge forward at its enemy, gaining a short-term attack bonus. This bonus is valid only for the next attack, but in the thick of the battle, it may be just enough:

```
// Example 02
class Knight : public Unit {
  public:
  Knight(double strength, double armor) :
  Unit(strength, armor), charge_bonus_(0) {}
  double attack() {
    double res = strength_ + sword_bonus_ + charge_bonus_;
    charge_bonus_ = 0;
    return res;
  }
  double defense() { return armor_ + plate_bonus_; }
  void charge() { charge_bonus_ = 1; }
  protected:
  double charge_bonus_;
  static constexpr double sword_bonus_ = 2;
  static constexpr double plate_bonus_ = 3;
};
```

The charge bonus is activated by calling the `charge()` member function and lasts for one attack, and then it is reset. When the player activates the charge, the game executes the code, which looks something like this:

```
Knight k(10, 5);
Ogre o(12, 2);
k.charge();
k.hit(o);
```

Of course, we would expect the veteran knight to be able to charge forward as well, but here we run into a problem - our code does not compile:

```
VeteranUnit vk(k, 7, 2);
vk.charge(); // Does not compile!
```

The root of the problem is that `charge()` is a part of the interface of the `Knight` class, while the `VeteranUnit` decorator is derived from the `Unit` class. We could move the `charge()` function into the base class, `Unit`, but this is a bad design - `Ogre` is also derived from `Unit`, and ogres cannot charge, so they should not have such an interface (it violates the *is-a* principle of public inheritance).

This is a problem that's inherent in the way we implemented the decorator object - both Knight and VeteranUnit are derived from the same base class, Unit, but they don't know anything about each other. There are some ugly workarounds, but it is a fundamental C++ limitation; it does not handle *cross-casting* well (casting to a type in another branch of the same hierarchy). But what the language takes with one hand, it gives with the other - we have much better tools to deal with this problem, and we are going to learn about these tools next.

Decorators the C++ way

We have encountered two problems while implementing a classic decorator in C++ - first of all, the decorated object did not take ownership of the original object, so both must be kept around (this may not be so much a problem as a feature if the decoration needs to be removed later, which is one of the reasons the decorator pattern is implemented this way). The other problem is that a decorated Knight is not really a Knight at all, but a Unit. We can solve the second problem if the decorator is itself derived from the class that is being decorated. This would imply that the VeteranUnit class does not have a fixed base class - the base class should be whatever class is being decorated. This description matches the **Curiously Recurring Template Pattern (CRTP)** to a tee (this C++ idiom was described earlier in this book in *Chapter 8, The Curiously Recurring Template Pattern*). To apply CRTP, we need to make the decorator into a template and inherit from the template parameter:

```cpp
// Example 03
template <typename U>
class VeteranUnit : public U {
  public:
  VeteranUnit(U&& unit,
              double strength_bonus,
              double armor_bonus) :
    U(unit), strength_bonus_(strength_bonus),
    armor_bonus_(armor_bonus) {}
  double attack() { return U::attack() + strength_bonus_; }
  double defense() { return U::defense() + armor_bonus_; }
  private:
  double strength_bonus_;
  double armor_bonus_;
};
```

Now, to promote a unit to the veteran status, we must convert it to the decorated version of the concrete unit class:

```cpp
// Example 03
Knight k(10, 5);
Ogre o(12, 2);
k.hit(o); // Hit!
```

```
VeteranUnit<Knight> vk(std::move(k), 7, 2);
VeteranUnit<Ogre> vo(std::move(o), 1, 9);
vk.hit(vo); // Hit!
VeteranUnit<VeteranUnit<Ogre>> vvo(std::move(vo), 1, 9);
vk.hit(vvo); // Miss...
vk.charge(); // Compiles now, vk is a Knight too
vk.hit(vvo); // Hit with the charge bonus!
```

This is the same scenario that we saw at the end of the previous section, but it now uses the template decorator. Notice the differences. First of all, a `VeteranUnit` is a class that's derived from a concrete unit such as `Knight` or `Ogre`. As such, it has access to the interface of the base class: for example, a veteran knight, `VeteranUnit<Knight>`, is a `Knight` too and has the member function `charge()` inherited from `Knight`. Second, the decorated unit explicitly takes ownership of the original unit - to create a veteran unit, we have to move the original unit into it (the base class of the veteran unit is move-constructed from the original unit). The original object is left in the unspecified moved-from state, and the only safe action that can be done on this object is a call to the destructor. Note that, at least for the simple implementation of unit classes, the move operation is just a copy, so the original object is usable, but you should not rely on it - making assumptions about the moved-from state is a bug waiting to happen.

It is worth pointing out that our declaration of the `VeteranUnit` constructor enforces and requires this ownership transfer. If we try to construct a veteran unit without moving from the original unit, it will not compile:

```
VeteranUnit<Knight> vk(k, 7, 2); // Does not compile
```

By providing only one constructor that accepts an r-value reference, that is, `Unit&&`, we require that the caller agrees to the transfer of ownership.

So far, for demonstration purposes, we have created all unit objects on the stack as local variables. In any non-trivial program, this is not going to work - we need these objects to stay around, long after the function that created them is done. We can integrate decorator objects and the memory ownership mechanism and ensure that the moved-from original units are deleted after a decorated version is created.

Let's say that ownership is managed throughout the program by unique pointers (each object has a clear owner at any given time). Here is how this can be accomplished. First of all, it is convenient to declare aliases for the pointers we need to use:

```
using Unit_ptr = std::unique_ptr<Unit>;
using Knight_ptr = std::unique_ptr<Knight>;
```

While any unit can be owned by the `Unit_ptr` pointer, we cannot call unit-specific member functions such as `charge()` through it, so we may need pointers to the concrete classes as well. As we will see next, we need to move the object between these pointers. Moving from a pointer to the derived class to the pointer to the base class is easy:

```
Knight_ptr k(new Knight(10, 5));
Unit_ptr u(std::move(k)); // Now k is null
```

Going in the other direction is a little harder; `std::move` will not work implicitly, just like we cannot convert from `Unit*` to `Knight*` without an explicit cast. We need a *moving cast*:

```
// Example 04
template <typename To, typename From>
std::unique_ptr<To> move_cast(std::unique_ptr<From>& p) {
  return std::unique_ptr<To>(static_cast<To*>(p.release()));
}
```

Here, we use `static_cast` to cast to the derived class, which works if the assumed relation (that the base object really is the expected derived object) is correct, otherwise, the results are undefined. We can test this assumption at runtime if we want to, using `dynamic_cast` instead. Here is a version that does the test, but only if asserts are enabled (we could throw an exception instead of the assert):

```
// Example 04
template <typename To, typename From>
std::unique_ptr<To> move_cast(std::unique_ptr<From>& p) {
#ifndef NDEBUG
  auto p1 =
    std::unique_ptr<To>(dynamic_cast<To*>(p.release()));
  assert(p1);
  return p1;
#else
  return std::unique_ptr<To>(static_cast<To*>(p.release()));
#endif
}
```

If all objects will be owned by instances of a unique pointer, then the `VeteranUnit` decorator has to accept a pointer in its constructor and move the object out of this pointer:

```
// Example 04
template <typename U> class VeteranUnit : public U {
  public:
  template <typename P>
  VeteranUnit(P&& p,
              double strength_bonus,
              double armor_bonus) :
```

```
    U(std::move(*move_cast<U>(p))),
    strength_bonus_(strength_bonus),
    armor_bonus_(armor_bonus) {}
  double attack() { return U::attack() + strength_bonus_; }
  double defense() { return U::defense() + armor_bonus_; }
  private:
  double strength_bonus_;
  double armor_bonus_;
};
```

The tricky part here is in the initialization of the base class U of VeteranUnit<U> - we have to move the unit from a unique pointer to the base class into a move-constructor of the derived class (there is no way to simply move the object from one unique pointer to another; we need to wrap it into the derived class). We have to do this without leaking any memory, too. The original, unique pointer, is released, so its destructor will do nothing, but our move_cast returns a new unique pointer that now owns the same object. This unique pointer is a temporary variable and will be deleted at the end of the initialization of the new object, but not before we use its object to construct a new derived object that is a VeteranUnit (the move-initialization of the unit object itself does not save any time versus copy in our case, but it is a good practice in the event a more heavyweight unit object provides an optimized move constructor).

Here is how this new decorator is used in a program that manages resources (units, in our case) by unique pointers:

```
// Example 04
Knight_ptr k(new Knight(10, 5));
    // Knight_ptr so we can call charge()
Unit_ptr o(new Ogre(12, 2));
    // Could be Orge_ptr if we needed one
Knight_ptr vk(new VeteranUnit<Knight>(k, 7, 2));
Unit_ptr vo(new VeteranUnit<Ogre>(o, 1, 9));
Unit_ptr vvo(new VeteranUnit<VeteranUnit<Ogre>>(vo, 1, 9));
vk->hit(*vvo); // Miss
vk->charge(); // Works because vk is Knight_ptr
vk->hit(*vvo); // Hit
```

Note that we did not redefine the hit() function - it still accepts a unit object by reference. This is correct because this function does not take ownership of the object - it merely operates on it. There is no need to pass an owning pointer into it - that would suggest a transfer of ownership.

Note that, strictly speaking, there is very little difference between this example and the last one - the moved-from unit should not be accessed either way. Practically speaking, there is a significant difference - the moved-from pointer no longer owns the object. Its value is null, so any attempt to operate on the original unit after it was promoted will become evident in very short order (the program will dereference a null pointer and crash).

As we have seen, we can decorate an already decorated class, as the effects of the decorators stack up. Similarly, we can apply two different decorators to the same class. Each decorator adds a particular new behavior to the class. In our game engine, we can print the results of each attack, whether or not there was a hit. But if the result does not match the expectations, we don't know why. For debugging, it might be useful to print the attack and defense values. We would not want to do this all the time for all units, but for the part of the code we are interested in, we could use a debugging decorator that adds new behavior to the units to print the intermediate results of the calculations.

The `DebugDecorator` uses the same design idea as the previous decorator - it's a class template that generates a class that's derived from the object to be decorated. Its `attack()` and `defense()` virtual functions forward the calls to the base class and print the results:

```
// Example 05
template <typename U> class DebugDecorator : public U {
  public:
  using U::U;
  template <typename P> DebugDecorator(P&& p) :
    U(std::move(*move_cast<U>(p))) {}
  double attack() {
    double res = U::attack();
    cout << "Attack: " << res << endl;
    return res;
  }
  double defense() {
    double res = U::defense();
    cout << "Defense: " << res << endl;
    return res;
  }
};
```

In this example, we left out the dynamic memory allocations and relied on moving the objects themselves for ownership transfer. There is no reason we cannot have both stackable decorators and unique pointers:

```
// Example 06
template <typename U> class VeteranUnit : public U {
  ...
};
template <typename U> class DebugDecorator : public U {
  using U::U;
  public:
  template <typename P>
```

```
    DebugDecorator(std::unique_ptr<P>& p) :
      U(std::move(*move_cast<U>(p))) {}
    double attack() override {
      double res = U::attack();
      cout << "Attack: " << res << endl;
      return res;
    }
    double defense() override {
      double res = U::defense();
      cout << "Defense: " << res << endl;
      return res;
    }
    using ptr = std::unique_ptr<DebugDecorator>;
    template <typename... Args>
    static ptr construct(Args&&... args) { return
      ptr{new DebugDecorator(std::forward<Args>(args)...)};
    }
};
```

When implementing decorators, you should be careful to not inadvertently change the behavior of the base class in unexpected ways. For example, consider this possible implementation of DebugDecorator:

```
template <typename U> class DebugDecorator : public U {
  double attack() {
    cout << "Attack: " << U::attack() << endl;
    return U::attack();
  }
};
```

There is a subtle bug here - the decorated object, in addition to the expected new behavior - the printout - hides a change in the original behavior - it calls attack() twice on the base class. Not only might the printed value be incorrect if two calls to attack() return different values, but also any one-time attack bonuses such as the knight's charge will be canceled.

DebugDecorator adds very similar behavior to each member function it decorates. C++ has a rich set of tools that are aimed specifically at improving code reuse and reducing duplication. Let's see if we can do better and come up with a more reusable, universal decorator.

Polymorphic decorators and their limitations

Some decorators are very specific to the classes they modify, and their behavior is narrowly targeted. Others are very general, at least in principle. For example, a debugging decorator that logs function calls and prints return values could be used with any function if we could only implement it correctly.

Such an implementation is pretty straightforward in C++14 or above using `variadic` templates, parameter packs, and perfect forwarding:

```
// Example 07
template <typename Callable> class DebugDecorator {
  public:
  template <typename F>
  DebugDecorator(F&& f, const char* s) :
    c_(std::forward<F>(f)), s_(s) {}
  template <typename ... Args>
  auto operator()(Args&& ... args) const {
    cout << "Invoking " << s_ << endl;
    auto res = c_(std::forward<Args>(args) ...);
    cout << "Result: " << res << endl;
    return res;
  }
  private:
  Callable c_;
  const std::string s_;
};
```

This decorator can be wrapped around any callable object or function (anything that can be called with the `()` syntax) with any number of arguments. It prints the custom string and the result of the call. However, writing out the callable type is often tricky - it is much better to get the compiler to do it for us using template argument deduction:

```
// Example 07
template <typename Callable>
  auto decorate_debug(Callable&& c, const char* s) {
  return DebugDecorator<Callable>(
    std::forward<Callable>(c), s);
}
```

This template function deduces the type of the `Callable` and decorates it with the debugging wrapper. We can now apply it to any function or object. Here is a decorated function:

```
// Example 07
int g(int i, int j) { return i - j; } // Some function
auto g1 = decorate_debug(g, "g()"); // Decorated function
g1(5, 2); // Prints "Invoking g()" and "Result: 3"
```

We can also decorate a callable object:

```
// Example 07
struct S {
```

```
  double operator()() const {
    return double(rand() + 1)/double(rand() + 1);
  }
};
S s; // Callable
auto s1 =
  decorate_debug(s, "rand/rand"); // Decorated callable
s1(); s1(); // Prints the result, twice
```

Note that our decorator does not take ownership of the callable object (we could write it in such a way that it does so if we wanted to).

We can even decorate a lambda expression, which is really just an implicitly typed callable object. The one in this example defines a callable object with two integer arguments:

```
// Example 07
auto f2 = decorate_debug(
  [](int i, int j) { return i + j; }, "i+j");
f2(5, 3); // Prints "Invoking i+j" and "Result: 8"
```

In our example, we decided to forward the callables both in the decorator class constructor and in the helper function. Often, the callables are passed by value instead and are assumed to be cheap to copy. In all cases, it is important that the decorator stores a copy of the callable in its data member. If you capture it by reference instead, there is a subtle error waiting to happen:

```
template <typename Callable> class DebugDecorator {
  public:
  DebugDecorator(const Callable& c, const char* s) :
    c_(c), s_(s) {}
  ...
  private:
  const Callable& c_;
  const std::string s_;
};
```

Decorating a function is likely to work fine, but decorating a lambda will fail (although not necessarily in an immediately visible way). The const Callable& c_ member is going to be bound to a temporary lambda object:

```
auto f2 = decorate_debug(
  [](int i, int j) { return i + j; }, "i+j");
```

The lifetime of this object ends at the semicolon at the end of this statement, and any subsequent use of f2 accesses a dangling reference (address sanitizer tools can help detect such errors).

Our decorator has some limitations. First, it falls short when we try to decorate a function that does not return anything, such as the following lambda expression, which increments its argument but returns nothing:

```
auto incr = decorate_debug([](int& x) { ++x; }, "++x");
int i;
incr(i); // Does not compile
```

The problem lies with the `void res` expression that is coming from the `auto res = ...` line inside the `DebugDecorator`. This makes sense since we cannot declare variables of the `void` type. This problem can be solved using `if constexpr` in C++17:

```cpp
// Example 08
template <typename Callable> class DebugDecorator {
  public:
  ...
  template <typename... Args>
  auto operator()(Args&&... args) const {
    cout << "Invoking " << s_ << endl;
    using r_t = decltype(c_(std::forward<Args>(args)...));
    if constexpr (!std::is_same_v<res_t, void>) {
      auto res = c_(std::forward<Args>(args)...);
      cout << "Result: " << res << endl;
      return res;
    } else {
      c_(std::forward<Args>(args)...);
    }
  }
  private:
  Callable c_;
  const std::string s_;
};
```

Before C++17, the most common alternative to if constexpr uses function overloading (the first argument is `std::true_type` or `std::false_type` depending on the branch of if constexpr provided by the corresponding function):

```cpp
// Example 08a
template <typename Callable> class DebugDecorator {
  public:
  ...
  template <typename... Args>
  auto operator()(Args&&... args) const {
    cout << "Invoking " << s_ << endl;
```

```
    using r_t = decltype(c_(std::forward<Args>(args)...));
    return this->call_impl(std::is_same<res_t, void>{},
                            std::forward<Args>(args)...);
  }
  private:
  Callable c_;
  const std::string s_;
  template <typename... Args>
  auto call_impl(std::false_type, Args&&... args) const {
    auto res = c_(std::forward<Args>(args)...);
    cout << "Result: " << res << endl;
    return res;
  }
  template <typename... Args>
  void call_impl(std::true_type, Args&&... args) const {
    c_(std::forward<Args>(args)...);
  }
};
```

The second limitation is that the `auto` return type of our decorator is deduced only *mostly* accurately - for example, if a function returns `double&`, the decorated function will return just `double`. Lastly, wrapping member function calls is possible, but requires a somewhat different syntax.

Now, the template mechanism in C++ is powerful, and there are ways to make our generic decorator even more generic. These ways also make it more complex. Code like this belongs in a library, such as the standard library, but in most practical applications a debugging decorator is not worth such effort.

The other limitation is that the more generic a decorator becomes, the less it can do. As it is, there are very few actions we could take that make sense for calling any function or member function (even to produce a good debug message in our decorator we might need to use compiler extensions, see *Example 09*). We could add some debug printouts, and print the result as long as it has the stream output operator defined. We could lock a mutex to protect a non-thread-safe function call in a multi-threaded program. Maybe there are a few more general actions. But, in general, do not get seduced by the pursuit of the most generic code for its own sake.

Whether we have somewhat generic or very specific decorators, we often have the need to add multiple behaviors to an object. We have seen one such example already. Now, let's review the problem of applying multiple decorators more systematically.

Composable decorators

The decorator property that we would like to have here has a name composability. Behaviors are composable if they can be applied to the same object separately: in our case, if we have two decorators, A and B. Therefore, A(B(object)) should have both behaviors applied. The alternative to composability is the explicit creation of the combined behaviors: to have both behaviors without composability, we would need to write a new decorator, AB. Since writing new code for any combination of several decorators would be impossible even for a relatively small number of decorators, composability is a very important property.

Fortunately, composability is not hard to achieve with our approach to decorators. The CRTP decorators we used in our game design earlier are naturally composable:

```
template <typename U> class VeteranUnit : public U { ... };
template <typename U> class DebugDecorator : public U { ...
};
Unit_ptr o(new DebugDecorator<Ogre>(12, 2));
Unit_ptr vo(new DebugDecorator<VeteranUnit<Ogre>>(o, 1, 9));
```

Each decorator inherits from the object it decorates and, thus, preserves its interface, except for the added behavior. Note that the order of the decorators matters since the new behavior is added before or after the decorated call. DebugDecorator applies to the object it decorates and provides debugging for it, so a VeteranUnit<DebugDecorator<Ogre>> object would debug the base portion of the object (Ogre), which can be useful as well.

Our (somewhat) universal decorators can be composed as well. We already have a debugging decorator that can work with many different callable objects, and we mentioned a possible need to protect these calls with a mutex. We can now implement such a locking decorator in a similar manner (and with similar limitations) to the polymorphic debugging decorator:

```
// Example 10
template <typename Callable> class LockDecorator {
  public:
  template <typename F>
  LockDecorator(F&& f, std::mutex& m) :
    c_(std::forward<F>(f)), m_(m) {}
  template <typename ... Args>
  auto operator()(Args&& ... args) const {
    std::lock_guard<std::mutex> l(m_);
    return c_(std::forward<Args>(args) ...);
  }
  private:
  Callable c_;
  std::mutex& m_;
};
template <typename Callable>
auto decorate_lock(Callable&& c, std::mutex& m) {
  return
    LockDecorator<Callable>(std::forward<Callable>(c), m);
}
```

Again, we will use the `decorate_lock()` helper function to delegate to the compiler the tedious work of figuring out the right type of the callable object. We can now use a mutex to protect a function call that is not thread-safe:

```
std::mutex m;
auto safe_f = decorate_lock([](int x) {
  return unsafe_f(x); }, m
);
```

If we want to protect a function by a mutex and have a debug printout when it's called, we do not need to write a new *locking debugging decorator,* but instead can apply both decorators in sequence:

```
auto safe_f = decorate_debug(
  decorate_lock(
    [](int x) { return unsafe_f(x); },
    m
  ),
  "f(x)");
```

This example demonstrates the benefits of composability - we do not have to write a special decorator for every combination of behaviors (think how many decorators you would have to write for any combination of five different primary decorators if they were not composable!).

This composability is achieved easily in our decorators because they preserve the interface of the original object, at least the part we are interested in - the behavior changes, but the interface does not. When a decorator is used as an original object for another decorator, the preserved interface is once again preserved, and so on.

This preservation of the interface is a fundamental feature of the Decorator pattern. It is also one of its most serious limitations. Our locking decorator is not nearly as useful as it may seem at first glance (so do not go around your code bolting a lock onto every call when you need to make the code thread-safe). As we will see next, not every interface can be made thread-safe, no matter how good the implementation is. That's when we have to change the interface in addition to modifying the behavior. This is the job for the Adapter pattern.

The Adapter pattern

We ended the last section with the notion that the decorator pattern has particular advantages that come from preserving the decorated interface and that these advantages can sometimes turn into limitations. The Adapter pattern is a more general pattern that can be used in such cases.

The Adapter pattern is defined very generally - it is a structural pattern that allows an interface of a class to be used as another, different interface. It allows an existing class to be used in code that expects a different interface, without modifying the original class. Such adapters are sometimes called

class wrappers since they *wrap* around a class and present a different interface. You may recall that decorators are also sometimes called **class wrappers**, much for the same reason.

However, Adapter is a very general, broad pattern. It can be used to implement several other, more narrowly defined patterns - in particular, the decorator. The decorator pattern is easier to follow, so we dealt with that first. Now, we will move on to the general case.

Basic Adapter pattern

Let's follow on from the final example from the last section - the locking decorator. It calls any function under a lock, so no other function protected by the same mutex can be called on any other thread at the same time. In some cases, this could be enough to make the entire code thread-safe. Often, it is not.

To demonstrate this, we are going to implement a thread-safe queue object. A queue is a moderately complex data structure, even without thread safety, but, fortunately, we do not need to start from scratch - we have `std::queue` in the C++ standard library. We can push objects onto the queue and take them from the queue in first-in-first-out order, but only on one thread - it is not safe to push two objects onto the same queue from two different threads at the same time, for example. But we have a solution for that - we can implement a locking queue as a decorator for the basic one. Since we are not concerned about the empty base optimization here (`std::queue` is not an empty class) and we have to forward every member function call, we do not need the inheritance and can use composition instead. Our decorator will contain the queue and the lock. Wrapping the `push()` method is easy. There are two versions of `push()` in `std::queue` - one moves the object and one copies it. We should protect both with the lock:

```
// Example 11
template <typename T> class locking_queue {
  using mutex = std::mutex;
  using lock_guard = std::lock_guard<mutex>;
  using value_type = typename std::queue<T>::value_type;
  void push(const value_type& value) {
    lock_guard l(m_);
    q_.push(value);
  }
  void push(value_type&& value) {
    lock_guard l(m_);
    q_.push(value);
  }
  private:
  std::queue<T> q_;
  mutex m_;
};
```

Now, let's turn our attention to getting elements off the queue. The standard queue has three relevant member functions - first, there is `front()`, which lets us access the front element of the queue, but does not remove it from the queue. Then, there is `pop()`, which removes the front element but returns nothing (it gives no access to the front element - it just removes it). Both of these functions should not be called if the queue is empty - there is no error checking, but the result is undefined.

Finally, there is the third function, `empty()`; it returns false if the queue is not empty, and then we can call `front()` and `pop()`. If we decorate them with locking, we will be able to write code like the following:

```
locking_queue<int> q;
q.push(5);
... sometime later in the program ...
if (!q.empty()) {
  int i = q.front();
  q.pop();
}
```

Each function is thread-safe by itself. The entire combination of them is not. It is important to understand why. First, we call `q.empty()`. Let's assume that it returns `false`, so we know there is at least one element on the queue. We go on to access it on the next line by calling `q.front()`, which returns 5. But this is just one of many threads in the program. Another thread is going through the same code at the same time (enabling this behavior is the point of the exercise). That thread, too, calls `q.empty()` and also gets `false` - as we just said, there is an element in the queue, and we have done nothing to remove it yet. The second thread also calls `q.front()` and gets 5 as well. That is already a problem - two threads each tried to take an element from the queue, but got the same one instead. But it gets worse - our first thread now calls `q.pop()` and removes 5 from the queue. The queue is now empty, but the second thread does not know about this - it called `q.empty()` earlier. Therefore, the second thread now calls `q.pop()` as well, this time on an empty queue. The best-case scenario here is that the program will crash right away.

We have just seen a specific case of a general problem - a sequence of actions, each of which is thread-safe, but is not thread-safe as a whole. In fact, this *locking queue* is entirely useless, and there is no way to write thread-safe code with it. What we need is a single thread-safe function that performs the entire transaction under one lock, as a single uninterruptible action (such transactions are called **atomic**). The transaction, in our case, is the removal of the front element if it's present, and some kind of error diagnostic if it's not. The `std::queue` interface does not provide such a transactional API.

So, now, we need a new pattern - one that transforms the existing interface of a class to our needs for a different interface. This cannot be done with the decorator pattern, but this is exactly the problem that the Adapter pattern solves. Now that we have agreed that we need a different interface, we just have to decide what it should be. Our single new `pop()` member function should do all of this - if the queue is not empty, it should remove the first element from the queue and return it, by copy or move, to the caller. If the queue is empty, it should not alter the state of the queue at all, but should somehow notify the caller that the queue was empty. One way to do this is to return two values - the element itself (if there is one) and a Boolean value that tells us whether the queue was empty or not. Here is the pop() part of the locking queue, which is now an adapter, not a decorator:

```
// Example 11
template <typename T> class locking_queue {
  ... the push() is unchanged ...
  bool pop(value_type& value) {
    lock_guard l(m_);
    if (q_.empty()) return false;
    value = std::move(q_.front());
    q_.pop();
    return true;
  }
  private:
  std::queue<T> q_;
  mutex m_;
};
```

Note that we do not need to change push() - the single function call already does everything we need, so that part of the interface is just forwarded one-to-one by our adapter. This version of pop() returns true if it removed an element from the queue, and false otherwise. If true is returned, the element is saved into the provided argument, but if false is returned, the argument is unchanged. If the element type T is move-assignable, a move will be used instead of copy.

This is, of course, not the only possible interface for such an atomic pop(). Another way would be to return both the element and the Boolean value as a pair. One significant difference is that there is now no way to leave the element unchanged - it's the return value and it always has to be something. The natural way is to default-construct the element if there isn't one on the queue (which implies a restriction on the element type T - it has to be default-constructible).

In C++17, the better alternative is to return a std::optional:

```
// Example 12
template <typename T> class locking_queue {
  ... the push() is unchanged ...
  std::optional<value_type> pop() {
    lock_guard l(m_);
    if (q_.empty()) return std::nullopt;
    value_type value = std::move(q_.front());
    q_.pop();
    return { value };
  }
};
```

Depending on the application code that needs this queue, one of the interfaces may be preferable, and so there are other ways to design it as well. In all cases, we end up with two member functions, push() and pop(), that are protected by the same mutex. Now, any number of threads can execute any combination of these operations at the same time, and the behavior is well-defined. This means that the locking_queue object is thread-safe.

Converting an object from its current interface to the interface needed by a particular application, without rewriting the object itself, is the purpose and use of the Adapter pattern. All kinds of interfaces may have to be converted, and so there are many different types of adapters. We will learn about some of them in the next section.

Function adapters

We have just seen a class adapter that changes the interface of a class. Another kind of interface is a function (a member or a non-member function). A function has certain arguments, but we may want to call it with a different set of arguments. This would need an adapter. One common application of such adapters is known as currying one (or more) of the function's arguments. All it means is that we have a function of several arguments, and we fix the value of one of these arguments, so we don't have to specify it on every call. One example would be if we have f(int i, int j), but we want g(i), which is the same as f(i, 5), only without typing the 5 every time.

Here is a more interesting example that we are actually going to work our way through and implement an adapter. The std::sort function takes an iterator range (the sequence to sort), but it can also be called with three arguments - the third one is the comparison object (by default, std::less is used, which, in turn, calls operator<() on the objects being sorted).

We want something else now - we want to compare floating-point numbers *fuzzily*, with tolerance - if the two numbers x and y are close enough to each other, then we don't consider one to be less than the other. Only when x is much less than y do we want to enforce the sorted order where x comes before y.

Here is our comparison functor (a callable object):

```cpp
// Example 13
struct much_less {
  template <typename T>
  bool operator()(T x, T y) {
    return x < y && std::abs(x - y) > tolerance);
  }
  static constexpr double tolerance = 0.2;
};
```

This comparison object can be used with a standard sort:

```cpp
std::vector<double> v;
std::sort(v.begin(), v.end(), much_less());
```

However, if we need this kind of sort often, we may want to curry the last argument and make ourselves an adapter that has just two arguments, the iterators, and the sorting function implied. Here is such an adapter - it is very simple:

```
// Example 13
template<typename RandomIt>
    void sort_much_less(RandomIt first, RandomIt last) {
    std::sort(first, last, much_less());
}
```

Now, we can call a sort function with two arguments:

```
// Example 13
std::vector<double> v;
sort_much_less(v.begin(), v.end());
```

Now, if we often call sort in this manner to sort the entire container, we may want to change the interface once again and make another adapter:

```
// Example 14
template<typename Container> void sort_much_less(Container&
    c) {
std::sort(c.begin(), c.end(), much_less());
}
```

In C++20, `std::sort` and other STL functions have variants that accept ranges; they are a generalization of our container adapter. Now, the code in our program looks even simpler:

```
// Example 14
std::vector<double> v;
sort_much_less(v);
```

It is important to point out that C++14 provides an alternative for writing such simple adapters that should, in general, be preferred; we can use a lambda expression, as follows:

```
// Example 15
auto sort_much_less = [](auto first, auto last) {
    return std::sort(first, last, much_less());
};
```

Of course, the comparison function much_less() is itself a callable, so it could be a lambda too:

```
// Example 15a
auto sort_much_less = [](auto first, auto last) {
    return std::sort(first, last,
        [](auto x, auto y) {
```

```
    static constexpr double tolerance = 0.2;
    return x < y && std::abs(x - y) > tolerance;
  }); };
```

The container adapter is just as easy to write:

```
// Example 16
auto sort_much_less = [](auto& container) {
  return std::sort(container.begin(), container.end(),
                   much_less());
};
```

Note that you cannot have both of these in the same program under the same name - lambda expressions cannot be *overloaded* in this manner; they are actually not functions at all, but rather objects (you can create an overload set from lambdas, as was shown in *Chapter 2, Class and Function Templates*).

Coming back to the matter of calling a function with some arguments fixed, or bound, to constant values, we should say that this is such a common need that the C++ standard library provides a standard customizable adapter for this purpose, std::bind. Here is an example that shows us how it is used:

```
// Example 17
using namespace std::placeholders; // For _1, _2 etc
int f3(int i, int j, int k) { return i + j + k; }
auto f2 = std::bind(f3, _1, _2, 42);
auto f1 = std::bind(f3, 5, _1, 7);
f2(2, 6);      // Returns 50
f1(3);      // Returns 15
```

This standard adapter has its own *mini-language* - the first argument to std::bind is the function to be bound, while the rest are its arguments, in order. The arguments that should be bound are replaced by the specified values. The arguments that should remain free are replaced by the placeholders _1, _2, and so on (not necessarily in that order; that is, we can also change the order of the arguments). The returned value is of an unspecified type and has to be captured using auto. The only thing we know about the return value is that it can be called as a function with as many arguments as there are placeholders. It can also be used as a function in any context that expects a callable, for example, in another std::bind:

```
// Example 17
...
auto f1 = std::bind(f3, 5, _1, 7);
auto f0 = std::bind(f1, 3);
f1(3);    // Returns 15
f0();        // Also returns 15
```

However, these objects are callables, not functions, and you will discover that if you try to assign one of them to a function pointer:

```
// Example 17
int (*p3)(int, int, int) = f3;    // OK
int (*p1)(int) = f1;              // Does not compile
```

In contrast, lambdas can be converted to function pointers if they have no captures:

```
auto l1 = [](int i) { return f3(5, i, 7); }
int (*p1)(int) = l1;              // OK
```

As useful as `std::bind` is, it does not free us from the need to learn how to write our own function adapters - its greatest limitation is that `std::bind` cannot bind template functions. We cannot write the following:

```
auto sort_much_less = std::bind(std::sort, _1, _2, much_less()); //
No!
```

This does not compile. Inside a template, we can bind the specific instantiation of it, but, at least in our sorting example, this really does not buy us anything:

```
template<typename RandomIt>
void sort_much_less(RandomIt first, RandomIt last) {
  auto f = std::bind(std::sort<RandomIt, much_less>,
                     _1, _2, much_less());
  f(first, last, much_less());
}
```

As we mentioned at the beginning of this section, decorators can be seen as a special case of the Adapter pattern. Sometimes, the distinction is not so much in a particular application of the pattern but in how we choose to view it.

Adapter or Decorator

Until now, we described the Decorator as a pattern we use to augment an existing interface, while the Adapter is used to convert (adapt) an interface for integration with code that expects a different interface. The distinction is not always clear.

For example, let us consider a simple class that adapts the result of the system call `std::time` to a printable date format (`std::chrono` provides this functionality, but it makes for an easy-to-follow example). The function `std::time` returns a value of the type `std::time_t` which is an integer containing the time in seconds since some standard moment in the past that is called the "start of the epoch." Another system function, `localtime`, converts this value to a struct that contains the date elements: year, month, and day (also hours, minutes, etc). The calendar calculations, in general, are rather non-trivial (which is why `std::chrono` is not as simple as we might wish) but for now, let us assume that the system library does the right thing and all we have to do is print the date in the right format. For example, here is how to print the current date in the US format:

```
const std::time_t now = std::time(nullptr);
const tm local_tm = *localtime(&now);
cout << local_tm.tm_mon + 1 << "/" <<
        local_tm.tm_mday << "/" <<
        local_tm.tm_year + 1900;
```

We want to create an adapter that converts a time in seconds to the date in a particular format and lets us print it; we will need separate adapters for the US format (month first), European format (day first), and ISO format (year first).

The implementation of the adapter is pretty straightforward:

```
// Example 18
class USA_Date {
  public:
  explicit USA_Date(std::time_t t) : t_(t) {}
  friend std::ostream& operator<<(std::ostream& out,
                                  const USA_Date& d) {
    const tm local_tm = *localtime(&d.t_);
    out << local_tm.tm_mon + 1 << "/" <<
            local_tm.tm_mday << "/" <<
            local_tm.tm_year + 1900;
    return out;
  }
  private:
  const std::time_t t_;
};
```

The other two date formats are similar except for the order in which we print the fields. In fact, they are so similar that we may want to refactor the code to avoid typing three almost identical classes. The easiest way to do this is to use a template and encode the field order in a "format code" which specifies the order in which we print the day (field 0), month (field 1), and year (field 2). For example, "format" 210 means year, then month, then day – the ISO date format. The format code can be an integer template parameter:

```
// Example 19
template <size_t F> class Date {
  public:
  explicit Date(std::time_t t) : t_(t) {}
  friend std::ostream& operator<<(std::ostream& out,
```

```
                                        const Date& d) {
    const tm local_tm = *localtime(&d.t_);
    const int t[3] = { local_tm.tm_mday,
                       local_tm.tm_mon + 1,
                       local_tm.tm_year + 1900 };
    constexpr size_t i1 = F/100;
    constexpr size_t i2 = (F - i1*100)/10;
    constexpr size_t i3 = F - i1*100 - i2*10;
    static_assert(i1 >= 0 && i1 <= 2 && ..., "Bad format");
    out << t[i1] << "/" << t[i2] << "/" << t[i3];
    return out;
  }
  private:
  const std::time_t t_;
};
using USA_Date = Date<102>;
using European_Date = Date<12>;
using ISO_Date = Date<210>;
```

Our little wrapper adapts a type (an integer) to be used in the code that expects dates in a particular format. Or does it decorate the integer with the operator<<()? The best answer is ... whichever one is more helpful to you to think about your particular problem. It is important to remember the purpose of speaking in the language of the patterns in the first place: we do it to have a compact and commonly understood way to describe our software problems and the solutions we choose. When multiple patterns appear to yield similar results, the description you choose lets you focus on the aspect that is most important to you.

So far, we have considered only adapters that convert runtime interfaces, which are the interfaces we call when the program is executed. However, C++ has compile-time interfaces as well - one of the prime examples that we considered in the last chapter was policy-based design. These interfaces are not always exactly what we need them to be, so we have to learn to write compile-time adapters next.

Compile-time adapters

In *Chapter 16, Adapters and Decorators*, we learned about policies, which are building blocks for classes - they let the programmer customize the implementation for a particular behavior. As an example, we can implement this policy-based smart pointer that automatically deletes the object it owns. The policy is the particular implementation of the deletion:

```
// Chapter 15, Example 08
template <typename T,
          template <typename> class DeletionPolicy =
                                       DeleteByOperator>
```

```
class SmartPtr {
  public:
  explicit SmartPtr(T* p = nullptr,
    const DeletionPolicy<T>& del_policy =
                              DeletionPolicy<T>())
  : p_(p), deletion_policy_(deletion_policy)
  {}
  ~SmartPtr() {
    deletion_policy_(p_);
  }
  ... pointer interface ...
  private:
  T* p_;
  DeletionPolicy<T> deletion_policy_;
};
```

Note that the deletion policy is itself a template - this is a *template* parameter. The default deletion policy is to use `operator delete`:

```
template <typename T> struct DeleteByOperator {
  void operator()(T* p) const {
    delete p;
  }
};
```

However, for objects allocated on a user-given heap, we need a different deletion policy that returns the memory to that heap:

```
template <typename T> struct DeleteHeap {
  explicit DeleteHeap(MyHeap& heap) : heap_(heap) {}
  void operator()(T* p) const {
    p->~T();
    heap_.deallocate(p);
  }
  private:
  MyHeap& heap_;
};
```

Then we have to create a policy object to use with the pointer:

```
MyHeap H;
SmartPtr<int, DeleteHeap<int>> p(new int, H);
```

This policy is not very flexible, however - it can handle heaps of only one type - `MyHeap`. We can make the policy more general if we make the heap type the second template parameter. As long as the heap has the `deallocate()` member function to return memory to it, we can use any heap class with this policy:

```
// Example 20
template <typename T, typename Heap> struct DeleteHeap {
  explicit DeleteHeap(Heap& heap) : heap_(heap) {}
  void operator()(T* p) const {
    p->~T();
    heap_.deallocate(p);
  }
  private:
  Heap& heap_;
};
```

Of course, if we have a heap class that uses another name for this member function, we can use a class adapter to make that class work with our policy, too. But we have a larger problem - our policy does not work with our smart pointer. The following code does not compile:

```
SmartPtr<int, DeletelHeap> p; // Does not compile
```

The reason is again the interface mismatch, only now it is a different kind of interface – the `template <typename T, template <typename> class DeletionPolicy> class SmartPtr {};` template expects the second argument to be a template with one type parameter. Instead, we have the `DeleteHeap` template with two type parameters. This is just like trying to call a function that has one parameter but uses two arguments - it won't work. We need an adapter to convert our two-parameter template into a one-parameter one, and we have to fix the second argument to a particular heap type (but we do not need to rewrite the policy if we have multiple heap types, we just need to write several adapters). We can create this adapter, `DeleteMyHeap`, using inheritance (and remembering to bring the constructors of the base class into the derived adapter class scope):

```
// Example 20
template <typename T>
struct DeleteMyHeap : public DeleteHeap<T, MyHeap> {
  using DeleteHeap<T, MyHeap>::DeleteHeap;
};
```

We could do the same using the template alias:

```
// Example 21
template <typename T>
using DeleteMyHeap = DeleteHeap<T, MyHeap>;
```

This first version is, obviously, much longer. However, we have to learn both ways of writing template adapters because the template alias has one major limitation. To illustrate it, let's consider another example where an adapter is needed. We will begin by implementing a stream insertion operator for any STL-compliant sequence container whose elements have such an operator defined. It is a simple function template:

```
// Example 22
template <template <typename> class Container, typename T>
std::ostream& operator<<(std::ostream& out,
                         const Container<T>& c) {
  bool first = true;
  for (auto x : c) {
  if (!first) out << ", ";
    first = false;
    out << x;
  }
  return out;
}
```

This `template` function has two type parameters, the container type and the element type. The container is itself a template with one type parameter. The compiler deduces both the container type and the element type from the second function argument (the first argument in any `operator<<()` is always the stream). We can test our insertion operator on a simple container:

```
// Example 22
template <typename T> class Buffer {
  public:
  explicit Buffer(size_t N) : N_(N), buffer_(new T[N_]) {}
  ~Buffer() { delete [] buffer_; }
  T* begin() const { return buffer_; }
  T* end() const { return buffer_ + N_; }
  ...
  private:
  const size_t N_;
  T* const buffer_;
};
Buffer<int> buffer(10);
... fill the buffer ...
cout << buffer; // Prints all elements of the buffer
```

But this is just a toy container and is not very useful. What we really want is to print elements of a real container, such as `std::vector`:

```
std::vector<int> v;
... add some values to v ...
cout << v;
```

Unfortunately, this code does not compile. The reason is that `std::vector` is not really a template with one type parameter, even though we used it as such. It has two parameters - the second is the allocator type. There is a default for this allocator, which is why we can write `std::vector<int>` and it compiles. But, even with this default argument, this is still a template with two parameters, while our stream insertion operator is declared to accept container templates with only one parameter. Again, we can solve the problem by writing an adapter (most STL containers are used with the default allocator anyway). The easiest way to write this adapter is with an alias:

```
template <typename T> using vector1 = std::vector<T>;
vector1<int> v;

...
cout << v; // Does not compile either
```

Unfortunately, this does not compile either, and now we can show the template alias limitation that we alluded to earlier - template aliases are not used in template argument type deduction. When the compiler attempts to figure out the template argument types for the call of `operator<<()` with the arguments `cout` and `v`, the template alias `vector1` is *invisible*. In this case, we have to use a derived class adapter:

```
// Example 22
template <typename T>
struct vector1 : public std::vector<T> {
  using std::vector<T>::vector;
};
vector1<int> v;

...
cout << v;
```

By the way, if you paid attention to the previous chapter, you may realize that we already encountered the problem of extra parameters to the template template parameters, and solved it by declaring these parameters as variadic templates:

```
// Example 23
template <typename T,
  template <typename, typename...> class Container,
  typename... Args>
std::ostream& operator<<(std::ostream& out,
```

```
                     const Container<T, Args...>& c) {
    ...
}
```

Now our `operator<<()` can print any container, so we no longer need to worry about adapters, right? Not quite: one of the containers we still cannot print is `std::array` which is a class template with one type and one non-type parameter. We could declare an overload just to handle this case:

```
// Example 23
template <typename T,
   template <typename, size_t> class Container, size_t N>
std::ostream& operator<<(std::ostream& out,
                         const Container<T, N>& c) {

   ...
}
```

But we may have yet another kind of container that does not fit either of these templates (whether because it has to or simply because it is part of legacy code that was written differently). Then, we have to use an adapter again.

We have now seen how we can implement decorators to augment class and function interfaces with the desired behavior, and how to create adapters when the existing interface is not suitable for a particular application. Decorator, and, even more so, Adapter, are very general and versatile patterns that can be used to solve many problems. It should come as no surprise that, often, a problem can be solved in more than one way, so there is a choice of patterns to use. In the next section, we will see one such case.

Adapter versus policy

The adapter and the policy (or strategy) patterns are some of the more general patterns, and C++ adds generic programming capabilities to these patterns. This tends to extend their usability and sometimes blurs the lines between the patterns. The patterns themselves are defined very distinctly - policies provide custom implementations while adapters change the interface and add functionality to the existing interface (the latter is a decorator aspect, but, as we have seen, most decorators are implemented as adapters). We also saw in the last chapter that C++ broadens the capabilities of policy-based design; in particular, policies in C++ can add or remove parts of the interface as well as control the implementation. So, while patterns are different, there is significant overlap in the types of problems they can be used for. It is instructive to compare the two approaches when a problem is, broadly speaking, amenable to both. For this exercise, we will consider the problem of designing a custom value type.

A value type, to put it simply, is a type that behaves mostly like an `int`. Often, these types are numbers. While we have a set of built-in types for that, we may want to operate on rational numbers, complex numbers, tensors, matrices, or numbers that have units associated with them (meters, grams, and so on). These value types support a set of operations such as arithmetic operations, comparisons, assignments, and copying. Depending on what the value represents, we may need only a limited subset of these operations - for example, we may need to support addition and multiplication for matrices, but no division, and comparing matrices for anything other than equality probably doesn't make sense in most cases. Similarly, we probably don't want to allow the addition of meters to grams.

More generally, there is often a desire to have a numeric type with a limited interface - we would like it if the operations that we do not wish to allow for the quantity represented by such numbers did not compile. This way, a program with an invalid operation simply cannot be written. To be general, our design has to allow us to build the interface piece by piece. For example, we may want a value that is comparable for equality, ordered (has the less-than operation defined), and addable, but without multiplication or division. This seems like a problem that is tailor-made for the Decorator (or, more generally, Adapter) pattern: decorators can add behaviors like comparison operator or addition operator. On the other hand, creating a type with a set of capabilities configured by plugging in the right policies is exactly what the Policy pattern is for.

Adapter solution

Let us examine the Adapter solution first. We will start with a basic value type that supports almost nothing in its interface, and then we can add the desired capabilities, one by one.

Here is our initial `Value` class template:

```
// Example 24
template <typename T> class Value {
  public:
  using basic_type = T;
  using value_type = Value;
  explicit Value() : val_(T()) {}
  explicit Value(T v) : val_(v) {}
  Value(const Value&) = default;
  Value& operator=(const Value&) = default;
  Value& operator=(basic_type rhs) {
    val_ = rhs;
    return *this;
  }
  protected:
  T val_ {};
};
```

The `Value` is copyable and assignable, both from the underlying type such as `int` and from another `Value`. We could have moved some of those capabilities into adapters as well if we wanted to have non-copyable values, but you will find this an easy change after making your way through the rest of the chapter.

For convenience, we will also make our Value printable (in any real situation you would likely want this to be a separate and configurable capability, but it makes the examples simpler without taking anything important away).

```
// Example 24
template <typename T> class Value {
  public:
  friend std::ostream& operator<<(std::ostream& out,
                                    Value x) {
    out << x.val_;
    return out;
  }
  friend std::istream& operator>>(std::istream& in,
                                    Value& x) {
    in >> x.val_;
    return in;
  }
  ...
};
```

We use the *friend factory*, which was described in *Chapter 12, Friend Factory*, to generate these functions. So far, all we can do with our Value is to initialize it, maybe assign it to another value, and print it:

```
// Example 24
using V = Value<int>;
V i, j(5), k(3);
i = j;
std::cout << i;      // Prints 5
```

There is nothing else we can do with this class - no comparisons for equality or inequality, no arithmetic operations. However, we can create an adapter that adds the comparison interface:

```
// Example 24
template <typename V> class Comparable : public V {
  public:
  using V::V;
  using V::operator=;
  using value_type = typename V::value_type;
  using basic_type = typename value_type::basic_type;
  Comparable(value_type v) : V(v) {}
  friend bool operator==(Comparable lhs, Comparable rhs) {
    return lhs.val_ == rhs.val_;
  }
  friend bool operator==(Comparable lhs, basic_type rhs) {
    return lhs.val_ == rhs;
```

```
    }
    friend bool operator==(basic_type lhs, Comparable rhs) {
      return lhs == rhs.val_;
    }
    ... same for the operator!= ...
};
```

This is a class adapter - it is derived from the class it is augmenting with new capabilities, so it inherits all of its interface and adds some more - the complete set of comparison operators. Note that it is common to use pass-by-value instead of reference when dealing with value types (passing by reference to const isn't wrong either, and some compilers may optimize either version to the same end result).

We are familiar with the way these adapters are used:

```
using V = Comparable<Value<int>>;
V i(3), j(5);
i == j; // False
i == 3; // True
5 == j; // Also true
```

That is one capability. What about some more? No problem - the `Ordered` adapter can be written very similarly, only it provides the operators <, <=, >, and >= (or, in C++20, operator <=>):

```
// Example 24
template <typename V> class Ordered : public V {
  public:
  using V::V;
  using V::operator=;
  using value_type = typename V::value_type;
  using basic_type = typename value_type::basic_type;
  Ordered(value_type v) : V(v) {}
  friend bool operator<(Ordered lhs, Ordered rhs) {
    return lhs.val_ < rhs.val_;
  }
  friend bool operator<(basic_type lhs, Ordered rhs) {
    return lhs < rhs.val_;
  }
  friend bool operator<(Ordered lhs, basic_type rhs) {
    return lhs.val_ < rhs;
  }
  ... same for the other operators ...
};
```

We can combine the two adapters - as we say, they are composable, and they work in any order:

```
using V = Ordered<Comparable<Value<int>>>;
// Or Comparable<Ordered<...>
V i(3), j(5);
i == j; // False
i <= 3; // True
```

Some operations, or capabilities, require more work. If our value type is numeric, such as `Value<int>`, we will want some arithmetic operations like addition and multiplication. Here is a decorator that enables addition and subtraction:

```
// Example 24
template <typename V> class Addable : public V {
  public:
  using V::V;
  using V::operator=;
  using value_type = typename V::value_type;
  using basic_type = typename value_type::basic_type;
  Addable(value_type v) : V(v) {}
  friend Addable operator+(Addable lhs, Addable rhs) {
    return Addable(lhs.val_ + rhs.val_);
  }
  friend Addable operator+(Addable lhs, basic_type rhs) {
    return Addable(lhs.val_ + rhs);
  }
  friend Addable operator+(basic_type lhs, Addable rhs) {
    return Addable(lhs + rhs.val_);
  }
  ... same for the operator- ...
};
```

The decorator is trivial to use:

```
using V = Addable<Value<int>>;
V i(5), j(3), k(7);
k = i + j; // 8
```

We can also combine `Addable` with other decorators:

```
using V = Addable<Ordered<Value<int>>>;
V i(5), j(3), k(7);
if (k - 1 < i + j) { ... yes it is ... }
```

But we have a problem that so far has been hidden only by good luck. We could have just as easily written:

```
using V = Ordered<Addable<Value<int>>>;
V i(5), j(3), k(7);
if (k - 1 < i + j) { ... }
```

There should be no difference whatsoever between this example and the previous one. Instead, we get a compilation error: there is no valid `operator<` to be used in the last line. The problem here is that the `i + j` expression uses the `operator+()` that comes from the `Addable` adapter, and this operator returns an object of type `Addable<Value<int>>`. The comparison operator expects the type `Ordered<Addable<Value<int>>>`, and will not accept the "partial" type (there is no implicit conversion from a base class to the derived one). The unsatisfactory solution is to require that `Addable` is always the top decorator. Not only it just feels wrong, but it also doesn't get us very far: the next decorator we will want is `Multipliable` and it is going to have the same problem. When something is both `Addable` and `Multipliable` we can't have both be on top.

Note that we had no problems with comparison operators returning `bool`, but once we have to return the decorated type itself, which is what `operator+()` does, the composability breaks down. To solve this problem, every operator that returns the decorated type has to return the original (outermost) type. For example, if our value type is `Ordered<Addable<Value<int>>>`, the result of adding two values should have the same type. The problem, of course, is that `operator+()` is provided by the `Addable` decorator which knows only about `Addable` and its base classes. We need an intermediate class in the hierarchy (`Addable<...>`) to return objects of its derived type (`Ordered<Addable<...>>`). This is a very common design problem, and there is a pattern for it: the Curiously Recurring Template Pattern, or CRTP (see the eponymous *Chapter 8, The Curiously Recurring Template Pattern*). Applying this pattern to our decorators takes some recursive thinking. We will introduce the two main ideas, then we just have to wade through a fairly large coding example.

First of all, every decorator is going to have two template parameters. The first one is the same as before: it is the next decorator in the chain, or `Value<int>` at the end of the chain (of course, the pattern is not limited to `int`, but we're simplifying our examples by staying with the same base type throughout). The second parameter is going to be the outermost type; we will call it the "final value type." Thus, all of our decorators are going to be declared like this:

```
template <typename V, typename FV> class Ordered : ...
```

But in our code, we still want to write

```
using V = Ordered<Addable<Value<int>>>;
```

This means we need a default value for the second template parameter. This value can be any type that we're not going to use elsewhere in our decorators; void will do nicely. We will also need a partial template specialization for this default type since, if the final value type is not specified explicitly, we have to somehow figure out what it is:

```
template <typename V, typename FV = void> class Ordered;
template <typename V> class Ordered<V, void>;
```

Now we're going to walk through our "nested" type Ordered<Addable<Value< int >>> step by step. At the outer layer, we can think of it as Ordered<T> where T is Addable<Value<int>>. Since we did not specify the second type parameter FV to the Ordered template, we are going to get the default value void and the template instantiation Ordered<T> is going to use the partial specialization of the Ordered template. Even thought we don't have the "final value type" FV specified, we know what that is: it's Ordered<T> itself.

Now we need to figure out the base class to inherit from. Since every decorator inherits from the type it decorates, it should be T which is Addable<U> (where U is Value<int>). But that's not going to work: we need to pass the correct final value type into Addable. So we should inherit from Addable<U, FV> where FV is the final value type Ordered<T>. Unfortunately, we do not have Addable<U, FV> written in the code: we have Addable<U>. What we need is to somehow figure out the type that would have been generated by the same template Addable but with a different second type argument (Ordered<T> instead of the default void).

This is a very common problem in C++ templates, and it has an equally common solution: template rebinding. Every one of our decorator templates needs to define the following template alias:

```
template <typename V, typename FV = void>
class Ordered : public ... some base class ... {
  public:
    template <typename FV1> using rebind = Ordered<V, FV1>;
};
```

Now, given the type T, which is an instantiation of one of the decorator templates, we can find out the type that would have been produced by the same template but with a different second template argument FV: it's T::template rebind<FV>. That is what our Ordered<V> needs to inherit from to pass the correct final value type to the next decorator:

```
// Example 25
template <typename V, typename FV = void>
class Ordered : public V::template rebind<FV> { ... };
```

This class template says that given a type `Ordered<T, FV>` we are going to inherit from the type T rebound to the same final value type FV and ignore the second template argument of T. The exception from this is the outermost type, where the template parameter FV is void but we know what the final value type should be, so we can rebind to that type:

```
// Example 25
template <typename V> class Ordered<V, void> :
  public V::template rebind<Ordered<V>> { ... };
```

Note the syntax, with the keyword `template`: some compilers will accept `V:: rebind<Ordered<V>>` but this is wrong, the standard requires this exact syntax.

Now we can put everything together. In the general case where our decorator is somewhere in the middle of the decorator chain, we must pass the final value type to the base class:

```
// Example 25
template <typename V, typename FV = void>
class Ordered : public V::template rebind<FV> {
  using base_t = typename V::template rebind<FV>;
  public:
  using base_t::base_t;
  using base_t::operator=;
  template <typename FV1> using rebind = Ordered<V, FV1>;
  using value_type = typename base_t::value_type;
  using basic_type = typename value_type::basic_type;
  explicit Ordered(value_type v) : base_t(v) {}
  friend bool operator<(FV lhs, FV rhs) {
    return lhs.val_ < rhs.val_;
  }
  ... the rest of the operators ...
};
```

The type alias `base_t` is introduced for convenience, it makes writing using statements easier. Note that we need the `typename` keyword before any type that depends on the template parameters; we did not need this keyword to specify the base class because the base class is always a type, so writing `typename` would be redundant.

The special case of the outermost type where the final value type is not specified and defaults to `void` is very similar:

```
// Example 25
template <typename V> class Ordered<V, void>
  : public V::template rebind<Ordered<V>> {
  using base_t = typename V::template rebind<Ordered>;
```

```
  public:
  using base_t::base_t;
  using base_t::operator=;
  template <typename FV1> using rebind = Ordered<V, FV1>;
  using value_type = typename base_t::value_type;
  using basic_type = typename value_type::basic_type;
  explicit Ordered(value_type v) : base_t(v) {}
  friend bool operator<(Ordered lhs, Ordered rhs) {
    return lhs.val_ < rhs.val_;
  }
  ... the rest of the operators ...
};
```

The specialization differs from the general case in two ways. In addition to the base class, the parameters of the operators cannot be of the type FV since it is void. Instead, we must use the type of the class generated by the template, which inside the template definition can be referred to simply as Ordered (the name of the template, when used inside the class, refers to the specific instantiation – you do not need to repeat the template arguments).

For decorators whose operators return a value, we need to make sure to always use the correct final value type for the return type. In the general case, this is the second template parameter FV:

```
// Example 25
template <typename V, typename FV = void> class Addable :
  public V::template rebind<FV> {
  friend FV operator+(FV lhs, FV rhs) {
    return FV(lhs.val_ + rhs.val_);
  }
  ...
};
```

In the specialization for the outermost decorator, the final value type is the decorator itself:

```
// Example 25
template <typename V> class Addable<V, void> :
  public V::template rebind<FV> {
  friend Addable operator+(Addable lhs, Addable rhs) {
    return Addable(lhs.val_ + rhs.val_);
  }
  ...
};
```

We must apply this technique to every decorator template. Now we can compose the decorators in any order and define value types with any subset of available operations:

```
// Example 25
using V = Comparable<Ordered<Addable<Value<int>>>>;
// Addable<Ordered<Comparable<Value<int>>>> also OK
V i, j(5), k(3);
i = j; j = 1;
i == j;          // OK - Comparable
i > j;          // OK - Ordered
i + j == 7 - k;    // OK - Comparable and Addable
i*j;               // Not Multipliable - does not compile
```

So far, all of our decorators added member or non-member operators to the class. We can also add member functions and even constructors. The latter is useful if we want to add a conversion. For example, we can add an implicit conversion from the underlying type (as written, `Value<T>` is not implicitly constructible from `T`). The conversion decorator follows the same pattern as all the other decorators but adds an implicit converting constructor:

```
// Example 25
template <typename V, typename FV = void>
class ImplicitFrom : public V::template rebind<FV> {
  ...
  explicit ImplicitFrom(value_type v) : base_t(v) {}
  ImplicitFrom(basic_type rhs) : base_t(rhs) {}
};
template <typename V> class ImplicitFrom<V, void> :
  public V::template rebind<ImplicitFrom<V>> {
  ...
  explicit ImplicitFrom(value_type v) : base_t(v) {}
  ImplicitFrom(basic_type rhs) : base_t(rhs) {}
};
```

Now we can use implicit conversions to our value type, for example, when calling functions:

```
using V = ImplicitFrom<Ordered<Addable<Value<int>>>>;
void f(V v);
f(3);
```

If you want an implicit conversion to the underlying type, you can use a very similar adapter but instead of the constructor, it adds the conversion operator:

```
// Example 25
template <typename V, typename FV = void>
class ImplicitTo : public V::template rebind<FV> {
```

```
  ...
  explicit ImplicitTo(value_type v) : base_t(v) {}
  operator basic_type(){ return this->val_; }
  operator const basic_type() const { return this->val_; }
};
template <typename V> class ImplicitTo<V, void> :
  public V::template rebind<ImplicitTo<V>> {
  ...
  explicit ImplicitTo(value_type v) : base_t(v) {}
  operator basic_type(){ return this->val_; }
  operator const basic_type() const { return this->val_; }
};
```

This allows us to do the conversion in the opposite direction:

```
using V = ImplicitTo<Ordered<Addable<Value<int>>>>;
void f(int i);
V i(3);
f(i);
```

This design gets the job done, there aren't any particular problems with it, other than the complexity of writing the adapters themselves: the recursive application of CRTP tends to send your brain into infinite recursion until you get used to thinking about this kind of template adapters. The other alternative is a policy-based value type.

Policy solution

We are now going to look at a somewhat different form of the policy-based design compared to what we saw in *Chapter 15, Policy-Based Design*. It is not as general, but when it works, it can provide all the advantages of the policies, in particular, the composability, without some of the problems. The problem remains the same: create a custom value type with a set of operations we can control. This problem can be tackled with the standard policy-based approach:

```
template <typename T, typename AdditionPolicy,
                      typename ComparisonPolicy,
                      typename OrderPolicy,
                      typename AssignmentPolicy, ... >
class Value { ... };
```

This implementation runs into the entire set of drawbacks of policy-based design - the policy list is long, all policies must be spelled out, and there aren't any good defaults; the policies are positional, so the type declaration requires careful counting of commas, and, as the new policies are added, any semblance of a meaningful order of policies disappears. Note that we did not mention the problem of different sets of policies creating different types - in this case, this is not a drawback, but the design intent. If we want a type with support for addition and a similar type but without addition, these have to be different types.

Ideally, we would like to just list the policies for the properties we want our value to have - I want a value type based on integers that support addition, multiplication, and assignment, but nothing else. After all, we did this with the Adapter pattern, so we would not settle for anything less now. As it turns out, there is a way to accomplish this.

First, let's think of what such a policy might look like. For example, the policy that enables addition should inject operator+() into the public interface of the class (and maybe also operator+=()). The policy that makes the value assignable should inject operator=(). We have seen enough of such policies to know how they are implemented - they have to be base classes, publicly inherited, and they need to know what the derived class is and cast it to its type, so they have to use CRTP:

```
template <
   typename T,    // The base type (like int)
   typename V>    // The derived class
struct Incrementable {
  V operator++() {
    V& v = static_cast<V&>(*this);
    ++v.val_;       // The value inside the derived class
    return v;
  }
};
```

Now, we need to give some thought to the use of these policies in the primary template. First of all, we want to support the unknown number of policies, in any order. This brings variadic templates to mind. However, to use CRTP, the template parameters have to be templates themselves. Then, we want to inherit from an instantiation of each of these templates, however many there are. What we need is a variadic template with a template template parameter pack:

```
// Example 26
template <typename T,
         template <typename, typename> class ... Policies>
class Value :
  public Policies<T, Value<T, Policies ... >> ...
{ ... };
```

The preceding declaration introduces a class template called Value, with at least one parameter that is a type, plus zero or more template policies, which themselves have two type parameters (in C++17, we can also write typename ... Policies instead of class ... Policies). The Value class instantiates these templates with the type T and itself and inherits publicly from all of them.

The `Value` class template should contain the interface that we want to be common for all our value types. The rest will have to come from policies. Let's make the values copyable, assignable, and printable by default:

```
// Example 26
template <typename T,
          template <typename, typename> class ... Policies>
class Value :
  public Policies<T, Value<T, Policies ... >> ...
{
  public:
  using base_type = T;
  explicit Value() = default;
  explicit Value(T v) : val_(v) {}
  Value(const Value& rhs) : val_(rhs.val_) {}
  Value& operator=(Value rhs) {
    val_ = rhs.val_;
    return *this;
  }
  Value& operator=(T rhs) { val_ = rhs; return *this; }
  friend std::ostream&
  operator<<(std::ostream& out, Value x) {
    out << x.val_; return out;
  }
  friend std::istream&
    operator>>(std::istream& in, Value& x) {
    in >> x.val_; return in;
  }
  private:
  T val_ {};
};
```

Again, we use the *friend factory* from *Chapter 12, Friend Factory,* to generate the stream operators.

Before we can indulge ourselves in implementing all of the policies, there is one more hurdle to overcome. The `val_` value is private in the `Value` class, and we like it this way. However, the policies need to access and modify it. In the past, we solved this problem by making each policy that needed such access into a friend. This time, we don't even know the names of the policies we may have. After working through the preceding declaration of the parameter pack expansion as a set of base classes, the reader may reasonably expect us to pull a rabbit out of the hat and somehow declare friendship to the entire parameter pack. Unfortunately, the standard offers no such way. The best solution we can suggest is to provide a set of accessor functions that should be called only by the policies, but there is no good way to enforce that (a name, such as `policy_accessor_do_not_call()`, might go some way to suggest that the user code should stay away from it, but the ingenuity of the programmer knows no bounds, and such hints are not universally respected):

```
// Example 26
template <typename T,
          template <typename, typename> class ... Policies>
class Value :
  public Policies<T, Value<T, Policies ... >> ...
{
  public:
  ...
  T get() const { return val_; }
  T& get() { return val_; }
  private:
  T val_ {};
};
```

To create a value type with a restricted set of operations, we have to instantiate this template with a list of policies we want, and nothing else:

```
// Example 26
using V = Value<int, Addable, Incrementable>;
V v1(0), v2(1);
v1++; // Incrementable - OK
V v3(v1 + v2); // Addable - OK
v3 *= 2; // No multiplication policies - won't compile
```

The number and the type of policies we can implement are limited mostly by the need at hand (or imagination), but here are some examples that demonstrate adding different kinds of operations to the class.

First of all, we can implement the aforementioned `Incrementable` policy that provides the two `++` operators, postfix and prefix:

```
// Example 26
template <typename T, typename V> struct Incrementable {
  V operator++() {
    V& v = static_cast<V&>(*this);
    ++(v.get());
    return v;
  }
  V operator++(int) {
    V& v = static_cast<V&>(*this);
    return V(v.get()++);
```

```
    }
};
```

We can make a separate `Decrementable` policy for the `--` operators, or have one policy for both if it makes sense for our type. Also, if want to increment by some value other than one, then we need the `+=` operators as well:

```
// Example 26
template <typename T, typename V> struct Incrementable {
  V& operator+=(V val) {
    V& v = static_cast<V&>(*this);
    v.get() += val.get();
    return v;
  }
  V& operator+=(T val) {
    V& v = static_cast<V&>(*this);
    v.get() += val;
    return v;
  }
};
```

The preceding policy provides two versions of `operator+=()` - one accepts the increment of the same `Value` type, and the other of the foundation type `T`. This is not a requirement, and we could implement an increment by values of some other types as needed. We can even have several versions of the increment policy, as long as only one is used (the compiler would let us know if we were introducing incompatible overloads of the same operator).

We can add the operators `*=` and `/=` in a similar manner. Adding binary operators such as comparison operators or addition and multiplication is a little different - these operators have to be non-member functions to allow for type conversions on the first argument. Again, the friend factory pattern comes in handy. Let's start with the comparison operators:

```
// Example 26
template <typename T, typename V> struct ComparableSelf {
  friend bool operator==(V lhs, V rhs) {
    return lhs.get() == rhs.get();
  }
  friend bool operator!=(V lhs, V rhs) {
    return lhs.get() != rhs.get();
  }
};
```

When instantiated, this template generates two non-member non-template functions, that is, the comparison operators for variables of the type of the specific Value class, the one that is instantiated. We may also want to allow comparisons with the foundation type (such as int):

```
template <typename T, typename V> struct ComparableValue {
  friend bool operator==(V lhs, T rhs) {
    return lhs.get() == rhs;
  }
  friend bool operator==(T lhs, V rhs) {
    return lhs == rhs.get();
  }
  friend bool operator!=(V lhs, T rhs) {
    return lhs.get() != rhs;
  }
  friend bool operator!=(T lhs, V rhs) {
    return lhs != rhs.get();
  }
};
```

More often than not, we will likely want both types of comparison at the same time. We could simply put them both into the same policy and not worry about separating them, or we could create a combined policy from the two we already have:

```
// Example 26
template <typename T, typename V>
struct Comparable : public ComparableSelf<T, V>,
                    public ComparableValue<T, V> {};
```

In the previous section, we combined all comparisons in a single adapter from the beginning. Here, we use a slightly different approach just to illustrate different options for controlling class interfaces with policies or adapters (both solutions offer the same options). The addition and multiplication operators are created by similar policies. They are also friend non-template non-member functions. The only difference is the return value type - they return the object itself, for example:

```
// Example 26
template <typename T, typename V> struct Addable {
  friend V operator+(V lhs, V rhs) {
    return V(lhs.get() + rhs.get());
  }
  friend V operator+(V lhs, T rhs) {
    return V(lhs.get() + rhs);
  }
  friend V operator+(T lhs, V rhs) {
```

```
      return V(lhs + rhs.get());
  }
};
```

As you can see, the problem of returning the "final value type" that we struggled with while writing adapters does not exist here: the derived class that is passed into each policy is the value type itself.

Explicit or implicit conversion operators for conversions to the base type can be added just as easily:

```
// Example 26
template <typename T, typename V>
struct ExplicitConvertible {
  explicit operator T() {
    return static_cast<V*>(this)->get();
  }
  explicit operator const T() const {
    return static_cast<const V*>(this)->get();
  }
};
```

This approach, at first glance, seems to solve most of the drawbacks of the traditional policy-based types. The order of the policies does not matter - we can specify only the ones we want and not worry about the other ones - what's not to like? There are, however, two fundamental limitations. First of all, the policy-based class cannot refer to any policy by name. There is no longer a slot for `DeletionPolicy` or `AdditionPolicy`. There are no convention-enforced policy interfaces, such as the deletion policy having to be callable. The entire process of binding the policies into a single type is implicit; it's just a superposition of interfaces.

Therefore, we are limited in what we can do using these policies - we can inject public member functions and non-member functions - even add private data members - but we cannot provide an implementation for an aspect of behavior that's determined and limited by the primary policy-based class. As such, this is not an implementation of the Strategy pattern - we are composing the interface, and, perforce, the implementation, at will, not customizing a specific algorithm (which is why we deferred the demonstration of this alternative policy-based design pattern until this chapter).

The second, closely related, limitation is that there are no default policies. The missing policies are just that, missing. There is nothing in their place. The default behavior is always the absence of any behavior. In the traditional policy-based design, each policy slot has to be filled. If there is a reasonable default, it can be specified, and then that is the policy unless the user overrides it (for example, the default deletion policy uses `operator delete`). If there is no default, the compiler won't let us omit the policy - we have to give an argument to the template.

The consequences of these limitations reach farther than you may think at first glance. For example, it may be tempting to use the `enable_if` technique we saw in *Chapter 15, Policy-Based Design*, instead of injecting public member functions through the base class. Then, we could have a default behavior that is enabled if none of the other options are. But it won't work here. We can certainly create a policy that is targeted for use with `enable_if`:

```
template <typename T, typename V> struct Addable {
  constexpr bool adding_enabled = true;
};
```

But there is no way to use it - we can't use `AdditionPolicy::adding_enabled` because there is no `AdditionPolicy` - all policy slots are unnamed. The other option would be to use `Value::adding_enabled` - the addition policy is a base class of `Value`, and, therefore, all of its data members are visible in the `Value` class. The only problem is that it does not work - at the point where this expression is evaluated by the compiler (in the definition of the `Value` type as the template parameter for the CRTP policies), `Value` is an incomplete type and we cannot access its data members yet. We could evaluate `policy_name::adding_enabled` if we knew what the policy name was. But that knowledge is exactly what we gave up in trade for not having to specify the entire list of policies.

While not, strictly speaking, an application of the Strategy pattern, the alternative to the policy-based design that we have just learned about can be attractive when the policies are primarily used to control a set of supported operations. While discussing the guidelines for policy-based design, we have mentioned that it is rarely worth it to use a policy slot just to provide the additional safety of the restricted interface. For such situations, this alternative approach should be kept in mind.

Overall, we can see that both patterns have their advantages and drawbacks: adapters rely on a more complex form of CRTP while the "slot-less" policies we just saw require us to compromise the encapsulation (we have to expose the value to the policies using something like our `get()` methods).

Such is the nature of the problems we have to solve as software engineers - once a problem becomes complex enough, it can be solved, frequently using more than one design, and each approach has its own advantages and limitations. There is no way we can compare every two patterns that can be used to create two very different designs that address the same need, at least not in a book of any finite size. By presenting and analyzing these examples, we hope to equip the reader with the understanding and insight that will be helpful in evaluating similarly complex and varied design options for real-life problems.

Summary

We have studied two of the most commonly used patterns - not just in C++, but in software design in general. The Adapter pattern offers an approach to solving a wide class of design challenges. These challenges have only the most general property in common - given a class, a function, or a software component that provides certain functionality, we must solve a particular problem, and build a solution for a different, related problem. The decorator pattern is, in many ways, a subset of the Adapter pattern, which is restricted to augmenting the existing interface of the class of a function with new behavior.

We have seen that the interface conversion and modification done by the adapters and decorators can be applied to interfaces at every stage of the program's life - while the most common use is to modify runtime interfaces so that a class can be used in a different context, there are also compile-time adapters for generic code that allow us to use a class as a building block or a component of a larger, more complex, class.

The Adapter pattern can be applied to many very different design challenges. The varied nature of these challenges and the generality of the pattern itself often mean that an alternative solution is possible. Such alternatives often use a completely different approach - an entirely different design pattern - but end up providing similar behavior. The difference lies in trade-offs, additional conditions, and limitations imposed by the chosen approach to the design, and the possibilities of extending the solution in different ways. To this end, this chapter offers a comparison of two very different design approaches to the same problem, complete with an evaluation of the strengths and drawbacks of both options.

The next, penultimate, chapter introduces a pattern that is large, complex, and has several interacting components - an appropriate pattern to be left for our grand finale - the Visitor pattern.

Questions

1. What is the Adapter pattern?

2. What is the decorator pattern and how does it differ from the Adapter pattern?

3. The classic OOP implementation of the decorator pattern is usually not recommended in C++. Why not?

4. When should the C++ class decorator use inheritance or composition?

5. When should the C++ class adapter use inheritance or composition?

6. C++ provides a general function adapter for currying function arguments, `std::bind`. What are its limitations?

7. C++11 provides template aliases that can be used as adapters. What are their limitations?

8. Both the adapter and policy patterns can be used to add or modify the public interface of a class. Give some reasons for preferring one over the other.

17

The Visitor Pattern and Multiple Dispatch

The Visitor pattern is another classic object-oriented design pattern, one of the 23 patterns introduced in the book *Design Patterns – Elements of Reusable Object-Oriented Software*, by Erich Gamma, Richard Helm, Ralph Johnson, and John Vlissides. It was one of the more popular patterns during the golden age of object-oriented programming since it can be used to make large class hierarchies more maintainable. In recent years, the use of Visitor in C++ declined, as large complex hierarchies became less common, and the Visitor pattern is a fairly complex pattern to implement. Generic programming - in particular, the language features added in C++11 and C++14 - makes it easier to implement and maintain the Visitor classes, while the new applications of the old pattern have served to rekindle some of the fading interest in it.

The following topics will be covered in this chapter:

- The Visitor pattern
- Implementations of Visitor in C++
- The use of generic programming to simplify the Visitor classes
- The use of Visitor for composite objects
- Compile-time Visitor and reflection

Technical requirements

The example code for this chapter can be found at the following GitHub link: https://github.com/PacktPublishing/Hands-On-Design-Patterns-with-CPP-Second-Edition/tree/main/Chapter17.

The Visitor pattern

The Visitor pattern stands out from the other classic object-oriented patterns due to its complexity. On the one hand, the basic structure of the Visitor pattern is quite complex and involves many coordinated classes that must work together to form the pattern. On the other hand, even the description of the Visitor pattern is complex - there are several very different ways to describe the same pattern. Many patterns can be applied to multiple kinds of problems, but the Visitor pattern goes beyond that - there are several ways to describe what it does that use completely different languages, talk about seemingly unrelated problems, and overall have nothing in common. However, they all describe the same pattern. Let's start by examining the many faces of the Visitor pattern, and then move on to the implementation.

What is the Visitor pattern?

The Visitor pattern is a pattern that separates the algorithm from the object structure, which is the data for this algorithm. Using the Visitor pattern, we can add a new operation to the class hierarchy without modifying the classes themselves. The use of the Visitor pattern follows the **open/closed principle** of software design - a class (or another unit of code, such as a module) should be closed for modifications; once the class presents an interface to its clients, the clients come to depend on this interface and the functionality it provides. This interface should remain stable; it should not be necessary to modify the classes in order to maintain the software and continue its development. At the same time, a class should be open for extensions - new functionality can be added to satisfy new requirements. As with all very general principles, a counter-example can be found where the rigorous application of a rule is worse than breaking it. Again, as with all general principles, its value lies not in being an absolute rule for every case, but rather a *default* rule, a guideline that should be followed in the absence of a good reason not to; the reality is that the majority of everyday work is *not special* and the result is better if this principle is followed.

When viewed this way, the Visitor pattern allows us to add functionality to a class or an entire class hierarchy without having to modify the class. This feature can be particularly useful when dealing with public APIs - the users of the API can extend it with additional operations without having to modify the source code.

A very different, more technical way to describe the Visitor pattern is to say that it implements **double dispatch**. This requires some explanation. Let's start with the regular virtual function calls:

```
class Base {
  virtual void f() = 0;
};
class Derived1 : public Base {
  void f() override;
};
class Derived2 : public Base {
  void f() override;
};
```

If we invoke the b->f() virtual function through a pointer to the b base class, the call is dispatched to Derived1::f() or Derived2::f(), depending on the real type of the object. This is the **single dispatch** - the function that is actually called is determined by a single factor, the type of the object.

Now let's assume that the function f() also takes an argument that is a pointer to a base class:

```cpp
class Base {
  virtual void f(Base* p) = 0;
};
class Derived1 : public Base {
  void f(Base* p) override;
};
class Derived2 : public Base {
  void f(Base* p) override;
};
```

The actual type of the *p object is also one of the derived classes. Now, the b->f(p) call can have four different versions; both the *b and *p objects can be of either of the two derived types. It is reasonable to want the implementation to do something different in each of these cases. This would be double dispatch - the code that ultimately runs is determined by two separate factors. Virtual functions do not provide a way to implement double dispatch directly, but the Visitor pattern does exactly that.

When presented this way, it is not obvious that the **double-dispatch** Visitor pattern has anything to do with the **operation-adding** Visitor pattern. However, they are exactly the same pattern, and the two requirements are really one and the same. Here is a way to look at it that might help - if we want to add an operation to all classes in a hierarchy, that is equivalent to adding a virtual function, so we have one factor controlling the final disposition of each call, the object type. But, if we can effectively add virtual functions, we can add more than one - one for each operation we need to support. The type of operation is the second factor controlling the dispatch, similar to the argument to the function in our previous example. Thus, the operation-adding visitor is able to provide double dispatch. Alternatively, if we had a way to implement double dispatch, we could do what the Visitor pattern does - effectively add a virtual function for each operation we want to support.

Now that we know what the Visitor pattern does, it is reasonable to ask, *why* would we want to do it? *What* is the use of double dispatch? And why would we want *another way* to add a virtual function substitute to a class when we can just add a *genuine* virtual function? Setting aside the case of the public API with unavailable source code, why would we want to add an operation *externally* instead of implementing it in every class? Consider the example of the serialization/deserialization problem. Serialization is an operation that converts an object into a format that can be stored or transmitted (for example, written into a file). Deserialization is the inverse operation - it constructs a new object from its serialized and stored image. To support serialization and deserialization in a straightforward, object-oriented way, each class in the hierarchy would need two methods, one for each operation. But what if there is more than one way to store an object? For example, we may need to write an object into a memory buffer, to be transmitted across the network and deserialized on another machine.

Alternatively, we may need to save the object to disk, or else we may need to convert all objects in a container to a markup format such as JSON. The straightforward approach would have us add a serialization and a deserialization method to every object for every serialization mechanism. If a new and different serialization approach is needed, we have to go over the entire class hierarchy and add support for it.

An alternative is to implement the entire serialization/deserialization operation in a separate function that can handle all classes. The resulting code is a loop that iterates over all objects, with a large decision tree inside of it. The code must interrogate every object and determine its type, for example, using dynamic casts. When a new class is added to the hierarchy, all serialization and deserialization implementations must be updated to handle the new objects.

Both implementations are difficult to maintain for large hierarchies. The Visitor pattern offers a solution - it allows us to implement a new operation - in our case, the serialization - outside of the classes and without modifying them, but also without the downside of a huge decision tree in a loop (note that the Visitor pattern is not the only solution to the serialization problem; C++ offers other possible approaches as well, but we focus on the Visitor pattern in this chapter).

As we stated at the beginning, the Visitor pattern is a complex pattern with a complex description. We can best handle this difficult pattern by studying concrete examples, starting from the very simple ones in the next section.

Basic Visitor in C++

The only way to really understand how the Visitor pattern operates is to work through an example. Let's start with a very simple one. First, we need a class hierarchy:

```cpp
// Example 01
class Pet {
  public:
  virtual ~Pet() {}
  Pet(std::string_view color) : color_(color) {}
  const std::string& color() const { return color_; }
  private:
  const std::string color_;
};
class Cat : public Pet {
  public:
  Cat(std::string_view color) : Pet(color) {}
};
class Dog : public Pet {
  public:
  Dog(std::string_view color) : Pet(color) {}
};
```

In this hierarchy, we have the `Pet` base class and several derived classes for different pet animals. Now we want to add some operations to our classes, such as "feed the pet" or "play with the pet." The implementation depends on the type of pet, so these would have to be virtual functions if added directly to each class. This is not a problem for such a simple class hierarchy, but we are anticipating the future need for maintaining a much larger system in which modifying every class in the hierarchy is going to be expensive and time-consuming. We need a better way, and we begin by creating a new class, `PetVisitor`, which will be applied to every `Pet` object (visit it) and perform the operations we need. First, we need to declare the class:

```cpp
// Example 01
class Cat;
class Dog;
class PetVisitor {
  public:
  virtual void visit(Cat* c) = 0;
  virtual void visit(Dog* d) = 0;
};
```

We had to forward-declare the `Pet` hierarchy classes because `PetVisitor` has to be declared before the concrete `Pet` classes. Now we need to make the `Pet` hierarchy visitable, which means we do need to modify it, but only once, regardless of how many operations we want to add later. We need to add a virtual function to accept the Visitor pattern to every class that can be visited:

```cpp
// Example 01
class Pet {
  public:
  virtual void accept(PetVisitor& v) = 0;
  ...
};
class Cat : public Pet {
  public:
  void accept(PetVisitor& v) override { v.visit(this); }
  ...
};
class Dog : public Pet {
  public:
  void accept(PetVisitor& v) override { v.visit(this); }
  ...
};
```

Now our `Pet` hierarchy is visitable, and we have an abstract `PetVisitor` class. Everything is ready to implement new operations for our classes (note that nothing we have done so far depends on what operations we are going to add; we have created the visiting infrastructure that has to be implemented once). The operations are added by implementing concrete Visitor classes derived from `PetVisitor`:

```
// Example 01
class FeedingVisitor : public PetVisitor {
  public:
  void visit(Cat* c) override {
    std::cout << "Feed tuna to the " << c->color()
              << " cat" << std::endl;
  }
  void visit(Dog* d) override {
    std::cout << "Feed steak to the " << d->color()
              << " dog" << std::endl;
  }
};
class PlayingVisitor : public PetVisitor {
  public:
  void visit(Cat* c) override {
    std::cout << "Play with a feather with the "
              << c->color() << " cat" << std::endl;
  }
  void visit(Dog* d) override {
    std::cout << "Play fetch with the " << d->color()
              << " dog" << std::endl;
  }
};
```

Assuming the visitation infrastructure is already built into our class hierarchy, we can implement a new operation by implementing a derived Visitor class, and all its virtual functions overrides for `visit()`. To invoke one of the new operations on an object from our class hierarchy, we need to create a visitor and visit the object:

```
// Example 01
Cat c("orange");
FeedingVisitor fv;
c.accept(fv); // Feed tuna to the orange cat
```

The latest example of the call is too simple in one important way - at the point of calling the visitor, we know the exact type of the object we are visiting. To make the example more realistic, we have to visit an object polymorphically:

```
// Example 02
std::unique_ptr<Pet> p(new Cat("orange"));
...
FeedingVisitor fv;
p->accept(fv);
```

Here we do not know at compile time the actual type of the object pointed to by p; at the point where the visitor is accepted, p could have come from different sources. While less common, the visitor can also be used polymorphically:

```
// Example 03
std::unique_ptr<Pet> p(new Cat("orange"));
std::unique_ptr<PetVisitor> v(new FeedingVisitor);
...
p->accept(*v);
```

When written this way, the code highlights the double-dispatch aspect of the Visitor pattern - the call to accept() ends up dispatched to a particular visit() function based on two factors - the type of the visitable *p object and the type of the *v visitor. If we wish to stress this aspect of the Visitor pattern, we can invoke the visitors using a helper function:

```
// Example 03
void dispatch(Pet& p, PetVisitor& v) { p.accept(v); }
std::unique_ptr<Pet> p = ...;
std::unique_ptr<PetVisitor> v = ...;
dispatch(*p, *v); // Double dispatch
```

We now have the most bare-bones example of the classic object-oriented visitor in C++. Despite its simplicity, it has all the necessary components; an implementation for a large real-life class hierarchy and multiple visitor operations has a lot more code, but no new kinds of code, just more of the things we have already done. This example shows both aspects of the Visitor pattern; on the one hand, if we focus on the functionality of the software, with the visitation infrastructure now in place, we can add new operations without any changes to the classes themselves. On the other hand, if we look just at the way the operation is invoked, the accept() call, we have implemented double dispatch.

We can immediately see the appeal of the Visitor pattern, we can add any number of new operations without having to modify every class in the hierarchy. If a new class is added to the Pet hierarchy, it is impossible to forget to handle it - if we do nothing at all to the visitor, the accept() call on the new class will not compile since there is no corresponding visit() function to call. Once we add the new visit() overload to the PetVisitor base class, we have to add it to all derived classes as well; otherwise, the compiler will let us know that we have a pure virtual function without an override. The latter is also one of the main disadvantages of the Visitor pattern - if a new class is added to the hierarchy, all visitors must be updated, whether the new classes actually need to support these operations or not. For this reason, it is sometimes recommended to use the visitor only on *relatively stable* hierarchies that do not have new classes added often. There is also an alternative visitor implementation that somewhat mitigates this problem; we will see it later in this chapter.

The example in this section is very simple - our new operations take no arguments and return no results. We will now consider whether these limitations are significant, and how they can be removed.

Visitor generalizations and limitations

Our very first visitor, in the previous section, allowed us to effectively add a virtual function to every class in the hierarchy. That virtual function had no parameters and no return value. The former is easy to extend; there is no reason at all why our `visit()` functions cannot have parameters. Let's expand our class hierarchy by allowing our pets to have kittens and puppies. This extension cannot be done using only the Visitor pattern - we need to add not only new operations but also new data members. The Visitor pattern can be used for the former, but the latter requires code changes. A policy-based design could have let us factor out this change into a new implementation of an existing policy if we had the foresight to provide the appropriate policy. We do have a separate chapter on *Chapter 15, Policy-Based Design* in this book, so here we will avoid mixing several patterns together and just add the new data members:

```
// Example 04
class Pet {
  public:
    ..
    void add_child(Pet* p) { children_.push_back(p); }
    virtual void accept(PetVisitor& v, Pet* p = nullptr) = 0;
  private:
    std::vector<Pet*> children_;
};
```

Each parent `Pet` object tracks its child objects (note that the container is a vector of pointers, not a vector of unique pointers, so the object does not own its children, but merely has access to them). We have also added the new `add_child()` member function to add objects to the vector. We could have done this with a visitor, but this function is non-virtual, so we have to add it only once to the base class, not to every derived class - the visitor is unnecessary here. The `accept()` function has been modified to have an additional parameter that would have to be added to all derived classes as well, where it is simply forwarded to the `visit()` function:

```
// Example 04
class Cat : public Pet {
  public:
    Cat(std::string_view color) : Pet(color) {}
```

```
  void accept(PetVisitor& v, Pet* p = nullptr) override {
    v.visit(this, p);
  }
};
class Dog : public Pet {
  public:
  Dog(std::string_view color) : Pet(color) {}
  void accept(PetVisitor& v, Pet* p = nullptr) override {
    v.visit(this, p);
  }
};
```

The visit() function also has to be modified to accept the additional argument, even for the visitors that do not need it. Changing the parameters of the accept() function is, therefore, an expensive global operation that should not be done often, if at all. Note that all overrides for the same virtual function in the hierarchy already have to have the same parameters. The Visitor pattern extends this restriction to all operations added using the same base Visitor object. A common workaround for this problem is to pass parameters using aggregates (classes or structures that combine multiple parameters together). The visit() function is declared to accept a pointer to the base aggregate class, while each visitor receives a pointer to a derived class that may have additional fields, and uses them as needed.

Now, our additional argument is forwarded through the chain of virtual function calls to the visitor, where we can make use of it. Let's create a visitor that records the pet births and adds new pet objects as children to their parent objects:

```
// Example 04
class BirthVisitor : public PetVisitor {
  public:
  void visit(Cat* c, Pet* p) override {
    assert(dynamic_cast<Cat*>(p));
    c->add_child(p);
  }
  void visit(Dog* d, Pet* p) override {
    assert(dynamic_cast<Dog*>(p));
    d->add_child(p);
  }
};
```

Note that if we want to make sure that there are no biological impossibilities in our family tree, the verification has to be done at run time - at compile time, we do not know the actual types of the polymorphic objects. The new visitor is just as easy to use as the ones from the last section:

```
Pet* parent; // A cat
BirthVisitor bv;
```

```
Pet* child(new Cat("calico"));
parent->accept(bv, child);
```

Once we have established the parenthood relationships, we may want to examine our pet families. That is another operation we want to add, which calls for another Visitor:

```
// Example 04
class FamilyTreeVisitor : public PetVisitor {
  public:
  void visit(Cat* c, Pet*) override {
    std::cout << "Kittens: ";
    for (auto k : c->children_) {
      std::cout << k->color() << " ";
    }
    std::cout << std::endl;
  }
  void visit(Dog* d, Pet*) override {
    std::cout << "Puppies: ";
    for (auto p : d->children_) {
      std::cout << p->color() << " ";
    }
    std::cout << std::endl;
  }
};
```

We have hit a slight problem, though, because as written, the code will not compile. The reason is that the `FamilyTreeVisitor` class is trying to access the `Pet::children_` data member, which is private. This is another weakness of the Visitor pattern - from our point of view, the visitors add new operations to the classes, just like virtual functions, but from the compiler's point of view, they are completely separate classes, not at all like member functions of the `Pet` classes and have no special access. Application of the Visitor pattern usually requires that the encapsulation is relaxed in one of two ways - we can either allow public access to the data (directly or through accessor member functions) or declare the Visitor classes to be friends (which does require changes to the source code). In our example, we will follow the second route:

```
class Pet {
  ...
  friend class FamilyTreeVisitor;
};
```

Now the family tree visitor works as expected:

```
Pet* parent; // A cat
...
```

```
amilyTreeVisitor tv;
parent->accept(tv); // Prints kitten colors
```

Unlike BirthVisitor, FamilyTreeVisitor does not need the additional argument.

Now we have visitors that implement operations with parameters. What about the return values? Technically, there is no requirement for the visit() and accept() functions to return void. They can return anything else. However, the limitation that they have to all return the same type usually makes this capability useless. Virtual functions can have covariant return types, where the base class virtual function returns an object of some class and the derived class overrides return objects derived from that class, but even that is usually too limiting. There is another, much simpler solution - the visit() functions of every Visitor object have full access to the data members of that object. There is no reason why we cannot store the return value in the Visitor class itself and access it later. This fits well with the most common use where each visitor adds a different operation and is likely to have a unique return type, but the operation itself usually has the same return type for all classes in the hierarchy. For example, we can make our FamilyTreeVisitor count the total number of children and return the value through the Visitor object:

```cpp
// Example 05
class FamilyTreeVisitor : public PetVisitor {
  public:
  FamilyTreeVisitor() : child_count_(0) {}
  void reset() { child_count_ = 0; }
  size_t child_count() const { return child_count_; }
  void visit(Cat* c, Pet*) override {
    visit_impl(c, "Kittens: ");
  }
  void visit(Dog* d, Pet*) override {
    visit_impl(d, "Puppies: ");
  }
  private:
  template <typename T>
  void visit_impl(T* t, const char* s) {
    std::cout << s;
    for (auto p : t->children_) {
      std::cout << p->color() << " ";
        ++child_count_;
    }
      std::cout << std::endl;
  }
  size_t child_count_;
};
FamilyTreeVisitor tv;
parent->accept(tv);
```

```
std::cout << tv.child_count() << " kittens total"
          << std::endl;
```

This approach imposes some limitations in multithreaded programs - the visitor is now not thread-safe since multiple threads cannot use the same Visitor object to visit different pet objects. The most common solution is to use one Visitor object per thread, usually a local variable created on the stack of the function that calls the visitor. If this is not possible, more complex options are available to give the visitor a per-thread (thread-local) state, but the analysis of such options lies outside of the scope of this book. On the other hand, sometimes we want to accumulate results over multiple visitations, in which case the previous technique of storing the result in the Visitor object works perfectly. Also note that the same solution can be used to pass arguments into the Visitor operations, instead of adding them to the `visit()` functions; we can store the arguments inside the Visitor object itself, and then we don't need anything special to access them from the visitor. This technique works particularly well when the arguments don't change on every invocation of the visitor, but may vary from one Visitor object to another.

Let's return for a moment and examine the `FamilyTreeVisitor` implementation again. Note that it iterates over the child objects of the parent object and calls the same operation on each one, in turn. It does not, however, process the children of the child object - our family tree is only one-generation deep. The problem of visiting objects that contain other objects is very general and occurs rather often. Our motivational example from the very beginning of this chapter, the problem of serialization, demonstrates this need perfectly - every complex object is serialized by serializing its components, one by one, and they, in turn, are serialized the same way, until we get all the way down to the built-in types such as `int` and `double`, which we know how to read and write. The next section deals with visiting complex objects in a more comprehensive way than what we have done so far.

Visiting complex objects

In the last section, we saw how the Visitor pattern allows us to add new operations to the existing hierarchy. In one of the examples, we visited a complex object that contained pointers to other objects. The visitor iterated over these pointers, in a limited way. We are now going to consider the general problem of visiting objects that are composed of other objects, or objects that contain other objects and build up to the demonstration of a working serialization/deserialization solution at the end.

Visiting composite objects

The general idea of visiting complex objects is quite straightforward - when visiting the object itself, we generally do not know all the details of how to handle each component or contained object. But there is something else that does - the visitor for that object type is written specifically to handle that class and nothing else. This observation suggests that the correct way to handle the component objects is to simply visit each one, and thus delegate the problem to someone else (a generally powerful technique, in programming and otherwise).

Let's first demonstrate this idea on the example of a simple container class, such as the Shelter class, which can contain any number of pet objects representing the pets waiting for adoption:

```
// Example 06
class Shelter {
  public:
  void add(Pet* p) {
    pets_.emplace_back(p);
  }
  void accept(PetVisitor& v) {
    for (auto& p : pets_) {
      p->accept(v);
    }
  }
  private:
  std::vector<std::unique_ptr<Pet>> pets_;
};
```

This class is essentially an adapter to make a vector of pet objects visitable (we have discussed the Adapter pattern in detail in the eponymous chapter). Note that the objects of this class do own the pet objects they contain - when the Shelter object is destroyed, so are all the Pet objects in the vector. Any container of unique pointers is a container that owns its contained objects; this is how polymorphic objects should be stored in a container such as std::vector (For non-polymorphic objects we can store objects themselves, but that won't work in our case, objects derived from Pet are of different types.)

The code relevant to our current problem is, of course, Shelter::accept(), which determines how a Shelter object is visited. As you can see, we do not invoke the Visitor on the Shelter object itself. Instead, we delegate the visitation to each of the containing objects. Since our Visitors are already written to handle Pet objects, nothing more needs to be done. When Shelter is visited by, say, FeedingVisitor, every pet in the shelter gets fed, and we didn't have to write any special code to make it happen.

Visitation of composite objects is done in a similar manner - if an object is composed of several smaller objects, we have to visit each of these objects. Let's consider an object representing a family with two family pets, a dog and a cat (the humans who serve the pets are not included in the following code, but we assume they are there too):

```
// Example 07
class Family {
  public:
  Family(const char* cat_color, const char* dog_color) :
  cat_(cat_color), dog_(dog_color) {}
  void accept(PetVisitor& v) {
```

```
    cat_.accept(v);
    dog_.accept(v);
  }
  private: // Other family members not shown for brevity
  Cat cat_;
  Dog dog_;
};
```

Again, visiting the family with a visitor from the `PetVisitor` hierarchy is delegated so that each `Pet` object is visited, and the visitors already have everything they need to handle these objects (of course, a `Family` object could accept visitors of other types as well, we would have to write separate `accept()` methods for them).

Now, at last, we have all the pieces we need to tackle the problem of serialization and deserialization of arbitrary objects. The next subsection shows how this can be done using the Visitor pattern.

Serialization and deserialization with Visitor

The problem itself was described in detail in the previous section - for serialization, each object needs to be converted to a sequence of bits, and these bits need to be stored, copied, or sent. The first part of the action depends on the object (each object is converted differently) but the second part depends on the specific application of the serialization (saving to disk is different from sending across the network). The implementation depends on two factors, hence the need for double dispatch, which is exactly what the Visitor pattern provides. Furthermore, if we have a way to serialize some object and then deserialize it (reconstruct the object from the sequence of bits), we should use the same method when this object is included in another object.

To demonstrate serialization/deserialization of a class hierarchy using the Visitor pattern, we need a more complex hierarchy than the toy examples we have used so far. Let's consider this hierarchy of two-dimensional geometric objects:

```
// Example 08
class Geometry {
  public:
  virtual ~Geometry() {}
};
class Point : public Geometry {
  public:
  Point() = default;
  Point(double x, double y) : x_(x), y_(y) {}
  private:
  double x_ {};
  double y_ {};
};
```

```
class Circle : public Geometry {
  public:
  Circle() = default;
  Circle(Point c, double r) : c_(c), r_(r) {}
  private:
  Point c_;
  double r_ {};
};
class Line : public Geometry {
  public:
  Line() = default;
  Line(Point p1, Point p2) : p1_(p1), p2_(p2) {}
  private:
  Point p1_;
  Point p2_;
};
```

All objects are derived from the abstract Geometry base class, but the more complex object contains one or more of the simpler objects; for example, Line is defined by two Point objects. Note that, at the end of the day, all our objects are made of double numbers, and, therefore, will serialize into a sequence of numbers. The key is knowing which double represents which field of which object; we need this to restore the original objects correctly.

To serialize these objects using the Visitor pattern, we follow the same process we used in the last section. First, we need to declare the base Visitor class:

```
// Example 08
class Visitor {
public:
  virtual void visit(double& x) = 0;
  virtual void visit(Point& p) = 0;
  virtual void visit(Circle& c) = 0;
  virtual void visit(Line& l) = 0;
};
```

There is one additional detail here - we can also visit double values; each visitor would need to handle them appropriately (write them, read them, and so on). Visiting any geometry object will result, eventually, in visiting the numbers it is composed of.

Our base Geometry class and all the classes derived from it need to accept this visitor:

```
// Example 08
class Geometry {
  public:
```

```
    virtual ~Geometry() {}
    virtual void accept(Visitor& v) = 0;
};
```

There is, of course, no way to add an `accept()` member function to double, but we won't have to. The `accept()` member functions for the derived classes, each of which is composed of one or more numbers and other classes, visit every data member in order:

```
// Example 08
void Point::accept(Visitor& v) {
    v.visit(x_); // double
    v.visit(y_); // double
}
void Circle::accept(Visitor& v) {
    v.visit(c_); // Point
    v.visit(r_); // double
}
void Point::accept(Visitor& v) {
    v.visit(p1_); // Point
    v.visit(p2_); // Point
}
```

The concrete Visitor classes, all derived from the base `Visitor` class, are responsible for the specific mechanisms of serialization and deserialization. The order in which the objects are broken down into their parts, all the way down to the numbers, is controlled by each object, but the visitors determine what is done with these numbers. For example, we can serialize all objects into a string using the formatted I/O (similar to what we get if we print the numbers into `cout`):

```
// Example 08
class StringSerializeVisitor : public Visitor {
public:
    void visit(double& x) override { S << x << " "; }
    void visit(Point& p) override { p.accept(*this); }
    void visit(Circle& c) override { c.accept(*this); }
    void visit(Line& l) override { l.accept(*this); }
    std::string str() const { return S.str(); }
    private:
    std::stringstream S;
};
```

The string is accumulated in `stringstream` until all the necessary objects are serialized:

```
// Example 08
Line l(...);
Circle c(...);
```

```
StringSerializeVisitor serializer;
serializer.visit(l);
serializer.visit(c);
std::string s(serializer.str());
```

Now that we have the objects printed into the s string, we can restore them from this string, perhaps on a different machine (if we arranged for the string to be sent there). First, we need the deserializing Visitor:

```
// Example 08
class StringDeserializeVisitor : public Visitor {
  public:
  StringDeserializeVisitor(const std::string& s) {
    S.str(s);
  }
  void visit(double& x) override { S >> x; }
  void visit(Point& p) override { p.accept(*this); }
  void visit(Circle& c) override { c.accept(*this); }
  void visit(Line& l) override { l.accept(*this); }
  private:
  std::stringstream S;
};
```

This Visitor reads the numbers from the string and saves them in the variables given to it by the object that is visited. The key to successful deserialization is to read the numbers in the same order as they were saved - for example, if we started by writing X and Y coordinates of a point, we should construct a point from the first two numbers we read and use them as X and Y coordinates. If the first point we wrote was the endpoint of a line, we should use the point we constructed as the endpoint of the new line. The beauty of the Visitor pattern is that the functions that do the actual reading and writing don't need to do anything special to preserve this order - the order is determined by each object and is guaranteed to be the same for all visitors (the object makes no distinction between the specific visitors and doesn't even know what kind of visitor is it). All we need to do is to visit the objects in the same order they were serialized in:

```
// Example 08
Line l1;
Circle c1;
// s is the string from a serializer
StringDeserializeVisitor deserializer(s);
deserializer.visit(l1); // Restored Line l
deserializer.visit(c1); // Restored Circle c
```

So far, we have known which objects are serialized and in what order. Therefore, we can deserialize the same objects in the same order. A more general case is when we don't know what objects to expect during deserialization - the objects are stored in a visitable container, similar to `Shelter` in the earlier example, which has to ensure that the objects are serialized and deserialized in the same order. For example, consider this class, which stores a geometry represented as an intersection of two other geometries:

```
// Example 09
class Intersection : public Geometry {
  public:
  Intersection() = default;
  Intersection(Geometry* g1, Geometry* g2) :
    g1_(g1), g2_(g2) {}
  void accept(Visitor& v) override {
    g1_->accept(v);
    g2_->accept(v);
  }
  private:
  std::unique_ptr<Geometry> g1_;
  std::unique_ptr<Geometry> g2_;
};
```

Serialization of this object is straightforward - we serialize both geometries, in order, by delegating the details to these objects. We cannot call `v.visit()` directly because we do not know the types of the `*g1_` and `*g2_` geometries, but we can let these objects dispatch the call as appropriate. But deserialization, as written, will fail - the geometry pointers are `null`, there are no objects allocated yet, and we do not know what type of objects should be allocated. Somehow, we need to encode the types of objects in the serialized stream first, then construct them based on these encoded types. There is another pattern that offers the standard solution for this problem, and that is the Factory pattern (it is quite common to have to use more than one design pattern when building a complex system).

There are several ways in which this can be done, but they all boil down to converting types to numbers and serializing those numbers. In our case, we have to know the complete list of geometry types when we declare the base `Visitor` class, so that we can also define an enumeration for all these types at the same time:

```
// Example 09
class Geometry {
  public:
  enum type_tag {POINT = 100, CIRCLE, LINE, INTERSECTION};
  virtual type_tag tag() const = 0;
};
class Visitor {
  public:
```

```
  static Geometry* make_geometry(Geometry::type_tag tag);
  virtual void visit(Geometry::type_tag& tag) = 0;
  ...
};
```

It is not essential that enum `type_tag` be defined inside the `Geometry` class, or that the `make_geometry` factory constructor be a static member function of the `Visitor` class. They can be declared outside of any class as well, but the virtual `tag()` method that will return the correct tag for every derived geometry type needs to be declared exactly as shown. The `tag()` overrides must be defined in every derived `Geometry` class, for example, the `Point` class:

```
// Example 09
class Point : public Geometry {
  public:
  ...
  type_tag tag() const override { return POINT; }
};
```

Other derived classes have to be similarly modified.

Then we need to define the factory constructor:

```
// Example 09
Geometry* Visitor::make_geometry(Geometry::type_tag tag) {
  switch (tag) {
    case Geometry::POINT: return new Point;
    case Geometry::CIRCLE: return new Circle;
    case Geometry::LINE: return new Line;
    case Geometry::INTERSECTION: return new Intersection;
  }
}
```

This factory function constructs the right derived object depending on the specified type tag. All that is left is for the `Intersection` object to serialize and deserialize the tags of the two geometries that form the intersection:

```
// Example 09
class Intersection : public Geometry {
  public:
  void accept(Visitor& v) override {
    Geometry::type_tag tag;
    if (g1_) tag = g1_->tag();
    v.visit(tag);
    if (!g1_) g1_.reset(Visitor::make_geometry(tag));
```

```
    g1_->accept(v);
    if (g2_) tag = g2_->tag();
    v.visit(tag);
    if (!g2_) g2_.reset(Visitor::make_geometry(tag));
    g2_->accept(v);
  }
  ...
};
```

First, the tags are sent to the visitor. The serializing visitor should write the tags along with the rest of the data:

```
// Example 09
class StringSerializeVisitor : public Visitor {
  public:
  void visit(Geometry::type_tag& tag) override {
    S << size_t(tag) << " ";
  }
  ...
};
```

The deserializing visitor has to read the tag (actually, it reads a `size_t` number and converts it to the tag):

```
// Example 09
class StringDeserializeVisitor : public Visitor {
  public:
  void visit(Geometry::type_tag& tag) override {
    size_t t;
    S >> t;
    tag = Geometry::type_tag(t);
  }
  ...
};
```

Once the tag is restored by the deserializing visitor, the `Intersection` object can invoke the factory constructor to construct the right geometry object. Now we can deserialize this object from the stream, and our `Intersection` is restored as an exact copy of the one we serialized. Note that there are other ways to package visiting the tags and the calls to the factory constructor; the optimal solution depends on the roles of different objects in the system - for example, the deserializing visitor may construct the objects based on the tag instead of the composite object that owns these geometries. The sequence of events that need to take place, however, remains the same.

So far, we have been learning about the classic object-oriented Visitor pattern. Before we see what the C++-specific twists on the classic pattern are, we should learn about another type of visitor that addresses some of the inconveniences in the Visitor pattern.

Acyclic Visitor

The Visitor pattern, as we have seen it so far, does what we wanted it to do. It separates the implementation of the algorithm from the object that is the data for the algorithm, and it allows us to select the correct implementation based on two run-time factors - the specific object type and the concrete operation we want to perform, both of which are selected from their corresponding class hierarchies. There is, however, a fly in the ointment - we wanted to reduce complexity and simplified the code maintenance, and we did, but now we have to maintain two parallel class hierarchies, the visitable objects and the visitors, and the dependencies between the two are non-trivial. The worst part of these dependencies is that they form a cycle - the Visitor object depends on the types of the visitable objects (there is an overload of the `visit()` methods for every visitable type), and the base visitable type depends on the base visitor type. The first half of this dependency is the worst. Every time a new object is added to the hierarchy, every visitor must be updated. The second half does not take much work from the programmer as new visitors can be added at any time and without any other changes - this is the whole point of the Visitor pattern. But there is still the compile-time dependency of the base visitable class, and, perforce, all derived classes, on the base Visitor class. Were the Visitor class to change, every file that uses one of the visitable classes would need to be recompiled. The visitors are, for the most part, stable in their interface and implementation, except for one case - adding a new visitable class. Thus, the cycle in action looks like this - a new class is added to the hierarchy of the visitable objects. The Visitor classes need to be updated with the new type. Since the base Visitor class was changed, the base visitable class and every line of code that depends on it must be recompiled, including the code that does not use the new visitable class, only the old ones. Even using forward declarations whenever possible does not help - if a new visitable class is added, all the old ones must be recompiled.

The additional problem of the traditional Visitor pattern is that every possible combination of the object type and the visitor type must be handled. Often there are cases when some combinations do not make sense, and certain objects will never be visited by some types of visitors. But we cannot take advantage of this as every combination must have a defined action (the action could be very simple, but still, every Visitor class must have the full set of `visit()` member functions defined).

The Acyclic Visitor pattern is a variant of the Visitor pattern that is specifically designed to break the dependency cycle and allow partial visitation. The base visitable class for the Acyclic Visitor pattern is the same as for the regular Visitor pattern:

```
// Example 10
class Pet {
  public:
  virtual ~Pet() {}
```

```
virtual void accept(PetVisitor& v) = 0;
...
};
```

However, that is where the similarity ends. The base Visitor class does not have the `visit()` overloads for every visitable. In fact, it has no `visit()` member function at all:

```
// Example 10
class PetVisitor {
  public:
  virtual ~PetVisitor() {}
};
```

So, who does the visiting then? For every derived class in the original hierarchy, we also declare the corresponding Visitor class, and that is where the `visit()` function is:

```
// Example 10
class Cat;
class CatVisitor {
  public:
  virtual void visit(Cat* c) = 0;
};
class Cat : public Pet {
  public:
  Cat(std::string_view color) : Pet(color) {}
  void accept(PetVisitor& v) override {
    if (CatVisitor* cv = dynamic_cast<CatVisitor*>(&v)) {
      cv->visit(this);
    } else { // Handle error
      assert(false);
    }
  }
};
```

Note that each visitor can visit only the class it was designed for - the `CatVisitor` visits only `Cat` objects, the `DogVisitor` visits only `Dog` objects, and so on. The magic is in the new `accept()` function - when a class is asked to accept a visitor, it first uses `dynamic_cast` to check whether this is the right type of visitor. If it is, all is well, and the visitor is accepted. If it isn't, we have a problem and must handle the error (the exact mechanism of error handling depends on the application; for example, an exception can be thrown). The concrete Visitor classes, therefore, must be derived from both the common `PetVisitor` base class and the class-specific base class such as `CatVisitor`:

```
// Example 10
class FeedingVisitor : public PetVisitor,
```

```
                        public CatVisitor,
                        public DogVisitor {
  public:
  void visit(Cat* c) override {
    std::cout << "Feed tuna to the " << c->color()
            << " cat" << std::endl;
  }
  void visit(Dog* d) override {
    std::cout << "Feed steak to the " << d->color()
            << " dog" << std::endl;
  }
};
```

Each concrete visitor class is derived from the common visitor base and from every per-type visitor base (CatVisitor, DogVisitor, and so on) for every type that must be handled by this visitor. On the other hand, if this visitor is not designed to visit some of the classes in the hierarchy, we can simply omit the corresponding visitor base, and then we won't need to implement the virtual function override either:

```
// Example 10
class BathingVisitor : public PetVisitor,
                       public DogVisitor
                         { // But no CatVisitor
  public:
  void visit(Dog* d) override {
    std::cout << "Wash the " << d->color()
            << " dog" << std::endl;
  }
  // No visit(Cat*) here!
};
```

The invocation of the Acyclic Visitor pattern is done in exactly the same way as with the regular Visitor pattern:

```
// Example 10
std::unique_ptr<Pet> c(new Cat("orange"));
std::unique_ptr<Pet> d(new Dog("brown"));
FeedingVisitor fv;
c->accept(fv);
d->accept(fv);
BathingVisitor bv;
//c->accept(bv); // Error
d->accept(bv);
```

If we try to visit an object that is not supported by the particular Visitor, the error is detected. Therefore, we have solved the problem of partial visitation. What about the dependency cycle? That is taken care of as well - the common `PetVisitor` base class does not need to list the complete hierarchy of visitable objects, and the concrete visitable classes depend only on their per-class visitors, but not on any visitors for other types. Therefore, when another visitable object is added to the hierarchy, the existing ones do not need to be recompiled.

The Acyclic Visitor pattern looks so good that one has to wonder, *why not use it all the time instead of the regular Visitor pattern?* There are a few reasons. First of all, the Acyclic Visitor pattern uses `dynamic_cast` to cast from one base class to another (sometimes called cross-cast). This operation is typically more expensive than the virtual function call, so the Acyclic Visitor pattern is slower than the alternative. Also, the Acyclic Visitor pattern requires a Visitor class for every visitable class, so twice as many classes, and it uses multiple inheritance with a lot of base classes. That second issue is not much of a problem for most modern compilers, but many programmers find it difficult to deal with multiple inheritance. Whether the first issue - the runtime cost of the dynamic cast - is a problem depends on the application, but it is something you need to be aware of. On the other hand, the Acyclic Visitor pattern really shines when the visitable object hierarchy changes frequently or when the cost of recompiling the entire code base is significant.

You may have noticed one more issue with the Acyclic Visitor pattern - it has a lot of boilerplate code. Several lines of code have to be copied for every visitable class. In fact, the regular Visitor pattern suffers from the same problem in that implementing either kind of visitor involves a lot of repetitive typing. But C++ has a special set of tools to replace code repetition with code reuse: that is exactly what generic programming is for. We shall see next how the Visitor pattern is adapted to modern C++.

Visitors in modern C++

As we have just seen, the Visitor pattern promotes the separation of concerns; for example, the order of serialization and the mechanism of serialization are made independent, and a separate class is responsible for each. The pattern also simplifies code maintenance by collecting all code that performs a given task in one place. What the Visitor pattern does not promote is code reuse with no duplication. But that's the object-oriented Visitor pattern, before modern C++. Let's see what we can do with the generic capabilities of C++, starting from the regular Visitor pattern.

Generic Visitor

We are going to try to reduce the boilerplate code in the implementation of the Visitor pattern. Let's start with the `accept()` member function, which must be copied into every visitable class; it always looks the same:

```
class Cat : public Pet {
  void accept(PetVisitor& v) override { v.visit(this); }
};
```

This function cannot be moved to the base class because we need to call the visitor with the actual type, not the base type - `visit()` accepts `Cat*`, `Dog*`, and so on, but not `Pet*`. We can get a template to generate this function for us if we introduce an intermediate templated base class:

```cpp
// Example 11
class Pet { // Same as before
  public:
  virtual ~Pet() {}
  Pet(std::string_view color) : color_(color) {}
  const std::string& color() const { return color_; }
  virtual void accept(PetVisitor& v) = 0;
  private:
  std::string color_;
};
template <typename Derived>
class Visitable : public Pet {
  public:
  using Pet::Pet;
  void accept(PetVisitor& v) override {
    v.visit(static_cast<Derived*>(this));
  }
};
```

The template is parameterized by the derived class. In this regard, it is similar to the **Curiously Recurring Template Pattern (CRTP)**, but here we do not inherit from the template parameter - we use it to cast the `this` pointer to the correct derived class pointer. Now we just need to derive each pet class from the right instantiation of the template, and we get the `accept()` function automatically:

```cpp
// Example 11
class Cat : public Visitable<Cat> {
  using Visitable<Cat>::Visitable;
};
class Dog : public Visitable<Dog> {
  using Visitable<Dog>::Visitable;
};
```

That takes care of half of the boilerplate code - the code inside the derived visitable objects. Now there is only the other half left: the code inside the Visitor classes, where we have to type the same declaration over and over again for every visitable class. We can't do much about the specific visitors; after all, that's where the real work is done, and, presumably, we need to do different things for different visitable classes (otherwise why use double dispatch at all?)

However, we can simplify the declaration of the base Visitor class if we introduce this generic Visitor template:

```
// Example 12
template <typename ... Types> class Visitor;
template <typename T> class Visitor<T> {
  public:
  virtual void visit(T* t) = 0;
};
template <typename T, typename ... Types>
class Visitor<T, Types ...> : public Visitor<Types ...> {
  public:
  using Visitor<Types ...>::visit;
  virtual void visit(T* t) = 0;
};
```

Note that we have to implement this template only once: not once for each class hierarchy, but once forever (or at least until we need to change the signature of the visit() function, for example, to add arguments). This is a good generic library class. Once we have it, declaring a visitor base for a particular class hierarchy becomes so trivial that it feels anticlimactic:

```
// Example 12
```

Notice the somewhat unusual syntax with the class keyword - it combines the template argument list with a forward declaration and is equivalent to the following:

```
class Cat;
class Dog;
using PetVisitor = Visitor<Cat, Dog>;
```

How does the Generic Visitor base work? It uses the variadic template to capture an arbitrary number of type arguments, but the primary template is only declared, not defined. The rest are specializations. First, we have the special case of one type argument. We declare the pure visit() virtual member function for that type. Then we have a specialization for more than one type argument, where the first argument is explicit, and the rest are in the parameter pack. We generate the visit() function for the explicitly specified type and inherit the rest of them from an instantiation of the same variadic template but with one less argument. The instantiation is recursive until we are down to only one type argument, and then the first specialization is used.

This generic and reusable code has one restriction: it does not handle deep hierarchies. Recall that each visitable class is derived from a common base:

```
template <typename Derived>
class Visitable : public Pet {...};
class Cat : public Visitable<Cat> {...};
```

If we were to derive another class from `Cat`, it would have to be derived from `Visitable` as well:

```
class SiameseCat : public Cat,
                   public Visitable<SiameseCat> {...};
```

We cannot just derive `SiameseCat` from `Cat` because it is the Visitable template that provides the `accept()` method for each derived class. But we can't use the double inheritance as we just tried either, because now, the `SiameseCat` class inherits from Pet twice: once through the `Cat` base and once through the `Visitable` base. The only solution to this, if you still want to use the templates to generate `accept()` methods, is to separate the hierarchy so each visitable class such as `Cat` inherits from `Visitable` and from a corresponding base class `CatBase` that has all the "cat-specific" functionality except for the visitation support. This doubles the number of classes in the hierarchy and is a major drawback.

Now that we have the boilerplate visitor code generated by templates, we can also make it simpler to define concrete visitors.

Lambda Visitor

Most of the work in defining a concrete visitor is writing code for the actual work that has to happen for every visitable object. There is not a lot of boilerplate code in a specific visitor class. But sometimes we may not want to declare the class itself. Think about lambda expressions - anything that can be done with a lambda expression can also be done with an explicitly declared callable class because lambdas are (anonymous) callable classes. Nonetheless, we find lambda expressions very useful for writing one-off callable objects. Similarly, we may want to write a visitor without explicitly naming it - a lambda Visitor. We would want it to look something like this:

```
auto v(lambda_visitor<PetVisitor>(
  [] (Cat* c) { std::cout << "Let the " << c->color()
                          << " cat out" << std::endl;
  },
  [] (Dog* d) { std::cout << "Take the " << d->color()
                          << " dog for a walk" << std::endl;
  }
));
pet->accept(v);
```

There are two problems to be solved - how to create a class that handles a list of types and corresponding objects (in our case, the visitable types and the corresponding lambdas), and how to generate a set of overloaded functions using lambda expressions.

The former problem will require us to recursively instantiate a template on the parameter pack, peeling off one argument at a time. The solution to the latter problem is similar to the overload set of the lambda expression, which was described in the chapter on class templates. We could use the overload set from that chapter, but we can use the recursive template instantiation that we need anyway, to build the overloaded set of functions directly.

There is going to be one new challenge in this implementation - we have to process not one but two lists of types. The first list has all visitable types in it; in our case, `Cat` and `Dog`. The second list has the types of lambda expressions, one for each visitable type. We have not seen a variadic template with two parameter packs yet, and for a good reason - it is not possible to simply declare `template<typename... A, typename... B>` as the compiler would not know where the first list ends and the second begins. The trick is to hide one or both lists of types inside other templates. In our case, we already have the `Visitor` template that is instantiated on the list of visitable types:

```
using PetVisitor = Visitor<class Cat, class Dog>;
```

We can extract this list from the `Visitor` template and match each type with its lambda expression. The partial specialization syntax used to process two parameter packs in sync is tricky, so we will work through it in steps. First of all, we need to declare the general template for our `LambdaVisitor` class:

```
// Example 13
template <typename Base, typename...>
class LambdaVisitor;
```

Note that there is only one general parameter pack here, plus the base class for the visitor (in our case, it will be `PetVisitor`). This template must be declared, but it is never going to be used - we will provide a specialization for every case that needs to be handled. The first specialization is used when there is only one visitable type and one corresponding lambda expression:

```
// Example 13
template <typename Base, typename T1, typename F1>
class LambdaVisitor<Base, Visitor<T1>, F1> :
  private F1, public Base
{
  public:
  LambdaVisitor(F1&& f1) : F1(std::move(f1)) {}
  LambdaVisitor(const F1& f1) : F1(f1) {}
  using Base::visit;
  void visit(T1* t) override { return F1::operator()(t); }
};
```

This specialization, in addition to handling the case where we have only one visitable type, is used as the last instantiation in every chain of recursive template instantiations. Since it is always the first base class in the recursive hierarchy of `LambdaVisitor` instantiations, it is the only one that directly inherits from the base Visitor class such as `PetVisitor`. Note that, even with a single `T1` visitable type, we use the `Visitor` template as a wrapper for it. This is done in preparation for the general case where we will have a list of types whose length is unknown. The two constructors store the `f1` lambda expression inside the `LambdaVisitor` class, using move instead of copy if possible. Finally, the visit (T1*) virtual function override simply forwards the call to the lambda expression. It may appear simpler, at first glance, to inherit publicly from F1 and just agree to use the functional calling syntax (in other words, to rename all calls to visit() to calls to operator() everywhere). This is not going to work; we need the indirection because the operator() instance of the lambda expression itself cannot be a virtual function override. By the way, the override keyword here is invaluable in detecting bugs in code where the template is not inherited from the right base class or the virtual function declarations do not match exactly.

The general case of any number of visitable types and lambda expressions is handled by this partial specialization, which explicitly deals with the first types in both lists, then recursively instantiates itself to process the rest of the lists:

```
// Example 13
template <typename Base,
          typename T1, typename... T,
          typename F1, typename... F>
class LambdaVisitor<Base, Visitor<T1, T...>, F1, F...> :
  private F1,
  public LambdaVisitor<Base, Visitor<T ...>, F ...>
{
  public:
  LambdaVisitor(F1&& f1, F&& ... f) :
    F1(std::move(f1)),
    LambdaVisitor<Base, Visitor<T...>, F...>(
      std::forward<F>(f)...)
  {}
  LambdaVisitor(const F1& f1, F&& ... f) :
    F1(f1),
    LambdaVisitor<Base, Visitor<T...>, F...>(
      std::forward<F>(f) ...)
  {}
  using LambdaVisitor<Base, Visitor<T ...>, F ...>::visit;
  void visit(T1* t) override { return F1::operator()(t); }
};
```

Again, we have two constructors that store the first lambda expression in the class and forward the rest to the next instantiation. One virtual function override is generated on each step of the recursion, always for the first type in the remaining list of the visitable classes. That type is then removed from the list, and the processing continues in the same manner until we reach the last instantiation, the one for a single visitable type.

Since it is not possible to explicitly name the types of lambda expressions, we also cannot explicitly declare the type of the lambda visitor. Instead, the lambda expression types must be deduced by the template argument deduction, so we need a `lambda_visitor()` template function that accepts multiple lambda expression arguments and constructs the `LambdaVisitor` object from all of them:

```
// Example 13
template <typename Base, typename ... F>
auto lambda_visitor(F&& ... f) {
  return LambdaVisitor<Base, Base, F...>(
    std::forward<F>(f) ...);
}
```

In C++17, the same can be accomplished with a deduction guide. Now that we have a class that stores any number of lambda expressions and binds each one to the corresponding `visit()` override, we can write lambda visitors just as easily as we write lambda expressions:

```
// Example 13
void walk(Pet& p) {
  auto v(lambda_visitor<PetVisitor>(
  [](Cat* c){std::cout << "Let the " << c->color()
                       << " cat out" << std::endl;},
  [](Dog* d){std::cout << "Take the " << d->color()
                       << " dog for a walk" << std::endl;}
  ));
  p.accept(v);
}
```

Note that, because of the way we declare the `visit()` function in the same class that inherits from the corresponding lambda expression, the order of the lambda expression in the argument list of the `lambda_visitor()` function must match the order of classes in the list of types in `PetVisitor` definition. This restriction can be removed, if desired, at the cost of some additional complexity of the implementation.

Another common way of dealing with type lists in C++ is to store them in a `std::tuple`: for example, we can use `std::tuple<Cat, Dog>` to represent a list consisting of the two types. Similarly, an entire parameter pack can be stored in a tuple:

```
// Example 14
template <typename Base, typename F1, typename... F>
class LambdaVisitor<Base, std::tuple<F1, F...>> :
  public F1, public LambdaVisitor<Base, std::tuple<F...>>;
```

You can compare examples 13 and 14 to see how to use `std::tuple` to store a type list.

We have now seen how the common fragments of the visitor code can be turned into reusable templates, and how this, in turn, lets us create a lambda visitor. But we have not forgotten the other visitor implementation we learned in this chapter, the Acyclic Visitor pattern. Let's see how it, too, can benefit from the modern C++ language features.

Generic Acyclic Visitor

The Acyclic Visitor pattern does not need a base class with a list of all visitable types. However, it has its own share of boilerplate code. First of all, each visitable type needs the `accept()` member function, and it has more code than the similar function in the original Visitor pattern:

```cpp
// Example 10
class Cat : public Pet {
  public:
  void accept(PetVisitor& v) override {
    if (CatVisitor* cv = dynamic_cast<CatVisitor*>(&v)) {
      cv->visit(this);
    } else { // Handle error
      assert(false);
    }
  }
};
```

Assuming that the error handling is uniform, this function is repeated over and over for different types of visitors, each corresponding to its visitable type (such as `CatVisitor` here). Then there is the per-type Visitor class itself, for example:

```cpp
class CatVisitor {
  public:
  virtual void visit(Cat* c) = 0;
};
```

Again, this code is pasted all over the program, with slight modifications. Let's convert this error-prone code duplication into easy-to-maintain reusable code.

We will need to create some infrastructure first. The Acyclic Visitor pattern bases its hierarchy on a common base class for all visitors, such as the following:

```cpp
class PetVisitor {
  public:
  virtual ~PetVisitor() {}
};
```

Note that there is nothing specific to the `Pet` hierarchy here. With a better name, this class can serve as a base class for any visitor hierarchy:

```
// Example 15
class VisitorBase {
  public:
  virtual ~VisitorBase() {}
};
```

We also need a template to generate all these Visitor base classes specific to visitable types, to replace the near-identical `CatVisitor`, `DogVisitor`, and so on. Since all that is needed from these classes is the declaration of the pure virtual `visit()` method, we can parameterize the template by the visitable type:

```
// Example 15
template <typename Visitable> class Visitor {
  public:
  virtual void visit(Visitable* p) = 0;
};
```

The base visitable class for any class hierarchy now accepts visitors using the common `VisitorBase` base class:

```
// Example 15
class Pet {
  ...
  virtual void accept(VisitorBase& v) = 0;
};
```

Instead of deriving each visitable class directly from `Pet` and pasting a copy of the `accept()` method, we introduce an intermediate template base class that can generate this method with the correct types:

```
// Example 15
template <typename Visitable>
class PetVisitable : public Pet {
  public:
  using Pet::Pet;
  void accept(VisitorBase& v) override {
    if (Visitor<Visitable>* pv =
        dynamic_cast<Visitor<Visitable>*>(&v)) {
      pv->visit(static_cast<Visitable*>(this));
    } else { // Handle error
      assert(false);
    }
```

```
  }
};
```

This is the only copy of the `accept()` function we need to write, and it contains the preferred error handling implementation for our application to deal with cases when the visitor is not accepted by the base class (recall that Acyclic Visitor allows partial visitation, where some combinations of the visitor and visitable are not supported). Just like for the regular Visitor, the intermediate CRTP base class makes it hard to use deep hierarchies with this approach.

The concrete visitable classes inherit from the common `Pet` base class indirectly, through the intermediate `PetVisitable` base class, which also provides them with the visitable interface. The argument to the `PetVisitable` template is the derived class itself (again, we see the CRTP in action):

```
// Example 15
class Cat : public PetVisitable<Cat> {
  using PetVisitable<Cat>::PetVisitable;
};
class Dog : public PetVisitable<Dog> {
  using PetVisitable<Dog>::PetVisitable;
};
```

It is, of course, not mandatory to use the same base class constructors for all derived classes, as custom constructors can be defined in every class as needed.

The only thing left is to implement the Visitor class. Recall that the specific visitor in the Acyclic Visitor pattern inherits from the common visitor base and each of the visitor classes that represent the supported visitable types. That is not going to change, but we now have a way to generate these visitor classes on demand:

```
// Example 15
class FeedingVisitor : public VisitorBase,
                       public Visitor<Cat>,
                       public Visitor<Dog>
{
  public:
  void visit(Cat* c) override {
    std::cout << "Feed tuna to the " << c->color()
              << " cat" << std::endl;
  }
  void visit(Dog* d) override {
    std::cout << "Feed steak to the " << d->color()
              << " dog" << std::endl;
  }
};
```

Let's look back at the work we have done - the parallel hierarchy of visitor classes no longer needs to be typed explicitly; instead, they are generated as needed. The repetitive `accept()` functions are reduced to the single `PetVisitable` class template. Still, we have to write this template for every new visitable class hierarchy. We can generalize this too, and create a single reusable template for all hierarchies, parameterized by the base visitable class:

```cpp
// Example 16
template <typename Base, typename Visitable>
class VisitableBase : public Base {
  public:
  using Base::Base;
  void accept(VisitorBase& vb) override {
    if (Visitor<Visitable>* v =
        dynamic_cast<Visitor<Visitable>*>(&vb)) {
      v->visit(static_cast<Visitable*>(this));
    } else { // Handle error
      assert(false);
    }
  }
};
```

Now, for every visitable class hierarchy, we just need to create a template alias:

```cpp
// Example 16
template <typename Visitable>
using PetVisitable = VisitableBase<Pet, Visitable>;
```

We can make one more simplification and allow the programmer to specify the list of visitable classes as a list of types, instead of inheriting from `Visitor<Cat>`, `Visitor<Dog>`, and so on, as we have done previously. This requires a variadic template to store the list of types. The implementation is similar to the `LambdaVisitor` instance we saw earlier:

```cpp
// Example 17
template <typename ... V> struct Visitors;

template <typename V1>
struct Visitors<V1> : public Visitor<V1> {};

template <typename V1, typename ... V>
struct Visitors<V1, V ...> : public Visitor<V1>,
                             public Visitors<V ...> {};
```

We can use this wrapper template to shorten the declarations of the specific visitors:

```
// Example 17
class FeedingVisitor :
  public VisitorBase, public Visitors<Cat, Dog>
{
  ...
};
```

If desired, we can even hide `VisitorBase` in the definition of the `Visitors` template for the single type argument.

We have now seen both the classic object-oriented Visitor pattern and its reusable implementations, made possible by the generic programming tools of C++. In the earlier chapters, we have seen how some patterns can be applied entirely at compile time. Let's now consider whether the same can be done with the Visitor pattern.

Compile-time Visitor

In this section, we will analyze the possibility of using the Visitor pattern at compile time, in a similar fashion to, say, the application of the Strategy pattern that leads to policy-based design.

First of all, the multiple dispatch aspect of the Visitor pattern becomes trivial when used in the template context:

```
template <typename T1, typename T2> auto f(T1 t1, T2 t2);
```

A template function can easily run a different algorithm for any combination of the T1 and T2 types. Unlike the run-time polymorphism implemented with virtual functions, dispatching the call differently based on two or more types comes at no extra cost (other than writing code for all the combinations we need to handle, of course). Based on this observation, we can easily mimic the classic Visitor pattern at compile time:

```
// Example 18
class Pet {
  std::string color_;
  public:
  Pet(std::string_view color) : color_(color) {}
  const std::string& color() const { return color_; }
  template <typename Visitable, typename Visitor>
  static void accept(Visitable& p, Visitor& v) {
    v.visit(p);
  }
};
```

The accept () function is now a template and a static member function - the actual type of the first argument, the visitable object derived from the Pet class, will be deduced at compile time. The concrete visitable classes are derived from the base class in the usual way:

```
// Example 18
class Cat : public Pet {
  public:
  using Pet::Pet;
};
class Dog : public Pet {
  public:
  using Pet::Pet;
};
```

The visitors do not need to be derived from a common base since we now resolve the types at compile time:

```
// Example 18
class FeedingVisitor {
  public:
  void visit(Cat& c) {
    std::cout << "Feed tuna to the " << c.color()
              << " cat" << std::endl;
  }
  void visit(Dog& d) {
    std::cout << "Feed steak to the " << d.color()
              << " dog" << std::endl;
  }
};
```

The visitable classes can accept any visitor that has the correct interface, that is, visit () overloads for all classes in the hierarchy:

```
// Example 18
Cat c("orange");
Dog d("brown");
FeedingVisitor fv;
Pet::accept(c, fv);
Pet::accept(d, fv);
```

Of course, any function that accepts the visitor arguments and needs to support multiple visitors would have to be made a template as well (it is no longer sufficient to have a common base class, which only helps to determine the actual object type at run time).

The compile-time visitor solves the same problem as the classic visitor, it allows us to effectively add new member functions to a class without editing the class definition. It does, however, look much less exciting than the run-time version.

More interesting possibilities arise when we combine the Visitor pattern with the Composition pattern. We have done this once already when we discussed the visitation of complex objects, especially in the context of the serialization problem. The reason this is particularly interesting is that it relates to the connection with one of the few *big-ticket* features missing in C++; namely, the reflection. Reflection in programming is the ability of a program to examine and introspect its own source and then generate new behavior based on this introspection. Some programming languages, such as Delphi or Python, have native reflection capability, but C++ does not. Reflection is useful for solving many problems: for example, the serialization problem could be easily solved if we could make the compiler iterate over all data members of the object and serialize each one, recursively, until we reach the built-in types. We can implement something similar using a compile-time Visitor pattern.

Again, we will consider the hierarchy of geometric objects. Since everything is now happening at compile time, we are not interested in the polymorphic nature of the classes (they could still use virtual functions if needed for runtime operations; we just won't be writing them or looking at them in this section). For example, here is the Point class:

```
// Example 19
class Point {
  public:
  Point() = default;
  Point(double x, double y) : x_(x), y_(y) {}
  template <typename This, typename Visitor>
  static void accept(This& t, Visitor& v) {
    v.visit(t.x_);
    v.visit(t.y_);
  }
  private:
  double x_ {};
  double y_ {};
};
```

The visitation is provided via the accept() function, as before, but it is class-specific now. The only reason we have the first template parameter, This, is to support both const and non-const operations easily: This can be Point or const Point. Any visitor to this class is sent to visit the two values that define the point, x_ and y_. The visitor must have the appropriate interface, specifically, the visit() member function that accepts double arguments. Like most C++ template libraries, including the **Standard Template Library (STL)**, this code is held together by conventions - there are no virtual functions to override or base classes to derive from, only the requirements on the interface of each class involved in the system. The more complex classes are composed of the simpler ones; for example, here is the Line class:

```
// Example 19
class Line {
  public:
  Line() = default;
  Line(Point p1, Point p2) : p1_(p1), p2_(p2) {}
  template <typename This, typename Visitor>
  static void accept(This& t, Visitor& v) {
    v.visit(t.p1_);
    v.visit(t.p2_);
  }
  private:
  Point p1_;
  Point p2_;
};
```

The Line class is composed of two points. At compile time, the visitor is directed to visit each point. That is the end of the involvement of the Line class; the Point class gets to determine how it is visited (as we have just seen, it also delegates the work to another visitor). Since we are not using runtime polymorphism anymore, the container classes that can hold geometries of different types now have to be templates:

```
// Example 19
template <typename G1, typename G2>
class Intersection {
  public:
  Intersection() = default;
  Intersection(G1 g1, G2 g2) : g1_(g1), g2_(g2) {}
  template <typename This, typename Visitor>
  static void accept(This& t, Visitor& v) {
    v.visit(t.g1_);
    v.visit(t.g2_);
  }
  private:
  G1 g1_;
  G2 g2_;
};
```

We now have visitable types. We can use different kinds of visitors with this interface, not just serialization visitors. However, we are focused on serialization now. Previously, we have seen a visitor that converts objects into ASCII strings. Now let's serialize our objects as binary data, continuous streams of bits. The serialization visitor has access to a buffer of a certain size and writes the objects into that buffer, one `double` at a time:

```cpp
// Example 19
class BinarySerializeVisitor {
  public:
  BinarySerializeVisitor(char* buffer, size_t size) :
    buf_(buffer), size_(size) {}
  void visit(double x) {
    if (size_ < sizeof(x))
      throw std::runtime_error("Buffer overflow");
    memcpy(buf_, &x, sizeof(x));
    buf_ += sizeof(x);
    size_ -= sizeof(x);
  }
  template <typename T> void visit(const T& t) {
    T::accept(t, *this);
  }
  private:
  char* buf_;
  size_t size_;
};
```

The deserialization visitor reads memory from the buffer and copies it into the data members of the objects it restores:

```cpp
// Example 19
class BinaryDeserializeVisitor {
  public:
  BinaryDeserializeVisitor(const char* buffer, size_t size)
    : buf_(buffer), size_(size) {}
  void visit(double& x) {
    if (size_ < sizeof(x))
      throw std::runtime_error("Buffer overflow");
    memcpy(&x, buf_, sizeof(x));
    buf_ += sizeof(x);
    size_ -= sizeof(x);
  }
  template <typename T> void visit(T& t) {
    T::accept(t, *this);
  }
  private:
  const char* buf_;
```

```
    size_t size_;
};
```

Both visitors process built-in types directly by copying them to and from the buffer while letting the more complex types decide how the objects should be processed. In both cases, the visitors throw an exception if the size of the buffer is exceeded. Now we can use our visitors to, for example, send objects through a socket to another machine:

```
// Example 19
// On the sender machine:
Line l = ...;
Circle c = ...;
Intersection<Circle, Circle> x = ...;
char buffer[1024];
BinarySerializeVisitor serializer(buffer, sizeof(buffer));
serializer.visit(l);
serializer.visit(c);
serializer.visit(x);
... send the buffer to the receiver ...

// On the receiver machine:
Line l;
Circle c;
Intersection<Circle, Circle> x;
BinaryDeserializeVisitor deserializer(buffer,
   sizeof(buffer));
deserializer.visit(l);
deserializer.visit(c);
deserializer.visit(x);
```

While we cannot implement universal reflection without language support, we can have classes reflect on their content in limited ways, such as this composite visitation pattern. There are also a few variations on the theme that we can consider.

First of all, it is conventional to make the objects that have only one *important* member function callable; in other words, instead of calling the member function, we invoke the object itself using the function call syntax. This convention dictates that the visit() member function should be called operator() instead:

```
// Example 20
class BinarySerializeVisitor {
  public:
    void operator()(double x);
```

```
    template <typename T> void operator()(const T& t);
    ...
};
```

The visitable classes now call the visitors like functions:

```
// Example 20
class Point {
  public:
  static void accept(This& t, Visitor& v) {
    v(t.x_);
    v(t.y_);
  }
  ...
};
```

It may also be convenient to implement wrapper functions to invoke visitors on more than one object:

```
// Example 20
SomeVisitor v;
Object1 x; Object2 y; ...
visitation(v, x, y, z);
```

This is easy to implement using a variadic template:

```
// Example 20
template <typename V, typename T>
void visitation(V& v, T& t) {
  v(t);
}
template <typename V, typename T, typename... U>
void visitation(V& v, T& t, U&... u) {
  v(t);
  visitation(v, u ...);
}
```

In C++17, we have fold expressions and do not need a recursive template:

```
// Example 20
template <typename V, typename T, typename... U>
void visitation(V& v, U&... u) {
  (v(u), ...);
}
```

In C++14 we can mimic fold expressions using a hack based on `std::initializer_list`:

```
template <typename V, typename T, typename... U>
void visitation(V& v, U&... u) {
  using fold = int[];
  (void)fold { 0, (v(u), 0)... };
}
```

This works, but it is not going to win any prizes for clarity or maintainability.

The compile-time visitors are, in general, easier to implement because we don't have to do anything clever to get multiple dispatch, as the templates provide it out of the box. We just need to come up with interesting applications of the pattern, such as the serialization/deserialization problem we just explored.

Visitor in C++17

C++17 introduced a major change in the way we use the Visitor pattern with the addition of `std::variant` to the standard library. The `std::variant` template is essentially a "smart union:" `std::variant<T1, T2, T3>` is similar to `union { T1 v1; T2 v2; T3 v3; }` in that both can store a value of one of the specified types and only one value can be stored at a time. The key difference is that a variant object knows which type it contains, while with a union the programmer is wholly responsible for reading the same type as what was written earlier. It is undefined behavior to access a union as a type that differs from the one used to initialize it:

```
union { int i; double d; std::string s; } u;
u.i = 0;
++u.i;              // OK
std::cout << u.d;      // Undefined behavior
```

In contrast, `std::variant` offers a safe way to store values of different types in the same memory. It is easy to check at runtime which alternative type is currently stored in the variant, and accessing a variant as the wrong type throws an exception:

```
std::variant<int, double, std::string> v;
std::get<int>(v) = 0;        // Initialized as int
std::cout << v.index();        // 0 is the index of int
++std::get<0>(v);          // OK, int is 0th type
std::get<1>(v);             // throws std::bad_variant_access
```

In many ways, `std::variant` offers capabilities similar to inheritance-based run-time polymorphism: both let us write code where the same variable name can refer to objects of different types at run time. The two major differences are: first, a `std::variant` does not require that all its types come from the same hierarchy (they need not be classes at all), and second, a variant object can store only one of the types listed in its declaration, while a base class pointer can point to any derived class. In other words, adding a new type to the hierarchy generally does not require recompilation of the code that uses the base class, while adding a new type to the variant requires changing the type of the variant object, so all code that refers to this object must be recompiled.

In this section, we will focus on the use of `std::variant` for visitation. This capability is provided by the aptly named function `std::visit` that takes a callable and a variant:

```cpp
std::variant<int, double, std::string> v;
struct Print {
  void operator()(int i) { std::cout << i; }
  void operator()(double d) { std::cout << d; }
  void operator()(const std::string& s) { std::cout << s; }
} print;
std::visit(print, v);
```

To use with `std::visit`, the callable must have an `operator()` declared for every type that can be stored in the variant (otherwise the call will not compile). Of course, if the implementation is similar, we can use a template `operator()`, either in a function object or in a lambda:

```cpp
std::variant<int, double, std::string> v;
std::visit([] (const auto& x) { std::cout << x;}, v);
```

We will now reimplement our pet visitors using `std::variant` and `std::visit`. First of all, the `Pet` type is no longer the base class of the hierarchy but the variant, containing all possible type alternatives:

```cpp
// Example 21
using Pet =
  std::variant<class Cat, class Dog, class Lorikeet>;
```

The types themselves do not need any visitation machinery. We may still use inheritance to reuse common implementation code, but there is no need for the types to belong to a single hierarchy:

```cpp
// Example 21
class PetBase {
  public:
  PetBase(std::string_view color) : color_(color) {}
  const std::string& color() const { return color_; }
  private:
  const std::string color_;
};
class Cat : private PetBase {
  public:
  using PetBase::PetBase;
  using PetBase::color;
```

```
};
class Dog : private PetBase {
  ... similar to Cat ...
};
class Lorikeet {
  public:
  Lorikeet(std::string_view body, std::string_view head) :
    body_(body), head_(head) {}
  std::string color() const {
    return body_ + " and " + head_;
  }
  private:
  const std::string body_;
  const std::string head_;
};
```

Now we need to implement some visitors. The visitors are just callable objects that can be invoked with every alternative type that might be stored in the variant:

```
// Example 21
class FeedingVisitor {
  public:
  void operator()(const Cat& c) {
    std::cout << "Feed tuna to the " << c.color()
              << " cat" << std::endl;
  }
  void operator()(const Dog& d) {
    std::cout << "Feed steak to the " << d.color()
              << " dog" << std::endl;
  }
  void operator()(const Lorikeet& l) {
    std::cout << "Feed grain to the " << l.color()
              << " bird" << std::endl;
  }
};
```

To apply a visitor to a variant, we call `std::visit`:

```
// Example 21
Pet p = Cat("orange");
FeedingVisitor v;
std::visit(v, p);
```

The variant p can contain any of the types we listed when we defined the type Pet (in this example, it's a Cat). We then invoke std::visit and the resulting action depends both on the visitor itself and on the type currently stored in the variant. The result looks a lot like a virtual function call, so we can say that std::visit allows us to add new polymorphic functions to a set of types (it would be misleading to call them "virtual functions" since the types do not have to even be classes).

Whenever we see a callable object with the user-defined operator(), we must be thinking about lambdas. However, the use of lambdas with std::visit is not straightforward: we need the object to be callable with every type that can be stored in the variant, while a lambda has only one operator(). The first option is to make that operator a template (polymorphic lambdas) and handle all the possible types inside:

```
// Example 22
#define SAME(v, T) \
  std::is_same_v<std::decay_t<decltype(v)>, T>
auto fv = [](const auto& p) {
  if constexpr (SAME(p, Cat)) {
    std::cout << "Feed tuna to the " << p.color()
              << " cat" << std::endl; }
  else if constexpr (SAME(p, Dog)) {
    std::cout << "Feed steak to the " << p.color()
              << " dog" << std::endl; }
  else if constexpr (SAME(p, Lorikeet)) {
    std::cout << "Feed grain to the " << p.color()
              << " bird" << std::endl; }
  else abort();
};
```

Here the lambda can be invoked with an argument of any type, and inside the body of the lambda, we use if constexpr to handle all types that can be stored in the variant. The disadvantage of this approach is that we no longer have compile-time validation that all possible types are handled by the visitor. The flip side of this is, however, that the code will now compile even if not all types are handled, and, as long as the visitor is not called with a type for which we have no action defined, the program will work fine. In this way, this version is similar to the acyclic visitor, while the previous implementation was similar to the regular visitor.

It is also possible to implement the familiar set of overloaded operator() using lambdas and the technique for creating overload sets we have seen in *Chapter 1, An Introduction to Inheritance and Polymorphism*:

```
// Example 22
template <typename... T> struct overloaded : T... {
  using T::operator()...;
};
```

```
template <typename... T>
overloaded( T...)->overloaded<T...>;
auto pv = overloaded {
  [](const Cat& c) {
    std::cout << "Play with feather with the " << c.color()
              << " cat" << std::endl; },
  [](const Dog& d) {
    std::cout << "Play fetch with the " << d.color()
              << " dog" << std::endl; },
  [](const Lorikeet& l) {
    std::cout << "Teach words to the " << l.color()
              << " bird" << std::endl; }
};
```

This visitor is a class that inherits from all the lambdas and exposes their operator (), thus creating a set of overloads. It is used just like the visitor where we explicitly wrote each operator ():

```
// Example 22
Pet l = Lorikeet("yellow", "green");
std::visit(pv, l);
```

So far, we have not used the full potential of std::visit: it can be called with any number of variant arguments. This allows us to perform an action that depends on more than two run-time conditions:

```
// Example 23
using Pet = std::variant<class Cat, class Dog>;
Pet c1 = Cat("orange");
Pet c2 = Cat("black");
Pet d = Dog("brown");
CareVisitor cv;
std::visit(cv, c1, c2);      // Two cats
std::visit(cv, c1, d);       // Cat and dog
```

The visitor has to be written in a way that handles all possible combinations of the types that can be stored in each variant:

```
class CareVisitor {
  public:
  void operator()(const Cat& c1, const Cat& c2) {
    std::cout << "Let the " << c1.color() << " and the "
              << c2.color() << " cats play" << std::endl; }
  void operator()(const Dog& d, const Cat& c) {
    std::cout << "Keep the " << d.color()
              << " dog safe from the vicious " << c.color()
```

```
                          << " cat" << std::endl; }
    void operator()(const Cat& c, const Dog& d) {
      (*this)(d, c);
    }
    void operator()(const Dog& d1, const Dog& d2) {
      std::cout << "Take the " << d1.color() << " and the "
                << d2.color() << " dogs for a walk"
                << std::endl; }
};
```

In practice, the only way it is feasible to write a callable for all possible type combinations is by using a template `operator()`, which works only if the visitor actions can be written in a generic way. Still, the ability to do multiple dispatch is a potentially useful feature of `std::visit` that goes beyond the double dispatch capability of the regular Visitor pattern.

Summary

In this chapter, we learned about the Visitor pattern and the different ways it can be implemented in C++. The classic object-oriented Visitor pattern allows us to effectively add a new virtual function to the entire class hierarchy without changing the source code of the classes. The hierarchy must be made visitable, but after that, any number of operations can be added, and their implementation is kept separate from the objects themselves. In the classic Visitor pattern implementation, the source code containing the visited hierarchy does not need to be changed, but it does need to be recompiled when a new class is added to the hierarchy. The Acyclic Visitor pattern solves this problem but at the cost of the additional dynamic cast. On the other hand, the Acyclic Visitor pattern also supports partial visitation - ignoring some visitor/visitable combinations - while the classic Visitor pattern requires that all combinations must at least be declared.

For all visitor variants, the tradeoff for extensibility is the need to weaken the encapsulation and, frequently, grant external visitor classes access to what should be private data members.

The Visitor pattern is often combined with other design patterns, in particular, the Composition pattern, to create complex visitable objects. The composite object delegates the visitation to its contained objects. This combined pattern is particularly useful when an object must be decomposed into its smallest building blocks; for example, for serialization.

The classic Visitor pattern implements the double dispatch at run-time - during execution, the program selects which code to run based on two factors, the types of the visitor and the visitable objects. The pattern can be similarly used at compile time, where it provides a limited reflection capability.

In C++17, `std::visit` can be used to extend the Visitor pattern to types not bound into a common hierarchy, and even to implement multiple dispatch.

This chapter on the Visitor pattern used to conclude this book dedicated to C++ idioms and design patterns. But, like new stars, the birth of new patterns never stops – new frontiers and new ideas bring with them new challenges to be solved and new solutions to be invented, and they evolve and develop until the programming community collectively arrives at something we can point to and say, with confidence, *this is usually a good way to handle that problem*. We will elaborate on the strengths of each new approach, consider its drawbacks, and give it a name so we can concisely refer to the entire set of knowledge about the problem, its solutions, and its caveats. With that, a new pattern enters our design toolset and our programming vocabulary. To illustrate this process, in the next and final chapter, we have collected some of the patterns that emerged to address problems specific to concurrent programs.

Questions

1. What is the Visitor pattern?

2. What problem does the Visitor pattern solve?

3. What is double dispatch?

4. What are the advantages of the Acyclic Visitor pattern?

5. How does the Visitor pattern help implement serialization?

18

Patterns for Concurrency

The last chapter is dedicated to a set of patterns for use in concurrent programs. Concurrency and C++ have a somewhat complex relationship. On the one hand, C++ is a performance-oriented language, and concurrency is almost always employed to improve performance, so the two are a natural fit. Certainly, C++ was used to develop concurrent programs since the earliest days of the language. On the other hand, for a language so often used for writing concurrent programs, C++ has a surprising dearth of constructs and features that directly address the needs of concurrent programming. These needs are mostly addressed by a wide range of community-developed libraries and, often, application-specific solutions. In this chapter, we will review common problems encountered in the development of concurrent programs and solutions that emerged from years of experience; together, these are the two sides of a design pattern.

The following topics are covered in this chapter:

- What is the state of concurrency support in C++?
- What are the main challenges of concurrency?
- The challenges of data synchronization and the C++ tools to meet them
- What is the design for concurrency?
- What are common patterns for managing concurrent workloads in C++?

Technical requirements

The example code for this chapter can be found on GitHub at the following link: `https://github.com/PacktPublishing/Hands-On-Design-Patterns-with-CPP-Second-Edition/tree/master/Chapter18`. Also, basic knowledge of concurrency in general as well as concurrency support in C++ are a pre-requisite.

C++ and concurrency

The concept of concurrency was introduced into the language in C++11, but concurrent programs were written in C++ long before that. This chapter is not meant to be an introduction to concurrency or even an introduction to concurrency in C++. This subject is well-covered in the literature (at the time of publication of this book, one of the works that are both general and up-to-date is the book *C++ Concurrency in Action* by Anthony Williams). Also, while concurrency is almost always used to improve performance, we will not directly address performance and optimization issues here; for that, you can refer to my book *The Art of Writing Efficient Programs*. We are going to focus on the problems that arise in the design of concurrent software.

There are, broadly speaking, three types of challenges we encounter when developing concurrent programs. First, how to make sure the program is correct even when multiple threads operate on the same data concurrency? Second, how to execute the work of a program on multiple threads to improve the overall performance? Finally, how to design software in a way that allows us to reason about it, understand its functions, and maintain it, all with the added complexity of concurrency.

The first set of challenges broadly relates to data sharing and synchronization. We will examine the related patterns first: the program must be first and foremost correct, and great performance in a program that crashes or produces results that cannot be trusted is useless.

Synchronization patterns

Synchronization patterns have one overarching purpose: to ensure correct operations on data shared by multiple threads. These patterns are critically important for the absolute majority of concurrent programs. The only programs that do not have any need for synchronization are the ones that execute several entirely independent tasks that do not involve any common data (except for, possibly, reading shared and immutable inputs) and produce separate results. For every other program, there is a need to manage some shared state, which exposes us to the danger of the dreaded data races. Formally, the C++ standard says that concurrent access to the same object (same memory location) without the appropriate synchronization that guarantees exclusive access for each thread results in undefined behavior. To be precise, the behavior is undefined if at least one thread can modify the shared data: if the data is never changed by any thread, then there is no possibility of a data race. There are design patterns that take advantage of that loophole, but let us start with the most widely known synchronization pattern. What comes to mind first when you hear about avoiding data races?

Mutex and locking patterns

If there is one tool for writing concurrent programs, it is a mutex. A mutex is used to guarantee exclusive access to the shared data accessed by multiple threads:

```
std::mutex m;
MyData data;
...
// On several threads:
m.lock();
transmogrify(data);
m.unlock();
```

The data-modifying operation `transmogrify()` must be guaranteed exclusive access to the shared data: only one thread may do this operation at any given time. The programmer uses a **mutex** (short for **mutual exclusion**) to ensure this: only one thread at a time can lock the mutex and enter the critical section (the code between `lock()` and `unlock()`).

The use of a mutex is sufficient to ensure correct access to the shared data, but this is hardly a good design. The first issue is that it is error-prone: if `transmogrify()` throws an exception, or if the programmer adds a check for the return value and exits the critical section early, the final `unlock()` is never executed and the mutex remains locked forever, thus blocking every other thread from ever accessing the data.

This challenge is easily addressed by a particular application of the very general C++ pattern we have already seen in *Chapter 5, A Comprehensive Look at RAII*. All we need is an object to lock and unlock the mutex, and the C++ standard library already provides one, `std::lock_guard`:

```
// Example 01
std::mutex m;
int i = 0;
void add() {
  std::lock_guard<std::mutex> l(m);
  ++i;
}
...
std::thread t1(add);
std::thread t2(add);
t1.join();
t2.join();
std::cout << i << std::endl;
```

The function add() modifies the shared variable i and, therefore, needs exclusive access; this is provided by the use of the mutex m. Note that if you run this example without the mutex, chances are you will get the correct result nonetheless because one of the threads will execute before the other. Sometimes the program will fail, and more often it won't. This doesn't make it correct, it just makes it hard to debug. You can see the race condition with the help of the **thread sanitizer (TSAN)**. If you are using GCC or Clang, add --sanitize=address to enable it. Remove the mutex from add() (*Example 02*), compile with TSAN, run the program, and you will see this:

```
WARNING: ThreadSanitizer: data race
...
Location is global 'i' of size 4 at <address>
```

There is a lot more information shown to help you figure out which threads have a data race and for which variable. This is a far more reliable way to test for data races than waiting for your program to fail.

In C++17, the use of std::lock_guard is slightly simpler since the compiler figures out the template argument from the constructor:

```
// Example 03
std::lock_guard l(m);
```

In C++20, we can use std::jthread instead of calling join() explicitly:

```
// Example 03
{
  std::jthread t1(add);
  std::jthread t2(add);
}
std::cout << i << std::endl;
```

Note that care must be taken to destroy the threads before using the result of the computation since the destructor now joins the thread and waits for the calculation to complete. Otherwise, there is another data race: the main thread is reading the value of i while it is being incremented (TSAN finds this race as well).

The use of RAII ensures that every time a mutex is locked it is also unlocked, but this does not avoid other errors that can happen when using mutexes. The most common one is forgetting to use the mutex in the first place. The synchronization guarantees apply only if every thread uses the same mechanism to ensure exclusive access to the data. If even one thread does not use the mutex, even if it's only to read the data, then the entire program is incorrect.

A pattern was developed to prevent unsynchronized access to the shared. This pattern usually goes by the name "mutex-guarded" or "mutex-protected" and it has two key elements: first, the data that needs to be protected and the mutex that is used to do so are combined in the same object. Second, the design ensures that every access to the data is protected by the mutex. Here is the basic mutex-guarded class template:

```
// Example 04
template <typename T> class MutexGuarded {
  std::mutex m_;
  T data_ {};
  public:
  MutexGuarded() = default;
  template <typename... Args>
  explicit MutexGuarded(Args&&... args) :
    data_(std::forward<Args>(args)...) {}
  template <typename F> decltype(auto) operator()(F f) {
    std::lock_guard<std::mutex> l(m_);
    return f(data_);
  }
};
```

As you can see, this template combines the mutex and the data guarded by it, and offers only one way to access the data: by invoking the MutexGuarded object with an arbitrary callable. This ensures that all data accesses are synchronized:

```
// Example 04
MutexGuarded<int> i_guarded(0);
void add() {
  i_guarded([] (int& i) { ++i; });
}
...
// On many threads:
std::thread t1(add);
std::thread t2(add);
t1.join();
t2.join();
i_guarded([] (int i) { std::cout << i << std::endl; });
```

These are the most basic versions of the patterns for the correct and reliable use of mutexes. In practice, the needs are often more complex, and so are the solutions: there are much more efficient locks than std::mutex (for example, spinlocks for guarding short computations, which you can find in my book *The Art of Writing Efficient Programs*), and there are also more complex locks such as shared and exclusive locks for efficient read-write access. Also, often we have to operate on several shared objects at the same time, which leads to the problem of safely locking multiple mutexes.

Many of these problems are solved by more complex variations of the patterns we have just seen. Some call for an entirely different approach to the synchronization of data accesses, and we will see several of those later in this section. Finally, some data access challenges are better solved at a much higher level of the overall system design; this will also be illustrated in this chapter.

Let us next review different approaches to data sharing that go beyond the commonly used mutex.

No sharing is the best sharing

While protecting shared data with a mutex does not seem that complicated, in reality, data races are the most common bugs in any concurrent program. While it may seem a useless truism to state that you cannot have data races accessing data you do not share, not sharing is a frequently overlooked alternative to sharing. To put it another way, it is often possible to redesign a program to avoid sharing some of the variables or to restrict access to shared data to a smaller part of the code.

This idea is the basis of a design pattern that is simple to explain but often hard to apply because it requires thinking outside of the box – the thread-specific data pattern. It is also known as "thread-local data," but the name invites confusion with the C++ `thread_local` keyword. To illustrate the idea, we consider this example: we need to count certain events that may be happening in multiple threads simultaneously (for this demonstration, it does not matter what is counted). We need the total count of these events in the entire program, so the straightforward approach is to have a shared count and increment it when a thread detects an event (in the demonstration, we count random numbers divisible by 10):

```
// Example 05
MutexGuarded<size_t> count;
void events(unsigned int s) {
  for (size_t i = 1; i != 100; ++i) {
    if ((rand_r(&s) % 10) == 0) { // Event!
      count([](size_t& i) { ++i; });
    }
  }
}
```

This is a straightforward design; it is not the best one. Notice that while each thread is counting events, it does not need to know how many events were counted by other threads. This is not to be confused with the fact that, in our implementation, each thread needs to know what the current value of the count is so it can correctly increment it. The distinction is subtle but important and suggests an alternative: each thread can count its own events using a thread-specific count, one for each thread.

None of these counts are correct, but it doesn't matter as long as we can add all counts together when we need the correct total event count. There are several possible designs here. We can use a local count for the events and update the shared count once before the thread exits:

```
// Example 06
MutexGuarded<size_t> count;
void events(unsigned int s) {
  size_t n = 0;
  for (size_t i = 1; i != 100; ++i) {
    if ((rand_r(&s) % 10) == 0) { // Event!
      ++n;
    }
  }
  if (n > 0) count([n](size_t& i) { i += n; });
}
```

Any local (stack-allocated) variable declared in a function that is being executed by one or more threads is specific to each thread: there is a unique copy of this variable on the stack of each thread, and each thread accesses its own variable when they all refer to the same name n.

We could also give each thread a unique count variable to increment and add them together in the main thread after all the counting threads are finished:

```
// Example 07
void events(unsigned int s, size_t& n) {
  for (size_t i = 1; i != 100; ++i) {
    if ((rand_r(&s) % 10) == 0) ++n;
  }
}
```

When calling this counting function on multiple threads, we have to take some precautions. Obviously, we should give each thread its own variable for the count n. This is not enough: due to the hardware-related effect known as "false sharing," we must also ensure that the thread-specific counts are not adjacent in memory (a detailed description of false sharing can be found in my book *The Art of Writing Efficient Programs*):

```
// Example 07
alignas(64) size_t n1 = 0;
alignas(64) size_t n2 = 0;
std::thread t1(events, 1, std::ref(n1));
std::thread t2(events, 2, std::ref(n2));
t1.join();
t2.join();
size_t count = n1 + n2;
```

The `alignas` attribute ensures 64-byte alignment for each count variable, thus ensuring that there is at least 64 bytes difference between the addresses of `n1` and `n2` (64 is the size of the cache line on most modern CPUs, including X86 and ARM). Note the `std::ref` wrapper that is needed for `std::thread` to invoke functions that use reference arguments.

The previous example reduces the need for shared data access to once per thread, while the last one does not have any shared data at all; the preferred solution depends on exactly when is the value of the total count needed.

The last example can be examined from a slightly different point of view; it would help to slightly rewrite it:

```
// Example 08
struct {
  alignas(64) size_t n1 = 0;
  alignas(64) size_t n2 = 0;
} counts;
std::thread t1(events, 1, std::ref(counts.n1));
std::thread t2(events, 2, std::ref(counts.n2));
t1.join();
t2.join();
size_t count = counts.n1 + counts.n2;
```

This does not change anything of substance, but we can view the thread-specific counts as parts of the same data structure rather than independent variables created for each thread. This way of thinking leads us to another variant of the thread-specific data pattern: sometimes, multiple threads must operate on the same data, but it may be possible to partition the data and give each thread its own subset to work on.

In the next example, we need to clamp each element in the vector (if an element exceeds the maximum value, it is replaced by this value, so the result is always in the range between zero and the maximum). The computation is implemented by this templated algorithm:

```
// Example 09
template <typename IT, typename T>
void clamp(IT from, IT to, T value) {
  for (IT it = from; it != to; ++it) {
    if (*it > value) *it = value;
  }
}
```

A production-quality implementation would ensure that the iterator arguments satisfy the iterator requirements and the maximum value is comparable with the iterator value type, but we omit all that for brevity (we had an entire chapter on concepts and other ways to restrict templates).

The `clamp()` function can be called on any sequence, and sometimes we will be lucky to have separate unrelated data structures we can process independently on multiple threads. But to continue this example, let us say that we have only one vector we need to clamp. All is not lost, however, as we can process non-overlapping parts of it on multiple threads with no risk of data races:

```
// Example 09
std::vector<int> data = ... data ...;
std::thread t1([&](){
  clamp(data.begin(), data.begin() + data.size()/2, 42);
});
std::thread t2([&](){
  clamp(data.begin() + data.size()/2, data.end(), 42);
});
...
t1.join();
t2.join();
```

Even though the data structure in our program is shared between two threads and both threads modify it, this program is correct: for each vector element, there is only one thread that can modify it. But what about the vector object itself? Isn't it shared between all threads?

We have already highlighted that there is one case when data sharing is allowed without any synchronization: any number of threads can read the same variable as long as no other thread is modifying it. Our example takes advantage of this: all threads read the size of the vector and other data members of the vector object, but no threads change them.

The application of the thread-specific data pattern must be carefully thought through and often requires a good understanding of the data structures. We must be absolutely certain that none of the threads attempt to modify the variables they do share, such as the size and the pointer to the data that are members of the vector object itself. For example, if one of the threads could resize the vector, that would be a data race even if no two threads access the same element: the size of the vector is a variable that is modified by one or more threads without a lock.

The last pattern we want to describe in this subsection applies when several threads need to modify the entire data set (so it cannot be partitioned) but the threads do not need to see the modifications done by other threads. Usually, this happens when the modifications are done as a part of the computation of some result, but the modified data itself is not the final result. In this case, sometimes the best approach is to create a thread-specific copy of the data for each thread. This pattern works best when such copy is a "throw-away" object: each thread needs to modify its copy but the result of the modifications does not need to be committed back to the original data structure.

In the following example, we use an algorithm to count unique elements in a vector that sorts the vector in place:

```
// Example 10
void count_unique(std::vector<int> data, size_t& count) {
  std::sort(data.begin(), data.end());
  count = std::unique(data.begin(),
                      data.end()) - data.begin();
}
```

Also, when we need to count only elements that satisfy a predicate, we erase all other elements first (std::erase_if is a C++20 addition, but is easy to implement in a prior version of C++):

```
// Example 10
void count_unique_even(std::vector<int> data, size_t& count) {
  std::erase_if(data, [](int i) { return i & 1; });
  std::sort(data.begin(), data.end());
  count = std::unique(data.begin(),
                      data.end()) - data.begin();
}
```

Both are destructive operations on a vector, but they are only means to an end: the altered vector can be discarded once we have our count. The simplest, and often the most efficient, way to compute our counts on several threads simultaneously is to make thread-specific copies of the vector. Actually, we did this already: both counting functions take the vector argument by value and, therefore, make a copy. Usually, this would be a mistake, but in our case, it is intentional and allows both functions to operate on the same vector concurrently:

```
// Example 10
std::vector<int> data = ...;
size_t unique_count = 0;
size_t unique_even_count = 0;
{
  std::jthread t1(count_unique, data,
                  std::ref(unique_count));
  std::jthread t2(count_unique_even, data,
                  std::ref(unique_even_count));
}
```

Of course, there is still concurrent access to the original data, and it is done without a lock: both threads need to make their thread-specific copies. However, this falls under the exception of read-only concurrent access and is safe.

In principle, avoiding data sharing when possible and using mutexes otherwise is sufficient to arrange race-free access to data in any program. However, this may not be an efficient way to accomplish this goal, and good performance is almost always the goal of concurrency. We will now consider several other patterns for concurrent access to shared data that, when applicable, can offer superior performance. We are going to start with synchronization primitives that go beyond a mutex and are specifically designed to allow threads to efficiently wait for some event.

Waiting patterns

Waiting is a problem that is frequently encountered in concurrent programs and takes many forms. We have already seen one: the mutex. Indeed, if two threads are trying to enter the critical section simultaneously, one of them will have to wait. But waiting is not the goal here, just an unfortunate side effect of exclusive access to the critical section. There are other situations where waiting is the primary objective. For example, we may have threads that are waiting for some event to happen. This could be a user interface thread waiting for input (little to no performance requirements) or a thread waiting on a network socket (moderate performance requirements) or even a high-performance thread such as a computing thread in a thread pool waiting for a task to execute (extremely high performance requirements). Not surprisingly, there are different implementations for these scenarios, but fundamentally there are two approaches: polling and notifications. We are going to look at notifications first.

The basic pattern for waiting for a notification is the **condition pattern**. It usually consists of a condition variable and a mutex. One or more threads are blocked waiting on the condition variable. During this time, there is one more thread that locks the mutex (thus guaranteeing exclusive access) and does the work whose completion the other threads are waiting for. Once the work is done, the thread that completed it must release the mutex (so other threads can access the shared data containing the results of this work) and notify the waiting threads that they can proceed.

For example, in a thread pool, the waiting threads are the pool worker threads that are waiting for tasks to be added to the pool. Since the pool task queue is a shared resource, a thread needs exclusive access to push or pop tasks. A thread that adds one or more tasks to the queue must hold the mutex while doing it and then notify the worker threads that there are tasks for them to execute.

Let us now see a very basic example of the notification pattern with just two threads. First, we have the main thread that starts a worker thread and then waits for it to produce some results:

```
// Example 11
std::mutex m;
std::condition_variable cv;
size_t n = 0;                    // Zero until work is done
// Main thread
void main_thread() {
  std::unique_lock l(m);
  std::thread t(produce);       // Start the worker
  cv.wait(l, []{ return n != 0; });
```

```
    ... producer thread is done, we have the lock ...
}
```

The locking in this case is provided by `std::unique_lock`, an object that wraps around a mutex and has a mutex-like interface with `lock()` and `unlock()` member functions. The mutex is locked in the constructor and almost immediately unlocked by the `wait()` function when we start waiting on the condition. When the notification is received, `wait()` locks the mutex again before returning control to the caller.

Many implementations of waiting and conditions suffer from what is known as spurious wake-up: wait can be interrupted even without notification. This is why we also check whether the results are ready, in our case, by checking the result count n: if it is still zero, there are no results, the main thread has been awakened in error and we can go back to waiting (note that the waiting thread must still acquire the mutex before `wait()` returns, so it must wait for the worker thread to release this mutex).

The worker thread must lock the same mutex before it can access the shared data, then unlock it before notifying the main thread that the work is done:

```
// Example 11
// Worker thread
void produce() {
    {
        std::lock_guard l(m);
        ... compute results ...
        n = ... result count ...
    } // Mutex unlocked
    cv.notify_one();              // Waiting thread notified
}
```

It is not necessary to hold the mutex the entire time the worker thread is active: its only purpose is to protect the shared data such as the result count n in our example.

The two synchronization primitives `std::conditional_variable` and `std::unique_lock` are standard C++ tools for implementing the waiting pattern with a condition. Just as with a mutex, there are many variations.

The alternative to notifications is polling. In this pattern, the waiting thread repeatedly checks whether some condition is met. In C++20, we can implement a simple example of polling wait using `std::atomic_flag` which is essentially an atomic boolean variable (prior to C++20 we could do the same with `std::atomic<bool>`):

```
// Example 12
std::atomic_flag flag;
// Worker thread:
void produce() {
```

```
  ... produce the results ...
  flag.test_and_set(std::memory_order_release);
}
// Waiting thread:
void main_thread() {
  flag.clear();
  std::thread t(produce);
  while (!flag.test(std::memory_order_acquire)) {} // Wait
  ... results are ready ...
}
```

Atomic operations such as `test_and_set()` make use of **memory barriers**: a kind of global synchronization flag that ensures that all changes made to the memory before the flag is set (release) are visible to any operation on any other thread that is executed after the flag is tested (acquire). There is a lot more to these barriers, but it is outside of the scope of this book and can be found in many books dedicated to concurrency and efficiency.

The most important difference between this and the previous example is the explicit polling loop for the waiting thread in *Example 12*. If the wait is long, this is highly inefficient since the waiting thread is busy computing (reading from memory) the entire time it waits. Any practical implementation would introduce some sleep into the wait loop, but doing so also comes at a cost: the waiting thread will not wake up immediately after the worker thread sets the flag but must finish the sleep first. These efficiency concerns are outside of the scope of this book; here we want to show the overall structure and the components of these patterns.

The boundary between polling and waiting is not always clear. For example, for all we know, `wait()` could be implemented by polling some internal state of the condition variable periodically. In fact, the same atomic flag we just saw can be used to wait for a notification:

```
// Example 13
std::atomic_flag flag;
// Worker thread:
void produce() {
  ... produce the results ...
  flag.test_and_set(std::memory_order_release);
  flag.notify_one();
}
// Waiting thread:
void main_thread() {
  flag.clear();
  std::thread t(produce);
  flag.wait(true, std::memory_order_acquire); // Wait
  while (!flag.test(std::memory_order_acquire)) {}
```

```
    ... results are ready ...
}
```

The call to `wait()` requires a corresponding call to `notify_one()` (or `notify_all()` if we have more than one thread waiting on the flag). Its implementation is almost certainly more efficient than our simple polling loop. After the notification is received and the wait is over, we check the flag to make sure it was really set. The standard says that this is not necessary and `std::atomic_flag::wait()` does not suffer from spurious wakeups, but TSAN in both GCC and Clang disagree (this could be a false positive in TSAN or a bug in the standard library implementation).

There are many other situations where waiting is needed, and the conditions we need to wait for vary widely. Another common need is to wait for a certain number of events to occur. For example, we may have several threads producing results and we may need all of them to complete their share of the work before the main thread can proceed. This is accomplished by waiting on a barrier or a latch. Prior to C++20, we would need to implement these synchronization primitives ourselves or use a third-party library, but in C++20 they became standard:

```
// Example 14
// Worker threads
void produce(std::latch& latch) {
  ... do the work ...
  latch.count_down();      // One more thread is done
}
void main_thread() {
  constexpr size_t nthread = 4;
  std::jthread t[nthread];
  std::latch latch(nthread); // Wait for 4 count_down()
  for (size_t i = 0; i != nthread; ++i) {
    t[i] = std::jthread(std::ref(latch));
  }
  latch.wait();   // Wait for producers to finish
  ... results are ready ...
}
```

The latch is initialized with the count of events to wait for. It will unlock when that many `count_down()` calls have been done.

There are many other applications of waiting, but almost all waiting patterns fall broadly into one of the categories we have seen in this section (a specific implementation can have a dramatic effect on performance in a particular case, which is you are far more likely to see custom application-specific versions of these synchronization constructs than you are to find non-standard containers or other basic data structures).

We are now going to see several examples of very specialized and very efficient synchronization patterns. They are not for all situations, but when they fit the need, they often offer the best performance.

Lock-free synchronization patterns

Most of the time, safely accessing shared data relies on mutexes. C++ also supports another type of synchronizing concurrent threads: atomic operations. Again, a detailed explanation is outside of the scope of this book, and this section requires some prior knowledge of the atomics.

The basic idea is this: some data types (usually integers) have special hardware instructions that allow a few simple operations such as reading or writing or incrementing the values to be done atomically, in a single event. During this atomic operation, other threads cannot access the atomic variable at all, so if one thread performs an atomic operation, all other threads can see the same variable as it was before the operation or after the operation but not in the middle of the operation. For example, an increment is a read-modify-write operation, but an atomic increment is a special hardware transaction such that once the read began, no other thread can access the variable until the write completes. These atomic operations are often accompanied by memory barriers; we have used them already to ensure that not just atomic but all other operations on all variables in the program are synchronized and free from data races.

The simplest but useful application of atomic operations is for counting. We often need to count something in programs, and in concurrent programs, we may need to count some events that can occur on multiple threads. If we are only interested in the total count after all threads are done, this is best handled by the "non-sharing" or thread-specific counter we saw earlier. But what if all threads need to know the current count as well? We can always use a mutex, but using a mutex to protect a simple increment of an integer is highly inefficient. C++ gives us a better way, the atomic counter:

```
// Example 15
std::atomic<size_t> count;
void thread_work() {
  size_t current_count = 0;
  if (... counted even ...) {
    current_count =
      count.fetch_add(1, std::memory_order_relaxed);
  }
}
```

There is only one shared variable in this example, count itself. Since we do not have any other shared data, we have no need for memory barriers ("relaxed" memory order means there are no requirements on the order of accesses to other data). The fetch_add() operation is an atomic increment, it increments count by one and returns the old value of count.

The atomic count can also be used to let multiple threads work on the same data structure without any need for locking: to do this, we need to make sure there is only one thread working on each element of the data structure. When used in this manner, the pattern is often referred to as the atomic index. In the next example, we have an array of data that is shared between all threads:

```
// Example 16
static constexpr size_t N = 1024;
struct Data { ... };
Data data[N] {};
```

We also have an atomic index that is used by all threads that need to store the results of their work in the array. To do so safely, each thread increments an atomic index and used the pre-increment value as the index into the array. No two atomic increment operations can produce the same value, therefore, each thread gets its own array elements to work on:

```
// Example 16
std::atomic<size_t> index(0);
// Many producer threads
void produce(size_t& n) {
  while (... more work ... ) {
    const size_t s =
      index.fetch_add(1, std::memory_order_relaxed);
    if (s >= N) return;      // No more space
    data[s] = ... results ...
  }
}
```

Each thread gets to initialize however many array elements it can and stops when it (and all other threads) fill the entire array. The main thread has to wait until all the work is done before accessing any of the results. This cannot be done with just the atomic index since it is incremented when a thread starts working on a particular array element, not when that thread is done with the work. We have to use some other synchronization mechanism to make the main thread wait until all the work is done, such as a latch or, in a simple case, joining the producer threads:

```
// Example 16
void main_thread() {
  constexpr size_t nthread = 5;
  std::thread t[nthread];
  for (size_t i = 0; i != nthread; ++i) {
    t[i] = std::thread(produce);
  }
  // Wait for producers. to finish.
  for (size_t i = 0; i != nthread; ++i) {
    t[i].join();
```

```
    }
    ... all work is done, data is ready ...
}
```

The atomic count is good when we don't rely on the value of the count to access the results that are already produced. In the last example, the producer threads did not need access to the array elements computed by other threads, and the main thread waits for all threads to complete before accessing the results. Often, this is not the case and we need to access data as it is being produced. This is where memory barriers come in.

The simplest but surprisingly powerful lock-free pattern that relies on memory barriers is known as the publishing protocol. The pattern is applicable when one thread is producing some data that is going to be made accessible to one or more other threads when it is ready. The pattern looks like this:

```
// Example 17
std::atomic<Data*> data;
void produce() {
  Data* p = new Data;
  ... complete *p object ...
  data.store(p, std::memory_order_release);
}
void consume() {
  Data* p = nullptr;
  while (!(p = data.load(std::memory_order_acquire))) {}
  ... safe to use *p ...
}
```

The shared variable is an atomic pointer to the data. It is often called the "root" pointer because the data itself may be a complex data structure with multiple pointers connecting its parts. The key requirement of this pattern is that there is only one way to access the entire data structure and this is through the root pointer.

The producer thread builds all the data it needs to produce. It uses a thread-specific pointer, usually a local variable, to access the data. No other thread can see the data yet because the root pointer does not point to it and the local pointer of the producer thread is not shared with other threads.

Finally, when the data is complete, the producer atomically stores the pointer to the data in the shared root pointer. It is often said that the producer atomically publishes the data, hence the name of the pattern, the publishing protocol.

The consumers must wait for the data to be published: as long as the root pointer is null, there is nothing for them to do. They wait for the root pointer to become non-null (the wait does not have to use polling, a notification mechanism is also possible). Once the data is published, the consumer threads can access it through the root pointer. Because there is no other synchronization, no thread can modify the data once it's published (the data may contain a mutex or some other mechanism to allow parts of it to be modified safely).

The atomic variable itself is insufficient for this pattern to guarantee no data races: all threads access not just the atomic pointer but the memory it points to. This is why we needed the specific memory barriers: when publishing the data, the producer uses the release barrier to not only initialize the pointer atomically but also ensure that all memory modifications that were done before the atomic write operations on the pointer become visible to anyone who reads the new value of the pointer. The consumer uses the acquire barrier to ensure that any operation on the shared data that is done after the new value of the pointer is read observes the latest state of the shared data as it existed at the moment the data was published. In other words, if you read the value of the pointer and then dereference it, you generally do not know if you will get the latest value of the data the pointer points to. But if you read the pointer with the acquire barrier (and the pointer was written with the release barrier), then you can be sure that you will read (acquire) the data as it was last written (released). Together, the release and acquire barriers guarantee that the consumer sees the shared data exactly as it was seen by the producer at the moment it published the address of the data in the root pointer.

The same pattern can be used to publish completed elements of a larger data structure shared between threads. For example, we can have a producer thread publish how many array elements it initialized with the results:

```
// Example 18
constexpr size_t N = ...;
Data data[N];      // Shared, not locked
std::atomic<size_t> size;
void produce() {
  for (size_t n = 0; n != N; ++n) {
    data[n] = ... results ...
    size.store(n, std::memory_order_release);
  }
}
void consume() {
  size_t n = 0;
  do {
    n = size.load(std::memory_order_acquire);
    ... n elements are safe to access ...
  } while (n < N - 1);
}
```

The idea is exactly the same as in the previous example, only instead of the pointer we use the index into an array. In both cases, we have one producer thread that computes and publishes data, and one or more consumer threads that wait for the data to be published. If we need multiple producers, we must use some other synchronization mechanism to ensure that they don't work on the same data, such as the atomic index we just saw.

In a program with multiple producer and consumer threads, we often have to combine several synchronization patterns. In the next example, we have a large shared data structure organized as an array of pointers to the individual elements. Several producer threads fill this data structure with results; we are going to use the atomic index to ensure that each element is handled by only one producer:

```
// Example 19
static constexpr size_t N = 1024;
struct Data { ... };
std::atomic<Data*> data[N] {};
std::atomic<size_t> size(0);       // Atomic index
void produce() {
  Data* p = new Data;
  ... compute *p ...
  const size_t s =
    size.fetch_add(1, std::memory_order_relaxed);
  data[s].store(p, std::memory_order_release);
}
```

Our producer computes the result, then fetches the current index value and, at the same time, increments the index so the next producer cannot get the same index value. The array slot data[s] is, therefore, uniquely reserved for this producer thread. This is enough to avoid sharing conflicts between producers, but the consumers cannot use the same index to know how many elements are already in the array: the index is incremented before the corresponding array element is initialized. For the consumers, we use the publishing protocol: each array element is an atomic pointer that remains null until the data is published. The consumers must wait for a pointer to become non-null before they can access the data:

```
// Example 19
void consumer() {
  for (size_t i = 0; i != N; ++i) {
    const Data* p =
      data[i].load(std::memory_order_acquire);
    if (!p) break; // No more data
    ... *p is safe to access ...
  }
}
```

In this example, the consumer stops as soon as it finds a data element that is not ready. We could continue scanning the array: some of the subsequent elements may be ready because they were filled by another producer thread. If we do, we have to somehow remember to come back to handle the elements we missed. The right approach depends on the problem we need to solve, of course.

The literature on lock-free programming is extensive and full of (usually) very complex examples. The concurrency patterns we have demonstrated are only the basic building blocks for more complex data structures and data synchronization protocols.

In the next section, we will see some of the much higher-level patterns that are applicable to the design of such data structures or even entire programs and their major components.

Concurrent design patterns and guidelines

Designing and implementing concurrent software is hard. Even the basic patterns for controlling access to shared data, such as the ones we saw in the last section, are complex and full of subtle details. Failing to notice one of these details usually results in hard-to-debug data races. To simplify the task of writing concurrent programs, the programming community came up with several guidelines. All of them arise out of earlier disastrous experiences, so take these guidelines seriously. Central to these guidelines is the concept of thread safety guarantees.

Thread safety guarantees

While this is not a pattern, it is a concept that is much broader in scope and one of the key design principles for any concurrent software. Every class, function, module, or component of a concurrent program should specify the thread safety guarantees it provides, as well as the guarantees it requires from the components it uses.

In general, a software component can offer three levels of thread-safety guarantees:

- **Strong thread safety guarantee**: Any number of threads can access this component without restrictions and without encountering undefined behavior. For a function, it means that any number of threads can call this function at the same time (possibly, with some restrictions on parameters). For a class, it means that any number of threads can call member functions of this class concurrently. For a larger component, any number of threads can operate its interfaces (again, possibly with some restrictions). Such components, classes, and data structures are sometimes called thread-safe.

- **Weak thread safety guarantee**: Any number of threads can access this component for operations that are specified to not alter the state of the component (for a class, this is usually `const` member functions). Only one thread can modify the state of the component at any time, and the locking or another way of ensuring such exclusive access is the responsibility of the caller. Such components, classes, and data structures are sometimes called thread-compatible because you can build a concurrent program from them using the appropriate synchronization mechanisms. All STL containers offer this level of guarantee.

- **No thread-safety guarantee**: Such components cannot be used in a concurrent program at all and are sometimes called thread-hostile. These classes and functions often have hidden global states that cannot be accessed in a thread-safe manner.

By designing each component to provide certain thread safety guarantees, we can divide the intractable problem of making the entire program thread-safe into a hierarchy of design challenges where the more complex components take advantage of the guarantees provided by the simpler ones. Central to this process is the notion of the transactional interface.

Transactional interface design

The idea of the transactional interface design is very simple: every component should have an interface such that every operation is an atomic transaction. From the point of view of the rest of the program, the operation either has not happened yet or is done. No other thread can observe the state of the component during the operation. This can be accomplished using mutexes or any other synchronization scheme that fits the need – the particular implementation can influence performance but is not essential for correctness as long as the interface guarantees transaction processing.

This guideline is most useful for designing data structures for concurrent programs. Here, it is so important that it is generally accepted that one cannot design a thread-safe data structure that does not offer a transactional interface (at least not a useful data structure). For example, we can consider a queue. The C++ standard library offers a `std::queue` template. As with any other STL container, it offers the weak guarantee: any number of threads can call `const` methods of the queue as long as no thread calls any non-`const` methods. Alternatively, any one thread can call a non-`const` method. To ensure the latter, we have to lock all accesses to the queue with an external mutex. If we want to pursue this approach, we should combine the queue and the mutex in a new class:

```
template <typename T> class ts_queue {
  std::mutex m_;
  std::queue<T> q_;
  public:
  ts_queue() = default;
  ...
};
```

To push another element onto a queue, we need to lock the mutex, since the `push()` member function modifies the queue:

```
template <typename T> class ts_queue {
  public:
  void push(const T& t) {
    std::lock_guard l(m_);
```

```
    q_.push(t);
  }
};
```

This works exactly as we want it to: any number of threads can call push() and every element will be added to the queue exactly once (the order is going to be arbitrary if multiple calls happen simultaneously, but this is the nature of concurrency). We have successfully provided the strong thread safety guarantee!

The triumph is going to be short-lived, unfortunately. Let us see what it takes to pop an element from the queue. There is a member function pop() that removes the element from the queue, so we can protect it with the same mutex:

```
template <typename T> class ts_queue {
  public:
  void pop() {
    std::lock_guard l(m_);
    q_.pop();
  }
};
```

Notice that this function does not return anything: it removes the oldest element in the queue and destroys it, but that's not what we need to find out what that element is (or was). For that, we need to use the function front() which returns a reference to the oldest element but does not modify the queue. It is a const member function, so we need to lock it only if we call any non-const functions at the same time; we are going to ignore this optimization possibility for now and always lock this call as well:

```
template <typename T> class ts_queue {
  public:
  T& front() const {
    std::lock_guard l(m_);
    return q_.front();
  }
};
```

If we call front() from multiple threads and don't call any other functions, this implementation is sub-optimal, but it is not wrong.

There is one special case we have neglected to mention: if the queue is empty, you should not call pop() or front() – doing so leads to undefined behavior, according to the standard. How do you know if it is safe to pop an element from the queue? You can check if the queue is empty. This is another const member function, and again we are going to over-protect it and lock every call to it:

```
template <typename T> class ts_queue {
  public:
  bool empty() const {
    std::lock_guard l(m_);
    return q_.empty();
  }
};
```

Now every member function of the underlying std::queue is protected by a mutex. We can call any of them from any number of threads and be guaranteed that only one thread can access the queue at any time. Technically, we have achieved the strong guarantee. Unfortunately, it is not very useful.

To see why, let us consider the process of removing an element from the queue:

```
ts_queue<int> q;
int i = 0;
if (!q.empty()) {
  i = q.front();
  q.pop();
}
```

This works fine on one thread, but we didn't need a mutex for that. It still (mostly) works when we have two threads, one of which is pushing new elements onto the queue and the other one is taking them from the queue. Let us consider what happens when two threads try to pop one element each. First, they both call empty(). Let us assume that the queue is not empty and both calls return true. Then, they both call front(). Since neither thread did a pop() yet, both threads get the same front element. This is not what was supposed to happen if we want each thread to pop an element from the queue. Finally, both threads call pop(), and two elements are removed from the queue. One of these elements we have never seen and will never see again, so we lost some of the data that was enqueued.

But this isn't the only way it can go wrong. What happens if there is only one element on the queue? Both calls to empty() still return true – a queue with one element is not empty. Both calls to front() still return the (same) front element. The first call to pop() succeeds but the second one is undefined behavior because the queue is now empty. It is also possible that one thread calls pop() before the other thread calls front() but after it calls empty(). In this case, the second call to front() is also undefined.

We have a perfectly safe and a perfectly useless data structure. Clearly, a thread safety guarantee is not enough. We also need an interface that does not expose us to undefined behavior, and the only way to do this is to perform all three steps of the pop operation (`empty()`, `front()`, and `pop()`) in a single critical section, i.e., without releasing the mutex between the calls. Unless we want the caller to supply their own mutex, the only way to do this is to change the interface of our `ts_queue` class:

```
// Example 20
template <typename T> class ts_queue {
  std::queue<T> q_;
  std::mutex m_;
  public:
  ts_queue() = default;
  template <typename U> void push(U&& u) {
    std::lock_guard l(m_);
    q_.push(std::forward<U>(u));
  }
  std::optional<T> pop() {
    std::lock_guard l(m_);
    if (q_.empty()) return {};
    std::optional<T> res(std::move(q_.front()));
    q_.pop();
    return res;
  }
};
```

The push() function is the same as it was before (we made the argument type more flexible, but this is not related to thread safety). The reason we did not need to change the push operation is that it is already transactional: at the end, the queue has one more element than it had at the beginning of the operation, and the state of the queue is otherwise identical. We just made it atomic by protecting it with a mutex (no other thread that also uses the same mutex correctly can observe our queue in its transitional non-invariant state).

The pop() operation is where the transactional interface looks very different. In order to provide a meaningful thread safety guarantee, we have to provide an operation that returns the front element to the caller and removes it from the queue atomically: no other thread should be able to see the same front element, therefore, we have to lock both front() and pop() on the original queue with the same mutex. We also have to consider the possibility that the queue is empty and we have no front element to return to the caller. What do we return in this case? If we decided to return the front element by value, we would have to default-construct this value (or return some other agreed-upon value that means "no element"). In C++17, a better way is to return a std::optional that holds the front element if there is one.

Now both pop() and push() are atomic and transactional: we can call both methods from as many threads as we want, and the results are always well-defined.

You may wonder why didn't `std::queue` offer this transactional interface, to begin with. First, STL was designed long before threads made it into the standard. But the other, very important, reason is that the queue interface was influenced by the need to provide exception safety. Exception safety is the guarantee that the object remains in a well-defined state if an exception is thrown. Here, the original queue interface does very well: `empty()` just returns the size and cannot throw an exception, `front()` returns the reference to the front element and also cannot throw, and finally `pop()` calls the destructor of the front element, which normally does not throw either. Of course, when accessing the front element, the caller's code may throw (for example, if the caller needs to copy the front element to another object) but the caller is expected to handle that. In any case, the queue itself remains in a well-defined state.

Our thread-safe queue, however, has an exception safety problem: the code that copies the front element of the queue to return it to the caller is now inside `pop()`. If the copy constructor throws during the construction of the local `std::optional` variable `res`, we are probably OK. However, if an exception is thrown when the result is returned to the caller (which can happen by move or copy), then `pop()` was already done, so we are going to lose the element we just popped from the queue.

This tension between thread safety and exception safety is often unavoidable and has to be considered when designing thread-safe data structures for concurrent programs. Regardless, it must be reiterated that the only way to design thread-safe data structures or larger modules is to ensure that every interface call is a complete transaction: any steps that are conditionally defined must be packaged into a single transactional call together with the operations that are needed to ensure that such conditions are met. Then, the entire call should be guarded by a mutex or some other way to ensure race-free exclusive access.

Designing thread-safe data structures is generally very hard, especially if we want good performance (and what is the point of concurrency if we don't?). That is why it is very important to take advantage of any use restrictions or special requirements that allow us to impose restrictions on how these data structures are used. In the next section, we will see one common case of such restrictions.

Data structures with access limitations

Designing thread-safe data structures is so hard that one should look for any opportunity to simplify the requirements and the implementation. If there is any scenario you don't need right now, think if you can make your code simpler if you do not support that scenario. One obvious case is a data structure that is built by a single thread (no thread safety guarantees needed) then becomes immutable and is accessed by many threads that act as readers (a weak guarantee is sufficient). Any STL container, for example, can operate in this mode as-is. We still need to ensure that no reader can access the container while it's still being filled with data, but that can be easily done with a barrier or a condition. This is a very useful but rather trivial case. Are there any other restrictions we can make use of?

In this section, we consider a particular use case that occurs quite frequently and allows for much simpler data structures. Specifically, we examine the situation when a particular data structure is accessed by only two threads. One thread is the producer, it adds data to the data structure. The other thread is the consumer, it removes the data. Both threads do modify the data structure but in different ways. This situation occurs rather frequently and often allows for very specialized and very efficient data structure implementations. It probably deserves recognition as a design pattern for concurrent designs, and it already has a commonly recognized name: "single-producer single-consumer data structure."

In this section, we are going to see an example of a single-producer single-consumer queue. It is a data structure that is frequently used with one producer and one consumer thread, but the ideas we explore here can be used to design other data structures as well. The main distinguishing feature of this queue is going to be that it is lock-free: there are no mutexes in it at all, so we can expect much higher performance from it.

The queue is built on an array of a fixed size, so, unlike a regular queue, it cannot grow indefinitely (this is another common restriction used to simplify lock-free data structures):

```
// Example 21
template <typename T, size_t N> class ts_queue {
  T buffer_[N];
  std::atomic<size_t> back_{0};
  std::atomic<size_t> front_{N - 1};
  ...
};
```

In our example, we default-construct elements in the array. If this is undesirable, we can also use a properly aligned uninitialized buffer. All accesses to the queue are determined by two atomic variables, back_ and front_. The former is the index of the array element that we will write into when we push a new element onto the queue. The latter is the index of the array element we will read from when we need to pop an element from the queue. All array elements in the range [front_, back_) are filled with elements currently on the queue. Note that this range can wrap over the end of the buffer: after using the element buffer_[N-1] the queue does not run out of space but starts again from buffer_[0]. This is known as a **circular buffer**.

How do we use these indices to manage the queue? Let us start with the push operation:

```
// Example 21
template <typename T, size_t N> class ts_queue {
  public:
  template <typename U> bool push(U&& u) {
    const size_t front =
      front_.load(std::memory_order_acquire);
    size_t back = back_.load(std::memory_order_relaxed);
    if (back == front) return false;
    buffer_[back] = std::forward<U>(u);
```

```
      back_.store((back + 1) % N, std::memory_order_release);
      return true;
    }
};
```

We need to read the current value of `back_`, of course: this is the index of the array element we are about to write. We support only one producer, and only the producer thread can increment `back_`, so we do not need any particular precautions here. We do, however, need to be careful to avoid overwriting any elements already in the queue. To do this we must check the current value of `front_` (we can read it before or after reading `back_`, it makes no difference). If the element `buffer_[back]` that we are about to overwrite is also the front element, then the queue is full and the `push()` operation fails (note that there is another solution to this problem that is often used in real-time systems: if the queue is full, the oldest element is silently overwritten and lost). After the new element is stored, we atomically increment the `back_` value to signal to the consumer that this slot is now available for reading. Because we are publishing this memory location, we must use the release barrier. Also note the modular arithmetic: after reaching the array element `N-1`, we're looping back to element 0.

Next, let us see the `pop()` operation:

```
// Example 21
template <typename T, size_t N> class ts_queue {
  public:
  std::optional<T> pop() {
    const size_t back =
      back_.load(std::memory_order_acquire);
    const size_t front =
      (front_.load(std::memory_order_relaxed) + 1) % N;
    if (front == back) return {};
    std::optional<T> res(std::move(buffer_[front]));
    front_.store(front, std::memory_order_release);
    return res;
  }
};
```

Again, we need to read both `front_` and `back_`: `front_` is the index of the element we are about to read, and only the consumer can advance this index. On the other hand, `back_` is needed to make sure we actually have an element to read: if the front and back are the same, the queue is empty; again, we use `std::optional` to return a value that might not exist. We must use acquire barrier when reading `back_` to make sure we see the element values that were written into the array by the producer thread. Finally, we advance `front_` to ensure that we don't read the same element again and to make this array slot available to the producer thread.

There are several subtle details here that must be pointed out. Reading `back_` and `front_` is not done in a single transaction (it is not atomic). In particular, if the producer reads `front_` first, it is possible that, by the time it reads `back_` and compares the two, the consumer has already advanced `front_`. That does not make our data structure incorrect, though. At worst, the producer can report that the queue is full when in fact, it is no longer full. We could read both values atomically, but this will only degrade the performance, and the caller still has to handle the case when the queue is full. Similarly, when `pop()` reports that the queue is empty, it may no longer be so by the time the call completes. Again, these are the inevitable complexities of concurrency: each operation reflects the state of the data at some point in time. By the time the caller gets the return value and can analyze it, the data may have changed already.

Another note-worthy detail is the careful management of the queue elements' lifetime. We default-construct all elements in the array, so the proper way to transfer the data from the caller into the queue during `push()` is by copy or move assignment (`std::forward` does both). On the other hand, once a value is returned to the caller by `pop()`, we never need that value again, so the right operation here is move, first into the optional and then into the caller's return value object. Note that moving an object is not the same as destroying it; indeed, the moved-from array elements are not destroyed until the queue itself is. If an array element is reused, it is copy- or move-assigned a new value, and assignments are two of the three operations that are safe to do on a moved-from object (the third one is the destructor, which we will also call eventually).

The single-producer single-consumer pattern is a common pattern that allows a programmer to greatly simplify their concurrent data structures. There are others, you can find them in books and papers dedicated to concurrent data structures. All these patterns are ultimately designed to help you write data structures that perform correctly and efficiently when accessed by multiple threads. We, however, must move on and finally tackle the problem of using these threads to get some useful work done.

Concurrent execution patterns

The next group of patterns for concurrency we must learn are execution patterns. These patterns are used to organize the computations done on multiple threads. You will find out that, just as with the synchronization patterns we saw earlier, all of these are low-level patterns: most solutions for practical problems must combine these patterns into larger, more complex, designs. This is not because C++ is ill-suited for such larger designs; if anything, it is the opposite: there are so many ways to implement, for example, a thread pool, in C++, that for every concrete application, there is a version that is ideally suited in terms of performance and features. This is why it is hard to describe these more complete solutions as patterns: while the problems they address are common, the solutions vary a great deal. But all of these designs have a number of challenges to resolve, and the solutions to those challenges usually use the same tools over and over, so we can at least describe these more basic challenges and their common solutions as design patterns.

Active object

The first concurrent execution pattern we are going to see is the Active Object. An active object usually encapsulates the code to be executed, the data needed for the execution, and the flow of control needed to execute the code asynchronously. This flow of control could be as simple as a separate thread that the object starts and joins. In most cases, we do not start a new thread for every task, so an active object would have some way to run its code on a multi-threaded executor such as a thread pool. From the caller's point of view, an active object is an object that the caller constructs, initializes with the data, then tells the object to execute itself, and the execution happens asynchronously.

The basic active object looks like this:

```cpp
// Example 22
class Job {
  ... data ...
  std::thread t_;
  bool done_ {};
  public:
  Job(... args ...) { ... initialize data ... }
  void operator()() {
    t_ = std::thread([this](){ ... computations ... }
  );
  }
  void wait() {
    if (done_) return;
    t_.join();
    done_ = true;
  }
  ~Job() { wait(); }
  auto get() { this->wait(); return ... results ...; }
};
Job j(... args ...);
j();      // Execute code on a thread
... do other work ...
std::cout << j.get();  // Wait for results and print them
```

In the simplest case shown here, the active object contains a thread that is used to execute the code asynchronously. In most practical cases you would use an executor that schedules the work on one of the threads it manages, but this gets us into implementation-specific details. The execution starts when `operator()` is called; we can also make the object execute as soon as it is constructed by calling `operator()` from the constructor. At some point, we have to wait for the results. If we use a separate thread, we can join the thread at that time (and take care to not attempt to join it twice if the caller calls `wait()` again). If the object represents not a thread but a task in a thread pool or some other executor, we would do the cleanup necessary for that case.

As you can see, once we settle on a particular way to execute code asynchronously, writing active objects with different data and code is a rather repetitive task. Nobody writes active objects the way we just did, we always use some generic reusable framework. There are two general approaches to implementing such a framework. The first one uses inheritance: the base class does the boilerplate work, and the derived class contains the unique task-specific data and code. Staying with our simple approach to active objects, we could write the base class as follows:

```
// Example 23
class Job {
  std::thread t_;
  bool done_ {};
  virtual void operator()() = 0;
  public:
  void wait() {
    if (done_) return;
    t_.join();
    done_ = true;
  }
  void run() {
    t_ = std::thread([this](){ (*this)(); });
  }
  virtual ~Job() { wait(); }
};
```

The base object Job contains everything needed to implement the asynchronous control flow: the thread and the state flag needed to join the thread only once. It also defines the way to execute the code by calling the non-virtual function run(). The code that is executed on the thread must be provided by the derived object by overriding operator(). Note that only run() is public, and operator() is not: this is the non-virtual idiom in action (we saw it in *Chapter 14, The Template Method Pattern and the Non-Virtual Idiom*).

The derived object is problem-specific, of course, but generally looks like this:

```
// Example 23
class TheJob final : public Job {
  ... data ...
  void operator()() override { ... work ... }
  public:
  TheJob(... args ...) {
    ... initialize data ...
    this->run();
  }
  auto get() { this->wait(); return ... results ...; }
};
```

The only subtlety here is the call to `run()` done at the end of the constructor of the derived object. It is not necessary (we can execute the active object later ourselves) but if we do want the constructor to run it, it has to be done in the derived class. If we start the thread and the asynchronous execution in the base class constructor, then we will have a race between the execution on the thread – `operator()` – and the rest of the initialization which continues in the derived class constructor. For the same reason, an active object that starts executing from the constructor should not be derived from again; we ensure that by making the object final.

The use of our active object is very simple: we create it, the object starts executing the code in the background (on a separate thread), and when we need the result we ask for it (this may involve waiting):

```
// Example 23
TheJob j1(... args ...);
TheJob j2(... args ...);
... do other stuff ...
std::cout << "Results: " << j1.get() << " " << j2.get();
```

If you've written any concurrent code in C++ at all, you will have definitely used an active object already: `std::thread` is an active object, it lets us execute arbitrary code on a separate thread. There are concurrency libraries for C++ where a thread is a base object and all concrete threads are derived from it. But this is not the approach chosen for the C++ standard thread. It follows the second way to implement a reusable active object: type erasure. If you need to familiarize yourself with it, reread *Chapter 6, Understanding Type Erasure*. Even though `std::thread` itself is a type-erased active object, we're going to implement our own just to demonstrate the design (the standard library code is rather hard to read). This time, there is no base class. The framework is provided by a single class:

```
// Example 24
class Job {
  bool done_ {};
  std::function<void()> f_;
  std::thread t_;
  public:
  template <typename F> explicit Job(F&& f) :
    f_(f), t_(f_) {}
  void wait() {
     if (done_) return;
     t_.join();
     done_ = true;
  }
  ~Job() { wait(); }
};
```

To implement the type-erased callable, we use `std::function` (we could also use one of the more efficient implementations from *Chapter 6, Understanding Type Erasure*, or implement type erasure ourselves following the same approach). The code supplied by the caller to be executed on a thread comes from the callable `f` in the constructor argument. Note that the order of the class members is very important: the asynchronous execution starts as soon as the thread `t_` is initialized, so other data members, in particular, the callable `f_`, must be initialized before that happens.

To use the active object of this style, we need to supply a callable. It could be a lambda expression or a named object, for example:

```
// Example 24
class TheJob {
  ... data ...
  public:
  TheJob(... args ...) { ... initialize data ... }
  void operator()() { // Callable!
    ... do the work ...
  }
};
Job j(TheJob(... args ...));
j.wait();
```

Note that, in this design, there is no easy way to access the data members of the callable `TheJob`, unless it was created as a named object. For this reason, the results are usually returned through arguments passed to the constructor by reference (the same as we do with `std::thread`):

```
// Example 24
class TheJob {
  ... data ...
  double& res_; // Result
  public:
  TheJob(double& res, ... args ...) : res_(res) {
    ... initialize data ...
  }
  void operator()() { // Callable!
    ... do the work ...
    res_ = ... result ...
  }
};
double res = 0;
Job j(TheJob(res, ... args ...));
j.wait();
std::cout << res;
```

Active objects can be found in every concurrent C++ program, but some uses of them are common and specialized, and so are recognized as concurrent design patterns in their own right. We will now see several of these patterns.

Reactor Object pattern

The Reactor pattern often uses for event handling or responding to service requests. It solves a specific problem where we have multiple requests for certain actions that are issued by multiple threads; however, the nature of these actions is such that at least part of them must be executed on one thread or otherwise synchronized. The reactor object is the object that services these requests: it accepts requests from multiple threads and executes them.

Here is an example of a reactor that can accept requests to perform a specific computation with caller-supplied inputs and store the results. The requests can come from any number of threads. Each request is allocated a slot in the array of results – that is the part that must be synchronized across all threads. After the slot is allocated, we can do the computations concurrently. To implement this reactor, we are going to use the atomic index to allocate unique array slots to each request:

```
// Example 25
class Reactor {
  static constexpr size_t N = 1024;
  Data data_[N] {};
  std::atomic<size_t> size_{0};
  public:
  bool operator()(... args ...) {
    const size_t s =
      size_.fetch_add(1, std::memory_order_acq_rel);
    if (s >= N) return false;  // Array is full
    data_[s] = ... result ...;
    return true;
  }
  void print_results() { ... }
};
```

The calls to `operator()` are thread-safe: any number of threads can call this operator simultaneously, and each call will add the result of the computation to the next array slot without overwriting any data produced by other calls. To retrieve the results from the object, we can either wait until all requests are done or implement another synchronization mechanism such as the publishing protocol to make calls to `operator()` and `print_results()` thread-safe with respect to each other.

Note that usually, a reactor object processes requests asynchronously: it has a separate thread to execute the computations and a queue to channel all the requests to a single thread. We can build such a reactor by combining several patterns we saw earlier, for example, we can add a thread-safe queue to our basic reactor to get an asynchronous reactor (we are about to see an example of such a design).

So far, we focused on starting and executing jobs, and then we wait for the work to complete. The next pattern focuses on handling the completion of asynchronous tasks.

Proactor Object pattern

The Proactor pattern is used to execute asynchronous tasks, usually long-running, by requests from one or more threads. This sounds a lot like the Reactor, but the difference is what happens when a task is done: in the case of the Reactor, we just have to wait for the work to get done (the wait can be blocking or non-blocking, but in all cases, the caller initiates the check for completion). The Proactor object associates each task with a callback, and the callback is executed asynchronously when the task is done. The Reactor and the Proactor are the synchronous and asynchronous solutions to the same problem: handling the completion of concurrent tasks.

A proactor object typically has a queue of tasks to be executed asynchronously or uses another executor to schedule these tasks. Each task is submitted with a callback, usually a callable. The callback is executed when the task is done; often, the same thread that executed the task will also invoke the callback. Since the callback is always asynchronous, care must be taken if it needs to modify any shared data (for example, any data that is accessed by the thread that submitted the task to the proactor). If there is any data shared between the callback and other threads, it must be accessed in a thread-safe way.

Here is an example of a proactor object that uses the thread-safe queue from the previous section. In this example, each task takes one integer as input and computes a `double` result:

```cpp
// Example 26
class Proactor {
  using callback_t = std::function<void(size_t, double)>;
  struct op_task {
    size_t n;
    callback_t f;
  };
  std::atomic<bool> done_{false}; // Must come before t_
  ts_queue<op_task> q_;           // Must come before t_
  std::thread t_;
  public:
  Proactor() : t_([this]() {
    while (true) {
      auto task = q_.pop();
      if (!task) {                    // Queue is empty
        if (done_.load(std::memory_order_relaxed)) {
          return;                     // Work is done
        }
        continue;                     // Wait for more work
      }
      ... do the work ...
```

```
      double x = ... result ...
      task->f(n, x);
    } // while (true)
  }) {}
  template <typename F>
  void operator()(size_t n, F&& f) {
    q_.push(op_task{n, std::forward<F>(f)});
  }
  ~Proactor() {
    done_.store(true, std::memory_order_relaxed);
    t_.join();
  }
};
```

The queue stores the work requests which consist of the input and the callable; any number of threads can call `operator()` to add requests to the queue. A more generic proactor might take a callable for the work request instead of having the computation coded into the concrete proactor object. The proactor executes all the requests in order on a single thread. When the requested computation is done, the thread invokes the callback and passes the result to it. This is how we may use such a proactor object:

```
// Example 26
Proactor p;
for (size_t n : ... all inputs ...) {
  p(n, [](double x) { std::cout << x << std::endl; });
}
```

Note that our proactor executes all callbacks on one thread, and the main thread does not do any output. Otherwise, we would have to protect `std::cout` with a mutex.

The Proactor pattern is used to both execute asynchronous events and perform additional actions (callbacks) when these events happen. The last pattern we explore in this section does not execute anything but is used to react to external events.

Monitor pattern

The Monitor pattern is used when we need to observe, or monitor, some conditions and respond to certain events. Usually, a monitor runs on its own thread that is sleeping or waiting most of the time. The thread is awakened either by a notification or simply by the passage of time. Once awakened, the monitor object examines the state of the system it is tasked to observe. It may take certain actions if the specified conditions are met, then the thread goes back to waiting.

We are going to see a monitor implementation that uses a timeout; a monitor with a condition variable can be implemented using the same approach but with the waiting on notification pattern as seen earlier in this chapter.

First, we need something to monitor. Let us say that we have several producer threads that do some computations and store results in an array using an atomic index:

```
// Example 27
static constexpr size_t N = 1UL << 16;
struct Data {... data ... };
Data data[N] {};
std::atomic<size_t> index(0);
void produce(std::atomic<size_t>& count) {
  for (size_t n = 0; ; ++n) {
    const size_t s =
      index.fetch_add(1, std::memory_order_acq_rel);
    if (s >= N) return;
    const int niter = 1 << (8 + data[s].n);
    data[s] = ... result ...
    count.store(n + 1, std::memory_order_relaxed);
  }
}
```

Our producer also stores the count of results computed by the thread in the count variable passed to it. Here is how we launch the producer threads:

```
// Example 27
std::thread t[nthread];
std::atomic<size_t> work_count[nthread] = {};
for (size_t i = 0; i != nthread; ++i) {
  t[i] = std::thread(produce, std::ref(work_count[i]));
}
```

We have one result count per thread, so each producer has its own count to increment. Why, then, did we make the counts atomic? Because the counts are also what we are going to monitor: our monitor thread will periodically report on how much work is done. Thus, each work count is accessed by two threads, the producer and the monitor, and we need to either use atomic operations or a mutex to avoid data races.

The monitor is going to be a separate thread that wakes up every now and then, reads the values of the result counts, and reports the progress of the work:

```
// Example 27
std::atomic<bool> done {false};
std::thread monitor([&]() {
  auto print = [&]() { ... print work_count[] ... };
  std::cout << "work counts:" << std::endl;
  while (!done.load(std::memory_order_relaxed)) {
    std::this_thread::sleep_for(
```

```
        std::chrono::duration<double, std::milli>(500));
    print();
  }
  print();
});
```

The monitor can be started before the producer threads, or at any time we need to monitor the progress of the work, and it will report how many results are computed by each producer thread, for example:

```
work counts:
1096 1083 957 1046 1116 -> 5298/65536
2286 2332 2135 2242 2335 -> 11330/65536
...
13153 13061 13154 12979 13189 -> 65536/65536
13153 13061 13154 12979 13189 -> 65536/65536
```

Here we used five threads to compute the total of 64K results, and the monitor reports the counts for each thread and the total result count. To shut down the monitor, we need to set the done flag and join the monitor thread:

```
// Example 27
done.store(true, std::memory_order_relaxed);
monitor.join();
```

The other common variant of the Monitor pattern is the one where, instead of waiting on a timer, we wait on a condition. This monitor is a combination of the basic monitor and the pattern for waiting on a notification that we saw earlier in this chapter.

The concurrent programming community has come up with many other patterns for solving common problems related to concurrency; most of these can be used in C++ programs but they are not specific to C++. There are C++-specific features such as atomic variables that influence the way we implement and use these patterns. The examples from this chapter should give you enough guidance to be able to adapt any other concurrent pattern to C++.

The description of execution patterns mostly concludes the brief study of C++ patterns for concurrency. Before you turn the last page, I want to show you a totally different type of concurrent pattern that is just coming to C++.

Coroutine patterns in C++

Coroutines are a very recent addition to C++: they were introduced in C++20, and their present state is a foundation for building libraries and frameworks as opposed to features you should use in the application code directly. It is a complex feature with many subtle details, and it would take an entire chapter to explain what it does (there is a chapter like that in my book *The Art of Writing Efficient Programs*). Briefly, coroutines are functions that can suspend and resume themselves. They cannot be forced to suspend, a coroutine continues to execute until it suspends itself. They are used to implement what is known as cooperative multitasking, where multiple streams of execution voluntarily yield control to each other rather than being forcibly preempted by the OS.

Every execution pattern we saw in this chapter, and many more, can be implemented using coroutines. It is, however, too early to say whether this is going to become a common use of coroutines in C++, so we cannot say whether a "proactor coroutine" will ever become a pattern. One application of coroutines, however, is well on the way to becoming a new pattern in C++: the coroutine generator.

This pattern comes into play when we want to take some computation that is normally done with a complex loop and rewrite it as an iterator. For example, let us say that we have a 3D array and we want to iterate over all its elements and do some computation on them. This is easy enough to do with a loop:

```
size_t*** a; // 3D array
for (size_t i = 0; i < N1; ++i) {
  for (size_t j = 0; j < N2; ++j) {
    for (size_t k = 0; k < N3; ++k) {
      ... do work with a[i][j][k] ...
    }
  }
}
```

But it's hard to write reusable code this way: if we need to customize the work we do on each array element, we have to modify the inner loop. It would be much easier if we had an iterator that runs over the entire 3D array. Unfortunately, to implement this iterator we have to turn the loops inside out: first, we increment k until it reaches N3; then, we increment j by one and go back to incrementing k, and so on. The result is a very convoluted code that reduced many a programmer to counting on their fingers to avoid one-off errors:

```
// Example 28
class Iterator {
  const size_t N1, N2, N3;
  size_t*** const a;
  size_t i = 0, j = 0, k = 0;
  bool done = false;
  public:
  Iterator(size_t*** a, size_t N1, size_t N2, size_t N3) :
```

```
      N1(N1), N2(N2), N3(N3), a(a) {}
  bool next(size_t& x) {
    if (done) return false;
    x = a[i][j][k];
    if (++k == N3) {
      k = 0;
      if (++j == N2) {
        j = 0;
        if (++i == N1) return (done = true);
      }
    }
    return true;
  }
};
```

We even took a shortcut and gave our iterator a non-standard interface:

```
// Example 28
Iterator it(a, N1, N2, N3);
size_t val;
while (it.next(val)) {
    ... val is the current array element ...
}
```

The implementation is even more convoluted if we want to conform to the STL iterator interface.

Problems such as this, where a complex function such as our nested loop must be suspended in the middle of the execution so the caller can execute some arbitrary code and resume the suspended function, are an ideal fit for coroutines. Indeed, a coroutine that produces the same sequence as our iterator looks very simple and natural:

```
// Example 28
generator<size_t>
coro(size_t*** a, size_t N1, size_t N2, size_t N3) {
  for (size_t i = 0; i < N1; ++i) {
    for (size_t j = 0; j < N2; ++j) {
      for (size_t k = 0; k < N3; ++k) {
        co_yield a[i][j][k];
      }
    }
  }
}
```

That's it; we have a function that takes the parameters necessary to loop over a 3D array, a regular nested loop, and we do something to each element. The secret is in that innermost line where "something" happens: the C++20 keyword `co_yield` suspends the coroutine and returns the value `a[i][j][k]` to the caller. It is very similar to the `return` operator, except `co_yield` does not exit the coroutine permanently: the caller can resume the coroutine, and the execution continues from the next line after `co_yield`.

The use of this coroutine is also straightforward:

```
// Example 28
auto gen = coro(a, N1, N2, N3);
while (true) {
  const size_t val = gen();
  if (!gen) break;
  ... val is the current array element ...
}
```

The coroutine magic happens inside the generator object that is returned by the coroutine. Its implementation is anything but simple, and, if you want to write one yourself, you have to become an expert on C++ coroutines (and do so by reading another book or article). You can find a very minimal implementation in *Example 28*, and, with the help of a good reference for coroutines, you can understand its inner working line by line. Fortunately, if all you want is to write code like that shown previously, you don't really have to learn the details of the coroutines: there are several open-source libraries that provide utility types such as the generator (with slightly different interfaces), and in C++23 `std::generator` will be added to the standard library.

While it is certainly easier to write the coroutine with a loop and `co_yield` than the convoluted inverted loop of the iterator, what is the price of this convenience? Obviously, you have to either write a generator or find one in a library, but once that is done, are there any more disadvantages to the coroutines? In general, a coroutine involves more work than a regular function, but the performance of the resulting code depends greatly on the compiler and can vary with seemingly insignificant changes to the code (as is the case for any compiler optimizations). The coroutines are still quite new and the compilers do not have comprehensive optimizations for them. That being said, the performance of coroutines can be comparable to that of the hand-crafted iterator. For our *Example 28*, the current (at the moment of this writing) release of Clang 17 gives the following results:

```
Iterator time: 9.20286e-10 s/iteration
Generator time: 6.39555e-10 s/iteration
```

On the other hand, GCC 13 gives an advantage to the iterator:

```
Iterator time: 6.46543e-10 s/iteration
Generator time: 1.99748e-09 s/iteration
```

We can expect the compilers to get better at optimizing coroutines in the future.

Another variant of the coroutine generator is useful when the sequence of values that we want to produce is not limited in advance and we want to generate new elements only when they are needed (lazy generator). Again, the advantage of coroutines is the simplicity of returning results to the caller from inside of the loop.

Here is a simple random number generator implemented as a coroutine:

```
// Example 29
generator<size_t> coro(size_t i) {
  while (true) {
    constexpr size_t m = 1234567890, k = 987654321;
    for (size_t j = 0; j != 11; ++j) {
      if (1) i = (i + k) % m; else ++i;
    }
    co_yield i;
  }
}
```

This coroutine never ends: it suspends itself to return the next pseudo-random number i, and every time it is resumed, the execution jumps back into the infinite loop. Again, the generator is a rather complex object with a lot of boilerplate code that you would be better off getting from a library (or waiting until C++23). But once that's done, the use of the generator is very simple:

```
// Example 29
auto gen = coro(42);
size_t random_number = gen();
```

Every time you call gen(), you get a new random number (of rather poor quality since we have implemented one of the oldest and simplest pseudo-random number generators, so consider this example useful for illustration only). The generator can be called as many times as you need; when it is finally destroyed, so is the coroutine.

We will likely see more design patterns that take advantage of coroutines develop in the coming years. For now, the generator is the only established one, and just recently at that, so it is fitting to conclude the last chapter of the book on C++ design patterns with the newest addition to our pattern toolbox.

Summary

In this chapter, we explored common C++ solutions to the problems of developing concurrent software. This is a very different type of problem compared to everything we studied before. Our main concerns here are correctness, specifically, by avoiding data races, and performance. Synchronization patterns are standard ways to control access to shared data to avoid undefined behavior. Execution patterns are the basic building blocks of thread schedulers and asynchronous executors. Finally, the high-level patterns and guidelines for the concurrent design are the ways we, the programmers, keep our sanity while trying to think about all the things that could happen before, after, or at the same time as one another.

Questions

1.   What is concurrency?

2.   How does C++ support concurrency?

3.   What are synchronization design patterns?

4.   What are execution design patterns?

5.   What overall guidelines for the design and the architecture of concurrent programs should be followed?

6.   What is a transactional interface?

Assessments

Chapter 1, An Introduction to Inheritance and Polymorphism

1. Objects and classes are the building blocks of a C++ program. By combining data and algorithms (*code*) into a single unit, the C++ program represents the components of the system that it models, as well as their interactions.

2. Public inheritance represents an *is-a* relationship between objects—an object of the derived class can be used as if it was an object of the base class. This relation implies that the interface of the base class, with its invariants and restrictions, is also a valid interface for the derived class. Unlike public inheritance, private inheritance says nothing about the interfaces. It expresses a *has-a* or *is implemented in terms of* relationship. The derived class reuses the implementation provided by the base class. For the most part, the same can be accomplished by composition. Composition should be preferred when possible; however, empty base optimization and (less often) virtual method overrides are valid reasons to use private inheritance.

3. A polymorphic object in C++ is an object whose behavior depends on its type, and the type is not known at compile time (at least at the point where the behavior in question is requested). An object that is referred to as a base class object can demonstrate the behavior of the derived class if that is its true type. In C++, polymorphic behavior is implemented using virtual functions.

4. Dynamic cast verifies at run time that the destination type of the cast is valid: it must be either the actual type of the object (the type the object was created with) or one if its base types. It is the latter part, checking all possible base types of an object, that makes dynamic casts expensive.

Chapter 2, Class and Function Templates

1. A template is not a type; it is a *Factory* for many different types with similar structures. A template is written in terms of generic types; substituting concrete types for these generic types results in a type generated from the template.

2. There are class, function, and variable templates. Each kind of template generates the corresponding entities—functions in the case of function templates, classes (types) from class templates, and variables from variable templates.

3. Templates can have type and non-type parameters. Type parameters are types. Non-type parameters can be integral or enumerated values or templates (in the case of variadic templates, the placeholders are also non-type parameters).

4. A template instantiation is the code generated by a template. Usually, the instantiations are implicit; the use of a template forces its instantiation. An explicit instantiation, without use, is also possible; it generates a type or a function that can be used later. An explicit specialization of a template is a specialization where all generic types are specified; it is not an instantiation, and no code is generated until the template is used. It is only an alternative recipe for generating code for these specific types.

5. Usually, the parameter pack is iterated over using recursion. The compiler will typically inline the code generated by this recursion, so the recursion exists only during compilation (as well as in the head of the programmer reading the code). In C++17 (and, rarely, in C++14), it is possible to operate on the entire pack without recursion.

6. Lambda expressions are essentially a compact way to declare local classes that can be called like functions. They are used to effectively store a fragment of code in a variable (or, rather, associate the code with a variable) so that this code can be called later.

7. Concepts impose restrictions on the template parameters. This can be used to avoid substituting types and instantiating a template that would lead to an error in the body of the template. In the more complex cases, concepts can be used to disambiguate the choice between multiple template overloads.

Chapter 3, Memory and Ownership

1. Clear memory ownership, and by extension, resource ownership, is one of the key attributes of a good design. With clear ownership, resources are certain to be created and made available in time for when they are needed, maintained while they are in use, and released/cleaned up when no longer needed.

2. Resource leaks, including memory leaks; dangling handles (resource handles, such as pointers, references, or iterators, pointing to resources that do not exist); multiple attempts to release the same resource; multiple attempts to construct the same resource.

3. Non-ownership, exclusive ownership, shared ownership, as well as conversion between different types of ownership and transfer of ownership.

4. Ownership-agnostic functions and classes should refer to objects by raw pointers and references if the corresponding ownership is handled through owning pointers. If the objects are owned by rich pointers or containers, the problem becomes more difficult. If the additional data contained in the rich pointer is not needed or a single element of a container is accessed, raw pointers and references are perfectly adequate. Otherwise, ideally, we would use a corresponding non-owning reference object like `std::string_view` or one of the views from the ranges library. If none is available, we may have to pass the owning object itself by reference.

5. Exclusive memory ownership is easier to understand and follow the control flow of the program. It is also more efficient.

6. Preferably, by allocating the object on the stack or as a data member of the owning class (including container classes). If reference semantics or certain move semantics are needed, a unique pointer should be used. For conditionally constructed objects, `std::optional` is a great solution.

7. Shared ownership should be expressed through a shared pointer such as `std::shared_ptr`.

8. Shared ownership in a large system is difficult to manage and may delay the deallocation of resources unnecessarily. It also has a nontrivial performance overhead, compared to exclusive ownership. Maintaining shared ownership in a thread-safe concurrent program requires very careful implementation.

9. Views such as `std::string_view`, `std::span`, and views from `std::ranges` are essentially non-owning rich pointers. A string view to a string is what a raw pointer is to a unique pointer: a non-owning object containing the same information as the corresponding owning object.

Chapter 4, Swap - From Simple to Subtle

1. The swap function exchanges the state of the two objects. After the swap call, the objects should remain unchanged, except for the names they are accessed by.

2. Swap is usually employed in programs that provide commit-or-rollback semantics; a temporary copy of the result is created first, then swapped into its final destination only if no errors were detected.

3. The use of swap to provide commit-or-rollback semantics assumes that the swap operation itself cannot throw an exception or otherwise fail and leave the swapped objects in an undefined state.

4. A non-member swap function should always be provided, to ensure that the calls to non-member swap are executed correctly. A member swap function can also be provided, for two reasons—first, it is the only way to swap an object with a temporary, and second, the swap implementation usually needs access to the private data members of the class. If both are provided, the non-member function should call the member swap function on one of the two parameters.

5. All STL containers and some other standard library classes provide a member function `swap()`. In addition, the non-member `std::swap()` function template has standard overloads for all STL types.

6. The `std::` qualifier disables the argument-dependent lookup and forces the default `std::swap` template instantiation to be called, even if a custom swap function was implemented with the class. To avoid this problem, it is recommended to also provide an explicit instantiation of the `std::swap` template.

Chapter 5, Comprehensive Look at RAII

1. Memory is the most common resource, but any object can be a resource. Any virtual or physical quantity that the program operates on is a resource.

2. Resources should not be lost (leaked). If a resource is accessed through a handle, such as a pointer or an ID, that handle should not be dangling (referring to a resource that does not exist). Resources should be released when they are no longer needed, in the manner that corresponds to the way they were acquired.

3. Resource Acquisition Is Initialization is an idiom; it is the dominant C++ approach to resource management, where each resource is owned by an object, acquired in the constructor, and released in the destructor of that object.

4. An RAII object should always be created on the stack or as a data member of another object. When the flow of the program leaves the scope containing the RAII object or the larger object containing the RAII object is deleted, the destructor of the RAII object is executed. This happens regardless of how the control flow leaves the scope.

5. If each resource is owned by an RAII object and the RAII object does not give out raw handles (or the user is careful to not clone the raw handle), the handle can only be obtained from the RAII object and the resource is not released as long as that object remains.

6. The most frequently used is `std::unique_ptr` for memory management; `std::lock_guard` is used to manage mutexes.

7. As a rule, RAII objects must be non-copyable. Moving an RAII object transfers the ownership of the resource; the classic RAII pattern does not support this, so most RAII objects should be non-movable (differentiate between `std::unique_ptr` and `const std::unique_ptr`).

8. RAII has difficulty handing release failures, because exceptions cannot propagate from the destructors, and hence there is no good way to report the failure to the caller. For that reason, failing to release a resource often results in undefined behavior (this approach is sometimes taken by the C++ standard as well).

Chapter 6, Understanding Type Erasure

1. Type erasure is a programming technique where the program, as written, does not show an explicit dependence on some of the types it uses. It is a powerful design tool when used for separating abstract behavior from a particular implementation.

2. The implementation involves either a polymorphic object and a virtual function call, or a function that is implemented specifically for the erased type and is invoked through a function pointer. Usually, this is combined with generic programming to construct such polymorphic objects or generate functions from a template automatically and ensure that the reified type is always the same as the one provided during construction.

3. A program may be written in a way that avoids explicit mention of most types. The types are deduced by template functions and declared as `auto` or as template-deduced typedef types. However, the actual types of objects that are hidden by `auto` still depend on all types the object operates on (such as the deleter type for a pointer). The erased type is not captured by the object type at all. In other words, if you could get the compiler to tell you what this particular auto stands for, all types would be explicitly there. But if the type was erased, even the most detailed declaration of the containing object will not reveal it (such as `std::shared_ptr<int>` —this is the entire type, the deleter type is not there).

4. The type is reified by the function that is generated for that type: while its signature (arguments) does not depend on the erased type, the body of the function does. Usually, the first step is casting one of the arguments from a generic pointer such as `void*` to the pointer to the erased type.

5. The performance of type erasure always incurs some overhead compared to invoking the same callable directly: there is always an extra indirection and the pointer associated with it. Almost all implementations use runtime polymorphism (virtual functions or dynamic casts) or the equivalent virtual table of function pointers, which increases both the time (indirect function calls) and memory (virtual pointers). The greatest overhead usually comes from additional memory allocations, necessary for storing objects whose size is not known at compile time. If such allocations can be minimized and the additional memory made local to the object, the total overhead at runtime may be quite small (the overhead in memory remains and is often increased by such optimizations).

Chapter 7, SFINAE, Concepts, and Overload Resolution Management

1. For each function call, it is the set of all functions with the specified name that are accessible from the call location (the accessibility may be affected by the namespaces, nested scopes, and so on).

2. It is the process of selecting which function in the overload set is going to be called, given the arguments and their types.

3. For template functions and member functions (and class constructors in C++17), type deduction determines the types of template parameters from the types of the function arguments. For each parameter, it may be possible to deduce the type from several arguments. In this case, the results of this deduction must be the same, otherwise, the type deduction fails. Once the template parameter types are deduced, the concrete types are substituted for the template parameters in all arguments, the return type, and the default arguments. This is a type substitution.

4. Type substitution, described previously, can result in invalid types, such as a member function pointer for a type that has no member functions. Such substitution failures do not generate compilation errors; instead, the failing overload is removed from the overload set.

5. This is only in the function declaration (return type, parameter types, and default values). Substitution failures in the body of the function chosen by the overload resolution are hard errors.

6. If each overload returns a different type, these types can be examined at compile time. The types must have some way to distinguish them, for example, different sizes or different values of embedded constants. For `constexpr` functions, we can also examine the return values (the function needs the body in this case).

7. It is used with great care and caution. By deliberately causing substitution failures, we can direct the overload resolution toward a particular overload. Generally, the desired overload is preferred unless it fails; otherwise, the variadic overload remains and is chosen, indicating that the expression we wanted to test was invalid. By differentiating between the overloads using their return types, we can generate a compile-time (`constexpr`) constant that can be used in conditional compilation.

8. C++20 constraints offer a more natural, easier-to-understand syntax. They also result in much clearer error messages when a called function does not meet the requirements. Also, unlike SFINAE, constraints are not limited to the substituted parameters of function templates.

9. The standard did not just define concepts and constraints in the language. It also offers a way of thinking about template restrictions. While a wide range of SFINAE-based techniques exists, the code is easier to read and maintain if the use of SFINAE is restricted to a few powerful approaches that resemble the use of concepts.

Chapter 8, The Curiously Recurring Template Pattern

1. While not very expensive in absolute numbers (a few nanoseconds at most), a virtual function call is several times more expensive than a non-virtual one, and could easily be an order of magnitude or more slower than an inlined function call. The overhead comes from the indirection: a virtual function is always invoked by a function pointer, and the actual function is unknown at compile time and cannot be inlined.

2. If the compiler knows the exact function that is going to be called, it can optimize away the indirection and may be able to inline the function.

3. Just like the runtime polymorphic calls are made through the pointer to the base class, the static polymorphic calls must be also made through a pointer or reference to the base class. In the case of CRTP and static polymorphism, the base type is actually a whole collection of types generated by the base class template, one for each derived class. To make a polymorphic call we have to use a function template that can be instantiated on any of these base types.

4. When the derived class is called directly, the use of CRTP is quite different from the compile-time equivalent of the virtual functions. It becomes an implementation technique, where common functionality is provided to multiple derived classes, and each one expands and customizes the interface of the base class template.

5. Strictly speaking, nothing new is needed to use multiple CRTP bases: the derived class can inherit from several such base types, each an instantiation of a CRTP base class template. However, listing these based together with the correct template parameter (derived class itself) for each

one becomes cumbersome. It is easier and less error-prone to declare the derived class as a variadic template with a template template parameter and inherit from the entire parameter pack.

Chapter 9, Named Arguments, Method Chaining, and the Builder Pattern

1. It is easy to miscount arguments, change the wrong argument, or use an argument of the wrong type that happens to convert to the parameter type. Also, adding a new parameter requires changing all function signatures that must pass these parameters along.

2. The argument values within the aggregate have explicit names. Adding a new value does not require changing the function signatures. Classes made for different groups of arguments have different types and cannot be accidentally mixed.

3. The named argument idiom permits the use of temporary aggregate objects. Instead of changing each data member by name, we write a method to set the value of each argument. All such methods return a reference to the object itself and can be chained together in one statement.

4. Method cascading applies multiple methods to the same object. In a method chain, in general, each method returns a new object and the next method applies to it. Often, method chaining is used to cascade methods. In this case, all chained methods return the reference to the original object.

5. The Builder pattern is a design pattern that uses a separate builder object to construct complex objects. It is used when a constructor is not sufficient or not easy to use to construct an object in its desired fully built state. The need for a builder can arise when the constructor of the object being built cannot be modified (a general object used for a particular purpose), when a desired constructor would have many similar arguments and be hard to use when the construction process is complex, or when the construction process is computationally expensive but some of the results can be reused.

6. The fluent interface is an interface that uses method chaining to present multiple instructions, commands, or operations that can be executed on an object. In particular, fluent builders are used in C++ to split complex object construction into multiple smaller steps. Some of these steps can be conditional or depend on other data.

Chapter 10, Local Buffer Optimization

1. Micro-benchmarks can measure the performance of small fragments of code in isolation. To measure the performance of the same fragment in the context of a program, we have to use a profiler.

2. Processing small amounts of data usually involve a correspondingly small amount of computing and are therefore very fast. Memory allocation adds a constant overhead, not proportional to the

data size. The relative impact is larger when the processing time is short. In addition, memory allocation may use a global lock or otherwise serialize multiple threads.

3. Local buffer optimization replaces external memory allocation with a buffer that is a part of the object itself. This avoids the cost, and the overhead, of an additional memory allocation.

4. The object has to be constructed and the memory for it must be allocated, regardless of whether any secondary allocations happen. This allocation has some cost – more if the object is allocated on the heap and less if it's a stack variable – but that cost must be paid before the object can be used. Local buffer optimization increases the size of the object and therefore of the original allocation, but that usually does not significantly affect the cost of that allocation.

5. Short string optimization involves storing string characters in a local buffer contained inside the string object, up to a certain length of the string.

6. Small vector optimization involves storing a few elements of the vector's content in a local buffer contained in the vector object.

Chapter 11, ScopeGuard

1. An error-safe program maintains a well-defined state (a set of invariants) even if it encounters an error. Exception safety is a particular kind of error safety; it assumes that errors are signaled by throwing expressions. The program must not enter an undefined state when an (allowed) expression is thrown. An exception-safe program may require that certain operations do not throw exceptions.

2. If a consistent state must be maintained across several actions, each of which may fail, then the prior actions must be undone if a subsequent action fails. This often requires that the actions do not commit fully until the end of the transaction is reached successfully. The final commit operation must not fail (for example, throw an exception), otherwise error safety cannot be guaranteed. The rollback operation also must not fail.

3. RAII classes ensure that a certain action is always taken when the program leaves a scope, such as a function. With RAII, the closing action cannot be skipped or bypassed, even if the function exits the scope prematurely with an early return or by throwing an exception.

4. The classic RAII needs a special class for every action. ScopeGuard automatically generates an RAII class from an arbitrary code fragment (at least, if lambda expressions are supported).

5. If the status is returned through error codes, it cannot. If all errors in the program are signaled by exceptions and any return from a function is a success, we can detect at runtime whether an exception was thrown. The complication is that the guarded operation may itself take place during stack unwinding caused by another exception. That exception is propagating when the guard class has to decide whether the operation succeeded or failed, but its presence does not indicate the failure of the guarded operation (it may indicate that something else failed elsewhere). Robust exception detection must keep track of how many exceptions are propagating

at the beginning and at the end of the guarded scope, which is possible only in C++17 (or using compiler extensions).

6. The ScopeGuard classes are usually template instantiations. This means that the concrete type of the ScopeGuard is unknown to the programmer, or at least difficult to specify explicitly. The ScopeGuard relies on lifetime extension and template argument deduction to manage this complexity. A type-erased ScopeGuard is a concrete type; it does not depend on the code it holds. The downside is that type erasure requires runtime polymorphism and, most of the time, a memory allocation.

Chapter 12, Friend Factory

1. A non-member friend function has the same access to the members of the class as a member function.

2. Granting friendship to a template makes every instantiation of this template a friend; this includes instantiations of the same template but with different, unrelated, types.

3. Binary operators implemented as member functions are always called on the left-hand-side operand of the operator, with no conversions allowed for that object. Conversions are allowed for the right-hand-side operand, according to the type of the argument of the member operator. This creates an asymmetry between expressions such as x + 2 and 2 + x, where the latter cannot be handled by a member function since the type of 2 (int) does not have any.

4. The first operand of the inserter is always the stream, not the object that is printed. Therefore, a member function would have to be on that stream, which is a part of the standard library; it cannot be extended by the user to include user-defined types.

5. While the details are complex, the main difference is that user-defined conversions (implicit constructors and conversion operators) are considered when calling non-template functions but, for template functions, the argument types must match the parameter types (almost) exactly, and no user-defined conversions are permitted.

6. Defining an in situ friend function (with the definition immediately following the declaration) in a class template causes every instantiation of that template to generate one non-template, non-member function with the given name and parameter types in the containing scope.

Chapter 13, Virtual Constructors and Factories

1. There are several reasons, but the simplest is that the memory must be allocated in the amount `sizeof(T)`, where T is the actual object type, and the `sizeof()` operator is `constexpr` (a compile-time constant).

2. The Factory pattern is a creational pattern that solves the problem of creating objects without having to explicitly specify the type of the object.

3. While in C++ the actual type has to be specified at the construction point, the Factory pattern allows us to separate the point of construction from the place where the program has to decide what object to construct and identify the type using some alternative identifier, a number, a value, or another type.

4. The virtual copy constructor is a particular kind of factory where the object to construct is identified by the type of another object we already have. A typical implementation involves a virtual `clone()` method that is overridden in every derived class.

5. The Template pattern describes the design where the overall control flow is dictated by the base class, with derived classes providing customizations at certain predefined points. In our case, the overall control flow is that of factory construction, and the customization point is the act of construction of an object (memory allocation and constructor invocation).

6. The Builder pattern is used when it is necessary (or just more convenient) to delegate the work of constructing an object to another class instead of doing the complete initialization in the constructor. An object that constructs other objects of different types depending on some run-time information using the factory method is also a builder. In addition to the factory itself, such builders, or factory classes, usually have other run-time data that is used for constructing objects and must be stored in another object – in our case, the factory object, which is also the builder object.

Chapter 14, The Template Method Pattern and the Non-Virtual Idiom

1. A behavioral pattern describes a way to solve a common problem by using a specific method to communicate between different objects.

2. The template method pattern is a standard way to implement an algorithm that has a rigid *skeleton,* or the overall flow of control, but allows for one or more customization points for specific kinds of problems.

3. The Template Method lets the sub-classes (derived types) implement specific behaviors of the otherwise generic algorithm. The key to this pattern is the way the base and the derived types interact.

4. The more common hierarchical approach to design sees the low-level code provide *building blocks* from which the high-level code builds the specific algorithm, by combining them in a particular flow of control. In the template pattern, the high-level code does not determine the overall algorithm and is not in control of the overall flow. The lower-level code controls the algorithm and determines when the high-level code is called to adjust specific aspects of the execution.

5. It is a pattern where the public interface of a class hierarchy is implemented by non-virtual public methods of the base class and the derived classes contain only virtual private methods (as well as any necessary data and non-virtual methods needed to implement them).

6. A public virtual function performs two separate tasks – it provides the interface (since it is public) and also modifies the implementation. A better separation of concerns is to use virtual functions only to customize the implementation and to specify the common interface using the non-virtual functions of the base class.

7. Once the NVI is employed, virtual functions can usually be made private. One exception is when the derived class needs to invoke a virtual function of the base class to delegate part of the implementation. In this case, the function should be made protected.

8. Destructors are called in *nested* order, starting from the most derived class. When the destructor for the derived class is done, it calls the destructor of the base class. By that time, the *extra* information that the derived class contained is already destroyed, and only the base portion is left. If the base class destructor were to call a virtual function, it would have to be dispatched to the base class (since the derived class is gone by then). There is no way for the base class destructor to call the virtual functions of the derived class.

9. The fragile base class problem manifests itself when a change to the base class unintentionally breaks the derived class. While not specific to the template method, it affects, potentially, all object-oriented designs, including ones based on the template pattern. In the simplest example, changing the non-virtual public function in the base class, in a way that changes the names of the virtual functions called to customize the behavior of the algorithm, will break all existing derived classes because their current customizations, implemented by the virtual functions with the old names, would suddenly stop working. To avoid this problem, the existing customization points should not be changed.

Chapter 15, Policy-Based Design

1. The Strategy pattern is a behavioral pattern that allows the user to customize a certain aspect of the behavior of the class by selecting an algorithm that implements this behavior from a set of provided alternatives, or by providing a new implementation.

2. While the traditional OOP Strategy applies at runtime, C++ combines generic programming with the Strategy pattern in a technique known as policy-based design. In this approach, the primary class template delegates certain aspects of its behavior to the user-specified policy types.

3. In general, there are almost no restrictions on the policy type, although the particular way in which the type is declared and used imposes certain restrictions by convention. For example, if a policy is invoked as a function, then any callable type can be used. On the other hand, if a specific member function of the policy is called, the policy must necessarily be a class and provide the required member function. Template policies can be used as well but must match the specified number of template parameters exactly.

4. The two primary ways are composition and inheritance. The composition should generally be preferred; however, many policies in practice are empty classes with no data members and can benefit from empty base class optimization. Private inheritance should be preferred unless the

policy must also modify the public interface of the primary class. Policies that need to operate on the primary policy-based class itself often have to employ CRTP. In other cases, when the policy object itself does not depend on the types used in the construction of the primary template, the policy behavior can be exposed through a static member function.

5. As a general rule, policies that contain only constants and are used to constrain the public interface are easier to write and maintain. However, there are several cases when injecting public member functions through the base class policies is preferred: when we also need to add member variables to the class or when the complete set of public functions would be difficult to maintain or lead to conflicts.

6. The primary drawback is complexity, in various manifestations. Policy-based types with different policies are, generally, different types (the only alternative, type erasure, usually carries a prohibitive runtime overhead). This may force large parts of the code to be templated as well. Long lists of policies are difficult to maintain and use correctly. For this reason, care should be taken to avoid creating unnecessary or hard-to-justify policies. Sometimes a type with two sufficiently unrelated sets of policies is better to be split into two separate types.

Chapter 16, Adapters and Decorators

1. The Adapter is a very general pattern that modifies an interface of a class or a function (or a template, in C++) so it can be used in a context that requires a different interface but similar underlying behavior.

2. The Decorator pattern is a more narrow pattern; it modifies the existing interface by adding or removing behavior but does not convert an interface into a completely different one.

3. In the classic OOP implementation, both the decorated class and the Decorator class inherit from a common base class. This has two limitations; the most important one is that the decorated object preserves the polymorphic behavior of the decorated class but cannot preserve the interface that is added in a concrete (derived) decorated class and was not present in the base class. The second limitation is that the Decorator is specific to a particular hierarchy. We can remove both limitations using the generic programming tools of C++.

4. In general, a Decorator preserves as much of the interface of the decorated class as possible. Any functions the behavior of which is not modified are left unchanged. For that reason, public inheritance is commonly used. If a Decorator has to forward most calls to the decorated class explicitly, then the inheritance aspect is less important, and composition or private inheritance can be used.

5. Unlike Decorators, adapters usually present a very different interface from that of the original class. Composition is often preferred in this case. The exception is compile-time adapters that modify the template parameters but otherwise are essentially the same class template (similar to template aliases). These adapters must use public inheritance.

6. The main limitation is that it cannot be applied to template functions. It also cannot be used to replace function arguments with expressions containing those arguments.

7. Template aliases are never considered by the argument type deduction when function templates are instantiated. Both adapter and policy patterns can be used to add or modify the public interface of a class.

8. Adapters are easy to stack (compose) to build a complex interface one function at a time. The features that are not enabled do not need any special treatment at all; if the corresponding adapter is not used, then that feature is not enabled. The traditional policy pattern requires predetermined slots for every pattern. With the exception of the default arguments after the last explicitly specified one, all policies, even the default ones, must be explicitly specified. On the other hand, the adapters in the middle of the stack do not have access to the final type of the object, which complicates the implementation. The policy-based class is always the final type, and using CRTP, this type can be propagated into the policies that need it.

Chapter 17, The Visitor Pattern and Multiple Dispatch

1. The Visitor pattern provides a way to separate the implementation of algorithms from the objects they operate on; in other words, it is a way to add operations to classes without modifying them by writing new member functions.

2. The Visitor pattern allows us to extend the functionality of class hierarchies. It can be used when the source code of the class is not available for modification or when such modifications would be difficult to maintain.

3. Double dispatch is the process of dispatching a function call (selecting the algorithm to run) based on two factors. Double dispatch can be implemented at runtime using the Visitor pattern (virtual functions provide the single dispatch) or at compile time using templates or compile-time visitors.

4. The classic visitor has a circular dependency between the visitor class hierarchy and the visitable class hierarchy. While the visitable classes do not need to be edited when a new visitor is added, they do need to be recompiled when the visitor hierarchy changes. The latter must happen every time a new visitable class is added, hence a dependency circle. The Acyclic Visitor breaks this circle by using cross-casting and multiple inheritance.

5. A natural way to accept a visitor into an object composed of smaller objects is to visit each of these objects one by one. This pattern, implemented recursively, ends up visiting every built-in data member contained in an object and does so in a fixed, predetermined order. Hence, the pattern maps naturally onto the requirement for serialization and deserialization, where we must deconstruct an object into a collection of built-in types, then restore it.

Chapter 18, Patterns for Concurrency

1. Concurrency is the property of a program that allows multiple tasks to execute at the same time or partially overlapping in time. Usually, concurrency is achieved through the use of multiple threads.

2. C++11 has the basic support for writing concurrent programs: threads, mutexes, and condition variables. C++14 and C++17 added several convenience classes and utilities, but the next major addition to concurrency features of C++ is C++20: here, we have several new synchronization primitives as well as the introduction of the coroutines.

3. Synchronization patterns are the common solutions to the basic problems of accessing shared data. Usually, they provide ways to arrange exclusive access to the data that is modified by multiple threads or is accessed by some threads while being modified by others.

4. Execution patterns are the standard ways to arrange asynchronous execution of some computations using one or more threads. These patterns offer ways to initiate the execution of some code and receive the results of this execution without the caller being responsible for the execution itself (some other entity in the program has that duty).

5. The most important guideline for design for concurrency is modularity; when applies specifically to concurrency, it means building concurrent software from components that satisfy certain restrictions on their behavior in concurrent programs. The most important of these restrictions is the thread safety guarantee: generally, it is much easier to build concurrent software from components that allow a wide range of thread-safe operations.

6. In order to be useful in concurrent programs, any data structure or component must provide a transactional interface. An operation is a transaction if it performs a well-defined complete computation and leaves the system in a well-defined state. A simplified way to identify which operations are and are not transactions is this: if a concurrent program executes each operation under lock but there are no order guarantees between the operations, is the state of the system guaranteed to be well-defined? If it isn't, then some of the operations should be executed as a sequence without releasing the lock. That sequence is a transaction; the operations that are the steps of the sequence are not transactions by themselves. It should not be the responsibility of the caller to arrange these operations in a sequence. Instead, the data structure or component should offer the interface for performing the entire transaction as a single operation.

Index

V

www.packtpub.com

Subscribe to our online digital library for full access to over 7,000 books and videos, as well as industry leading tools to help you plan your personal development and advance your career. For more information, please visit our website.

Why subscribe?

- Spend less time learning and more time coding with practical eBooks and Videos from over 4,000 industry professionals

- Improve your learning with Skill Plans built especially for you

- Get a free eBook or video every month

- Fully searchable for easy access to vital information

- Copy and paste, print, and bookmark content

Did you know that Packt offers eBook versions of every book published, with PDF and ePub files available? You can upgrade to the eBook version at packtpub.com and as a print book customer, you are entitled to a discount on the eBook copy. Get in touch with us at customercare@packtpub.com for more details.

At www.packtpub.com, you can also read a collection of free technical articles, sign up for a range of free newsletters, and receive exclusive discounts and offers on Packt books and eBooks.

Other Books You May Enjoy

If you enjoyed this book, you may be interested in these other books by Packt:

Template Metaprogramming with C++

Marius Bancila

ISBN: 978-1-80324-345-0

- Understand the syntax for all types of templates
- Discover how specialization and instantiation works
- Get to grips with template argument deduction and forwarding references
- Write variadic templates with ease
- Become familiar with type traits and conditional compilation
- Restrict template arguments in C++20 with constraints and concepts
- Implement patterns such as CRTP, mixins, and tag dispatching

C++20 STL Cookbook

Bill Weinman

ISBN: 978-1-80324-871-4

- Understand the new language features and the problems they can solve

- Implement generic features of the STL with practical examples

- Understand standard support classes for concurrency and synchronization

- Perform efficient memory management using the STL

- Implement seamless formatting using std::format

- Work with strings the STL way instead of handcrafting C-style code

Packt is searching for authors like you

If you're interested in becoming an author for Packt, please visit `authors.packtpub.com` and apply today. We have worked with thousands of developers and tech professionals, just like you, to help them share their insight with the global tech community. You can make a general application, apply for a specific hot topic that we are recruiting an author for, or submit your own idea.

Share your thoughts

Now you've finished *Hands-On Design Patterns with C++ (Second Edition)*, we'd love to hear your thoughts! Scan the QR code below to go straight to the Amazon review page for this book and share your feedback or leave a review on the site that you purchased it from.

`https://packt.link/r/1-804-61155-7`

Your review is important to us and the tech community and will help us make sure we're delivering excellent quality content.

Download a free PDF copy of this book

Thanks for purchasing this book!

Do you like to read on the go but are unable to carry your print books everywhere?

Is your eBook purchase not compatible with the device of your choice?

Don't worry, now with every Packt book you get a DRM-free PDF version of that book at no cost.

Read anywhere, any place, on any device. Search, copy, and paste code from your favorite technical books directly into your application.

The perks don't stop there, you can get exclusive access to discounts, newsletters, and great free content in your inbox daily

Follow these simple steps to get the benefits:

1. Scan the QR code or visit the link below

https://packt.link/free-ebook/9781804611555

2. Submit your proof of purchase
3. That's it! We'll send your free PDF and other benefits to your email directly